WSP

2010 / 2014

THE PERILS

OF DIVERSITY

Immigration & Human Nature

BYRON M. ROTH

Second Edition

WASHINGTON SUMMIT PUBLISHERS

2010 / 2014

Washington Summit Publishers
P. O. Box 1676
Whitefish, MT 59937

email : info@WashSummit.com
web: www.WashSummit.com

Cataloging-in-Publication Data is on file
with the Library of Congress

ISBN: 978-1-59368-034-3
eISBN: 978-1-59368-007-7

Printed in the United States of America
10 9 8 7 6 5 4 3 2
Second Edition

For Sophie Elizabeth, Philip Harold,
Andrew Nicholas, Ari Samuel,
Emma Lida, Gabriel David, & Lia Ruth

ACKNOWLEDGEMENTS

The author of a work such as this owes a powerful debt of gratitude to the multitude of scholars and scientists upon whose effort and integrity he relies. In the case of this book, dealing as it does with many contentious issues, I owe a special debt to those who have maintained an unerring commitment to their callings as scientists and scholars. Those callings are privileged ones and carry with them the crucial duty to pursue the truth so far as it is possible for it to be discerned. Unfortunately, that duty, especially in the social sciences, has often been compromised in recent decades, sometimes to avoid the penalties that can be imposed on those who challenge conventional wisdom. Additionally, it is often asserted that some knowledge, especially as it relates to human beings, should not be pursued because it might be dangerous or, alternatively, that the truth about human nature is so relative that it cannot be achieved. While the hope for ultimate, unchanging knowledge is indeed a chimera, the diligent pursuit of the truth about the world in which we live is not; it is, in fact, the absolute obligation of any serious scholar and the bedrock upon which any hope of human betterment must rest. For that reason, I wish to express my profound gratitude to those scholars, many cited in the following pages, who have honorably pursued their calling, often at considerable personal and professional cost.

I would also like to thank my wife Doris for her forbearance, for her encouragement and for her incisive judgment in critiquing this work as it unfolded. She is indeed a worthy friend and partner in just about everything I do. For that she has my undying gratitude.

I would also like to thank my lifelong friend, Edward Stern, whose comments on an earlier version were of great value, especially as he did not agree with everything I had to say. Furthermore, I wish to acknowledge the role of Louis Andrews, editor of Washington Summit Publishers, for his willingness to pursue this work, and his diligent efforts to get it speedily into print. His efforts were all the more remarkable in that he was confronted with extraordinary health difficulties after he began this work. For his courage and fortitude throughout, he has my lasting admiration and gratitude.

Finally I wish to express my deep gratitude to my father-in-law and my friend, Philip A. Ernst, whose effort, foresight and optimism during his life have provided me with the means and freedom to undertake this work and without which it could not have been completed. This book is, in a small way, my tribute to him.

I have dedicated this book to my grandchildren in recognition that they must deal with the consequences of the decisions made by those who came before. I hope they will not judge us harshly.

CONTENTS

United States Immigration Since 1965 | 311

European Immigration in the Postwar Era | 385

THE PERILS OF DIVERSITY

Chapter 1

IMMIGRATION AND HUMAN DIFFERENCES

Introduction

DURING THE PAST FOUR DECADES, both Europe and the United States have undergone and continue to undergo demographic changes of unprecedented proportions. Large numbers of people from Third-World countries have migrated from their impoverished homelands to the developed countries of Europe and the European-settled nations of the United States, Canada, and Australia. While this seismic shift in demography is widely recognized in the west and viewed with considerable apprehension by large numbers of citizens, those who hold elite positions in politics, industry, academia, and journalism do not share this apprehension. In fact, these elites are encouraging these immigration trends and strongly disparage and condemn the vast majority of citizens who view these changes with alarm.[1]

The immediate cause of the mass migration in recent years has been explosive population growth in the second half of the 20th century. World population grew from 2.5 billion in 1950 to 6.8 billion in 2009; so today it is more than 2.5 times what is was in 1950. The UN projects a world population of more than 9 billion people by 2050. Almost all of the recent and projected growth occurred and will occur in the less developed regions of the world. The population of

Africa, which includes much of the Middle East, almost quadrupled from 227 million in 1950 to over one billion in 2005 and is expected to double to 1,998 million by 2050. A similar rapid growth in Latin America, which includes Mexico, produced in the same period a rise from 167 million to 582 million, with population expected to grow to 729 million by mid-century. Mexico grew by four times from 27 million in 1950 to 109 million in 2009 and is expected to grow to 128 million by 2050.[2]

These massive increases in population have not been accompanied by sufficient economic growth in the less developed regions; the consequence has been great pressure for the migration of people to the more developed regions. Modern media has lent impetus to the pressure to migrate, since today, even poor people in impoverished societies see graphic evidence of the enormous gap between their conditions and those in the richer countries. Given modern improvements in transportation, large-scale migration can only be prevented by stringent border controls and highly selective immigration policies, at least until such times as economic conditions improve in the less developed areas of the world. The governments in most developed countries have not taken such restrictive measures and therefore have invited, by relative inaction, large-scale immigration. The reasons governments have not responded in ways to slow immigration are the subject of much of this chapter. The likely consequences of that inaction are the subject of this book.

There has been, to be sure, considerable discussion at the academic and policy level about the implications of these inflows of people and the best way to deal with them. That discussion, however, has taken place uninformed, largely, by empirical data and theoretical perspectives from the social and biological sciences. Rather, the discussion has been framed as an argument between multiculturalists, on the one hand, and assimilationists, on the other, about how to assure that immigrants and their children flourish in their new environment. There has been little discussion of the potential impact of such massive immigration on the social fabric and cultural heritage of the host countries, especially when the immigrants possess different cultural values, motivations, and talents.

Many proponents of large scale immigration seem to assume, at the outset, that human beings are more or less identical social atoms who can be moved from one society to another without in any important way altering themselves or the societies they enter. In this view, societies have a social reality of their own which transcends the human groups that happen to live in them. But that is a fairly radical view, of very recent origin. Far more common, in the past, was the view that societies are organic systems very much shaped by the particular human beings who inhabit them. In this latter view, large scale migrations must alter, in important ways, either the migrant or the host country, or both.

Multiculturalism Versus Assimilationism

The argument between assimilationists and multiculturalists is whether it is the immigrant or the culture that should change. However, there has been virtually no discussion among assimilationists of the extent to which it is possible for immigrants to make the changes necessary for successful assimilation. It is assumed, that with the appropriate societal effort, assimilation will come about relatively swiftly and smoothly. Likewise, there has been little discussion among multiculturalists as to the nature of the changes necessary to bring about the new multicultural society they envision. It is assumed that if all groups are provided appropriate respect and equal opportunity, coexistence will be relatively easy to achieve.

The multiculturalists argue that trying to impose the values and mores of the host country on an immigrant explicitly demeans the culture of the immigrant and, by extension, the immigrant himself. Such disparagement of the immigrant culture is said to produce deleterious psychological effects, such as low self-esteem, which interfere with the ability of the immigrant to thrive and prosper in his new country. Immigrants are encouraged, in this view, to retain the culture of their home country, even occasionally encouraged to keep their native tongue, citing Switzerland and Canada as successful multilingual societies. The net result, according to multicultural doctrine, is that the host country will in time become a vibrant mélange of cultural communities that live in harmony, and respect each other's values and practices, however different. They will be tied together by their allegiance to the political ideals of the host country rather than a common ancestry, heritage, culture, and language. The motto "in diversity is strength," highlights this bold optimism. The multicultural view is clearly in the ascendance in the debate over immigration in all the countries of Europe and of European origin.[3]

Assimilationists, who are clearly in the minority among academics, journalists, and other elites, argue that the melting pot pattern common to the immigrant experience in the United States until the 1970s is a better formula for the successful integration of immigrants. In this view, immigrants should cast aside as quickly as possible the cultural and linguistic baggage of their homelands and adopt the patterns of their host countries. By doing so they will integrate into the larger society, as did previous immigrant groups. They, and certainly their children, will be able to take advantage of the enormous opportunities available.[4]

While the above sketch is an oversimplification of both of these views, I believe it does reflect the essence of those positions. What is disturbing is that these positions are taken as self-evident by their advocates who seem uninterested in serious theoretical and empirical evidence that would support their view or provide guidance for its successful implementation. After all, the effects of large scale immigration are largely irreversible (barring major civil violence). Even the most disastrous natural and man-made catastrophes do not permanently alter the fundamental nature of societies. The citizens of Western Europe who survived the upheavals of World War I and II returned to a way of life that was poorer, to be sure, but otherwise not much different than it had been before the wars. Much had changed, but much more remained the same. This is very unlikely to be the case if one ethnic or cultural group replaces another; such demographic changes may alter a society profoundly and irreversibly. Edmund Burke, reflecting on the changes being wrought by the French Revolution, had grave misgivings about what was transpiring across the channel from his native Britain. According to Burke, every society is an organic whole that has evolved over centuries by often costly and violent trial and error. We only witness those societies that managed over time to survive; we are left to ponder the ruins, if any remain, of those that at some point made a fatal error and simply ceased to exist as coherent social entities. Quoting Burke:

> [V]ery plausible schemes, with very pleasing commencements, have often shameful and lamentable conclusions.... The science of government being...a matter that requires experience, and even more experience than any person can gain in his whole life, however sagacious and observing he may be, it is with infinite caution that any man ought to venture upon pulling down an edifice that has answered in any tolerable degree for ages the common purposes of society...[5]

It is imprudent and unwise for leaders to pursue a course of massive immigration without sound reasoning and powerful evidence about its consequences. Unfortunately they have provided neither. They certainly have not consulted the social sciences for, if they did, they would soon discover that the evidence for both the multiculturalist and the assimilationist positions is either nonexistent or contradictory.

For instance, the multiculturalists' assertion of the damaging psychological effects on individuals if the general population does not hold their group in high esteem is completely at variance with more than forty years of research in the social sciences. In fact, the consensus among most researchers is that self-esteem is utterly unrelated to a person's group membership, and is unrelated to how the group is viewed by the larger society. Black children, for instance, do not suffer from low self-esteem; in most studies they exhibit higher self-esteem than those in other ethnic or racial groups. The status of an ethnic group relative to other ethnic groups has no discernible effect on an individual's self-esteem.[6]

Multiculturalists further ignore the historical record that suggests that social harmony among different ethnic and language groups is at best rare, and where it exists, tenuous. The history of Europe, whatever else it is, is one long tale of religious and ethnic conflict, almost ceaseless war, and the slaughter and the destruction it entails. The enlightenment, and the scientific advances it engendered, did nothing to mitigate this tale of horrific and bloody conflict, with the twentieth century exhibiting the most lethal and unsparing carnage in European history. In addition, in the twentieth century, class conflict was raised to a level in Europe and Asia never seen before. Communist rulers in Europe and Asia effectively divided their societies along economic lines and managed over the century to slaughter even more people than the ethnically based World Wars I and II.[7]

The breakup of the British Empire led to bloody civil strife throughout the former colonies among the disparate peoples held together by British force of arms. The civil war that led to the partition of India and Pakistan left an estimated one million dead in its wake. Similar terrible and murderous turmoil in Southeast Asia, in for example Cambodia and Vietnam, followed the withdrawal of the European colonial powers. Among the former European colonies in Africa, even today, civil strife is rampant.

In the wake of the fall of Communism those multiethnic societies that had been held together by authoritarian dictators quickly fell asunder. Czechoslovakia divided in a peaceful and largely amiable way. Yugoslavia, on the other hand, was torn by vicious civil war and genocidal ethnic cleansing. Iraq, after the fall of Saddam Hussein, presents a similar case. The ongoing Israeli-Palestinian conflict is a different and bloody example of the difficulties of establishing harmony among groups of differing cultures and religions. Even Belgium, (the seat of the European Union Parliament) is in danger of splitting into its Dutch-speaking and French-speaking halves.[8] Canadians of French and English ancestry are grappling with similar problems.

In addition, there is a fundamental inconsistency at the base of the multiculturalist program, in that it applauds ethnic minorities who maintain their cultural traditions, but looks askance at majority populations who wish to do the same. Political elites in all Western societies take a negative view of those who wish to preserve their traditional values and patterns of living and question whether those patterns can be sustained in the face of large numbers of newcomers who do not share those values or are actually hostile to them.

This is particularly clear when those cultural traditions clash with those of recent immigrant groups. In Europe, for instance, many Muslims are deeply offended by religious artworks depicting in a favorable light the Crusader victories over Muslims. Some are even offended by any public display of Christian symbolism. Should the host population have to honor the sensitivities of immigrants by censoring what appears in textbooks or on the walls of public buildings? Many devout Muslims are offended by the way European schoolgirls dress. Should school dress codes reflect this concern?

Should British law allow polygamous unions among Muslims and provide taxpayer support for two or three spouses and their children and provide subsidized housing for such large families, as is the case in England? Is it xenophobia that explains the objections by native British citizens to whom such a practice is alien and offensive in light of traditional British customs?[9] The widespread rioting in various Muslim countries over the Danish cartoon depictions of Mohammed found offensive by Muslims led to serious discussion in Europe as to whether such depictions should be censored for demeaning the Muslim population. Do a free press and a tradition of political and religious satire trump the religious sensitivities of newcomers, or is it to be the other way around?

If the native population finds the ways of immigrants offensive, whose views should prevail? Do Europeans have the right to interfere with arranged marriages, often made against the wishes of young women, on the grounds that freedom of marital choice is a right of all European citizens? As mentioned above, polygamy, recognized under Islamic *sharia* law, is not uncommon and is tolerated in France and England, and no doubt in many other European countries, though it is unlawful in those countries.[10]

The leader of the UMP party in France claimed that the authorities were "strangely lax" in dealing with the estimated 30,000 polygamous families living in France.[11] Similarly, African Muslim immigrants often take their female children back to their native countries for the genital mutilation required by their customs, a practice that is repugnant to Westerners and completely illegal in all Western societies. Should European citizens change their laws to allow exceptions for certain religious groups out of tolerance for their religious beliefs? Should they be chastised for failing to respect customs, such as arranged marriage, polygamy and female mutilation, which they find repugnant? Should immigrants be encouraged to abandon those practices which most Europeans view as barbaric?

These questions are not mere idle speculation. Under a legal clause that allows individuals to resolve disputes by agreeing to abide by the judgment of arbitration panels, Muslim clerics in the UK are now ruling on a variety of matters using Islamic *sharia* law. What is more, these rulings are considered binding under UK law and can be enforced by Britain's regular courts. The *sharia* courts have issued rulings on domestic matters and even criminal cases involving domestic violence. Some difficulties can arise with this arrangement. Consider a case where a young woman is physically abused for refusing an arranged marriage. She now has the choice of taking her complaint to a secular British court or taking it to arbitration before an Islamic court. But how can it be determined that her choice of arbitration was freely chosen and not coerced by the same men, her brothers or father for instance, who attacked her? Once a ruling is issued by an Islamic court, it cannot be appealed to a secular court unless the woman can prove that her submission to arbitration was coerced.

The *Daily Mail* reported in June 2009 that according to the think-tank Civitas, there were at least 85 working sharia tribunals operating in the country, some "17 times higher than previously accepted." The Civitas study explained that the courts "operate behind doors that are closed to independent observers and their decisions are likely to be unfair to women and backed by intimidation." The Mail quotes the author of the report, Islamic specialist Denis MacEoin: "Among the rulings we find some that advise illegal actions and others that transgress human rights standards as applied by British courts." Among the "examples set out in this study is a ruling that no Muslim woman may marry a non-Muslim unless he converts to Islam and that any children of a women who does should be taken from her until she marries a Muslim." Other rulings "approve polygamous marriage and enforce a woman's duty to have sex with her husband upon demand."[12]

In an earlier September 2008 article, the *Daily Mail* reported that, at the time, there were *sharia* courts in five major English cities that had existed for about one year, and had already dealt with six cases of domestic violence. In all six cases the men were chastised by the Clerics and required to take classes in anger management. In all six cases the women withdrew their complaints from the police and the investigations were halted without having determined the seriousness of the abuse or the reasons it was taken to the *sharia* court. In another case, involving a Muslim man's estate, the proceeds were distributed among his three daughters and two sons, with his sons, however, receiving twice the amount as the daughters as prescribed by Islamic law. British law requires that an estate be divided equally among all of a person's offspring, unless a will specifies otherwise.[13] Having agreed to have the estate settled by the Islamic court, the females had no recourse to appeal the ruling to a secular court unless they could have proven that their agreement to arbitration was coerced. But given the position of women in most Islamic societies, how likely are authorities to discover that the agreement was coerced? Even more important, how can a society remain cohesive if its citizens, depending on their ethnicity, are bound by different laws? What do laws dealing with inheritance or domestic violence mean if various groups can opt out of them?

In a democratic republic, people ought to have the right to shape their societies as they think best. They are, of course, limited in so doing by constitutional restrictions necessary to protect the minority from the depredations of the majority. But within those limits they ought to have wide latitude in the sorts of behaviors they wish to encourage and discourage in their dealings with each other. They have the right to determine what sort of things their children are taught, what values they should cherish, what cultural heroes they should honor, and what language they speak. It is, of course, on such shared cultural values, and other conventions and beliefs, that a nation's cohesion is based, and that make it distinct from other nations. To what extent can a minority culture eschew those values and still be considered members of the same national community? At what point does cultural pluralism undermine the cultural and legal integrity of the host society, and at what cost in social harmony? These are hardly trivial questions and those who support multicultural approaches to immigration do not seriously address them.

In fact, the social science evidence that a harmonious society composed of identifiable ethnic groups with different cultural and religious backgrounds can be arranged is, almost without exception, negative. Has some new type of social engineering appeared that would allow this historic pattern to be broken? Has some new sort of human being been born who will not repeat the follies of his ancestors? Will the world find a way to emulate the example of the Swiss? Policy makers should be trying to understand how the Swiss have managed to preserve their experiment in multicultural harmony for so long, when so many others have failed so utterly. Perhaps Switzerland can be a model for the new multicultural societies? On the other hand, maybe Switzerland is a special case that cannot be copied. Switzerland, for all its ethnic harmony, is, in effect, a confederation of separate but closely related European ethnicities who reside in different cantons, who speak their own languages (French, German, Italian, and Native Swiss), and maintain their ethnic customs and tastes. It would be reasonable to ask if such an arrangement could be widely duplicated in very different settings, but few in the multicultural camp appear interested in such a question.

Similarly, the assimilationists who support mass immigration seem equally nonchalant about the evidence for their position. Clearly, the history of immigration to the United States has been fortunate and largely successful. But in the past virtually all successful immigration was from European cultures very similar to that of the original English settlers. In addition, those settlers usually came with similar skills and abilities, often better than those of the earlier settlers, and generally had little difficulty in competing with them. Once in America, they could easily blend in, there being few physical or social features which set them apart. Usually they came in small numbers over an extended period of time and were forced to acquire the language of their host country if they expected to thrive. This was because (except for German and French speakers in some areas) no one group could sustain communities sufficiently large as to be economically independent and thereby sustain their native language for general commerce. As a counterexample, the French community in Quebec did possess sufficient size and was therefore able to maintain its language as well as its ethnic identity.

The United States was so vast and the opportunities it offered so generous that group conflict was generally muted. Conflict among immigrant Europeans was generally limited to the crowded multiethnic coastal cities, and those who wished to avoid those conflicts could migrate to the interior, often gravitating to ethnic enclaves. Even in those less crowded settings, however, conflict was not uncommon, though it usually took the form of political differences over the place of religion in society and the nature of education. Is this an immigration pattern that could be replicated today in modern societies when the immigrant groups come in large numbers from vastly different cultural and ethnic backgrounds compared to the residents of their host countries? Can this model work in crowded Western Europe where land for housing is limited and where unemployment remains at chronically high levels? In other words, is the American immigration experience prior to 1965 an exceptional one? Can it be the model for future immigration cycles or are the conditions today so different as to make the model inapplicable? These are questions that need to asked, but rarely are.

Other very serious questions arise, but are also rarely addressed. Do the very generous social welfare benefits and affirmative action policies of all modern Western societies create different incentives for people to migrate from those who existed in the past, when migration was far riskier and the chances of success much smaller? Milton Freedman, an ardent proponent of open markets, argued that generous welfare benefits were incompatible with a successful immigration policy. His point was that without the prod of economic necessity, the motivation to assimilate is seriously reduced. Another question concerns the place of religious differences today in the creation of a harmonious society. Given the history of Jews in Europe, what is the likely consequence of the large movement of fundamentalist Muslims into the secular societies of Europe and the United Kingdom? It should be recalled that it was not long ago that Protestants and Catholics tore Europe apart over their differences regarding how to worship their common deity. Today religious conflict is common in almost every region of the world where people of different faiths reside inside common borders and who, unlike most in the West, take their religious beliefs very seriously.

Also missing from the assimilationists perspective is the fact that non-Europeans were not nearly so welcomed in the United States as those of European origin. All sorts of exclusionary practices were placed in the way of Asian immigrants of Chinese and Japanese descent. In the early years they were not able, except occasionally, to successfully assimilate. Part of the reason was that America refused to admit sufficient Asian women, so Asian men rarely married or formed families. In addition, they were usually barred from owning land, and were often relegated to segregated communities.[14]

American Indians were generally excluded and no real attempt was made to bring them into the fold, nor did they exhibit any strong desire to do so. Generally, the European and Native American populations remained hostile toward each other and the history of their relations is hardly a model for the blending of disparate peoples. While that animosity no longer exists, Native Americans maintain their cultural distinctions largely on separate reservations. This is hardly a model consistent with assimilation.

Perhaps the most troubling failure, at least to date, has been the failure to fully integrate the black descendants of African slaves into American society. While many black Americans have fully assimilated into the American middle and elite classes, a very large number continues to languish in underclass communities whose way of life is alien to most other Americans. Needless to say, this failure is one of the most disturbing problems confronting America and continues to trouble the nation four decades after the exclusion and subjugation of black Americans was repudiated in the Civil Rights Act of 1964, an act supported by a vast majority of Americans of European descent.

Social Science and Group Differences

The idea that different groups of people are virtually identical and interchangeable serves as the basis of the immigration policies of all Western nations and is accepted by both multiculturalists and assimilationists. But is this idea correct? If group differences exist and have important social implications, it would appear only logical to inquire into how those differences might affect the harmonious integration of immigrants into the larger society, or their peaceful coexistence with other groups. But to ask such questions is to step into the minefield created by the proponents of the doctrine of political correctness. In fact, there is a lot of research on subjects that would undoubtedly have a bearing on immigration, but this research has been carried out by a relatively small group of scientists. To carry out their research, these researchers, many of them distinguished scientists, have had to bear the burden of violating the strongest taboo in mainstream social science—engaging in research into the genetic factors explaining group differences.

In general, mainstream "legitimate" social scientists accept the fact that genes play a role in a variety of human characteristics, such as IQ, aggressiveness, criminality, depression, anxiety, altruism, and risk-taking, to name but a few. Much of the evidence has been known for years because of wide-ranging research with identical twins reared together compared to those reared apart. What these studies show, without serious doubt, is that many human characteristics are the product, in considerable measure, of heredity. This position is being confirmed by new studies of DNA prompted by the mapping of the human genome. Put bluntly, the evidence that genes are significant determinants of behavior is at this point scientifically almost irrefutable. In general, most mainstream social scientists have accepted this scientific reality and have given up the untenable positions promoted during most of the twentieth century that all human traits are the product of learning and other environmental factors, and that genes play no part.[15]

On the other hand, social scientists, in the main, have refused to acknowledge that genetic factors may play a role in racial and ethnic differences. Most readers have heard this often enough, and know quite well the social penalties associated with claiming that this or that ethnic group is more intelligent or aggressive than another. To do so is to expose oneself to the charge of boorishness, ignorance, lack of sophistication, or racism and xenophobia. As Richard Herrnstein put it, expressing such views is seen as obscene, and a form of modern blasphemy.[16] When one examines the arguments challenging the evidence for group differences, however, one finds that they are tendentious and generally make no sense. Those arguments were hardly plausible decades ago when they were first advanced, but are much less so today in light of the numerous genetic studies demonstrating

DNA patterns clearly associated with race and ethnicity, studies which will be examined in due course.

Those who argue that genes play a role in human characteristics such as IQ, do *not* deny that environment is important or that genetically predisposed traits cannot be modified. It is well established, for instance, that diet and education can modify IQ. The debate among scientists studying these issues concerns not whether environment can affect outcomes, but how much those outcomes can be modified. The same kinds of questions are being posed as new knowledge of genetic effects on disease become clear. There is evidence, for instance, that blacks are more prone to hypertension than whites and that the genetic components to these differences, at present, cannot be modified. But there seem, in addition, important environmental and lifestyle factors relating to hypertension that can be modified. This raises questions about the extent of interaction between genes and environment, and may lead to recommendations, for instance, that certain people, because of genetic predispositions, can reduce risks by modifying their behavior or changing their exposure to some environmental factors.

In this context it is important to recognize that the term IQ relates to two separate things. On the one hand, it refers to an underlying general intelligence or "g" factor that determines people's ability to understand and solve conceptual problems. On the other hand, it also refers to various practical measures used to obtain estimates of general intelligence (g). These measures of IQ are made up of subtests of abilities that correlate with general intelligence. For instance, tests that measure mathematical skills, vocabulary, pattern recognition, and reaction times all relate to general IQ, and, in general, are related to each other, but nevertheless individuals with the same general IQ can score differently on the various subtests. IQ tests therefore are instruments used to measure an ability (g) reflecting the way the brain functions. In a sense IQ tests are akin to the rulers used to measure height, but because of the complexity of IQ are not quite as reliable.

This issue has come to prominence in recent years because of a general phenomenon, known as the Flynn Effect, of a worldwide and substantial increase in measured IQ since IQ testing began early in the 20th century. A variety of explanations have been offered to explain this rise, including improved diet, greater exposure to schooling, and a number of other factors. No one explanation or any a combination of explanations seem compelling. In addition, since the increase has occurred so rapidly and widely, it seems unlikely to result from genetic changes. Furthermore the increase in general IQ is the result of improved performance in some subtests, while other subtests have hardly changed at all.

James Flynn, for whom the effect is named, has recently suggested that modern life, including modern communication technology, has lead young people, especially, to acquire certain skills that earlier generations never developed, and in addition, to develop other skills at an earlier age. He doubts that people today are actually smarter than they were two generations ago, but that they may have mental habits that enable them to think about certain things in different and better ways. When the Flynn Effect was first identified, many suggested that the effect provided disconfirmation of genetic explanations for IQ differences. But as Flynn himself points out, there is no inconsistency between genetic influences on IQ and the fact that environmental factors can affect IQ.[17] Perhaps most significant to the arguments put forth in this book is that the Flynn Effect operates indiscriminately and effects all groups more or less equally, and has not resulted in reduced group differences in IQ.

Perhaps new genetic research and brain imaging techniques may make it easier to measure brain functioning directly and obtain actual physical tests of mental ability, but this would not diminish the fact that environmental factors can influence and modify IQ. Indeed, research into genetic factors may help identify early interventions in diet or other conditions that may lead to improved IQ in some children. This is not mere speculation, as is suggested by the condition known as phenylketonuria or PKU. Children born with this condition lack an enzyme necessary for normal development resulting in, among other things, severe mental retardation. Fortunately, the condition can be overcome by providing the newborn with a special diet to compensate for the enzyme deficit. This example provides a profound reason why opposition to the genetic study of IQ is seriously misguided.

Perhaps the best known of the arguments against the existence of genetic group differences is the claim that most genetic variation occurs within groups rather than between groups, with only a small percentage of human genetic variation accounted for by differences between groups. This is true. However, anyone with the slightest familiarity with statistics knows that within-group differences are almost always greater than between-group differences for most human variables. Consider height and weight as examples. Among human beings there is very great variability in both those factors, much greater than the difference in average height and weight between, say, men and women, and in fact the differences between the sexes accounts for only a small fraction of the variability in human height and weight. Does anyone, on that basis, deny that men are, in general, taller and heavier than women or that these differences do not have practical and important consequences? Of course not; such a suggestion is patently absurd. But it is equally absurd to suggest that because genetic differences between racial and ethnic groups account for a small fraction of the total variation among human beings, they are therefore of no consequence. The overall variation in IQ is considerably greater than the IQ difference between any two groups, but any teacher with any experience knows the vast gulf between what can be successfully taught to groups differing by ten or fifteen IQ points.

Equally bizarre is the claim that no group differences along racial lines can exist because race is not a meaningful scientific concept, but is merely a socially constructed one useful to dominant racial groups. Some have supported this claim with the assertion that human traits vary continuously and not discreetly. For example skin color varies continuously, and there are no sharp breaks in skin color when one examines the whole spectrum of human variation. This is, of course, correct, but wholly beside the point. Races are usually defined as populations originating in large geographic areas, and it was always known that intermediate populations existed, with intermediate characteristics. Furthermore, races are not defined by any one trait but rather by a constellation of characteristics that can be easily measured. When we look at different human beings, we may be very much aware of the continuous nature of human traits, but can, nonetheless, clearly make racial distinctions. Those distinctions are not merely subjective. Geneticists have found patterns of genetic markers that are virtually error-free in distinguishing individuals from different racial groups, as well as those with mixed racial background.[18]

Why then are such arguments put forward? They are part of the general reluctance to admit any legitimacy to the notion of inherent group differences. The most common explanation for this reluctance is that knowledge of group differences is dangerous, that such knowledge can be used by dominant groups to deny opportunities to less favored groups. The gist of the argument appears to be that if one asserts that Americans of African descent, for instance, have lower IQs on average than Americans of European descent, then one is therefore condoning the blanket denial of opportunities to black Americans. But the ugly motivation here is merely asserted; it is hardly a logical necessity. Is an honest scientific effort to explain the black-white education gap in genetic terms necessarily an indication of bias or of a desire to deny opportunities to black individuals? Might it not, quite reasonably, be an effort to find ways to improve black performance? Is an attempt to understand different disease patterns among different ethnic and racial groups motivated by a desire to denigrate those groups? Yet exceptionally respected scholars have been so charged, when they have had the temerity to engage in such research. It is unreasonable to attribute motives in this way, especially when no other evidence is produced to bolster the charge of bigotry. These are *ad hominem* arguments that have no legitimacy whatsoever in scholarly discourse.

It should be emphasized just how illegitimate is the use of *ad hominem* arguments. To claim that a person, who is "bad," by someone's definition, cannot possibly be telling the truth is so patently false that it is hard to understand the motives of those who use it. Werner Von Braun led the Nazi effort to build the V1 and V2 missiles that rained destruction and death on innocent civilians and he was, therefore, in some people's minds, a very bad man. But that had nothing whatever to do with his mastery of ballistics and rocketry that enabled him to put humans on the Moon. Albert Einstein's theories led directly to the development of nuclear weapons that killed tens of thousands of innocent people. Einstein himself proposed the development of the atomic bomb out of fear that the Germans would get it first. Was Einstein a bad man? Were his theories false? In fact, if personal moral failings were sufficient to undermine a person's contribution to knowledge, much of the philosophic and scientific basis of our current worldview would have to be abandoned.[19]

A variation of the above argument is that while the scientist might act out of honest and benign motives, his ideas could, in the wrong hands, be put to malignant ends. In this view, the general public will not understand the subtleties of the scientific argument and will use it to justify illegitimate discrimination on the basis of prejudices reinforced by such scientific explanations. As Harvard Psychologist Steven Pinker put it, the "claim of racial differences would...embolden racist kooks and unsavory political movements."[20] But if a scientist were to limit his research to avoid those possibilities, he would invariably find himself limited to the most trivial of subjects. What would modern genetics, chemistry, physics or biology look like today if scientists limited their research out of concerns that their findings might be abused by deranged kooks? Obviously, scientific findings can be used for ill as well as for good. But there are very few people who would jettison the fruits of science on that account. Those who wish to do so are free to close their own eyes, but they ought not to, cloaked in the respectable garments of scholars and scientists, be free to lie and thereby blind those lacking expertise in these important matters.

Another common argument against asserting genetic differences is that since slavery and discrimination in the past were justified by the supposed inferiority of Africans, it is morally reprehensible to argue that at least on some measures Africans appear on average inferior to Europeans. This fear appears to have a sound basis, but on closer inspection it is rather specious, as is apparent by paraphrasing the argument. Since some people in the past used a particular trait or weakness of a group of people to justify the oppression of those people, it is immoral to acknowledge that the trait or weakness may have been real. It is not, however, the recognition of the trait or weakness which is morally repugnant, but the oppression itself, whatever the excuse given for it. If a person kills another and says he did it because his victim had red hair, we rightly condemn the killer for his action, not for his aesthetic judgment. We would hardly hold someone morally defective if he agreed with the murderer that the victim, in fact, had red hair. Likewise if someone were to claim the right to enslave someone because he had a lower than average IQ, we would rightly deny his right to enslave that person even if we agreed with his judgment about the person's intelligence.

In other words, if we agree that an act is wrong, it is wrong no matter what assertions are made to justify the act, and the moral taint lies with excusing the act, not in agreeing with the assertion, especially if the assertion appears to be true. In America and Europe today there exist very strong sanctions for discriminating against people based on their race and ethnicity. Those sanctions exist in law and in public opinion. We rightly condemn those who would discriminate against a person because of his race or ethnicity, and that is true no matter what characteristics we correctly or incorrectly think are more or less common in the person's group. To suggest that most people would use a group characteristic such as average IQ to deny opportunities to an individual member is an ugly assertion and, without substantiation, no more than an assertion. It is more than a little ironic that many social scientists find it acceptable to claim that white Americans are so mean-spirited, unfair and devious that they would use any pretext to visit harm on nonwhites, a charge which is presented without evidence, while at the same time arguing that any statement about blacks or other minorities as a group, even if well-substantiated, is morally reprehensible.

Another common claim is that false beliefs about genetic differences were a cause of the Holocaust, and making such claims today may lead to similar behavior in the future. But this argument is historically inaccurate. Despite the despicable Nazi propaganda depicting Jews as less than human, the widespread animus against Jews in Europe early in the twentieth century was most assuredly not because the general public thought that Jews were an inferior race, intellectually or otherwise. To the contrary, most Europeans were astounded by the meteoric rise of Jews in almost all fields of endeavor, once the universities and professions were opened to them, and they were allowed to compete with other Europeans. Almost all of the anti-Semitic commentators in the late 19th and early 20th centuries acknowledged the superior talents of the Jews.[21] What troubled them was a sense that Jewish influence would undermine European traditions, or that non-Jews had an unfair disadvantage given the success of the Jews, especially in light of the Jews' obvious social cohesiveness. Arthur de Gobineau, often called the father of modern racism, and whose theories heavily influenced Nazi racial thought, was himself not anti-Semitic. In talking of the Jews after their arrival in ancient Palestine, Gobineau remarked that, "They became a people that succeeded in everything it undertook. A free, strong and intelligent people, and one which before it lost, sword in hand, the name of an independent nation, had given to the world as many learned men as it had merchants..."[22]

Research over the last thirty years suggests that Eastern European Jews have very high average IQs, with estimates ranging from 110 to 117, considerably higher than the European average of 100.[23] Perhaps it was their intellectual prowess, along with other personal traits, that enabled Jews to dominate a wide spectrum of professions in the sciences and academia, and to achieve prominence in the visual and literary arts, journalism, and in business enterprises of all sorts. Some clearly saw this success as resulting from unsavory practices, from conspiracies favoring Jewish interests, or from moral defects of one sort or another. Would knowledge, based in sound science, that Jewish success was the result of innate intelligence have made Europeans more, or less, resentful of that success?

Another factor explaining anti-Semitism was that Jews were seen by many as a closed and clannish group. Jews, at the time, were highly endogamous in their marriage patterns and exhibited considerable nepotism. These are not uncommon among minority groups who find themselves in less than welcoming societies. But those practices tended to create the impression that Jews' allegiance was to their coreligionists and not to any particular nation. In other words, they were viewed as cosmopolitans whose loyalty could not be trusted. This charge was exacerbated by the prominent role Jews played in the various Communist and Socialist parties during and after the First World War, a prominence no doubt reflecting the talent Jews brought to almost all the fields they embraced. In short, a lot of people disliked Jews, and said so openly, but only rarely claimed that Jews were in some sense genetically inferior.

A similar hostility, often punctuated by violence, has been exhibited against ethnic Chinese living in various Southeast Asian countries (the Overseas Chinese) who have achieved great success and prominence in various countries of Southeast Asia. As with the Jews in Europe, it was their success, and not any supposed inferiority, which produced the widespread hostility they encountered.[24] Similarly, the genocidal massacre of almost one million Tutsis by the Hutus was motivated by the unfair advantage by which the Tutsi were thought to have gained their superior social standing in Rwanda. In fact, as Amy Chua has documented in, *World on Fire,* such conflicts are common worldwide between what she calls "market-dominant minorities" and less successful majorities.[25]

To put it another way, groups differ in their relative success in society, and that success often gives rise to hostility among those who do not do as well, especially if the successful group is new to the society, has displaced many people from desirable positions and is clearly recognized as ethnically distinct. The perverse genius of the communists was their ability to create hostility toward successful members of society who were not ethnically distinct, but whose modest success was attributed to all sorts of moral failings. The Kulaks under the Russian Communists suffered almost as cruelly as did the Jews under Hitler, and for much the same reason. There is very little reason to believe that explaining well-known group differences in genetic terms will lead to hostility. It is, after all, the differences themselves that give rise to hostility; what causes those differences seems hardly of much significance.

Group Differences and Political Correctness

It is important to emphasize the significance of group differences in immigration policy, and reiterate some of the points already raised. The historical record makes it clear that it is very difficult for large and recognizably different groups to live side by side in harmony. It is also clear from the historical record that if the groups differ in relative success, social harmony is even more difficult to achieve. It is therefore extremely important when assessing immigration policy to consider group differences and their potential impact.

Such a concern would have been obvious to all serious scholars at the beginning of the twentieth century. Few scholars would have questioned the widely held belief that the differences so apparent in the world's various societies reflected differences in the innate characteristics of their inhabitants. This was a common view throughout history, and was given added weight by Charles Darwin's theory of evolution. Francis Galton's work on hereditary genius and the early work of psychologists on the measurement of intelligence seemed to reinforce the scientific basis of this popular understanding of human cultural variation.[26]

This view of racial difference that came to dominate thought in the late 19th century was not without dissenters. Enlightenment thinking, so prominent during the preceding century, tended to support the idea of racial equality and played a prominent role in the ideology supporting the French Revolution. This view also played an important role in the American Declaration of Independence, but did not inform the Constitution of the new nation inasmuch as it allowed for the continued practice of slavery.[27]

By the late 19th century, however, few people would have questioned the assertion that if large numbers of Africans, for instance, were to migrate to Europe and be set up in separate communities for themselves, they would reproduce many of the characteristics common to African communities. Of course, it was widely believed that small groups would and could assimilate fairly readily to European culture, as had been the common experience in Europe at the time. However, most Europeans would have been surprised if more than a small number of those immigrants rose to high status in their societies.

Europeans who migrated to other continents, even if small in number, almost invariably preserved their own ways, and with very few exceptions, did not attempt to integrate into the cultures they colonized. In whatever continent they settled, Europeans set up communities that were almost identical, in physical appearance and in social customs, to their native communities. This was because they believed that European culture was materially and morally superior to other cultures. It was also the case that their superior power and wealth allowed them to settle almost anywhere without any need to assimilate to the native cultures they colonized. Whenever European migration involved large numbers it drastically altered the cultures in which Europeans settled. In other words, they turned those societies into multicultural societies that came to resemble European cultures in many respects, at least as long as they remained in sufficient numbers.

If one were to ask thoughtful people in the late 19th century to speculate about the prospects of the large scale migration of the more primitive of the world's inhabitants to the more civilized countries of Europe or Asia, they would have expressed grave reservations. Given the great disparities believed to exist between the races in ability and temperament, they would have doubted that assimilation of large groups of racially distinct people could be successfully accomplished. In addition, they would have doubted, given the evidence of ingroup favoritism and ethnic war, that such a large migration could have peaceful consequences.

In the 1930s, the early 20th century intellectual consensus regarding the hereditary sources of group differences came into question, and by the 1950's it had been largely abandoned in favor of the view that all human differences resulted from a variety of environmental factors and were, in fact, the product of learning. This was not so much the result of new evidence, but rather a shift in sentiment among scientists.[28] This change reflected new social attitudes among American social scientists about the place of blacks in American society. It also reflected widespread political concern in Europe and America about the rise of the Nazi party, and, in particular, the apparent popular appeal of its racial doctrines. The new consensus among social scientists that arose in the prewar years became nearly unanimous among educated people in the 1960s and remains so to this day. This is so, in spite of the fact that it has been under serious challenge since the 1970s by theoretical advances in evolutionary theory and empirical evidence. Both theory and evidence suggest that genes play a powerful role in shaping human nature and in accounting for human differences, including those between the races. Arthur Jensen's 1969 article arguing for a partially genetic explanation for black-white IQ differences in school performance can be seen, in retrospect, as seminal in this regard.[29] Since then, evidence from evolutionary and developmental psychology, from biology and anthropology, has tended to cast serious doubt on the mid-century consensus that all differences are the result of environmental factors.[30]

In the last decade, developments in population genetics, spurred in part by the mapping of the human genome, have tended to provide further evidence for powerful genetic influences on human biology and psychology.[31] Recent studies have begun to throw into question the long held assumption that evolution, which was generally thought to proceed at a very gradual rate, could not explain differences among human groups during the last 50,000 years when the first modern humans are thought to have migrated out of Africa, since that seemed too short a time for natural selection to produce meaningful differences. Oddly, many of those who so argued readily accepted the argument that all the variation in human skin color and physiognomy were produced in this same brief span of evolutionary time. Recent evidence suggests that, in fact, evolution continues and natural selection does seem to have produced significant differences of relatively recent origin among human populations.[32]

All of which has led reasonable people to ask whether the original rejection of the early twentieth century view of human variation was premature, resting as it did more on ideological grounds than scientific ones. It has also led reasonable people to ask what, if any, impact this will have on the success of various immigration strategies. Formulating immigration policy in the absence of sound scientific knowledge regarding human differences would be irresponsible in the extreme.

While there has been a great deal of serious scientific work on group differences, the proponents of political correctness have managed to achieve a stranglehold over honest discussion of this research. Some of the most incisive work in the social sciences ranging over a wide range of topics is placed off-limits and treated as heretical. Distinguished scholars and scientists such as Arthur Jensen, Linda Gottfredson, Richard Herrnstein, Charles Murray, and Richard Lynn have all been characterized as racist for their work on intelligence. Similarly demonized has been J. Philippe Rushton for his prolific work on group differences and ethnic conflict, Frank Salter for his work on ethnocentrism and Kevin MacDonald and Albert Lindemann for their groundbreaking work on anti-Semitism. These are but a few of the distinguished scientists and only a small number of the topics they have researched that have been, and continue to be, suppressed. Every one of these scientists has been abused by mainstream social scientists and their work all but ignored by the mainstream media and intellectual elites. Those attempting, for instance, to understand anti-Semitism or racism are accused of condoning those practices. It is reminiscent of the attacks on early medical researchers promoting the use of inoculation as a means of preventing smallpox who were accused of trying to facilitate its spread.[33] Such an assertion was preposterous at the time. On similar grounds, it is equally preposterous to condemn scientists studying racism with the claim they are really trying to promote it.

A consequence of this censorship is that public policy is uninformed by the most significant scientific knowledge about a host of issues and is, in effect, placed in a straitjacket imposed by political correctness. This has led to wasteful and often disastrous policies. Responsible decision-making requires at the minimum a reasonable estimate as to the likely consequences of this or that decision. To act without seeking such information is therefore irresponsible, especially when the consequences could have enormous ramifications for human well-being and societal harmony. And yet the scientific debate surrounding these issues has quite literally been banned in mainstream intellectual circles, on the claim that such debate violates in some serious way the West's democratic ethos.

No one familiar with the research examining the genetic basis of ethnic conflict could possibly have been surprised by the vicious ethnic slaughter which broke out in the wake of the United States' toppling of Saddam Hussein. No one even marginally familiar with the massive research into the genetics of IQ differences could imagine that ethnic and racial gaps in educational success could be eliminated by government fiat (as is supposed in The No Child Left Behind Act). No one familiar with the powerful relationship between IQ and economic success could have thought that all people, even those with limited and spotty employment history, possessed the human capital to maintain the income required for homeownership.

Physical scientists, until now, have not had to contend with political correctness, but that is changing. The recent completion of the mapping of the human genome and very recent advances in the ability to decode individual genes has led many geneticists, especially those concerned with the genetic components of disease, to explore racial differences. This research has not always been welcomed, even though it promises to lead to better diagnosis of diseases, which are more common in some races, and in better treatments, some of which are more effective in some races than in others.[34]

Bruce Lahn, for instance, a University of Chicago geneticist, analyzed the genetic pattern for two genes implicated in brain size (and perhaps intelligence), taken from individuals of different racial groups. His research indicated that one of these genes was common among people from Asia and Europe, but not among people from Africa, and seems to have arisen about 40,000 years ago. This is roughly within the time frame during which the first modern humans are thought to have appeared in Europe. The other gene he isolated occurs mainly in people from Europe and the Middle East and was thought to have arisen about 6,000 years ago. Lahn speculated that the first may have been selected for conditions in northern latitudes and the second may have been the product of, or the explanation for, large-scale agriculture and the rise of early civilizations. These changes imply quite recent evolutionary developments. Other researchers have discovered similar, quite recent, changes.[35] The clear implication of the research is that these may be among those many genes thought to influence the various differences among the three large racial groups found in Africa, Asia, and Europe.

This point was not lost on Lahn's colleagues, and many of them found reason to object to his work. As a consequence of many personal attacks, Dr. Lahn abandoned the study of brain differences.[36] In explaining the hostility Lahn encountered, Harvard evolutionary psychologist Steven Pinker notes that findings of a genetic basis for racial differences would put into question "the assumption that all group-wide social differences (e.g., in crime, poverty, and health) are caused by discrimination or a rigged economic system. It would be an enormous challenge to the unspoken consensus of mainstream left-of-center politics during the past fifty years..."[37] Part of that mainstream consensus is support for very liberal immigration policies, especially from third world countries. Evidence of important group differences might require serious reconsideration of those immigration policies that are supported almost unanimously by intellectuals in all Western countries. This sort of ostracism of those who dissent on this issue is not practiced only by those on the left. Kevin Lamb was summarily fired from his job as managing editor of the conservative newsweekly *Human Events* when it was discovered that he was writing for, and editing in his free time, *The Occidental Quarterly*, a journal "that specializes in research and analysis on issues involving race, ethnicity, politics and culture..." He was fired because the journal in question was termed "white supremacist" since it promotes the idea that Western Civilization is a product of the unique nature of European peoples.[38]

But if Pinker is correct, then the argument about group differences is really an ideological disagreement and not a scientific one. Scientific debate requires at the very least an impartial examination of theory and fact and civil discourse among participants, and this has certainly not been the case in the debate over group differences and immigration policy. Immigration advocates in all Western societies have attempted to shut down debate on the issue, rather than engage in it.

In American academic circles and in elite circles generally, it is clearly forbidden to discuss group differences without putting oneself or one's career in jeopardy. Lawrence Summers, hardly a right-wing ideologue, was forced to resign as president of Harvard University for suggesting a possible genetic explanation for differences in scientific achievement between the sexes. His suggestion is hardly exceptional, and, in fact, is based on well-established research that has been well known for years. One of the best-known explanations is that most characteristics are more widely distributed among men than among women; i.e., there are more males than females at the extreme tails, top and bottom, of the bell curve. Therefore, it is perfectly reasonable to argue that among those scientists who have made extraordinary contributions, there are likely to be more men than women.[39] Similarly, those who advanced a genetic explanation for group differences in social and economic success, such as Richard Herrnstein and Charles Murray, have been almost completely marginalized in elite academic circles. Christopher Brand, a highly respected British scholar, published a book on group IQ differences that produced such uproar among his critics that his publishers canceled his contract and went so far as to recall all the books it had already distributed to bookstores.[40] He was subsequently dismissed from his position at Edinburg University, although the university eventually settled with him for unlawful dismissal. Similar tales are legion.

The case of Nobel Prize geneticist James Watson, arguably the preeminent living scientist, is particularly troubling. In a long interview published in the *London Sunday Times,* Watson commented on Western policies with respect to Africa that "are based on the fact that their intelligence is the same as ours—whereas all the testing says not really." Further, "there is no firm reason to anticipate that the intellectual capacities of people geographically separated in their evolution should prove to have evolved identically. Our wanting to preserve equal powers of reason as some universal human heritage of humanity will not be enough to make it so." For these perfectly defensible statements (they are supported by overwhelming scientific evidence) he was widely vilified and relieved of his duties at the research laboratory that was largely his own creation.[41]

This narrow-minded denigrating of differing scientific views has become so widespread that otherwise thoughtful scholars find themselves taking positions that are close to absurd. A case in point is Jared Diamond, who in his widely acclaimed book, *Guns, Germs and Steel*, argues that all societal differences can be explained in terms of resources and geography, are, in others words environmentally determined. While this is hardly a novel view, Diamond introduces material that is certainly valuable to the argument. In an earlier time such a scholar would have welcomed thoughtful challenges as an opportunity to clarify and strengthen his argument. In fact, there is a large body of scholarly work by accomplished scientists which challenges Diamond's position and suggests that, while environmental factors are important, so, too, are genetic factors. For instance, the relationship between IQ and wealth is well established for intrasocietal differences, and a strong case has been made that IQ has an important impact on income differences between societies.[42]

Diamond does not discuss this literature or attempt to refute it. The word "intelligence" does not even appear in the index of his book, and he cites none of the prominent scientists who have argued that genes may play a prominent role in human social organization. In fact, he makes the rather preposterous claim, contradicted by overwhelming scientific evidence that "'Stone Age' peoples are on average probably more intelligent, not less intelligent, than industrialized peoples."

He gives as evidence the most cursory anecdotal stories based on his personal encounters with individuals. Those who disagree are labeled loathsome and racist.[43] In other words, anyone who questions Diamond's politically correct view is simply dismissed *ad hominem.*

In an early chapter of *Guns, Germs and Steel,* Diamond describes the relative ease with which a few hundred Spanish soldiers overcame an army of tens of thousands of Inca warriors. The most important element, by all accounts, in the conquest of the Americas by Europeans was the inexperience of Amerindians with European diseases. This is a topic taken up in a later section. But the initial astounding success of the European invaders, at least in the case discussed by Diamond, did not depend on that factor. Diamond attributes much of that success to the fact that the Spaniards were armed with steel and rode into battle on well-trained horses, while the Incas fought mainly with simple stone weapons and on foot. He explains this phenomenon as a result of the superior technology, social organization, and knowledge that the Europeans were able to acquire during their much longer history of agriculture. But Diamond rejects, out of hand, the idea that during those thousands of years during which Europeans lived in agricultural empires, they may have evolved in somewhat different ways from people still living as hunters and gatherers, or who like the Incas, had only recently emerged from that way of life. Could such differences, perhaps, help to explain the extraordinary success of the Spaniards?

The disparagement of research on human differences does not merely result in social disapproval and ostracism. It can also result in the denial of both promotion and tenure to scholars by their colleagues who may disapprove of their research. For instance, all universities that receive government funding must establish "Institutional Review Boards" to oversee and approve any research involving human subjects. Not surprisingly, these faculty boards are not above imposing their ideological views on the approval process.[44] It behooves a young scholar who must do research to win tenure and promotion to stick to "approved" areas. One consequence is that much valuable research never gets done.

In a truly extraordinary paper reviewing the enormous strides made in neuroscience (in brain-imaging and in genetic mapping) tying IQ to clearly heritable brain structures, scientists Jeremy Gray and Paul Thompson suggest that racial differences in brain anatomy and function are likely to emerge in future research. They find this possibility so disturbing that they suggest that research in this area should be very carefully planned and executed. In fact, the restrictions they recommend are so onerous as to make such research all but impossible to perform. In not so subtle terms they seem to be suggesting that the information widely available to knowledgeable scientists should be carefully monitored lest it get into the "wrong" hands.[45]

The attacks on those engaged in controversial work are so intense as to impose a debilitating self-censorship on the part of scientists. Some like Lahn merely move on to other things. Many simply avoid controversial topics. And sometimes important research is consciously suppressed if it is inconsistent with politically correct wisdom. A particularly disturbing case is the work of Harvard Political Scientist Robert Putnam, a supporter of mass immigration as "inevitable but also desirable, a proven asset in terms of creativity and economic growth." His highly regarded book, *Bowling Alone,* emphasized the significance of interpersonal trust in promoting what he called *social capital* (as a corollary of *human capital*) for economic growth. His work has been extremely influential among policy makers and leaders in both the United States and England, especially in regard to immigration policy.[46]

Putnam, beginning in 2000, headed a team that surveyed approximately 30,000 individuals in 43 communities across the United States. The study was an attempt to assess the effects of ethnic diversity on communal trust and social capital. His group found that, contrary to expectations, greater ethnic and racial diversity had serious negative consequences for communities (the research will be discussed in a later chapter) and drastically reduced the trust important to the economic and social well-being of communities. The first report of these results was made in a speech given in Scandinavia in 2006, some five years after the project had been completed. To date, this research has yet to be published in a scientific journal, where its detailed results and methods can be examined by other scientists. In effect, this extremely important work, especially in its implications for immigration policy, was suppressed for at least five years.[47] In explaining this delay, Putnam told the *Financial Times* that he was hoping to find proposals to compensate for the negative effects of diversity, saying it "would have been irresponsible to publish without that."[48] His expressed concern was, according to *The Guardian,* that his research "could be seized upon by right-wing politicians hostile to immigration."[49] The withholding of this information was a serious and egregious breach of scientific integrity, which requires that important results be made public, especially if they disconfirm the researcher's initial hypothesis. It is made even worse by Putnam's considerable influence among policy makers and the substantial support of his work by important tax-exempt foundations.[50]

In America social research conflicting with politically correct thinking is suppressed; in Europe it is criminalized. If American researchers are confronted by social sanctions and institutional restraints in questioning the doctrine of group equality or the positive value of diversity, violators in European countries in which there are no constitutional guarantees of free speech face legal, even criminal, sanctions. Rather than respond to the critics of multiculturalism and mass immigration, European governments resort to increasingly aggressive attempts to silence them. They do so with totally unjustified and scurrilous claims that government critics are motivated by mean-spirited, racist, and xenophobic concerns. The EU has put in place a large propaganda campaign to stamp out "Islamophobia." Under the purported desire to reduce prejudice and racism, some European governments have passed increasingly stringent hate-speech codes governed by human rights commissions that harass critics and threaten them with criminal sanctions. These commissions actively support civil rights and "anti-racist" organizations that threaten criminal and civil suits against individuals who criticize immigration policy.

The leaders of the British National Party, for instance, a party that opposes large-scale immigration, were put on trial merely for campaigning on their party's platform. The pretext for their prosecution was that they were trying to promote hatred of immigrants and racial minorities, but any fair reading of what they said made clear the charges were merely attempts to silence and outlaw the party.[51] Similarly, the separatist and anti-immigration party in Belgium, the *Vlaams Blok* (The Flemish Block), the largest party in Belgium, was outlawed because, in the view of the Belgian election commission, to oppose immigration is, by definition, criminally racist and therefore outside the range of legitimate politics.[52] The party reconstituted itself as the *Vlaams Belang* (The Flemish Interest) and remains one of the largest parties in Belgium and is still under legal assault. In 2000, the Austrian people gave Jorg Haider's Freedom Party 27% of the vote largely because of its anti-immigration stance, and it formed a ruling coalition with the Social Democratic party that had obtained 33% of the vote. All the EU nations issued statements condemning the Austrian people's support of a xenophobic and racist party. They issued a statement that "they would 'not promote or accept any bilateral official contacts at a political level' with any Austrian government that includes the Freedom Party."[53] In other words, if people freely elect leaders who oppose mass immigration they can expect their country to be vilified and boycotted by EU member states. Such actions completely vitiate democratic debate about immigration policy.

Geert Wilders, leader of the immigration restrictionist Dutch Freedom Party, (PVV), is being prosecuted for "inciting hatred against Muslims" after the Amsterdam Court of Appeals ruled that his prosecution should be pursued; he could be imprisoned if found guilty. The charge is based on the fact that he made a 15 minute film entitled Fitna which features footage of inflammatory speeches by Muslim clerics, quotations from the Koran interspersed with images of terrorists' acts such as the destruction of the World Trade Center, a deadly bus bombing in England, and an equally deadly train bombing in Spain.[54] While it warns of the threat of fanatical Islam, it does not advocate, in any way, violent action against individual Muslims. The reader can form his own opinion by viewing it online at the Google website and other places.[55] An opinion poll conducted in late February 2009 found that his party would, if elections were conducted at the time, be the largest party in the Netherlands, in large measure due to public disapproval of his prosecution.[56]

Similar attacks on less prominent figures are a constant threat to people who disagree with EU policies on immigration. In addition, there is a totalitarian campaign to punish dissidents with the loss of employment. Large numbers of people have lost their jobs merely for being members of the British National Party (BNP), a perfectly legitimate and legal political party. The most notorious example was that of the English National Ballet's prima ballerina Simone Clarke. When her membership in the party was disclosed, her performances were disrupted by "anti-Fascist" protesters and she was forced to leave the ballet company. Rather than having the protesters forcibly removed and arrested if they persisted, thereby supporting the political freedom of their talented star, the ballet company simply abandoned her. It is hard to imagine an aspiring artist or academic risking his career by uttering incorrect views on immigration or joining with any group opposing government policy in this area.[57]

When a conservative Member of Parliament, Baroness Warsi, raised concerns about immigration, she was denounced as "pandering to the BNP." The charge was patently ridiculous. Warsi is a Muslim of Asian ancestry and a founding member of *Operation Black Vote*. As A. Miller correctly observes, "By raising an issue of importance to the majority of British citizens (including non-white citizens) she had joined the league of 'Fascists.'" This attack was "a clear threat to her position. And, by extension, it was a threat to the livelihood of any dissenter to the prevailing, and increasingly stifling political ideology." Such actions, actively supported by the government, create a "climate of fear and resentment among the general public."[58]

But that appears to be the point. Immigration policy is remarkably similar in all Western countries in its encouragement of large-scale Third-World immigration, while at the same time, in all countries, the native population, by wide majorities, opposes those policies. In England, for instance, some 75% of the population believes that laws on immigration should be much tougher or immigration stopped altogether. Only 6% thought laws should be more lenient. In addition, when asked if their government was in control of immigration, fully 82% thought that it was not. Furthermore, 80% thought their leaders were misleading them about the magnitude and costs of immigration.[59]

Even respected scholars who publish on the genetics of racial differences are liable to state prosecution in countries like Canada that lack free-speech protections. J. Philippe Rushton was investigated by the Ontario police for possible prosecution for a paper he presented on racial differences at an academic conference in 1989. According to Jonathan Rauch, writing in Reason magazine, the police "launched a six-month investigation of Rushton under Canada's hate-speech prohibition. They questioned his colleagues, demanded tapes of his debates and media appearances, and so on." If prosecuted and convicted, Rushton might have been imprisoned for two years for "using questionable source data." Rauch explains "In the end, the attorney general decided not to prosecute and settled for denouncing Rushton's ideas as 'loony.'"[60]

Similar repressive measures are common in other countries where authors who express unapproved views are liable to suppression by government human rights commissions and, in addition, can be sued for libel by offended parties. A particularly notorious case involved Mark Steyn, (a Canadian author who resides in the United States) who published a best-selling book *America Alone,* which questioned the wisdom of large-scale Muslim immigration to western countries. An excerpt from that book was published in *Mclean's,* the most widely read news magazine in Canada, the result of which was that a number of Canadian Human Rights Commissions charged him with using language "likely to expose a person or persons to hatred or contempt," and called for censorship of his work. Steyn and *Mclean's* were required to incur the expense of defending themselves, which came to hundreds of thousands of dollars, or acquiesce in what were obvious attempts to suppress free speech on the immigration issue. The group that filed the complaint, the Canadian Islamic Congress, incurred no such expense since, once the complaint was accepted, the Canadian Government covered all costs of the prosecution. A similar complaint was filed with the Ontario Human Rights Commission against Ezra Levant who published the Danish Mohammad cartoons in his magazine, *The Western Standard.* The complaint was brought by a Muslim Cleric and by the Edmonton Council of Muslim Communities. The Cleric eventually dropped the charge, but as Levant explained, "he saddled the taxpayers with a half million dollars in costs and me with almost a hundred grand." Levant is still being legally pursued by the Edmonton group.[61]

It is not merely government human rights commissions that can harass authors and repress free speech, but individuals pursuing libel claims can also do so, and a number of particularly egregious cases have taken place in Britain. A book, *Alms for Jihad*, by American authors Robert O. Collins and J. Millard Burr, dealt with funding for terrorist activities by businesses and charities associated with the Saudi Banker, Khalid bin Mahfouz. When Mahfouz threatened to sue for libel, the publisher of the book, Cambridge University Press, agreed not only to "pulp the book, but also issue a public apology, payment of substantial damages, legal fees, and a pledge to contact libraries worldwide with a request that they remove *Alms for Jihad* from their shelves."[62] The authors of the book protested these actions and defended their scholarship, refused to apologize and wished to defend their work in court—all to no avail. The reason for the truly incredible capitulation by Cambridge University Press is that British libel law is extremely favorable to complainants and some judges have been quite harsh in their treatment of defendants. Stanley Kurtz reports that as many as 36 books "containing passing mentions of

Mahfouz's financial activities have been suppressed by the threat or the reality of British libel suits."[63]

A case in point involved Rachel Ehrenfeld's book *Funding Evil* in which she contended that Mr. Mahfouz was involved in the funding of Hamas and Al Qaeda. Bin Mahfouz sued in Britain for libel. The Judge in this case was Sir David Eady, who handles many such suits and has a reputation of ruling in favor of complainants.[64] Even though Ehrenfeld is an American and the book was published in America, the British court ruled that the suit could be heard in their court since it had been purchased online in Britain. In the event, Judge Eady found for bin Mafouz and ordered Ehrenfeld to apologize, "retract, pay hundreds of thousands of dollars in damages, and destroy all copies of her book." The idea that a foreign complainant, in this case a Saudi national, could bring suit against another foreigner, in this case an American author, has earned Britain the honor as the prime destination for *libel-tourists* such as bin Mahfouz.[65] It is interesting that it has recently come to light that French, British and American intelligence agencies had documentation that bin Moufouz "was one of the architects of a banking scheme constructed for the benefit of Osama bin Laden."[66] *The Washington Times* makes the point that it was this sort of evidence upon which Ehrenfeld based her case. But since, under British law, the burden of proof rests with the defendant in libel cases she was required to demonstrate the veracity of such evidence. How does one establish the truth of government intelligence agency reports? Does not reliance on such reports demonstrate good faith scholarship and the absence of deception with the intent to defame?[67] Ehrenfeld did not comply with the court's ruling, but is now unable to travel or do research in England because of it.

The number of similar cases is legion. Before her death as an exile in New York City, the famous journalist Oriana Fallaci was being sued in France, Italy, Switzerland, and other countries by groups attempting to suppress her negative view of Islam in the West.[68] Former film star and animal-rights activist Brigitte Bardot was fined 5,000 Euros in 2004 for for statements opposing the Islamization of France in her best-selling book *A Cry in the Silence*. The charges were brought by a French anti-racism organization and the League for Human Rights. According to the BBC, she had "previous convictions for inciting racial violence after criticizing in print the Muslim practice of slaughtering sheep."[69] In June of

2008 she was again convicted of racism and fined 15,000 Euros and ordered to pay 1,000 Euros to the anti-racist groups that brought the charges. Her crime was commenting in a letter in 2006 to interior minister, Nicolas Sarkozy, that she was "tired of being led by the nose by this population that is trying to destroy us, destroying our country by imposing its acts." The acts she was talking about were the slaughtering of sheep during the Muslim feast of Aid el-Kebir.[70]

Many of these hate crime laws were originally designed to silence those who denied the extent of the Holocaust, such as David Irving, who was imprisoned in Austria for his claim that the number of Jewish deaths was greatly exaggerated. The consequence of criminalizing holocaust denial was to open the door for various groups to prevent insults to their beliefs. The wholesale abandonment of freedom of speech that currently limits debate in most European countries seems a very high price to pay to silence a renegade World War II scholar whom few people took seriously in any case.[71]

The absurdity of the prosecution of Bardot for saying what is, in fact, a widespread opinion among Frenchmen, makes it easy to dismiss the seriousness of such charges, but as the previous cases indicate, they dramatically reduce the freedom to criticize government policies, especially in regard to the immigration of large numbers of people from non-European ethnic groups, cultures and races.

Mark Steyn explains the cumulative effects of these libel and antiracism laws. If a writer approaches a publisher with a book criticizing immigration, he will be reminded that the book cannot be sold in Canada. "So there goes ten percent of the North American market. And we won't be able to license a British edition since some big shot Saudi prince will sue in a London court. And we won't be able to sell French and German translation rights because it runs afoul of European xenophobia legislation." The consequence is that such a book will never reach the public, as it may not make economic sense to publish it.[72]

These attacks on the critics of immigration as promoting "hate" are ludicrously hypocritical. While major news outlets regularly report on fiery sermons by Muslim Imams condemning homosexuals, Christians, and Jews, and proclaiming the legitimacy of violent Jihad against non-Muslim infidels, almost all have been ignored by the authorities even though they clearly violate European hate-speech laws.

A remarkable example is the case of the British television Channel 4 that aired a documentary entitled *Undercover Mosque* in January 2007. In the program, preachers and teachers were shown espousing extreme Muslim doctrines such as the killing of homosexuals and apostates who leave the Muslim faith to adopt another religion. Rhetoric included, "Take that homosexual and throw him off a mountain" and "whoever changes his religion from al-Islam to anything else—kil him!"[73] It also showed a teacher arguing for the inferiority of women and the need to force them to wear the traditional veil, using violent means if necessary. The West Midlands police, in whose jurisdiction the mosques were filmed, attacked the broadcaster, Channel 4, of the program rather than the clerics preaching violence against innocent Britons. The police and the Crown Prosecution Service issued a press release claiming the program had misrepresented the views of the clerics by heavy editing to give them a more sinister meaning, and reported the television station to the broadcasting regulator, Ofcam, for possible sanctions. When Channel 4 sued the police for libel, the police were forced to issue a public apology admitting they had been wrong. It seems the police had spent 14,000 British Pounds in an investigation, initially of the clerics depicted, but then of the television station to determine whether the program directors should be prosecuted for stirring up racial hatred. In the legal settlement with Channel 4, the police agreed to pay 100,000 British Pounds in damages and legal fees. What this says about the priorities of British authorities needs no elaboration.[74]

All of which raises the question that must baffle any thoughtful observer. Why have governments taken a position so contrary to the expressed wishes of the overwhelming majority of their citizens, and engaged in clearly undemocratic attacks on their critics, all in defense of a policy that has so few benefits and so many tangible costs? Crime rates in almost all Western countries have risen dramatically in recent years, largely due to the unassimilated children and grandchildren of immigrants. In many non-European ethnic communities, welfare dependency, unemployment, and school failure are significantly higher than they are among the native Europeans. Adding to the burden of immigration are the increasingly costly measures taken to prevent terrorist attacks, virtually all of which are undertaken by Muslim immigrants or their European-born children.

To counter the concerns of citizens about these real costs, governments make the claim that immigration is needed to bolster the social security needs of an aging European population. But this claim has been shown to be false, since many immigrants are older individuals, often the parents of younger immigrants, who are admitted under family unification provisions. Many of these individuals are unemployable due to their age and lack of fluency in the language of their host country. In addition, large numbers of immigrants and their children occupy the lowest economic levels and have high rates of unemployment and welfare dependency. The net result is that immigration increases to a relatively small degree the number of workers who contribute to retirement funds, but this hardly compensates for the government expenditures that immigrants require.

The C. D. Howe Institute, a highly respected Canadian think tank, published an analysis of the extent to which immigration can alter the age structure of Canada's population. The authors of the report, Yvan Guillemette and William Robson, conclude that "no conceivable amount of immigration with an age profile such as Canada currently experiences can significantly affect the coming shift in the ratio of older to working-age Canadians." They point out that even the attempt to solve the problem by admitting only a much younger immigrant population would not be effective because "the number of young people Canada would have to attract is preposterously large…" They conclude, "Whatever the benefits of immigration to Canada's economy and society…immigration cannot relieve Canada of the challenges of an aging population."[75]

The failure of governments to respond in coherent ways to the legitimate concerns of their citizens invites a reasonable skepticism that there may be more nefarious reasons for their immigration policies than those given. It could, of course, be the simple arrogance of an elite class that has completely lost touch with the common man and that believes itself so superior as to justify completely ignoring his concerns. Or perhaps they simply do not care what impact their policies have on the people and societies they control. How else to explain the fact that all Western societies have refused to tighten immigration controls and therefore have allowed large numbers of potentially hostile Muslims into their midst? With all the supposed concern about terrorism, and all the indignities imposed on common citizens for security reasons, the authorities refuse to take the one step which would greatly reduce the threat of terrorist attacks, namely, to institute a more selective immigration policy, with special scrutiny given to Muslim men from countries known to harbor citizens hostile to the West.

In most European countries and in many areas of the United States, whole communities have been transformed and, in many cases, immigrants of very different habits and social patterns have displaced the indigenous population. Almost all polls show that people are extremely concerned by these changes. A poll conducted by the Pew Foundation in 47 countries involving interviews with more than 45,000 people found overwhelming majorities in favor of further restrictions and controls over immigration. These opinions are not limited to people in the West, but are just as strong, and in many cases stronger, in the countries of Asia, Africa, South America, and the Middle East as they are in Europe and the North America. These views are more influenced by concerns with the preservation of native cultures than with attitudes toward immigrants. Significant majorities of the citizens of England and France, for instance, express positive attitudes toward immigrants from Third World Countries. Similarly, in Canada and the United States, majorities of citizens express positive attitudes toward immigrants from Latin America and Asia. Nevertheless, citizens of these countries favor further restrictions on immigration by majorities of 75% in England, 68% in France, 62% in Canada and 75% in the United States. In most Western countries, therefore, these results suggest that concern with immigration is not, as is so often charged, based in xenophobia, but rather a concern that the pace of immigration poses a threat to native folkways.[76]

It is worth noting that virtually every war America has fought during the twentieth century has been justified in part to "preserve the American way of life." Were the presidents and generals who directed those wars acting out of mean-spirited xenophobia? Were the soldiers who died in those efforts equally motivated by a fear and hatred of foreigners? These questions require no answer. Yet common citizens who believe that an influx of large numbers of immigrants into a community threatens their traditional way of life, a perfectly rational belief, are maligned for their "intolerance."

On the basis of such false charges, the overwhelming desires of the populations of the West have been ignored and have utterly no influence upon elite opinion that supports even more expansive immigration, and upon political leaders who implement immigration policies totally at variance with the wishes of their populations. Why is this happening and why it is happening now?

The Convergence of Left and Right on Mass Immigration

The main reason appears to be that the traditional political battle lines in western nations between left and right are not applicable to issues of multiculturalism and immigration. The left-right dichotomy is usually defined, at least in the sphere of economics, as pitting the interests of large industrialists and financiers against those of workers or, more simply, between the haves and the have-nots. This is especially clear in Europe, with those on the left quite openly identifying themselves as socialists, and those on the right openly speaking for business interests. In addition, the left and right have usually split between those favoring national self-interest (the right) and those who favor an international perspective (the left). Academicians have in general, at least in recent decades, generally aligned themselves with the left. In the case of the doctrine of multiculturalism and mass immigration, however, the political leaders of both the left and the right, and virtually all academicians, are unanimous in their support. The consequence is that the members of the general public, who are most affected by immigration, have no parties to represent their interests and are left with a powerful sense of disenfranchisement for the simple reason that on issues of immigration they are, in fact, disenfranchised. A case in point is the 2008 United States Presidential elections, where both nominees favored even more liberalized immigration policies than those then in existence, and this in spite of the overwhelming opposition to these policies by the electorate.

In the age of globalized industry and markets, multinational enterprises have a vested interest in reducing the significance of national borders and restraints on trade and on the movement of workers. Many of the advanced industries run by global corporations have matured to the point where it is extremely difficult for them to achieve greater efficiencies through expansion and mechanization. These corporations compete fiercely on a global scale and are run by elites whose remuneration is tied directly to their profitability, which in turn drives their stock prices. The most expedient means, therefore, for corporate leaders in mature industries to earn greater financial rewards is to drive up profits by driving down wages. This they have done by relocating factories and jobs through off shoring to places with much lower standards of living. Many industries, however, such as the hotel and restaurant trades, agriculture, janitorial and landscaping services, meat-packing, the building industry, to name but a few, can most easily effect productivity gains from the importation of cheap labor through legal and illegal immigration from third world countries. Of course, those who hold securities in these firms, in America and in the world at large, share in the benefits of these productivity gains.

Since these approaches to lowering labor costs have become common practice, the wages of chief executives have skyrocketed. Lou Dobbs reports that CEO salaries went from "being forty-two times that of the average blue-collar worker's pay in 1980..." to "431 to 1..." today. And the practice of rewarding CEOs with stock options increases their compensation as their company's stock price improves.[77] At the same time the average income of middle-aged men has remained stagnant or actually declined in real, noninflationary terms.[78] Much of the reason is increased competition from Hispanic, largely immigrant, low-wage workers. Noted economist Edwin S. Rubenstein, research director for the Hudson Institute, writing in October of 2008 makes the point that "since January 2001 Hispanic employment has increased by 4,413,000, or 27.4 percent, while non-Hispanic employment grew by 3,066,000, or 2.5 percent. He notes that even the loss of more than a million jobs in the United States has not "staunched the rate at which Hispanics are displacing non-Hispanics in the workforce."[79]

Clearly the people in managerial positions have powerful incentives to lobby government for policies on immigration that enable them to improve the bottom lines of their corporations. Dobbs reports that in 1968 there were 68 lobbyists in Washington, but today they number 34,000. According to Dobbs, from "1998 to 2004 lobbyists spent nearly 13 billion dollars to not only influence legislation, but in many cases to write the language of the laws and regulations they support."[80] Not surprisingly, many of these dollars are spent to influence Congress to increase legal immigration and to ignore illegal immigration, and Congress has clearly obliged them.

Large-scale, Third-World immigration to Western nations clearly puts downward pressure on working-class wages in the West, as the law of supply and demand requires. While it is clear why corporations should support liberal immigration policies, why should leftists, who claim to speak for the workingman? To answer that question requires a brief digression to examine the way in which Marxist thought has been transformed in recent years so as to embrace multicultural doctrine and mass immigration.

Marx defined social life as resulting from the conflict among economic classes, with those in the ruling classes using their favored position to exploit those beneath them. Among the most important tools of that exploitation was the erection of various ideologies to make their behavior appear benign. One of these purported Capitalist ideologies now goes by the name of "meritocracy," which argues that influence and economic benefits are distributed according to the abilities and ambitions of individuals. Marxist thinking attributes such ideas to the "false consciousness" imposed on the masses as a way of justifying their exploitation.

Why this sort of thinking is so popular among intellectual elites is a subject best left for another place, but more than a few commentators have suggested that its appeal lies in being a sort of secular Christianity, and it is especially appealing to European elites, who in large measure have abandoned traditional religious faith and are often quite hostile to it. In the Christian view, all men are equal in the eyes of God and all are eligible for salvation. In secular Marxism, the equality of all men means that there can be no justification for one man or group to live a more fulfilling life than any other.

A good many things follow from this view. Communism as a social system was one of them. If the dominant class, the owners of industry during Marx's time, in the 19th century, could be overturned and the state run by the exploited class of workers, or proletarians as Marx called them, then a much more just distribution of economic goods could be arranged. This could not be done democratically since the capitalists had the resources to control the political process and would never allow the workers an honest understanding that would allow them to take action in the political arena. Democracy as it was practiced in Europe was, according to Marxists, only an empty form, a "sham democracy," which perpetuated the rule of the oppressor class. Revolution was therefore necessary to remove the capitalist rulers, and once removed the masses would have to undergo massive reeducation to remove the false understandings under which they labored. In the short run, this would require dictatorial control by a revolutionary cadre, but in time, would end in a utopian situation where the state would wither away for lack of any important function.

Part of the reeducation of the masses would be to reshape them into new men, men lacking the material selfishness which capitalism inspired. People had to be restored to their basic communal nature that existed in an earlier time and where all goods were shared equally, according to the dictum "from each according to his abilities, to each according to his needs." This is one of the reasons the state will "wither away," it will become unnecessary since without human greed and selfishness, the need for police would disappear. Only people with mental deficiencies would commit crime, and they could be treated in mental hospitals, not punished in jails.

Furthermore, in this view, states would be unnecessary since once Communism became global, the sources of war, namely, the greed of the capitalist classes, would cease to exist and so would the justification of the nation state. A global world economy based on communist principles would therefore be a world of liberty, global equality and fraternity, a peaceful world with abundant resources for all. The vast resources stolen by capitalists in the form of profits and the avoidance of the huge wastes of war would provide more than enough to support all people of the world in reasonable comfort.

This is, of course, an oversimplification and, in brief form, almost a caricature, but it does boil down the essence of Marxist thinking on human equality, on economic motivation, on the purposes of education, on the malleability of human nature, and on the sources of war and crime. It is not hard to understand why people would find this philosophy appealing, as did a great many well-educated people all over the world.

Those who disagreed with Marx did so on the grounds that, firstly, his portrayal of human nature as completely malleable was simply false; they pointed to the fact that trying to remake men in the Marxist vision wherever it was tried required the most brutal totalitarian methods. A second argument is that the Marxist vision of human equality cannot be squared with the Western vision of human freedom. The reason is straightforward. People who are free to use their talents to pursue their own self-defined ends will end up in very different circumstances, for the simple fact that people differ markedly in their talents and motives. Critics of Marx also disagreed with his utopian assessment of human fraternity and doubted that his vision of a peaceful world under benevolent leaders could ever be attained.

While most thoughtful observers were well aware of the malfunctioning of the Soviet Union, its collapse made glaringly clear the utopian nature of Marxism as applied to the economic sphere. People simply could not be made to work as hard for the good of all as they would for themselves and their own families. People who could not, because of communist rules, benefit themselves by harder work, simply did not work very hard. In time the Soviet Union fell further and further behind the West in productivity and wealth. Furthermore, the predicted withering away of the state under communism did not, in fact, transpire. Rather, all Communist states required massive, and often brutal, repression of their people and nowhere tolerated democracy or freedom of expression.

No one should be deluded, however, into thinking that the failure of Communism as an economic and political system has discredited Marxist thinking among its former sympathizers. It has certainly not done so among a great many of the intellectuals in America or Europe's dominant political class. Multiculturalism, for instance, is clearly an outgrowth of Marxist thinking, with ethnic groups replacing economic classes as the primary actors in the conflict that defines modern societies. Whites of European stock are the oppressor class, and the various less fortunate racial and ethnic groups are the exploited classes. Another important product of Marxist thinking is its disparagement of nationalism and its promotion of global internationalism. It is, perhaps, the driving idea behind the formation of a political European Union, as opposed to a merely economic common market. And it certainly explains the faith of the left in world organizations such as the UN and the World Court. It also explains the left's embrace of large-scale Third-World immigration to the industrial democracies, which serves to dilute white European influence and to reduce distinctions among nation states.[81]

According to Daniel Mahoney, many of these ideas originated with the writings of influential French left-wing thinkers such as Foucault, Derrida, and Lacan who sought to "subvert—to deconstruct—traditional wisdom and established social institutions. Egalitarian moralism coexisted with a fanatical repudiation of the idea of the Truth…"

Further, these ideas created a "new authoritarianism…more illiberal than anything found in the old order since it showed limitless contempt for habits, practices and judgments that had long served to support civilized human existence."[82] Mahoney quotes Dominique Schnapper, writing in the French journal *Commentaire* which was founded by her illustrious father, Raymond Aron. According to Schnapper such thinking has transformed "the democratic principle of human and civic equality...into a passion for equality that perceives every distinction...as discriminatory, every difference as inegalitarian, every inequality as inequitable."[83] This reflects Aristotle's assertion that the corruption of democracy results when people falsely believe that people "who are equal in any respect are equal in all respects; because men are equally free, they claim to be absolutely equal."[84]

The attachment of the many intellectuals to this view explains their support for programs of international multiculturalism that deny any difference between people and culture. It also explains their concern for the world's oppressed minorities, a concern that trumps their concern for their own countrymen. To favor one's own over others is viewed as a base chauvinism. Therefore, the inconsistency of supporting mass immigration while at the same time claiming a concern for the working poor disappears if one defines the working poor in international terms, rather than in chauvinistic, national ones. Put in other terms, a true Marxist should show a concern for all the struggling masses of mankind; to be more concerned for your own working classes is a retrograde nationalism, best eschewed. This change of focus explains, in large measure, the left's abandonment of the workingman and joining with corporate interests on the issue of immigration. It is, of course, also the case that the parties of the left increase their power by importing Third-World immigrants who overwhelmingly become constituents of those parties. The net result is that people who oppose massive immigration have no place to turn for support on either the right or the left of the political spectrum.

The Role of Philanthropic Foundations

In order to fully understand the convergence of opinion among elites, it is essential to understand the role that major philanthropic foundations, such as the Ford and Carnegie Foundations, have played in the immigration debate and their role in the promotion of the doctrine of multiculturalism. These foundations have very large endowments, in the billions of dollars, and by targeting funds to selective causes they can have far-reaching effects. The enormous resurces of foundations allow them to approach problems on many levels. They fund the research of individual scholars, set up think tanks, and support academic programs in order to muster expertise and evidence for dealing with issues of concern to them. They fund the publication of journals and books, promote the production of radio and television presentations, and sponsor educational programs of all sorts in order to influence public opinion. Perhaps most important, they fund organizations and advocacy groups that represent their views on issues. These satellite organizations are able to influence political policy through appearances at legislative hearings, by direct lobbying of legislators, and political actions of various sorts. The large foundations have a global reach and can bring an international perspective to issues demanding one and they often host international conferences. To these conferences they invite politicians, business leaders, academics, and scientists. All of these efforts are framed in terms of a disinterested concern with bringing to bear the best information about any question.

A consequence of all these activities, and many others, is that foundations, especially the largest, play a major role in defining what are, and what are not, important issues of public policy and in defining who are, and who are not, reputable contributors to speak to those issues. The people invited to their conferences almost invariably share a concern with the issues addressed and more often than not share a similar worldview. Almost all are highly educated, most are leaders in their fields and most are comfortable financially. Furthermore, the directors of large foundations move freely back and forth from positions in academia, politics, industry, and advocacy groups. They are, in short, the sorts of people almost always identified as *elites*. It is hardly surprising that on a wide range of issues, ranging from global warming to the benefits of mass immigration, there emerges a consensus of opinion accepted by the vast majority of leaders in business, industry, and academia.[85]

The enormous influence of foundations, however, may not always be in disinterested public service, but may reflect, perhaps inadvertently, the interests of those who support the foundations and even more the interests of the bureaucrats who direct them. Joan Roelofs, in her highly informative book, *Foundations and Public Policy: The Mask of Pluralism*, argues that the Carnegie and Rockefeller foundations promoted, early in the 20th century, the ideology of progressivism as a means to counter the growing influence of socialist ideas. According to Roelofs, "progressives gradually transformed notions of class struggle and social classes into 'social problems' and tasks for social scientists." In this way, according to Roelofs, the foundations diverted attention from the injustices of capitalism.[86] The economic problems people confronted could best be dealt with by amelioration rather than revolution.

The Rockefeller and Carnegie foundations created the Social Science Research Council in 1923, according to Roelofs, to "create scientific politics as a tool of political reform, based on integrated social science."[87] In the 1930s, both foundations supported studies in international relations and they also founded the Council on Foreign Relations and the influential journals, *Foreign Affairs* and *Foreign Policy*. In the 1940s the Ford Foundation became active in social science funding; its behavioral science division created the Center for the Advanced Study in the Behavioral Sciences and the important journal *Behavioral Science*. According to Roelofs, Ford spent $23,000,000 for social science projects between 1951 and 1957.[88]

While much of the research supported by foundations in the first half of the 20th century was aimed at the amelioration of social problems, the focus shifted significantly during and after World War II. At the end of that conflict the United States seemed poised to become the dominant world power and in a position to shape the world consistent with American values and interests. The consolidation of Russian Communism in Eastern Europe and triumph of Communism in China put those ambitions in jeopardy. The proliferation of nuclear weaponry meant that the United States could not, at any reasonable cost, hope to counter Communist influence by direct military confrontation.

For that reason, The United States mounted a two-pronged effort to contain Communism and prevent its spread. The first prong involved the economic and military support of governments confronting communist insurgencies. The Vietnamese War was a result of this policy of containment. The second prong involved a major intellectual offensive to demonstrate the superiority of free-market democracy for the nonindustrialized nations of the world. This effort was supported by government grants to academics and a variety of democratic and free-market advocacy groups in America and throughout the world. It was in this effort that foundations played a major, perhaps a decisive role, since they could promote American ideas through honest scholarship and not be viewed as merely mouthing government propaganda. The social sciences at the time were still relatively undeveloped and seemed the logical venue to mount this sort of intellectual offensive. This, in large measure, explains the massive funding of social science research by the Ford and other foundations in the aftermath of World War II. [89]

Part of this effort was an attempt to address the social problems that undermined America's claim to moral superiority, especially the glaring example of discrimination against blacks in the United States. Foundations had already supported groups like the NAACP since early in the century. The Carnegie Foundation, for instance, supported the large-scale research directed by Swedish economist Gunnar Myrdal that resulted in the 1944 publication of *An American Dilemma*.[90] That extremely influential book sought to demonstrate that the various social problems facing black Americans were the direct result of their ill-treatment by white Americans and American institutions. The Ford Foundation's support, to take another case, for the NAACP during the litigation over school desegregation was critical to its success.[91] During the 1960s, spurred in part by the urban riots of that decade, the Ford Foundation, in particular, awarded large grants to various civil rights organizations and related efforts. Quoting Roelofs,

> Millions were given to a variety of civil rights organizations: the National Urban League ($17.8 million between 1966 and 1977); the Southern Regional Council ($8.6 million between 1953 and 1977); and open housing organizations ($11.3 million between 1961 and 1977). Grants for civil rights litigation amounted to $18 million, mostly for the NAACP and the NAACP-LDEF.[92]

The Ford Foundation's efforts were guided, in the main, by the conclusion of *An American Dilemma* that all the difficulties of black Americans were the result of prejudice and discrimination. Research that questioned this view, such as the position that IQ differences played a role, while common among social scientists, was simply not supported by the foundations.

The funding for civil rights organizations continues to the present time and has expanded under the banner of human rights, with generous support of advocacy groups that take positive positions on immigration and multiculturalism. Among the largest of these are the Mexican American Legal Defense and Educational Fund (MALDEF), the National Council of La Raza, the National Lawyers Guild, and the American Civil Liberties Union. People with fairly radical leftwing views staff all of these groups. They all take positions opposing restrictions on immigration, the strengthening of border security, and sanctions on businesses employing illegal aliens. In addition, they advocate liberalized asylum policies. They support the idea that human rights principles require that illegal aliens should be accorded the same constitutional rights as citizens. As will be discussed in later chapters, these groups have played a major role in all legislation dealing with immigration in recent years. In addition, they have taken legal actions to expand the rights of illegal aliens and limit the government's ability to restrict illegal immigration. These positions put them in diametric opposition to the vast majority of Americans, including many Hispanics.[93]

The transformation of the major foundations' support for civil rights for black Americans into support for multicultural policies reflects their elite ethos and sense of mission to deal with the world's ills, especially the plight of the impoverished masses of the world. From this perspective migration is one of the surest ways in which the lives of those impoverished people can be improved, and enlightened opinion, therefore, requires support of their effort to migrate. Migrations are seen as inevitable and, from the multicultural perspective, desirable. The bureaucrats who run foundations see themselves, according to Roelofs, as being a vanguard able to "innovate by breaking through creaky political machinery and unenlightened public opinion." Roelofs quotes James Josephs, president of the umbrella organization, the Council on Foundations:

> [Foundations] have the unique advantage of being somewhat insulated from public opinion and political constituencies. Consequently, grant-makers can take pride in their ability to fund innovative programs and work on the frontlines of social problems without concern for popular opinion or building political mandates.[94]

The Ford Foundation, in particular, seems to have accepted this vanguard role in dealing with immigration, and has been extremely generous in the funding of pro-immigration advocacy groups. Between 1968 and 1992, it gave $18 million to MALDEF and $10 million to La Raza. Between 1983 and 1989, Ford alone gave more than $6.5 million to the ACLU, and it also gave millions to dozens of pro-immigration organizations, both large and small, and it continues to do so.[95]

A small sampling of Ford's activities in the few years since 2006 reveals an extraordinary concern with immigration. It gave $2,675,000 to the Center for Community Change that promotes civic engagement among immigrants. It gave $400,000 to the Florida Immigrant Advocacy Center, $600,000 to the Immigrant legal Resource Center, $1,000,000 to the National Alliance of Latin American and Caribbean Communities, $950,000 to La Raza, $300,000 to MALDEF, $1,100,000 to the National Immigration Forum, $860,000 to the National Immigration Law Center, $460,000 to the Mississippi Immigrants Rights Alliance, and $1,245,000 to the Puerto Rican Legal Defense and Education Fund. In addition, it gave $9,170,000 to the Four Freedoms Fund to strengthen the immigrant rights movement in the United States.[96]

Other foundations also provide support for mass immigration advocacy groups. The Bill and Melinda Gates Foundation (currently the largest American foundation) has, since 2000, given more than $26 million to the National Council of La Raza, largely in support of its Charter Schools program.[97] Contributors to MALDEF and LA Raza include many major foundations and a host of American Corporations. MALDEF raised more than $4.5 million from contributors and special events, and had a total income of almost $6 million in 2004.[98] La Raza had income of more than $42 million in 2007, including $11.5 million in the form of federal grants.[99]

Billionaire George Soros has established and funded the Open Society Institute (OSI) that operates over 30 branches worldwide. The OSI supports multiculturalism and the focus of much of its funding deals with the treatment of minorities and especially the status of Muslims in Europe. It carries on major research programs dealing with immigrant issues. Its legal arm files various lawsuits against governments that, in the Institute's view, violate the provisions of the European Court of Human Rights or the United Nations' Convention on Refugees. OSI reports that The Open Society Institute and the Soros Foundations Network spent more than $417 million in 2006 supporting various programs and initiatives.[100]

It should be stressed that the above organizations are merely the best known; there are many other organizations, academic programs, religious groups, and labor organizations that support current immigration policies. Almost the entire intellectual establishments of the left and right have joined the mass immigration coalition and have adopted multicultural orientations.

It is not merely foundations that contribute to immigration causes; many business and industry organizations spend vast sums in lobbying efforts to oppose the limitation of illegal immigration, reductions in special visas for foreign workers or efforts to require employers to use *E-Verify* to determine the legal status of workers. In a truly eye-opening report, Eric Ruark, senior researcher at FAIR (Federation for American Immigration Reform), has documented the huge funds expended by the hospitality, construction, agricultural, financial, and technology industries, and a host of others that have a clear economic interest in efforts to influence legislation relating to immigration.[101] Ruark documents these efforts related to three bills in the period between 2006 and mid-2008. Two of these bills dealt with "comprehensive" immigration reform.

The provisions of these bills included "an amnesty to the estimated 13 million illegal aliens,...created new unskilled guest worker programs, allowing hundreds of thousands of new aliens to enter the United States labor market each year" and various other provisions such as increasing the number of H-1B guest workers, who possess technical skills, in, for instance, computer programming.[102] The third bill would have eliminated the E-Verify citizenship verification system set up by the Department of Homeland Security that allows employers to check the social security status of potential employees. The system is, by all accounts, easy to use, taking about 5 minutes on the Web and has been used on a voluntary basis "by some 92,000 employers with a 99.5% accuracy rate."[103] It hardly speaks to the seriousness of a Congress that claims a concern with the employment of illegal aliens that this verification system has not been made mandatory. It does, however, clearly demonstrate the power of business lobbies that benefit from inexpensive labor.

In all, $345 million were expended in lobbying efforts for these three bills. The United States Chamber of Commerce spent close to $44 million during this short period of time. The Business Roundtable invested almost $10 million on two of the three bills. The Altria Corporation (formally Philip Morris) expended close to $23 million. (Poor people, often immigrants, smoke more than higher income people). Exxon-Mobil spent over $12 million and IBM expended almost $8 million for lobbying. The Associated Builders and Contractors spent over $4 million, undoubtedly to maintain and expand the supply of labor in their industry. The financial Services Roundtable spent

$7.5 million.[104] (Much of the money made in the subprime mortgage business was made in loans to immigrants, both legal and illegal.)[105] One could go on, but just about every major corporation is on the list. Significant numbers of educational and medical organizations are included. It is interesting that the American Federation of State, Local and Municipal Employees, AFL-CIO, expended more than $21 million to help assure amnesty to some 13 million illegal immigrants.[106] It seems that the AFL-CIO is less concerned with the competition posed by those additional low-wage workers, since few would qualify for such employment, and is more interested with the work that the poor generate for its employees in various federal, state, and local agencies.

Finally, all the major religious groups in America, if they take any position at all on immigration, are uniformly in favor of liberal immigration policies. A perusal of the websites of the United States Conference of Catholic Bishops (USCCB), the Hebrew Immigrant Aid Society (HIAS), supported by a wide variety of Jewish organizations, the United Methodist Committee on Relief (UMCOR) and the Lutheran Immigration and Refugee Service (LIRS), reveals that all take a strong and active role in promoting liberal immigration policies. All support immigration reform, including amnesty for illegal aliens, and oppose most enforcement efforts to curtail illegal immigration. Similar positions are taken by a large number of smaller religious groups. Churches and synagogues with millions of members preach that supporting restrictions on immigration is mean-spirited and inhumane and, for that reason, is inconsistent with the fundamental teachings of their faiths. Since a wide majority of Americans oppose current immigration policy when giving opinions to polling organizations, it is questionable how effective religious preaching is on this issue. However, there can be little question that they tend to stifle open questioning of current immigration trends among congregants, at least in their services, meetings and educational programs.[107]

Opposing all of these powerful forces are the average citizens of all western countries who overwhelmingly voice discontent with current immigration policies, and obviously have little in the way of lobbying clout. The main motivation of the great mass of these people is their desire to preserve their heritage and not see their national borders dissolved and their particular traditions swept aside by massive waves of immigration. The common venue for popular discontent is talk-radio in America and the Internet, internationally. Only a handful of organizations argue in favor of immigration restriction and these are small and have very limited resources. Two of the best known are the Federation for American Immigration Reform (FAIR) and the Center for Immigration Studies (CIS). In 2005, FAIR received some $695,000 and CIS received $395,000 in foundation support. Numbers USA, a similar organization, received all of $75,000 in grants. Almost all of the support for these organizations came from various Scaife family foundations that generally support conservative causes.[108] In the above report dealing with lobbying efforts, only 2% was spent by organizations, such as FAIR, that support restrictions on immigration.

In addition, there are a handful of influential and highly informative American websites that take positions critical of current immigration policies, namely, *Vdare* (vdare.com) run by Peter Brimelow, *American Renaissance* (amren.com) run by Jared Taylor, *View From the Right* (amnation.com) run by Lawrence Auster, and Steve Sailer's *iSteve* (isteve.blogspot.com). *Gene Expression* (gnxp. com), an important website on genetics, does not generally address immigration, but contains informed discussions of recent research on the genetics of group differences, including differences in IQ and temperament. None of these sites obtain significant foundation support and are almost entirely supported by individual contributors. The same can be said about the *Brussels Journal* (brusselsjournal. com), a European website dealing with European immigration issues, *Galliawatch,* (galliawatch.blogspot.com), a website that provides insights into immigration issues in France, and *Honest Thinking* (honestthinking.org), a website reporting on issues in Scandinavia. Other groups and websites take similar positions, but all are small and almost totally dependent on individual contributions, as they receive virtually no support from large foundations.

The extremely well financed and radical left-wing organization, the Southern Poverty Law Center (SPLC), which advertises itself as supporting "civil rights," lists virtually all immigration-restriction organizations as "hate groups" and lumps them together with skinheads, neo-Nazis and white supremacists. The Center reports more than $200 million in assets and an annual operating budget of more than $38 million.[109] It regularly puts out alerts to local media about the presence of such "hate" groups in their communities that, all too often, are taken at face value by local journalists and result in highly misleading news articles about these groups. The

SPLC in its publications and media alerts slanders totally legitimate organizations and highly informative websites on a regular basis, and, by extension the great majority of American citizens who endorse similar views.[110]

The consensus among elites is that the popular resistance to mass immigration is an ignorant xenophobia that should be ignored in setting public policy. As Francis Fukayama explains, "Postmodern elites, particularly in Europe, feel that they have evolved beyond identities defined by religion and nation and have arrived at a superior place."[111] Esteemed British philosopher Roger Scruton observes that such elites dominate European national parliaments and the bureaucracy of the European Union. It is this domination that "is partly responsible for the acceptance of subsidized immigration, and for the attacks on customs and institutions associated with traditional and native forms of life." A typical member of this elite class, according to Scruton, himself hardly a stranger to this class, "repudiates national loyalties and defines his goals and ideals *against* the nation..." (Italics in original). He sees himself "as a defender of enlightened universalism against local chauvinism." It follows than that such a person defines "his political vision in terms of cosmopolitan values that have been purified of all reference to the particular attachments of a real historical community."[112]

Not surprisingly, the multicultural program these elites promote is, by its very nature, profoundly undemocratic, in that it imposes changes on society that citizens most assuredly do not want and which they resist when given the opportunity to do so. Hence the extraordinary repression of dissent in the immigration debate and the totalitarian imposition of political correctness wherever elites have power, such as in American universities and in most European political parties.

Nobel Prize winning novelist Doris Lessing, no enemy of the left, argued in a 1992 article that political correctness is "immediately evident as a legacy of Communism...a continuation of that old bully, the Party line." She argues: "millions of people, the rug of Communism pulled out from under them, are searching frantically, and perhaps not even knowing it, for another dogma." They are rabble-rousers using the "most dirty and often cruel tactics" and are "no less rabble-rousers because they see themselves as anti-racists or feminists or whatever."[113]

It is difficult to disagree with Lessing that the totalitarian methods and utopian ambitions of multiculturalism clearly have their roots in Communist ideology. The multicultural program is, to be sure, spectacularly utopian. It supposes that, given the proper conditions, national and ethnic identities can be suppressed and eventually wither away as people come to see themselves as citizens of the world. This is truly an extravagant vision, but one the elites of the West have demonstrably embraced. They seem not willing to ask what the consequences would be if their vision is flawed. Marxist visionaries were wrong in thinking that they could remake people to love and to work hard for other people's children as for their own. Are today's visionary multiculturalists wrong in thinking they can eradicate ethnic solidarity and the group strife it so often engenders?

Communist totalitarians committed grave crimes against millions of people in their attempt to eliminate human self-interest in their plans for a just economic order. Left-wing intellectuals in the West defended the barbarities of Communism for years because they viewed its ends as noble. Today, intellectuals of all political stripes excuse the excesses of their governments in promoting large-scale immigration. After all, the goal of world harmony and universal justice is as noble as the goal of economic equality. Will today's governments pursue those noble goals with a ruthlessness similar to their communist predecessors? This is not an idle concern. Many today call the tactics of European multiculturalists a "soft" totalitarianism. However, the willingness of governments to put people in jail or deprive them of their livelihoods for disagreeing with government policies can hardly be characterized as soft. It should be recalled that in its last years, the Soviet Union rarely murdered opponents, but used tactics similar to the ones being used today in Europe.

A world without borders would be one without refuge from despotic rule. Despotic governance was the rule throughout most of recorded history, and it is still the rule for the majority of the world's citizens. The Soviet Union built walls to keep its people from seeking refuge in the West. What if there had been no "West" in which to seek refuge? The last time Western Europe was united was under Nazi rule, and people who opposed that rule were simply murdered, as were millions of undesired minorities who were trapped in the boundaries of that multicultural empire. Whether people would be better off without independent nation states, living under the rule of a world government, or in large supernational blocs such as the EU is by no means clear. In fact, history and reason suggest that just the opposite would be the case. Most utopian dreams when implemented have, in fact, been real-life nightmares for the vast majority. One is hard-pressed to think of an exception.

Future Prospects: A Perfect Storm

A recent report sponsored by the Educational Testing Service (the company that produces a wide variety of educational tests, including the SAT) analyzed recent trends in education, workforce requirements and globalization and predicted a "perfect storm" for our society should current trends continue.[114] In a nutshell, the problem is that while the emerging global economy requires a more educated and highly trained workforce, current projections indicate a decline in education and skills among Americans. The authors argue that unless these trends are corrected, America will be less competitive in the world economy and Americans consequently will experience a declining standard of living.

Such a decline, according to the authors, will be especially troubling since not all groups will share the impact equally. In particular, Americans of European and Asian descent will thrive, while those of African and Hispanic background are likely to fall further behind than is currently the case. These predictions are based on the differing educational attainments of the aforementioned groups. Americans of European descent approximate, in general, the average educational attainment of other industrial societies, while Asian-Americans tend to surpass those averages. Just the opposite is the case for black and Hispanic-Americans, who lag far behind in their educational success. While enormous efforts have been invested in the attempt to close the gap between blacks and whites since the 1964 Civil Rights Act, so far these attempts have failed. The most recent initiative to address the problem, namely, the 2001 No Child Left Behind Act, seems, at least at this point, unlikely to prove any more successful than past attempts. In fact, there was no change in the gap between whites and blacks and whites and Hispanics, between 2004 and 2008 in NAEP test results.[115]

Many recent immigrants, as would be expected, arrive with very little education and limited linguistic ability, especially proficiency in English, and a good number are illiterate. The problem is that the children and grandchildren of Hispanic immigrants are not moving up educationally. While most second- and third-generation Hispanics are proficient in English, their educational attainments lag far behind those of whites and Asian-Americans. The authors of the report explain these problems as a result of blacks and Hispanics failing to acquire the basic literacy and mathematical skills fundamental to educational success, and recommend, with some urgency, that the educational establishment find a way to deal with these deficits. The authors rely on data collected by ETS in the National Adult Literacy Survey (NALS) that measured prose, document and quantitative literacy. Each of these literacy measures is broken into five ability levels. The authors point out that most well-paying occupations in the professions, managerial positions, and skilled trades require proficiency at the two highest levels. Those in the middle level will fare moderately well, while those in the bottom two levels, (which include 52% of all Americans) will probably only find employment in a limited range of manual and service trades that do not pay very well. According to the authors, "Performance in Levels 3 and higher is considered to be a minimum standard for success in the labor market."[116]

The worldwide consulting firm of McKinsey and Company echoed these concerns, especially their economic consequences, in a recent report. The authors of that report estimate that if the achievement gap between racial groups in the United States had been closed by 1998, the United States GDP (gross domestic product) in 2008 "would have been between $310 Billion and $525 billion higher, or roughly 2 to 4% of GDP." In addition, they estimate that if educational levels (in mathematics and science) in the United States had been raised to the levels found in "such nations as Finland and Korea US GDP would have been between $1.3 trillion and $2.3 trillion higher, representing 9 to 16 percent of GDP."[117] This international achievement gap "is imposing on the US economy an invisible yet recurring economic loss that is greater than the output shortfall in what has been called the worst economic crisis [in 2008-2009] since the Great Depression." In other words, these gaps "have created the equivalent of a permanent national recession in terms of the gap between the actual and potential output in the economy."[118]

The authors of the McKinsey report conclude optimistically that these problems can be solved by better research resulting in improved education. It is interesting that the oft-noted educational shortfall of the United States relative to other advanced societies usually fails to take the racial gaps into account. Erling Boe and Sujie Shin, of the University of Pennsylvania Graduate School of Education, analyzed international educational performance among major industrial societies. When ranked among 22 of the world's industrialized nations, the United States' performance is indeed middling. However, when compared to the major nations comprising the G7 group (United States, Canada, France, Germany, Italy Japan and the UK), United States' students perform at a par with the European students. They and other western nations fall significantly below Japan in science and mathematics. Perhaps most striking is their finding that when scores are broken down by race and ethnicity, they found that United States' white students significantly *outperform* the other Western nations. Compared to Japanese students, white American students perform significantly better in reading, somewhat but not much below Japan in science, and considerably below Japan in mathematics.[119] These data suggest that improving American educational performance will not be easy, or even possible. Certainly the data make clear that European educational practices offer little in the way of guidance. Unfortunately, none of these studies includes China, which is quickly becoming a major international competitor for the United States and other Western countries.

The problems created by the educational trends outlined in the *A Perfect Storm* are not likely to be simply economic, but portend serious social problems because of the stark group differences in performance. Fifty-eight percent of native-born whites score in the top three quintiles and seventy-four percent of native-born Asians do so. Alternately, only twenty-two percent of native-born blacks and thirty-two percent of native-born Hispanics fall into the top three categories. Given those figures, large majorities of black and Hispanic Americans lack the rudimentary skills necessary for all but the least remunerative occupations.

Political correctness forces these otherwise candid researchers to skirt what is probably the main explanation, namely, IQ differences, and to hide behind euphemisms such as "the lack of literacy skills." Surely the authors know, or should know, that basic literacy and mathematical skills are almost perfectly correlated with IQ, for the simple reason that that is what IQ tests measure. Linda Gottfredson, who has done path-breaking work on IQ and occupational attainment, analyzed the NALS data in great detail and estimates that entry into level three requires an IQ of approximately 98, which is the average for all Americans.[120] Put another way, the job prospects for those below average in IQ are not good and become less so as desirable jobs become more complex and many simpler jobs are mechanized or sent offshore.

The literacy skills of these four groups mirror almost perfectly what would be predicted given the IQ of these groups. The average for Americans of European descent is approximately 102, while Asian Americans score somewhat higher in the range of 105 to 107. Blacks, on the other hand, average about 85 and Hispanics fall in the range of 87 to 90. The figure for Hispanics in the U.S. is somewhat obscured by the fact that California, which has the largest Hispanic population, bans the use of IQ tests. The figure is based on smaller American samples and on average IQs obtained from samples in Mexico and other Latin American countries.[121]

While the reasons for these IQ differences are much debated, it is sufficient to point out that they are extremely reliable predictors of educational success and occupational achievement, and are extremely persistent over time. Group IQs can be raised by exposure to education and by improved nutrition, but there appears to be a limit to how effective these factors are in closing IQ gaps. Americans of African descent do not suffer malnutrition relative to other Americans and, at least in recent decades, have had available similar levels of education, and yet the IQ gap today is little different from what it was when first measured early in the twentieth century. Hispanics may yet benefit from their exposure to education in American schools and probably better nutrition, but as yet this has not been the case. Third-generation Hispanics still, on average, lag significantly behind whites and Asians, and on some measures, behind blacks. For instance, third-generation Hispanics drop out of high school at twice the rate of whites, and do so somewhat more frequently than black Americans.[122] The authors of *A Perfect Storm* predict that as the size of the Hispanic population grows and comes to represent most of the growth in the labor force, American productivity and wealth will decline and income disparities will grow larger. To suggest that the problems produced by these gaps can be overcome by by a pedagogical breakthrough is to, in effect, sidestep the issue.

The issue, which the ETS authors completely ignore, is, of course, our current immigration policy, which is enormously biased in favoring Hispanic immigration. Not only do the family-unification provisions of the current policy favor recent immigrants, but also the failure to enforce border security allows an enormous number of illegal immigrants to enter, most from Latin America, whose children become automatic citizens upon being born here. The "perfect storm" these authors foresee is the utterly predictable consequence of our current immigration policies and it is disingenuous, in the least, not to address those policies.

This perfect storm is magnified by the ability of multinational corporations to export all manner of work, including intellectual work, to countries such as India and China with many millions of educated people. Robert Blinder, a Princeton University Economist and former member of the Federal Reserve, has been analyzing this phenomenon for a number of years. His work suggests that as many as 40 million jobs are potentially at risk of being outsourced via Internet connections and other sources of communication. Many of these jobs require advanced training and include computer programmers, graphics designers, radiologists, accountants, and financial analysts, to name a few. Blinder argues that the only jobs not in danger are service sector jobs which are impractical to move for one reason or another, such as surgeons, cosmetologists, carpenters, landscapers, teachers, and others. Blinder also makes the point that general education will not be the overall solution for people as it has in past decades. Rather, individuals will have to tailor their educations to the particular skills that cannot be easily exported.[123]

The problem in a nutshell is that there is now a global labor market at all skill levels, and people living in poor countries will gladly work for salaries that could not sustain an individual, much less a family, in the United States or Western Europe. In the long run, of course, national wealth disparities among most nations will tend to diminish, but in the meantime, people in Western nations are going to face employment competition of an unprecedented nature. It is reasonably safe to assume that people in the two highest literacy levels will find the means to cope and to settle in those occupations not under threat from outsourcing. But what about the lowest three levels? People in level three in the past often found well-paid factory work in industry, as clerical workers, and in a variety of skilled trades. Unfortunately, much of this type of work has been, and continues to be, moved offshore.

The future that these developments portend is not one consistent with the vision of the founding fathers who built their republic on a model that included large numbers of independent yeoman farmers and skilled tradesmen. Rather the future of America is likely to come to resemble South American oligarchies, in which there are extremely successful elites, relatively small middle classes, and large masses of people whose main work is to provide services for the more successful members of society. These class distinctions in Latin America, moreover, are quite clearly related to ethnic and racial differences.

America is not alone in facing serious consequences brought on by unexamined immigration policies. Europe and all European-derived nations face similar problems to a greater or lesser degree. Most critics of European immigration policy focus on the difficulty of assimilating North Africans and Western Asians, many of whom are Muslim, due to religious differences and the potential social conflict produced by those religious differences. Left out of these discussions is the fact that, according to the best estimates, Middle Eastern and West Asian societies (that include India, Bangladesh, and Pakistan) have populations whose average IQs range between 85 and 90, with some having averages considerably below that range.[124] As will be seen in Chapter 7, these figures are reflected in the academic performance of the native-born children of immigrants in European schools. A notable exception is students of Indian descent. As in the case of Hispanic immigrants to America, these differences between immigrants and host populations will probably decline somewhat through improved education and nutrition, but there is little reason to believe that these gaps will close to the point of being socially unimportant.

Europeans, therefore, face the problem of assimilating people of very different religious and social values who, in addition, are unlikely to achieve the economic success of native Europeans. This is by now glaringly evident in France where large numbers of the children of North Africans perform poorly in school, have bleak economic prospects, and have failed to integrate into French society. Similar difficulties are widespread throughout Europe. Invoking the nostrum of better education as the answer to these growing problems is as disingenuous for European elites as it is for American ones.

It is important to understand the significance of these IQ gaps, since they are often dismissed as trivial and unimportant, and their persistence over time is generally not emphasized. An IQ difference of ten or fifteen points, for instance, results in widely differing numbers of those at the top and the bottom of the distributions, due to the normal distribution or bell curve for IQ. Whereas 50% of the individuals drawn from a European population will have IQs above 100, the figure drops to 25% for those whose group mean is 90, and only about 16% for those whose group mean is 85. The figures for IQs associated with success in higher education, roughly a minimum IQ of about 110 (equivalent to literacy levels 1 and 2 according to Gottfredson's estimates), are even more striking. Approximately 25% of the European host population will surpass that figure, but only about 10% of the population of the typical North African and West Asian country, and an even smaller percentage of those from the countries of sub-Saharan Africa.[125]

These figures are not only important for economic success, but suggest a host of other problems associated with immigration. It has by now been well established that IQ correlates very highly with rates of criminality and antisocial behavior and with other maladaptive behaviors such as illegitimacy. These correlations are, furthermore, found worldwide.[126] Challenges to social harmony are exacerbated if some immigrant groups exhibit, and come to be associated with, a host of social pathologies, as is currently the case in America and Europe. High crime and illegitimacy rates are common among Third-World immigrants to industrial societies, and it is possible that these phenomena are linked to cultural and intellectual differences. It is also possible that ethnic groups are somewhat different in their temperamental makeup in impulse control and aggressiveness, and these may simply compound the problems posed by cultural and ability differences. This is a very important and highly controversial question, which will be explored in Chapters 3 and 4.

All of which suggests that, without dramatic changes in patterns of immigration, considerable economic and social disparities among groups are likely to persist and to grow more apparent as immigration swells the ranks of those less academically talented. A related question is what these figures mean for democratic governance. Can democracy thrive when only a small percentage of the population has the capacity and skills associated with middle-class employment? Are the autocratic societies of North Africa the natural byproduct of societies where an insufficient fraction of the population has the intellectual wherewithal to deal with political and economic complexity?

If people from North Africa and Southwest Asia replace European people, will European civilization, including its democracy and wealth, be replaced by some new civilization with very different dynamics and values? Will America be the same if it becomes a confederation of different ethnic groups with different values and aptitudes? Given current immigration policies these are the most important questions the Western world must attempt to assess. Such a demographic realignment would be epochal in nature and would have ramifications in every corner of the globe. When coupled with the rise of China and India as world superpowers, it heralds a new chapter in world history that will shape the destiny of mankind for centuries to come. Thoughtful people would not hesitate to consider what these epochal changes portend for their progeny. Neither would they hesitate to openly consider the full consequences of the current immigration policies which, if left on their present course, will prove to be irreversible and quite possibly tragic.

Notes

1   Bat Ye'or, *Eurabia: The Euro-Arab Axis* (Madison, New Jersey: Fairleigh Dickinson University Press, 2005); Bruce Bawer, *While Europe Slept: How Radical Islam is Destroying the West from Within* (New York: Doubleday, 2006); Peter Brimelow, *Alien Nation: Common Sense About America's Immigration Disaster* (New York: Harper Collins, 1995); Patrick J. Buchanan, *State of Emergency: The Third World Invasion and Conquest of America* (New York: St. Martin's Press, 2006); Melanie Phillips, *Londonistan* (New York: Encounter Books, 2006); Mark Steyn, *America Alone: The End of the World as We Know It* (Washington, D.C.: Regnery Publishing, 2006); Tom Tancredo, *In Mortal Danger: The Battle for America's Border and Security* (Nashville, Tenn.: WND Books, 2006).

2   United Nations, World Population Prospects: The 2008 Revision, 1, 40.

3   K. Anthony Appiah, The Limits of Pluralism, *in Multiculturalism and American Democracy, ed.* Arthur M. Melzer, Jerry Weinberger, and M. Richard Zinman (Lawrence, Kansas: University Press of Kansas, 1998), 37–54; Stanley Fish, Boutique Multiculturalism, in Melzer, et. al., *Multiculturalism and American Democracy*, 69–90; Charles Taylor, The Politics of Recognition, in *Multiculturalism: Examining the Politics of Recognition*, ed., Charles Taylor (Princeton, New Jersey: Princeton University Press, 1994), 25–74; Susan Wolf, Comment, in Taylor, *Multiculturalism*, 75–86.

4   James Ceaser, Multiculturalism and American Liberal Democracy, in Melzer, et. al. *Multiculturalism and American Democracy*; Tamar Jacoby, Defining Assimilation for the 21st Century, *In Reinventing the Melting*

Pot: The New Immigrants and What It Means to be an American, ed., Tamar Jacoby (New York: Basic Books, 2004), 3–16; Lorraine Pangle, Multiculturalism and Civic Education, in Melzer, et. al., *Multiculturalism and American Democracy;* Stephen Thernstrom, Rediscovering the Melting Pot—Still Going Strong, in Jacoby, *Reinventing the Melting Pot,* 47–60.

5   Edmund Burke, *Reflections on the Revolution in France* (1790) published in one volume along with Thomas Paine, *The Rights of Man* (Garden City, New York: Doubleday, 1961), p. 74.

6   Roy F. Baumeister, Jennifer D. Campbell, Joachim I. Krueger, and Kathleen D. Vohs, Does High Self-esteem Cause Better Performance, Interpersonal Success, Happiness or Healthier Lifestyles, *Psychological Science in the Public Interest,* 4:1, (2000), 1–44. Byron M. Roth, Self-Esteem, Ethnicity and Academic Performance among American Children, In Craig L. Frisby and Cecil R. Reynolds, eds., *Comprehensive Handbook of Multicultural School Psychology* (Hoboken, New Jersey: Wiley, 2005), 577–610.

7   Stephane Courtois, Nicolas Werth, Jean-Louis Panne, Andrezej Paczkowski, Karel Bartosek and Jean-Louis Margolin, *The Black Book of Communism: Crimes, Terror, Repression,* Translated by Jonathan Murphy and Mark Kramer (Cambridge, Mass: Harvard University Press, 1999).

8   James McConalogue, Immigration: Heaping Up the Funeral Pyre, *BrusselsJournal.com*, August 8, 2006, online at brusselsjournal.com.

9   Sue Reid, Polygamy UK: This Special Mail Investigation reveals how thousands of Men are Milking the Benefits System to Support Several Wives, *Daily Mail*, February 24, 2009.

10 Melanie Philips, *Londonistan*, 2006; Nina Bernstein, In Secret, Polygamy Follows Africans to N.Y., *New York Times*, March 23, 2007.

11 Colin Randall, Migrant Polygamy helped Cause Riots, *Telegraph,* November 17, 2005.

12 Steve Doughty, Britain has 85 *Sharia* Courts: The Astonishing Spread of the Islamic Justice Behind Closed Doors, *Mail Online*, June 29, 2009, online. The study referred to is: Denis MacEoin, Sharia Law or One Law for All (London: Civitas: The Institute for the Study of Civil Society, 2009).

13 Mathew Hickley, Islamic Sharia Courts in Britain are now 'Legally Binding', *Mail Online*, September 15, 2008.

14 Thomas Sowell, *Ethnic America* (New York: Basic Books, 1981), 136–142.

15 Ulric Neisser, Gwyneth Boodoo, Thomas J. Bouchard, A. Wade Boykin, Nathan Brody, Stephen J. Ceci, Diane F. Halpern, John C. Loehlin, Robert Perloff, Robert J. Sternberg and Susana Urbina, Intelligence: Knowns and Unknowns, *American Psychologist*, Vol. 31, No. 2, (1996), 77–101.

16 Richard Herrnstein, Still an American Dilemma, *The Public Interest*, No. 98 (Winter, 1990), pp. 3–17.

17 James Flynn, Beyond the Flynn Effect: A Lecture by James Flynn, Psychometrics Centre, University of Cambridge, April 17, 2009.

18 Noah A. Rosenberg, Jonathan K. Pritchard, James A. Weber, Howard M.

Cann, Kenneth K. Kidd, Lev A. Zhivotovski and Marcus W. Feldman, Genetic Structure of Human Populations, *Science* Vol. 34. No. 1 (2002), 2381–2385; Benjamin F. Voight, Sridhar Kudaravalli, Xiaoquan Wen and Jonathan K. Pritchard. A Map of Recent Positive Selection in the Human Genome, *PLoS Biol* 4:3, (2006), 446–458; Nicholas Wade, *Before the Dawn: Recovering the Lost History of Our Ancestors*. (New York: Penguin Press, 2006), 185–88; Scott Williamson, Melissa J. Hubisz, Andrew G. Clark, Bret A. Payseur, Carlos D. Bustamante and Rasmus Nielson, Localizing Recent Adaptive Evolution in the Human Genome, *PLoS Genetics* 3:6 (2007).

19   Paul Johnson, *Intellectuals: From Marx and Tolstoy to Sartre and Chomsky* (New York: Harper Collins, 2007).

20   Darth Quixote, 10 Questions for Steven Pinker, *Gene Expression*, July 4, 2006.

21   Kevin MacDonald, *Separation and Its Discontents: Toward an Evolutionary Theory of Anti-Semitism* (Bloomington Ind.: Firstbooks Library, 2004), originally published in 1998 by Praeger, Westport, CT; Albert S. Lindemann. *Esau's Tears: Modern Anti-Semitism and the Rise of the Jews* (Cambridge: Cambridge University Press, 2000);
Yuri Slezkine, *The Jewish Century* (Princeton, New Jersey; Princeton University Press, 2004).

22   Michael D. Biddis, *Gobineau: Selected Political Writings* (New York: Harper and Row, 1970), 78.

23   Gregory Cochran, Jason Hardy, and Henry Harpending, Natural History of Ashkenazi Intelligence. *Journal of Biosocial Science*. 38, (2006) 659–663.

24   Thomas Sowell, *Ethnic America*, 1981.

25   Amy Chua, *World on Fire: How Exporting Free Market Democracy Breeds Ethnic Hatred and Global Instability* (New York: Anchor Books, 2003).

26   Carl N. Degler, *In Search of Human Nature: The Decline and Revival of Darwinism in American Social Thought* (Oxford: Oxford University Press, 1991).

27   Degler, *In Search of Human Nature*, 72–73; Peter Gay, *The Enlightenment: An Interpretation, Volume 2. The Science of Freedom* (New York: Norton, 1969), 328–343.

28   Degler, *In Search of Human Nature*.

29   Arthur R. Jensen, How Much Can We Boost IQ and Scholastic Achievement? *Harvard Educational Review* 39 (1969), 1–123.

30   Degler, *In Search of Human Nature*, 1991, 310–349; Wade, *Before the Dawn*.

31   Wade, *Before the Dawn*.

32   Noah Rosenberg, A., Jonathan K. Pritchard, James A. Weber, Howard M. Cann, Kenneth K. Kidd, Lev A. Zhivotovski and Marcus W. Feldman, Genetic Structure of Human Populations, *Science*, 34:1 (2002), 2381–2385; Benjamin F. Voight, Sridhar Kudaravalli, Xiaoquan Wen and

Jonathan K. Pritchard. A Map of Recent Positive Selection in the Human Genome, *PLoS Biol* 4:3 (March 2006), 446–458; Scott Williamson, Melissa J. Hubisz, Andrew G. Clark, Bret A. Payseur, Carlos D. Bustamante and Rasmus Nielson. Localizing Recent Adaptive Evolution in the Human Genome, *PLoS Genetics* 3:6 (2007).

33   Jennifer Lee Carrell, *The Speckled Monster: A Historical Tale of Battling Smallpox* (New York: Penguin Group, 2004).

34   Wade, *Before the Dawn.*

35   Rosenberg, et. al., Genetic Structure of Human Populations; Voight, et. al., A Map of Recent Positive Selection in the Human Genome; Wade, *Before the Dawn,* 2006, 185–88; Williamson, et. al. Localizing Recent Adaptive Evolution in the Human Genome.

36   Antonio Regalado, Head Examined: Scientist's Study of Brain Genes Sparks a Backlash, *Wall Street Journal,* June 16, 2006, A1, online.

37   Darth Quixote, 10 Questions for Steven Pinker, 8.

38   Kevin Lamb, Forced Out: The Price of Speaking Freely in Multicultural America, *Middle American News,* June 2005, online.

39   Jacob Sullum, Brain Storm: Can we Talk About Sex Differences in Math and Science Aptitude Without Yelling? *Reason Online,* January 21, 2005.

40   Ruth Bell and Ehsan Masood, Race and IQ, Psychologist in Inquiry over Teaching Conduct. *Nature,* 381, 6578, (1996), 105.

41   Charlotte Hunt-Grubbe, The Elementary DNA of Dr. Watson, *The Sunday Times,* October 14, 2007.

42   Richard Lynn and Tatu Vanhanen, *IQ and the Wealth of Nations* (Westport, Conn: Praeger, 2002).

43   Jared Diamond, *Guns, Germs and Steel: A Short History of Everybody for the Last 13,000 Years* (London: Vintage, 2005), 19.

44   Stephen Ceci, Douglas Peters and Jonathan Plotkin, Human Subjects Review, Personal Values, and the Regulation of Social Science Research. *American Psychologist,* Vol. 40, No. 9, (1985), 994–1002.

45   Jeremy R. Gray and Paul M. Thompson, Neurobiology of Intelligence: Science and Ethics, *Nature reviews: Neuroscience,* 5, (2004), 471–482.

46   Madeleine Bunting, 2007, Immigration is Bad for Society, But Only Until a New Solidarity is Forged, *The Guardian,* June 18, 2007.

47   Robert D. Putnam, E pluribus Unum: Diversity and Community in the Twenty-First Century, The 2006 Johan Skytte Prize Lecture. *Scandinavian Political Studies,* 30:2, (2007).

48   John Lloyd, Study paints bleak picture of ethnic diversity, *Financial Times,* October 8, 2007.

49   Bunting, Immigration is bad for society.

50   Putnam, E Pluribus Unum.

51   A. Miller, The New British McCarthyism, *Taki's Magazine,* February 4, 2007.

52   Court Rules Vlaams Blok is Racist, *BBC News*, 9/11/2004.

53   David Pryce-Jones, Heil Haider?, *National Review*, 52, May 6, 2000.

54   Cnaan Lipshitz, Dutch MP behind film on Radical Islam: Decision to Prosecute me is Political, *Haaretz*, January 23, 2009, online at haaretz.com.

55   Google Vidio: Fitna the Movie: Geert Wilders' Film about the Quran (English), online at video.google.com.

56   Dutch News—*Radio Netherlands Worldwide—English*, Wilders' Freedom Party leads Polls, March 1, 2009.

57   A. Miller, The New British McCarthyism.

58   *Ibid.*

59   Public Wants Much Harsher Immigration Policy, Says Poll, *Times Online*, August 20, 2006.

60   Jonathan Rauch, The Truth Hurts: The Humanitarian Threat to Free Speech, *Reason*, April 1993, online at reasononline.com.

61   Stanley Kurtz, Not Without a Fight, *The New Criterion*, *Special Pamphlet, Free Speech in an Age of Jihad: Libel Tourism, Hate Speech & Political Freedom*. Summer 2008, 7–9.

62   *Ibid.*, 5

63   *Ibid.*, 6.

64   Battling Censorship, Editorial, *The Washington Times*, July 20, 2007.

65   Kurtz, *Not Without a Fight*, 5–7.

66   Battling Censorship, Editorial, *Washington Times*, July 20, 2007.

67   *Ibid.*

68   Kurtz, Not Without a Fight, 13.

69   Bardot Fined for "Race Hate" Book, *BBC News*, June 10, 2004.

70   Brigitte Bardot Fined for Racism, *The Independent*, June 3, 2008.

71   Mark Steyn, The Lamps are Going Out. *The New Criterion*, *Special Pamphlet, Free Speech in an Age of Jihad*, 32–33.

72   *Ibid.*

73   John Plunkett, Ofcom back Channel 4 over Mosque probe, *The Guardian*, Novemeber 19, 2007.

74   Leigh Holmwood, Dispatches damages to go to charity, *The Guardian*, May 15, 2008.

75   Yvan Guillemette and William B. P. Robson, *No Elixir of Youth: Immigration Cannot Keep Canada Young* (Backgrounder, No. 96, September 2006), Ottawa, Canada: The C. D. Howe Institute, 2006, 2.

76   Richard Wike and Juliana Menasce Horowitz, *World Publics Welcome Global Trade—But Not Immigration: 47–Nation Pew Global Attitudes Survey*, The Pew Global Attitudes Project, October 4, 2007.

77   Lou Dobbs, *The War on the Middle Class* (New York: Penguin Group, 2006), 37.

78   Isabel Sawhill and John E. Morton, *Economic Mobility: Is the American Dream Alive and Well* (Washington D.C.: The Pew Charitable Trusts, 2007).

79   Edward S. Rubenstein, National Data: September Data Shows Immigrants Displacing American Workers-Especially Blacks. *Vdare*, October 5, 2008.

80   Lou Dobbs, *The War on the Middle Class* (New York: Penguin Group, 2006), 37.

81   Fjordman, Political correctness: The revenge of Marxism, *Gates of Vienna*, June 14, 2006; Jamie Glazov, Symposium: The death of Multiculturalism? *Front Page Magazine*, September 8, 2006; Paul E. Gottfried, *The Strange Death of Marxism: The European Left in the New Millennium* (Columbia, MO: University of Missouri Press, 2005); William S. Lind, Political Correctness: A Short History of an Ideology, Free Congress Foundation, 2004; Phillips, *Londonistan;* Mark Steyn, *America Alone.*

82   Daniel J. Mahoney, 1968 and the Meaning of Democracy, *The Intercollegiate Review, 43:2, Fall 2008, 10–11.*

83   *Ibid.,* 11. The quotation is Mahoney's translation from Dominique Schnapper, *Relativisme* in Commentaire, 31:121 (Spring 2008) 126–130.

84   Loomis, Louise Ropes, ed., *Aristotle, On Man in the Universe* (New York: Walter J. Black, 1943), 348.

85   Joan Roelofs, *Foundations and Public Policy: The Mask of Pluralism* (Albany, New York, State University of New York Press, 2003), 2–6.

86   *Ibid.,* 28.

87   *Ibid.,* 35

88   *Ibid.,* 34–38.

89   *Ibid.,* 159–60.

90   Gunnar Myrdal, with Richard Sterner and Arnold Rose, *An American Dilemma: The Negro Problem and Modern Democracies, 20th Anniversary Edition* (New York: Harper and Row, 1962).

91   Roelofs, *Foundations,* 111.

92   *Ibid.,* 111.

93   William R. Hawkins, *Importing Revolution, Open borders and the Radical Agenda* (Monterey, Virginia: The American Immigration Control Foundation, 1994), 114.

94   Roelofs, *Foundations,* 12.

95   Hawkins, *Importing Revolution.*

96   Ford Foundation, Database, Grants.

97   Bill and Melinda Gates Foundation, Grants.

98   MALDEF, *2003–2004, Annual Report.*

99   National Council of La Raza, *2007, Annual Report.*

100   Open Society Institute, *2006 Annual Report.*

101   Eric Ruark, *Immigration Lobbying: A Window Into the World of Special Interests,* (Washington, D.C.: Federation for American Immigration Reform, January 2008).

102   *Ibid.,* 4.

103   *Ibid.,* 5.

104   *Ibid.,* Appendix A1–C9.

105 Steve Sailer, America's Minority Mortgage Meltdown/ Diversity Recession: The Smoking Gun, *Vdare,* October, 10, 2008; Steve Sailer, The Minority Mortgage Meltdown (Contd.): How the Community Reinvestment Act Fits In, *Vdare,* February 1, 2009.

106 Ruark, *Immigration Lobbying,* Appendix A1–C9.

107 An excellent source of news on the views of major religious organizations is the Pew Forum on Religion & Public life, online at pewforum.org. Searching the site for "immigration" resulted in more than 500 news items on the topic.

108 *Media Transparency, Recipients,* online at mediatransparency.org/recipientsgrants.

109 Southern Poverty Law Center, *2007 Annual Report.*

110 Southern Poverty Law Center, The Intelligence Project.

111 Francis Fukuyama, Identity and Migration, *Prospect Magazine,* Vol. 131, February 2007, 7.

112 Roger Scruton, Roger Scruton on immigration, multiculturalism and the need to defend the nation state. Speech by Roger Scruton, Antwerp, 23 June, 2006. *Brussels Journal,* 7/8/2007.

113 Doris Lessing, Questions You Should Never Ask a Writer. *New York Times,* June 26, 1992. Reprinted by the *New York Times,* October 13, 2007.

114 Irwin Kirsch, Henry Braun, Andrew Sum, and Kentaro Yamamoto, *America's Perfect Storm: Three Forces Changing Our Nation's Future.* Princeton, NJ: Educational Testing Service, 2007.

115 Bobby D. Rampey, Gloria S. Dion and Patricia L. Donahue, The Nation's Report Card: Trends in Academic Progress in Reading and Mathematics 2008, April 2009, National Center of Education Statistics, U.S. Department of Education; Sam Dillon, 'No Child' Law Is Not Closing a Racial Gap, New York Times, April 28, 2009.

116 Kirsch, et. al., *America's Perfect Storm,* 12.

117 McKinsey & Company, The Economic Impact of the Achievement Gap in America's Schools, April 2009, 17.

118 *Ibid..,* 18.

119 Erling E. Boe and Sujie Shin, Is the United States Really Losing the International Horse Race in Academic Achievement? *Phi Delta Kappan,* 86, 9 (May 2005), 688–695.

120 Linda S. Gottfredson, Why g Matters: The Complexity of Everyday Life, *Intelligence,* 24:1 (1997) 79–132.

121 Richard Lynn and Tatu Vanhanen, *IQ and the Wealth of Nations.* Westport Conn.: Praeger, 2002. Richard Lynn, *Race Differences In Intelligence: An Evolutionary Analysis* (Augusta, Georgia: Washington Summit Publishers, 2006); Richard Lynn, *The Global Bell Curve: Race, IQ, and Inequality Worldwide* (Augusta, Georgia: Washington Summit Publishers, 2008).

122 *Hispanics: A Statistical Portrait* (Oakton, Virginia: New Century Foundation, 2006).

123 Alan S. Blinder, Offshoring: The next industrial revolution, *Foreign Affairs*, March/April. (2006).

124 Lynn, and Vanhanen, *IQ and the Wealth of Nations;* Lynn, *Race Differences in Intelligence*. Lynn, *The Global Bell Curve*.

125 These percentages are based on estimates of IQ from Lynn and Vanhanen, *IQ and the Wealth of Nations* which is discussed at length in a later section. The calculations for percentages above various thresholds are easily determined by consulting a table for the normal distribution, if one has the mean and standard deviation for a population.

126 Robert A. Gordon, Everyday Life As an Intelligence Test: Effects of Intelligence and Intelligence Context, *Intelligence*, 24(1), (1997) 203–320; Richard J. Herrnstein and Charles Murray, *The Bell Curve: Intelligence and Class Structure in American Life*. (New York: Free Press, 1994); Lynn, *The Global Bell Curve*. J. Philippe Rushton, *Race, Evolution and Behavior: A Life History Perspective*. (New Brunswick, New Jersey: Transaction Publishers, 1995).

Chapter 2

FUNDAMENTAL PRINCIPLES OF THE EVOLUTION OF SOCIAL BEHAVIOR[1]

IN ORDER TO HAVE A CLEAR UNDERSTANDING of the likely impact of large migrations on existing societies, it is important to have a firm grasp of those aspects of human nature that are likely to influence human interaction. During the past thirty years, a considerable amount of scientific literature has accumulated which deals with the evolution of animal and human social behavior. It is safe to say that this movement is one of the most dynamic in the social sciences. That dynamism has accelerated in the last decade with new advances in genetic research bolstering and providing powerful empirical support for earlier theory and research. This chapter deals with the basic principles governing the evolution of social behavior and is meant as a brief introduction to this material.

Evolution: Stability, and Change

The cornerstone of modern physics and chemistry is that all material things are composed of a small number of fundamental elements held together by, as yet, not fully understood forces. It follows, therefore, that in any environment, common things will be those whose constituent elements are most readily available, are easily and quickly assembled and that, once assembled, are resistant to disintegration.

Put another way, the variety of things existing at any moment in time is dependent upon the likelihood and rapidity of their creation and their vulnerability to disintegration—either spontaneously or due to contact with other things.

It was Charles Darwin's genius to recognize that these, now almost self-evident, premises about the nature of material things apply as well to living things. According to Darwin, all the forms of life we see around us today exist because they are stable arrangements resistant to disintegration by the forces of nature, among which must be counted the actions of other living things. An important difference between living and nonliving things is that the stability of living things applies to their forms and not the individuals that take those forms. Unlike inanimate stable objects, living objects continuously disintegrate and are not preserved, but rather their forms are preserved, though not always precisely, through the process of reproduction.

It is important to emphasize that the creation of living things is dependent upon coded information in the form of genes that do not resemble the things they create. Codes, by definition, are not identical to the things they represent and are almost always more concise. This is important because it means that the genetic codes responsible for reproduction are simpler and more compact than the organisms whose construction they direct, much as computer programs are simpler than the output they create. Most computer programs consist of strings of binary elements whose complexity resides in their arrangement and not in the diversity of their constituent elements. In addition, most computer programs are more compact than their output; a fairly short segment of a computer program can, through nested iteration, for instance, produce a sequence of output that is infinitely long. The genetic code is also based on the sequence of a few constituent elements; namely, the bases of DNA.

Most of us are aware that the truly wondrous visual displays on our computer monitors may be produced, in many cases, by fairly compact codes, yet we are nevertheless in wonder at the display. Similarly, it is hardly surprising that before human beings understood that inheritance was based on coded forms they found it difficult to accept the notion put forward by Darwin that the wondrous variety of life could have arisen by chance. Even more remarkable was the fact that Darwin uncovered and advanced his thesis, and supported it convincingly, without knowledge of the genetic codes governing inheritance.

Genes have two functions. First, they are miniature automated factories that build amino acids in precise sequences that allow them to be assembled into the complex protein molecules that comprise all known organisms. Second, genes also make copies of themselves that they pass into the living things they create. If they could not do the latter, genetic codes could arise by chance and assemble organisms, but those organisms would disappear from the Earth once they disintegrated and would not reappear until such time as an identical code again arose by chance. By placing copies of themselves into the organisms they create, they, the genes, become potentially self-sustaining and potentially immortal. They are only potentially self-sustaining since they are dependent on "their" organism surviving long enough to pass them on in additional offspring. Organisms capable of surviving and passing on their genes are said to be "fit" in the Darwinian sense. It is important to stress that the fitness of an organism refers to the fitness of the "form" of that organism and, by extension, the genetic code that produces that form.

This way of looking at evolution was popularized in the 1970s by Richard Dawkins and Edward O. Wilson in their groundbreaking books, *The Selfish Gene* and *Sociobiology: The New Synthesis*.[2] Both authors based their thinking on the seminal 1964 mathematical treatment by William D. Hamilton.[3] In Dawkins' colorful and instructive language, it is the genes who are struggling for survival—and possible immortality—by attempting to find their way into successful "vehicles" or "survival machines" that take living form. Those genetic fragments fortunate enough to combine with other genetic fragments to build successful or fit organisms come to dominate the living world.[4]

From this perspective, chickens are the method by which chicken genes assure their survival. By extension, human beings are the mechanisms by which human genes assure theirs. The fitness of an organism, in this view, is how efficiently it performs the function of preserving the gene combinations that direct its fabrication.

When people talk about the survival of the fittest they are, given the meaning of fitness, speaking tautologically. The organic forms in the world today are those that have remained fit since the initial accidental creation of their ancestors. The point is that large numbers of potentially self-sustaining organisms lacked that fitness and no longer exist. Why some organisms survive and reproduce and others fail to do so is the question which the theory of natural selection addresses.

The fact that codes reproduce themselves accounts for the survival of existing forms or "lineages" of living things, but it does not explain the evolution of the wide variety of living things. That variety arises from the fact that genetic codes, when replicating themselves, sometimes do so imperfectly. Such failures in the transcription process are known as mutations. Most mutations are generally unimportant, since there appears to be a good deal of redundancy in the genetic code. Slight changes may not be important. Important transcription errors or mutations, however, can often seriously damage an organism. This is so because any surviving creature is the end result of a very long and unlikely series of genetic accidents. All its parts must work together and enable it to survive in its environment. Any single accidental change in the genetic code is very unlikely to produce an organism as well adjusted as the original.

The sheer improbability of beneficial mutations arising purely by chance led many thoughtful people to reject Darwin's original thesis on the origin of different species, and to argue that some sort of intelligence must be guiding evolution and the creation of new forms. This objection to evolutionary theory fails to take into account the extraordinary time frame during which evolution has played out. It is now known (though it was not in Darwin's day) that three billion years have elapsed since the first elementary forms of life appeared. This time frame allows for an almost infinite number of transcription errors to occur and for an enormous number of them to enter into a variety of successful organisms. This is all the more reasonable given the brief lives and rapid reproduction of the simplest creatures, and explains why they are so much more numerous among the living things than the more complex creatures that evolved out of them.

It should be added, parenthetically, that the truthfulness of the Darwinian theory of natural selection is not dependent on the accidental origin of species. Even if one supposes that complex creatures arose by design, the principle that some would reproduce themselves erroneously would still lead over time to new varieties. Similarly, over time and in different environmental conditions, some organisms would survive and reproduce more prolifically than others and some would go extinct. In other words, natural selection operates as a fundamental feature of nature and operates on living things whatever their origins.

To summarize to this point: the theory of evolution argues that the variety of current life forms is the result of mutations producing variant forms that have differential probabilities of surviving and reproducing. Those probabilities are, in turn, dependent on the conditions of the environment in which the particular life form is found. Organisms adapted to their environments thrive; those ill-adapted, diminish. Put in Darwinian terms, the environment—nature—acts as a filter allowing some genetic assemblages to pass into the future, while others are held back. From among the multitude of forms that arise, nature selects those destined for posterity. And since environments change, organisms that win the favor of nature in one time or place may go extinct in a different time and place. Nature is a fickle suitor.

Sexual Reproduction

Evolutionary change tends to increase the diversity of living forms. Given the variety of sources of sustenance in most environments, mutations allow for forms to arise that can carve out a niche for themselves and flourish side by side with other forms living next to them in slightly different niches. Variety therefore allows for the more efficient exploitation of any given environment. Life is extraordinarily opportunistic, or more accurately, the genes that create living things are extraordinarily opportunistic. Genes that change too easily, however, cease to exist in their original form, even if they produce favorable changes in the organisms they construct. Therefore, only conservative genes resistant to mutation should be widespread in existing life forms. On the other hand, a gene in an organism produced by a favorable mutation in some other gene, benefits from its bearer's ability to exploit new niches in the environment. It can, in effect, ride piggyback on the new organisms created by these mutated genes. In fact, there are genes known as mutators that can induce mutations within sister genes in an organism.[5]

In asexual organisms, mutations are the only source of variation in organisms. For such organisms, fitness involves living long enough to generate clones or otherwise generate copies of themselves that, with the exception of those containing the occasional mutation, are identical, uniform copies of the original. Since the original worked well in its niche, so will the identical copies or clones. This holds, however, only as long as the environment remains unchanged. Asexual organisms can adapt to new circumstances only because, in general, they reproduce at an extraordinary rate and can therefore create many novel forms through mutation.

Sexual reproduction, on the other hand, is almost always associated with larger and more complex creatures that cannot reproduce as prodigiously as simple organisms. It takes considerable time and energy to create a large creature, which limits reproductive numbers. Sexual reproduction arose, and it has persisted despite the complications it entails, because it produces greater diversity and greater opportunities to fully exploit the environment for large and complex organisms. By mixing together the genes of two slightly different organisms, new and slightly different offspring are regularly produced in each generation. The important point here is that the differences produced are regular and slight. If the changes were not slight the chances that the offspring would survive in their parents' environment would be severely reduced. Slight variations, however, allow for survival in the original habitat and may allow for the exploitation of new or changed environments in which parents might not survive or flourish. An important additional advantage of sexual reproduction is that it reshuffles an organism's immune defenses against disease. By doing so, it complicates the task of the evolution of microorganisms trying (figuratively) to decode and break through an organism's immune system. If all organisms in a species had identical immune systems, it would be easier for disease agents to evolve so as to overcome their defenses.[6]

Most sexually reproduced organisms have two sets of chromosomes, each set of which they received whole from one of their two parents. Cloned organisms have only one set of chromosomes and are said to be haploid; sexual reproducers have two and are said to be diploid. It will be readily apparent that if each sexually reproducing parent passes on both sets of chromosomes, their children will have four sets, their grandchildren eight, and so on. This will not do and it does not happen that way. Rather, sexual reproducers produce intermediate chromosomal forms. These intermediate forms or "gametes" (sperm and eggs) contain only one set of chromosomes. When one such gamete is combined with another, they produce individuals with the requisite two. The process of gamete formation is known as meiosis.

In meiotic division the diploid set of chromosomes splits in two. Before splitting, however, during the process known as "crossing over," genetic material is exchanged, generating a new set of chromosomes made up of elements of the originals. In other words, the set an individual got from his mother or father is not passed on unchanged in his gametes, but rather each contains a mixture of maternal and paternal genes. In order for this process to work the chromosomes must "match up." In other words, although the component genes making up the maternal and paternal chromosomes may differ, they must occupy the same region or locus on the chromosome. Such chromosomes are said to be homologous. Genes that can occupy the same site on homologous chromosomes, and guide the formation of some bodily structure or substance, are denoted homologous genes. Different versions of homologous genes are referred to as alleles.[7]

Sometimes, as in the case of eye color, one allele (brown) is said to be "dominant" over the other (blue), which is said to be recessive. The dominant gene determines the bodily outcome, or phenotype, if it appears at either one or both chromosomal sites. Only if both maternal and paternal chromosomes contain the recessive alleles will the recessive gene be expressed as a phenotype. In technical terms the genotypes brown-brown and brown-blue produce the expressed character or "phenotype" of brown eyes. Only the genotype blue-blue will be expressed by the phenotype of blue eyes. Dominance is not always operative and sometimes the phenotype expressed is intermediate between the phenotypes produced by homologous genotypes. In addition, there can be more than two alleles available for any chromosomal locus.[8]

Many inherited characteristics such as body size are controlled by alleles at more than one chromosomal locus. Such "polygenic" characteristics can produce characteristics, such as height, that are continuously variable, rather than discrete in the way of eye color. In addition, it is most common for such continuously variable characteristics to be normally distributed in the well-known normal distribution or bell curve. The bell curve is the mathematical representation of the binomial distribution that represents, among other things, the outcome of a large number of chance binary occurrences.

For instance, height in human beings appears to be determined by a variety of chromosomal loci that can be occupied by one or more alleles. It is most unlikely in the random assortment of sexual reproduction that an offspring will be dealt out all of the alleles that promote great height, or conversely, all those who would make the individual extremely short. It is far more likely that a person will receive a random mix of alleles, some promoting greater, and others, lesser stature. The result of this random mixing of alleles will be a normal distribution of individuals; a few will be very tall or very short, most will be of intermediate height. Suppose, for example, there exist only two alleles at twenty loci that determine height. The determination of height therefore could be likened to tossing a coin at each locus in turn to determine which allele—the one promoting greater or the one promoting lesser stature—is selected. Being very short would be as likely as throwing a string of twenty tails. Being very tall, as likely as throwing a string of twenty heads. Throwing approximately half heads and half tails is most likely, and for that reason most people are of moderate or intermediate height.

Of course, the pool of alleles any person receives is limited to those possessed by his parents. Taller parents tend to have children who are also taller and shorter parents, likewise, shorter children. Within these constraints considerable randomness, nevertheless, remains. The well-known phenomenon of "regression to the mean" is produced by this randomness. Because of regression to the mean, parents who are unusually tall, for instance, will tend to have children who are somewhat less tall. This is because the outcome of the randomizing process that produces very tall people is probabilistically very unlikely. When those alleles are reshuffled in the production of gametes, the new combinations are less likely to be as deviant from the average, since there are so many more combinations producing average heights than unusual ones.

Gene-Environment Interactions

The phenotypic expression of a gene can be modified by many factors, the most important of which are the actions of other genes and the physical and social environment in which the organism operates. For instance, in humans, sex is determined by the presence or absence of male hormones during fetal development. The presence of such hormones is in turn determined by the genetic makeup of the individual. If male hormones (androgens) are present, the individual will be physically male and at maturity show male behavioral patterns, such as being attracted to females. In the absence of androgens during fetal development, the organism will be physically and behaviorally female. The sex-determining genes, therefore, can modify the expression of the host of other genes producing male and female forms. Experimental studies with animals demonstrate that sex reversals can be induced by artificially altering the hormonal makeup of the fetal environment. The most likely explanation for the phenomena of transsexuality and homosexuality in humans is that sometime fairly late during gestation the fetal hormonal environment deviated, for as yet unknown reasons, from that dictated by the sex-determining genes. The result is a physical male or female with many of the behavioral traits and emotions normally associated with the opposite sex.[9]

Environmental conditions can also influence the phenotypic expression of genes. For instance, the presence of important nutrients is crucial for normal development. Genes build bodies from the nutrients available and the full phenotypic expression of characteristics cannot be achieved if the requisite nutrients are unavailable or in short supply. In humans, malnutrition clearly influences such things as height and IQ. Malnutrition can also delay the genetically programmed onset of puberty. Seasonal variations obviously regulate the expression of genes controlling growth and development in plants. Similarly, a wide variety of genetically controlled behaviors in animals, such as the expression of mating behavior, migration and hibernation, are also influenced by seasonal variations. Exposure to radiation and other mutagens can influence the mutation rate of genes, often producing debilitating and sometimes lethal effects.

It should be emphasized that while environmental conditions can influence the expression of genes, it cannot change an organism's genetic makeup in a systematic way. An exception is exposure to radiation that induces mutations, but these are generally random and unsystematic. The idea that the environment can alter genes and that such changes can be passed to offspring (that characteristics acquired during the lifetime of parents can be inherited by children) is known as Lamarchianism and has long been rejected by geneticists. Exposing an organism to a cold environment, for instance, cannot change its genes so as to make it more cold tolerant. The most famous case of this idea was the effort of Trofim Lysenko, agricultural minister under Joseph Stalin, who tried to extend wheat from warmer climates to more northern latitudes by exposing them to extreme cold. This effort proved to be a costly failure, both for the Soviet Union and the Chinese Communists who also tried it on a large scale.[10]

While the environment can effect gene expression, the alternative is also true. The expression of a gene can alter the environment in such a way as to have a feedback effect that further influences genetic expression. When a beaver builds a dam he remakes the environment to allow the expression of genetically determined behaviors that would be unlikely to appear in the setting before it was altered. Humans have been spectacularly successful in altering their environment, and in doing so, have produced technological and cultural changes that have changed in important ways, the expression of human genetic propensities. These changes and their impact will be discussed in the following two chapters. But the phenomenon can also be seen in everyday life. For instance, if a child inherits characteristics that contribute to well-coordinated physical movement, it is likely that he will display athletic abilities that induce him or his parents to encourage further development of those activities. Similarly, a child who demonstrates, spontaneously, specific musical abilities will likely be encouraged to apply those abilities in such a way as to enhance their display. Likewise, children who are naturally docile are likely to draw out less discipline from parents and teachers than those who are naturally more restless and irritable.

David Rowe, in his influential book, *The Limits of Family Influence*, demonstrates that as children grow older they tend to express more of their genotypic characteristics and fewer of those characteristics associated with their upbringing.[11] This finding is based on studies of adopted children that show that children come to resemble their birth parents more than their adoptive parents as they pass through adolescence in, for instance, such things as intelligence. The reason is that as children grow older they have greater freedom to gravitate to those environments that reflect their natural proclivities. High school students, for example, tend to associate with peer groups of individuals with similar interests and ability. Similarly, spouses tend to share a wide range of characteristics, both cultural and genetic; a phenomenon known as assortative mating. Such associations tend to create environments that reinforce already existing tendencies. Intelligent children associate with intelligent friends who reinforce each other's interests and who in turn contribute to their making greater use of their natural abilities. For similar reasons, children with aggressive and antisocial proclivities seek out each other, and that often leads to gang formation. If one is inclined to aggressive activity, he is well advised to have allies similarly inclined.

Gene-environment interactions are now beginning to merit greater research. An important recent example involves research that examined the question of why some, but not all, children who are seriously maltreated grow up to be violent or antisocial. These researchers found that a particular allele of a gene for encoding a neurotransmitter had a protective effect. Those maltreated children who had that particular allele were less likely to exhibit antisocial behavior in later life than those carrying a different allele.[12]

Inbreeding, Outbreeding, Genetic Disease, and Human Marriage Patterns

As mentioned previously, positive genetic mutations are relatively rare; most mutations are either unimportant or damaging when expressed. A problem arises, therefore, in attempting to understand how genetic diseases can remain in a population for extended periods of time. How can a mutation that causes the death of an organism remain in the gene pool? The explanation is found in the fact that most such diseases are caused by recessive genes. A lethal allelic mutation, if recessive, can be passed down from generation to generation since it is only expressed phenotypically in lethal form when it occupies both sites on a chromosomal locus. The medical practice of genetic counseling involves detection of lethal or debilitating recessives in individuals and advising them to avoid reproduction with others known to carry or likely to carry similar recessives. In general, mutant alleles are either lethal or debilitating if expressed and reduce the fitness of those who carry them. That is why very few debilitating alleles are dominant. Dominant alleles are phenotypically expressed in all who carry them, even in single dose, and are therefore always exposed to elimination by natural selection. Lethal and debilitating recessives survive since they are only occasionally exposed to the rigors of natural selection. Nevertheless, though it may take time, debilitating recessives should decline in a population and eventually be eliminated under the pressure of natural selection.

An important exception to the above generalization is that debilitating alleles, both dominant and recessive, can survive if they are only expressed after an organism has completed his reproductive and parental activities. Such "late acting lethals" can be passed from generation to generation, since, if they do not curtail reproduction or hinder the success of offspring, they do not reduce an organism's fitness. This may explain the host of "diseases of aging" that in recent years have come into greater focus as humans increasingly live to relatively older ages.[13]

Similarly, a debilitating or lethal recessive allele, if it does not curtail reproduction completely, may continue if it is linked to, and is compensated by, beneficial characteristics. The most famous such case is a recessive allele that, if it appears on only one chromosome, serves to protect against malaria, but if it appears on both chromosomes produces sickle-cell anemia. This allele is most common in tropical regions inhabited by malaria-spreading anopheles mosquitoes. In a similar light, recent research suggests that the high IQ of Eastern European (Ashkenazi) Jews may be linked to recessive genes associated with inherited diseases common in that population. The idea here is that among Ashkenazi Jews, high IQ may, in the past, have conferred a significant reproductive advantage that enabled genes that foster high IQ to remain in the population even if they, in some cases, have debilitating effects in a number of serious diseases common to this population.[14]

In general, sexually reproducing organisms carry a number of lethal or damaging recessives, and it is dangerous for them to mate with close kin who are likely to carry the same lethal recessives. For instance, brothers and sisters may carry a lethal recessive on a chromosomal site passed on by their father or their mother. If they mate, approximately one quarter of their children will receive the recessive allele in double dose and will therefore suffer the phenotypic consequence of the debilitating or lethal allele. Many miscarriages are attributed to such effects. Natural selection, therefore, penalizes those who engage in incestuous mating. Humans clearly have cultural prohibitions against incest, and may also inherit a natural distaste for incestuous relations. A study of children raised communally in Kibbutz communities in Israel found no marriages among those raised together. This suggests a mechanism of "negative imprinting," first proposed by Westermark in 1891 that disinclines individuals who are raised together from viewing each other as desirable sexual partners.[15]

Some animals may also inherit similar propensities against incest. However, the capacity to detect close relatives may not be necessary in most cases. Many animals are able to avoid incest by the simple mechanism of dispersal before they attain sexual maturity. Among lions, for instance, young males are driven from their parental pride at an early age, thereby preventing them from mating with their sisters and mothers.

While mating among individuals whose genes are very similar is reproductively wasteful, so also is mating with those who are genetically distant. Sexual reproduction requires that the chromosomes from each parent "mesh," that is, be homologous. In other words, if the chromosomal locus directing the assembly of a blood constituent on one chromosome is matched with a chromosome in which that locus directs the formation of a chemical necessary for vision, both functions will likely suffer. Dogs cannot mate with horses, but even if one could artificially bring together gametes from each, no offspring could be produced. Closely related organisms such as donkeys and horses can mate, and can produce offspring in the form of mules, but in that case the mules are sterile, because horses and donkeys have a different number of chromosomes. As a consequence, the effective formation of gametes during meiosis cannot be carried out, since the chromosomal loci do not coincide properly. The chromosomal structures of more distantly related organisms simply cannot work together to produce a living product.

Therefore, organisms who cannot identify their own kind for purposes of reproduction, or who have not evolved other mechanisms to constrain reproductive choices, are unlikely to leave many offspring. Animals should for these reasons, exhibit a tendency to prefer mating with organisms fairly similar to themselves, that is, of the same species, but not those too closely related, namely, those likely to carry identical lethal recessives.

This undoubtedly explains the widespread human pattern of exogamy, that is, outmarriage, often accompanied by cousin marriage. Among hunters and gatherers, for instance, marriage within the tribe is often proscribed, and men seek wives from neighboring tribes. This practice means that neighboring groups are often fairly closely related. A good many of the children in neighboring tribes will be the children of sisters and brothers and therefore cousins. This practice illustrates that while sibling incest is to be avoided, marriage to other relatives is often preferred. Cousin marriages and uncle-niece marriages are extremely common in North Africa and Southwest Asia. One advantage of such practices is that the individuals born into those groups are more closely related, sometimes much more closely related than they would be by more random mating. For reasons to be discussed later in this chapter, the more closely related people are, the more likely they are to assist each other.[16] Another reason animals and humans may prefer mating with closely related others is that their offspring may preserve the beneficial combinations of traits that have enabled their parents to thrive that would likely be broken up by outbreeding.[17] Patrick Bateson attempted to determine experimentally the preferred breeding partners of Japanese quail. In his experiment he allowed quail to choose mates among those very closely related and those more distantly related. He found that in both males and females the preferred genetic distance for mates was approximately equivalent in humans to the marriage of first cousins.[18]

The practice, common among many human groups, of marrying first cousins does not appear to exact a high price in genetic disorders. First cousins share approximately one-eighth of their genes by virtue of having common grandparents. If one of those grandparents carries a lethal or severely debilitating recessive gene, it would, on average, express itself phenotypically in one-sixteenth, or 6.25 percent, of the offspring of marriages between first cousins. By contrast, such damaging effects would appear, as mentioned earlier, in fully twenty-five percent of the offspring of brother-sister pairings. The latter effect would be easily detected by early human groups and would give rise to social rules on the inadvisability of such pairings. In the case of first cousin marriage, however, the morbidity rate is sufficiently small that it would hardly be detectable, especially when embedded in the background noise of the high miscarriage and child mortality rates common in earlier times. It should be stressed that the 6.25 percent figure is probably an overestimate of the damaging consequences of such consanguineous pairings. Lethal recessives are generally rare and may not be carried by either grandparent of a closely related couple. A large study of a number of populations found an excess mortality of 4.4% attributable to first cousin marriage.[19]

An interesting example is provided by the Rothschild family. For a number of generations, the men who controlled the family's fortune only married their female cousins with no obvious detrimental effect. Since inbreeding tends to promote the survival of rare combinations of genes, perhaps the rare combination of genetic traits that enabled the Rothschilds to accumulate prodigious wealth were preserved by their marriage patterns. If such keen financial acumen could be taught, there would probably be many more families like the Rothschilds. A different explanation, though not necessarily incompatible with the genetic explanation, is that such marriage practices keep wealth within a close family circle and less likely, therefore, to be diluted in a few generations.[20]

K versus r Reproductive Strategies

Population biologists distinguish between r and K reproductive strategies. Organisms that deploy the r strategy reproduce at a very high rate and provide little assistance to offspring, while K strategists reproduce at a low rate and usually invest heavily in assisting their young. (The small letter r denotes the natural rate of increase for an animal when no constraints are present; the capital letter K denotes the carrying capacity of the animal's environment setting limits on population growth.)[21] Edward Wilson explains that the first strategy is more common among creatures occupying habitats with "fluctuating environments and ephemeral resources," where favorable conditions may be short-lived and unpredictable.[22] In order to succeed, such a species needs to reproduce rapidly and to disperse its offspring widely so that at least some will end up in favorable circumstances. Such a strategy is common among seed plants, insects, and many fish that scatter their seed (or offspring) willy-nilly in hopes that some will survive and start the process all over again.

K strategists, on the other hand, are more common in habitats that are more predictable and longer lasting, and that after time are likely to be saturated with a variety of life forms. In such a setting "it is more important for a genotype to confer competitive ability, in particular the capacity to seize and hold a piece of the environment and to extract the energy produced by it."[23] Such an organism should be expected to reproduce in limited fashion and assist offspring in dealing with the competition they face in a fully populated environment. K strategists are generally longer-lived, larger and more complex than r strategists.

K and r strategies represent a continuum, generally correlated with complexity, ranging from species exhibiting prolific reproduction with little parental care (common in fish and insects) to those species, such as birds and mammals, that reproduce in very limited numbers and lavish extensive care on their young. It is also important to consider the ecological conditions that determine the carrying capacity of the environment. If environments change drastically from generation to generation, going erratically from feast to famine and back to feast again, those who can take advantage of good times by reproducing at a greater rate should have a fitness advantage. On the other hand, in times of scarcity, those who are more prudent and show greater parental care are less likely to find their line going extinct.

Over evolutionary time, species will tend to evolve in the direction of reproductive rates that have in the past proved fitness enhancing. It is important here to distinguish mechanisms that operate over evolutionary time and those operating in the lifetime of an individual. Some animals can make adjustments in their own lifetimes based on environmental signals related to, for instance, population density and climate. In most cases these sorts of adjustments will be automatic. Human beings are the exception and possess the capacity to make refined estimates and regulate their reproduction accordingly. Human beings have over time evolved into relatively conservative K strategists who commonly adjust their reproduction to anticipated environmental conditions.

Among human beings, prior to modern times, the most important environmental conditions determining reproductive strategies were disease and food scarcity. Where diseases, especially those of childhood, carry off large numbers of children, reproduction should be maximized consistent with an r strategy. That is especially the case for those living in disease-prone tropical climates. This tendency is reinforced where food is naturally fairly plentiful as it usually is in tropical locales. On the other hand, one would expect somewhat lower reproductive rates (closer to the K rate) where scarcity is the primary problem, as it is in more temperate climatic zones. Very often this limitation on reproduction occurs naturally among humans since malnourished women may cease ovulating or be prone to miscarriages. In addition, the later weaning of children in times of scarcity may contribute to more widely spaced births. In particularly difficult circumstances, infanticide of newborns may be the only option for parents to preserve the lives of children born earlier.

One should also expect somewhat different mating patterns in climates promoting different reproductive strategies. In tropical climates where food is plentiful, men are less important to the survival of the young. In such cases polygamy is likely to be common and marriages less long-lasting. In harsher climates where food is scarce, men are often critical for the survival of young. In these settings monogamy should be the rule and marriages somewhat more secure. As will be seen in a later chapter, marriage patterns do indeed reflect these predictions, though moderated by a good many other factors.

In modern industrial societies people tend to drastically curtail reproduction. This has important implications for human evolution and is of considerable importance in questions relating to immigration. In particular, it means that people who migrate from simpler to more complex industrial societies are likely to continue to reproduce at their accustomed rate and not at the rate of the host population. The consequence is that the immigrant population, at least initially, will grow at a much faster rate than is usually anticipated by the host population. If, in addition, the immigrant group persists in a pattern of marriage for women at relatively young ages, population growth will be exaggerated. Policies promoting assimilation will tend to reduce the effect of these reproductive phenomena, whereas policies promoting multiculturalism, which encourage people to maintain their traditional practices, will tend to prolong them.

Races and Species

Species are generally defined as groups of animals within which sexual reproduction results in surviving and reproducing organisms. Among asexual reproducers such a definition makes no sense and asexual species are usually differentiated on the basis of anatomy or behavior. In asexual cases, species arise from mutant forms that diverge to the point that they come to occupy different niches and become significantly different in form or habit. In such cases, the distinction of types into species is largely a function of human determination. In the case of certain bacteria, for instance, mutant forms are unlikely to merit the status of separate species unless they affect human life very differently.[24]

The definition of a species among sexual reproducers is not so arbitrary. Mutant forms of organisms that can continue to reproduce with nonmutant forms will share a large number of genetic similarities. However, if mutant forms occupy different geographical areas or widely disparate niches, or have nonoverlapping breeding seasons, they may lack opportunities for mating and start to diverge more and more from each other. If, over time, their chromosomal structures become sufficiently different, mating may fail to produce offspring. At that point we are confident in defining each population as a separate species that can be said to share in and contribute to its own common gene pool.

Within species it is not uncommon for populations to become separated geographically so that they never or rarely mate, but if they do, they can produce viable offspring. Such populations are defined as races. The distinction between races and species, however, is not always clear-cut or easy to make. Among populations that never mate with each other by virtue of geographic separation or very different mating habits, races can only be distinguished from species by artificial propagation carried out by human researchers.

The important point of the above is that different species and races are more than populations distinguished arbitrarily by human beings to satisfy human interests. Species, and to a lesser extant, races, are populations of organisms that, because they do not intermingle their genes, draw those genes from separate gene pools, and over time are likely to become ever more divergent and incompatible as they become more finely tuned to their separate environments. [25]

A gene pool is therefore a set of genes that more or less randomly contributes to the genetic characteristics of a set of organisms. The set of those organisms drawn from a specific gene pool is a species or a race. The gene pool (and by extension the species or race) evolves as the proportion of various alleles in the gene pool fluctuates over time. Phenotypic expressions of genes that enable their possessors to survive and reproduce will cause an increase in the proportion of those genes in the gene pool at the expense of those genes that produce less successful phenotypes.

Occasionally a mutation will enter a gene pool and spread, even if it confers no selective advantage. If it is not debilitating it can spread through the population and may in some cases replace an existing allele due to normal chance variation. This is a phenomenon known as "genetic drift." If there are three competing alleles in a gene pool, for instance, and they are passed on randomly, then their relative proportion in the population will fluctuate over time simply due to chance. Over an extended period, the proportion of one may fall to zero, in which case it ceases to exist in the gene pool. It may, on the other hand, come to replace the other alleles completely, in which case, it is described as fixed.[26]

The significance of genetic drift is that not all evolution (the replacement of one allele by another) is produced by natural selection. In other words, not all evolutionary changes necessarily produce organisms that are more fit. It is important to emphasize, however, that while genetic drift can produce changes in a gene pool in the absence of natural selection, natural selection is far more potent in producing widespread and rapid change. For instance, a change in climate or the availability of a food source may, in a few generations, drastically alter a gene pool.

The loss or fixation of alleles due to genetic drift is far more likely in populations that are small, since in large populations it would take a very long time for any allele to be either completely eliminated or become fixed. Since in prehistoric times human populations were relatively small, human populations came to diverge through genetic drift even if there do not appear to be environmental factors forcing such changes.[27] This appears to be the case with certain physical features, such as eye color, that differ among human populations and races, but do not appear to confer any selective advantage. Furthermore, in small populations, the likelihood that new mutations will arise is necessarily more limited than in large populations.

For that reason, population size matters a great deal in evolution. Favorable and unfavorable mutations, and unlikely gene combinations, are more likely to appear in large populations than in small ones, and are less likely to be eliminated by genetic drift. A mutation or gene combination that has no obvious selective advantage in a particular setting, may remain in a large gene pool and be available should that mutation have beneficial consequences in some new setting. For example, a mutation that improves mathematical reasoning might confer no advantage in a population lacking mathematical knowledge, but might be highly advantageous in a more advanced culture where it might serve to improve its carrier's fitness. It then would be expected to spread rapidly in the population. Similarly, a gene that improves reading comprehension would have no value in an illiterate culture, but much value in a literate one.

Evolutionary scientist John Hawks argues that the rapid growth in human communities following the advent of agricultural technology was of primary significance in the recent evolutionary history of human beings. The large populations, sustained by agricultural empires, allowed for a dramatic increase in human diversity due to a greater likelihood of potentially beneficial mutations. Furthermore, the large size of the gene pools in these civilizations made it less likely that those mutations would be lost due to genetic drift. The consequence, according to Hawks, was a notable acceleration in human evolution since the emergence of humans out of the hunter and gatherer way of life.[28]

Smaller populations have an advantage over large ones, on the other hand, in that characteristics that are fitness-enhancing (shaped by natural selection rather than genetic drift) are likely to persist, especially where inbreeding is common and many individuals carry the same set of genes. A rare combination of genes that improves the survival and reproductive prospects of an individual can spread more quickly throughout a small inbred group than in a large diverse population where it might be broken up and lost. This phenomenon explains what are known as "founder effects." If two individuals from an existing population leave it and start a family in a region separated from the original one, they will, in effect, give rise over time to a gene pool lacking the variation of the one they left. They will be founders who will leave their own genetic mark on future generations. If one or both of those individuals possess a rare combination of debilitating genes, then the line they found will be short-lived. On the other hand, if they possess a rare combination of fitness-enhancing genes, then their line should flourish. The problem is that those unique characteristics of the founders may only be fitness enhancing in environments very similar to that of the founders. For that reason small populations lacking in genetic diversity are more vulnerable to extinction than large, genetically diverse populations.

Sexual Differences and Sexual Selection

The fundamental distinction between the males and females of most species is that males provide sperm and females eggs. The eggs of the female, in addition to genetic material, also carry nutrients critical for the early growth of the fetus. They are therefore larger than sperm, which are really little more than vehicles for the carrying of chromosomal material to the eggs. The female egg therefore requires more biological work and more time to produce, a consequence of which is that eggs are much scarcer than sperm. The law of supply and demand—that dictates that if something is desirable or necessary, it will be in greater demand to the extent that it is scarce—produces the expected result. Females possess something over which we would expect males to compete, and that they most assuredly do.

In species in which parental care on the part of the female is sufficient and males contribute only sperm, some males can impregnate many females and others will, necessarily, impregnate few. It follows that those males who are successful in gaining access to many females will leave many sons who possess characteristics similar to their own. The consequence is that, in many species, males who are large and physically powerful will have a clear selective advantage and should become, over time, increasingly large in comparison to females. In the case of primates such as Langur Monkeys and Baboons, who can possess large harems, almost all of their energy goes to first winning over a harem and then policing it against possible interlopers. The males in these species are, therefore, physically far larger and more aggressive than the females. Male gorillas that control a harem of moderate size grow almost twice as large as females. Edward Wilson refers to the differences between males and females as sexual dimorphism.[29]

The females in such species seem indifferent to which male comes to control them, and in fact benefit from the fitness that powerful males confer on their own sons. The size disparities between males and females reach an upper limit when countervailing effects come into play. For instance, an extremely large male would have to devote so much time and energy feeding himself, that he would lose whatever advantage he gained by defeating other males. They would simply wait until he is off feeding himself to take advantage of his females.

Where polygamy is practiced among humans, physical strength and competence at aggressive contests are common features of successful men, as are social competence and personal flamboyance. In such societies weaker men often find themselves permanent bachelors. From a raw, calculating Darwinian perspective, a woman in that type of society might prefer to share with other females the favors of a powerful polygamous male who may provide her with sons who share their father's propensities, rather then accept a monogamous union with a weaker, less desirable male whose sons might, like their father, lack the qualities to provide many grandchildren. Of course, in most societies practicing polygamy, a woman rarely has any choice in the matter and is merely taken as a prize by a powerful male. Equally often, she is exchanged by her male relatives to obtain women, or for some other economic or political benefit.

In many species, especially humans, large harems are the exception since it is rarely possible for one male to provide for more than a few mates; therefore, sexual dimorphism tends to be somewhat muted. In the case of humans, for instance, males are only moderately larger and stronger than females, suggesting that humans, in general, are mildly polygamous. The extent of that polygamy depends largely on environmental factors determining, for instance, how many mates a male can support and how easily a harem can be defended. In environments rich in food resources where females and offspring can provide for themselves, societies may be moderately polygamous. In such circumstances, powerful and aggressive males have a clear fitness advantage. They can produce many offspring, while their weaker neighbors may produce none. On the other hand, where the environment is more difficult and a male is critical for the survival of a female's offspring, monogamy is more likely. In this case, we would expect males to compete, not for many females, but for access to more desirable females. In either case, we should expect males to evolve in the direction of becoming specialized competitors for the female's eggs.

That competition can take a variety of forms and often leads to fairly complex "courtship" rituals that determine whether mating will take place. A female who is prepared to mate usually advertises this fact, by chemical or visual signals, which attracts available males in the neighborhood. In most cases the female is selective, and bases her choice on her estimate of the worth of a suitor as indicated by his courtship behaviors. These rituals often take time and consume energy, time and energy that could be put to use producing and caring for offspring. Wouldn't males and females who, when ready, merely accepted the first mate to come along, leave more offspring than those who used time and energy in courtship activities? The answer is no, if their promiscuous couplings produce offspring who may fail to survive and prosper. Clearly, therefore, among the things that make a sexually reproducing animal fit is the capacity to select mates with whom it is likely to produce healthy and successful offspring.

Additionally, among the animals where extensive parental care is required, we would expect animals to be selective in seeking out mates with the potential for providing such care. For example, the rearing of young sparrow hawks is a time and energy-consuming business requiring the full-time efforts of both parents. Since sparrow hawks are predators relying on small game, it is critical that they be good at hunting if their offspring are to be reared successfully. David Barash describes an aerial mating ritual in sparrow hawks. As he watched, they flew in "elaborate loops alternating with power dives. They had a small mouse which one of them had caught, and at different points in the exhibition, one of the birds would drop its prize and the other would gracefully swoop down and snatch it in mid-air." According to Barash, such routines provide an opportunity for potential mates to size up each other's competence as hunters, as well their general health and physical robustness.[30]

Edward Wilson characterizes such courtship rituals as involving either intrasexual competition or epigamic competition. Intrasexual competition involves the competition, most often among the males, for access to females. Epigamic competitive behaviors, on the other hand, are displays, such as the aerial display of the sparrow hawk, designed to win the favor of a prospective mate, male or female. In general, these epigamic displays allow for the demonstration of physical health and competence, and therefore the likelihood that healthy and competent offspring will result.[31] Often intrasexual and epigamic competition will overlap. In species in which males must fight each other for access to females, the fact of success in fighting is evidence of genetic worth. A male who wins in such struggles is more likely to have sons who will also triumph. Males who, by a show of fearless bravado, can intimidate others without actually having to fight are likely to be especially successful and especially desirable to the female.

Males who lose in such competitions may never reproduce at all. Such is not the case for females, who even if they cannot find the most desirable mate, will rarely fail to reproduce. This would explain why female competition, though it may be intense in some species, rarely reaches the level found in the males. It also explains why female competition, if it exists at all, generally takes the form of epigamic displays of fitness rather than the aggressive combat of intrasexual competition. From this perspective, sports for human males and females provide an opportunity for individuals to display physical competence. Men's athletic competition often takes the form of demonstrating aggressive potential, whereas women's athletic competitions allow for the display of physical grace and dexterity. Dancing is a rare case, allowing both sexes to display grace and physical competence without aggressive displays, and for that reason is an almost universal aspect of human mating rituals.

As a sidelight, it is interesting that studies of attractiveness in humans done by psychologists indicate that facial features and body physique are considered pleasing if they are relatively close to the group average and do not deviate too much from the norm.[32] This suggests that physical traits may be used by both sexes as a sort of proxy for general wellbeing. In other words, if there is nothing peculiar in the way one's body or face is shaped, there is little reason to expect that less visible aspects of the body suffer peculiarities and potential defects. Bodily symmetry, for instance, has been shown to be related to judgments of attractiveness. Physical asymmetries, in which right features differ from left features, tend to be more pronounced in people who have suffered difficulties, such as illnesses, during gestation or in early childhood. When asked to explain their esthetic judgments, people rarely cite symmetry and are usually perplexed by the request.[33]

Once a species has evolved a way of judging the merits of prospective mates, the characteristics associated with desirable mates become, in and of themselves, desirable, whether or not they continue to have any real survival or reproductive value. Those who possess desirable traits are likely to pass on those traits to offspring who will themselves, by virtue of inheriting those traits, be more desirable. In human terms, finding a spouse generally considered attractive, for whatever reason, makes it more likely that your children will be attractive and therefore more likely that you will have grandchildren. The investment necessary to secure an attractive mate is, therefore, a sound reproductive strategy. In like manner, the investment necessary to convey or to feign those characteristics is equally sound. It is hardly surprising that the fashion, cosmetic, and fitness industries thrive, in one form or another, in most societies.

Evolutionary Stable Strategies: The Battle of the Sexes

In those cases where paternal care is important, such as is common in humans, epigamic displays should include demonstrations of the male's ability to acquire crucial resources and, in addition, his likely loyalty to a female and her offspring. In such a situation a male who is able to demonstrate honesty and loyalty, or one who can successfully feign such attributes, is more likely to win a mate than one who cannot. This leads to the "Battle of the Sexes" game outlined by Maynard Smith.[34] It is a simplified game theory model depicting the interactions within a population of males and females attempting to maximize their genetic fitness by employing alternative mating strategies. For instance, if all females are "coy" and wait until they are quite certain of a male's loyalty, males would have to commit themselves to extended courtship and the expenditure of considerable resources demonstrating that commitment. In the process a good deal of time is lost and loyal males may lose interest in trying to please such a female. This sets the stage for a female who is "fast" and less discriminating. As long as most males are honest, a fast female can have an offspring (a major gain in fitness) without the costs of the mating ritual, but still have the support of the honest and loyal male. This strategy on the part of the female, however, provides an opening for an occasional cad or dishonest suitor feigning loyalty, who can gain an offspring and then leave, without entailing any of the costs of providing support for the offspring. Furthermore, he is free to play the field in search of other fast females. Therefore, genes for male dishonesty should spread in the population, but only to the point where their numbers are so large that it is unlikely that a fast female will find an honest suitor. At that point, the probable costs of fastness become great, and females who remain coy will have an advantage over fast females, and in time females will tend to shift to more coy strategies.

That, in turn, reduces the fitness of cheating males who have a hard time finding fast females, especially if they obtain a reputation as cads. Under such circumstances, more males will adopt honesty, if only out of necessity. But, over time, as more males become honest, fastness on the part of females once again has an advantage. And so it goes. In Smith's model, behavior will fluctuate in such fashion, with coyness and fastness coexisting among females, and cheating and honesty coexisting in males. This is said to produce a set of "evolutionary stable strategies" that, while waxing and waning, are likely to persist in a population. Evolutionary stable strategies are sometimes referred to as "frequency dependent." In the Battle of the Sexes game, for instance, the fitness value of the strategies adopted by one sex is determined by the frequency with which alternative strategies are utilized by the other sex.

The implications of the above are obvious in explaining the consequences of the sexual revolution of the 20th century in the West. The availability of female contraception and safe abortion dramatically reduced the costs of sexual freedom among prudent women. But the rise in the number of fast women drove up the advantages of playing the cad. The consequence is that women who were not so prudent often found themselves with offspring but without husbands. The result has been a dramatic rise in illegitimacy, especially among younger and less intelligent girls who are less likely to exhibit either prudence or discernment in cad-detection.

Adults in almost all preindustrial societies recognize the powerful motives effecting people's choice of mates and these motives often conflict with the interests of parents and the community at large. In communities with scarce resources, people have a profound interest in seeing that children are provided for, lest they become a burden on everyone. They, therefore, place tight controls on when and with whom their children, and especially their daughters, may mate. For that reason, arranged marriage is the rule in most nonindustrial societies, with young people given some freedom of choice in the matter, as in early modern Europe, or none, as in the more traditional cultures of the Middle East and Southwest Asia. Political and economic considerations often play a more prominent role than the desires of young people.

In Muslim societies, very tight control over women is exercised by men, and women who violate these controls are subject to extremely harsh punishment, including death (honor killings), banishment and gang rape.[35] The last punishment is reserved for women seen as promiscuous and is legally sanctioned in some communities.[36] Even women who are raped are spurned as impure and often blamed for allowing themselves to get into situations where rape was possible.[37] Women in traditional Muslim societies are expected to remain in the home and cover themselves when they must go out in public, lest they tempt men by their physical appearance. This is, of course, completely at variance with practices in all industrial societies where women are given as much freedom in everyday life and in marital choice as are men.

The reasons for the differing treatment of women in different types of societies will be taken up in the next chapter. For now it is enough to point out that if immigrants from such traditional societies do not adopt the values of their host countries, their treatment of women will be a source of continual tension between them and members of their host societies. Of course, people wishing to maintain their traditional way of life will be disinclined to accept the freedom possessed by women in industrial societies and see such freedom as undermining their traditional values, as it surely does. If not fully integrated into their host culture, young men from such societies will tend to view the behavior and attitudes of Western women in terms of shameless promiscuity.

These attitudes clearly impede assimilation since immigrant women who wish to adopt Western ways are often restrained, sometimes violently, by more traditional male family members who see such behavior as morally repugnant. The practice of honor killings has deeply shocked western people.[38] Similarly shocking to most modern people is the widespread incidence of gang rape in, for instance, France's

North African slums where women, who are seen as "loose" for wearing modern attire or having intimate relations before marriage, are thought of as fair game for gang rape by adolescent males.[39]

Authorities who adopt a wide-ranging multicultural philosophy, such as those in Europe, have a difficult time squaring these practices with their faith in multicultural tolerance. As of this writing, however, French elites have largely attempted to avoid the issue and certainly have made no attempt so far to put an end to the gang rape endemic in the French slums or "banlieues" that surround all of France's major cities. The reasons for this grotesque failure are hard to fathom, but it surely puts in question the goodwill of those who preach tolerance for what, to most Europeans, is plainly intolerable.

Inclusive Fitness, Altruistic Behavior, and Group Conflict

In all animals, the behaviors associated with parental care are regulated by biological mechanisms, much as are courtship behaviors. Like all instinctive behavior, parental care involves programmed sequential responses to specific stimuli that are monitored and regulated by brain structures that have been shaped during the course of evolution. Little, if any, learning seems to be required for appropriate parental responses in most species; the obsessive devotion to the young so visible among many birds has its counterpart in many other species. Human beings are no different and most parents bestow great effort on the well-being of their children. Of course, human beings do so for reasons of love and affection toward their children, but that begs the question of why they love their children, and why so selflessly.

Among organisms that are born unable to care for themselves and which require parental care, genes that program parents to care for their young will soon displace those that fail to do so. This view explains why many animals, including humans, will go to extraordinary lengths to assure the safety of their young. Some social scientists, especially behaviorists, suggest that humans have the capacity to learn to care for their children and have no need for genetic programming. But the mere fact that we could function without such genes does not mean we do not possess them. All other mammals have such genetic programming. On what grounds and by what evolutionary mechanism would such genes disappear from the gene pool of early hominids? Such genes are virtually fixed in all other primates. It is hard to imagine any set of circumstances that would render genes promoting parental care decreasing and lost through the action of natural selection. For these reasons, it is safe to assume that humans are as genetically programmed to exhibit the parental care and affection as other primates. It remains for geneticists to isolate the specific genes in the human genome that program this behavior, perhaps in a search for an understanding of the rare instances where they seem to fail and produce abusive parents.

William D. Hamilton, in a groundbreaking analysis, made the point that genes promoting parental care, when passed to offspring, preserve themselves in those offspring. In other words, the gene complex that programs parental concern is protecting itself, since it is likely to be lodged in those offspring. By this reasoning, Hamilton asked, shouldn't gene complexes arise for showing care and concern for siblings and parents with whom we share fifty percent of our genes and to whom we are as closely related as to our own children? By similar logic shouldn't such genes induce us to show concern for the well-being of, let us say, grandchildren and nieces and nephews, to the extent that nieces and nephews also carry those same genes?[40]

An individual is as closely related to nieces and nephews as he is to his grandchildren. In both cases he shares approximately one quarter of those genes that make him a unique individual among those who share a common gene pool. For this reason, any particular gene in a person has a twenty-five percent chance of also being carried by a niece or nephew as by a grandchild. A gene complex that induces a person to care for and protect these close relatives helps to preserve itself in them. Shouldn't an organism, following Hamilton's insight, be programmed to show concern about the welfare of any organism with whom he shares many genes?

Hamilton's answer is, in short, yes. From the perspective of what Hamilton termed "inclusive fitness," measuring the fitness of an animal only through its own offspring is unsatisfactory. Rather, fitness should be measured to include all organisms who share substantial numbers of genes in common. Remember, it is genes that are preserved and not the individuals who carry them. A combination of genes that predisposes you to look after close relatives is fit, because it preserves itself in those relatives. Such genes are using you, figuratively speaking, for their own ends; you are, in Dawkins' terms, acting as an agent for your selfish genes.

Most examples of altruistic behavior in animals can be understood in terms of inclusive fitness. The practice of adoption, common among humans, and sometimes practiced by other species, is a good example. Adoption, when it is not the result of mistaken identity, seems somewhat paradoxical. How could such a tendency survive the pruning of natural selection that ought to favor those who devote all their energies to their own children rather than the children of strangers? The paradox is resolved when we recognize that most adoption, among animals and humans, especially in earlier times, was not the adoption of strangers but rather of close kin, often of grandchildren and nieces and nephews. If animals, including humans, live in inbred groups as they so often do, then all are closely related, and adoption would reflect the principle of inclusive fitness.

Some other instances of altruistic behavior seem equally paradoxical. Primatologist Michael P. Ghiglieri reports that Chimpanzees forage for food, either singly or in small groups, and if an individual happens upon a tree that has a large supply of fruit, he will signal its presence by "pant-hoots" that often bring a large number of chimps to the site. Ghiglieri reports that such hooting "sometimes produced an impressive din that lasted for at least ten minutes."[41] Why should a Chimpanzee create such a ruckus in order to share food when in so doing he exposes himself to the considerable danger of predators by all the noise? He gets no obvious benefit himself and clearly exposes himself to danger. By the logic of evolution, those predisposed to such altruistic hooting should, over many generations, begin to suffer from their generosity and leave fewer offspring like themselves, while their more selfish compatriots should live and reproduce and become an increasing proportion of the population. But, since hooting has remained dominant in the gene pool, this is not the case. Similarly, group living animals who signal the presence of predators by warning calls expose themselves to greater risk than those who silently scurry at the first sight of danger, leaving others to satisfy the appetite of the predator. These examples, like adoption, are best understood as revealing the operation of inclusive fitness. Since most group-living species live in inbred groups, altruistic behavior directed toward close kin can be understood as conferring inclusive fitness on animals.[42]

Inclusive fitness has its limits. If it did not, then of course, all creatures, and especially those in the same species, should be equally concerned for each other, since they share many genes in common. Altruism should be the rule rather than the exception, which is clearly not the case. The reason is that organisms, and by extension the genes that build them, are in constant competition with each other for scarce resources. This is especially true of members of the same species, since they tend to occupy the same ecological niche and require similar resources. When, therefore, should an animal act altruistically and when competitively? When are other animals from the same species to be treated as kin and when as competitors?

The line between kin and nonkin is likely to be differently drawn in different species and differing circumstances. Hamilton has suggested that the line is best understood as maximizing fitness in cost/benefit terms. Our own offspring, for instance, are twice as closely related to us as are our nieces and nephews and therefore we should be twice as concerned with sons and daughters as with nieces and nephews. Aiding nieces and nephews hurts our own sons and daughters, since to some extent, cousins are often in competition with each other.[43]

Sibling rivalry seems a special case of this balancing of motives. Sibs, who share fifty percent of their genes on average, clearly have an interest in helping and protecting each other, and generally do so when out in the world at large. Within the family, however, where there is little likelihood of danger from parents, the selfish gene rears its ugly head. Sibs clearly have an interest in the fifty percent of the genes they share with each other, but have a somewhat greater interest in their own one hundred percent.

At some point aiding a relative who is sufficiently far removed from us will incur a greater potential loss than gain. Any aid I give to the children of third cousins' benefits my genes in small fashion, since those children are less likely to carry them, and the aid I give them must be taken from my own children. In addition, the children of third cousins will undoubtedly be in competition for the same resources and mates as my own children, especially if we all live in the same geographic area. In general we would expect an animal's altruistic behavior to decline fairly sharply as relatedness and the associated benefit-to-cost ratio of altruistic behavior declines.

Put another way, genes for very generalized and indiscriminate altruism would in time succumb to those sets of alleles inducing greater discrimination. However, generalized altruism can remain in a population since it is often fitness-enhancing. This is explained by Robert Trivers in the concept of "reciprocal altruism."[44] Trivers made the point that it often makes sense for animals, even those not related, to help others if they can reasonably expect help in return. The reason for this is straightforward. If an altruistic act is less costly to the altruist than it is beneficial to the recipient, then over time, those who engage in mutual aid gain in overall fitness. For example, an animal who comes across a food resource he cannot possibly consume completely, loses little by sharing it with another, and gains if the act is reciprocated at some future time. He may gain a great deal if he resides in a group where food sharing is common; one act of food sharing will be paid back many times by others in the group. Similarly, warning calls can also be seen as acts based in reciprocal altruism. The mutual grooming of primates who remove lice and other parasites from each other is another example.

Human friendship is a highly elaborated form of reciprocal altruism, very often among males requiring mutual self-defense, and among females who can benefit by aid in child-rearing. The problem with reciprocal altruism, however, is that free-riders can take advantage of altruists, unless free-riders can be identified and shunned. It makes no sense to scratch the back of a stranger if one suspects he won't scratch yours. Reciprocal altruism is most pronounced, therefore, in humans and other complex animals that have the mental capacity to recognize each other and remember past behavior so that they can identify and punish free-riders. Among such species, free-riding should tend to disappear, but not completely, especially if a group is fairly large. In such cases free-riders can find others who have not yet identified them as such. If they benefit from their behavior, their numbers will grow. In others words, free-riding will be fitness-enhancing and genes for free riding should spread in a population.

This is another example of the phenomenon of evolutionary stable strategies, as in the "Battle of the Sexes" game discussed earlier. As free-riding becomes more common in a population it becomes less successful, since individuals burned by strangers will tend to become more cautious in bestowing altruistic acts. Over time an equilibrium should be established in which a limited number of free-riders or cheats can sustain themselves in a population of reciprocal altruists or trusting souls. Put another way, the strategies of being trusting and being a cheat can therefore coexist as "evolutionary stable strategies" whose proportions fluctuate around some equilibrium value. That equilibrium will in turn be dependent on the size of the group, the memory capacity of its members, the value of the aid provided, and the punishment meted out to cheats or free-riders. The ubiquity of crime and punishment in all human groups is evidence in humans of the operation of this model. The model also explains why crime is much more common in large cities with anonymous populations than in small towns and rural areas where everyone knows all the players.

Inclusive fitness appears to be a special case of reciprocal altruism that operates independent of the ability to remember specific acts of cheating or free-riding. An organism that carries genes predisposing him to aid kin can be fairly sure that close kin, such as parents and children and siblings, also carry those genes. For that reason if he aids close kin he can be reasonably assured that aid will be reciprocated. Strangers, on the other hand, and those with whom one is not closely related may well be free-riders, and aiding them would be wasteful and potentially dangerous. The example of the hooting chimps illustrates this point. Their altruism, as clear as it relates to close kin, does not extend to unrelated chimpanzees. Ghiglieri reports that the chimps patrol the borders of their territory and will kill other chimps, often infants with mothers, if they are found infringing on their normal feeding territory.[45]

In fact, killing within species is quite common although its extent has only recently been brought to light. The reason is that most of the reports in the literature on animal behavior dealt with groups of animals that were generally highly inbred. Most contests within such groups, such as the competition between males for access to females, generally stops short of lethal action, and is generally broken off when one party gains the upper hand. This occurs because most males competing in these small groups are close kin, very often brothers and cousins. The genes that predispose male animals to compete over mates are partially offset and kept in check by genes that predispose animals to protect close relatives.

In these groups we may mistake behaviors driven by kin selection as a generalized desire to spare members of the same species, that is, as a sort of taboo on murder within species. An additional reason why animal combat is often ritualized and stops short of mortal combat is plain prudence. Members of the same species are often equally matched for combat and therefore deadly fights are likely to be harmful, even to the winners. This interpretation is given support by the fact that killing within species is most common when members are not equally matched.

Infanticide is a striking example of such behavior. Brian C. R. Bertram reports that this is a fairly regular practice among African lions. Lion prides are made up of two or three adult males, a similar number of adult females, and their offspring. When the male offspring approach maturity they are driven out of the pride by the older males while female offspring remain within the pride. These males, who are closely related, remain together as a troop and roam the savanna until they are in a position to overpower and drive out the adult males from an existing pride, and take it over for themselves. Thus there is a relatively constant turnover of males, with females remaining fairly constant.[46] Bertram reports instances where newly installed males systematically kill off the nursing infants found in the pride, and in doing so they bring the females into heat more quickly owing to the end of nursing. In addition, by killing the nursing offspring, the newly installed males eliminate the competition for their own sons and daughters who are likely to follow after the infanticide.

This sort of behavior has been observed in other carnivores, such as tigers, pumas, brown bears, coyotes and wild dogs. Sometimes it involves not only the killing, but the cannibalizing of the murdered infants. In fact, it is quite common, and not limited to males. Dominant females have been observed killing the infants of subordinates. An interesting sidelight here is that the subordinate female whose young are killed often proceeds to assist the dominant female, who gains doubly by her murder; she eliminates competition for her own offspring who, in turn, receive more extensive care. Intraspecies killing of infants is therefore fairly common and suggests that it is the unevenness of the contests between adults and infants that makes it so.[47]

Similar infanticide has been observed among many primates.[48] Sarah Hrdy reported on infanticide among the Langur monkeys she studied in India. In the case of Langurs, one dominant male controls a harem of many females and their offspring. A harem of females is valuable and often contested, and not surprisingly, harems often change hands. The newly ascendant male cannot take full advantage of his harem if many females are nursing offspring. Rather than wait for nursing to take its natural course, the new male proceeds to murder the infants in methodical fashion.[49]

Few of our primate relatives are immune to such behavior. It has been observed among baboons, gorillas, and our closest relatives, the chimpanzees.[50] Diane Fossey sums up her observations of gorillas: "Given the long period of dependency of the gorilla infant upon its mother and the violent means by which silverbacks [male gorillas] acquire their harems, it seems likely that all sexually mature males at some time in their lives carry out infanticide."[51]

It is hardly surprising, in light of the above, that among humans, infanticide and accidental death are far more common in families with stepfathers than those in which fathers reside with their natural offspring. Researchers Martin Daly and Margo Wilson report that young children raised in stepparent homes in the United States were seven times more likely to suffer physical abuse than those raised by genetic parents and, even more strikingly, the incidence of "fatal abuse was on the order of 100-fold." They go on to report that "Canadian and British data tell much the same story, with a large excess of stepchildren among reported child abuse victims and an even larger excess among children fatally abused."[52]

Human Group Solidarity and Conflict: War and Territorial Behavior

Primitive human groups are generally quite small, numbering from about fifty to one hundred individuals who are invariably close kin—bands of brothers and cousins, as it were. Not surprisingly, they exhibit a high degree of altruism, based both in inclusive fitness and reciprocity. Their solidarity is demonstrated in high relief when they engage in hostilities, as they often do, with other bands. The ferocity and genocidal nature of such conflicts, and their regularity among hunter-gatherer groups, is well-documented.[53]

Lawrence A. Keeley in his *War Before Civilization* argues that while most anthropologists subscribe to the "myth of the peaceful savage," the ethnographic evidence clearly contradicts that view. He presents powerful evidence that people living before the advent of civilization are much more likely to suffer the ill effects of war. Death, maiming and the destruction of crucial resources are much more common among hunters and gatherers than among civilized peoples. The high war-related mortality among primitive groups is often overlooked because the absolute number of casualties is relatively small in comparison to the wars of civilized nations. However, when primitive war is examined in terms of the percentage of people affected, the numbers are much higher than among civilized people. Small bands of hunters and gatherers often engage in frequent battles, small-scale raids, and ambushes, sometimes many times during a year. In addition, a much greater proportion of adult males are involved in this regular fighting than is common in civilized societies. As a consequence, the casualties can mount quickly.[54]

Adding to the toll is the fact that primitive warriors seldom take prisoners; male captives are almost always killed immediately or shortly after the fighting ends. No quarter is given or expected. In addition, if a group is successful in the decisive defeat of an enemy it will often attack the enemy's home village and slaughter all the inhabitants left behind, including women and children. Frequently, the women are raped before being killed, though often young women are taken as war prizes. In addition, some groups are notoriously brutal, torturing captives mercilessly before they are killed, as they almost always are. It is not uncommon for victims to be mutilated and parts taken as trophies for display as signs of merit by the victorious warrior. Such gratuitous displays of cruelty are no doubt designed to inspire fear in potential enemies, but are otherwise inexplicable except as evidence of a complete lack of empathy and utter contempt for the enemy.[55]

The picture that emerges from Keeley's account is one of small, closely related kin groups, who view other similar groups as almost nonhuman, which perhaps explains their cruelty in dealing with captives. It should be stressed that such brutal, genocidal behavior is most common among groups that share few kinship ties. Groups with such ties, such as those practicing marriage exchange, are likely to show some restraint when they fight, which they, nevertheless, often do.[56]

The causes of these disputes relate to the theft of resources, the abduction or rape of women, the betrayal of agreements, the death or injury of an individual, or territorial disputes. Keeley also demonstrates that fighting is likely to be more intense and frequent during times of temporary scarcity or where population growth begins to surpass the carrying capacity of an area. While Keeley does not invoke evolutionary explanations, all of this, including the genocidal murder of innocents, is perfectly consistent with the theory of inclusive fitness.[57]

Sigmund Freud is famous for having argued that all human behavior can be explained in terms of sex and aggression, or of love and hate. What Freud did not fathom, however, was that both these motives are the necessary consequence of the struggle for genes to preserve themselves and to eliminate real and potential rivals. The brutal murder of competing outsiders is the mirror image of self-sacrifice for one's own family and close kin. It must be recalled that hunters and gatherers live in territories from which they gather the sustenance essential to their survival. Groups that are successful will grow in size and require more territory and may begin to infringe on the territories of neighboring groups. If they are successful in wresting control of this territory, it necessarily reduces the resources of their neighbors who will over time be reduced in size. Primitive life is thus a very real zero-sum game in the evolutionary sense. If one group grows at the expense of another, such that it can mount a significantly larger fighting force, it may well attack the main habitations of the neighbor and attempt to massacre all inhabitants. Those who manage to escape may be absorbed in other tribal groups, but the gene pool from which they came has quite literally gone extinct, and genocide effected. Keeley presents considerable evidence that this is the intent in many of the wars launched by primitive people.[58]

Strangers who venture into a territory held by a resident band are almost always viewed with caution and fear, and are often killed outright. Strangers are easily identified as nonkin by physiognomic features, by language or dialect, by dress and body decorations, and a host of other ways. The us-them dichotomy is so pervasive among hunters and gatherers, and indeed among all human groups, that it is hard to deny that it is a fundamental feature of human nature.

The spontaneous development among young males in civilized societies of gangs and gang warfare seems the natural outgrowth of these powerful impulses. That these gangs are often formed on the basis of ethnicity or race strengthens this interpretation. Furthermore, they mimic the hunter and gatherer model in what they fight over. The admiration and possession of young women is a primary motive, as it is for the many primitive bands and tribes. The territories gangs defend are valuable in being places where they can maintain a monopoly on highly lucrative criminal behavior, whether it is drug dealing, theft, or extortion. Almost all major cities in America are populated with numerous gangs, which often recruit along ethnic lines. Prisons are particularly fertile grounds for gang formation and conflict, where the recruiting almost always takes on a racial or ethnic character.

The tribal nature of much gang competition is particularly clear in Los Angeles, where the recent influx of Latinos has begun to displace blacks as the predominant minority group. According to Paul Harris, reporting in the London Observer, there are "an estimated 120,000 gang members across five counties [that] battle over turf, pride and drugs. It is a city of violence as a new race war escalates between Hispanic gangs and older black groups, each trying to ethnically cleanse the other." [59]

Similar territorial defense is common among adolescent immigrants in many European cities, although immigrant gangs more often defend neighborhoods against police and attack natives of the host country, rather than each other.[60] Fjordman, the prolific and highly reliable essayist, reports on an epidemic of rape of native women in major Swedish and Norwegian cities by gangs of young men of North African descent.[61] In Oslo, two out of three rapes in 1999 were committed by men of non-Western background, even though this segment makes up only 14% of Oslo's population. Among the victims, 80% were women of Norwegian heritage.[62] Such behavior mirrors the rape of women from rival tribes so common among primitive peoples. Whether this behavior reflects the same evolutionary-based motives is a question of considerable interest and will be explored in the next chapter. Whatever the source of gang formation and gang-related violence and rape, it unquestionably complicates the problem of integrating immigrant groups into host societies, and seriously exacerbates frictions between immigrants and native populations.

The Nation State and Inclusive Fitness

Most simple societies are bound together by inclusive fitness, since they are to a large degree merely extended families. Societies can grow larger on the basis of inclusive fitness only if they can convince their members that they are part of an extended kin group or clan, and draw their commonalities from a common gene pool. In premodern times, the distances between various groups made intermarriage and a widespread commingling of genes impossible. Large societies tended to be confederations of unrelated people from separate regions held together by mutual and often temporary convenience, or by coercion. One thinks of the shifting alliances of the Greek city-states as an example of one based on convenience and the Roman Empire as an example of one based on coercion. Very often those confederations bolstered a sense of common ancestry through myths of origin and sagas of heroic figures from the past. The founding of the Hebrew nation as related in the story of Abraham's encounter with God implies a common genetic ancestry, as do the heroic legends of the Greeks and Vikings. Most of the world's religions deal with questions of the physical origins of the world and the linking together of people through a common founding lineage.

However, the unity of a large society based on a presumed extended kinship is constantly threatened by the centripetal forces of more local loyalties, since the kinship claimed by large societies is often more mythic than real. Such confederations are, therefore, highly unstable and increasingly come to be held together by physical force without any pretense of common ancestry. That is, of course, what is meant by an empire and what distinguishes it from a tribe or a nation. A nation, especially a modern nation-state, is somewhat of a combination of a tribe and an empire in that it ties people together on the basis of both coercion and common ancestry. To the extent that a sense of common ancestry, of genetic relatedness, is real and not fictitious, the society can rely more on the power of inclusive fitness and less on naked force to bind its population together.

It is well to keep in mind that the history of the European nations was one of ever greater consolidation of separate ethnicities, often involving great violence. This was the case even though Western European populations share a common ancestry with the Neolithic peoples that inhabited those regions thousands of years ago. In effect, modern Europeans are drawn from the same distinctive gene pool as those prehistoric peoples. Genetic studies suggest that more recent migrants, mainly from the Middle East, have contributed relatively little (about 20%) to the European gene pool as it exists today.[63]

Nevertheless, it took centuries, and it was not until quite recently that the European states were able to fashion a unified population where marriage across ethnic lines became common. Before transportation brought people from separate regions into regular contact with each other, this was not possible. In France, for instance, it was not until the twentieth century that the transfer of allegiance from region to nation was complete. Once the intermingling of regional populations became sufficient to foster near universal intermarriage, a nation could be transformed into one sharing a common gene pool and, in effect, one based in common ancestry. This is clearly what happened to the various nations of Europe and indeed of almost all nations of sufficient age. These nations are made up of closely related peoples, and comprise a fairly large, but nevertheless identifiable gene pool— an extended clan or tribe as it were. Where this genetic consolidation didn't happen, as in Yugoslavia and Czechoslovakia, ethnic allegiance trumped national allegiance with the expected outcome.

Modern war, as exemplified in all its horror by World War I, demanded nearly universal participation of most young men and was especially reliant on this sense of shared ancestry and the solidarity it inspired. When young men went to war for the nation (for the fatherland or motherland), it was not mere propaganda that induced them to feel a brotherhood with each other. The genes that promote group loyalty and bravery in young men induced a fervent belief that the losses on the battlefield were compensation for the preservation of the integrity of the nation. It is commonly noted that the horrific and often senseless losses of that war marked the beginning of the decline of national allegiance among European peoples that is so evident today, especially among elites. Such national feeling and allegiance managed, almost by inertia, to motivate Europeans through World War II. That experience, however, shook to the foundations most Europeans' devotion to their nations and explains the revulsion engendered today, in so many, at the very thought of national and patriotic feeling. The power of inclusive fitness to exact sacrifice has its limits. One is forced to conclude that, at least for Europeans in the twentieth century, it had been extended well beyond its limits. One is reminded of the poignant words attributed to the South Carolina soldier at Appomattox. As he reflected on the carnage and destruction visited on his defeated nation, he spoke as if for all his comrades when he remarked that, "It is a serious thing to love a country."[64] For the millions of young men who witnessed the horrors of World Wars I and II, it was indeed a serious and a terrible thing to love their nations.

The formation of the United States as a nation-state is very different from almost all others. While in the beginning it clearly traced its history and traditions to England, subsequent English and European settlers came from so many different backgrounds that for them America had no common history and was ancestral to none. This was true even for Englishmen who came from quite different regions and brought very different customs with them and settled in distinct geographical areas in America. However, most Europeans arrived at a time when geographic mobility allowed for intermingling and intermarriage to become common and to become increasingly common as the nation grew. Nevertheless, the country suffered a devastating civil war between rival regions that in some measure reflected ethnic differences.[65] It must be recalled that the founding fathers of the United States maintained their primary allegiance to their separate states, and drew up a constitution with those allegiances clearly in mind. After the Civil War, and to some extent because of it, a vast intermingling of population occurred that in a few generations created a national gene pool for those of European descent. However, this intermingling did not include the Jewish European immigrants arriving early in the twentieth century, who maintained a separate gene pool, by mutual consent, from the other Europeans. By the late twentieth century, within three or four generations after their arrival, this separation crumbled, much to the chagrin of Jewish religious leaders. The United States is still divided by race, however, and rates of interracial marriage, especially between blacks and whites, remain quite low, too low to create a truly common gene pool in the near term. It is hardly unreasonable to attribute at least part of the tensions between whites and blacks to this failure. A conclusion hard to avoid is that until such time as a nation is molded into a population of common ancestry, it remains in constant danger of schism along ethnic and racial lines.

The historical evidence is clear that the critical problem in fashioning a well-functioning nation-state is the necessity of binding together the population into a cohesive whole whose allegiance is to the state. In general, any allegiances above and beyond the immediate family work at cross-purposes to this enterprise. In the extreme case of totalitarian states, even family allegiances are seen as threatening loyalty to the state. Tribal and clan attachments must be restricted if the state is to function effectively. Similarly, religion is tolerated as long as it does not challenge the authority of the state. The history of Europe and China, indeed, of every region of the world in which the nation state came into being, is one of almost ceaseless conflict between the centralizing rulers and the fractionating forces of clan and tribe and religious allegiance.[66]

Empires, since they stretch over very large areas encompassing many ethnic populations, have a harder time than more genetically homogenous nations in restraining ethnic tensions and can do so only by overwhelming force. Loyalty in empires is difficult to maintain and is almost always conditional on the empire providing physical and economic security. Niall Ferguson in his book *The War of the World*, concluded that the most intense and brutal violence in recent history involved ethnic clashes among groups that were part of empires in the midst of disintegration and decline.[67] This interpretation is completely consistent with the theory of inclusive fitness outlined above. People are intensely concerned with the welfare of kin and those they can reasonably view as kin, and will engage in genocidal conflict if they perceive other groups as threatening their own. During times of economic and political turmoil, if unrestrained by superior force, these powerful instincts come to be expressed in all their ferocity. The widespread social turmoil and violence in vast areas of the world formerly ruled by the English and European empires is testament, if one were needed, to the truth of the above assertion.

The answer to the famous question posed by Rodney King, "Why can't we all just get along?" is quite simply that we are not programmed to get along, but rather to view people different from ourselves with varying degrees of suspicion and hostility. Harvard political scientist Robert Putnam found, to his dismay, that multicultural communities in America are rife with distrust. Speaking to a reporter for the Financial Times he said his research indicated that, "[t]he effect of diversity is worse than had been imagined." This is the case even after adjusting for the factors of class, income, and urban versus rural residence. Putnam found that "the more people of different races living in the same community, the greater the loss of trust."[68] He reports that the greater ethnic diversity in society the less trust people had in each other, even people of their own race. "In more diverse setting, Americans distrust not merely people who do not look like them, but even people who *do*." In addition, "inhabitants of diverse communities tend to withdraw from collective life, to distrust their neighbors, regardless of the color of their skin, to withdraw even from close friends, to expect the worst from their community and its leaders, to volunteer less, give less to charity and work on community projects less often, to register to vote less." He adds that "in colloquial language, people living in ethnically diverse settings appear to 'hunker down'—that is, to pull in like a turtle."[69]

From the perspective of inclusive fitness, unfamiliar others are potential free-riders and, out of a concern that they will be exploited by others, people reduce considerably their altruistic attitudes and behavior in a general way in more diverse communities. This loss of trust is a symptom of a breakdown in social cohesion and is surely a forerunner of the sort of ethnic conflict that is always likely to break out if allowed to do so. This is undoubtedly the reason why multicultural nation-states are forever promoting tolerance and ever more punitive sanctions for the expression of ethnic hostility, even going so far to as to discourage the expression of opinion about the reality of ethnic and racial differences. Currently these measures are directed at the host population when they express reservations about the wisdom of mass immigration, but this will surely change as it becomes ever more obvious that it is the presence of competing ethnic groups that is creating the tension and not the expressed reservations of the majority population. The real danger for modern democracies is that in their zeal to promote multicultural societies, they will be forced to resort to the means that have characterized all empires attempting to maintain their hegemony over disparate peoples.

Empires cannot be democracies, for if they were, people would choose to separate themselves into ethnically distinct jurisdictions or states. This happened after the breakup of the Hapsburg Empire in the wake of WWI. A similar pattern resulted when the USSR dissolved and the separate nationalities that had been submerged reestablished their independent identities. For similar reasons a democratic multiethnic nation cannot survive unless it can drastically reduce ethnic identity through widespread assimilation, and concomitant intermarriage. The traditional nation-state based in ethnicity does not face this problem and can therefore survive and remain democratic, and has only a limited need for coercion. This, of course, is not to deny that a state can accommodate small, relatively powerless groups who fail to assimilate, but the key here is that they must be small and powerless. The Jews of Western Europe are a tragic case of a group that, while small, was perceived as powerful.

In summary, the modern nation-state is a relatively new phenomenon in that it can comprise a very large population in a cohesive society based in considerable measure in a common ancestry. That shared ancestry, buttressed by a shared cultural heritage, means that it is less reliant on coercion than other large societies lacking a shared ancestry and heritage. Because of the workings of inclusive fitness, people of the same ethnic background normally exhibit greater empathy for, and understanding of, each other than they do for people from other groups. It may not be accidental that the most successful welfare states are the Scandinavian nations that were highly homogenous until recently. In the current immigration debate and its assumptions about a multicultural society based on ideology, rather than ancestry and heritage, it is well to keep these things in mind. In the attempt to reduce conflict by replacing ethnic and national loyalties with ideological loyalties, it is wise to consider that such loyalties can generate conflicts every bit as deadly and tragic.

In the utopian vision of those who promote a universal altruism, ethnic and national loyalties would be replaced with a loyalty to all of mankind. But can one really love and be loyal to everyone? Would the world be a better place if parents had no more affection for their own children than those of total strangers? Would the world be a better place if people cared as much for strangers as for their friends and neighbors? What would a friend or a neighbor be in such a case? In such a world people might be excused if they chose to care for no one. The end result would be a society in which people exhibited an indifference to the welfare of their neighbors and a profound sense of alienation from the larger community. This was recognized more than 2000 years ago by Aristotle in his critique of Plato's *Republic* and its communal nature. "That which is common to the greatest number has the least care bestowed upon it. Everyone thinks chiefly of his own, hardly at all of the common interest...everybody is more inclined to neglect the duty which he expects another to fulfill." He goes on to reject Plato's notion of collective family life: "Each citizen will have a thousand sons who will not be his sons individually, but anybody will be equally the son of anybody and will therefore be neglected by all alike." Further "which is better to say 'mine' about every one... of the other citizens, or to use the word 'mine' in the ordinary and more restricted sense.... How much better it is to be the real cousin of somebody, than to be a son after Plato's fashion!"[70]

But the vision of universal altruism is plainly utopian and can never, thankfully, be realized. People need and want families and friends and allies and that will not change if national loyalties are undermined in the interests of multicultural tolerance. What may be undermined is the shared sense of national community within nations that took centuries of human misery to bring into being. Is it really wise to abandon the moderately harmonious communities, so created, on a fashionable whim, only to find that we must start the painful process all over again?

Notes

1   Parts of this Chapter appeared in Byron M. Roth, *Prescriptions for Failure: Race Relations in the Age of Social Science* (New Brunswick, New Jersey: Transaction Publishers, 1994). The author wishes to thank The Social and Policy Center of Bowling Green State University that holds the copyright to that book, for permission to use this material.

2   Richard Dawkins, *The Selfish Gene, New Edition* (Oxford: Oxford University Press, 1989); Edward O. Wilson, *Sociobiology: The New Synthesis* (Cambridge Mass.: Belknap Press, 1975).

3   William D. Hamilton, The Genetical Evolution of Social Behavior, I, II, *Journal of Theoretical Biology* 7 (1964) 1–52, Reprinted in William D. Hamilton, *Narrow Roads of Gene Land: The Collected Papers of W .D. Hamilton*, I, II (Oxford: W. H. Freeman, 1995).

4   Dawkins, *Selfish Gene*, 21–44.

5   *Ibid.*, 44.

6   Matt Ridley, *The Red Queen: Sex and the Evolution of Human Nature*. (New York: Penguin, 1993), 76–79; George C. Williams, *Sex and Evolution* (Princeton, New Jersey: Princeton University Press, 1975).

7   Louis Levine, *The Biology of the Gene, 3rd Edition* (St. Louis, Missouri: C. W. Mosby company) 1980, 73, 93.

8   *Ibid.*, 100–108.

9   Lee Ellis and M. Ashley Ames, Neurohormonal Functioning and Sexual Orientation: A Theory of Homosexuality-Heterosexuality, *Psychological Bulletin*, 101:2 (1987), 241–251.

10   Paul Johnson, *A History of the Modern World from 1917 to the 1980s* (London: Weidenfeld and Nicolson, 1983).

11   David C. Rowe, *The Limits of Family Influence* (New York: Guilford Press, New York, 1994).

12   Avshalom Caspi, Joseph McClay, Terrie E. Moffitt, Jonathan Mill, Judy Martin, Ian W. Craig, Alan Taylor, and Richie Poulton, Role of Genotype in the Cycle of Violence in Maltreated Children, *Science* 297:5582 (2002) 851–4; Avshalom Caspi, and Terrie E. Moffitt, Gene-Environment Interactions in Psychiatry: Joining Forces with Neuroscience, Nature reviews: *Neuroscience*. 7, (2006) 583–590.

13   Dawkins, *Selfish Gene*, 40–1.

14   Gregory Cochran, Jason Hardy and Henry Harpending, Natural History of Ashkenazi Intelligence, *Journal of Biosocial Science*. 38, (2006) 659–93.

15   Patrick Bateson, Optimal Outbreeding, in *Mate Choice*, ed., Patrick Bateson (Cambridge Mass.: Cambridge University press, 1983), 257–78. Talmon-Garber, Yonina G., *Family and Community in the Kibbutz* (Cambridge, Mass.: Harvard University Press, 1972).

16   Steven Sailer, Cousin Marriage Conundrum: The Ancient Practice Discourages Democratic Nation-Building. *The American Conservative*. January 13, 2003, 20–22.

17 Bateson, *Optimal Outbreeding*, 259–62.

18 *Ibid.*, 268–69.

19 Allen. H. Bittles and James V. Neel, The Costs of Human Inbreeding and their Implications for Variations at the DNA level, *Nature Genetics*, 8 (1994) 117–121.

20 Ferguson, Niall, *The House of Rothschild* (London: Penguin Books, 1998).

21 Wilson, *Sociobiology*, 40.

22 *Ibid.*, 47.

23 *Ibid.*, 48.

24 Ronald A. Fisher, *The Genetical Theory of Natural Selection* (New York: Dover Publications, 1958), 135–37.

25 Fisher, *Genetical Theory*, 137–43; John Maynard Smith, *The Theory of Evolution*. (Cambridge, Mass.: Cambridge University Press, 1975), 216–230.

26 Levine, *Biology of the Gene*, 470–473; Wilson, Sociobiology, 33.

27 Christopher Wills, *The Runaway Brain: The Evolution of Human Uniqueness* (London: Harper Collins, 1994), 202–210; Frank Salter, *On Genetic Interests: Family, Ethnicity and Humanity in an Age of Mass Migration* (New Brunswick, New Jersey: Transaction Publishers, 2007), 96–97.

28 John Hawks, Why Human Evolution Accelerated.

29 Wilson, *Sociobiology*, 158–167.

30 David Barash, *The Whisperings Within: Evolution and the Origins of Human Nature* (New York: Harper and Row, 1979), 83.

31 Wilson, *Sociobiology*, 158–162.

32 David Myers, *Psychology, 3d Ed.* (New York: Worth publishers, 1992), 580: Ridley, *Red Queen*, 296.

33 David M. Buss, *Evolutionary Psychology: The New Science of the Mind.* 2nd Ed. (Boston, Mass.: Pearson, 2000), 121.

34 John Maynard Smith, *Evolution and the Theory of Games* (Cambridge, Mass.: Cambridge University Press, 1982).

35 IRIN, News.org, Pakistan: Honour Killings Continue, Despite Law, March 8, 2007, online at *IRIN, News.org;* Jordan: Honour Killings Still Tolerated, March 11, 2007, online at *IRIN, News.org.*

36 John Lancaster, Pakistan Court Will Reopen Rape Case: Fresh Inquiry is Ordered as Suspects are Detained, *Washington Post*, June 29, 2005.

37 *Middle East Times Online*, Saudi Gang Rape Victim Faces 90 Lashes, March 5, 2007.

38 Bruce Bawer, *While Europe Slept: How Radical Islam is Destroying the West from Within* (New York: Doubleday, 2006), 21–25.

39 Rose George, Revolt Against the Rapists, *Guardian Unlimited*. April 5, 2003, online; Rosie Goldsmith, R., France in Shock Over Gang Rape, BBC News online, July, 26, 2001; Bruce Crumley and Adam Smith, Sisters in hell, *Time*, November 24, 2002, online; Jonathan Mann, Muslim Women Rebel in France, CNN.com transcript of feature aired on May 24, 2004, online; Christina Ho, Gang Rapes and the 'Cultural Time Bomb,

review of Paul Sheehan, *Girls Like You; Four Young Girls, Six Brothers and a Cultural Time Bomb.* (Sydney, Australia: Pan Macmillan, 2006), *Australian Review of Public Affairs*, September, 25 2006, online.

40 Hamilton, *Genetical Evolution of Social Behavior,* 47–48.

41 Michael P. Ghiglieri, The Social Ecology of Chimpanzees, *Scientific American*, 252:6, (1985) 110.

42 John Maynard Smith referred to inclusive fitness as "kin-selection." The term is used to indicate that kinship plays a selective role in survival of kin and non-kin in a way similar to the selective role played by nature in natural selection. Smith, *Theory of Evolution*, 195.

43 Hamilton, *Genetical Evolution of Social Behavior,* 44–5.

44 Robert L. Trivers, The Evolution of Reciprocal Altruism, *Quarterly Review of Biology*, 46, (1971) 35–57. *Reprinted in Selected Readings in Sociobiology*, ed. James H. Hunt (New York: McGraw-Hill), 1980, 38–68.

45 Ghiglieri, *Social Ecology of Chimpanzees,* 111–112.

46 Brian C. R. Bertram, The Social System of Lions, *Scientific American*, 232, (1975), 54–65.

47 Robert W. Elwood and Malcolm C. Ostermeyer, Infanticide by Male and Female Mongolian Gerbils: Ontogeny, Causation and Function, In *Infanticide: Comparative and Evolutionary Perspectives*, ed. Glen Hausfater and Sara Blaffer Hrdy (New York: Aldine, 1984), 367–386; Craig Packer and Anne E. Pusey, Infanticide in Carnivores, in Hausfater and Hrdy, *Infanticide,* 31–42.

48 Carolyn M. Crockett and Ranka Sekulic, Infanticide in Red Howler Monkeys, In Hausfater and Hrdy, Infanticide, 173–192; Lysa Leland, Thomas T. Struhsaker and Thomas M. Butynski, Infanticide by Adult Males in Three Primate Species of Kibale Forest, Uganda: A Test of Hypotheses, in Hausfater and Hrdy, *Infanticide*, 151–172.

49 Sara Blaffer Hrdy, Assumptions and Evidence Regarding the Sexual Selection Hypothesis: A Reply to Boggess, in Hausfater and Hrdy, *Infanticide*, 315–319.

50 D. Anthony Collins, Curt Busse, and Jane Goodall, in Hausfater and Hrdy, Infanticide, 193–216; Dian Fossey, Infanticide in Mountain Gorillas (Gorilla gorilla beringei) in Hausfater and Hrdy, *Infanticide,* 217–236.

51 Fossey, in Hausfater and Hrdy, *Infanticide,* 222.

52 Martin Daly and Margo Wilson. Violence Against Stepchildren. *Current Directions in Psychological Science*, 5, (1996), 78.

53 Napolian A. Chagnon, *Yanomamo: The Fierce People* (New York: Holt, Rinehart and Winston, 1977); Lawrence H. Keeley, *War Before Civilization: The Myth of the Peaceful Savage* (Oxford: Oxford University Press, 1996); Mervyn Meggitt, *Blood Is Their Argument.* (Palo Alto, Calif: Mayfield, 1977).

54 Lawrence H. Keeley, *War Before Civilization*, 29.

55   *Ibid.*, 83–94.
56   *Ibid.*, 65.
57   *Ibid.*, 138–41.
58   *Ibid.*, 92–3.
59   Harris, Paul (2007). Gang Mayhem Grips LA, Observer, March 18, 2007. *Observer*, Guardian Co., UK, online.
60   Bawer, *While Europe Slept*, 37–40, 208–12.
61   Fjordman, Norwegian Authorities Still Covering Up Muslim Rapes, *Gates of Vienna*, July 27. 2006 online at gatesofvienna.blogspot.com.
62   Aftenposten, Oslo Rape Statistics Shock, September 5, 2001, online at aftenposten.no/English.
63   Salter, *On Genetic Interests: Family,* 52–53; Ornella Semeno, et. al., The Genetic Legacy of Paleolithic Homo Sapiens in Extant Europeans: A Y Chromosome Perspective, *Science*, 290, (2000) 1155–9; Brian Sykes, *The seven daughters of Eve (New York: W. W. Norton and Company. NY, 2001).*
64   Avery O. Craven, *The Coming of the Civil War* (Chicago: University of Chicago Press, 1966) 322.
65   David Hacket Fischer, *Albion's Seed: Four British Folkways in America* (New York: Oxford University Press, 1989).
66   Hugh D. R. Baker, *Chinese Family and Kinship*, (New York: Columbia University Press, 1979), 107–161.
67   Niall Ferguson, *The War of the World: Twentieth Century Conflict and the Descent of the West* (New York: The Penguin Press, 2006), xxxvii–xli.
68   John Lloyd, Study Paints Bleak Picture of Ethnic Diversity, *Financial Times*, October 8, 2007, online.
69   Robert D. Putnam, E pluribus Unum: Diversity and Community in the Twenty-First Century, The 2006 Johan Skytte Prize Lecture. *Scandinavian Political Studies,* 30:2, (2007), 148–151.
70   Louise Ropes Loomis, ed., Aristotle, *On Man in the Universe* (New York: Walter J. Black, 1943), 275.

Chapter 3
TECHNOLOGY, SOCIAL STRUCTURE, AND HUMAN EVOLUTION

Introduction

THIS CHAPTER DEALS WITH EXPLANATIONS of the evolution and differentiation of human groups since the period about fifty thousand years ago when modern humans migrated out of Africa. It examines the effect of differential climate and social organization in shaping human abilities and temperament. For most of that time humans lived in small hunter-gatherer groups and did not exhibit advances which would distinguish them in important ways from other primates. About ten thousand years ago, however, humans began in isolated places to emerge from the hunter-gather way of life and began the transition to the agricultural way of life which in time led to the emergence of large civilizations. During the last five hundred years, the scientific revolution ushered in the industrial way of life whose final patterns we are only beginning to decipher. This chapter and the one that follows examine how these epochal changes in social organization have influenced human evolution. The answer to that and related questions have enormous significance for the success or failure of various social schemes and are likely to be crucial for anticipating the likely impact of large movements of people seeking a better life in societies very different from the ones they leave.

Recent immigrant patterns to the United States and Europe are radically different from past patterns. In the first place, recent patterns are far more massive, especially for Europe, than any that occurred before. Secondly, immigrant populations today, much more than in the past, differ in culture, race, and ethnicity from the populations of their host countries. As such they are transforming monocultural and monoracial societies into multicultural and multiracial ones. This presents special challenges, especially if the immigrants come from countries with considerably lower average IQs than those to which they migrate. Problems are compounded if those immigrants come from countries characterized by high rates of criminal violence. Obviously, immigrants may not be representative of their home countries, and the IQ and crime common to their home countries may be the result of environmental factors specific in those home countries that are not present in the United States and Europe. If that is the case, these differences should present relatively minor problems for the integration of immigrants. On the other hand, if these differences reflect genetic differences in ability and temperament, and if immigrants are representative of the populations from which they come, those differences could pose very serious obstacles to successful integration. Before attempting to resolve such questions it will be useful to examine the data that gives rise to these concerns.

Statistical Differences for IQ and Criminal Violence of Host and Donor Countries

According to the Office of Immigration Statistics of the U. S. Department of Homeland Security, the following are the 10 most common countries of origin of individuals who obtained legal residency in the United States in 2007, the most recent data available. These countries contributed approximately 51% of all documented immigrants in that year. The IQ averages are taken from Richard Lynn's and Tatu Vanhanen's, *IQ and Global Inequality*.[1]

The figure for Haiti is an estimate since no direct measures are available and it is based on the IQs found in similar nearby countries. These figures indicate that the majority of immigrants come from countries with an average IQ between 80 and 90, which is considerably below the average of 98 for the United States. The notable exceptions are the countries of Korea and China, with IQ averages higher than the United States, and Vietnam, which is somewhat lower. When one examines the data for all the countries that contribute immigrants to the United States, this subset is quite representative and indicates a considerable disparity of about two-thirds of a standard deviation between the population of the countries contributing the most immigrants to the United States and that of the United States population. This is smaller than the disparity that currently exists between blacks and whites in the United States, but is, nevertheless, considerable in its likely impact.

Table 3.1. Individuals Obtaining Legal Permanent Resident Status by Country of Birth in 2007[2]

Country	Number	% of Total	IQ
Mexico	148,640	14.1%	88
China	76,655	7.3%	105
Philippines	72,596	6.9%	86
India	65,353	6.2%	82
Columbia	33,187	3.2%	84
Haiti	30,405	2.9%	67
Cuba	29,104	2.8%	85
Vietnam	28,691	2.7%	94
Dominican Republic	28,024	2.7%	82
Korea	22,405	2.1%	106

Of course, since immigration is always selective, these differences may not exist between immigrants and natives resident in the United States. Furthermore, the immigrant flows from some countries may be more selective than others. For instance, most immigrants from India spoke English before immigrating, indicating that they are a fairly select group as the great majority of Indians do not speak English at home. On the other hand, the close proximity of Central America to the United States suggests that immigration may be less selective for immigrants from this region. This is an important and complex issue that will be discussed more fully in Chapters 5 and 6 dealing with United Sates immigration patterns.

The situation for the EU is somewhat different in that about half of European immigrants come from other European countries.

The bulk of the immigrant populations of Western Europe come from Eastern and Western Europe, Turkey, the Arab countries of the Middle East, the Indian Subcontinent (India and Pakistan), North Africa, and sub-Saharan Africa. In general, the Eastern Europeans countries have IQs similar to Western Europe. Sub-Saharan African countries tend to fall about two standard deviations below Europe, with average IQs of about 70. The rest average between 85 and 90, so that in general they fall about two-thirds of a standard deviation below that of European natives. In effect, there is about the same disparity between the native populations of Europe and the United States and the non-European countries of origin of their immigrant populations. Of course, the selective nature of migration means that host country populations may differ significantly from immigrants.

The IQ data employed above comes from the most comprehensive analysis of the distribution of worldwide IQ, undertaken by Richard Lynn and Tatu Vanhanen in their books, *IQ and the Wealth of Nations* and *IQ and Global Inequality.* These estimates are based on numerous samples from a large number of countries on all the continents of the world. The authors demonstrate that a country's economic status is strongly correlated with the average IQ of its population.[3] Recently, economists Garett Jones and Joel Schnieder performed an exhaustive analysis involving a large number of important variables and confirmed Lynn's and Vanhanen's findings. They argue that the best explanation for the robust relation between IQ and economic growth may simply be that "national average IQ is a better measure of general human capital than any of the other measures tested...."[4]

Lynn's and Vanhanen's earlier book, *IQ and the Wealth of Nations,* not unexpectedly, came in for a great deal criticism.[5] A good deal of that criticism came in the form of general challenges to the validity and reliability of IQ in general. Much of the same criticism had been leveled at Herrnstein and Murray's 1994 book, *The Bell Curve.* As discussed previously, most of that criticism has long since been refuted. The liberal American Psychological Association (APA), in response to the controversy surrounding the *Bell Curve,* created a task force to examine the questions raised and in 1996 acknowledged the validity and reliability of IQ tests. In addition, the task force endorsed the idea that IQ is to a significant extent heritable, though it remained agnostic on the issue of genetically determined racial differences.[6] More recently, in an 2005 article in the authoritative

APA journal *Psychology, Public Policy and Law*, J. Philippe Ruston and Arthur R. Jensen presented an exhaustive review of the literature on race and IQ over thirty years, and effectively refuted the critiques of the link between race and IQ, which is by now well established.[7] The scientific evidence they present is clear and not seriously open to dispute, though, of course, politically correct commentators have been, and will continue to be, unmoved by the scientific evidence.

However, given the wide-ranging nature of *IQ and the Wealth of Nations*, it is worth reviewing the responses of the authors to these critiques. In particular, were questions relating to the estimates Lynn and Vanhanen made for countries for which they had no direct measures of IQ and made estimates based on data from neighboring countries. In their more recent book *IQ and Global Inequality*, the authors were able to obtain actual average IQ measures for an additional 32 countries, some of which had been estimated in the earlier book. In comparing the actual and estimated average IQs for 25 countries, they found a correlation coefficient of 0.913, which is about as close a relationship as that between two tests of IQ taken at different times by the same person.[8] These data clearly validate their method of estimation and suggests that when used on other countries for which measures do not exist, will produce, in most cases, accurate results.

The authors also addressed the question of the reliability of their samples. "In the present study we have 71 countries and subcategories within countries for which there are two or more scores. The correlation between the two extreme IQs (namely, the highest and the lowest) is 0.92 and is highly statistically significant."[9] They also examined the validity of their IQ measures by comparing them with international tests taken by students in a large number of countries. In the author's words, "our national IQs are highly correlated with national scores in tests of mathematics and science in ten independent data sets. The correlations range between 0.79 and 0.89. These correlations could not be present if our critics were correct in dismissing national IQs as meaningless...IQs correlate well with educational achievement across nations just as they do for individuals within nations."[10]

They did not directly respond to the issue of how representative their samples are for the countries they included. This does not represent a serious problem for the industrialized countries of the world, where such testing is fairly widespread. In smaller, less developed countries, this does present a problem, and in large countries with extensive rural populations, such as India and China, the problem is even greater. However, their study included 10 independent measures for China and 10 for Hong Kong. For Japan, they had 22 independent measures. In the case of the Indian subcontinent they included 12 for India and three for Pakistan. Nevertheless, it is likely that in China under Communist rule, in particular, rural populations are probably underrepresented. Without actual data it is difficult to determine the effect of this problem, but in all likelihood the greater inclusion of the rural population would reduce the IQ for China. However, since rural populations usually suffer poorer nutrition and more limited education than developed areas, they are likely to benefit in coming decades from China's rapid development. The very great similarity in the measured IQs of about 105 for the East Asian countries of China, Japan, Korea, and Taiwan suggests that in the future the actual IQ for the total population of China will probably approximate the general East Asian figure as life in rural China improves.

Susan Barnett and Wendy Williams, in their harsh criticism of *IQ and the Wealth of Nations*, nevertheless acknowledged the difficulty of obtaining representative samples. "Building a representative IQ estimate for any single country is clearly a tremendously difficult task, requiring extensive preliminary work to understand the distribution of individuals within the population by age, education, socioeconomic status, and so on, as well as extensive testing for each subgroup. Establishing representative IQ data for all 81 countries in the primary group here is, thus, a Herculean challenge..."[11] In fact, the sort of representative samples that would satisfy these criteria would be an *impossible* task, even if many researchers were willing to engage in such controversial work and could find sufficient funding to carry it out. In light of the current ideological state of the social sciences, it simply could not be done. Rather, Lynn and Vanhanen made strenuous efforts to obtain reasonable estimates from as many sources as possible, and within these limitations have produced, at least to this author, an extremely valuable contribution to social science understanding. In this particular case, as is so often true when trying to grapple with difficult questions, attempting to achieve perfection would have resulted in achieving nothing at all.

As discussed above, some immigrant flows may be more selective than others. For instance, the children of Mexican immigrants have IQs similar to those of their home country and IQs have not changed appreciably in the second and third generation of Mexican-Americans. The same appears to be true of the immigrants to Europe from the Arab countries who exhibit similar levels of achievement whether they remain in their home countries or migrate to Europe. IQ is, however, influenced by nutrition and education, and the very low figures for sub-Saharan Africa are partly explained by those variables. The figures for African immigrants should, if this is the case, rise after they have resided in their host countries a generation or so. This partially explains the higher IQ figure (approximately 85) for Americans of African descent, along with the fact that there has been considerable mingling of African and European populations during the centuries of their coexistence on the American continent. Immigration from Asia appears to be more selective, since it usually requires air travel which is beyond the means of extremely poor people. In addition, as will be discussed in Chapter 6, a good many immigrants from India and East Asia come under employment visas for highly skilled and educated individuals. For purposes of this book, the high IQ of East Asians given by Lynn and Vanhanen are, if anything, probably underestimates of the immigrant population of East Asians residing in Western countries. Later Chapters will confirm this hypothesis by the educational performance of the children of East Asians in the schools of all Western countries.

Parenthetically, it is worth noting that the superior performance of East Asians on IQ tests appears to be mainly related to measured abilities in visual and mathematical tests; they do not, in general, surpass Europeans and sometimes do less well in subtests related to verbal abilities.[12] This, of course, helps to explain their stellar performance in scientific fields and the extreme overrepresentation of Asian students in the most prestigious scientific universities in the West.

These differences in intellectual ability are quite pronounced and while they may diminish over time, they are likely to remain socially relevant. They are reflected in the relative academic and economic performance of the various groups and the ease with which they assimilate into their host countries. Asians, often referred to in the United States as model minorities, generally perform as well, and often better, than Americans of European descent in school and in the economic sphere. Those of African descent tend to lag behind in those areas, while others, such as Hispanics, tend to fall midway in their performance between blacks and whites. Barring fairly large rates of intermarriage, these relative rankings are unlikely to change. Any attempt to reduce the difficulties the various immigrants groups face in assimilating into modern Western societies that do not take these differences into account are likely to fall short in effectiveness.

Similar differences exist in rates of antisocial violence. The most reliable measure of comparative rates of criminality is usually reflected in homicide rates. The following table of homicide rates by world region is based on information provided by the World Health Organization.[13]

Table 3.2. Global Homicide for Selected Regions

Global Region Homicide Rate per 100,000 People	
African Region	22.2
Region of the Americas	19.3
European Region	8.4
Western Pacific Region	3.4

The above table includes four of the six regions listed by the World Health Organization. Intentionally excluded here were the WHO regions of Southwest Asia (which includes India and Pakistan), and the Eastern Mediterranean (which includes the Arab States). These were excluded because the countries reporting homicide statistics were far too few to be representative. In the case of the Eastern Mediterranean, only Kuwait and Israel reported results. In the case of Southwest Asia, neither India nor Pakistan did. All the other regions included reports from a sufficient sample of nations to make the regional estimates meaningful. The figures provide evidence of considerable regional and racial differences in criminal violence. Homicide rates for the Western Pacific Region (which includes China and Japan) are quite low in comparison with European rates, and are both much lower than those of Africa and the Americas. The American region includes Canada and the United States, which are populated largely by people of European descent, and have much lower homicide rates (1.4 and 6.9, respectively) than do the nations of South and Central America, whose regional rates are as high or higher than those of Africa. The significant difference between the United States and Canada is explained, in considerable measure, by the higher proportion in the United States of people of African and Hispanic descent. These relative ratings given by the World Health Organization are largely consistent with homicide statistics reported by the United Nations.[14] Caution is required, since not all countries in all regions reported data, and the data that was reported is, in many cases, of doubtful validity. Nevertheless the rank ordering, if not the absolute rates, of the regions seem quite reasonable.

As is the case with IQ, the patterns of antisocial behavior common in the native countries of immigrants often persist in their host countries and are reflected in crime rates there. In both the United States and Europe, Africans have the highest rates of crime and Asians the lowest. In America, crime rates for Hispanics are fairly high, especially for the children of immigrants, which is consistent with the patterns common in their countries of origin. In Europe, the children of immigrants from the Muslim countries of the Middle East and Pakistan exhibit fairly high rates of crime, but we have little data on crime and homicide patterns in their countries of origin.[15] However, these rates of criminality are consistent with anecdotal evidence of a high degree of violent behavior in Muslim communities worldwide. Middle Eastern peoples are organized on the basis of the extended family, clan and tribe far more than on the nation state. This is reflected in the pattern of violence in the Muslim World that commonly involves family and tribal feuds, often commingled with religious strife. The high degree of endogamy among these people, as previously argued, probably accounts for their high degree of ingroup altruism and helps to explain their outgroup enmity. Given the worldwide problem of terrorism initiated by many in the Muslim community, these questions are extremely important and will be examined more fully in later chapters. Though not reported in the data above, crime rates in Eastern Europe are higher than in Western Europe, which is consistent with the fact that recent immigrants from Eastern Europe tend to have elevated rates of crime in their host countries.

The high rates of criminal violence common to the countries of Mexico, the Caribbean and Central America may pose especially difficult problems for the United States which draws most of its immigrant population from those countries. Europe may face similar dilemmas in dealing with the immigrant populations coming from the countries of sub-Saharan Africa and the Middle East. The current criminality among the Eastern Europeans in Western Europe may decline, as occurred among earlier European immigrants to America. The IQ data for most Eastern Europeans suggests that they will have a relatively easy time in assimilating, and as they do, their rates of criminality will probably diminish.

The potential differences between immigrant populations and those of their host countries in IQ and criminality are hardly trivial matters. These differences may well produce significant strains in societies that can only be reduced by fairly radical social and legal changes in the host countries, especially in the areas of education and law enforcement. They are also likely to have an impact on policies relating to social welfare and affirmative action. For this reason, it is important to try to determine the sources of these differences. In particular, it is important to know whether they are reflective of the temporary strains of adjustment to new societies that all immigrants confront and, therefore, should resolve themselves fairly readily. If they are based in persistent cultural patterns that assimilation will correct, then policies based in multicultural doctrine may inhibit assimilation and interfere with this adjustment process. On the other hand, if these behavioral differences are partially genetic in nature, they are unlikely to be altered in the short term, if at all. The following sections are an attempt to provide answers to these important questions. The evolution of modern humans will be examined along with the origins of the regional and racial differences among human groups that exist today. An important element of that analysis will be an attempt to determine the origins of the obvious physical differences between racial groups, as well as the roots of any differences in ability and temperament.

The Origin of Modern Human Races

While there is a general consensus that human beings evolved from the lower primates that existed in Africa, there is disagreement about the origins of truly modern humans and the origins of existing racial groups. The most widely accepted theory is the recent African replacement model, which argues that truly modern humans arose in Africa sometime between 100,000 and 200,000 years ago, and migrated out of Africa some 50,000 years ago. In this theory, they completely replaced the archaic humans, such as the Neanderthals, who had left Africa at a much earlier time, perhaps 1 million years ago. It is also posited that this replacement was complete and involved no substantial interbreeding. This theory, sometimes referred to as the African Eve theory, is supported by genetic evidence suggesting a common maternal ancestor in Africa some 200,000 years ago, and is heavily dependent on computer models based on hypothetical mutation rates.[16]

An alternative theory, with few supporters today, the multiregional model, argues that archaic humans left Africa between one and two million years ago, spread around the world and evolved slightly differently from each other under the different pressures of their respective locations in the world. Supporters of this theory argue that the 50,000 years or less allowed by the recent replacement model seems too short a period of time to account for these differences.[17] The multiregional model argues that over millennia, the separate populations maintained sufficient contact with each other to allow enough gene flow to prevent their differentiation into distinct species. Research on the dental structure of Africans and Eurasians, for instance, supports the argument of such contact going back more than a million years[18] This theory gains its support mainly from the similarities found by physical anthropologists between characteristics of the archaic types and modern peoples living in those regions today. The multiregional model should not be confused with the 19th century theory of polygenic origins which argued that the modern races descended from different species of prehuman hominids.[19]

While recent genetic evidence appears to rule out the multiregional model, which today has few supporters, an important variation on that model has been offered by Gregory Cochran and Henry Harpending who posit a theory of "introgression" in which physically modern humans coming out of Africa intermingled with the existing archaic populations and acquired important genes from those individuals. In the process, they became better suited to their new environments and eventually replaced the archaic populations while retaining some of their archaic characteristics.[20] Cochran and Harpending argue that an explosive growth in innovation including "cave painting, sculpture, jewelry, dramatically improved tools and weapons" appeared in Europe when migrating Africans came into contact with archaic Neanderthal types some 30,000 to 40,000 years ago. They suggest that this innovative progress provides evidence that modern humans acquired important characteristics from Neanderthals, since such innovations are not evident among the artifacts of the modern humans who remained in Africa.[21]

The fact that the migration out of Africa began about 50,000 years ago, is explained by the fact that, at that time, there was a period of relative warming, which led to a retreat of the northern glaciers allowing for the northern migration of human beings. Before that time, for millions of years, much of the Northern Hemisphere was covered with glacial ice and frozen tundra making it unsuitable for large-scale human existence. This warming lasted about 20,000 years and was followed by a return of glacial ice, probably driving most humans to more southerly regions. About 11,000 years ago, the current interglacial period began, allowing humans once again to venture north in large numbers.[22]

All theories hypothesize that the much harsher climate these early migrants encountered in northern latitudes had profound evolutionary effects that produced the physical differences so apparent today. The lighter skin of northern peoples for instance, is speculated to have arisen because of the need for Vitamin D from sunlight, which is less strong in northern than in tropical regions. However, as Cochran and Harpending report, the genetic changes producing lighter skin color among Asians were different from those producing lighter skin in Europeans. "In most cases the mutations involve changes in different genes, and even when the same gene is involved," the mutations common in Europe are different from those common in Asia."[23] Similarly, the thicker, stockier build of Europeans and Asians is thought to have arisen out of the need to provide protection against the bitter cold of northern latitudes. The epicanthic fold and other facial features that give Asians their distinctive appearance are thought to have arisen from the need of early hunters to scan a glaring, ice-covered landscape. It is also assumed that lacking the year-round vegetation of the tropical regions, these early humans in northern regions relied on hunting to provide sustenance during the long winter months.[24]

Part of the reason for the wide acceptance of the recent African replacement theory is that it is consistent with the commonly held belief that racial differences are small and mainly superficial, suggesting as it does a very recent origin of the main racial groups. The introgression theory argues that these changes are more plausibly explained by the incorporation of archaic genes that had a much longer time to evolve. They argue that beneficial mutations acquired in Africa could spread throughout the human species, while those acquired from archaic populations that were useful in particular environments could be quickly acquired and incorporated into the modern gene pool.

All of these theories explain the differentiation of races in terms of their geographic separation and adjustment to different environments. If members of a species come to occupy different environments, these new settings will produce changes by natural selection, since some genes will confer a greater fitness advantage in one setting than in another. In most cases the changes will be gradual, resulting first in changes in the proportion of specific genes in their respective gene pools. If the fitness advantage of these genes continues over time, eventually the favored genes will completely eliminate competing alleles and will become fixed. As discussed earlier, genetic drift could produce the same result by chance, but over a much longer period of time.

While such differentiation is generally thought to be gradual, it could have come about fairly abruptly in certain circumstances. The recent African replacement model is based, to a large extent, on such abrupt changes. For instance, founder effects could quickly transform a population. Founder effects arise if a few people migrate away from their natal group and found a new population. Such a population would be small, and if they possess unique gene complexes, fixation of their alleles, if favorable, could occur rapidly in a few generations. Similarly, "bottlenecks" can also be responsible for rapid evolutionary change. A bottleneck is an environmental event that produces a massive die-off in a population, leaving only a few survivors who, in effect, become the founders of a new population. If those few individuals possessed unique genes or gene complexes that enabled them to survive the catastrophe that killed their neighbors, then many of their progeny are likely to possess similar genes. In this scenario, in a relatively short time, these new genes will be fixed in what has become a new smaller gene pool, significantly different from the original.[25]

Bottlenecks might account for some of the important racial differences thought to have resulted from climatic change. For example, if a population of early modern or premodern humans migrated significantly far north during a short period of moderating temperatures, they might have become isolated from other similar populations by a rapid return of colder climate, for instance, especially if barriers made a southern retreat impossible. If conditions were sufficiently harsh, many, perhaps most, would have succumbed. Those who survived such a bottleneck might have done so because they possessed characteristics different from those who did not, and became founders of a new population.

It is interesting to note that the progeny of founders will necessarily possess many genetic characteristics of the founders that may have had little to do with the founder's survival. Many gene and gene complexes are linked to others because of some past benefit or, in some cases, merely by happenstance. These genes could readily become fixed in a new population even if they conferred no fitness benefits. Many racial differences, such as differences in facial features, could have arisen in this way.

In assuming mechanisms of rapid evolution, the prevailing recent African replacement theory, especially its emphasis on climate as the primary cause of racial differences, has some problems. According to the theory, the first migrants moved out of Africa into the Middle East and from there spread north and east. Subsequent waves of migrants are thought to have followed similar routes. In the early phases of this migration, during the warming trend between 50,000 and 30,000 years ago, some may have traveled north into what is now Europe, and then east into Asia. Others likely followed the coasts and made their way around the Indian subcontinent and into Southeast Asia. From there, many may have traveled south and populated the islands of the South Pacific. At the time, such overseas migration may have been facilitated by the fact that the ice age that returned about 30,000 years ago would have resulted in reduced sea levels that connected many of these currently separate islands. Those that remained separated would be larger and the sea distances between them would have been reduced. It was during the last stages of this time period that Asians are thought to have migrated across the Bering Strait and populated the Americas.[26]

Given these hypothetical migration patterns, what mechanisms account for the changes in the early African migrants who followed the coastal route, and who hypothetically drove the existing archaic populations along those routes to extinction? The climate of the southern coastal regions of the Eurasian continent is not markedly different from that of Africa. Neither were there important differences in the availability or type of vegetable or animal food. Why, then, aren't the inhabitants of these coastal regions Africans, or at least closely related to modern Africans? Some isolated groups do appear closely related to Africans, such as the Andaman Islanders, but most are not.[27]

The Cochran and Harpending introgression theory posits that those who traveled north benefited by incorporating genes of the archaic populations who had survived the harsh climate of northern Eurasia, especially behavioral characteristics that were critical for survival in the north. They argue "that even limited gene flow from Neanderthals (and perhaps other archaic humans) would have allowed anatomically modern humans to acquire most of their favorable alleles."[28] Consistent with this theory (though not explicitly posited by the authors), those African migrants who traveled the southerly coastal route, on the other hand, may have mingled their genes with archaic people who had never faced the harsh conditions of the north. This may explain the differences which exist between northern Eurasians, such as the Europeans and Chinese, and the populations of southern Eurasia, such as the people of Southeast Asia, southern India, and the Pacific Islands.

Very recently, genetic mapping has begun to allow for the dating of evolutionary events, such as founder effects and bottlenecks, enabling researchers to estimate in what time periods new genetic features appeared and became fixed. These estimates are based on computer models that make assumptions about the rate of mutational change and these assumptions are open to dispute. As with all new techniques, these sometime produce conflicting results, and to this point have not been able to resolve the differences between the prevailing recent African replacement theory and the introgression theory.[29] In truth, the evolution of today's existing modern human groups is still unclear, and whether the racial differences common today arose independently among African migrants or involved the acquisition of characteristics of more archaic origin is hardly a settled question. It is clear, however, that by the end of the last ice age, and certainly by 4000 or 5000 years ago, modern humans with all their racial diversity came to populate all the habitable regions of the world.

Technology and the Success of Homo Sapiens

Whatever their origins, there is broad agreement that modern human beings can all trace their ancestry to primates in Africa. There can be no question that modern humans are related to existing primates, such as the great apes and chimpanzees. Genetic mapping indicates that humans share between 97% and 99% of their genes with chimps, their closest living relatives.[30] Pointing out that humans are closely related to primates is not to deny the great differences between them. A one or two percent difference represents substantial genetic divergence and, given the nature of the differences, even more substantial phenotypic differences. Among the more obvious differences are the fully upright gait of human beings, the ability to communicate verbally in complex ways, and an extended capacity to anticipate the future and plan for it.

An upright gait, in conjunction with an opposable thumb, allows human beings to make use of tools in ways unprecedented in the animal kingdom. Their ability to communicate has allowed humans to amass information about their world and pass it across geographic and generational lines. The ability to plan, to think ahead, has allowed humans to develop complex responses to changing ecological conditions. These capacities allow human beings to alter their environment in truly extraordinary ways. The ability to think—to manipulate symbols—means that human beings live in a world that is as much ideational as physical. Only human beings can imagine a life beyond the present in a world ordered by different rules. For many human beings, ideas—such as the ideas of god and heaven and universal justice—are as important in guiding behavior as is the ground beneath their feet. In similar fashion, only human beings could have imagined a world composed of invisible atoms and organisms, and devised strategies to cope with such imagined entities. It should be clear that the mental capacities that enable human beings to master scientific understanding are also responsible for their ability to imagine forces and spirits affecting the physical world. The witch doctor and the scientist are both the product of the human ability to manipulate symbols, to talk and reflect upon events and upon human actions that are only potentially possible; in short, to make use of imagination.

The extraordinary planning and tool-making capacities of human beings, when compared to other primates, should not be underestimated, but neither should they blind us to the important similarities between humans and other primates. If we accept the estimate that truly human communities have existed for at most 200,000 years, we must acknowledge the reality that for most of that time human beings did not distinguish themselves in socially or materially important ways, from the other primates. For thousands of years, tools existed in the most rudimentary form. Broken rocks and sticks represented the ultimate human technology for most of human existence. Wheels, writing, astronomy, etc., are all developments of the last few thousand years. The proverbial man on the Moon looking down on Earth some 30,000 thousand years ago, would have found little to marvel at in human existence. He would have noted an upright, highly communicative ape that, in the main, was not especially more successful than his more primitive cousins.

Prehistoric men, based on the available evidence, lived like modern hunter-gatherers. Hunters and gatherers have been, until recently, located in geographically isolated regions and lived in small, kin-based groups not unlike apes and other social primates. If such groups of humans survived during the thousands of years of prehistory, it could not have been because they had the tools and knowledge common today. They, like their primate cousins, were forced to rely on the same mechanisms that enabled those primates to survive, among which must be counted the biological and psychological characteristics shaped by natural selection. It is simply not credible to imagine that the small genetic changes that separated humans from the other primates—allowing upright posture and symbolic thought—were accompanied by the wholesale loss of fitness-conferring characteristics formed during millions of years of primate evolution.

The size of these early human groups, as with all organisms, was limited by the needs of the organism and the resources available. The size of a territory for a group is constrained by the fact that the energy needed to obtain food, for instance, cannot, for any appreciable period of time, exceed the energy value of the food obtained. It will not do for an animal to expend 3000 calories in pursuit of food that yields only 2000. Human population densities are therefore constrained by the resources that human technology allows humans to exploit. Hunter-gatherers, having very limited technology, must—like other primates—survive on the limited resources a territory naturally provides. It was not until humans developed agricultural technology and animal husbandry in the last 5,000 to 10,000 years that group size could increase appreciably. Agriculture allowed for the beginnings of civilized life and all the technological advances associated with that way of life. It was the agricultural revolution that allowed humans to alter their environment for vastly greater human exploitation and enormous gains in evolutionary fitness. Our figurative man on the Moon would, upon noticing this remarkable development, have noted that human beings began, almost immediately, to outdistance their primate cousins, both in numbers and in geographic dispersal. Clearly, a biological revolution was under way.

The relationship between technology and population size is not unidirectional. Technological improvements, like agriculture, allow for greater population densities, but greater population densities in turn accelerate technological improvement. Mere size matters a great deal. Innovations are somewhat like beneficial mutations, and their spread through a population is likely to be similar. It is a basic principle of population genetics that the likelihood that a beneficial mutation will survive in a population—reach a stable equilibrium in a gene pool—is directly related to population size. In a small group it may never arise or become established. Many mathematical geniuses were undoubtedly born in prehistory, but with whom could they have shared their insights? Most innovations depend on prior developments. How could our hypothesized mathematical genius have expressed that genius and shared it with others in the absence of a system of written numerals, for example?

The use of sticks and rocks as tools for prying and breaking is common among primates other than man, but the idea of chipping a rock or flint so as to make its edge sharper and more useful is a purely human invention.[31] Yet even this simple insight appears to have taken many hundreds of generations to become common. There is a synergistic, cascading effect in technology, in which technological developments tend to foster further developments. This is obvious, today, when technological change comes fast and furious, but it clearly was not obvious in earlier times. It is not unreasonable to argue that human beings in all times and places tend to accept the world as it is and to think that it could not be otherwise. Those who can imagine a different world are historically very unusual, and therefore innovations are rare events. As population density increases, however, so does the likelihood that similar creative types will come into contact and communicate with each other. Population density acts as a catalyst for technological change. By allowing for vastly greater population densities, agriculture heralded a host of cultural innovations, including writing, numeration, metallurgy, astronomy, large-scale architecture, to name only the most obvious early developments of agricultural civilizations.

Agriculture facilitated creative innovation, furthermore, by allowing a greater division of labor. Large-scale agriculture, in particular, required the coordination of large numbers of people over extended periods of time. The relative efficiency of agricultural methods for food production freed human minds and hands for the various new tasks upon which the agricultural way of life depended. As these societies expanded, so did their need for specialized skills and the number of people trained in them, which in turn spurred further innovations. The upshot was an explosion of new knowledge and technological developments. The agricultural way of life produced a steady stream of innovations wherever it arose. During this period, writing and mathematics were refined, and philosophic and religious systems were elaborated. Metallurgical, architectural, administrative and military arts grew at an astounding rate.

The transition from small scale hunter-gathering societies to large agricultural empires was limited to the relatively warm climates of middle latitude. An altogether different trajectory was taken by the populations in the much colder regions of central Eurasia. In these "steppe" regions a way of life grew up dependent on a form of nomadic pastoralism. According to William McNeill, "[i]n all probability, nomadism developed into a fully independent way of life only after human beings had learned to live largely on animal milk and milk products, thus tapping a new food source..."[32] Among the domesticated animals, the horse played a prominent role as a means of transportation for rapid movement across the vast stretches of grassland that make up the steppe.

The Eurasian steppe region was for thousands of years inhabited jointly by scattered small settlements in well-watered oases and by nomadic pastoralists. Nevertheless, their superior dairying practices allowed them to spread out into regions far beyond their ancestral homeland in the steppe region of southwest Russia between the Black and the Caspian Seas. Archeological research, inaugurated by Russian archeologist Victor Sarianidi, has uncovered settlements with the massive architecture usually associated with civilized life. These settlements in what is now Turkmenistan arose about four thousand years ago, roughly coincident with the civilizations that arose in the Middle East. While most of the steppe region is unsuitable for agriculture, there are limited areas, oases in the sea of grass as it were, that have sufficient water to support true agriculture. Presumably these large civilization-like settlements grew up out of these isolated oases. Little is known about these people since they left no written records and, for unknown reasons, disappeared after a fairly short existence.[33]

Nevertheless, the steppe people were spectacularly successful conquerors. We can be sure of their military prowess, since from the beginning of the written histories of the settled world these steppe peoples were a continual threat to that world. In wave after wave they moved east and west out of the steppes as fierce warriors who conquered the settled regions of East Asia and the Mediterranean. By the time of these recorded invasions, they had mastered the technology of horse warfare which allowed them to assemble large groups of mounted warriors who could quickly attack and outmaneuver traditional armies of foot soldiers. At first they rode in chariots, but in time invented the stirrup that allowed them to wield weapons on horseback. These were the barbarian tribes that continuously threatened the Chinese and Roman Empires and eventually conquered both within a short span of time. Their most recent incarnation was as the Mongol horsemen who, beginning in the 12th century, swept into Europe, China, India and the Middle East under the leadership of Genghis Khan. At their height they were the most successful conquerors in all recorded history, their empire encompassing most of the Eurasian landmass. Yet little is known about their societies and their everyday way of life.[34]

One of the most remarkable consequences of these invasions was the spread of the Indo-European language group which appears to have originated with the Kurgan people living in what is today southwest Russia and the Ukraine, in the steppe region between the Caspian and Black Seas. It is theorized that they began to expand out of their homeland about BC 4,000 and by conquest imposed their language which became the source of most of the languages spoken in Western Europe, Turkey, Iran and much of India. Roughly half the population of the world today speak languages that are part of this Indo-European language group. Cochran and Harpending argue that the success of these Kurgan peoples was based on the fact that they carried the variant gene (the 13910-T) that allows for lactose digestion, and they could benefit, therefore, from the development of a dairying tradition that is 4 to 5 times more nutritionally efficient than simply raising cattle for meat. As a consequence, they could support a much larger population in the same territory as nondairying pastoralists and could readily conquer them by mere force of numbers. In doing so, they spread their language and in turn spread their gene for lactose metabolism among the peoples of Western Eurasia.[35]

Their way of life apparently promoted, on a sporadic basis, rapid population growth that spurred migration out of their harsh native habitat into the more settled and richer regions of Eurasia. Once they mastered the art of mounted fighting, their spread intensified; local sedentary agriculturalists were no match for the fierce hordes of horse soldiers who descended upon them. Villagers who resisted their advance were slaughtered mercilessly, and no doubt accounted for the lack of resistance that speeded up their conquests. According to Cochran and Harpending, the genetic evidence suggests that, most of the time they did not slaughter and replace existing populations but subdued them and as a ruling elite imposed their language on them.[36]

Kevin MacDonald has argued that the steppe population, including the Mongols and related peoples, evolved a particular "North Eurasian and Circumpolar culture." He argued that this culture was quite different from those that arose in the settled regions of the Middle East and China. In this view, Greco-Roman civilization was a product of North Eurasians who invaded and displaced the people in the fairly undeveloped regions of the Northern Mediterranean. The invasions of North Eurasians into the densely populated regions of the Middle East, while altering what MacDonald calls the "Middle Old World Culture," did not replace it. In this view, Greco-Roman civilization is a rather pure product of North Eurasians and speakers of Indo-European languages. The Middle Old World Culture, while it assimilated many features and patterns of the North Eurasian invaders, retained its fundamental character. Consistent with this is the fact that the gene for lactose utilization remained uncommon in the middle East. In addition, their languages form a group distinct from the Indo-European group. On the other hand, since there was, at the time, no advanced civilization in Europe north of the Mediterranean, whatever civilization arose there had to be the product of these Northern invaders.[37]

The clash between the Greco-Roman Culture with the Middle Old World Culture is recorded in the history of the Persian wars. These wars halted the advance of the Middle Eastern armies into Europe by the forces of Classical Greece some four hundred years before the birth of Christ. The contention between these cultures over the Mediterranean basin continued and formed an important element of world history and continues to influence world events today.

The interaction of the steppe Nomads with the civilization of China resembled that of the Middle East. Though China was conquered on two separate occasions by steppe armies, and ruled by them for extended periods, Chinese culture was not greatly altered. More than 90% of the population of modern China today belongs to the Han ethnic group that has predominated for more than two thousand years.[38] As was the case in the Middle East, China, and the Far East, in general, retained their separate linguistic patterns and never incorporated the gene for lactose utilization. Perhaps this goes some way in explaining the considerable differences between the cultures and peoples of Europe, the Middle East and East Asia.

In one of the most remarkable demographic changes in history, the steppe population declined in the 14th and 15th centuries and the region remains today very sparsely settled and its people no longer threaten the settled regions of the world. William McNeill argues that this massive depopulation resulted from the spread of bubonic plague throughout the region rendering it inhospitable to large-scale settlement. Whatever the reason for their demise as a mighty warrior force, these people left an indelible mark on the world's civilizations and their gene pools. Perhaps modern genetic science will provide some answers about the nature of that mark, so much of which is obscure.[39]

The Mongol conquests of the 13th and 14th Centuries, before the depopulation of the steppes, greatly facilitated communication among all the great and by then mature Eurasian civilizations, and allowed for the exchange of innovative ideas and practices. Many of the ideas and inventions that played a prominent role in Europe during the Middle Ages came by way of China, India and the Moslem world. The isolation of the civilizations of the Americas and those of sub-Saharan Africa may in large part explain their backwardness relative to those on the Eurasian landmass. This exchange of ideas may have facilitated the dramatic rise of a European civilization distinct from Roman civilization.

The above analysis is bolstered by the trajectory of European history. By the year 1000 AD, after a period of turmoil and stagnation following the fall of Rome, innovation in Europe began to appear, most spectacularly in the construction of the daring and still enthralling Gothic cathedrals that were built all over the continent. At this time, however, China was, by most accounts, the more advanced of the World's civilizations, both technologically and in terms of social organization. Well before the European voyages of discovery, the Chinese had mounted monumental explorations throughout Asia, including major expeditions to Africa. For reasons that are almost inexplicable, China's rulers rejected the outward-looking attitude that motivated these voyages and turned inward in the middle of the second millennium, and as a consequence, China remained scientifically and technological stagnant for almost four centuries, centuries during which Europe came to dominate the world.[40]

About five hundred years ago, shortly after the Mongol incursions, Europeans began to achieve real and steady growth in knowledge and technological innovation. The most obvious sign of these were the voyages of discovery that culminated in the colonization of America. Other obvious signs were major refinements in mechanical devices such as windmills and the development of timekeeping instruments. A steady increase in scientific devices—the telescope, the microscope, the vacuum pump—occurred. There were great strides made in scientific knowledge, especially in mathematics and astronomy. These innovations, which we now call the scientific revolution, led in time to practical applications in industry and to the development and application of steam power, which heralded the industrial age. This industrial revolution had consequences for the human species as dramatic, perhaps even more dramatic, than those of the agricultural revolution.

The steam engine changed forever the relationship of the human species to its environment. Prior to that invention almost all work was performed by men and beasts who had to be fed. Food was the main energy for work, and that energy derived from the sun. The earliest hunter-gatherers survived by eating plants that sunlight made possible and the animals that ate those plants. The agriculture revolution was important because it enabled humans to arrange their environment to make more efficient use of solar energy in the form of concentrated and useful-to-man vegetation. The industrial revolution enabled men to transcend the limits of food-based biological energy and to make productive use of coal, oil and gas to generate the heat that the steam engine could convert into motion to perform useful work. Prior to the steam engine, the nonbiological use of energy was limited to wind energy for sailing ships and to a much lesser degree by windmills and waterwheels. With these few exceptions, work prior to the industrial revolution was done by humans and animals who got their energy in the form of food.

It is important to distinguish between Darwinian success and human well-being. Gregory Clark in his *A Farewell to Alms* argued that during all the years prior to industrialization, human populations were confined in a Malthusian trap.[41] For this reason, Darwinian fitness as measured in population growth cannot be equated with any improvement in living standards for the average human being. Improved agricultural technology that allowed for population growth may have initially improved living conditions by creating more nutritious crops or expanded regions open to agriculture. However, eventually, as population grew, per capita consumption declined to earlier levels and the lot of the vast majority returned to earlier or even less desirable levels. Ironically, famine, war and pestilence, by reducing population, often improved the well-being of those who survived. This certainly seems to have been the case in Europe following the devastating effects of the Black Death in the 14th century. Clark argued that living standards in China and Japan were somewhat lower than in Europe for the average peasant, since the Asian societies practiced better hygienic practices that allowed for greater population densities, with the consequence of lower average economic living standards.[42] In many ways, the life of a peasant in agricultural societies was harsher and more arduous than it was for the typical inhabitant of hunter-gatherer societies. The main benefit of most technological improvements accrued to the elites who could parasitize a larger population base. The industrial revolution changed this human equation drastically in allowing for both rapid population growth *and* improved living standards. Humanity for the first time was able to escape the Malthusian trap.

From the perspective of our observer on the Moon the results have been astounding. Prior to the industrial revolution human populations waxed and waned with hardly discernible growth following the increases facilitated by the introduction of the agricultural revolution. With the spread of industrialization, population growth shot upward explosively. On a graph marked off in millennia, starting some hundred thousand years ago, the trend of human population would be almost horizontal until about five thousand years ago, which would then show a very slight trend upward for the next five thousand years. Then, beginning about one hundred years ago, it would turn upward almost vertically. Measured in terms of the biological fitness of Homo sapiens, the last one hundred years are nothing short of astounding.

The acceleration of technological innovation during this period has been equally astounding and can be traced, as in earlier times, to the increase in population and the proportion of the population devoted to the tasks of innovation. With vastly more hands and minds at work and able to quickly communicate with each other, new ideas were generated at a rate inconceivable only a few centuries earlier.

In the final analysis, the power, both political and economic, of any settled society, is a function of the size of its population and the productivity of its people. The size and productivity of an agricultural society is directly related to the amount of cultivated land under its control. The larger the area under cultivation, the larger can be its workforce and its armies. It is hardly surprising that those first agricultural empires that began to expand, in China and the Middle East, were able to conquer their smaller neighbors with relative ease. Their greater food resources enabled them to mount larger armies and more sophisticated armaments for conquering the smaller and weaker societies on their borders. The lands and populations of those weaker societies were then put to use by the conquering power. The similarities in the rise of the Roman and Chinese civilizations, and by extension all the major agricultural civilizations, is no accident.

Rapid Evolutionary Change Driven by Technological Changes

All technological innovations alter in some degree the ecological niche occupied by the human species. Such alterations in the "nature" of the human environment must in turn alter the calculus of natural selection. Whenever the human species changes its relationship to the environment, it inadvertently sets in motion a chain of events likely to alter the species itself. Human evolution occurs because of the effect of nature on the differential survival and reproductive rates of human forms; this does not change when much of nature is shaped by humans.

A well-researched example of technologically induced evolution is the relation between the incidence of sickle-cell anemia and the clearing of land for agriculture. Lands opened for agriculture in tropical and semitropical climates often became inundated with stagnant pools of water hospitable to Anopheles mosquitoes which transmit malaria to human beings. While such mosquitoes also thrive in humid areas of the temperate regions, they only do so during the summer months and do not, therefore, represent a yearlong threat to existence. Sickle cell anemia is produced by a recessive gene that only has seriously debilitating effect when received in double dose. As a recessive, however, it alters the chemistry and shape of red blood cells in such a way as to make them less useful to the malaria plasmodium.

In such form, therefore, it confers resistance to malaria. The net result is that the sickling gene, while rare in populations not exposed to malaria, became common in those regularly exposed to that disease. By altering their environment (making it suitable for agriculture) humans altered themselves (made sickle cell anemia common).[43]

A second, more significant example of gene-technology interaction is the advent of epidemic disease. Epidemic diseases are caused by bacteria and viruses that spread among humans in dense populations. Most are thought to be mutations of bacteria and viruses residing in domestic animals, but many are the result of contact with wild animals. When such diseases first appear in a population they are often extremely virulent, and may lead to massive die-offs, as occurred in Europe during the plague epidemics in Classical Rome and later in Europe beginning in the 14th century. Those who survive usually develop immune responses that make them unlikely to be infected a second time. This is why such bacteria cannot sustain themselves in small, isolated populations. Once an isolated group is invaded by such a germ, all potential hosts are quickly exhausted, either because they are dead or have acquired immunity. Without new human hosts to attack, the mutated infectious agents go extinct, or find suitable hosts in nearby animal populations.[44]

In large, interconnected human populations, on the other hand, bacteria and viruses can spread from one community to another for an extended period of time. Over time, the bacteria and their hosts tend to make genetic adjustments to each other. The bacteria mutate into less virulent form, so that they can reside for much longer in each attacked host, and the humans who survive probably pass on immune systems somewhat better able to cope with such attacks. In time many, though not all, of these "diseases of civilization" come to be known as childhood diseases—smallpox, measles and whooping cough—since if they reoccur in a community, only the children will lack the immunity conferred by the earlier infection. Some diseases, such as influenza, are caused by agents that mutate so rapidly that it is not possible for human hosts to develop immunity for more than a year or so. Others evolve into chronic, endemic diseases, such as syphilis, whose agent can reside and spread through a host who may live a long time before succumbing to the cumulative effects of the pathogens. Of course, if any of these microbes enter a community with little or no experience with infectious diseases, the mortality can be catastrophic, as it was for the aboriginal populations of the Americas in their first encounters with Europeans.[45]

A final example of technology-gene interaction is that of milk production and lactose utilization. Europeans are among the few populations in the world that consume large quantities of milk and milk products. Most Asians do not drink milk as adults and rarely consume cheese and other products made from milk. The reasons are interesting and straightforward. Most of the world's adults cannot digest milk lactose and therefore derive no nutritional benefit from milk-drinking. In addition, a substantial number of people are lactose intolerant and are made ill when they consume milk. Why are Europeans different?[46]

William Durham explains that human infants produce an enzyme called lactase that enables them to break down the complex sugar, lactose, in human milk, so that it can be absorbed in the intestines. At about the time of weaning, the typical child stops producing lactase and as a consequence the lactose cannot be broken down and, therefore, passes through the body undigested. However, some people possess a mutation that allows them to continue to produce lactase into adulthood. The percentage of such people in a wide sample of societies ranges from 0 to 100%. These percentages correlate neatly with the extent to which a society practices dairying agriculture, and with how important it is in their diet. For instance, the percentage among Jews, and other people of Middle Eastern descent, is about 25 percent, whereas the percentage of Northern Europeans is approximately 90 percent.[47]

Durham relates this finding to climatic differences that allow, and have allowed for some time, Middle Eastern populations to have a relatively secure year-round supply of grain, as did the Chinese through rice cultivation, whereas Northern Europeans did not. As a consequence, Northern Europeans had to supplement their diet for thousands of years with other natural resources, such as the large game that were common in northern latitudes. With the advent of agriculture, the domestication of animals allowed for greater nutritional security in northern climes. It also allowed for the domestication of milk-producing animals by the steppe Nomads who came to settle Northern Europe. But this latter resource would have been of no use in a population incapable of benefiting from milk production. The upshot is that there were strong selective pressures in such circumstances favoring a gene, or gene complex, for the continued manufacture of lactase into adulthood. This argument is bolstered by the fact that groups in Africa such as the Tutsi, who practice dairying and have few other sources of nutrition, are close to 100 percent lactase producers, whereas others who do not practice dairying, such as the Bantu, are almost devoid of such types.[48]

These findings explain current dietary and culinary preferences. The French and the Swiss, for instance, (both having high numbers of lactase producers), cook with a good deal of butter and cream. The Italians, with somewhat fewer lactase producers, rely more on olive oil in their cooking. All of these people, however, are heavy consumers of cheese in which the lactose is broken down during the production process, making it valuable to all those in the population, even those who do not produce lactase. The Chinese, on the other hand, do not make use of milk or cheese in their cuisine for the simple reason that they never developed a dairying tradition that, even if they never used milk, would have allowed for the consumption of cheese and other dairy products. It seems that the Italians borrowed the habit of eating cheese by way of imitating their more northerly neighbors, whereas the Chinese lacked such neighbors from whom to copy this valuable practice.

These examples make clear that cultural modifications of the environment can alter gene frequencies in a population, and that these changes can occur relatively quickly in the timeframe of evolution. The agricultural and pastoral ways of life have existed for only a few thousand years for the overwhelming majority of mankind. Could similar technologically driven changes have had an impact on other, more psychological features of the human genome?

Climate, Evolution, and Human Psychology

The environmental differences between sub-Saharan Africa and other warm habitats of modern humans and more northern latitudes are stark. It would be surprising if these differences did not give rise to differences in social organization, technology and cultural practices. As discussed earlier, cultural innovation advanced at a snail's pace in the earliest human groups, and only did so, in many cases, when prodded by necessity. Where clothing was necessary for survival, its manufacture spread fairly rapidly; where clothing was not necessary, its manufacture was rudimentary at best. What other adaptations to different climates were common? How did these adaptations effect social organization? Did they lead to changes in the gene pools of populations residing in different climatic zones?

Perhaps the most ambitious attempt to make such connections has been the highly controversial work of Philip Rushton and Richard Lynn, both of whom have separately theorized a relationship between climate and intelligence. Rushton has extended the climate theory to include a host of cultural and psychological characteristics. These theories are extremely controversial because they link racial differences in ability and temperament to the very different climatic conditions of tropical Africa, the Americas, the semitropical regions of southern Eurasia and North Africa, and the colder climates of northern Eurasia including Europe, northeast Asia and the steppe lands. While there is broad agreement among social scientists that climate accounts for most of the physical differences among the races, such as skin color, body shape, facial features, etc., most deny that climate can affect human abilities and temperament. How could it be that climate produced so many physical differences among people, but left the nervous and endocrine systems completely untouched? An avalanche of new research in genetic variation makes such a claim increasingly implausible. What is emerging from these studies is that natural selection continues to operate and has done so differently for the populations of the Americas, Africa, Europe and Asia.[49]

Rushton, in particular, argues, that important psychological changes were induced by climatic differences and are readily apparent in measurable differences between the races. In tropical Africa, life and death were (and still are) commonly dependent on diseases that were not understood, could not be predicted, and could not be avoided. Unpredictable diseases were, therefore, more crucial to survival in these habitats than were food sources, which in tropical regions were, in general, regularly and abundantly available. In such conditions, Rushton argues, humans will adopt a reproductive strategy closer to the r than the K end of the r-K range possible for humans. The r-strategy involves having somewhat more children, beginning child-rearing at an earlier age and investing somewhat less in each offspring, since in an unpredictable tropical environment these would be fitness-conferring strategies. The environment will provide resources for all who survive, but infant mortality will be high owing to diseases over which human beings, until very recently, had virtually no control.[50]

In northern climates, on the other hand, the critical factor in survival was the availability of food and shelter from cold, and not, as in tropical climates, the incidence of disease. Disease does not appear to have presented a serious danger for human survival in northern, temperate zones until such time as men lived in dense communities where communicable diseases could be quickly and easily spread. Infant mortality was more likely to result from malnutrition and exposure than from disease. In such a setting, a human reproductive strategy should tend toward the K end of the human range. Having fewer children, starting at a later age, and investing maximally in each one should, over the long haul, be more consistent with evolutionary fitness. The children whose parents had the foresight and prudence to anticipate their future needs and reproduced accordingly were more likely to survive than those whose parents reproduced without restraint or discrimination.[51]

Perhaps the most controversial element of Rushton's thesis is his hypothesis that the different requirements of tropical versus temperate climates produced differences in intelligence and character. He argues that in tropical areas fitness will be less influenced by prediction and planning and the postponement of gratification than in areas of harsher climate. People in northern latitudes relied very heavily on the nutrition provided by the large game populating these regions in earlier times. The barren conditions of the north required different hunting techniques than those used in tropical jungle environments. In particular, group hunting was common and would involve considerable coordination among a sizable group of men. Group hunting of this sort was fairly common among the North American Plains Indians. It is also common among canines such as wolves, where pack-hunting allows them to take down large animals that would be impossible for a lone wolf. These animals are well known for the sociality and communicative expressiveness useful in pack-hunting. Perhaps these characteristics make them particularly attractive to humans and may account for their relatively early domestication and evolution into the dogs of today.

The need for coordination and planning in harsh climates could, according to Rushton, account for the average IQ differences found among African, European, and Asian populations, with Asians having the highest and Africans the lowest, average IQ.[52] Rushton also argues that in tropical climates where most children will have sufficient dietary resources, but many will die of disease, reproductive behavior need not be as conservative as in harsher northern climates, since promiscuity is less costly. He presents data demonstrating that, for instance, the average age of sexual maturity differs for the main racial groupings, with the Asians maturing latest and the Africans earliest. Furthermore, he argues that marriage patterns should be more conservative and marriages more secure in more northerly climes. This prediction is confirmed by demographic data relating to marriage among the populations of sub-Saharan Africa, Europe and Northern Asia.[53]

Another prediction relates to the fact that the loss of a male provider may be catastrophic for a family in harsh regions. As a consequence, men should be more prudent about their safety, and avoid unnecessary, violent confrontations with other men. On the other hand, in tropical climates, the children of imprudent men are likely to survive the loss of a father and carry their father's genes. In northern climates the children of imprudent men will likely perish, as will the genes they inherit. Once again, the demographic data support Rushton's prediction. Interpersonal violence is much more common among Africans than among Asians, with Europeans falling in the middle. In general, Europeans on a host of measures fall in an intermediate position between Asians and Africans. Rushton presents many other behavioral examples and a sizable body of evidence consistent with his hypothesis.[54]

Edward M. Miller has offered an additional factor to account for Rushton's data. He argues that in tropical environments with abundant food sources, hunter-gatherer males can more easily adopt polygamy, since females can often provide food for themselves and their own offspring. Similarly, the need for shelter and firewood for heat are much more limited in tropical than in temperate climates. Miller concludes that in such settings men who maximize reproduction by finding many consorts will prove more fit than those who devote their energies to one female and her young. Men should, therefore, reach sexual maturity earlier, be more aggressive in their intrasexual conflicts with other men over females, and be less inclined to monogamous attachments. They should also exhibit somewhat less attachment and provide fewer resources for any particular offspring, since they are likely to have many and may not live with them or their mother. In short, they are more likely to be "promiscuous cads" than trustworthy dads.[55]

Douglas White and Michael Burton, in a paper on the causes of polygamy, provide support for Miller's thesis and for the climate theory in general.[56] They based their analysis on data from 142 societies summarized in the Standard Cross-Cultural Sample.[57] Polygamy was strongly correlated with climatic conditions affecting the ease or difficulty of obtaining secure sources of nutrition. They found, for instance, that societies in resource-rich tropical savannas exhibited a high degree of general polygamy, with only 1 out of 42 societies being strictly monogamous, and only 7 being mainly monogamous. The remainder exhibited widespread polygamy, with 23 exhibiting *general polygamy*, defined as one in which polygamy is "preferred by most men, and attained by most men of sufficient years or wealth." By way of contrast, in resource-poor polar or desert highlands, monogamy was far more common, being prescribed in 9 and preferred in 10 out of a total of 51 societies. In those harsh climates polygamy was generally limited to leaders or the wealthy, with general polygamy occurring in only 7 out of the 51 societies. Not surprisingly, polygamy was very strongly correlated with warfare where the aim was the capture of women for purposes of marriage or concubinage.[58]

Consistent with the above data, Pierre L. van den Berghe reports that societies in which women did most of the work, or worked as much as men, were overwhelmingly polygamous, with 87 out of 88 such societies being classified as polygamous. In contrast, in societies where men did most or all of the work, 8 out of 42 were monogamous. It is important to stress, however, that in the latter societies, polygamy was still quite common.[59]

Climate theory posits important, though hypothetical, interactions between environment, culture (namely, marital arrangements and paternal behavior), human abilities (IQ), and temperament (favoring either prudence or aggressiveness). For instance, climate theory predicts that criminality should be highest among Africans and lowest among Asians, since successful aggression is more likely to be fitness-enhancing in tropical climates. Similarly rape should show a similar pattern, since if females can care for their own young, rape is fitness-enhancing for men, whereas it would not be if females needed male assistance. These predictions are consistent with criminal statistics in the United States and reflect worldwide patterns.[60] In an astonishing study by the South African Medical Research Council, some 1738 men in KwaZulu-Natal and Eastern Cape Provinces were interviewed. The study found that 25% admitted to having committed rape, and most had committed the crime during their teens. The survey included men of all races, though it did not provide a racial breakdown.[61] However, South Africa's population is composed of approximately 88% black African and mix-race individuals, with the remaining population being white or Indian/Asian.[62]

A serious problem for climate theory is that most extant hunter-gather societies are located in tropical or semitropical regions. In the Northern regions of Eurasia, in particular, most such societies have been superseded by more complex ones. For that reason, climatic effects may be confounded by social effects. In other words, many, perhaps most, of the differences between Africa, for instance, and Eurasia could be the result of the considerable differences in the sort of societies common to those regions. These regions are climatically quite moderate and they had more advanced societies than those found in southern Africa.

Another problem with climate theory is posed by the indigenous hunter-gatherer peoples of North America. They were confronted with very harsh winter conditions, and yet exhibit many of the behavioral characteristics common among such groups in tropical regions. For instance, Native Americans have an average IQ of about 86, considerably higher than sub-Saharan Africans, with estimated IQ of about 70, but well below that found in Northern Eurasia. In addition, with the exception of such groups as the Eskimo, polygamy is quite common, and warfare among these groups is very similar in purpose and intensity as among tropical peoples.

Richard Lynn, in particular, acknowledges this difficulty, but argues that the East Asians, who migrated into the Americas, especially those who traveled into Central and South America, did not experience the extreme cold common in the northernmost regions. In addition, life was somewhat easier in North America than in Asia, in large part because of the abundance of large game unaccustomed to human predation. Lynn assumes that the Asians who made this migration had the same IQ as the East Asians of the time, which he assumes was lower than it is today. He points out that American aborigines and Asians share the same intelligence profile "consisting of strong visualization abilities and weaker verbal abilities." However, because of the abundance of large game (useful for food, clothing and shelter) they faced less selective pressure than the East Asians. While the population of the northern reaches of North America did experience conditions as harsh as Northern Asia, Lynn argues that its much smaller size was not as conducive for the origin and spread of the beneficial mutations selected for in harsh climates.[63] This argument is augmented if it is assumed that the bulk of the population moved south during the coldest periods and moved back into the northern regions only in fairly recent times. The more sophisticated and densely populated cultures of pre-Columbian Central America lend credence to this latter assumption.

Culturally Driven Evolution: The Ashkenazi Jews

While it is certainly reasonable to suppose that climate had an effect on human psychological characteristics, it is, however, only one aspect of the environment likely to have an impact on human evolution. Another aspect of the human environment, namely, the economic and social organization of a society, is also likely to have had evolutionary effects. Population geneticist Marcus Feldman made the point that, "if we ask what are the most important evolutionary events of the last 5,000 years, they are cultural, like the spread of agriculture, or extinctions of populations through war and disease."[64] The hunter-gatherer and the agricultural way of life are so different that it is hard to imagine that they did not influence human evolution. Talents and skills that are highly desirable and therefore rewarded in settings common to one epoch are often useless or even undesirable in a different one, and go unrewarded or punished. Furthermore, not all agricultural societies developed in the same way and often produced markedly different cultural patterns. The intense grain-based and irrigation-dependent agriculture of the Middle East is very different from the more dispersed rain-dependent agriculture of Europe. Animal husbandry is also different in those regions. The agricultural and animal husbandry practiced throughout China differed in important ways from both those of the Middle East and Europe. For instance, in much of China, rice cultivation differs from grain production in either the Middle East or Europe, and no dairy culture has developed. Can the cultural differences of those regions have been shaped by the needs, both technological and social, of these differing agricultural practices? Could these differences have had selective effects on individual characteristics that may be differentially rewarded in different settings, producing differences in the proportion of various alleles in their respective gene pools? This might well explain, as will be discussed in the next chapter, the fact that the peoples of northern Africa and southern Eurasia have characteristics, IQ in particular, midway between northern Eurasians and sub-Saharan Africans.

In an important paper, Gregory Cochran, Jason Hardy and Henry Harpending, explore this question as it relates to the extraordinarily high IQ of the Ashkenazi Jews residing in Northern Europe. According to those authors, the average IQ of the Ashkenazi is approximately 115, or one standard deviation higher than their European neighbors. The authors point out that this is "the highest average IQ of any ethnic group." Significantly, "no similar elevation of intelligence was observed among Jews in classical times, nor is it seen in Sephardic and Oriental Jews today."[65]

The authors explain that from about the eighth century AD until recently, the Jews who lived in Europe did so as a distinct ethnic and cultural group with very low rates of exogamy, and they occupied a very restricted range of occupations, very different from others in Europe at the time. Nevertheless, even though they were highly endogamous, there was sufficient intermingling over the centuries so that today these Jews are, according to Cochran, et. al., "essentially European and not Middle Eastern."[66] In other words, they share more genes with Europeans than with Middle Easterners. However, they still differ in an important, if highly selective, subset of genes. These relate to two inherited disease clusters common among Ashkenazi Jews, but uncommon among Europeans and Sephardic Jews. Since these diseases are often lethal, how did they become common among the Ashkenazi? Normally, lethal genes are removed from a population by natural selection, unless, like the gene for sickle cell anemia, they confer some countervailing, selective benefit.

That is the explanation the authors propose. For a variety of reasons, Jews segregated themselves, and were segregated by others, into a very limited range of occupational niches, many of which demanded a fairly high degree of intellectual prowess. In the period after the fall of Rome, Jews were disproportionately involved in long-distance trade, often highly so, acting as intermediaries between the Muslim and Christian worlds. Over time, they become moneylenders, tax-farmers, and estate managers and were overrepresented in various business enterprises, including the operation of mills and taverns.[67] Success in these fields required a good deal of intelligence, and if success conferred reproductive fitness, then genes promoting intelligence should have experienced a selective advantage. The authors argue that throughout this period, economic success did, in fact, improve the survival of adults and children, and promoted larger family size, due mainly to healthier living conditions and greater nutritional security.[68]

Genes that contribute to IQ should therefore have increased in this population even if, in some circumstances, they produced deleterious effects. The authors hypothesize that the two disease clusters common among Ashkenazim are caused by genes that seem promising as catalysts for greater intelligence. The first cluster includes Tay-Sachs disease that is fatal when homologous, but not when heterozygous. The mutation is implicated in promoting nerve growth and neural complexity.[69]

The second cluster involves mutations interfering with gene repair mechanisms and includes the BRCA genes implicated in breast and other cancers. The authors cite research suggesting that BRCA1 and 2, by allowing certain mutations in germ cells to go uncorrected, appear to have been positively selected for over millions of years of primate evolution, since they seem to have promoted greater brain size. The authors also point out that the BRCA genes usually produce harmful effects late in life and may have had little impact on relative reproductive success, especially when viewed in conjunction with the host of infectious diseases that took such a heavy toll, particularly among the poor.[70] In addition, when the BRCA mutations appear in males they seem to have hardly any negative consequences. This suggests that these genes may have deleterious effects only in conjunction with other genes (such as sex determining genes) or certain environmental conditions.

If this admittedly speculative hypothesis is confirmed by further research, it would mean that important genetic changes of a psychological nature can occur in relatively short periods of historical time and that social factors can drive such changes. It is at least possible, and worth exploring, whether social factors can select for other characteristics in such a way as to create meaningful psychological differences between groups living in different circumstances. For example, if a society values and rewards physical aggressiveness, will biologically conditioned aggressiveness tend to increase in the gene pool of that society? Was the extraordinary economic growth in Europe in the last few centuries the product, at least in part, of the sort of individuals who were favored by natural selection and came to populate that region as has been proposed by Gregory Clark?[71]

Explaining Human Variation in Psychological and Behavioral Traits

The explanation for population differences in lactose utilization discussed earlier provides a useful model of the nature of the scientific explanation for other human differences. That explanation involved five crucial elements, outlined below.

1. Measurable phenotypic difference among various populations. In this case the ability, as an adult, to digest milk lactose.

2. Biological and physiological correlates explaining these differences. In this case the persistence into adulthood of the production of the enzyme lactase, essential for the digestion of lactose. People with this trait benefit from milk consumption; those without it, do not.

3. A genetic correlate tied directly to the trait in question. In this case, two single nucleotide polymorphisms create an allele of the gene LCT that directs the production of lactase into adulthood. Adults who possess this allele produce lactase and can benefit from milk-drinking, those with the alternative allele cannot.

4. Measurable differences in populations in the proportion of individuals who carry this allele. In this case, the allele is carried in large numbers by the populations of Europe and in small numbers in other areas such as Asia and Africa.

5. A testable hypothesis explaining the evolution of this variation. In this case, a reliance on milk producing animals because they are available and are needed due to the absence of other food sources for a good part of the year.

Is the above model for lactose utilization applicable to complex human traits such as intelligence, or temperamental characteristics such as risk taking, a proneness to violence or a tendency to exhibit empathy in dealing with others? Taking, as an example, intelligence, the model requires the above five elements.

1. Measurable phenotypic differences among populations. In this case, are there measurable differences in the proportion

of individuals capable of solving complex analytic problems with relative ease? IQ tests, verbal, nonverbal and behavioral (such as reaction time tests) have proven to be valid and reliable measures of this ability and show clear differences among groups present in higher degree in some populations than in others.

2. Biological and physical correlates for these differences. In the case of IQ a number of such correlates have been identified including brain size relative to body size, the anatomy of particular brain structures, the rapidity with which the brain processes neural impulses, and the metabolism of various neurotransmitters. Much of this work is, at this point, tentative, since many of the research techniques, such as brain imaging technology, are of fairly recent origin. Nevertheless, important and promising work on the causes of schizophrenia, for instance, implicates a number of such neurological and neurochemical substrates for the condition. This sort of research is crucial for the development of treatments, and possible prevention, of the disease. Schizophrenia has, in turn, been shown to correlate with general intelligence, so that similar biological substrates are putatively implicated in regulating brain activities associated with intelligence.[72] Brain-imaging technology has allowed for the examination of various areas of the brain during various mental tasks and shows clear patterns differentiating those who have difficulty with these tasks from those who do not.

3. Genetic correlates of intelligence have been found, and the evidence is growing rapidly. The gene COMT, involved in the metabolism of dopamine, an important neurotransmitter, is one such correlate. People with one variant have a more difficult time on memory tasks than others. Daniel Weinberger, who is involved in this research, remarked "it's as if they get poorer gas mileage out of their prefrontal cortex if they have this genetic background."[73] Similarly, various alleles of the gene CHRM2, that also influences dopamine metabolism, have been shown to correlate with certain aspects of IQ, such as the ability to organize things logically. Recent research on various alleles of the gene DTNB1, that predicts susceptibility to schizophrenia, and whose biological action is unknown,

have been correlated to IQ measures.[74] There are, undoubtedly, many other genes linked to IQ. Quoting researcher Danielle Dick, whose research involved examining variations of the gene CHRM2 which has been implicated in intelligence: "If we look at a single marker, a DNA variation might influence IQ scores between two and four points, depending on which variant a person carries." Her research discovered that, "the variations had cumulative effects, so that if one person had all of the 'good' variations and another all of the 'bad' variations, the difference in IQ might be 15 to 20 points." She adds that "Perhaps as many as 100 genes or more could influence intelligence. I think all the genes involved have small cumulative effects on increasing or decreasing IQ and I suspect overall intelligence is a function of the accumulations of these genetic variants..."[75] Researchers at UCLA, using brain scanner technology, examined identical and fraternal twins and found that those with thicker myelin sheaths processed nerve signals faster. The researchers concluded that "myelin integrity was determined genetically in many parts of the brain that are key for intelligence."[76]

4. Are there measurable differences in populations with regard to the commonality of the alleles associated with IQ? Due to the sensitive nature of this issue, few researchers have actually done this sort of study, but they have done so with regard to those same alleles in their attempts to understand different population's susceptibilities to schizophrenia and other mental diseases. In addition, databases exist allowing for the examination of population differences in the distribution of various alleles. ALFRED, a database compiled at Yale University, includes numerous studies of such differences. The International HapMap Project, in addition, has an extensive database comparing allele frequencies in four research groups of people of Chinese, Japanese, African and European descent, respectively. An examination of the relative frequency of IQ-related alleles shows clear population differences. For instance, one allele of the gene DTNBP1, showed a strong and consistent relationship to IQ.[77] It appeared in 93% of the Asian (Chinese and Japanese) samples, 82% in the European sample, and

63 percent of the African sample. Similarly, frequencies for alleles of the gene CHRM2 showed considerable variation among populations. One allele, for instance, appears in 45 percent of the African sample, 80% in the European sample and 100 percent in both the Japanese and Chinese samples.[78] Clearly, populations differ in the allele frequency for genes implicated in cognitive functioning.

5. Are there testable hypotheses explaining the origins and evolution of these phenotypic and genotypic differences? Clearly, there are. Rushton's climate theory discussed earlier is certainly one such theory. There are others, of which one relating to social structure is discussed in the next chapter.

Antisocial Behavior

The same sort of reasoning can be applied to a host of other phenotypic traits and behaviors that differ among populations. Criminal propensity, as indicated by the crime rates discussed at the beginning of this chapter, is one such behavior that differs markedly among populations. It should be emphasized that what in a modern society is considered criminal may have been normal and fitness-enhancing in many less advanced societies. Such behavior has been shown to have a significant genetic component. This has been demonstrated in a large number of studies comparing identical to fraternal twins, with genetics accounting for approximately 50% to 60% of the variance in the samples studied.[79] Philip Rushton, for example, examined a large sample of twins in the United Kingdom and estimated that approximately 50% of the variance in criminal violence was explained genetically. He found, furthermore, that the environmental factors that did influence criminality were not the product of common, shared upbringing within families, but rather were the result of an individual's own idiosyncratic choices. Individuals predisposed to criminal behavior, for instance, tended to reinforce those predispositions in their choice of friends and preferred activities.[80] For example, such individuals are often motivated by a tendency to seek novelty and risk, and therefore are more likely to, among other things, take drugs, gamble, and frequent bars known for casual sexual encounters. Of course, in doing such things, they often expose themselves to violent encounters with drug dealers, disgruntled gamblers and jealous boyfriends.

During most of the 20th Century, criminologists overwhelmingly subscribed to the paradigm that criminality was solely attributable to various social and environmental factors. Earlier theories that argued that there were individuals possessing inherited criminal tendencies were rejected by most mainstream criminologists. There continues to be reluctance in the field to investigate possible neurological and genetic influences on criminal behavior.[81] This was, and continues to be, the case even though noted researchers beginning in the 1930s were reporting studies on large cohorts of individuals studied longitudinally which showed consistently that criminal behavior tended to be more common in related individuals, but these findings were usually attributed to similarities in family structure, upbringing or other environmental factors.[82]

The last decade has seen the beginning, however, of a notable paradigm shift in that more and more criminologists are now inclined to view genetic factors as important contributors to criminal behavior. This change is largely the result of a large and growing number of research reports using modern genetic analysis and brain imaging technologies that demonstrate beyond any doubt that genes play a major role in the etiology of crime. This new paradigm most emphatically rejects the idea that there are genes for criminality; without exception researchers argue that certain genes can influences specific traits, such as risk taking or lack of self control, that in particular social environments are more likely to produce criminal behavior. Researchers taking this new view argue that genes and environments interact to produce criminal behavior and neither alone provides sufficient explanatory power. Furthermore, it seems clear that the genetically influenced traits do not in themselves produce criminality and in some cases can lead to behaviors that are viewed as desirable. As a corollary to this way of thinking, many behaviors that are antisocial or criminal in modern societies may have had significant advantages in less technologically advanced societies, which explain their existence. The fact that they remain in modern populations, albeit in relatively small degree, suggests that they may still possess fitness-conferring advantages. As discussed in the last chapter, males in tribal societies who were successful in aggressively competing for females were often far more successful than less aggressive types. In many tribal societies such behavior was often admired. Today, of course, similar behavior is considered antisocial, especially if it leads to violent confrontations that result in injury or death.

Most of the research along these lines is still in its infancy, having begun in only the last decade or so, since it is only in recent years that new techniques have allowed for the in depth analysis of genetic and nervous system functions. Nevertheless, it has in a short time produced impressive results. Much of the earlier research tying criminal behavior to inheritance relied on studies of identical and fraternal twins, and often included studies of adopted children. While many of these studies were extremely convincing to some, others questioned their validity on grounds that it was impossible to adequately control for environmental factors. Newer studies based on clearly measurable linkages between particular gene sequences, personality traits and criminal behavior are much harder to refute and add considerable weight to the findings of the earlier twin studies.

In large measure, researchers have tended to study traits such as impulsiveness, aggression, risk taking, lack of empathy and other traits that, in certain environmental circumstances, act as precursors to criminal and antisocial behavior. Since most of these traits are linked to emotional responses regulated by hormonal agents regulated by subcortical areas of the brain, much research has focused on genes related to hormonal functioning. In addition, since control of emotional responses is linked to various cortical or "higher function" brain regions, much research has focused on genes related to these areas. Since so much of this research is new and sometimes contradictory, what follows will necessarily be limited in scope to the most robust of the findings produced in recent years. It should be added that since IQ is closely tied to antisocial behavior, the effects of IQ should always be considered when evaluating the research results, though this factor is not always measured or reported upon in much of the research. In addition, owing to the sensitive nature of this research, very little in the way of ethnic or racial differences is reported. This will no doubt change in the future, but for now this question, so vital to the issues raised in this book, must remain largely speculative.[83]

A fairly common behavioral disorder, and perhaps the one most extensively studied, is the condition known as attention deficit hyperactivity disorder (ADHD) that predisposes individuals to an increased risk of antisocial behavior. The condition is found in about 3-5% of all children, usually appearing before the age of seven, and is most common among males. It is associated with a host of educational and behavioral problems, and often leads to educational failure even among people with normal or above normal IQ. Children with the condition are hyperactive, impulsive and have difficulty focusing their attention on tasks assigned to them. A substantial percentage of these 3–5% of the children diagnosed with ADHD (between 20 to 40%) develop more serious antisocial patterns of behavior. According to the National Institute of Mental Health, "these children frequently lie or steal, fight with or bully others, and are at a real risk of getting into trouble at school or with the police. They violate the basic rights of other people, are aggressive toward people and/or animals, destroy property, break into people's homes, commit thefts, carry or use weapons, or engage in vandalism."[84]

One particular allele of a gene (DRD4) regulating the reception at specific brain sites of the neurotransmitter dopamine is strongly associated with ADHD. The more common allele of DRD4 has four repetitions of a specific base pair, whereas the ADHD-related allele has seven repetitions. The latter allele is very common among the natives of South America, somewhat common in the populations of Europe and Africa and almost completely absent from those in China. As yet, the specific way in which this allele predisposes children to ADHD is not known.

It is important to add that ADHD, as are most complex human disorders, is polygenic in nature, and is likely the product of a variety of genes and possible environmental conditions. For instance, a variant of the DAT1 gene involved in dopamine regulation has been implicated in ADHD, but the results to date are inconsistent.[85] Since a condition such as ADHD is probably polygenic, no one gene is likely to have a very high correlation with the condition. In time it may be possible to detect other genes related to ADHD that will allow for greater precision in predicting the disorder and in perhaps finding ways, either pharmacological or environmental, to ameliorate its effects. The current use of Ritalin, while perhaps overused, does seem to relieve somewhat the symptoms of ADHD.

The allele linked to ADHD appears to be an allele of recent origin and seems to have remained at a stable frequency in the various populations in which it is found. Harpending and Cochran suggest that it is most likely a gene that induces certain behaviors that are fitness-enhancing in some settings, but negative in others. As such, it appears to be a frequency dependent gene that produces an evolutionary stable strategy in conjunction with the alternative 4-repeat allele. Harpending and Cochran point out that if it were merely fitness-reducing, as it appears to be in most modern settings, it would have long since gone extinct, and ask, "what is the niche in human societies for males who are energetic, impulsive (namely, unpredictable) and noncompliant?" Their answer is that such characteristics would be fitness-enhancing in those societies where male bravado, aggression and coalitional violence are rewarded with a reproductive advantage. The Yanomamo represent just such a society and not surprisingly have a high frequency of the 7-repeat allele.[86]

Another widely studied gene, "monoamine oxidase A" (MAOA) that regulates the level of neurochemicals, serotonin in particular, in the brain, has also been implicated in a host of behavioral problems. The gene takes on many forms depending on the number of repeated base pairs it possesses. For purposes of simplicity it is usually dichotomized into two alleles, one of which produces a high level of serotonin (the high-activity gene or MAOA-H), and another that produces low levels of serotonin (the low activity gene or MAOA-L). Low levels of serotonin have been linked to a host of characteristics including impulsivity, risk-taking, alcohol, nicotine and other drug addictions, depression, and violence. The low activity gene is relatively common and occurs in about a third of European males. The MAO gene is located on the X chromosome, of which men carry only one, while women carry two. This means that if a man carries the gene it will necessarily be fully expressed, since there is no second X chromosome to carry an alternative allele, which might moderate its influence. Women, with two X chromosomes, can have alternative versions of the gene, i.e., be heterozygous at this site, with the effect that the expression of the low activity allele may be attenuated. This may be one of the reasons females who carry the low allele gene rarely develop the antisocial characteristics commonly found in men.[87]

However, the gene in question can by no means be characterized as a criminal gene. This is obvious, if only because nowhere near one third of European males engage in criminal behavior even though that many carry the low MAOA gene. Clearly, other genes and environmental factors must be involved. For instance, an allele of a gene that codes for tryptophan hydroxylase, which influences the effects of serotonin, has been shown to be implicated in aggressive behavior and unprovoked anger.[88] Furthermore, research by Richard

Sjoberg and associates indicated that the negative effect of the low allele version is magnified in males with high testosterone levels as measured in the cerebrospinal fluid of subjects. This may be another reason why women tend not to be adversely affected by the low MAOA gene. In light of this finding, it is interesting to note that while testosterone in males is almost invariably related to dominance behavior in men and other mammals, it does not always produce aggressive behavior.[89] Sjoberg, et al. suggest that their findings "offer a plausible explanation for previous inconsistencies in studies of the relationship between testosterone and male aggression."[90]

The interplay of environmental and genetic factors is illustrated by the work of Avsholem Caspi and Terrie Moffitt, in a long-term research project on a large cohort of New Zealand children. They found no differences in antisocial behavior between those carrying the MAOA-H and the MAOA-L genes. They did, however, find a strong relationship between abuse during childhood and antisocial behavior in adolescence. Only a subset of abused children exhibited criminal behavior, while others seemed unaffected by their earlier maltreatment; those with the MAOA-L gene seemed more affected by the abuse. Among the males who had suffered abuse during childhood *and* carried the high activity gene MAOA-H, about 35% exhibited antisocial behavior, and about 20% were convicted of a violent crime. However, among the males who had been mistreated and carried the low activity allele MAOA-L approximately 80% exhibited antisocial behavior and 30% were convicted of a violent crime. The authors remark that, "these findings may partly explain why not all victims of maltreatment victimize others and provide epidemiological evidence that genotypes can moderate children's sensitivity to environmental insults." It is important to stress that in this study the low activity gene did not predispose individuals to antisocial behavior, but rather seemed to heighten the effect of parental abuse or neglect.[91]

The Caspi and Moffitt research has been replicated by a number of studies on adolescents in Italy, the United States and Sweden.[92] All of these studies included only whites of European background. One study in the United States was able to partially replicate the result, but found that it only held for white males, and not for nonwhites.[93] Two studies failed to replicate the finding at all, regardless of race. They found that childhood abuse or trauma was a significant risk factor for adolescent antisocial behavior but found no evidence of an exacerbating effect of the MAOA gene.[94] Young and associates, who reported on one of the failed attempts to replicate the finding, reported no difference in the incidence of the MAOA-L gene among racial groups, with whites, blacks and Hispanics all having an incidence of about 32%. Their sample, however, was quite small and it is unclear whether this finding can be generalized to the larger population.[95] Some of these inconsistencies may be accounted for by the fact that the studies included females that may have reduced the ability to detect significant differences, since as previously mentioned, the presence of high levels of testosterone increases the negative effect of the risky allele. Clearly, more research is needed to clarify the effect of the MAOA-L on criminal behavior. As mentioned earlier, this gene is likely only one of a yet undiscovered constellation of genes and environmental variables that together account for a heightened susceptibility to criminality.

An interesting sidelight of the above was a finding by epidemiologist Rod Lea. He reported that in attempting to find genetic correlates for the nicotine addiction common among the native Maori of New Zealand, he found a surprisingly high incidence of the low activity MAOA gene among them. In fact, it is twice as common among Maori men as among men of European origin, appearing in 60% of Maori compared to 32% in European men. Lea speculated that this, along with the environmental stresses common among the Maori, may help to explain their relatively high level of criminal violence. In a news report on this finding a journalist chose to call the low MAOA variant of the gene, a "warrior gene," a term which, unfortunately, subsequently gained wide currency.[96] While Maori make up about 14% of the New Zealand population, they are responsible for more than half the criminal offenses in that country.[97]

Recent brain imaging research by Meyer-Lindenberg and associates sheds light on the operation of the MAOA gene. These researchers focused on brain areas known to regulate emotional responses in individuals.[98] The subjects in their study, divided into MAOA low and high groups, had no history of violence, criminality or psychological disorders. Subjects were shown various images designed to evoke emotional reactions while various regions of their brains were monitored for neural responses. Males in the low MAOA group showed greater reactivity to emotional stimuli in brain regions (the limbic area and the amygdala, in particular) known to trigger emotional responses. Furthermore, they exhibited reduced activity in those cortical (prefrontal) regions known to regulate and moderate the subcortical regions giving rise to emotional responses. Females did not exhibit these patterns.[99]

These results suggest that MAOA-L carriers may be more affected by emotional or stressful conditions than MAOA-H carriers. Perhaps they are more prone to alcohol and tobacco addiction because they use these drugs to reduce their sensitivity to stress. It may also explain why they are more prone to violence, since they seem to have more difficulty regulating their emotional reactions. This interpretation helps to explain the Caspi and Moffitt findings. Children with the MAOA-L gene, when exposed to the stress of abusive upbringing, seemed to have been more traumatized by it than MAOA-H carriers and responded in less productive, often antisocial, ways.

A recent study may be particularly pertinent to the concerns of this book since it suggests that the MAO-L gene is related to gang membership. Kevin Beaver and coworkers, using a subsample of about 2000 of the more than 90,000 of those who participated in the National Longitudinal Study of Adolescent Health for whom genetic data existed, found "males with the low MAO genotype, compared to males with the high MAO genotype, were 1.94 times more likely to be gang members, and they were also 1.82 times more likely to have used a weapon in a fight." In addition, among the small number of male subjects (54) who reported gang membership, "male gang members who carried the low MAO activity alleles were 4.37 times more likely to use a weapon when compared with male gang members who carried the high activity alleles." No such relations were found for females.[100]

To summarize to this point, antisocial behavior has been shown to have clear genetic precursors by twin and family studies, and by recent research pointing to specific genes associated with such tendencies. Antisocial criminality and a host of other behavior problems have been linked to the MAOA-L gene that occurs in a substantial minority of European populations, and to the DRD4 dopamine receptor gene, that is far less common in that population but more common in others. It should be stressed that most people who carry these genes exhibit no criminality at all and may in fact exhibit traits that many find admirable. They are often quite fearless risk-takers and novelty-seekers and as such will excel in many endeavors, especially in athletics and military pursuits. What some would characterize as reckless and imprudent, others might see as daring, venturesome and heroic—features that many people seek out and admire in leaders. To the extent that MAOA-L individuals react more powerfully to mistreatment by others, it may well be an essential component of democratic society. Carriers may be less willing to suffer tyrants passively. It is intriguing to speculate on what may have been the incidence of the MAOA-L gene among the founding fathers of the American Republic. Perhaps scientists will one day be able to answer that question? It may well be that these genes are very much fitness-enhancing among hunters and gatherers, such as the Maori and the Yanomamo, as well as among the inhabitants of the early empires bent on conquest. The fact that they remain in the gene pool of people today strongly suggests that, in conjunction with other genes, they have, at least until recently, been fitness-enhancing, and may still be so today.

For the purposes of this author, it would be worthwhile to know whether some groups carry this gene more frequently than others. More specifically, it would be important to determine whether they are part of a constellation of genes that may in fact be differentially represented in various groups, and thereby explain existing differences among groups in phenotypically expressed criminal and antisocial behaviors in industrial societies. Unfortunately, at present, it is difficult to carry out such research and obtain funding to do so, given the present ideological resistance to recognizing group differences in criminality. According to criminologist John Paul Wright "linking race to criminal behavior runs the risk of public repudiation, professional exile, and even career death.... For this reason, many criminologists are loath to examine the connection between race and crime outside the modern sociological paradigm that holds that race is merely a social construct...'just a social invention.'"[101]

Psychopathic Personality Disorder

Moffitt and coworkers, in early research involving the New Zealand cohort discussed above, reported a clear distinction between what they called childhood-onset delinquency and adolescent-onset delinquency. Adolescent-onset delinquency was fairly common, representing about 25% of the cohort. These people seemed otherwise normal and relatively well-adjusted. By their late twenties, they had overwhelmingly ceased to engage in antisocial behavior. The childhood-onset delinquents, who represented about 7% of the cohort, were much more likely to commit violent crimes and did so at a much earlier age. This latter group exhibited a number of difficulties, including "neurological abnormalities, low intellectual ability, reading difficulties, hyperactivity, poor scores on neuropsychological tests..." Their average IQ was 17 points lower than the adolescent-onset delinquents. These troubled individuals were far more likely to persist in criminal activity into adulthood.[102]

This finding is consistent with longitudinal studies in "career criminality" going back over a half a century. Two studies of large male cohorts in Philadelphia found very similar results. The first study dealt with 9,945 boys born in 1945, while the second involved 13,160 boys born in 1958. The findings in both cases were remarkably consistent. In both studies about one-third of the subjects had some contact with the police, but only about 6 to 7%, were habitual offenders with multiple arrests for serious crimes. In the first study, this small group was responsible for 63% of all serious crimes in the whole 1945 cohort. They accounted for "71 percent of the murders, 73 percent of the rapes, 82 percent of the robberies and 69 percent of the aggravated assaults." In the later 1958 cohort, the 7% defined as habitual offenders "accounted for 60 percent of the murders, 75 percent of the rapes, 73 percent of the robberies and 65 percent of the aggravated assaults." Similar findings were reported for young men in Sweden and Racine, Wisconsin.[103]

Many career criminals match the profile of criminal psychopaths. The key ingredient required for the clinical diagnosis of psychopathy is a lack of empathy—an emotional callousness toward the feelings of others. This is not a characteristic associated with the MAOA-L gene, and appears to be independent of it. Viding and associates use the term "callous-unemotional traits" to describe this feature of the psychopathic personality and provide powerful evidence that it is under genetic control. They claim that it can be reliably diagnosed in children as young as seven years old.[104] This claim is consistent with the Moffit, et. al. finding that the early-onset delinquents displayed antisocial behavior at an early age and this is, in fact, a general phenomenon among career criminals.[105] The neural mechanisms underlying empathetic responses have been studied by a number of researchers using brain-imaging techniques. This research suggests that empathetic responses involve specific subcortical areas of the brain, in particular the amygdala, that enable a person to imagine the pain or discomfort of others from their facial expressions.[106] Psychopaths exhibit reduced responses to such empathy-inducing stimuli and often have dysfunctions in the implicated brain areas. A lack of empathy and potential psychopathological behavior therefore appears to be readily identifiable, to involve specific brain structures and neural circuitry, and, to some degree, to be inherited. As yet, no specific gene complex has been associated with psychopathic behavior. Given what is known, however, it is reasonable to suppose that genes predisposing individuals to this characterological anomaly will in time be found. According to respected criminologist Matt DeLisi, "Virtually everything that is known about career criminality strongly implicates at least a partially genetic etiological basis."[107]

It is important to stress that while it is likely that psychopaths make up a large proportion, perhaps most, of habitual career criminals, it is not the case that all psychopaths, or even a substantial portion of them, are criminals in the sense that they have committed crimes and been incarcerated. The reason for that is that while career criminals generally have below average IQs, that is not the case for psychopaths who are represented equally throughout the IQ spectrum. Put another way, while the correlation between low IQ and career criminality is quite high, such is not the case for the correlation between traits associated with psychopathy and IQ.

This is important since it is often difficult to detect psychopathic individuals because they often do not display antisocial behaviors, especially if they are above average in intelligence. Many of the world's worst tyrants were intellectually brilliant, but horribly cruel people who were totally indifferent to the pain they inflicted on others. When coupled with low IQ, on the other hand, psychopathic types seem predisposed to criminal violence and commit violent crime greatly disproportionate to their numbers.[108] Clearly, any increase in the percentage of these psychopathic types will have a dramatic effect on crime rates in a society and have serious ramifications for the quality of life in those societies.

It is important to stress the distinction between simple antisocial behavior and psychopathic criminality, since the latter, though relatively rare, is particularly disruptive to life in modern societies. Since psychopaths lack empathy and a moral sense, they cannot be relied upon to treat others fairly. Unlike more common antisocial traits, psychopathic traits seem immune to environmental amelioration; type of upbringing, for instance, has no discernible effect on their development. This often leads to instrumental aggression and premeditated crime, as opposed to the MAOA-L condition that is more likely to produce reactive aggression, namely, aggression triggered by the behavior of others or by environmental circumstances. Psychopaths, when criminal, are especially vicious and calculating in their violence. For instance, if they engage in rape, they may kill their victims to avoid arrest and would be completely unmoved by pleas from their victims. But even when psychopaths exhibit no criminality they represent a real threat so society, since their lack of any moral sense enables intelligent psychopaths to feign a host of emotional expressions so that they are often seen as pleasant and affable people, which makes it easy for them to manipulate others to their advantage.[109] They are, in short, ideal con-men, and it should be no surprise that many rise, especially if very intelligent, to great heights in the political and economic spheres.

Whether or not such predispositions are likely to be more fitness-enhancing in some social environments than in others is an intriguing question. Perhaps in the realm of hunters and gatherers it may, as previously suggested, have such an advantage in enabling individuals to fight and kill more effectively. In more complex societies it would seem advantageous, but only when accompanied by intelligence and reasonable prudence. Wanton and open disregard for others is unlikely to go unpunished in ordered societies with effective police functions. However, even when accompanied by prudence and intelligence it has a destructive effect in modern societies that depend on honest dealings between citizens and restraint in the pursuit of self-interest.

It is important to recall a point made earlier. Genes which seem to predispose individuals to criminality may only do so in combination with other genes and with particular social circumstances. It is also possible, though it appears unlikely, that there are not any significant differences among groups in the prevalence of such genes. However, it is important to keep in mind that, in America at present, IQ is the best overall predictor of criminality.[110] For that reason groups may differ in their likelihood of criminality not because of differences in the prevalence of certain temperamental genes linked to criminality, but simply because of the very real group differences in IQ. In the case of psychopathy, this seems quite clear, in that it appears to be expressed quite differently depending on a person's IQ.

At this point it is important to stress two important and well-established facts. The first is that groups differ in their level of criminal behavior. The second is that criminal behavior has clear genetic components, including IQ. Whether or not group differences in criminality can be traced to genetic differences other than IQ is, at this point, an unresolved question. Likewise is the question of whether such genetic differences have their origins in different cultural and physical environments making them more, or less, fit. These are empirical questions, however, and it is reasonable to assume that they will be amenable to scientific resolution. Until such questions are resolved, however, it would seem only prudent to consider the implications of such potential temperamental differences in formulating immigration policy.

Notes

1   Richard Lynn and Tatu Vanhanen, *IQ and Global Inequality: A Sequel to IQ and the Wealth of Nations* (Augusta, Georgia: Washington Summit Publishers, 2006).
2   Kelly Jeffreys and Randall Monger, *Annual Flow Report: U. S. Legal Permanent Residents: 2007*. U.S. Department of Homeland Security, Office of Immigration Statistics, March 2008.
3   Lynn and Vanhanen, IQ and Global Inequality; Richard Lynn and Tatu Vanhanen, *IQ and the Wealth of Nations* (Westport: Conn. Praeger, 2002).
4   Garett Jones and W. Joel Schneider, Intelligence, Human Capital, and Economic Growth. *Journal of Economic Growth*, 11:1 (2006) 71–93.
5   Astrid Oline Ervik, IQ and the Wealth of Nations, Book Review, *The Economic Journal*, June 2003, F406–F408; Susan M. Barnett and Wendy Williams, National Intelligence and the Emperor's New Clothes, *Contemporary psychology*, 2004, 49:1, 389–396.
6   Ulric Neisser, Gwyneth Boodoo, Thomas J. Bouchard, A. Wade Boykin, Nathan Brody, Stephen J. Ceci, Diane F. Halpern, John C. Loehlin, Robert Perloff, Robert J. Sternberg and Susana Urbina, Intelligence: Knowns and Unknowns, *American Psychologist*, 31:2, (1996), 77–101.
7   J. Philippe Rushton, and Arthur R. Jenson, Thirty years of research on race differences in cognitive ability, *Psychology, Public Policy, and Law*, 1:2, (2005) 235–294.
8   Lynn and Vanhanen, *IQ and Global Inequality*, 54–55.
9   Ibid., 61–62.
10   Ibid., 70–71.
11   Barnett and Williams, National Intelligence and the Emperor's New Clothes, 392.
12   J. Philippe Rushton,. *Race, Evolution and Behavior: A Life History Perspective* (New Brunswick, New Jersey: Transaction Publishers, 1995), 134.

13   Etienne G, Krug, Linda L. Dahlberg, James A. Mercy, Anthony B. Zwi and Rafael Lozanzo (Eds.) *World Report on Violence and Health*. Geneva: World Health Organization, 2002.

14   United Nations Office on Drugs and Crime (2003). *Eighth United Nations survey of crime trends and operations of criminal justice systems, covering the period 2001–2002* (2003), 28–29.

15   Crime Figures for Immigrant communities in the United States and Europe are discussed at length in chapters 6 and 7, respectively.

16   J. Philippe Rushton, *Race, evolution and behavior* 1995, 219; James Shreeve, *The Neandertal Enigma: Solving the Mystery of Modern Human Origins* (New York: Avon, 1995), 88; Milford H. Wolpoff, Bruce Mannheim, Alan Mann, John Hawks, Rachel Caspari, Karen R. Rosenberg, David W. Frayer, George W. Gill and Geoffrey Clark, Why *Not* the Neandertals? *World Archaeology* 36(4):527–546.

17   Alan G. Thorne and Milford Wolpoff, The Multiregional Evolution of Humans, revised paper, *Scientific American*, 13, 2 (2003), 46–53. John Hawks and Milford H. Wolpoff, Sixty Years of Modern Human Origins in the American Anthropological Association, *American Anthropologist*, 105, 1 (2003), 87–98.

18   M. Martinon–Torres, J.M. Bermudez de Castro, A. Gomez–Robles, J.L. Arsuaga, E. Carbonell, D. Lordkipanidze, G. Manzi, and A. Margvelashvili, Dental Evidence on the Hominin Dispersals During the Pleistocene, *Proceedings of the National Academy of Science*, August 7, 2007, online.

19   Thorne and Wolpoff, The Multiregional Evolution of Humans, 46–53; Hawks and Wolpoff, Sixty Years of Modern Human Origins, 87–98.

20   Gregory Cochran and Henry Harpending. *The 10,000 Year Explosion: How Civilization Accelerated Human Evolution* (New York: Basic Books, 2009), 25–64.

21   Ibid., 30.

22   Fred S. Singer and Dennis T. Avery, *Unstoppable global warming*, (Rowman and Littlefield, New York, 2007), xiv.

23   Cochran and Harpending. *The 10,000 Year Explosion*, 91.

24   Rushton, *Race, Evolution and Behavior*, 228–230.

25   Eldra P. Solomon, Linda R. Berg and Diana W. Martin, *Biology, 6th Edition*, (Toronto: Brooks/Cole, 2002), 395.

26   Wade, *Before the Dawn*, 74–94.

27   Ibid., 86.

28   Cochran and Harpending. *The 10,000 Year Explosion*, 64.

29   Vinayak Eswaran, Henry Harpending, and Alan R. Rogers. Genomics Refutes an Exclusively African Origin of Humans. *Journal of Human Evolution*. 49:1 (2005) 1–18

30   Vincent Sarich and Frank Miele, *Race: The reality of human differences* (Boulder, Col.: Westview Press, 2004).

31   Dora Biro, Norika Inoue–Nakamura, Rikako Tonooka, Gen Yamakoshi, Claudia Sousa and Tetsuro Matsuzawa, Cultural Innovation and Transmission of Tool Use in Wild Chimpanzees: Evidence from Field Experiments, *Animal Cognition*, 6:4. (2003), online; Thomas Breuer, Mireille Ndoundou–Hockemba and Vicki Fishlock, First Observation of Tool Use in Wild Gorillas. PLoS Biol 3:11 (2005), online; Craig B. Stanford, Caleb Gambaneza, John Bosco Nkurunungi and Michele L. Goldsmith. Chimpanzees in Bwindi–Impenetrable National Park,

Uganda, Use Different Tools to Obtain Different Types of Honey, *Primate*, 41.3 (2003) 337–341, online.

32 William H. McNeill, The Steppe, *Encyclopaedia Britannica*, 2007, 5, online.

33 John Noble Wilford, In Ruin, Symbols on a Stone Hint at a Lost Asian Culture, *New York Times*, May 13, 2001, online.

34 William H. McNeill, *The Rise of the West: A History of the Human Community* (Chicago: Chicago University Press, 1963), 484–494.

35 Cochran and Harpending. *The 10,000 Year Explosion*, 175–186.

36 Ibid., 184.

37 Kevin MacDonald, *The Culture of Critique: An Evolutionary Analysis of Jewish Involvement in Twentieth-Century Intellectual and Political Movements*, (Bloomington Ind: Firstbooks Library, 2002), xxiv–xxviii). Originally published in 1998 by Praeger, Westport, Conn.

38 L. Luca Cavelli-Sforza, The Chinese Human Genome Diversity Project, *Proceedings of the National academy of Science*, 95, September 1998, 11501–11503.

39 William H. McNeill, *Plagues and peoples*. (Anchor Press/Doubleday, Garden City, New York, 1976), 191–196.

40 Richard Duchesne, Asia First? The *Journal of the Historical Society*, VI: I (2006), 75; J. M. Roberts, *The Penguin History of the World* (London: Penguin, 1995), 441.

41 Gregory Clark, *A farewell to Alms: A brief economic history of the world* (Princeton, New Jersey: Princeton University Press, 2007).

42 Ibid., 105.

43 William H. Durham, *Coevolution: Genes, Culture and Human Diversity*. (Stanford Calif.: Stanford University Press, 199), 123–146.

44 Diamond, *Guns, Germs and Steel*, 203–210; William McNeill, Plagues and Peoples (Garden City New York: Doubleday, 1976), 1–14.

45 Diamond, *Guns, Germs and Steel*, 210–214.

46 Durham, *Coevolution*, 228–29.

47 Ibid., 226–37.

48 Ibid., 233–7; Cochran and Harpending, *10,000 Year Explosion*, 77–78.

49 Patrick D. Evans, Sandra L. Gilbert, Nitzan Mekel-Bobrov, Eric J. Vallender, Jeffrey R. Anderson, Leila M. Vaez-Azizi, Sarah A. Tishkoff, Richard R. Hudson, Bruce T. Lahn, Microcephalin, a Gene Regulating Brain Size, Continues to Evolve Adaptively in Humans, *Science*, 309: 5741, (2005), 1717–1720; Mekel-Bobrov, Nitzan, Sandra L. Gilbert, Patrick D. Evans, Eric J. Vallender, Jeffrey R. Anderson, Richard R. Hudson, Sarah A. Tishkoff, Bruce T. Lahn, Ongoing Adaptive Evolution of ASPM, a Brain Size Determinant in Homo Sapiens, *Science* 309: 5741 (2005), 1720–1722; Rosenberg, Genetic Structure of Human Populations; Voight, Benjamin F. Voight, Sridhar Kudaravalli, Xiaoquan Wen and Jonathan K. Pritchard. Voight, et. al., A Map of Recent Positive Selection in the Human Genome, *PLoS Biol* 4:3 (March 2006), 446–458; Wade, *Before the Dawn*, 185–88; Eric T. Wang, Greg Kodama, Pierre Baldi, and Robert K. Moyzis, Global Landscape of Recent Inferred Darwinian Selection for Homo Sapiens *PNAS*, 103:1 (2006), 135–140, online; Scott Williamson, Melissa J. Hubisz, Andrew G. Clark, Bret A. Payseur, Carlos D. Bustamante and Rasmus Nielson. Localizing Recent Adaptive Evolution in the Human Genome, *PLoS Genetics* 3:6 (2007), online.

50 Rushton, *Race, Evolution and Behavior*, 249–250.
51 Ibid., 228–31.
52 Ibid., 113–146.
53 Ibid., 155–157.
54 Ibid., 113–183.
55 Edward M. Miller, Paternal Provisioning Versus Mate Seeking in Human Populations, *Personality and Individual Differences*, 17:2 (1993) 227–255.
56 Douglas R. White and Michael L. Burton, Causes of polygyny: Ecology, Economy, Kinship and Warfare, *American Anthropologist*, 90:4 (1988), 871–887.
57 George P. Murdock and Douglas R. White, Standard Cross–Cultural Sample, *Ethnology*, 8 (1969) 329–369.
58 White and Burton. Causes of Polygyny, 871–887.
59 Pierre L. Van den Berghe, *Human Family Systems: An Evolutionary* View (*New York*: Elsevier, 1979), 66.
60 Krug, et. al. *World report on violence and health;* Byron M. Roth, *Prescription for Failure: Race Relations in the Age of Social Science* (New Brunswick, New Jersey: Transaction Publishers, 1994), 221–229.
61 *BBC News*, South African Rape Survey Shock, June 18, 2009, online.
62 CIA, *The World Factbook: Statistics and Analysis for Every Country on the Planet* (New York: Barnes and Noble, 2006), 548.
63 Richard Lynn, R*ace Differences in Intelligence: An Evolutionary Analysis,* (Augusta, Georgia: Washington Summit Publishers, 2006), 240–243.
64 Nicholas Wade, Humans Have Spread Globally, and Evolved Locally, *The New York Times*, June 26, 2007, online.
65 Gregory Cochran, Jason Hardy and Henry Harpending, Natural History of Ashkenazi Intelligence, *Journal of Biosocial Science*, 38, 2006. 660, online.
66 Ibid., 673.
67 Ibid., 668–70. Paul Johnson, *A History of the Jews*, (New York: Harper and Row, 1987), 246–259. Kevin MacDonald. *A people That Shall Dwell Alone: Judaism As a Group Evolutionary Strategy, with Diaspora Peoples*, (Lincoln Neb.: Writers Club Press, 2002), 170–209. Originally published in 1994 by Praeger, Westport, Conn.
68 Cochran, et. al., Natural History of Ashkenazi Intelligence, 670.
69 Ibid., 676.
70 Ibid, 681.
71 Clark, *A farewell to Alms*.
72 Janneke R. Zinkstok, Odette de Wild, Therese AMJ van Amelsvoort, Michael W. Tanck, Frank Baas and Don H. Linszen. D. H., Association Between the DTNBP1 Gene and Intelligence: A Case–Control Study in Young Patients with Schizophrenia and Related Disorders and Unaffected Siblings, *Behavioral and Brain Functions* 3:19 (2007), online; Katherine E. Burdick, Todd Lencz, Birgit Funke, Christine T. Finn, Philip R. Szeszko, John M. Kane, Raju Kucherlapati, and Anil K. Malhotra, Genetic Variation in DTNBP1 Influences General Cognitive Ability, *Human Molecular Genetics* 15:10 (2006), 1563–1568.
73 NIH/National Institute of Mental Health. Dopamine–dampening gene linked to prefrontal inefficiency, schizophrenia. *Science Daily,* May 29, 2001, online.
74 Zinkstok, et. Al., Association Between the DTNBP1 Gene and Intelligence.
75 Washington University School of Medicine in St. Louis, February 27, 2007., online at nootropics.com. Dick was commenting on the following:

Danielle M. Dick, Fazil Aliev, John Kramer, Jen C. Wang, Anthony Hinrichs, Sarah Bertelsen, Sam Kuperman, Marc Schuckit, John Nurnberger Jr, Howard J. Edenberg, Bernice Porjesz, Henri Begleiter, Victor Hesselbrock, Alison Goate and Laura Bierut Association of *CHRM2* with IQ: Converging Evidence for a Gene Influencing Intelligence, *Behavior Genetics*, 37, 2, March 2007.

76   Mark Wheeler, Study Gives More Proof that Intelligence is Largely inherited: UCLA Researchers Find that Genes Determine Brain's Processing Speed, *USLA Newsroom*, March 17, 2009, online at newsroom,ucla.edu.

77   Burdick, et. al., Genetic Variation in DTNBP1 Influences General Cognitive Ability.

78   These percentages were determined by consulting International Hapmap Project online for the CHRM2 gene, RefSNP rs1115781.

79   Linda Mealey, The Sociobiology of Sociopathy: An Integrated Evolutionary Model, *Behavioral and brain science* 18:3, (1995) 523–599. Essi Viding and Uta Frith, Genes for Susceptibility to Violence Lurk in the Brain, *Proceedings of the National Academy of Sciences*, 103:16 (2006) 6085–86.

80   J. Philippe Rushton, David W. Fulker, Michael C. Neale, David K. B. Nias and Hans J. Eysenck. Altruism and Aggression: The Heritability of Individual Differences, *Journal of Personality and Social Psychology*, 50 (1986), 1192–1198.

81   John Paul Wright, Danielle Boisvert, Kim Dietrich, and M. Douglas Ris, The Ghost in the Machine and Criminal Behavior: Criminology for the 21st Century, in Anthony Walsh and Kevin Beaver,(Eds.) *Biosocial Criminology: New Direction in Theory and Research* (New York: Routledge, 2009), 73–89, 73–74.

82   Matt DeLisi, Neuroscience and the Holy Grail: Genetics and Career Criminology, in Walsh and Beaver, *Biosocial Criminology*, 209–224, 210–213.

83   John Paul Wright, Inconvenient Truths: Science, Race and Crime, in Walsh and Beaver, Biosocial Criminology, 137–153.

84   Margaret Strock, Attention Deficit Hyperactivity Disorder, Public Information and Communications Branch, National Institute of Mental Health (NIMH), 1996.

85   Kevin M. Beaver, *The Nature and Nurture of Antisocial Outcomes* (El Paso, Texas: Scholarly Publishing LLC, 2008), 36–44.

86   Henry Harpending and Gregory Cochran, In Our Genes, *PNAS*, 99:1 (2002) 10–12, online.

87   Ronald Bailey, Born to be wild, *Reason Magazine*, August 7. 2002, online; Viding and Frith, Genes for Susceptibility to Violence Lurk in the Brain, 6085–86.

88   Richard J. Davidson, Katherine M. Putnam, and Christine L. Larson, Dysfunction in the Neural Circuitry of Emotion Regulation—A Possible Prelude to Violence, *Science*, 280, 5479, (2000), 591–594.

89   Allan Mazur, Testosterone and Violence Among Young Men, in Walsh and Beaver, *Biosocial Criminology*, 190–208.

90   Richard L. Sjoberg, Francesca Ducci, Christina S. Barr, Timothy K. Newman, Liliana ll'Osso, Matti Virkkunen and David Goldman., A Non- Additive Intereaction of a Functional MAO–A VNTR and Testosterone Predicts Antisocial Behavior, *Neurpsychopharmacology* (2008) 33, 425–430.

91   Avshalom Caspi,, Joseph McClay, Terrie E. Moffitt, Jonathan Mill, Judy Martin, Ian W. Craig, Alan Taylor, and Richie Poulton, Role of Genotype in the Cycle of

Violence in Maltreated Children, *Science* 297:5582 (2002) 851–4

92   Debra L. Foley, L, Lindon J. Eaves, Brandon Wormley, Judy L. Silberg, Hermine H. Maes, Jonathan Kuhn and Bruce Riley, Childhood Adversity, Monoamine Oxidaze A Genotype, and Risk for Conduct Disorder, *Archives of General Psychiatry* 61:7 (2004) 738–744; Giovanni Frazzetto, Giorgio D. Lorenzo, Valeria Carola, Luca Proletti, Ewa Sokolowska, Alberto Siracusano, Cornelius Gross and Alfonso Troisi, Early Trauma and Increased Risk for Physical Aggression During Adulthood: The Moderating Role of MAOA Genotype. *PLoS One* 2:5 (2007), e486, online; J. Kim–Cohen, Caspi, A., Taylor, A., Williams, B., Newcombe, R., Craig, I. W. and Moffitt, T.E, MAOA, Maltreatment, and Gene–Environment Interaction Predicting Children's Mental Health: New Evidence and a Meta–Analysis, *Molecular Psychiatry,* 11 (2006), 903–913; Kent W. Nilsson, Richard L. Sjoberg, Mattias Damberg, Jerzy Leppert, John Ohrvik, Per Olof Alm, Leif Lindstrom and Lars Oreland, Role of Monoamine Oxidase A Genotype and Psychosocial Factors in Male Adolescent Criminal Activity, *Biological Psychiatry* 59:2 (2006) 121–127.

93   C. S. Widom and L. M. Brzustowicz, MAOA and the Cycle of Violence: Childhood Abuse and Neglect, MAOA Genotype, and Risk for Violent and Antisocial Behavior, *Biological Psychiatry,* 2006, 60(7): 684–9.

94   D. Huizinga, B.C. Haberstick, A. Smolen, S. Menard, S. E. Young, R. P. Corley, M. C. Stallings, J. Grotpeter, J. K. and Hewitt, Childhood Maltreatment, Subsequent Antisocial Behavior, and the Role of Monoamine Oxidase A genotype, *Biological Psychiatry,* 60:7 (2006), 677–83; Susan E. Young, Andrew Smolen, John K. Hewitt, Brett C. Haberstick, Michael C. Stallings, Robin P. Corley, and Thomas J. Crowley. Interaction Between MAO–A Genotype and Maltreatment in the Risk for Conduct Disorder: Failure to Confirm in Adolescent Patients, *American Journal of Psychiatry,* 163, (2006), 1023.

95   Young, et al. Interaction Between MAO–A Genotype and Maltreatment, 1023.

96   Lewis, P., The World Today, ABC Radio (Transcript) August 9, 2006, online.

97   A. J. Becroft, Maori Youth Offending: Paper Addressing Some Introductory Issues by His Honor Judge A. J. Becroft, Principal Youth Court Judge. Ngakia Kia Puawai Conference, 8–10 November, 2005; *New Zealand Herald,* Maori Crime Rate Concerns Government. October 28, 2005, online; TVNZ. Police Tackling Maori Crime Rates. November 10, 2005, online.

98   Davidson, Putnam and Larson, Dysfunction in the Neural Circuitry of Emotion Regulation.

99   Andrea Meyer–Lindenberg, Joshua W. Buckholtz, Bhaskar Kolachana, Ahmad R. Hariri, Lukas Pezawas, Giuseppe Blasi, Ashley Wabnitz, Robyn Honea, Beth Verchinski, Joseph H. Callicott, Michael Egan, Venkata Mattay and Daniel R. Weinberger. Neural Mechanisms of Genetic Risk for Impulsivity and Violence in Humans, *PNAS* 103:16 (March, 2006), 6269–6274.

100 Kevin M. Beaver, Matt DeLisi, Michael G. Vaughn and J.C. Barnes, Monoamine Oxidase A Genotype is Associated with Gang Membership and Weapon Use, *Comprehensive Psychiatry,* 2009, Article in Press, online at sciencedirect.com.

101 Wright, Inconvenient Truths, 138.

102 Terrie Moffitt, Avshalom Caspi, Nigel Dickson, Phil Silva and Warren Stanton. Childhood–Onset versus Adolescent–Onset Antisocial Conduct Problems in Males: Natural History for Ages 3 to 18 Years, *Development and Psychopathology* 8 (1996), 399–424.

103 DeLisi, Neuroscience and the Holy Grail, 210–211.
104 Essi Viding, R. James R. Blair, Terrie E. Moffitt and Robert Plomin, Evidence for Substantial Genetic Risk for Psychopathy in 7–Year–Olds, *Journal of Child Psychology and Psychiatry* 46:6 (2005), 592–597.
105 DeLisi, Neuroscience and the Holy Grail, 212.
106 R. J. R. Blair, J. S. Morris, C. D. Frith, D. I. Perrett and R. J. Dolan, Dissociable Neural Responses to Facial Expressions of Sadness and Anger, *Brain* 122, (1999), 883–893; Laurie Carr, Marco Iacoboni, Marie–Charlotte Dubeau, John C. Mazziotta andGian Luigi Lenzi. Neural Mechanisms of Empathy in Humans: A Relay from Neural Systems for Imitation to Limbic Areas, *PNAS*, 100:9 (April 29, 2003) 5497–5502; Tania Singer, Ben Seymour, John O'Doherty, Holger Kaube, Raymond J. Dolan and Chris D. Frith, Empathy for Pain Involves the Affective But Not the Sensory Components of Pain, *Science*, 303:5661, (2004), 1157–1162.
107 DeLisi, Neuroscience and the Holy Grail, 212.
108 David Rose, Lives of crime. *Prospect Magazine*, 125. (2005), online; Byron M. Roth, Crime and Childrearing, *Society*, 34:1, (1996), 39–45.
109 R. J. R. Blair, Neurocognitive Models of Aggression, the Antisocial Personality Disorders and Psychopathy, *J. Neurol. Neurosurg. Psychiatry*, 71 (2001) 727–731.
110 Robert A. Gordon, Scientific Justification and the Race–IQ–Delinquency Model, in Timothy F. Hartagel and Robert A. Silverman eds. *Critique and Explanation: Essay in Honor of Gwynne Nettler* (New Brunswick, New Jersey: Transaction Books, 1986); James Q. Wilson and Richard J. Herrnstein, *Crime and Human Nature* (New York: Simon and Schuster, 1985), 155. The fundamental question to be addressed in this chapter is whether the dramatic changes in human living arrangements that have taken place over the last five thousand years have had an appreciable effect on the human gene pool. Put another way, does the social arrangement of a society influence natural selection in a form that might be called societal selection? Did the people living in agricultural empires evolve differently from those who remained in the hunter-gather way of life? Are people living in industrial societies undergoing natural selection of a somewhat different character than in earlier societies? Perhaps most important is whether these changes can influence psychological characteristics such as intelligence and temperament. The attempt to answer these questions will require an examination of the nature, in turn, of hunter-gatherer, agricultural, and industrial societies.

Chapter 4
CULTURAL CHANGE AND HUMAN EVOLUTION

THE FUNDAMENTAL QUESTION to be addressed in this chapter is whether the dramatic changes in human living arrangements that have taken place over the last five thousand years have had an appreciable effect on the human gene pool. Put another way, does the social arrangement of a society influence natural selection in a form that might be called societal selection? Did the people living in agricultural empires evolve differently from those who remained in the hunter-gather way of life? Are people living in industrial societies undergoing natural selection of a somewhat different character than in earlier societies? Perhaps most important is whether these changes can influence psychological characteristics such as intelligence and temperament. The attempt to answer these questions will require an examination of the nature, in turn, of hunter-gatherer, agricultural, and industrial societies.

The Hunter-Gatherer Way of Life

It is reasonable to assume that the earliest social organizations of Homo sapiens resembled the hunter-gatherers whose societies have been studied in the last two centuries. Included in this category are those small scale horticulturists who supplement their diet by maintaining small gardens in what is known as slash-and-burn agriculture. All hunter-gatherer societies necessarily include many common features due to a profound lack of technology, but they also are differentiated by the ecological circumstances peculiar to each group. Climate, the material and nutritional resources available, and other factors, affect the features of primitive existence. If social settings can influence the selection of personality characteristics, some characteristics may be more common in some primitive groups than others. Similarly, some traits may be more common in simple societies than in more complex agricultural and industrial societies. This would not be very important if all human groups made the transition to more complex societies at the same time and all, therefore, had been exposed for the same length of time to whatever selective effects complex social organizations impose. But not all groups made this transition simultaneously, and the hunter-gatherer groups most frequently studied never actually made that transition at all. The point is that we might expect differences between groups that made the transition thousands of years ago, and those who did so only recently, and those who never made that transition.

Common to all hunter-gatherer groups is a very limited division of labor based on the twin biological variables of age and sex. The very young serve as apprentices to adults, and the very old, as helpers. Women are responsible for the care of infants and the education of young girls. They also tend to gardens and contribute a large share to the gathering of plant food. Men are usually responsible for the training of older boys and for hunting most game animals, and are, without exception, responsible for collective defense and war-making. With such a limited division of labor, there is little opportunity for specialized talents based on genetic traits to be developed and expressed. Without phenotypic expression there can be no selective advantage to such traits.

Many traits which are likely to be important among hunters and gatherers may not confer any obvious selective advantage. For instance, beauty, grace, and intelligence are generally prized in women, but given the overall equality of material resources available in many settings, all women are likely to reproduce at a similar rate. Therefore, those traits can provide little, if any, reproductive advantage to their possessors. Among men, on the other hand, physical prowess and intelligence in hunting and in war are valuable, and will confer fitness if they lead to greater reproductive success through polygamy or more youthful reproduction. This is most likely in tropical climates where polygamy is more practical than in harsher climates. But even in harsh climates, these physical traits will confer fitness benefit to the extent that they provide better nutrition to families and greater protection from animal and human predation. In these settings, attractive females may achieve a fitness benefit if they are able to attach themselves to able males.

The subsistence level of hunter-gatherers and their limited technology means that wealth cannot be accumulated. Food, the most important commodity, cannot usually be gotten in sufficient quantity to act as a store of wealth for purposes of barter. In some environments food is plentiful, is available to all, but generally cannot be safely stored for any length of time.

Property in the form of land or watering sites is communally held and protected, and could not be taken or held by an individual even if he had the inclination to claim sole ownership. As a consequence, class distinctions do not exist in hunter-gatherer societies.

Furthermore, the ownership of enslaved males is virtually nonexistent in hunter-gatherer societies for economic reasons. If a slave's work must go in large measure to feeding himself, it makes little practical sense to attempt to impose slavery on others. But even more important, given the fact that most hunting and gathering tribes are relatively equal in strength to their neighbors, a slave could escape and return to the tribe from which he was captured. Attempting to prevent escape might simply not be worth the effort. This is the most likely explanation for the fact that most male captives taken in primitive war are slain.

This is not the case with female captives, who are often spared and married to one of the men in the raiding group. In many cases this amounts to a form of slavery. Women are considerably easier to restrain due to their limited strength and size, and attempts to flee might be punished by death. In such circumstances, prudence may dictate that a female captive accept her new situation as permanent and attempt to make do as best she can. In many primitive groups her status will improve as she bears children with her captor and comes to be seen more as the mother of his children than as merely a war prize. In practical terms her life may not be any different than if she had been given willingly to her captor in a peaceful exchange ceremony. In many cases, she would have had no more choice in the latter circumstance than in the former one. According to Lawrence Keeley, among the Indians of North America, the "social position of captive women varied widely among cultures, from abject slaves, to concubines, to secondary wives, to full spouses."[1] Men, therefore, who can enslave women benefit in terms of fitness. The women, for the most part, gain no particular fitness advantage, unless their captors are more fit than the alternate mates available. If the latter is the case, she gains an advantage in having potentially more successful children.

Very few psychological traits, therefore, other than an aggressive temperament and modest intelligence, seem likely candidates for fitness enhancement among hunter-gatherer men. Furthermore, the fitness benefits of these traits are moderated by the fact that most hunter-gatherer groups are really extended families, and the sharing of resources between their more capable and less capable members is common. One does not let one's brothers or parents die because they are less successful than you are at obtaining food. Skill at hunting or in war rarely leads to a more lavish or a more secure standard of living. In fact, social life among hunters and gatherers within their own bands or groups is largely democratic and lacking in coercion. In general, leadership in such societies is rewarded honorifically and most practically by marriage to desirable women. In these societies the most important evolutionary effect will be an advantage to male leaders who convert leadership into fitness by acquiring more than one wife. Those characteristics of leaders, such as physical strength and aggressiveness, bravado and reasonable intelligence, should increase in the hunter-gatherer gene pool. This selective advantage is exaggerated in those settings where it is easy for a man to support more than one wife and her children. Laura Betzig, in an exhaustive examination of the ethnographic record of a large number of preindustrial societies, concluded that "the most often cited motives for violence among men involve women."[2] This is consistent with Keeley's analysis of the causes of primitive war.[3]

A case in point is the Yanomamo, a well-researched group living in the Amazon jungle of South America. The Yanomamo are not pure hunter-gatherers, but practice a relatively simple slash-and-burn agriculture, and most agricultural work is performed by women. Polygamy is common, and successful men have considerable reproductive advantage over others. Yanomamo men are known for their extreme aggressiveness and engage in frequent raiding of neighboring villages, the primary purpose of which is stealing women. Women who are captured expect men to mistreat them and come to accept that mistreatment. Napoleon Chagnon, who has studied the Yanomamo most intensively, titled his book about them, *Yanomamo: The Fierce People*.[4] Their way of life is centered on acquiring young females in war. Men, if they are to be successful, need strong allies to capture women and prevent their own women from being stolen. Men, therefore, tend to exchange daughters or sisters with successful men for purposes of cementing advantageous fighting alliances. In effect, powerful men are not only more likely to gain wives through success in war, but, in addition, be offered more wives because of that success. Headmen tend to have more wives and consequently more children, often twice as many, than lower status males.[5] Clearly, the Yanomamo culture acts to select in favor of greater male aggression. More aggressive and powerful men who survive to maturity have many times more children than do their weaker and more timid neighbors, many of whom die young or never reproduce at all.

The fitness advantage of raiding other villages for women of childbearing age is a common feature of many societies. Among hunters and gatherers, living in close proximity, such raiding rarely takes the form of full-scale war of the sort common in more complex societies. The reasons, discussed in Chapter 2, are twofold and based in prudence and kinship. Since hunters and gatherers sharing an environment are likely to be of about equal size, no one group is likely to be measurably stronger in a military sense than any other. Simple prudence suggests that battles between equals ought to be mitigated, since the likelihood of gain, in the form of wives, is likely to be offset by the potential for serious injury and death. Among the Yanomamo, confrontations tend to be brief and are broken off when either side sustains more than minimal casualties. Of course injuries are common, since confrontations are common, and death often results, but it is rare that one group attempts to overwhelm the other. A second reason violence is somewhat muted has to do with inclusive fitness. People living in groups in close proximity to one another are likely to have kinship ties with each other. A wife gotten from another group either by purchase or by theft has relatives in that group and is likely to maintain sympathies toward her natal group. Furthermore, men may have sisters and therefore nieces and nephews in other groups, and would for reasons of inclusive fitness be ill-inclined to see them killed. The genocidal slaughter of populations does not become a common feature of war until the advent of agriculture allows some groups to grow in size and achieve strategic dominance over their smaller and weaker neighbors.

Culture-gene interaction in a society like the Yanomamo should produce a cascading effect, driving the population to ever greater levels of male aggressiveness. However, as among animals, such a tendency is limited by countervailing effects. Pure aggressiveness, unless tempered by intelligence and prudence, not to mention physical strength and coordination, is dangerous and often lethal. Nevertheless, in these groups, effective violence is clearly fitness enhancing.

In reflecting on Keeley's discussion, covered earlier, of the abuse, torture and murder of prisoners among primitive warriors, one has to wonder if the lack of empathy among these men is in some way conducive to effective violence and is, therefore, in itself, fitness enhancing. In other words, perhaps an utter lack of empathy for the enemy may make it easier to kill than would otherwise be the case. In Keeley's bloodcurdling descriptions of the sort of torture meted out to helpless captives, one is struck by its similarity to the behavior of psychopathic criminals in modern societies. As discussed earlier, psychopaths are characterized as emotionally unresponsive and callous, exhibiting a total disregard and a complete lack of empathy for those they harm. Could it be that the psychopathic personality type is more common among hunters and gatherers than among peoples living in more complex civilizations?

Perhaps the early agricultural empires that developed the capacity to launch large armies still retained men more akin temperamentally to those of the hunter-gather way of life from which they had recently emerged. Could a tendency for psychopathic violence explain the wholesale slaughter of innocents following their conquest as described in the Old Testament? Could it make somewhat more explicable the truly horrific treatment meted out to people who defied the Romans, as well as the atrocities attributed to the somewhat earlier soldiers of Alexander the Great? Or the ferocity of the Mongol hordes who swept into Europe during the centuries after the fall of Rome, or of the Viking raiders so instrumental in the shaping of Feudal Europe? The horrific human sacrifices among the civilizations of Mesoamerica seem to fit a similar pattern.

The question remains whether such violent and psychopathic types are fewer in number or influence in more mature societies. Certainly the terrible brutality and wanton cruelty common in the religious strife in preindustrial Europe should disabuse anyone that such behavior is limited to simple societies. Atrocities during modern war and civil turmoil are common even today, as is evidenced by the savage history of the twentieth century. That history should make one hesitant to attribute savage viciousness to the primitive way of life. On the other hand, with many exceptions, much of the slaughter in twentieth century war was highly impersonal; only occasionally did people come face to face with their adversaries. Furthermore, the savage torture of innocents so common in the Communist and Fascist regimes of the past century was often carried out by specialized, often psychopathic, agents. It was not common for most combatants in, for instance, the two world wars of the twentieth century, to torture or kill captives, although it happened often enough. Most people in modern societies were repelled by the atrocities which did occur, and these were widely and almost universally condemned. There is more than a little irony in all this. As Keeley points out, "killing of enemy civilians by bombardment or by systematic starvation via blockade is to some degree acceptable under international law, but murdering them with small arms is considered completely vile. In modern warfare, the more personal the cruelty or destruction, the more likely it is to be regarded as reprehensible."[6]

It is important to note, however, that the brutal behavior of early conquerors, involving the wholesale slaughter and mutilation of rebellious groups, such as was practiced by the Romans, was rarely hidden or denied. In fact, the atrocities were often advertised so as to intimidate potential adversaries and were seen as a rudimentary adjunct to the conquest and pacification of subject peoples. The atrocities of Hitler, Stalin, and the Japanese during World War II, while every bit as vicious as those of the Romans and involving far greater numbers, were, in contrast, usually carefully hidden and camouflaged whenever possible. Hunters and gatherers, on the other hand, when commenting on the vicious torture of captives, appear to view it as a rather mundane and routine consequence of human conflict. Do these changes in public sentiment regarding the treatment of captives merely reflect changes in cultural norms, or do they reflect more fundamental changes in human nature? Culture certainly affects human behavior, but human beings in turn shape culture. What is considered natural in any society is, in other words, to some degree determined by the nature of the people who inhabit that society.

Freud suggested that aggressive violence and cruelty are common in all men, but are restrained by the repression of civilized life. He argued that this is why atrocities are common in war zones where civilization has broken down.[7] An alternative explanation might be found in the declining fitness value of such brutality in more civilized settings. Linda Mealey argues that the sort of behavior common to psychopathic personality types may be more fitness-promoting in some environments than in others, and therefore should be more common is some populations than in others.[8] In other words, are psychopaths more common in primitive than in advanced societies? Perhaps as societies become more complex and more ordered, the fitness benefit of psychopathic violence declines. This possibility will be addressed in a later section of this chapter.

If the sort of behavior under discussion was largely the product of socialization in a particular culture, then socialization into a new culture would shortly eliminate it, and it would have little significance for the problems associated with immigration from less advanced to more advanced societies. On the other hand, if it has significant genetic correlates, then immigration from one culture to another could be fraught with serious dangers for both the host population and the immigrant. It is important to point out that psychopaths, who account for only 3% to 4% of the population in most Western societies, are hugely overrepresented among chronic criminal offenders who are estimated to account for more than 50% of the crime in those societies.[9] Obviously, even a small increase in the percentage of psychopathic types in modern societies will have serious and potentially devastating ramifications for the fabric of those societies. This raises complex and important questions which deserve exploration in contemplating any immigration policy, especially from less complex to more complex societies. It is also amenable to scientific verification. It requires, first, a determination that the complex differences in empathetic responses detectable by brain imaging techniques discussed in the last chapter have genetic correlates, and secondly, whether those correlates are more common in some human groups than in others.

Agricultural Kingdoms of Recent Origin in Africa

When Europeans first explored Africa they discovered a number of preindustrial societies utilizing agricultural technology that had grown to a size sufficient to merit the title of kingdoms or states. They encompassed large areas, some having populations in the tens of thousands and many were highly stratified and hierarchical. They cannot properly be described as civilizations since they lacked many of the attributes associated with civilization such as a written language and, as a consequence, had no literature, no body of philosophic writings, and no written law. They also lacked the refined division of labor associated with all known civilizations. Without written records it is difficult to determine their origins, but it appears that most were quite young and arose within the last five or six centuries.

This late development of complex societies in Africa can be explained, in large part, by the late arrival of agricultural technologies. According to Oxford historian J. M. Roberts, technological and cultural enrichment came earliest to Africa by cultural diffusion from the Middle East, especially Egypt. Among the improvements reaching Africa was the technology of iron-working which allowed for more effective weapons and tools. These technologies migrated South at a very slow pace. According to Roberts, it was not until 500 AD that "hunting and gathering areas were broken up by the coming of herdsmen and farmers" in more southerly regions. Agricultural development was hindered by the failure to adopt the plow, most likely because the diseases in Africa prevented the domestication of draft animals, such as oxen and horses.[10]

It wasn't until much later that the advanced agricultural crops from the Middle East, and bananas from Polynesia reached the Continent. According to Roberts, "Africa south of the Sahara seems almost inert under the huge pressures exercised on it by geography, climate and disease."[11] In general, Africa's agriculture was not terribly productive, relying for the most part on unrewarding crops and depending on intensive human hand labor, and, in any case, it did not arrive until thousands of years after it originated on the Eurasian Continent.

The myths of origins of these recent agricultural kingdoms suggest that they were founded by people who migrated into their current habitat and subdued the indigenous tribes already living there. If these earlier warrior tribes possessed agricultural technology and iron weapons, they could rather easily have subdued the indigenous populations whose territories they invaded. Unlike hunter-gathers, a people utilizing agriculture can expand and exploit a fairly large territory. In addition, if the invaders possessed the weaponry which would allow a few men to control the behavior of many, conquered men could be put to work as slaves or serfs. The females of a conquered tribe could be enslaved and exploited sexually for their value in expanding the size and power of the conquering group. In such circumstances, the conquerors could become a parasitic military caste specializing in the conquest and enslavement of weaker groups.

It should be emphasized that the above is merely a hypothetical description of the growth and development of these agricultural kingdoms, but it is entirely consistent with the ethnographic literature on these primitive agricultural societies and with their own myths. It is also consistent with the history of such societies in Europe and Asia in their formative stages. Indeed, the Old Testament is the story of a group of Semitic people expanding and conquering its neighbors and establishing the kingdom of Israel in much the way as is hypothesized above.

Perhaps the most striking difference between these primitive African kingdoms and their hunter-gatherer counterparts is in their intrasocietal relations. Hunter-gatherer groups are highly egalitarian and communal, as would be expected in inbred, extended families. Laura Betzig, in her important work on this topic, examined a large number of these states or kingdoms in Africa and elsewhere, especially those organized into administrative regions with clear hierarchical chains of command. She found that such societies were consistently despotic, with rulers treating their subjects with contempt, and demanding an extraordinary degree of obeisance from them. Betzig defines a despotic society as one in which the ruler or ruling class can "kill subjects for trivial or no cause with impunity."[12] In all but the simplest of these societies, rulers had that right and exercised it, regularly murdering and brutally punishing and torturing anyone who displeased them. In some cases, rulers had to abide by certain ritual rules, but in no sense did there exist the rule of law as most Westerners would understand it; rules were enforced arbitrarily and punishments meted out with little restraint.[13]

This despotic behavioral pattern is consistent with the above hypothetical description of the emergence of these societies in the conquest of weaker and unrelated strangers. Unlike in hunter-gatherer groups, where male slaves were of no use to the winners, in these agricultural kingdoms captives could be put to work as slaves. It is reasonable to assume that these conquered men were held in contempt by their captors, and in all likelihood, spared immediate slaughter only with the understanding that their lives were held hostage to the whim of their captors. As time passed, the origins of the ruler-subject relationship may have become obscure, but not the crucial aspect of that relationship, which was a cruel, almost psychopathic, despotism.

Betzig's analysis makes it very clear that not only did subjects owe physical work and obedience to their rulers; they also owed them virtually unlimited access to their women. In these societies, ruling elites, depending on their position in the hierarchy, could literally take any women they wanted, even those already married to their subjects. Supreme rulers in such societies had hundreds, even thousands, of wives and consequently huge numbers of offspring. In addition to the great disparities between rulers and ruled, most of these societies exhibited an extreme degree of restraint on women's freedom, especially those in the noble harems. They were kept isolated and any contact with men was severely punished, often with death. It is possible that this practice of the sequestration of women was a product of cultural diffusion from the Middle East, where such practices are common, even today. On the other hand, Betzig cites the Incas as practicing an extreme form of this sort of isolation and restraint on women.[14] Chinese emperors, to cite another example, often had thousands of wives who, while they might have lived in reasonable comfort, were, nevertheless, prisoners in the noble harem. Betzig concludes that rulers in the past used their power in a maximum effort to increase their fitness at the expense of their subjects. This final point is driven home by the fact that rulers often kept women sequestered, even those in whom they had no personal interest, for the sole purpose of denying their male subjects access to them.

In summary, as hunter-gatherers adopted agriculture, at least as evidenced by these early kingdoms, the primary motives of powerful men seem hardly to have changed at all. Whereas the typical successful hunter and gatherer rewarded himself with two or three wives, the ruling elites in primitive agricultural societies rewarded themselves with dozens, and if they were powerful enough, with many more. In addition, they seemed intent on limiting the reproductive opportunities of subject men. Clearly, the operation of inclusive fitness is in powerful evidence among these groups. Ruling castes likely saw themselves as ethnically distinct from their subjects, whom they treated with the utter mercilessness usually reserved for nonkin enemies. To the extent that their power resided in their numbers, they exploited subject females for the purpose of producing more men like themselves, among whom many may well have had similar despotic dispositions. It is well to recall, in this context, the biblical story of Exodus, a central feature of which was Pharaoh's order to kill all the male infants born among his potentially rebellious Hebrew slaves, but to spare females.

It is an open question whether these societies would have evolved into the sorts of agricultural empires as did most agricultural societies of more ancient origin. It is also an open question whether their relatively short duration precluded significant genetic changes that would differentiate them from their hunter-gatherer forebears. This would explain, in part, their relative lack of technological progress and innovation. From Betzig's description, the nature of these societies served mainly to magnify preexisting temperamental and behavioral tendencies.

Classical Agricultural Civilizations

The Agricultural way of life first emerged in the fertile crescent of the Middle East during the few millennia following the retreat of the last glaciers in the Northern Hemisphere, about 10 to 12 thousand years ago. Within a short time, agriculture arose in China and the Indian subcontinent. It is unclear whether agricultural technology arose independently in these areas or spread by cultural diffusion from the Middle East. It seems to have arisen independently considerably later in the Americas. It arrived very late in Africa. Perhaps more difficult is the question of why agriculture arose at the time that it did. Certainly climate improved very much after the retreat of northern glaciations. Climate during the period from 9,000 to 5,000 years ago in the ancient world was warmer and wetter than it had been before and more so than it is today.[15] It is reasonable to suppose that, due to this climate change, human populations expanded and may have in some places grown dense enough to require the search for more efficient food production. Another explanation might reside in small but important changes in the genotype of the people in these regions, which might have hastened the adoption of an alternative, agricultural way of life.

If the origins of agriculture remain obscure, it is clear that once agriculture was adopted it allowed for a dramatic increase in population densities which were the crucial ingredient for the rise of the earliest civilizations. Once a society masters the agricultural way of life, its greater population gives it a clear advantage in contests with smaller, less developed communities. It is therefore likely to spread fairly quickly by conquest within limited geographical regions. Successful agricultural empires evolved into the forms which are familiar to us from well-known historical examples, such as Rome and China. They grew on the conquest and often the enslavement of the people of neighboring societies. Genetic evidence supports this explanation for China. An analysis of Y Chromosomal and mitochondrial chromosomal differences indicate that both the Northern and Southern Han populations share common Y (male) chromosomal features, but quite different mitochondrial (female) features. This pattern indicates that as the Chinese expanded south, the migrants, most likely soldiers, displaced the indigenous males and took their women as wives. As the authors of this study point out, this is consistent with the historical evidence of the expansion of China.[16]

The Chinese and Roman empires were able to generate large, well-organized armies fitted with better weapons than their neighbors. They grew in size and wealth and ceased to do so only when they had pretty much run out of new territory worth conquering. This pattern continued until about the time of Christ when the Roman Empire dominated in the West and the Chinese Empire dominated the East.

Major civilizations also grew up near the Indus and Ganges rivers in northern India. A similar pattern emerges in the history of the civilizations of Mesoamerica somewhat later. The same type of consolidation, as discussed earlier, seems to have been underway in Africa when it was disrupted by European intrusion and conquest.

Wherever these civilizations arose they shared many features which set them apart from earlier societies. The primary feature is the much greater human densities that resulted directly from the food surpluses that agricultural allowed. These densities were of sufficient size to give rise to cities. It is in cities that we see the origins of specialized priestly, military, and managerial ruling castes, which had both the time and motivation to create social innovations of a far-reaching sort. Perhaps the most important of these were written languages and mathematical systems. They all developed a relatively sophisticated cosmology and complex religious systems, including a heroic literature depicting their origins. They also developed a monumental architecture and an active pursuit of improved technology. The latter impulse, often spurred by military necessity, led to the development of sophisticated metallurgy, improved land transportation, sea navigation, and more widespread trade. In all of these societies there arose a division and specialization of labor unknown in simpler societies. Lastly, the size and diversity of these societies required some body of written law for the settling of disputes, at least among elites. All of these things ushered in a dramatically different way of life for their inhabitants. A central question is whether these conditions created systematic selective pressures on their populations so as to alter in some meaningful way the gene pools from which they were drawn.

Probably the most important factor in attempting to assess the above question is to note that the gene pool of agricultural empires was much larger and more varied than in earlier societies. Perhaps the ruling classes could have maintained their caste-like genetic isolation from those they conquered early in their rise. However, the evidence of social circulation in these civilizations makes it unlikely that they maintained that isolation for long.[17] The conquered peoples would certainly have been moved and used where they were needed to man armies, build state edifices and roads, and expand agriculture. For that reason it is unlikely that conquered groups would have been able to maintain their genetic integrity. Such a large intermingling of formerly isolated gene pools would have both benefits and costs in terms of fitness. However, the benefits would tend to spread in the new and larger gene pool while the genetic costs would in time tend to diminish from the effects of natural selection. Sheer size, in addition, allowed for the spread and maintenance of neutral genes by way of genetic drift, which may have had no selective advantage initially, but may have become, over time, desirable.[18]

Class Differences

Sexual selection, as addressed by Laura Betzig, probably had a significant effect on the gene pool of these societies. Agricultural empires allowed ruling males to promote their own fitness at the expense of their male subjects. In all of these empires rulers enjoyed almost unlimited access to their female subjects. Chinese emperors kept huge harems and acted almost as male analogs of queen bees that do all the reproducing for their hives. The Mongol Genghis Khan is said to have been extraordinarily prolific; it is estimated that some 8% of the inhabitants of Eastern Eurasia are probably descended from him alone.[19] Inca rulers had similar prerogatives. The Bible informs us that the Hebrew King Solomon took many wives of various nationalities, having had "seven hundred wives, princesses and three hundred concubines."[20]

In almost all of these societies, men in elite classes, and not merely rulers, were in a position to have multiple wives. Elite Romans were almost chaste when compared to their Middle-Eastern, Asian, and Mesoamerican counterparts. Even in Rome, however, where marriage was monogamous, Roman law allowed a man to maintain concubines who, along with their children, were granted specific rights. However, wealthy Romans had large numbers of slaves, of whom many were female house servants, and no doubt many were sexually exploited. It would be hard, otherwise, to account for the large number of manumitted Roman slaves without assuming that many were the sons and daughters of their owners. The fitness advantage for powerful men in Europe was moderated with the rise of Christianity which tended to suppress polygamous practices, but hardly eliminated the reproductive advantage of socially successful men. They tended to marry more often and at younger ages, to maintain mistresses, and to remarry more often upon the death of wives than their less successful counterparts.[21]

In sharp contrast, men in the laboring classes could hardly ever support more than one wife, and often not even one. Most agricultural societies depended on the use of animal-drawn plows which involved work done exclusively by men. In societies which used plows, women could not fend for themselves as they could in simpler hunter-gatherer societies, and were, therefore, dependent on male providers. Douglas White and Michael Burton, in their wide-ranging analysis of polygamy, found that the presence of the plow correlated strongly with monogamy.[22] Most men were either slaves or serfs who worked the land of wealthy landowners or for the state itself. Many of these, especially male slaves, could not marry at all. Free farmers with small holdings were usually taxed so heavily that they could rarely rise above a subsistence level. Even if they could provide for a wife, men in the laboring classes would have a hard time finding one, since so many were monopolized by elites in polygamous unions or in concubinage.

There can be little doubt that in these early agricultural empires there were powerful fitness effects benefiting elite males. Whatever innate characteristics enabled them to achieve elite status were thus spread widely in the population. Among those characteristics, at least in the early years of these empires, were likely to have been a martial temperament and military prowess, including a certain fearlessness and the sort of bravado likely to attract followers and, not least, a singular brutality in dealing with enemies. These are the same characteristics that conferred fitness in hunter and gatherer societies, but they were magnified enormously by the introduction of agriculture and the accumulation of wealth and power that it allowed. Ronald Fisher, in his *Genetical Theory of Natural Selection*, noted that these are the "heroic" martial qualities celebrated in the mythic literature of all empires.[23]

This may well explain, in part, the rapid expansion of these societies as well as their eventual failure. A society that can reproduce, in great quantities, the sort of men who ruled these empires could readily build effective fighting forces and could motivate them with the expectation of bounteous booty. Successful participation in military enterprises was rewarded by a share of the winnings, including land, slaves, and women of reproductive age, and in many cases by admission to the ruling class itself. Once those empires had reached the limits of their expansion, however, it would hardly be surprising that such types would fall out among themselves and drag their societies into almost endless and devastating civil wars. The wars which ravaged Europe and the Middle East after the fall of the Roman Empire might well have had their origins in the widespread dispersal of heroic types, from the empire itself and from those people who eventually toppled it.

In addition to class differences in access to mates, there were major class differences in mortality from disease and privation, both of which played a role in shaping the gene pools in these empires. Those who rose into the upper ranks of such societies, whether man or woman, reaped considerable fitness advantages. The children of the wives and concubines of such men generally had superior living conditions compared to the poor and were more likely to thrive. They were less likely to die of starvation and exposure, or from the types of diseases to which the lower classes were exposed.

In his *Plagues and Peoples*, historian William McNeill argues that in the large agricultural societies that relied on irrigation, such as existed in the Middle East and southern China, workers were often exposed to water-born diseases that nonlaboring classes did not encounter. Even in the rain-watered agriculture common in the temperate climate of Europe and northern China, agricultural workers often lived in close contact with farm animals and were, therefore, more likely to contract parasitic and other diseases. The problem was compounded if densities were such as to bring them into contact with animal and human wastes. Shortages of firewood in winter, in addition, often forced the poor to sleep in communal beds where various diseases could be more readily passed onto others by body contact. Similarly, firewood shortages might reduce the use of cooking to destroy bacteria in food. And of course the lack of fresher foods often meant that the poor suffered from illnesses either directly or indirectly caused by vitamin deficiencies. McNeill suggests that the strict rules governing contact between upper and lower casts in India may have had their origins in disease prevention. Among the lowest castes were those who carried away human and animal wastes and those who slaughtered animals. Both occupations expose workers to great disease risk, and outlawing physical contact between them and upper castes can be seen as a form of disease prophylaxis designed to protect the higher castes.[24]

It is reasonable to assume that these class differences in reproductive success and mortality had some effect in shaping the temperament of rulers and ruled. Survival in these societies required men in the lower classes to submit to authority and resist the impulse to strike out at those who treated them unfairly. The sort of bravado, daring, and fearlessness so important to success in hunter-gatherer societies, would be deadly in these more ordered, hierarchical settings. A willingness to work hard and submit with forbearance to authority, namely, to express a real or feigned docility, was more likely to be fitness-enhancing than a defiant spirit of independence. This suggests that important differences in temperament should begin to distinguish the men of different social positions. The heroic qualities of earlier martial societies would continue to be a prerequisite for the acquisition of elite positions, but those same qualities would be lethal in those relegated to the laboring masses or slaves.

The above hypothetical temperamental distinctions were likely to have grown more complex as these societies matured and the division of labor expanded. A far greater diversity of human traits came into demand and could be converted into improved status and living conditions. Many other skills and talents—in administration, skilled craftsmanship, and intellectual activities—to name but a few, were often rewarded and could be convertible to reproductive advantage. This is even more likely to be true as wealth—in the form of land, slaves or exchangeable commodities—could be preserved and passed to succeeding generations. In other words, successful parents could pass on their accumulated wealth and its advantages to children who likely carried their fitness-conferring genes.

Despite the clear-cut fitness benefits of specialized talents, the impact of cultural selection on the gene pool of agricultural societies was, nevertheless, limited. The reason is that only a small subset of those with genetically influenced talents would have been able to express those talents phenotypically and use them to rise in agricultural society. Societies with limited technology cannot utilize all the men with socially useful traits, and the genetically conditioned skills of the great majority were therefore never expressed. There was too much need for tedious labor and too little demand for specialized talent. Most men, therefore, many undoubtedly possessing great potential, were left to languish in the laboring mass. In effect, the vast majority of genotypes for special talents never appeared as phenotypic characteristics to be acted upon by selective forces. As a consequence, those genotypes may have risen somewhat in the gene pool, but not nearly to the extent that would have been the case if all such genetically linked talents could have been developed and provided fitness advantages for all their possessors.

Nevertheless, the division of labor did allow for the emergence of a small middle-class where sheer necessity tended to promote prudence and foresight in those men for whom it was possible to acquire a wife and children. This is especially the case where skills and talents took years of training before they could be used to acquire economically rewarding employment. The well-known features of middle-class morality, which stress a conservative prudence and the postponement of gratification, may well have their genetic corollaries in the temperamental characteristics of the individuals in the emerging middle classes. Without such characteristics it is hard to see how an individual could ever rise out of the laboring classes, even if he possessed considerable talent. In addition, the sexual and marital mores associated with the middle class may have their origins in the shortage of potential wives. This shortage would have been the product of the almost universal tendency in most classic agricultural societies for elite males to take more than one wife, as was common in China, or concubines, as in Rome. As Marcia Guttentag and Paul Secord demonstrated in their *Too Many Women,* when women are in short supply men are more likely to put great value on them and devote greater effort to their maintenance and that of their children. They are also likely to be more constant in their marital arrangements, since finding a replacement is problematic. These tendencies were fortified as agricultural societies matured and erected legal structures regulating marital and inheritance practices. Even people with very small estates were likely to want them preserved and passed to offspring, and for both men and women that would have provided a powerful incentive to expect fidelity from their spouses. [25]

As a sidelight on the above, it has long been noted by sociologists that mores extolled by the middle classes are less pronounced in the lower and upper classes. The upper classes need not be so prudent and frugal to rise economically, since they achieve their position by virtue of birth. Members of the lower class often eschew such mores since they may conclude, not unreasonably, that economic advancement is, for them, at best a chimera.

The possibilities for upward mobility for women in these agricultural empires were quite different from what they were for men. All women who possessed desirable characteristics, such as beauty, wit, and intelligence, whatever their social origins, were likely to gain access to the higher classes through marriage. The children of these women were likely to thrive and possess the fitness-enhancing traits which allowed their mothers and fathers to rise in these societies. This would undoubtedly have given rise to even greater genetic disparities between classes.

As these societies matured, their middle classes took on more administrative functions, and opportunities for those with prudence and intelligence tended to increase. The Chinese example of widespread examinations for entry into elite positions would seem to be consistent with this interpretation. The kind of discipline and willingness to forego gratification required for the successful completion of those examinations are inconsistent with many of the temperamental characteristics common among hunter-gathering peoples. While not as well regulated, the schools which grew up in classical Greece and Rome represented a parallel development. The success of these endeavors is clearly evident in the speeches, literary writings, and artistic expressions of classical Greece and Rome, as they are in the literary and artistic productions of educated men in imperial China. It is hardly surprising that refined artistic productions are widely viewed as important features necessary for a society to be considered a true civilization.

Equally important as a mark of those civilizations is a growing dependence on the rule of law and lesser tolerance for despotism. This is especially the case as societies developed more highly refined divisions of labor and depended more, out of necessity, on economic exchange between strangers and less on tribal and family relations. The codification of the rules of exchange and the penalties imposed on those who violated them come to play an increasing role in the everyday workings of advanced civilization. Traits that facilitate trust should become more critical for success and free-riding less tolerable and more frequently punished than in relationships among closely related individuals where inclusive fitness tends to moderate reactions to free-riding. For similar reasons, the sort of egoistic and psychopathic indifference to the suffering of strangers should become less tolerable when many dealings are, of necessity, between strangers. Likewise, impulsivity and indiscriminate violence are counterproductive in societies regulated by law and are likely to produce results that reduce fitness. While these developments are likely to involve only modest changes in a society's gene pool, such changes could, nevertheless, have had quite large effects on the everyday nature and functioning of those societies. That violent criminals, psychopaths and free-riders still exist suggests either that these traits, to the extent that they have genetic components, have modest fitness advantages as low-level stable strategies even in advanced societies. For instance, democracies are particularly vulnerable to psychopathic con-men possessing charm and intelligence. Perhaps that explains why even the most highly developed societies produce beguiling leaders who lead their peoples into dangerous adventures and seem indifferent to the tragedies that predictably follow. It is otherwise difficult to fathom, for instance, the mentality of the leaders who allowed the carnage of World War I to continue for years after its futility became obvious to most reasonable people.

Another change is evident in agricultural societies after they cease to grow by the conquest of weaker societies, and that involves a gradual change in the relations between rulers and ruled. The most important of these changes, clearly evident in Europe after the decline of Rome, is a phasing out of slavery and the introduction of somewhat less brutal arrangements between the laboring classes and their rulers. The reasons for this are varied, but certainly an important factor is that the laborers ceased to be ethnically-distinct conquered peoples but rather were, generally, of the same ethnic and cultural background as their rulers. As a result, the force of inclusive fitness comes into play and tempers, somewhat, the use of coercion in the relations of men to their masters and reciprocity takes a more prominent place in their relations. Slavery gave way to serfdom, in which the serf owed service and obedience to his master, but who in turn was provided with protection and granted limited freedom in his domestic affairs.

Slavery was never a significant feature of the economy of China. This is perhaps best understood by the ethnic unity common to the Chinese people: the growth of the Chinese Empire involved the subjugation of people who, for the most part, were quite similar genetically and not alien groups as was the case for Rome. Under Chinese imperial rule, all workers were obliged to provide service to the emperor or a lord in a system of *corvee* similar to the service demanded of serfs in Medieval Europe. As in Europe, obligations were somewhat, if widely unbalanced, based in reciprocity.[26]

In both Europe and China, philosophic traditions evolved that reflect these changed relations. Confucianism is an extraordinarily elaborate formulation outlining the obligations owed by the parties in almost every conceivable social relationship: child to parent, husband to wife, and master to servant. In all cases the obligations travel both ways; the child owes absolute obedience to the father, but the father in turn is required to care for the needs of the child.[27] A similar philosophic tradition arose in Christian Europe, sometimes defined as "the great chain of being."[28] This sought to order all things, including the various classes of men, in a coherent hierarchy from the lowest of animals to the exalted place of angels ruled over by a benevolent and all-knowing deity. In the midst of the great hierarchy were placed the ranks of the humans from the meanest serf to the free peasant to the masters and the nobles who stood above them. In both Confucianism and Medieval Christianity, this ordering was characterized as natural and fitting. In the Middle Ages, not to know one's place and its rights and obligations was as unnatural as not understanding your sex and its rights and obligations. Noblesse oblige was fully understood and recognized among the ruling elites of Europe and China, though often honored more in the breach than in the practice.

The attribution of the decline of slavery to the workings of inclusive fitness is bolstered by the fact that it did not decline in the Middle East which had access to a steady supply of slaves from Africa, slaves who were quite obviously ethnically distinct. It is also consistent with the resurrection of slavery after the discovery of the Americas. If the abolition of slavery in Europe were simply the result of more enlightened thinking, its reintroduction in the Americas could hardly have been so readily accepted by educated European elites.

As discussed in the previous chapter, the thousand years between the fall of Rome and the age of discovery was a time during which technology and social relations were relatively static. The feudal systems in China and Europe, while they were terribly inequitable by modern standards, were, nevertheless, sufficiently tolerable to the laboring masses to remain workable arrangements for a very long time, by historical standards. If one considers communism to be a reincarnation of feudalism, with the state replacing the emperor, then it has lasted an even longer time in China than in Europe, though it appears, at least at present, to be on its way out.

A final point should be made. Agricultural civilizations, while exhibiting many similarities, nevertheless, vary in important ways; Chinese civilization is, after all, different from European civilization, and both differ from those of the Indian subcontinent and of the Muslim Middle East. Whether or not such differences have effects on their gene pools is an open question, as is the effect of differing gene pools on cultural differences. For instance, Asian infants tend to be more docile than Caucasian infants, and such differences appear to carry over into adulthood.[29] Are these differences the product or the cause of the cultural differences between East and West or are they unrelated? Are the historically noted differences among pastoral peoples, such as those of the Eurasian steppe and the more settled agricultural peoples of the Middle East, the product of genes, culture or an interaction of both? These questions go well beyond the scope of this particular book. Nevertheless, these issues are important and will be addressed in limited fashion when discussing the patterns of immigration particular to the United States and to the various European countries.

In summary, it seems reasonable to assert that the gene pools of populations living for extended periods of time in mature agricultural societies would contain a higher proportion of those genes associated with intelligence, and related characteristics such as artistic and musical ability, and traits related to skilled craftsmanship. Genes that promote characteristics that allow men to follow orders, postpone gratification, to cooperate with nonkin, and focus on long-term goals should also rise. On the other hand, there should be a reduced share of genes promoting promiscuous sexuality and impulsive violence, both of which would have been imprudent in these sorts of societies. These changes may well account for the differences between racial groups in average IQ and criminality outlined at the beginning of the last chapter. As discussed earlier, since almost all advanced civilizations arose in temperate climatic zones, a good deal of those racial differences attributable to climate may have their source in the selective effect of differing cultural environments. Perhaps harsh climatic conditions selected those traits that enabled people to develop agricultural societies in the first instance, but in time those societies became in turn the driving selective force in the further evolution of those traits, making them even more pronounced and more widespread within the population.

The Origins and Spread of Industrialization

The above hypothesis is consistent with the thesis of economic historian Gregory Clark concerning the origins of the industrial revolution in his widely acclaimed book, *A Farewell to Alms*. According to Clark, the industrial revolution originated in England in 1800 and spread fairly rapidly to the rest of Europe because of demographic changes that had taken place during the previous centuries. He bases his theory on inheritance records in England which demonstrate that "economic success translated powerfully into reproductive success, with the richest individuals having more than twice the number of surviving children at death as the poorest."[30] This is clearly a very large reproductive advantage and would markedly increase the presence of the genes carried by better-off individuals very quickly, certainly within a few centuries. It provides additional support for the Cochran and Harpending argument, in their study of Ashkenazi Jews, that genetic change can occur very quickly if under strong selective pressure. Clark argues that preindustrial England was caught in a Malthusian trap that kept its population at a stable level of about 6 million people between 1300 and 1750.[31] This is explained by the fact that during this time almost all arable land had been brought into cultivation and could not support a larger population given the existing agricultural technology. This was one of the primary reasons that England provided a vast source of migration to newly discovered lands during the period from the 16th century through the 19th century. An important consequence "was that England was a world of constant downward mobility. Given the static nature of the economy and the opportunities it afforded, the abundant children of the rich had to, on average, move down the social hierarchy. The craftsmen of one generation supplied many laborers of the next, merchants' sons became the petty traders, large landowners' sons ended up as smallholders."[32]

The social consequence was that English society became more and more populated by the descendants of people who had been successful in the relatively mature and stable agrarian society that had evolved during the previous 5 or 6 centuries. He argues that these people had characteristics and values associated with the middle class that were acquired either culturally or genetically, though his invocation of reproductive success suggests that he favors, if equivocally, the idea that genetics played an important role. During these centuries violence declined and middle-class orientations became more common. "Thrift, prudence, negotiation, and hard work were becoming values for communities that previously had been spendthrift, impulsive, violent, and leisure loving."[33] He does not deny the significance of the scientific revolution as crucial to industrialization, but rather that it could not have been implemented without the human capital which had accumulated over the years. In particular, he cites rising rates of literacy as an important factor. However, surprisingly, he does not include IQ in the qualities that produced the greater human capital that, in turn, led to both the scientific and industrial revolutions. This is so, even though he thinks "it is plausible that through the long agrarian passage leading up to the industrial revolution man was becoming *biologically* better adapted to the modern economic world [italics in original]."[34]

This latter conclusion is consistent with the arguments made earlier in this chapter. Also consistent with those arguments is evidence he presents that "the reproductive success of the class that engaged in warfare on a large scale in the pre-industrial era, the aristocracy, was much poorer than for economically successful commoners..."[35] While Clark focuses on England and, in particular, its role in the emergence of industrial society, many of his arguments about changes in human nature could well apply to other reasonably stable agrarian societies as existed in Europe, Japan, China and India. This would explain the very rapid spread of industrialization in the rest of Europe once introduced in England, and its relatively swift adoption by Japan in the early 20th Century and in China and India, at the end of that century. It would also explain why industrialization has had a much more difficult time being established in Africa and other less advanced societies. In attempting to explain the current divergence between the rich and poor nations of the world, Clark presents considerable evidence of the lack of efficiency of labor in less advanced societies. "Poor countries used the same technology as rich ones. They achieved the same levels of output per unit of capital. But in doing so they employed so much more labor per machine that they lost most of the labor cost advantages with which they began."[36]

Clark could have strengthened his argument considerably had he included IQ differences in his analysis. The very rapid rise of productivity in the East Asian countries of Japan, Korea and China, when contrasted to the conditions in Africa and many other regions of the world, seems to reflect IQ differences. India's economic growth seems to contradict this interpretation, given its relatively low average IQ. However, this can be explained by the fact that India's huge population allows for the tapping of large numbers of moderate to high IQ people capable of employing modern technology effectively. Furthermore, India's depressed IQ could be the result of poor nutrition and relatively low levels of education in rural areas. India has a literacy rate of 60% compared to a rate of 91% for China.[37] It remains to be seen if improvements in these areas result in higher IQ that would allow India's current economic dynamism to spread throughout the country.

In concluding this section, it is worth noting, that while the thrust of this book is premised on the existence of fixed (generally genetic) regional population differences, it is not dependent on any particular explanation as to how they arose. In that light it is important to emphasize that the existence of those differences, while admittedly speculative, are readily amenable to empirical test. It is well within the realm of modern genetic science to determine if there are genes or gene complexes associated with various abilities and temperamental characteristics. This effort is currently under way and considerable progress has already been made. It is equally within the realm of modern genetic techniques to determine whether these genes are more frequent in some populations and in some social classes than in others. That such is the case with IQ, for instance, is all but settled scientifically, though it is widely denied by cultural trendsetters, who seem almost uniformly to ignore the scientific literature in this area.[38]

Life in Industrial Societies

The defining characteristic of industrial societies is that more and more of the physical work of society is performed by machines. Today, even technical work that in the past required human mental activity, such as lab analysis, architectural working drawings, machine-tool operations and navigational reckoning, to name but a few, are routinely carried out by computers, and this trend is intensifying. One practical consequence of industrialization has been an enormous increase in labor specialization with an equally dramatic increase in human productivity. These consequences have in turn allowed for an explosion in scientific knowledge and technological innovation.

Concomitant with the industrial revolution, and in large measure owing to it, has been the emergence of the nation state as the dominant social and political structure. As discussed earlier, the nation-state has the important effect of broadening the range of inclusive fitness by fostering a sense of national kinship. For reasons to be discussed, industrialization facilitated the very broad democratic franchise that is the predominant political form of industrialized nation-states.

In addition, industrialization promoted the rise of capitalism as the dominant economic system of the modern nation-state. In a capitalist system, reciprocity—or reciprocal altruism—becomes the dominant form of relations between individuals. One consequence is reduced reliance on coercion. A second consequence is that reciprocity replaces almost completely relations based in kinship, tribe and caste. This is because economic efficiency in the industrial society is best served when people are selected on the basis of their training for specific tasks rather than on their ethnic or family connections. In addition, the great wealth and productivity of industrial societies allows for very generous welfare provisions.

The most immediate biological effect of industrialization has been a great reduction in death rates stemming from agricultural innovations that provided better nutrition and also by great strides in medicine, especially in public health. These changes led to an explosive growth in population. The initial alarm occasioned by this population explosion has been tempered by the reduced population growth in all societies after they have passed through the early stages of industrialization. In all these societies, birthrates tend to fall within a few generations after the initial decline in death rates. There are many reasons for this "demographic transition." In industrializing societies, social success usually requires urban living; people untouched by industrialization in rural areas tend to continue reproductive patterns common in preindustrial times. As populations become urbanized, however, reproductive rates decline due to, among other reasons, the higher costs of living in cities. Additionally, children cease to represent the assurance of support for parents in old age as they often do in rural, farming communities. This is because of the mobility of people required in industrialized societies; children often live far from parents, and even if they live close to parents, they rarely live or work in extended family-owned farms or workshops. This, in part, explains the establishment of government-sponsored social security schemes and other welfare programs that in the past were the purview of families and villages.

Today in America, birthrates are about equal to death rates and population growth would stabilize, were it not for immigration. Birthrates of about 2.1 births per woman produce stable population in most industrialized nations. In most European countries birthrates have fallen below replacement levels, and are well below two births per woman. The populations in those countries would decline were it not for immigration. It is hoped, and expected, that the demographic transition to lower birthrates will, sometime in this century, occur in most societies currently undergoing industrialization and serve to avert the worst consequences of runaway population growth. China has already passed through this stage and now has a fertility rate of 1.6.[39]

One important consequence of rapid population growth is that the population becomes younger, resulting in a large cohort of young people in adolescence and early adulthood that German sociologist Gunnar Heinsohn terms a "youth bulge." Heinsohn defines such a bulge as one where at least thirty percent of the men in a society fall into the 15 to 30 year age group. Such a large group of young men are in intense competition for meaningful roles in society and are biologically predisposed to aggressive violence when compared to older males. Heinsohn attributes much of the violence in history to periods during which there was an oversupply of ambitious and often violent young males, and an insufficient supply of older males to restrain them. "This trouble may take many forms—an increase in domestic crime...revolutions, riots and civil wars."[40] James Wilson in his *Thinking about Crime* made a similar point in attributing the dramatic rise in crime in the United States in the 1960s to the coming of age of the baby boom males.[41] The problems of a youth bulge may be compounded if there is a shortage of females available to these men as a result of selective abortion favoring males, as in China and India, or where older males remove many young females from the marriage market through polygamy, as in many Moslem societies.

Societies that have passed through the demographic transition tend to have older populations, to be more orderly and to have lower crime rates. They also have large numbers of retirees requiring support from a shrinking supply of younger workers. If these societies try to compensate by encouraging immigration from Third- World countries, they often introduce a youthful, rapidly growing population with the problems attendant on a youth bulge. For instance, within the Hispanic population of the United States in 2005, the 15-29 year old age group represented 26% of the population. The age group 14 years and below made up about 29% of the population. That percentage will be lower if continued immigration brings in additional older Hispanic-Americans. On the other hand, it may in fact be larger since many undocumented immigrants fall into the under-thirty age group. In other words, a youth bulge may already exist or will soon emerge in the United States' Hispanic population.[42] A similar problem has arisen in Europe as immigration from North Africa and elsewhere has produced a marked increase in the young male population.

The consequence is an almost inevitable increase in disorder and crime, especially violent crime. This is likely to be exacerbated in those societies unaccustomed to high crime rates and loathe to apply the sort of law enforcement practices necessary to limit criminal behavior. In other words, since a society's approach to crime is based on its past experience, it may take some time for it to adjust to new patterns and higher levels of crime. Of course, such an adjustment will be hindered if leaders insist on characterizing concern with crime as evidence of xenophobia and racism. The problem is exacerbated if an immigrant group, in general, is more prone to criminal violence than the host population, whether for genetic or cultural reasons. Clearly, this is a phenomenon of great consequence for immigration policy and will be examined in depth in later chapters dealing with the special circumstances of the United States and Western Europe.

The demographic transition resulting from reduced fertility in industrial societies is thought to be somewhat of an embarrassment to evolutionary theory. The reason is that for the first time in history, material well-being, on a societal scale, is not being converted into biological fitness through greater reproduction. Human beings are deviating from the general tendency for organisms to maximize reproduction commensurate with the resources available, a tendency which hitherto appeared to be as genetically programmed in humans as it appears to be in other organisms. However, there is nothing paradoxical about this. Genetic programming does not, in most cases, determine human behavior, but rather inclines humans to behave in certain ways depending on circumstances. Human reasoning capacity enables humans to ascertain the nature of their circumstances and to determine, based on their assessment, what actions are most consonant with their goals. Humans are clearly predisposed to enjoy sexual activities, but it would be foolish to argue that they are, like animals with lesser brain capacities, driven blindly to engage in them. Even fairly simple organisms will desist from sexual behavior in times of severe danger or hardship, and, of course, many animals refuse sexual advances until certain courtship signals have been received.

Humans tend to be relatively prudent K reproducers. Industrialization, by improving living conditions and creating wide opportunities, allows people choices that were nonexistent in the past. Technology in the form of contraception, furthermore, allows modern humans to separate their desire for sexual gratification from their desire to have children. In addition, modern medicine has so reduced infant mortality that people can now expect that most of their offspring will live to maturity. If they wish for two children, or think that they can support only two, they needn't have three or four as their ancestors did, out of the expectation that one or more would die in childhood. The demographic transition is best understood as resulting from these changes. It takes a generation or two before individuals adjust their reproductive behavior to new technologies and opportunities. What needs explaining is not why people limit their reproduction, but rather why they continue, in an admittedly egoistic age, to continue in their desire to live in families and devote the greatest energies of their productive years to raising offspring.

Family Life and the Role of Women in Industrial Society

Industrial societies not only allow couples to limit their reproduction, but they also tend to reward such limitations. The industrial way of life rewards those who acquire specialized skills and deliver those skills to areas of highest demand. Success requires extensive training and high mobility, both of which are difficult for large families. People of average wealth, therefore, tend to limit children so as to maximize the training they can provide for them.

In addition, since people often move out of their place of birth for training and employment, they come to rely less on aid from relatives. In preindustrial societies, people live in stable communities and are tied securely by family commitments and protections; nepotism is an important feature in such settings. Today, however, such is not the case and even should someone wish to aid a relative, people today are rarely in a position to do so. This is especially so in aiding relatives seeking employment. Most employers today, for reasons of economics, or law, seek individuals with the specialized skills they need. Writing computer programs is not like hauling water, which any strong body can do. In the case of simple physical work—the work most common in preindustrial eras—hiring a relative or a friend entails little economic loss, while in the case of specialized work, the costs can be considerable. The upshot is that the extended family ceases to serve an important economic or social welfare function, and its significance declines.

It is not only the extended family that loses much of its significance, but the nuclear family as well. The economic efficiency possible with the division of labor leads more and more tasks, which in the past were performed by families, to be taken up by specialists. Specialists provide training for children, food, clothing, repair of homes and cars, and entertainment. The consequence of the decline in the economic functions of the family has been that it has become a unit based largely on affection. Affectionate marriage is founded in friendship and sexual attraction, and since it has few other important functions, tends to dissolve if that attraction and friendship wanes. The consequent rise in divorce is abetted by the economic independence of women, also a consequence of industrialization. As modern medicine and modern contraceptive technology reduced the tasks of childbearing and child-rearing, women have been released for other tasks. Not surprisingly, the majority of women have turned to the marketplace that amply rewards those with marketable skills and talents. This has given women the independence to leave unsatisfying marriages. It has also allowed men to opt out of such marriages without fear that their children will suffer inordinately. This has set in motion a self-reinforcing cycle. As marriages became less secure, women have increasingly devoted their energies to obtaining the training for independence after divorce, an independence which facilitates many divorces in the first place. The resulting instability of marriages is another important reason individuals, especially women, are inclined to reduce the number of dependent children they produce.[43]

The Political Structure of Industrial Society

A corollary of industrialization has been the development of the modern democratic state, which generally includes a wide franchise and considerable personal freedom from despotic control. The franchise in early modern democracies was generally limited to self-supporting male householders, but over time it has been extended to include all adults. Democratic forms are pervasive, all modern states hold elections, even one-party dictatorships, though all involved know they are fraudulent. In addition to elections and personal freedom, modern states attempt to limit the impact of economic disparities among their citizens. Much of the history of the twentieth century can be viewed as a clash of ideologies over how, and to what extent, this should be accomplished. Central to this argument is the place of individual freedom and economic equality as defining features of democracy. The political left has argued that democracy is based on the notion of equality between citizens and that large economic disparities between citizens vitiate democracy. It follows from this view that the truly democratic state should reduce or eliminate economic disparities, even if that requires curtailing individual freedom of action. The political right, on the other hand, has argued that legal rather than economic equality is the source of democracy, and that denying people the freedom to pursue their economic interests is antithetical to democracy. In essence, the left urges limiting freedom for egalitarian ends, while the right maintains the supremacy of freedom over equality.

In general, both those on the left and the right, if thoughtful, acknowledge that there is a tension between freedom and equality. This follows directly from the fact of human variation in talent and interests, much of which is genetically influenced. Given the freedom to pursue their own economic interests, human beings will quite naturally produce economic disparities. Those on the right have argued that depriving individuals of the freedom to pursue their economic interests would undermine the productivity of those individuals and impoverish their societies. Only the Communists denied the importance of economic incentives for productivity, and the societies they built have been economic failures. As was pointed out earlier, innovation is generally rare, and anything which reduces innovation, such as depriving individuals the rewards of innovating, is likely to reduce the efficiency of a society. The left is less moved by this argument and expresses more concern with the unfairness of economic inequality and emphasizes the cost in social disharmony which it often produces.

What is it about industrial society that seems to favor the emergence of democracy? The most straightforward answer involves the economic advantages of allowing people freedom of action over enslaving them, on the one hand, and the economic and political advantages of a wide franchise on the other. Productivity in industrial societies is so great that those who wish to take advantage of the labor of others are better off rewarding them with a share of their efforts than by attempting to coerce or enslave them. Part of the reasons for the failures of the communist command economies is that they wasted enormous manpower and resources on the apparatus of coercive control. Those resources and manpower can be put to far more productive ends in reward-based economies. In addition, the most productive members of modern societies engage in activities which are largely self-directed and are not amenable to close supervision by overseers. Slavery in the United States, for instance, worked effectively in the South's agriculture enterprises, like cotton and tobacco growing that employed gang labor, where it was possible for a few overseers to monitor many slaves and derive the benefits of efficiency of scale.[44] In the modern case, it would take as many overseers of slave scientists or slave educators as scientists or educators themselves. When most work involves individually directed work, slavery simply becomes inefficient. In addition, much important creative work is today performed for the satisfaction it provides and is often self-motivated. For instance, much important scientific work is carried out by tenured full professors in science whose salary is rarely affected by their scientific output, but who, nevertheless, continue to work, some long after retirement age, out of simple intrinsic interest and the social rewards such work provides. Coercion would severely limit the satisfaction of this sort of work and thereby reduce the incentives to perform it.

The explanation for the extremely broad franchise in all industrial democracies is not so straightforward. In general, it follows from the need for trained and educated workers. In a modern society most people need to be educated and, given the modest differences in native ability, not many people are willing to accept the notion that only an elite have the knowledge necessary for rule. In earlier times it was far less difficult for elites to make such a claim when the great bulk of people were illiterate. Furthermore, to take advantage of modern technology, societies need to allow open communication. Attempting to deny the majority the vote in the modern age with rapid and universally available means of communication would be difficult to justify. Of course, the downside of a wide franchise is that it gives the vote to people who may, for reasons of ability or temperament, contribute very little in the form of taxes. As such they have little incentive to be concerned with profligacy in government, and may in fact benefit from it. Aristotle in his *Politics* warned that democracy cannot survive if the majority attempts to confiscate the goods of the wealthy. He argued that the sure consequence would be the ruin of the state. [45]

The dictatorships of the twentieth century were all police states and suffered the inefficiencies inherent in such states for the reasons discussed above. One should not lose sight that most of these dictatorships were, at least initially, popular and usually had the support of the majority of their citizens. The despotisms of the left were supported by the poor who saw in them the hope of economic advantage. The despotisms of the right promised, by and large, to protect the middle and upper classes—the owners of assets—from the depredations of the poor.

Despotisms of the left generally fail, we now know, because their inefficiencies produce dissatisfaction among their poor supporters. Trying to maintain control through police action only increases the inefficiency of those despotisms and further decreases their support. The despotisms of the right collapse when those in the middle classes who supported them out of fear of the poor, no longer have such fear.

To elaborate on this last point: people own assets either through productive effort, by theft and confiscation of one sort or another, by inheritance, or by some lucky circumstance. In newly emerging industrial societies those earning assets by their own productivity are relatively few and, together with other asset-owners, they act to protect themselves against those without assets. They fear democracy and turn to strong men to protect their interests. This was certainly the case in the various Fascist regimes in Europe and their close relatives in Latin America. North America was an exception in that the land was so plentiful and opportunities so great that a large-impoverished peasantry never developed. America's founders based their democracy on the assumption of a population consisting largely of yeoman farmers and skilled tradesmen, all of whom would in some degree be holders of assets. As industrialization proceeds, more and more people become productive asset owners due to the great strides in productivity which industrialization allows, while those without assets decline. When the poor are no longer in the majority, the fear of democracy by the higher economic classes subsides.

However, this progression may be aborted if large numbers of the poor are unable to acquire economically rewarding skills. This may be the result of limited access to education and training. It may also be the result of a lack of native abilities among the poor, so that they are unable to take advantage of training and education, even when widely available. The compromised democracies of Latin America may reflect this reality. If large numbers of the poor fail to become holders of assets, the middle and upper classes may have more to fear from democracy than from oligarchy. Democracy seems the most practical and efficient form of political organization for the modern industrial state, but only if human talents are normally distributed in the population. If the population is divided into large classes of considerably different talent, democracy may be unable to gain a secure footing or may be lost.

This argument is bolstered by a recent and highly original work by Finnish political scientist, Tatu Vanhanen, outlined in his book, *The Limits of Democratization*.[46] In a comprehensive analysis of 172 countries he found a strong positive correlation between measures of the distribution of significant resources and democratization. In other words, in countries in which important economic resources are widely distributed, democracy is common; in countries where resources are held by only a small percentage of the population, or are controlled by the state, as in Communist countries, democracy is rare. He furthermore demonstrated that the distribution of resources is highly correlated with average national intelligence, the major exceptions being Communist states such as China and North Korea, and those still plagued with some of the negative vestiges of Communism, as are some in Eastern Europe.

To further explore the relationship between national IQ and democracy, Vanhanen broke down 172 nations into 7 IQ categories, ranging from those with national IQs below 80 (levels 1 and 2, and those with IQs above 95 (levels 6 and 7). In addition to his own measure of democracy, he included 13 measures of "the quality of democracy and deficiencies in democratic governance," garnered from a variety of sources such as those published by Freedom House and the World Bank.[47] Almost none of the countries in the lowest levels can be called democratic, while almost all countries in the highest levels, with the exception of Communist states, are clearly democratic. In addition, they differ in the quality of governance. "For example, political violence, coups d'etat, other illegal political interventions, irregularities in elections, deficits in the rule of law, restrictions on freedom of expression, assembly, and association, corruption, and insecurity of individual people seem to be much more common in countries with low levels of national IQ than in countries with high levels."[48] Based on these data, it is reasonable to argue that a national IQ of about 90 is a minimal threshold for the emergence and maintenance of democracy.

The situations in the countries in the middle 3 levels, ranging in IQ from 80 to 95, are somewhat ambiguous. These include almost all the countries of the Middle East, Latin America and South Asia. Those at the higher end (level 5) are more likely to be democratic than those at the lower end (level 3). However, in this range, factors idiosyncratic to individual countries, such as the degree of ethnic and religious homogeneity, the experience of decolonization, and the differing responses to the collapse of communism, seem important in determining whether they achieve true democratic form. For instance, nearly all Middle Eastern countries lack democracy, whereas most of those in Latin America, with national IQs similar to the Middle East, are democratic, though almost all suffer democratic deficits of one sort or another. The problems in the Middle East are largely the result of their very recent modernization based on oil wealth that has resulted in, according to Vanhanen, "the concentration of economic power resources (oil) as well as the means of violence in the hands of government and on the control of intellectual power resources."[49] Latin America, on the other hand, while largely democratic, is plagued by "extreme economic inequalities, which tend to coincide with ethnic divisions." For these reasons "it may not be reasonable to solve these problems satisfactorily, and therefore it is not reasonable to expect the disappearance of democratic deficits in Latin America."[50] The particular circumstances of the other major groups of countries in the middle range of national IQ are far too varied and complex to be treated fairly here.

These findings are consistent with the above explanation of the rise of democracy with the advent of industrialization. Industrialization allowed a larger number of people to express their genetic abilities than was possible before industrialization, thus enabling them to acquire the economic resources and the power that such resources provide. In effect, the middle class came to represent a substantial element, and in some cases a majority, of the population. When resources are widely distributed, no one group or faction can easily monopolize political control. Democracy seems to be the most effective way of resolving the competing interests of varying groups of relatively equal power; the alternative would be almost continual strife and political instability as various factions attempted to seize control. It is important to emphasize the historical fact, however, that industrialization started in European countries with high national IQs. In the emerging countries of the Third World, those with high national IQ, especially in Asia, have tended to evolve in a similar way in the direction of democracy (China and North Korea being exceptions), whereas those with low national IQ have not. The reason seems plain: if few people have the intellectual capability to acquire skills, important resources will be relegated to the few with higher abilities and the conditions essential for democratic governance, namely, the wide dispersal of resources and power, can never materialize. As Vanhanen put it, "People in countries with low national IQs are not as able to organize themselves, to take part in national politics, and to defend their interests and rights against those in power as people in countries of higher national IQ."[51]

These results are perfectly consistent with Aristotle's observation, and general historical experience, that democracies can thrive only in the presence of a substantial middle class. Industrialization, in promoting the growth of a large middle class in Europe and America, almost inadvertently also promoted democratization. A similar pattern appears to be occurring today in the industrializing countries of East Asia. However, since human beings differ markedly in their ability to acquire resources it is, according to Vanhanen, "probably never possible to achieve the same level and quality of democracy in all countries or regions of the world."[52] For those countries with the lowest national IQ, which includes most of those in sub-Saharan Africa, true democracies may not be possible and it might, according to Vanhanen, "be useful to consider how to establish a less democratic but more functional political system."[53] The dilemmas this issue poses in relation to a changing world order will be taken up in Chapter 8.

Evolution in Industrial Societies

Economic and honorific rewards in industrial society tend to flow to those who perform tasks not easily mechanized. This, of course, rewards those people who can easily acquire such skills and penalizes those who have difficulty doing so. Furthermore, as transportation and communication improve, national economies have become increasingly globalized. This means that many jobs can be exported to countries with lower standards of living. The net effect of mechanization and globalization is to limit economic rewards to those whose skills have not been mechanized and which cannot easily be exported. Skilled technicians capable of repairing machinery are likely to do well in modern societies, as are gifted nurses and surgeons. Draftsman, however, are gradually being replaced by sophisticated computer programs. The manufacture of machinery, as opposed to its repair, can often be transferred to lower income regions of the world, and can often be partially or wholly mechanized.

A consequence of the above has been a vast increase in human mobility, both geographically and socially. In an agricultural society the overwhelming majority of people is engaged in agriculture and tends to be tied to the lands they farm. Craftsmen were usually tied to the shops they owned, often by inheritance. In industrial societies, people gravitate to the factories and offices where their skills are needed and economically rewarded. Young people tend to gravitate toward the best educational institutions consistent with their abilities. Those who are successful experience considerable social mobility relative to their parents and to siblings lacking their skills.

Geographic and social mobility has the effect of increasing social stratification and segregation based on inherited abilities and acquired skills. Since people tend to marry those with whom they interact, this means that people are likely to marry those with similar abilities and skills and not, as in times past, those in the towns or regions of their birth, or in the social circle of their parents. When people married the children of their parents' acquaintances, by choice or through arranged marriage, they were often mismatched in terms of ability, due to regression to the mean. The parents may have been relatively equal, but their children were apt to be less so. In addition, the relationship between favorable genetic traits and economic success is likely to be greater than in earlier societies, since genes favoring various desired skills and attributes are more likely to be expressed phenotypically in modern societies where the division of labor promotes the exploitation of a wide variety of favorable traits by those who posses them.

Universal schooling just about guarantees that any person with desirable genetic attributes, intelligence and impulse control in particular, can develop skills and find a niche. The result is that social status is more likely to be linked to genes in industrial societies than in earlier times. A curious consequence of these trends is that there tends to be an inverse relationship between social class and reproductive fitness in industrial societies. There are a number of reasons for this. Ronald Fisher in his now classic, *The Genetical Theory of Natural Selection*, argued that economic success is usually a consequence of limited reproduction. People who do well in industrial societies postpone reproduction while they acquire the education and skills necessary for economic well-being. Women destined for the upper classes, therefore, tend to marry later and begin reproduction later than do women of more limited ambition and ability.[54]

Reproduction at a younger age often translates into greater reproduction, and sometimes, into more successful reproduction. In the modern welfare state, furthermore, women can reproduce and support children outside of marriage. Women in the lower classes who do not pursue advanced education are able to reproduce at a young age and do not need to wait for suitable husbands. It is not at all uncommon for poor women in their thirties to be grandmothers, while their better-educated age-mates have only recently given birth to their own children. If every woman were to give birth to only two children, those who do so at an earlier age will have far more progeny in the long run than those who postpone birth.

The above relationship is well established and has been long known if not much discussed. Part of the reason is that concern with this pattern has often been associated with various eugenic schemes to limit reproduction in the lower classes, schemes widely unpopular in democratic societies. Furthermore, these trends are of very recent origin—having been common for fewer than one hundred years in most societies—and have not had time to produce noticeable effects. Another part of the reason is that the numbers of well-off as a proportion of the total is almost opposite to what it is in agricultural societies. The number of poor is relatively small and even if their reproduction is significantly greater in proportion to that of the better-off, the effect is obscured by the much greater absolute numbers produced by the middle and upper classes.

Nevertheless, the effects of this demographic pattern should become more noticeable as time passes. For one, the size of the less productive classes may grow simply because of their more rapid reproduction. Secondly, as the skills required by industrial societies become more specialized and as more routine tasks become mechanized, the number of people who can find well-paid employment may decline. Clearly one of the major tasks of future industrial societies will be how to maintain social peace between those with marketable skills that are richly rewarded and the potentially growing class of people lacking such skills, whose work may increasingly involve providing relatively routine services for the more advantaged classes. The egalitarian ethos of democracy requires that individuals maintain a sense that they contribute in meaningful ways to the support of their families in reasonable security and hold respected positions in their communities. While such goals are not incompatible with many people holding relatively simple service employment, it is necessary that there be such employment available and that it can provide reasonable support for families.

For this reason it is important to consider the impact of immigration on people's ability to find employment which allows them to satisfy reasonable economic and social expectations. On this count, current immigration policies give one pause. One has to question the wisdom of bringing into the workforce large numbers of low-skilled wage earners who compete directly with native low-skilled individuals. If the current immigrants are unable to advance, over a few generations, into more skilled employment, they will merely exacerbate the problems associated with a large class of people relegated to the lower rungs of society. This was, of course, the major concern of the authors of *The Perfect Storm* discussed in Chapter I.

People unable to meet the minimum goals of economic security and social respect are likely candidates for demagogic appeals. The economic turmoil in Europe following World War I was certainly a factor in the rise of European Communism which appealed to the grievances of those suffering economic hardship and psychological demoralization. The rise of Fascism was certainly, in part, a response of the classes who had much to lose by the establishment of a communist program. While modern productivity makes it unlikely that those failing to find productive work will suffer extreme material hardship, it is difficult to envision how they can be spared the demoralization often associated with economic superfluity. Should the numbers of such people become sufficiently large, the foundations of popular democracy may be fatally compromised.

Of course, none of the above observations are new. The ever present tensions between the wealthy, the middle class and the poor have been well understood since the beginnings of political philosophy and were clearly articulated by Aristotle some 2300 years ago. "Thus it is manifest that the best political community is formed by citizens of the middle class." The reason is plainly stated: "where some possess much and the rest nothing there may arise an extreme democracy, or a pure oligarchy..." In both cases, tyrannies are likely to arise. In democracies tyrannies are promoted by demagogues who prey on the envy of the poor. In oligarchies they arise out of the contempt and fear of the poor by the rich.[55] Aristotle's understandings were based on the study of the constitutions of more than 150 cities.[56] But they apply equally to states larger than the relatively small city-states common in Aristotle's time. A state without a substantial middle class is one "not of freemen, but masters and slaves, the one despising, the other envying...nothing can be more fatal to friendship and good fellowship." It is on such good fellowship, however, that successful states are based. The middle class makes for the most stable societies, since in their relative material equality they can maintain relations of friendship since they do not "covet their neighbors' goods, nor do others covet theirs."[57]

Stratification in Multiracial Societies

The problems created by meritocratic social systems are exacerbated if wealth and honor are differentially distributed in ways noticeably related to race. There are a number of reasons why this is so. If social standing is correlated with racial differences, grievances of an economic nature become entwined with the perceptions of nepotistic favoritism. In agricultural societies with strong tribal traditions, nepotism is the rule, and differences in the success or failure of various tribes is seen, often correctly, as evidence of tribal nepotism and outgroup discrimination. In industrial societies, especially within bureaucratic hierarchies, such nepotism is rarely possible. It does occur, of course, within small enterprises dominated by a particular ethnic group, but rarely has severe economic consequences for those outside those groups.

Nevertheless, the perception that income and occupational disparities among groups are the result of nepotistic practices is hard to dispel. This perception, furthermore, may not be dispelled even among those highly successful members of less talented groups, since their children are unlikely to achieve to the same degree as their parents. Since people have a profound interest in the well-being of their children, the downward mobility of a child may be particularly painful and give rise to feelings of deep-seated resentment toward society as a whole. But the reason for such downward mobility is easily explained by regression to the mean.

Highly successful people from a less talented group, if their success is based on inherited characteristics, represent a fairly unlikely set of favorable genes from within their group's gene pool. When their children regress to the mean, they will necessarily regress to the mean of their own ethnic gene pool and not the gene pool of the larger society. This is the most obvious explanation for the disappointing finding that black children whose parents fall in the top of the income distribution do less well academically, on average, than white children whose parents fall at the bottom of the income distribution.[58] This is clearly dispiriting to parents, many of whom may be reluctant to except the "luck of the draw" explanation and look to less benign explanations.

In most western societies, all sorts of rules and regulations are set up to restrict discrimination on the basis of race and ethnicity. In addition, affirmative action programs were instituted in the belief that past discrimination had conditioned people in minority groups from even attempting to enter various occupations. Affirmative action was initially designed to dispel these beliefs by requiring firms to demonstrate that they were taking affirmative measures to recruit people from minority populations. Unfortunately, the program was corrupted when the government began using statistics on the percentage of minority group members in firms and assuming that any deviation from proportional representation was necessarily the result of discrimination. Adding to this trend were court rulings on "disparate impact" that made any selection practice that produced differences in hiring and promotion, on its face, discriminatory. The net result was that companies began to hire and promote many minority individual merely to avoid penalties for charges of discrimination.[59] What had begun as an attempt to create equality of opportunity became a program for equality of result. Put another way, since differences in talent among groups exist, differences that governments refused to acknowledge, any disparities were attributed to discrimination that could only be overcome by additional incentives to increase "diversity" in schools and in the workforce. It is difficult to determine whether these stratagems are well-meaning and truly reflect the belief that groups are, in fact, equal in marketable skills, or are more disingenuous and merely attempts to reduce the social dangers which the obvious outcomes of such differences pose.

Affirmative action has produced understandable resentment in individuals who have been displaced by less capable individuals in school admissions and in hiring. In addition, it has often proven to be counterproductive for many members of minority groups who are admitted into schools for which they were not prepared to compete effectively and drop out of school in large proportions relative to members of those same minority groups not admitted through affirmative action.[60] In addition, by requiring firms to hire individuals in order to obtain an acceptable level of diversity rather than strictly based on objective standards, productivity must necessarily decline because of the mismatch between the ability requirements of a position and the personnel in those positions. To these losses in productivity must be added the substantial costs incurred by governments to enforce diversity standards and the compliance costs of firms necessary to avoid lawsuits and government penalties. According to respected economist Edwin Rubenstein, the combined costs of affirmative action in 2007 amounted to "8 percent of GDP...that implies a $1.1 trillion economic loss from affirmative action programs..." Part of the reason for the high price is that affirmative action programs that were originally targeted to limit discrimination against blacks, now cover all minority groups, including the large number of immigrants, especially Hispanics, who have entered the population since the inception of affirmative action.[61] Even if one doubts the size of Rubenstein's figure, an examination of his data suggests that the costs can in no way be considered trivial. This might all be worthwhile in the name of fairness and justice, if employment and income disparities were the result of discrimination, but that explanation is becoming increasingly difficult to defend. It is hard to deny, today, that these differences result from disparities in education and training that are in turn produced by native differences in aptitude and temperament.

When there are stark differences in economic performance among ethnic groups, tensions invariably arise and often turn violent. Those tensions take different forms in democratic societies and are often determined by whether the economically weaker group is in the minority or the majority. When it is a distinct minority, and lacks political power, people in a disadvantaged group may become disillusioned and embittered and express their resentment in a variety of ways. At least some of the crime, for instance, committed by aggrieved minorities in Western Europe and the United States has its origins in such resentment. It is hard to determine how common this motive is, but it seems clear enough when criminal acts target members of the majority in gratuitously violent ways.

On the other hand, when the economically weaker group is in the majority, that resentment can turn into widespread, sometimes genocidal violence. Amy Chua, in her important book, *World on Fire*, focuses on the phenomenon of "market-dominant minorities," which she defines as "ethnic minorities who, for widely varying reasons, tend under market conditions to dominate economically, often to a startling extent, the 'indigenous' majorities around them."[62] These appear in countries on all continents of the world. Her main thesis is that globalization has, in recent years, tended to amplify economic disparities and the resentments they produce. Global markets create powerful new avenues to success for those in a position to take advantage of the opportunities created.

According to Chua, the almost inevitable result in free-market democracies is a popular backlash which can take one of three forms. The first is an attack on the free market itself, in such a way as to undermine the advantages of the successful minority. This often takes the form of restrictions on the ownership of firms, access to education and the licensing of professionals. These restrictions all favor the majorities at the expense of the minority and are, in essence, affirmative action policies for indigenous majorities. The second form of backlash targets democracy, in which the successful minority forms an alliance with government leaders to suppress popular discontent. In the crony capitalism which results, the enterprising minority is allowed to exploit their advantage as long as government officials can share in the economic spoils. The third "and most ferocious kind of backlash is majority-supported violence aimed at eliminating the market-dominant minority."[63]

As Chua observes, there are many reasons for the dominance of these minorities, but in a substantial majority of cases the reasons can be found in differences in human capital, especially IQ. For reasons left unexplained, Chua never mentions IQ, though in most cases it is hard to ignore. For instance, in virtually every country in Southeast Asia, ethnic Chinese are overwhelmingly more successful than the local populace. Richard Lynn reports that the ethnic Chinese in Southeast Asia have an average IQ of 105, while natives of the region have an average IQ of 89.[64] Furthermore, Chinese dominance in trade in Southeast Asia is no recent phenomenon, but reflects a pattern going back centuries, centuries during which China itself remained economically and technologically stagnant.

In Burma, for instance, the Chinese account for about 5% of the population but they "dominate commerce at every level of society." In the Burmese cities of Mandalay and Rangoon they own nearly all the "shops, hotels, restaurants, and prime commercial and residential real estate."[65] In Vietnam, in the wake of the Vietnam War, Chinese entrepreneurs were targeted by the Communist rulers, "arresting and brutalizing thousands and confiscating their property." Yet in recent times, as Vietnam has reintroduced market liberalization, the Chinese, who represent 3% of the population and who are concentrated in the capital of Ho Chi Minh City, "control roughly 50% of the city's market activity, dominate light industry, import-export, shopping malls, and private banking."[66] In Thailand, among the "seventy most powerful business groups...all but three were owned by Thai Chinese."[67] In the Philippines, ethnic Chinese, "just 1 to 2 percent of the population, control all the Philippines' largest and most lucrative department store chains, major supermarkets and fast food chains." In addition, "with one exception, all of the Philippines principal banks are now Chinese-controlled."[68]

Not surprisingly, these economic disparities have led to popular discontent directed at the ethnic Chinese. In Indonesia, for instance, the dictator Suharto oversaw a market liberalization in the 1980s and 1990s that benefited Chinese entrepreneurs and Suharto himself in a classic case of crony capitalism. By the late 1990s, the Chinese, who made up 3% of the population, "controlled approximately 70% of the private economy." On the occasion of the resignation of General Suharto, three days of rioting broke out in Jakarta and ethnic Indonesians looted and burned Chinese businesses and homes, and gang-raped 150 Chinese women. In all, more than 2000 people died, including many of the rioters. The result was that wealthy Chinese fled the country and took their capital with them. The general sentiment among the population was that the harm done to the economy was well worth it "to get rid of the Chinese."[69] Chua reports that the sort of hatred and "deep anti-Chinese resentment" expressed by Indonesians is common throughout Southeast Asia. This hatred is "rooted not just in poverty but in feelings of envy, insecurity and exploitation." She reports that throughout the region Chinese "are repeatedly subject to kidnapping, vandalism and violence."[70]

It should be stressed that in all of these countries most of the Chinese inhabitants are hardly wealthy; many are middle class and often struggle to maintain their status. The point is that when one looks at the upper tail of the bell curve, the Chinese, with a group average IQ of 105, will have many times more individuals with extraordinary abilities than will those in the general population of Southeast Asia with a group IQ of 89, a full standard deviation lower than the Chinese. Of course, other factors may play a role in the economic success of the Chinese, but those would seem mainly to magnify the effects of the IQ disparities between the Chinese and the native groups.

The examples presented in Chua's comprehensive treatment make clear just how pervasive this phenomenon is. In Chapter 1 the tragic case of the Jews as a market-dominant minority in Europe was discussed. It is hardly surprising, given the parallels between them, that the ethnic Chinese in Southeast Asia have earned the title of the *Jews of Asia*. In many African countries Indians, sometimes called the *Jews of Africa* are heavily represented as merchants and tradesmen and have often been the target of African mobs, resentful of their relative success. In Tanzania in the 1980s they faced "bitter anti-Indian brutality." In Zambia they were "targeted in bloody mass riots in the mid-1990s." In Kenya in the 1980s the Indians were "confronted with the unleashed hatred of some of Kenya's 16 million African majority. Looters and rioters targeted Indian shops and businesses and smashed what could not be taken."[71] Idi Amin, the notoriously brutal dictator of Uganda in the 1970s, expelled all the Indians after confiscating their property and requiring them to leave almost penniless.[72] Currently the white Europeans in Zimbabwe are undergoing brutal suppression under the dictatorship of Robert Mugabe. They are being driven off their farms and often murdered in the process by thugs under the direct control of Mugabe.[73] Similar confiscations may come to the white minority in South Africa. They are currently under a siege of criminal violence and those who have the wherewithal are fleeing the country.

Many black African groups fit the mold of market-dominant minorities and are not spared the wrath of majorities by their skin color. The Ibo of Nigeria and the Tutsi of Rwanda are two well-known examples. According to Chua, such successful African groups do not "dominate their respective economies to anywhere near the extent that, say, the Chinese do in Southeast Asia." Nevertheless, "with varying degrees of intensity, all of these African groups have been the objects of widespread resentment." In Nigeria in the 1960s, for instance, "tens of thousands of Ibo were slaughtered indiscriminately by furious mobs."[74]

In Rwanda, the Tutsi, who make up perhaps 10% of the population, have long held an economically dominant position over the majority Hutu. Under Belgian colonial rule they were favored over the Hutu in education and administrative appointments. When the Hutu majority mounted a liberation campaign in the 1950s, they targeted the Tutsi as agents of the Belgians and systematically engaged in violent attacks against them, both before and after they gained independence in 1962. The lingering resentment toward the Tutsi took a particularly ugly turn in the 1990s when Hutu demagogues called openly for the slaughter of the Tutsi. The result of that campaign is all too well known. Hutu mobs, directed by the government and military, turned on their Tutsi neighbors in a fury of pillage, arson, rape, unspeakable torture and murder that targeted men, women and children, indiscriminately. According to Human Rights Watch, at least 500,000 Tutsis, approximately 75% of the Tutsi population, were murdered in this government sponsored slaughter which cannot possibly be characterized as anything other than genocide. Even after the bulk of the killings had taken place, the government continued to hunt down and kill Tutsis in an attempt to totally annihilate them.[75]

The point is that tension between ethnic groups is ubiquitous, but is greatly exacerbated when the groups have very different economic and political power. The above examples illustrate the danger when politically weak groups have strong economic power. When economically weak groups have little or only limited political power, their resentment toward the majority can take a variety of forms. As mentioned earlier, a good deal of the disproportionate crime committed by ethnic minorities in western societies may in some unknown degree reflect this resentment. Occasionally the resentment results in riots, especially in minority dominated areas, where the weaker minority turns its anger against more successful minorities in their midst. In the Los Angeles riots after the Rodney King affair, blacks and Hispanics looted and burned the Korean businesses in their neighborhoods. In the riots in Crown Heights section of Brooklyn, blacks targeted the orthodox Jews who lived among them. More generally, the resentment is expressed in a generalized feeling that the majority intentionally deprives them of opportunities. Governments of all Western democracies have developed a wide variety of programs to counteract this perceived discrimination. The problem, of course, is that these are ineffective if the economic disparities are not caused by discrimination. The failure of these programs leads inevitably to calls for more radical solutions, and a greater demoralization among disaffected minorities, without in any way reducing the sense of resentment. It is difficult to escape the conclusion that this is an intractable problem that is simply not amenable to solutions by democratic governments.

A second problem for multicultural societies, while not as severe as ethnic strife discussed above, is a general erosion of trust among individuals in the population. Francis Fukuyama has made a very strong case that the general trust which citizens feel in their everyday relations is an important ingredient for economic success. Those societies balkanized by tribal or class affiliations are considerably less economically successful than those in which people feel themselves part of one community with shared values and interests. The reasons are straightforward. Modern industrial economies are based in reciprocal altruism and to the extent that individuals feel that they can rely on others, as a matter of course, to fairly reciprocate their efforts, they need not waste energies and resources attempting to detect and punish free-riders. When a handshake can serve as well as a written contract, economic transactions are smoother and more efficient.[76]

Robert Putnam has coined the phrase "social capital" as shorthand for the economic benefits of such communal trust and argues that it is every bit as important as physical and human capital to a dynamic economy. Multiracial and multicultural societies tend toward less trustful relations and less economic dynamism. Putnam, in the major study mentioned in Chapter 1, oversaw thousands of interviews in hundreds of American communities. He found that on a wide variety of measures, the movement of ethnic or racial groups into communities tended to undermine the trust which previously characterized relations in those communities. In his words, "In the short to medium run...immigration and ethnic diversity challenge social solidarity and inhibit social capital."[77] He speculates that in the long run, however, as these new groups acclimate themselves to their new setting and as the host population adjusts to the ways of the newcomers, new forms of community solidarity will be created and social trust restored.

He bases this belief in the historical record of immigrant assimilation and societal accommodation which followed in the wake of immigration to the United States during most of its history. He also believes that in the long run the skills and values that immigrants bring will foster the sort of economic innovation and dynamism that accompanied earlier patterns. The loss of social capital is, therefore, according to Putnam, only a temporary hindrance to economic welfare which will be amply compensated by future robustness. But, as discussed earlier, there is much reason to question whether the earlier immigration experience can be repeated, given current circumstances and the very different cultural and racial makeup of current immigrant groups. It is also reasonable to question whether the skills and attributes brought by current immigrants match the needs of our current economy in ways consistent with historical patterns. If Putnam's expectations prove overly sanguine, the result could well be a gradual but real decline in the nation's standard of living and all the attendant ills such a decline would entail.

A third major problem for multiracial societies relates to their welfare policies. Most successful people in industrial societies are well aware that their success is dependent on the exploitation of inherited capacities over which they had little control. They are also fully aware of regression to the mean (even if they do not use that terminology) and know that in most families there is a considerable range of talent.

Not all siblings and cousins are equally successful and, as often as not, the differences are the result of differences in talent and not in motivation. Similarly all parents are aware that their children may not fare equally well, and some might not do as well as they do. Most parents, therefore, devote considerable resources in an effort to equalize the life chances and the well-being of their offspring.

Such understandings and concerns tend to produce an attitude favorable to social welfare policies that ameliorate the effects of differential talent. Most people seem to adopt an attitude that "but for the grace of god" (or genetic luck), I or my children might find ourselves in such circumstances. This is obviously the case in most people's attitudes toward the physically disabled and certainly carries over and expresses itself in sympathy for the poor, especially those who appear to be making an effort to help themselves. In many ways this is simply nepotism and kin favoritism stretched to include very large numbers of people with whom people feel a sense of community. Almost all Western societies take measures to see that all low-income families are provided with assistance for decent housing, food, healthcare and other basic needs. But such "noblesse oblige" is unlikely to be extended to those who are not, and cannot, be viewed as members of the community, especially in societies composed of groups or tribes whose allegiances do not extend to the whole society.

If the poor in such societies see themselves as an aggrieved ethnic group or tribe, they may express demands for compensation that the larger society does not feel any obligation to satisfy. Furthermore, if the offspring of immigrants fail in large numbers to integrate, and if many turn to criminal activities, any sympathy for their circumstances is likely to turn to outright antipathy. Of course, elites attempting to maintain the status quo will attempt to satisfy both groups, but in time will have an increasingly difficult time doing so, especially if the aggrieved group is relatively small. To satisfy those demands will require doing things the majority opposes and such elites may find themselves engaging in ever more undemocratic methods to satisfy minority demands. This of course leads to greater and greater dissatisfaction and the real possibility of majority revolt against the ruling elites.

On the other hand, another danger arises if the aggrieved group becomes sufficiently large that it becomes practically impossible to satisfy their demands at the expense of a diminishing majority, especially if economic productivity fails to grow, or even diminishes. This could well produce civil disturbances and revolutionary demands by the weaker groups. In the face of such civil strife, the majority may resort to the sort of harsh social control, and reduced civil liberties, that they see as necessary to maintain order. It was such social unrest which produced the Fascist regimes of the twentieth century. Those who oversee a nation's immigration policy would be well advised to maintain a good deal of caution when anticipating the consequences of wide scale indiscriminate immigration from the poorer to the richer countries of the world.

In summary, industrial societies, from the biological perspective, have too short a history to have had much impact on the evolution of human beings. The major biological effects of industrialization have been dramatic decreases in death rates, which give rise to explosive population growth followed by a demographic transition where population stabilizes and then begins a gradual decline. Equally important has been the rise of a meritocracy which allows almost all genotypes that affect social success to be expressed phenotypically. This gives rise to social stratification very largely based in genetics. While this will not usually lead to social disharmony in monoracial societies, it could easily do so in multiracial societies where genetically advantageous traits are unevenly distributed among the various groups in society.

Notes

1   Lawrence H. Keeley, *War Before Civilization: The Myth of the Peaceful Savage* (Oxford: Oxford University Press, 1996), 86.
2   Laura L. Betzig, *Despotism and Differential Reproduction* (New York: Aldine, Hawthorne, 1986), 88.
3   Keeley, *War Before Civilization*.
4   Napolian A. Chagnon, *Yanomamo: The Fierce People* (New York: Holt, Rinehart and Winston), 1977.
5   Pierre L. van den Berghe, *Human Family Systems: an Evolutionary View* (Prospect Heights, Illinois: Waveland Press, 1979), 146.
6   Keeley, *War Before Civilization*, 62.
7   Sigmund Freud, *Civilization and its discontents* (New York: Norton 1961).
8   Linda Mealey, The Sociobiology of Sociopathy: An Integrated Evolutionary Model, *Behavioral and Brain Science* 18:3, (1995), 523–599.
9   Ibid, 523.
10   J. M. Roberts, *The Penguin History of the World*. (London: Penguin, 1995), 461; Jared Diamond, *Guns, Germs and Steel: A Short History of Everybody for the Last 13,000 Years*. (London: Vintage, 2005) 186.
11   Roberts, *Penguin History*, 461.

12   Ibid, 89.
13   Ibid, 39–61.
14   Ibid, 81.
15   Fred S. Singer and D. T. Avery, *Unstoppable Global Warming* (New York: Rowman and Littlefield, 2007), xiv.
16   Bo Wen, Hui Li, Daru Lu, Xifeng Song, Feng Shang, Ungang He, Feng li, Yang Gao, Xianyun Maoo, Liang Zhang, Ji Qian, Jingze Tan, Jianzhong Jin, Wei Huang, Ranjan Deka, Bing Su, Ranajit Chakraborty and Li Jin, Genetic Evidence supports Demic Diffusion of Han Culture, *Nature*, 431, September 16, 2004, 302–305.
17   T. Frank, Race Mixture in the Roman Empire, *American Historical Review*, 21:4 (1916), 689–708.
18   John Hawks, Eric Wang, Gregory Cochran, Henry C. Harpending and Robert K. Mpyziz, Recent Acceleration of Human Adaptive Evolution, *Proceedings of the National Acadmey of Sciences (PNAS)*, 104, 52, December 17, 2007.
19   Tatiana Zerjal, Yali Xue, Giorgio Bertorelle, R. Spencer Wells, Weidong Bao, Suling Zhu, Raheel Qamar, Qasim Ayub, Aisha Mohyuddin, Songbin Fu, Pu Li, Nadira Yuldsheva, Ruslan Ruzibakiev, Juijin Xu, Qunfang Shu, Ruofu Du, Huanming Yang, Methew E. Hurles, Elizabeth Robinson, Tudevdagva Gerelsaikhan, Bumbein Dashnyam, S. Qasim Mehdi and Chris Tyler–Smith, The Genetic Legacy of the Mongols, *American Journal of Human Genetics*, 72, 2003, 717–721.
20   Betzig, *Despotism and Differential Reproduction*, 69–86.
21   Ibid, 69–86.
22   Douglas R. White and Michael L. Burton, Causes of polygyny: Ecology, Economy, Kinship and Warfare., *American Anthropologist*. 90:4 (1988), 871–887.
23   Ronald A. Fisher, *The Genetical Theory of Natural Selection* (New York: Dover, 1958), 264–269.
24   William H. McNeill, *Plagues and Peoples* (Garden City New York: Doubleday, 1976), 75.
25   Marcia Guttentag and Paul Secord, *Too Many Women: The Sex Ratio Question* (Beverly Hills, Calif.: Sage, 1983).
26   Hugh Thomas, *World History, Revised Edition* (New York: HarperCollins, 1996), 54–55, 108.
27   Hugh D. R. Baker, *Chinese Family and Kinship* (New York: Colombia University Press, 1979), 10–11.
28   Arthur A. Lovejoy, *The Great Chain of Being: The Study of the History of an Idea* (Cambridge, Mass: Harvard University Press, 1960).
29   Daniel G. Freedman, *Human Infancy: An Evolutionary Perspective* (Hillsdale, New Jersey: Lawrence Erlbaum, 1974), 148–159.
30   Gregory Clark, *A Farewell to Alms: A Brief Economic History of the World* (Princeton, New Jersey: Princeton University Press, 2007), 113.
31   Ibid, 267.
32   Ibid, 113.
33   Ibid, 166.
34   Ibid, 187.

35   Ibid, 122.

36   Ibid, 345.

37   *CIA World Fact Book* (New York: Barnes and Noble, 2006), 125, 279.

38   Richard J. Herrnstein and Charles Murray, *The Bell Curve: Intelligence and Class Structure in American Life* (New York: Free Press, 1994); Richard Lynn, *Race Differences in Intelligence: An Evolutionary Analysis* (Augusta, Georgia: Washington Summit Publishers, 2006); J. Philippe Rushton and Arthur R. Jenson, Thirty years of research on race differences in cognitive ability, *Psychology, Public Policy, and Law*, 1:2, (2005) 235–294.

39   L. Hedegaard, Interview: A Continent of Losers, Sappho (2007). The interview was with Gunnar Heinsohn.

40   Ibid.

41   James Q. Wilson, *Thinking About Crime* (New York: Vintage Books, 1985), 20–23.

42   U. S. Census Bureau. *Statistical Abstract of the United States*, 2008, Section 1, Population, (2007), 15.

43   Edward Shorter, *The Making of the Modern Family* (New York: Basic Books, 1977).

44   Robert William Fogel and Stanley L. Engerman, *Time on the Cross: The Economics of American Negro Slavery* (Boston: Little, Brown, 1974), 5.

45   Louise Ropes Loomis, ed., *Aristotle, On Man in the Universe*, (New York: Walter J. Black, 1943), 302.

46   Tatu Vanhanen, *The Limits of Democratization: Climate, Intelligence and Resource Distribution* (Augusta, Georgia: Washington Summit Publishers, 2009).

47   Ibid, 153–156, 169.

48   Ibid, 253.

49   Ibid, 266.

50   Ibid, 263.

51   Ibid, 270.

52   Ibid, 260.

53   Ibid, 266.

54   Fisher, *Genetical Theory*, 247–274.

55   Loomis, *Aristotle*, 337–338.

56   Ibid, 247.

57   Ibid, 337–338.

58   Rushton and Jensen, Thirty years of research.

59   Byron M. Roth, *Prescription for Failure: Race Relations in the Age of Social Science*. (New Brunswick, New Jersey : Transaction Publishers, 1994) 120–122.

60   Ibid, 264–267.

61   Edwin S. Rubenstein, Cost of Diversity: The Economic Costs of Racial and Cultural Diversity, October 2008, Issue Number 803 (Augusta Georgia: National Policy Institute, 2008), 1–2.

62   Amy Chua, *World on fire* (New York: Anchor Books, 2004), 6.

63   Ibid, 11.

64   Richard Lynn, *The Global Bell Curve: Race, IQ, and Inequality Worldwide* (Augusta, Georgia: Washington Summit Publishers, 2008), 237.

65 Chua, *World on Fire*, 25, 29.
66 Ibid, 34.
67 Ibid, 35.
68 Ibid, 36–37.
69 Ibid, 43–45.
70 Ibid, 47.
71 Ibid, 114
72 Michael T. Kaufman, Idi Amin, Murderous and Erratic Ruler of Uganda in the 70s, Dies in Exile. *New York Times*, August 17, 2003.
73 Peta Thornycroft, Invaders Cripple Zimbabwe Farms, Telegraph.co.uk, October 7, 2001; Peta Thornycroft, Robert Mugabe's Mobs Invade Last White Farms, *The Telegraph*, April 18, 2008; Louis Weston, Zimbabwe's Last White Farmer Forced to Quit, *The Telegraph.co.uk*, June 26, 2008.
74 Chua, *World on Fire*, 112.
75 Human Rights Watch, Leave None to Tell the Story: Genocide in Rwanda, 1999, hrw.org/reports/1999/Rwanda.
76 Francis Fukuyama, *Trust: The Social Virtues and the Creation of Prosperity* (New York: Free Press, 1995).
77 Robert D. Putnam, E Pluribus Unum: Diversity and Community in the Twenty–First Century, The 2006 Johan Skytte Prize Lecture, *Scandinavian Political Studies*, 30:2, (2007), 138.

Chapter 5

HISTORIC PATTERNS OF IMMIGRATION TO THE UNITED STATES

Introduction

THE EUROPEAN POWERS with important naval strength all established colonies in the Americas shortly after Columbus' discovery in 1492. The Spanish, the paramount navel power of the time, established colonies in Central America, northern South America, and numerous Islands in the Caribbean and had a substantial presence in Florida and small missionary outposts in what is now the American southwest.[1]

Portugal, a small nation, but with a substantial naval presence in the world, colonized the large area of South America now known as Brazil. The primary interest of these earlier conquerors was in the gold and silver ostentatiously displayed by native rulers, whose armies they subdued with relative ease. In a short time they, especially the Spanish, exported huge quantities of silver that enormously enhanced their power and influence. The new lands also proved especially well-suited for the production of sugar, a commodity in great demand in Europe, and the Spanish and Portuguese established large plantations in Brazil and on many of the Caribbean Islands. Initially they employed native labor, but in time came to depend on imported African slaves, as so many of the natives succumbed to European infectious diseases with which they had no experience.

The Dutch, perhaps the dominant world trading power at that time, wished to establish supremacy in trade in the new territories; they were major importers of slaves, especially to the sugar plantations in Brazil and the Caribbean, and had established trading bases in the Caribbean and in New Amsterdam. The English and French, who came somewhat later, took some of the Caribbean Islands, but mainly concentrated their colonization in those areas of North America not already taken by the others. However, according to historian J. M. Roberts, throughout the 1500s, "the English were too weak and the French too distracted" to undertake serious settlements. These efforts accelerated after 1600 with the English establishing substantial colonies along the Atlantic coast in New England and Virginia. The French settled in what is now Canada, along the St Lawrence River and the Great Lakes, and all along the Mississippi River.[2]

An early attempt by the English to settle in America was undertaken in 1587 in the Roanoke Colony on the North Carolina coast, but failed a few years after the colonizers arrived. The first settlers encountered unexpected difficulties and desperately needed reinforcement from England. Unfortunately, the expedition to provide reinforcement was detained because of the war with Spain, and when it did finally arrive, they found that the original settlers had disappeared and seemed to have abandoned the settlement. None of the original settlers or any other of their remains were ever found.[3] The most likely explanation is that they were taken captive by native tribes. Given the normal course of primitive war, the men were likely slain and the women taken as captive mates by the natives.[4]

Later English attempts were more successful and permanent communities were established in Virginia in 1607 and in New England in 1620. The initial settlements were dangerous and fraught with terrible difficulty. For instance, during the first few years, the mortality among settlers approximated 50%.[5] By this time the Dutch had established the New Netherlands, which included the area around the lower Hudson River, the Delaware valley and what is now New Jersey. In general, the English colonies were considerably more successful than those set up by the French and Dutch. J. M. Roberts offers two reasons for their success. First, the English, unlike the French or Dutch, sent whole communities with many intact families in the hope of establishing self-sustaining settlements. Secondly, the discovery and cultivation of tobacco in Virginia provided a valuable crop much in demand in Europe that promoted vigorous trade between Europe and the British-American colonies. For these reasons, large numbers of English migrants had established permanent and self-sustaining communities along the Atlantic seaboard by the mid 1600s.[6] The growing population of New England continuously encroached on the Dutch settlement to the south and eventually, after a series of armed conflicts in Europe between England and the Netherlands, including hostilities in North America, the territory of New Netherland came under English control in 1674.[7]

Approximately a hundred years later at the end of the Seven Years War, which raged in Europe and the Americas, the Treaty of Paris of 1763 was adopted. In that treaty, the French ceded all of their lands on continental North America to Britain. In addition, Spain, an ally of France, ceded Florida to the English, and in return was given the lower Mississippi valley around New Orleans. That territory was later acquired by France and subsequently sold to America in the Louisiana Purchase during the administration of President Jefferson. The result of the Seven Years War, called the French and Indian War in America, was that on the eve of the American Revolution virtually all the inhabited regions of North America were in the hands of the British. Paul Johnson characterized this outcome as "one of the greatest territorial carve-ups in history.[8]

In trying to understand the massive waves of migration to America that took place during the four centuries after the founding of the first English colonies, historians generally look to three explanatory factors: push, pull, and transportation factors. Push factors are those of an economic, political, or religious nature which induce people to consider undertaking the arduous and often dangerous task of uprooting themselves and their families. When circumstances in a region become intolerable for large numbers of people, or if the outlook for their future appears especially bleak, many people may consider such drastic actions. Where they go in their search for a better life is dependent on pull factors which make some destinations more promising than others. Most great migrations involve people from one region seeking refuge in a variety of alternative locations.[9]

In the early settlement of America, two push factors were of paramount significance. The first was a desire for religious freedom. At this time England was marked, as was all of Europe, by religious conflict between Catholics and Protestants, occasioned by the

Protestant Reformation of the 16th century. Henry VIII of England had broken with the Pope in 1534 and established the Anglican Church with himself at the head. But the new Anglican Church was to be the national Catholic Church of England and was no more tolerant of Protestant dissenters than was the Catholic Church headed by the Pope. The people who founded the Plymouth Colony in 1620 were Puritan dissenters who sought a place where they could freely practice their faith and build a community based upon it.[10]

The second powerful push factor was population pressure that drove up land prices and rents. This was to represent the most powerful motive which lasted well into the early 20th Century. Land scarcity in Europe was produced by a complex of factors. World population grew robustly in the centuries before 1350. The United States Census Bureau estimates that world population was 200 million people at the time of the birth of Christ and remained fairly steady for the next seven centuries. From 700 to 1350 world population doubled to an estimated 400 million.[11] The population of Europe contributed to the worldwide trend and grew rapidly, after falling substantially in the few centuries after the fall of Rome. J. C. Russell estimates that European population, which had stood at 27.5 million during the height of the Roman Empire, fell to 18 million in 650 AD, grew to 38.5 million in 1000 AD, and then to 73.5 million by 1340.[12]

The bubonic plague that arose on the Eurasian landmass in the middle of the 14th century dramatically reduced Eurasian population. For Europe, it fell from the estimated 73 million in 1340 to 50 million during the next 100 years. Europe recovered fairly rapidly, however, and according to Fernand Braudel, had grown to a population of approximately 100 million by 1650. Population continued to grow, reaching almost 200 million by 1800, and then 400 million by 1900.[13] In other words, Europe's population quadrupled in the 250 years during the period of massive immigration to the Americas. Of course, these population estimates are fairly speculative, especially early in this period, and were different in the various regions. Nevertheless, the pattern of a rapidly growing population is clear, and is generally accepted by most population historians.

The rapid rise in population is partly explained by the adjustment of European populations to the epidemic diseases discussed in Chapter 3. It is also partly explained by the adoption of more efficient agricultural practices, especially in England and the Low Countries.

These involved the consolidation of small holdings, and the taking over of common lands, previously available to peasants, into larger holdings that could be more efficiently farmed. Furthermore, new crops like turnips and potatoes became common as did the raising of livestock fed on grains and cereals grown on the same farms.[14] These measures, that benefited mainly large landowners, assured a more secure food supply and no doubt reduced the severity of ever threatening famines. However, these land consolidations threw many peasants from land they previously held under traditional feudal rights and forced them to eke out livelihoods as renters or laborers on land owned by others. Coming at the time of rapidly growing population, many peasants were forced to migrate to cities in search of industrial work or to America and other European colonies where land was available and relatively cheap.

The difficulties of the rural populations were compounded by what has come to be called the Little Ice Age, a period of global cooling that lasted from 1300 to 1850. While global temperatures were only a few degrees cooler than they are today, the effect was most severe in the northern latitudes where much of Europe is located. Not only was Europe cooler, but more important for farmers, weather become more variable and highly unpredictable. Periods of relative warmth would be followed by decades or more of intense cold. Likewise, periods of low rainfall and drought would be followed by damp, wet conditions. Such changes meant that crops that did well in one set of conditions would fail when conditions changed, and most peasant farmers did not have the resources to make the adjustments necessary for economic survival. In addition, there were marked regional differences in the severity of the problems these climate variations posed to peasant farmers.[15] For instance, England, which grew its own wine prior to this period, had to abandon its vineyards during this time because of cold and wet weather.[16]

In general, grain production was severely reduced in Northern Europe and food shortages became a common occurrence. Local crop failures often led to devastating famines since transportation rarely allowed for the rapid and effective transfer of food to people succumbing to starvation. It was not until the widespread adoption of root crops like turnips and potatoes in the mid-1700s that peasants had a food supply secure from stormy or excessively cold weather. Irish peasants, in particular, relied on potatoes and with that new nutritional resource their population grew rapidly, only to be tragically reduced by the potato blight that struck in the mid 1800s.[17]

It is difficult to determine the precise effects of the Little Ice Age on migration patterns. It certainly exacerbated the population pressure on the land in the north where productive land became scarce during this period. Since the climate was highly variable over time and in different places, it produced internal migrations of people abandoning areas where farming could not provide even meager nutrition. For instance, there were large movements of people out of the mountainous Alpine regions that suffered especially harsh conditions, with many of their villages and farmlands being destroyed by advancing glaciers.[18] These people migrated to the lowland areas adjacent to the Alps bordering on the Rhine in southwest Germany known as the Rhineland. This migration increased greatly the population pressures in that area which, not surprisingly, became a major source of immigrants to the American colonies in the 1700s.

An additional factor adding to the peasant's misery was the almost constant warfare, much of it caused by religious strife. Armies ravaged land and pillaged food supplies leaving peasants in desperate circumstances. Overpopulation and the scarcity of land no doubt contributed to the extent and intensity of warfare in this period. When population growth, colder climate, and war are considered together, it becomes clear that the lack of safe and productive land was a powerful factor pushing people to migrate and made the risks of doing so seem eminently acceptable. The relative warmth and productivity of the land in places like Virginia made it seem a virtual paradise when compared to Europe. Virginia lies at about 37 degrees north latitude, whereas Northern Europe and England lay between 50 and 60 degrees north latitude.

For an understanding of where people look to go when they are forced to migrate, a number of *pull* factors are prominent. Perhaps the most important of these is the presence of people of similar ethnicity and background to those considering migration. People are naturally drawn to locales that already have settled people who speak their language, eat their food and, in general, abide by similar customs. The reasons are rooted in sentiment and practicality. If people of similar ethnic background reside in a place, they are likely to welcome and assist those trying to immigrate. This is especially true if family and kin networks are already in place. Once Protestant communities were established in America, for instance, they drew similar like-minded people from Europe.

Of almost equal importance among the factors which pull people to an area are the economic and political circumstances immigrants are likely to find when they arrive. It is of little use to go to a place where one's prospects are not much better than if one stayed at home. It is not surprising that America became a magnet for Europeans. It had an abundance of productive land that was cheap by European standards. In addition, there was a growing appetite for labor to work the land. It was of little use to own vast tracts of land in a wilderness, and the people who held land grants in America were happy to accommodate immigrant workers.

In addition to push and pull factors, there is the vital factor of transportation. Migration is not an option if there is not some means by which people can practically transport themselves from one place to another. Not only must transportation be feasible, it must also be within the economic means of potential migrants, and it must not be so fraught with danger as to deter most reasonable people. In addition to the availability of physical means of transport, there must be economic incentives to those who are in the position to provide such services. Overland travel often required horses and carriages, places of lodging, guides, and people to protect travelers from the depredations of thieves and marauders. Without a network of such services, overland travel that could not be accomplished by foot in a few days would have been all but impossible for most potential migrants, especially for those with families.

Overseas travel, in particular, was even more difficult, and harder to develop. Marianne Wokeck in her important book, *Trade in Strangers* outlined the critical role played by shipping merchants in the development of large-scale migration to America. A massive expenditure of capital was needed to build and provision the boats capable of transporting people great distances. In addition, an infrastructure was required to move people to points of embarkation, and house and feed them while they waited for ships to sail. Only if there were profits to be made in the transport of people would businessmen and entrepreneurs make the investment necessary to do so. In the case of migration to America, shipping agents were motivated by a desire to find profitable cargo for the ships going to America to transport the sugar, tobacco, and furs bound for Europe. This was especially the case for those merchants who were not engaged in the triangular trade involving the transport of manufactured goods to Africa in exchange for slaves destined for the Americas. The business of transporting migrants to America proved a lucrative enterprise, and shipping merchants eagerly spread word to potential migrants of the great advantages to be found in America.[19]

The technological changes in transportation of the last few centuries have altered migratory patterns in profound ways. The earliest settlers to the Americas, for instance, made the dangerous 4 to 8 week journey from England on sailing vessels. Shipwrecks were not uncommon and diseases could often take a heavy toll on migrants forced into close proximity in cramped and unsanitary shipboard conditions. In addition, the per-capita costs of these journeys were quite high, since the need to acquire, provision and man such ships incurred significant costs which figured into the fares paid by a relatively small contingent of passengers. In addition, the travel from home to seaports was usually time-consuming and expensive, especially for those from regions not regularly served by river or overland transportation.

The advent of ocean-going steam vessels which began regular service in the late nineteenth century dramatically reduced the difficulty and dangers of overseas migration. Voyages were reduced to ten days or less, and for that reason disease aboard ships was greatly reduced, as was the danger of shipwreck. Furthermore, such vessels could accommodate hundreds of immigrants, thereby reducing considerably the per capita costs of such travel. By the late twentieth century, with the advent of commercial jet aircraft, safe overseas travel was reduced to hours, and migration became economically feasible to a much wider segment of the population.

Migratory patterns, in summary, are influenced by a complex of factors: those pushing people to leave their homes, those pulling them to this or that destination, and the practical means of actually making the move. These factors, in addition, produce certain uniformities in patterns of immigration. In general, the more expensive the move, the more truncated will be the economic stratification of the migrant population. The poorest people simply cannot afford to move and the richest have no desire to do so. In addition, pull factors include the demand for certain types of skills or labor in host countries, and if the need is great, employers are often willing to underwrite some or all of the transportation costs. This was obviously true in the case of the transport of African slaves brought to the South and the Chinese employed in building the western railroads, but it was also true for large numbers of immigrants who came as indentured workers. In that case, the costs of passage were assumed by employers in exchange for a fixed period of labor.

Such factors played a role in whether people came as single individuals, as members of families or as part of organized groups of settlers. The earliest migrants came as part of religious groups like the Puritans who settled in New England, or to establish commercial outposts, as was the case in Virginia. Once outposts had been established, large numbers of single men migrated as tradesmen and laborers. Once conditions became more settled and the journey less treacherous, intact families were more likely to attempt the move.

The Four Phases of Immigration to the North American Colonies

While immigration to North America was a continuous process, there were four clearly distinguishable phases marked by differences in the political and technological circumstances in which immigration occurred, as well differences in the ethnic makeup of the immigrants. The first phase took place during the 150 years from the time of the first English settlements to the American War of Revolution. Migrants in this phase were mainly people from Great Britain, Africa, and the German-speaking people of the Rhineland. Migration was greatly curtailed during the revolution and during the first two decades of the nineteenth century. Travel from Europe in those decades was made prohibitively dangerous because of the maritime activity of England and France during the Napoleonic Wars. In addition, immigration from Africa fell drastically after the importation of African slaves was prohibited in 1808.

The second major immigration phase took place in the years between 1820 and 1880, and involved a much larger stream of immigrants from more varied regions, though still overwhelmingly from Northwest Europe. Total immigration rose from 599,125 people in the 1830s to 2,812,191 in the 1870s. The great bulk of the people came from Germany, Ireland (especially during the potato famine of the 1840s and 1850s), and the United Kingdom. Toward the end of this period a sizable influx originated in Canada, as well as the Scandinavian countries of Norway and Sweden. With the notable exception of the Germans, the overwhelming percentage of these immigrants were English speaking peoples. In addition, almost all were Protestants of various denominations.[20]

The third phase, lasting from 1880 until 1924, was ushered in by the widespread availability of steam-powered ocean-going vessels and overland railroads. These technological advances greatly reduced the cost, duration, and hardship of long-distance travel, and provided many people who had reason to migrate the means to do so for the first time. They also provided enormous profits to those who could make those movements possible for much larger numbers of people. Immigration to the United States jumped from 2.8 million in the 1870s to 5.3 million in the 1880s. It fell back in the 1890s because of serious economic problems in the United States, but jumped again to 8.8 million in the first decade of the twentieth century. It fell to some 5.7 million in the second decade, largely due to the dislocations of World War I. Before it was drastically reduced in the mid-1920s, some 4.1 million immigrants arrived in the early 1920s. These numbers are particularly striking considering that the total population of the United States was some 50 million at the start of the period in 1880, and had swelled to more than 120 million by the late 1920s, with approximately half that increase attributable to the arrival of immigrants and their natural increase.[21]

In addition to much larger numbers, this third phase heralded the first influx of people from Eastern and Southern Europe. The great bulk of the people from Eastern Europe came from Germany, the Austrian-Hungarian Empire, and from the countries that became the Soviet Union. The two largest groups of these immigrants were identified as Poles and Jews. The largest group from Southern Europe was Italian, coming mainly from southern Italy. In addition, for the first time a sizable number of Asians (approximately 750,000 in all) arrived in America, mainly on the West Coast. Unlike the earlier immigrant groups from England and Northern Europe, few of these people were Protestants and most spoke no English upon their arrival. Given the numbers and circumstances of this migration it is not hard to see how sentiment to stem the flow of migrants would grow and produce the restrictions put in place in the early 1920s that culminated in the landmark Immigration Act of 1924.

The most recent and fourth phase of immigration began with the passage of the 1965 Immigration Act and is still with us. The characteristics of this phase were influenced by the advent of cheap air travel, which made migration possible for large numbers of Asians. It was, and continues to be, influenced by the fact that the majority of immigrants in this phase, unlike earlier ones, arrive by overland routes, primarily from Latin America. It is also characterized by massive numbers, equal in absolute, if not relative size, to those of the previous phase. In the decade of the 1950s, before the 1965 Act, some 2.5 million immigrants arrived, mostly from Europe. That number doubled to 5 million in the 1970s after the passage of the 1965 act and the people who came were overwhelmingly from Asia and Latin America. In the 1980s the immigrant numbers grew to 7.3 million with only about 10% originating in Europe. In the 1990s immigration grew to more than 10 million, and it appears that it will approximate that figure in the first decade of the 21st Century.[22] These figures do not include the estimated 10 to 20 million who came without legal immigrant status and who remain in the country as undocumented or illegal aliens.

Immigration before the Revolution

Three distinct groups made their way to the American Colonies prior to the establishment of an independent United States. The majority were English in background and language. A second major group was the large number of Africans of varying ethnicity who were forcibly transported as slaves. The third large group was large numbers of German-speaking people from the Rhineland, the area bordering on the Rhine River separating France and Germany.[23]

As outlined by Pulitzer Prize-winnign historian David Fischer in his *Albion's Seed*, the English-speaking people came in four distinguishable migratory waves from particular areas of England and took up residence in different geographical regions in America. Even though they came from the same home country, there were notable differences among them, and these differences tended to persist in the colonies where they settled. Being the first settlers, the patterns they established left an imprint on their regions, many of which persist even today.

The Puritans who settled New England, for instance, came predominantly from the counties east of London, from the area known as East Anglia. They were largely middle-class commoners of strong Protestant (mainly Calvinist) faith whose primary motive was to escape persecution from authorities for their dissent from the

Church of England. Their communities were powerfully influenced by their Christian faith and were not particularly open to those of different beliefs. Catholics, for instance, were not welcome. Their distaste for nobility, given their mistreatment in England, was marked and they consciously discouraged the immigration of those of noble rank.[24] As the cost of the journey excluded most of the very poor, their social ranking was fairly attenuated. However, the availability of inexpensive land and the relative freedom of their social structure allowed for considerable personal mobility. Despite their distaste for those of noble rank, they were hardly egalitarian, and firmly believed in the correctness of social hierarchy.[25] Their sense of hierarchy, however, contained a strong element of what today we call meritocracy, and they often provided financial assistance allowing poor, capable young men to attend the newly established Harvard College.[26] Their migration took place mainly during the eleven years between 1630 and 1641. After that period, it came to an end because many Puritans sailed home, and others who might have come, remained in England, to participate in the civil strife which racked England in the mid-1600s. It is estimated that approximately 20,000 people sailed to New England in this eleven-year period, and by the year 1700 New England's population had grown to 100,000. It is hardly surprising that they had a major impact on the region, given the homogeneity of their cultural background and the strength of their religious convictions.[27]

A quite different pattern emerged in the peopling of Virginia and the regions around the Chesapeake Bay. The migration which set the cultural pattern in this region took place primarily between 1640 and 1675. The migrants came primarily from the south and west of England, from areas close to London. Unlike the Puritan migration, there were clear class distinctions among the migrants. The primary movers of this migration were individuals of considerable wealth, and often superior education. Many of these were the younger sons of aristocratic families who, because of the custom of primogeniture, could not remain on their families' estates. They were quite comfortable with the official Anglican faith, and were motivated to migrate for economic rather than religious reasons. They brought with them a large number of workers, the majority of whom, perhaps 75%, came as indentured laborers and servants, though there were sizable numbers of skilled artisans as well. Almost all immigrants, whatever their class, came for the economic opportunities available in America. Fischer estimates that the total migration to the mid-Atlantic region in the in

17th Century involved approximately 125,000 people, and the total population of the area grew to 250,000 by the end of that century, making it over twice the size of the New England population.[28]

Given the social origins of the people who settled around the Chesapeake, it is not surprising that the society they created was considerably more hierarchical than that of New England and that its leadership took a decidedly aristocratic form. Unlike those in New England, they had not been driven from their homes by elite persecution, and they held no basic animosity toward their homeland. The elite families maintained close relations with their families still in England and tended to a high degree of endogamy, marrying others in their class. They thus recreated the social pattern they had left behind.[29] The hierarchical and conservative bent of Virginian culture may explain in part the relative equanimity with which the region adopted and grew comfortable with the customs and practices attendant on slave-holding. There can also be little doubt that the differing cultural patterns in the North and South played a role in the tensions that eventually gave rise to the Civil War some two centuries later.

A third distinct group of English people settled the areas of Pennsylvania, Delaware and New Jersey that bordered on the Delaware River. Many were Quakers or Friends who, like the Puritans, had suffered considerable persecution from the Anglican Church. They arrived in large numbers between 1675 and 1725. They came predominantly from an area in the north of England close to Scotland, known as the North Midlands. Fischer estimates that this migration totaled approximately 23,000 people by 1715, and that the region's population grew to 170,000 people by 1750.[30] As with the Puritans, these immigrants tended to come from the "lower middle ranks of English society."[31] More so than the Puritans, they eschewed the notion that wealth or birth conferred social worth, and tended to emphasize worth based in moral behavior. In this sense they were egalitarians, and generally welcomed religious and morally upright people of whatever origins.[32] For this reason, most German-speaking immigrants gravitated to this region and by 1725 made up 23% of the population of Pennsylvania.[33] The egalitarianism of the Quakers was directly related to their church organization which had no professional clergy. "They repudiated all sacraments, ceremonies, churches, ordinations and tithes, and maintained no ministers in the usual sense..."[34] Not surprisingly, the Quakers were among the first to decry slavery and to attempt to outlaw it in the territories they occupied.[35]

A fourth major migration of English people took place between 1717 and the outbreak of the Revolutionary War, a century after the first English immigrants. This migration involved about 250,000 to 300,000 people from the lands bordering on the Irish Sea. The largest group was about 150,000 of Scottish descent who came from Northern Ireland or Ulster. Fischer estimates that approximately 75,000 migrated directly from the Scottish Lowlands near the border with England and about 50,000 from the northern border region of England. These people had much in common and came for similar reasons, and the majority came in intact families. All were Protestants and suffered various degrees of persecution from the official Anglican Church of England. The largest group, those from Northern Ireland, are called the Scots-Irish in America, while in Britain they are referred to as Ulster Scots, and are to be distinguished from the Irish Catholics who came in much greater numbers in the late 19th and early 20th Centuries.[36]

The presence of Scots in Northern Ireland was part of the effort to subdue Ireland and bring it under English control. This involved centuries of bitter conflict that had been generally unsuccessful. However, by the year 1600, the English had succeeded in pacifying the Ulster region of Northern Ireland by killing or driving out most of the native Irish Catholic inhabitants. To consolidate their rule over the area, and prevent the Irish from returning, the English encouraged the migration of Protestant Scots and English from the border region to the area.[37]

The border peasants were well-disposed to make the relatively easy journey across the thirty miles or so of the Irish Sea. The border region between England and Scotland where they lived suffered from years of border wars between England and Scotland, and in addition suffered the depredations of warlords who dominated the highlands of Scotland and regularly pillaged lowland communities. Furthermore, during the 17th Century, the Anglican Church of England became increasingly intolerant to Scottish Presbyterians and Englishmen who adopted Protestant faiths at variance with the established church. Most of the peasants were tenant farmers of one sort or another and practiced an inefficient and outdated agriculture on small plots of poor soil. The extreme poverty of the tenant farmers in feudal arrangements was somewhat compensated for by the security of the system: traditional practice limited the rights of landlords to raise rents beyond reasonable amounts. This traditional system began changing in the 1500s as farming became part of the emerging market economy. It became more efficient, and property often changed hands with many holdings being held by absentee landlords who had no traditional relationship to the peasants who worked their land. The consequence was rising rents that forced many tenants off lands their families had farmed for years. Under these circumstances, many of these dispossessed people were happy to migrate to Ulster's fertile land and the promise of greater opportunity.[38]

Many thousands of Scots, and a smaller number of English people, migrated to Ulster, and during the first decades of the 17th Century, managed to establish a thriving colony. In 1641, however, the displaced Irish rose up and attempted to drive out the Scots and English whom they saw, correctly, as usurpers of their traditional lands. The rebellion lasted 11 years and was finally broken by an English campaign led by Oliver Cromwell that resulted in the deaths of more than a third of Ireland's 1.5 million people.[39] According to noted historian James Leyburn, by the year 1700, the English and Scottish settlement of Ulster was thriving again, but it was "the very success of the Plantation that led to events which caused many of the Ulstermen to leave their homes for the New World."[40] The proximate cause of the migration to America, beginning in 1717, was rising rents demanded by landlords, often absentee ones, of tenant farmers. Without the protection of feudal traditions, nothing prevented landlords from opening their lands to the highest bidders. During most of the 17th Century rents had been low as landlords were anxious to attract tenants to improve their holdings. Leases typically ran for 31 years and provided an inducement for farmers to invest sweat and capital in improving their lands. However, in the early years of the 1700s, landholders began putting their lands on the open market and forced many of the original lease-holders off the land. The precipitating factor was parliament's decision to abolish taxes on sheep-raising, which induced landholders to lease out large tracts to ranchers. Sheep-raising "became so much more lucrative than ordinary tillage that many landlords...began to consolidate their farms and expel their tenantry at the end of their leases."[41]

The result was a mass migration of these people to America. They left with no small sense of bitterness toward the English authorities for what they saw, correctly, as their betrayal in being displaced from lands that they had done so much to improve. Joining them were those who came directly from lowland Scotland and from Northern England who were driven by the same sort of factors that had driven the Scots to Ireland: high rents, short leases with little security and almost constant civil strife. While religion played a role, the predominant motive for all these migrants was economic necessity.[42] All of these border people shared the same culture and suffered the same sort of oppressive treatment by landholders, and harbored a profound distrust of the society that denied them the security of outright ownership of property. It is hardly surprising that they played a prominent part of the eventual war with England.[43]

They were pulled to America by very positive reports from those already there, especially to the colony of William Penn. "Land was cheap, authorities well disposed, the country vast, its soil fertile beyond all expectation. More than this, the colonies wanted men."[44] The size of the colonies and its growing economy by the early 1700s required a constant infusion of labor. Those already settled in the colonies were willing to pay substantial sums to bring workers from overseas and the Ulstermen were seen as good recruits. Much of the land had been granted by the English Government to individuals who were required to fill them with settlers in order to make their patents final. A thriving trade in indenture contracts developed and shipowners and immigration agents benefited greatly from this need for labor. A majority of those who came did so as indentured servants.[45]

Almost all these immigrants came through the port of Philadelphia, as they found the region hospitable, especially in regard to its religious tolerance.[46] The immigrants moved west, either immediately or as soon as their period of indenture was complete, and tended to settle in the *backcountry*, further inland from the already settled coastal regions. They spread into the sparsely settled interior of Pennsylvania and, as this area began to fill with settlers, moved south into the Appalachians, the Shenandoah Valley, the Piedmont region of Virginia, and the Carolinas.[47]

They brought with them their cultural forms, including an intense loyalty to kinsmen and clan which served as a protective force in the border region back home and played the same role in the backcountry of America where they often found themselves in warfare with the Indian tribes upon whose lands they infringed.[48] Fischer argues that, in addition, on "both sides of the British border there had been a strong antipathy to state churches, religious taxes and established clergy." These attitudes played an important role in the formation of their religious observance in America.[49] Not surprisingly, they were prominent among the pioneers who ventured west following the American Revolution.

German-Speaking Immigrants

While a number of people from Continental Europe came to America during the colonial period from non-English speaking countries such as Holland, France and the Scandinavian countries, the most numerous were the German-speaking people of the Rhineland. The Rhineland was the term given to the region in what are now northern Switzerland, eastern France, and southwest Germany. It bordered the Rhine River and included numerous people from more than 350 fragmented territories and principalities in Switzerland, the Palatinate in Germany, and Alsace and Lorraine in France.[50] The region, particularly in the German areas, had been ravaged by war, especially during the Thirty Years War of 1614–1648, "nearly destroying the demographic, political, social, and economic fabric of the area."[51] The Swiss Cantons escaped much of this devastation because of Swiss neutrality, but suffered under the harsh conditions produced by the Little Ice Age. Many of these principalities were run by despotic petty rulers who imposed all sorts of bureaucratic and religious restrictions that made the life of peasants particularly onerous. Various military expeditions continued to devastate the region, which was compounded by epidemic diseases that soldiers introduced into populations weakened by malnutrition.[52] Clearly, there were a host of "push" factors driving people from the region throughout this period.

According to economist and Nobel laureate Aaron Fogleman, people from this region migrated to America in three distinct phases, and came for somewhat different reasons. The first were organized religious "pietistic" sects who came to America in groups to escape religious persecution in the period 1683–1709. They were induced to come in part by the active recruiting of William Penn. Though small in actual numbers (perhaps only 300 people), their cohesive communities grew through later immigration and natural increase to became stable elements in the New World. The more well-known of these groups were the Mennonites, the Moravians, and the Amish.[53]

The second phase of German migration occurred between 1709 and 1714 and resulted from a disastrous agricultural failure in the Rhineland in 1709. The British government had been actively recruiting in this area in the hopes of bringing workers to develop a ship-building industry on the Hudson River. The push of the 1709 crop failure coupled with the pull of employment and (at one point) the promise of free passage, induced a large number to attempt to migrate to America, though only about 2400 actually completed the journey, with most settling along the Hudson river, north of New York City.[54]

These numbers were dwarfed by the migrations from the region in the mid-1700s. Between 1717 and 1775, at least 80,000 immigrants from the Rhineland arrived in Philadelphia alone. Beginning in the early 1700s, as peace returned to the area, rulers attempted to encourage inmigration and imposed onerous regulations to prevent emigration. The region was still largely feudal, composed of small principalities. Most of these people were peasant farmers and artisans whose status as serfs obligated them to pay rents, taxes, and provide services to the local rulers. Peasants got little in return from their rulers. As in England, and throughout Europe at this time, princes took over the traditional common lands and converted them to tax and rent-yielding parcels. An additional problem was that inheritance practices in the region, unlike those in England, required that all children receive a share of inheritable land and individual holdings grew smaller over time, so that most peasants were simply unable to pay the rents and taxes demanded. The net result was extreme population pressure caused by natural increase and in-migrations from the upland Alps that created land shortages and downward pressure on wages.[55]

The consequence was a massive emigration from the region throughout the 18th century, with an estimated 900,000 people leaving the area. These numbers are particularly impressive given the fact that in order to prevent emigration, most principalities imposed heavy fees to release peasants from their feudal obligation so that they had, in effect, to buy their freedom. Most emigrants were induced to take up residence in new and underpopulated areas controlled by the Austrian, Prussian, and Russian governments, who offered many incentives including promises of religious freedom, paid transportation, and extended periods of tax relief.[56]

Most Rhineland migrants, therefore, went east; only some 10 to 15% of the total went to the British colonies in North America. The transportation costs to America were much higher for the Rhinelanders than for those coming from England. Migration routes usually required river transport down the Rhine to the Dutch port of Rotterdam. From there migrants had to sail to ports in Great Britain and finally make the long trip across the Atlantic. Such journeys could take 4 to 6 months, as opposed to the 4 to 6 weeks for the transatlantic routes of those leaving directly from the British Islands. Merchants often took more people than were suitable for their ships and often stinted on provisions. These very long journeys, in crowded and unsanitary conditions, led to relatively high death rates.[57] Furthermore, in the days of sail power, weather could force long delays requiring the unanticipated expenses of prolonged stays in port cities. A consequence was that migrants often ran out of money before their journey ended and had to indenture themselves to continue or be left stranded in foreign ports. Migrants had little bargaining power and were often forced to accept very undesirable indenture contracts.

When they finally arrived in America, most commonly in Philadelphia, they were held hostage by the shipping agents until buyers could be found for their indentures. If they were fortunate, family, friends, religious groups, or generous benefactors would lend them the funds to purchase their own contracts. Otherwise they were forced to work for strangers for periods, usually of 3 to 7 years, to liquidate their debts.[58] In some cases, intact families could arrange for the indenture of an adolescent child who could often secure a sum sufficient to pay for all the family's travel expenses.[59] These adolescent indentures were similar to apprenticeships, a common arrangement for young people at the time, in both Europe and America, and were often advantageous for the young immigrant. It promised training in a particular trade, rapid language acquisition, and other practical advantages and was an arrangement, therefore, that need not burden the conscience of parents. Needless to say, the practice was open to abuse by unscrupulous masters.

Most of the Rhinelanders who arrived in Pennsylvania tended to remain in Philadelphia and counties close to that city, especially those who came earlier when land was still relatively cheap. The high cost of the journey meant that many of the early immigrants were moderately well-off middle-class families. By the middle of the 18th Century, however, as the transportation network bringing people from the Rhineland grew in size and sophistication, shipping merchants began offering passage on credit in exchange for the indenture contracts described above. This allowed people of lesser means to migrate, who continued to come generally as intact families and often came in groups from particular regions. Most would have preferred to settle with those of their home districts, but by this time land prices had grown considerably, especially close to Philadelphia. As a consequence they tended to settle in regions further west wherever land could be had at moderate prices, but tended to gravitate toward regions with already established German-speaking communities. In general, they maintained close relations with neighbors and family members from their home villages for reasons of mutual aid, even though their need for affordable land often meant they were spread out geographically. Those in indentured service went to the homes or shops of their masters, but when their service was complete they tended to follow the settlement patterns of the other German speakers.[60]

The consequence was that most German-speaking individuals in Pennsylvania and in other states as well, tended to live in communities that were more segregated ethnically than most other groups.[61] This tendency was reinforced by the Rhinelanders' desire to maintain their religious practices, and this was facilitated by living in close proximity to local churches that maintained doctrines of the Reformed Churches of their countries or districts of origin.[62] Those who spread further in search of affordable land moved west and south down the Appalachians and settled in the backcountry areas alongside the Scots-Irish who were migrating to these areas at the same time. However, they continued to remain in relatively segregated German-speaking communities centered on their church. According to Fogleman, in 1790, after this initial wave of German immigration had passed, "almost all of the immigrants and their descendants still spoke German, married other Germans, went to German churches and lived near or next to German neighborhoods."[63]

By the time of the Revolution some 80,000 Rhinelanders had immigrated to the New World through the port of Philadelphia and some 30,000 through other ports, for a total of 110,000, with most in Pennsylvania.[64] They, therefore, represented a sizable portion of the population, especially in the regions where they settled. By 1790, they made up some 8.6% of the white population of the United States.[65]

It is instructive that language did not appear to hinder in any serious way these immigrants' overall success or their ability to adapt to the culture of the British Colonies. Not surprisingly, a great deal of their interaction involved dealings with other German immigrants, but most achieved sufficient fluency for their dealing with non-German colonials. Of course, most of the day-to-day work on farms and workshops at that time did not require much communication. In addition, the large number of young indentured servants would have learned English as a matter of course. There seems to have been a fairly high level of literacy among the immigrants, and a number of German language presses provided general news and information so that by the 1660s they had become a significant political bloc in Pennsylvania elections.[66] Nevertheless, there remained significant numbers of communities where

German was the language of commerce, church and school well into the 19th century. In some states with large German populations, such as Pennsylvania and Ohio, legislators allowed instruction in public schools in the German language if a majority of parents in a community so desired.[67] As will be seen in a later section, this led to considerable social tension by the end of that century. This is important in light of current immigration patterns, in that it suggests that immigrant communities, if sufficiently large and geographically concentrated, can sustain their distinctive linguistic and cultural patterns without fully assimilating into the dominant culture. This even though there was little or no racial difference between them and the dominant English.

The African Transports

The largest numbers of non-English speakers making up the stream of people to the English colonies were the Africans brought into the territory as slaves. They were part of the almost 10 million Africans forcibly transported from their homes to the Western Hemisphere from the 16th to the middle of the 19th century. The great bulk of the slaves were transported to South America and the Caribbean, primarily to work on sugar plantations, as sugar and related products like rum became the most profitable exports from the Americas.[68] Fewer than 5% were transported to the North American colonies.[69]

While African slaves came to the colonies as early as the 1600s, the overwhelming majority of these individuals came in the 18th century and slave imports peaked in the first decade of the 19th century before the practice was prohibited after 1808. In all, about 350,000 were transported before this prohibition. In addition, it is estimated that as many as 50,000 may have been brought in illegally in the decades before the outbreak of the Civil War.[70] The transport of slaves was part of the triangular slave trade which brought manufactured goods from Europe to Africa in exchange for slaves who were transported to the Americas and then returned to Europe with agricultural products, such as sugar and tobacco from the American colonies.[71]

The slaves came mainly from West Africa. Major points of embarkation were located in Dahomey, Benin, Sierra Leone, Angola, and Mozambique. These regions were occupied by the sort of despotic kingdoms described in Chapter 4 and contained sizable slave populations. It is reasonable to suppose that the first trade involved the exchange of many of these slaves for European goods, especially firearms. According to Toyan Falola, the region was undergoing a period of political consolidation involving wars conducted by large states to extend their authority and territory and not initially to capture slaves. However, given the voracious demand for slaves and the incentives for warring kingdoms to acquire firearms, slave-taking became, over time, a primary purpose of military campaigns. This is consistent with the fact that the Europeans never mounted slave-raiding campaigns but relied on the native kingdoms to bring slaves to the trading ports. The extent of the death and destruction of the wars and raids spurred by the slave trade is impossible to determine, but given the ferocity of primitive warfare it was in all likelihood very high.[72] How many slaves died in captivity while waiting to board ships is also unknown, but is also likely to have been substantial.

In addition to the mortality on the African Continent, the long voyage to the Americas (the Middle Passage) took an additional toll, with estimated mortality of 15%, considerably higher than the rate for European migrants, estimated at 10%. In addition, mortality after landing, estimated as high as 15%, most likely from diseases contracted on-board ship, was equally common for African slaves and European immigrants.[73]

By 1800, almost 1 million Africans were residing in the North American colonies, and the large majority was native-born. The demographic pattern in the Continental colonies was remarkably different from the Caribbean Islands, mainly due to the appalling death rates in the Caribbean and much higher fertility rates on the mainland. Part of this was the result of imbalanced sex ratios; male slaves far outnumbered females in the Caribbean. According to historian Robert Fogel, "if the United States had duplicated the demographic experience of the West Indies, its black population in 1800 would have been only 186,000" rather than the 1,000,000 that in fact it was.[74]

Immigration from 1820 to 1880

By the time of the signing of the Constitution, the population of the United States had grown to about 4 million people. The first census in 1790 gave a figure of 3,930,000 of whom 3,172,000 were Europeans and 757,000 were African Slaves.[75] Among the Europeans, 85% were

English-speaking people with ancestry in the British Isles. Most of the rest were German-speakers (8.6%), Dutch (3.1%) or French (2.3%).[76]

A good proportion of this growth in population was due to the high levels of fertility for all groups in American society. Among people of European descent, fertility was twice as high as in Europe. Individual women gave birth to far more children and those children survived in greater numbers. The explanation is found in the fact that owing to the availability of land, couples married at younger ages and women therefore had greater opportunities to give birth, especially during their earlier years when such births were likely to be healthy.[77] In addition, America's population was largely rural at the time and life outside cities was generally much less disease-ridden. As discussed earlier, the climate of the southern colonies was far more forgiving than that of England and Northern Europe. General prosperity and rich farmland allowed for better nutrition and the virtual elimination of the famines that continued to plague Europe.

TABLE 5.1. IMMIGRANTS AS A PROPORTION OF
TOTAL POPULATION

Decade	Immigrants	Population	% of Population
1820–1829	128,502	9,638,453	1.33%
1830–1839	538,381	12,866,020	4.18%
1840–1849	1,427,337	17,069,453	8.36%
1850–1859	2,814,554	23,191,876	12.14%
1860–1869	2,081,261	31,443,321	6.62%
1870–1879	2,742,137	39,818,449	6.89%
1880–1889	5,248,568	50,151,783	10.47%
1890–1899	3,694,294	62,947,714	5.87%
1900–1909	8,202,388	75,994,576	10.79%
1910–1919	6,347,380	91,972,266	6.90%
1920–1929	4,295,510	105,710,620	4.06%
1930–1939	699,375	122,775,046	0.57%
TOTAL	**38,219,687**	**643,579,577**	**5.94%**

The American Revolution itself, the Napoleonic Wars, and hostilities between Britain and the United States greatly curtailed immigration in the first decades of the country's independence. Official government statistics on immigration compiled from 1820 indicate that the pace of immigration remained relatively low in the 1820s and does not appear to have been much different from what it had been before the Revolution. In all, about 143,000 migrants arrived during the 1820s, with an annual average of about 10,000 in the beginning of the decade and rising to about 25,000 by the end. Table 5.1 below gives the immigration figures for the decades up to and immediately following the Immigration Act of 1924, after which immigration was drastically curtailed. A number of factors in the United States and Europe explain the fluctuations in these figures. The economic depression of the 1890s suppressed immigration, as did the outbreak of World War I in Europe in the period 1914–1918. Immigration during the 1920s would probably have surpassed the figure for the first decade of the twentieth century had it not been for the restrictions imposed by Congress in the early 1920s that culminated in the 1924 Immigration Act.

During the early years of the republic the population was growing very rapidly, trebling its population in the forty years from 1790 to 1830, and almost all of this growth was due to natural increase. In addition, during that time the Louisiana Purchase doubled the geographic size of the nation. Europe in this period was also witnessing spectacular population growth, producing growing shortages of land and inflated rents. These produced powerful economic push factors driving Europeans to look to migration for relief from what were becoming intolerable conditions. In addition, the lure of open land and high labor demand in the United States acted as powerful incentives that increasingly made the United States a particularly attractive destination for migrants. Finally, as transatlantic travel became more organized and somewhat safer, the means to immigrate grew better in each decade of the 19th century. By the 1870s steamships had all but replaced sailing vessels and that, in great measure, explains the dramatic upsurge from the 1880s onward. The last column in Table 5.1 gives the percentage of immigrants arriving in each decade in relation to the population at the beginning of that decade.

It is noteworthy that the extraordinary growth by natural increase of Americans meant that even with the massive number of immigrants, the percentage of new arrivals in each decade never climbed much above 10% of the existing population. Cumulatively the foreign born percentage of the population ranged around 13% to 14% during this period.[78]

Of course, the immigrants arriving in the United States, many of whom were young adults, experienced relatively high fertility rates similar to natives, so that when the children of the foreign-born are added to the above figures, the size of an immigrant community was much greater than these percentages suggest. This led many natives to fear that immigration threatened their way of life, and gave rise to the anti-immigration sentiment known pejoratively as *nativism,* particularly in the period prior to the Civil War and later in the first decades of the twentieth century. This sentiment was, to a significant extent, influenced by the size of the immigrant influx, by people's perception of the likely integration of immigrants, and by the economic and political conditions in the United States. The overwhelming majority of the immigrants in the second major wave of immigration from 1820 to 1880 came from Ireland, from what is now Germany, and to a lesser extent from the Scandinavian countries. What follows is an examination of the somewhat different patterns common among these groups.

Irish immigration during 19th century should be distinguished from the Scots-Irish immigration of the colonial era, because of the origins of the immigrants and their pattern of settlement in the United States. In the years leading up to the Civil War, the Irish made up approximately 35% of all immigrants to the United States. These people were almost exclusively Catholics and were "pushed" to migrate out of economic necessity. In the fifty years prior to 1840, the population of Ireland almost doubled, producing an extreme scarcity of land and high rents. At the same time, the United States was undergoing the beginning of industrialization and needed labor to build railroads, canals, and other types of infrastructure. The promise of jobs acted as the primary "pull" factor in this migration. In addition, transatlantic shipping from Irish ports to America, especially Canada, had grown rapidly and allowed for an uncomplicated and relatively inexpensive journey. The British at the time were developing a significant lumber industry in Canada, and provided incentives, in the way of greatly reduced fares, to encourage the migration of labor to Canada from the British Isles. Once in Canada, many of these migrants could easily travel to New England and many did so.[81] Also, at this time, the development of prepaid tickets made it easier for immigrants already in America to bring in relatives, which they did in large numbers. These factors tended to increase the migration of those who would have been too poor to do so in the first, colonial phase. However, in contrast to earlier waves of immigrants, very few in the 19th century came as indentured servants. The majority came as single individuals rather than as members of existing families.

Most who came were unskilled and tended to work as laborers, if male, and domestic servants, if female. As few had the resources to purchase land, most remained in urban locations where labor demand was high. They settled predominantly in New England, New York and New Jersey, and were heavily concentrated in Boston, New York, Hartford, Jersey City and Newark, to name but a few of the cities they inhabited.[82] While the migration out of Ireland in the early years of the 19th century was prompted by a search for economic opportunity, in the later period between 1845 and 1855, it was prompted by the starvation and desperation occasioned by the potato famine in Ireland during those years. The situation was so calamitous that Ireland lost about 3 million people in this period, half to deaths attributable to the effects of famine and half to emigration.[83] Table 5.2 below provides an account of immigration from Ireland in the 19th century, clearly showing the huge increase in the 1840s occasioned by the potato famine. This table also illustrates that, even after the famine years, Irish immigration was still quite substantial well into the 20th century, but represented a diminishing percentage of all immigrants.

There are a number of important features about the Irish immigrant community which are of note. First was the very high proportion of the immigrants who were classified as laborers and domestic servants. Sixty-three percent of the Irish immigrants were in these occupational categories in 1850, and 50% in 1880. This, of course, largely reflects their occupational experience in their home country. There was, however, considerable upward mobility across generations, with only about 10% of first generation Irish-Americans falling into the lowest occupational categories.[85] In general, that progress was somewhat limited by the Irish's failure to take advantage of schooling in America. Irish children attended public and private schools in about equal numbers, but fewer than 1% graduated from high school in the first decade of the twentieth century.[86] A second feature of the Irish community was their considerable strength in city politics, no doubt owing to their high early concentration relative to other groups in rapidly expanding urban centers. This in turn explains their high representation in civil service occupations such as policemen, firemen, and public schoolteachers. These occupations were an important and relatively secure entrance to middle-class life and respectability.

TABLE 5.2. IRISH IMMIGRATION IN THE 19ᵀᴴ AND 20ᵀᴴ CENTURIES

Decade	Irish Immigrants[84]	All Immigrants	% Irish
1820–1829	51,617	128,502	40.17%
1830–1839	170,672	538,381	31.70%
1840–1849	656,145	1,427,337	45.97%
1850–1859	1,029,486	2,814,554	36.58%
1860–1869	427,419	2,081,261	20.54%
1870–1879	422,264	2,742,137	15.40%
1880–1889	674,061	5,248,568	12.84%
1890–1899	405,710	3,694,294	10.98%
1900–1909	344,940	8,202,388	4.21%
1910–1919	166,445	6,347,380	2.62%
1920–1929	202,854	4,295,510	4.72%
1930–1939	28,195	699,375	4.03%
Total	4,579,808	38,219,687	11.98%

A third important feature of the Irish immigrant experience was the very high percentage of young single people in the 14 to 25 year age bracket, especially those who came in the second half of the 19th century. This age category rose from about 45% in the 1850s and 1860s to more than 60% by the end of the 19th century and into the 20th century.[87] No other important immigrant group exhibited such a large age imbalance. This produced the sort of "youth bulge" discussed earlier, and probably explains, almost in its entirety, the reputation of the Irish for pugnacity, insobriety, and general rowdiness. They were displaying the near universal pattern of behavior common to young men with insufficient adult male supervision. This youth bulge also contributed to rising crime rates in urban centers, a major factor in the tensions between native-born groups, who tended to live in rural areas or small towns and cities, and the mass of new Irish immigrants who tended to reside in the large cities.

German-speaking people made up the largest ethnic group to migrate to the United States during the 19th century. During that century, almost 5 million Germans came to America, outnumbering the approximately 3.8 million Irish who did so. Unlike the earlier German-speakers from the Rhineland, these immigrants came from almost all areas of Germany. They are particularly interesting in that they represented the largest group of people who spoke a language other than English, and their assimilation into the English-speaking culture of the United States may prove instructive in understanding later immigrant patterns involving non-English speakers. As can be seen in Table 5.3, they came in substantial numbers throughout the 19th and early 20th century, but represented a declining percentage of all immigrants by the end of this period.

TABLE 5.3. GERMAN IMMIGRATION
IN THE 19TH AND 20TH CENTURIES

Decade	German Immigrants[89]	All Immigrants	% German
1820–1829	5,753	128,502	4.48%
1830–1839	124,726	538,381	23.17%
1840–1849	385,434	1,427,337	27.00%
1850–1859	976,072	2,814,554	34.68%
1860–1869	723,734	2,081,261	34.77%
1870–1879	751,769	2,742,137	27.42%
1880–1889	1,445,181	5,248,568	27.53%
1890–1899	579,072	3,694,294	15.67%
1900–1909	328,722	8,202,388	4.01%
1910–1919	174,227	6,347,380	2.74%
1920–1929	386,634	4,295,510	9.00%
1930–1939	110,107	699,375	17.03%
Total	6,000,431	38,219,687	15.70%

Unlike the earlier German migrants before the Revolutionary War, many of whom migrated to a variety of other countries, the bulk of all German emigrants came to the United States, no doubt owing, in large part, to improved transatlantic travel. As with the Irish, population pressure was the primary push factor, though the Germans did not suffer the catastrophic agricultural failures that drove the Irish, and a substantial proportion came as intact families. They tended to settle in the Midwest, in the "German triangle" formed by the cities of Saint Louis, Cincinnati, and Milwaukee. In contrast to the Irish, many (about 25%) turned to farming, while a significant number (37%) worked at skilled trades, with a minority working as common laborers.[88] Because of their concentration in the Midwest and their tendency to remain in place, they often were the dominant group in many small towns and cities and were able to persist in the traditional ways of the culture they left behind. This was of particular importance with respect to language. Two-thirds of 19th century German immigrants were Protestant, and a third were Catholic. A good many of the churches, both Catholic and Protestant, conducted their services in German.[90] In addition, German instruction in public schools was quite common throughout the 19th century wherever the German population was large. In many private and church schools, no English was even taught. According to historian Roger Daniels, there were "hundreds of thousands of students in German-language parochial schools before" World War I. Toward the end of the 19th century many states became alarmed by this development and began to require public school instruction in English. The antagonism toward the use of German became near universal during World War I. By the 1920s, German instruction had been almost eliminated in parochial schools and was completely eliminated in public schools.[91] It is not clear what the consequences would have been had this movement against German-speaking not materialized, or if America had avoided involvement in the European war.

Among those immigrants identified as Germans, it is estimated that about 5%, or some 250,000, were Jews. They differed considerably from other Germans, not only in religion, but in occupation and areas of settlement. Almost none went into farming and few, with the exception of tailors, were skilled artisans. Many worked as itinerant peddlers who over time became small shopkeepers. A few became major merchants and were the founders of many important department store chains. Though very few were engaged in major banking and other financial ventures, they tended to have had high visibility in these roles. In general, the German Jews were quite successful. According to Daniels, "more of the first generation entered into business or other middle-class occupations than any other nineteenth-century immigrant group."[92] About a fourth of the German Jews settled in New York City, but they had a substantial presence in most East Coast and Midwest cities. In general, they spread out into the country wherever retail opportunities presented themselves in rapidly expanding population centers, selling manufactured goods and provisions of all sorts. The relative success of the German Jews and the lack of religious persecution they experienced played an important role in making the United States the most attractive destination for the millions of Jewish migrants who left Eastern Europe after the 1880s.[93]

The third major groups of immigrants to arrive in the years prior to the 1880s were those with origins in the Scandinavian countries. The majority came from Sweden, but sizable numbers came from Norway and Denmark. They numbered about 2.15 million people, less than half the number of those who came from either Ireland or Germany. They were overwhelmingly Protestant and tended to settle in the Middle West and the Great Plains, moving to the edge of the expanding settled territory of the United States. As Table 5.4 illustrates, the vast majority arrived after the Civil War.

As with most other groups during this period, population pressure, and the poverty often accompanying it, served as the impetus to migration. Those who emigrated did so almost exclusively to the United States. At first, most were rural people looking to establish farms in America, and, they settled in the Midwest where land was plentiful. Swedes were concentrated in Minnesota and Illinois, while Norwegians were concentrated in North Dakota, Wisconsin, and Minnesota. As the century wore on, more and more of the immigrants came as tradesmen and laborers from urban areas. Many settled in cities, with Chicago being home to a large number of Swedes. Similarly a large contingent of Norwegians settled in Brooklyn, New York. It should be realized that population growth in Europe impelled a mass exodus from rural areas. Many rural people migrated to America, but many moved to cities in their native countries.

Scandinavia had not yet experienced the full impact of industrialization common in, for instance, England, and employment opportunities in Scandinavian cities were limited. Many of these new urban dwellers were therefore drawn to America, especially as they became aware of the opportunities across the sea by reports from countrymen who had immigrated earlier.[94] As was the case with the Germans, these people came speaking languages other than English. Those who came from Sweden made up a majority of Scandinavian immigrants who came mostly in intact families, many in organized groups. They came for economic reasons, but also to escape the stifling influence of the Swedish Lutheran Church. More than a third settled in the two states of Minnesota and Illinois and most of these took up farming. However, a large number settled as laborers (the men) and domestic servants (the women) in towns. In Chicago in 1900 about 9% of the population were Swedes, and Swedish was commonly spoken and facilitated a thriving Swedish press. However, the Swedes were simply too few in numbers and too dispersed geographically to maintain their linguistic traditions along generational lines, as was possible for many German communities.[96]

TABLE 5.4. SCANDINAVIAN IMMIGRATION
IN THE 19TH AND 20 CENTURIES

Decade	Scandinavian Immigrants[95]	All Immigrants	% Scandinavian
1820–1829	264	128,502	0.21%
1830–1839	2,076	538,381	0.39%
1840–1849	13,060	1,4727,337	0.91%
1850–1859	25,429	2,814,554	0.90%
1860–1869	96,490	2,081,261	4.64%
1870–1879	208,101	2,742,137	7.59%
1880–1889	671,783	5,248,568	12.80%
1890–1899	390,729	3,694,294	10.58%
1900–1909	488,208	8,202,388	5.96%
1910–1919	238,275	6,347,380	3.75%
1920–1929	204,735	4,295,510	4.77%
1930–1939	16,922	699,375	2.42%
Total	2,356,072	38,219,687	6.16%

The Norwegians, more than other Scandinavians, tended to settle in enclaves among other Norwegians, and many tried to preserve their traditions and language. Their arrival late in the century, when states had already made English the official language of public schools, however, made it difficult for them to promote their native language among their offspring. Given their relatively small numbers in the United States, that would have been difficult in any case, and there appears to have been no concerted effort by them to oppose the linguistic policies of the public schools.[97]

Danish immigrants made up about 15% of Scandinavian migrants and numbered in total some 300,000 people. Due to their relatively small number, and the fact that they dispersed widely in their habitat, the Danes did not, in general, form ethnic communities. As a consequence they tended to assimilate fairly rapidly, which is evidenced by their fairly high rate of marriage outside their own group.[98]

The Social Impact of Antebellum Immigration:
Nativism and the Civil War

As Table 5.1 illustrates, rates of immigration remained low until the 1830s, after which they grew to vary large numbers throughout the rest of the century. Its impact was greatest, however, in the years leading up to the Civil War. It was not until the first decade of the twentieth century that immigration would involve numbers so large in proportion to the native population. It is hardly surprising that in both eras it gave rise to profound anti-immigration sentiment.

During the antebellum period, the United States was experiencing explosive economic growth, which was part cause and part effect of the mass migration to the United States. The Northern states, to a much greater degree than the Southern states, were rapidly becoming industrialized and urbanized. For instance, New York and Philadelphia had approximately 100,000 inhabitants in 1820. By 1860 Philadelphia had grown to 500,000 and New York to almost a million, and both had become major centers of trade and manufacture. A good deal of the growth of these cities resulted from Irish and, to a lesser extent, German immigration. No such urban growth or industrialization occurred in the South, which remained largely rural and agricultural.[99]

The massive immigration, as discussed earlier, was encouraged by the shipping industries, which could profitably fill their boats with immigrants going to America, and then make the return voyage with the American products in demand in Europe. Mass immigration was also encouraged by industrial interests, backed by state governments engaged in massive infrastructure projects, such as the building of railroads and canals, and the building of factories and housing occasioned by the economic boom in the North. At the time, all such projects required the infusion of massive amounts of human labor, which mass immigration provided and provided at an increasingly lower cost. Midwest farmers also benefited from the rapid population growth which fueled demand for their goods and which, owing to the newly built canals and railroads, they could easily ship east to satisfy the demand.[100]

Early in this period, native laborers and craftsmen benefited from the surge in the demand for their services. However, as the cities filled with ever more immigrants seeking work, native laborers and craftsmen began to suffer declining living standards and reduced economic security. Immigrants were willing to work for lower wages since, if they were single, as they often were, they needed less. Even if they had families, the lower wages they demanded could provide for far better living standards, in comparison, than was the norm in their native lands. This was especially true for those who had come from rural backgrounds, as did most of those from Ireland, but it was also true for the Germans who often came as skilled tradesmen. Robert Fogel points out that by 1860, 69% of the labor force of New York City was foreign-born. In addition to the glut of labor which drove down wages, the rise of manufactured goods produced in new factories also put downward pressure on the income of skilled craftsmen producing competing goods in small workshops. It was during this period of phenomenal economic growth that, according to Fogel, "native-born mechanics and tradesmen suffered one of most severe economic disasters in American history, rivaling, if not exceeding, the economic blow suffered by urban labor during the Great Depression of the 1930s."[101]

This economic catastrophe for native workers was compounded by a "wave of devastating epidemics" brought mainly from Europe by immigrants. Fogel argues that in the period shortly after independence, the Northern cities of the United States had become the healthiest in the world. The very high fertility of American women in that period is merely one example of this phenomenon. By that time, many of the diseases that had plagued earlier settlers, such as diphtheria and smallpox, had declined radically. According to Fogel, "Such other diseases as cholera, tuberculosis, dysentery, and typhoid...were still unknown in America, or had not yet reached alarming proportions."[102] By the 1850s, however, these diseases had become widespread in crowded Northern cities and made those cities as deadly as European cities were at the time. This is reflected, according to Fogel, in the fact that life expectancy in 1860 had dropped by ten years compared to what it had been at the beginning of the century.[103] Needless to say, the loss of an adult in a young family, common enough in these years, was not only emotionally traumatic, but economically devastating at a time when there was no government support to help those in depressed circumstances.

The labor glut in large cities prior to the Civil War was exacerbated by a rise in free black labor which began to compete with immigrant laborers. Blacks represented a third labor pool which further undercut wages, since blacks were willing to work for less than new immigrants. The resentment and animosity toward blacks came to a head during the Civil War, although these had been growing before the war. During the numerous strikes which plagued New York City during the war, blacks were often recruited to replace striking white workers, which added greatly to the tensions in the already overcrowded, crime- and disease-ridden city and fueled the resentment of those living in what can only be described as squalid conditions.[104] The extent of these tensions led directly to the New York Draft Riots in July of 1863, in the days immediately following the Battle of Gettysburg, and seven months after Lincoln signed the Emancipation Proclamation.

The immediate cause of the riots was the imposition of a draft lottery for the Union Army. This incensed the Irish immigrants on two grounds. The first was a condition that the draft could be avoided by the payment of a $300 fee. Since few immigrants could possibly afford this amount, the draft was seen as a direct assault on the city's poor, especially the Irish poor. Secondly, the Emancipation Proclamation changed the official goal of the war, which had been to preserve the Union, to now include the freeing of the slaves, and this was a goal most New Yorkers and especially the Irish did not support.[105] Two days after the beginning of the lottery, riots broke out and lasted for four days, before being brought to an end by an emergency dispatch of Union troops fresh from the Gettysburg killing grounds. The rioters, mainly Irish, but including German immigrants, attacked all those in positions of authority including the police and ransacked and burned symbols of established, usually Republican, power. As such it was clearly a civil insurrection, and was so seen at the time. In addition, it specifically targeted blacks, who were seen as economically threatening and who were also blamed, along with the Republicans, for the miseries of the war.[106] It is unknown how many people were killed. The police gave a number of more than a thousand people, but Edward Spahn estimates that the "likely figure is between 120 and 150."[107]

The rising tensions produced by mass immigration and the economic distress it brought to the urban poor led to a variety of social movements in response. Labor unrest often resulted in strikes in an attempt to attenuate the effects of the labor glut. A land reform movement flourished, promoting the idea of providing free land in the new territories to all who would settle there, in the hope that such frontier settlement might act as a safety valve for distressed urban dwellers. At the same time, government lands were auctioned off to the highest bidders and served as a primary source of federal revenue. Amid all this workers turned to the major political parties, the Whigs and the Democrats, for some sort of relief. The abject failure of either party to provide such relief, or to even take the concerns of urban workers seriously, led to a large-scale defection from the traditional parties and to the formation of new political organizations more responsive to urban needs.[108]

The most successful were local parties, often called American or *Know-Nothing* parties, which were united in a strong anti-immigrant and anti-Catholic posture. Their anti-immigrant bias needs no explaining, while their anti-Catholicism had three sources. Most obviously, is the fact that the Irish were Catholic and were the main economic competitors for native-born workers. As important perhaps, was that Catholic-Protestant enmity that was an endemic feature of European social life did not automatically disappear when Europeans crossed the Atlantic. A third source of tension centered on the issue of education. Protestants were in favor of the establishment of state-funded public schools, whereas Catholics wanted state funds for parochial schools.[109]

The derogatory term Know-Nothings, attached to the American Party, derived from the fact that the party had its origins in ethnic, religious, or trade groups who formed benevolent associations for purposes of social insurance, such as helping to support widows and orphans. They were, in effect, nascent labor unions which were unlawful at the time. Members of such groups were instructed to say that they knew nothing of the policies of those organizations, if asked. According to Fogel, such secrecy was necessary "in an era of anticonspiracy statutes, which made it a crime for workers to combine for the purpose of compelling employers to raise wages or institute any other reform."[110]

By the 1850s the Know-Nothings and the American Party had coalesced into a formidable political force and won major elections in numerous Northern cities. At its height in the mid-1850s, the American Party had five members in the Senate and 43 Congressmen in the 34th Congress (1855-1857), though it disappeared from the scene during the Civil War.[111] These successes crippled the Democratic and Whig parties in the North and led to the dissolution of the two-party system which had dominated American politics for most of the early 19th century. The major significance of this, in hindsight, was that it opened the way for the antislavery movement to achieve political power in the name of the Republican Party. Prior to the 1850s, antislavery forces had only limited success politically against the entrenched forces of the Whig and Democratic parties. These parties were truly national parties, with major constituencies in the North and South, but could only remain so by downplaying regional differences, and most glaringly by turning a blind eye to the slave system of the South and accepting it as an enduring feature of American life. The willingness of both parties to accommodate the slave system came to a head in the Kansas-Nebraska Act, which allowed for slavery if the inhabitants of those states voted in favor of it. This repealed the "Missouri Compromise," which defined Kansas and Nebraska as Northern and banned slavery outright in them. As Senator Salmon Chase of Ohio put it, this act was "an atrocious plot to exclude from a vast unoccupied region immigrants from the Old World and free laborers from our own states."[112] This sentiment took hold among distressed Northern workers who feared that their option of employment by moving west would be foreclosed by competition from slave labor in those new territories should slavery be approved by the inhabitants. It should be clear that the anger over the Kansas-Nebraska act was not motivated by pro-black or antislavery sentiment, but rather by economic concerns. This was to become obvious during the New York Draft Riots discussed above. Nevertheless, by highlighting the economic threat to northern workers, the abolitionists in the Republican party were able to redirect the anger of urban laborers from immigrants to the "Slave Power" of the South and clearly led to the identification of the Republicans with the antislavery movement. Their success in this endeavor is evidenced by the election of the Republican Abraham Lincoln as President in 1860.

While the election of a Republican President was the immediate cause of the secession of a number of states of the Deep South, Lincoln's election alone would not necessarily have led to the Civil War. Lincoln had, after all, won the election with only 40% of the popular vote in a four-way race. Furthermore, the Republican Platform of 1860 explicitly acknowledged "the right of each state to order and control its own domestic institutions according to its own judgment exclusively." However, in its third plank it quite vigorously denied the right of any state to secede, calling such an action treasonable and stated that "it is the imperative duty of an indignant people sternly to rebuke and forever silence" such claims to secession.[113] When the South Carolinians fired on Fort Sumter, they made, to say the least, a miscalculation of enormous and tragic proportions. That miscalculation stemmed in part from their not taking seriously the Republican threat to use force to prevent secession.

This miscalculation can be partially attributed to their failure to realize how far the North and South had drifted apart economically and demographically since the 1820s. In those years, as discussed earlier, the North had become increasingly industrialized and urbanized. For instance, the North in 1860 had 10 times the factory production capacity as the South.[114] In addition, while about 25% of the North's population was urban in 1860, that figure was only 7% for the South. The North had also grown in size relative to the South. For instance, in 1830, before the advent of mass immigration, the South had a total population of 4.4 million, of whom 2.75 million were free whites, whereas the North had a population of 8.45 million, virtually all of whom were free whites. The population of the North was twice the size of the South, but the white population of the North was approximately 3 times that of the South. By 1860, largely owing to immigration, that ratio had risen to 4 to 1. The North's population had grown in those thirty years to more than 22 million, while the white population of the South had grown to only 5.5 million.[115] As a consequence of these population disparities the North was able to field an army of some 1,600,000 to the South's 750,000, and was able to sustain casualties of 642,000 compared the South's 450,000.[116] Given the differences that had existed in 1830, an invasion of the South, even with the North's larger economic and demographic base, would have been a risky undertaking with no assurance of success. Without the gross economic and population disparities that had grown up by 1860, it is doubtful that any president, no matter how committed to preserving the Union, would have contemplated war, and it is even more unlikely that he could have gained support for it from his constituents in the North.

In summary, the massive immigration of the antebellum years led to a dramatic decline in the economic and physical wellbeing of urban Northerners. This led, in turn, to deep frustration with, and eventual dissolution of, the existing national two-party system and its replacement by regional parties. The Republicans became the antislavery party of the North; the Democrats became the proslavery party of the South. In addition, to the extent that immigration contributed to the growing population gap between North and South it had, to an unknowable degree, strengthened the hands of those prepared to prevent secession by violent means. An important contention of this book is that large-scale immigration is bound to have consequences for a nation, not all of which are easily foreseeable. It is doubtful that even the most thoughtful observers in the 1830s and 1840s could have foreseen the chain of events which led up to, and made possible, the enormous tragedy that unfolded in the 1860s. Scholars have debated and will continue to debate whether the moral quagmire that was slavery could have been resolved peacefully.[117] It is also debatable whether the politicians and the powerful interests of the time could have, or would have, taken actions to alter the pace of immigration and thereby mitigate its more damaging effects. There can be little doubt, however, that the mass migrations from Europe played a role, perhaps a decisive role, in what was the most important and the most traumatic event in American history.

Immigration in the Period 1880–1924

During the Civil War and the Reconstruction era, patterns of immigration remained relatively unchanged, with large numbers of Irish, Germans and Scandinavians arriving in each decade of the 1860s and 1870s. In the 1880s, however, immigration grew dramatically, almost doubling to 5.2 million people in the 1880s compared to the 2.8 million who came in the 1870s. Much of this rise in immigration was seen as necessary to replenish the labor force diminished by the Civil War, and was particularly supported by the dominant Republican Party. Immigration fell back to 3.7 million in the 1890s, due to a severe economic depression in the United States, but grew to 8.8 million in the first decade of the 20th century. Immigration was somewhat curtailed in the second decade of the 20th century due to the War in Europe, though it still reached a figure of 5.7 million. In the 1920s, about 1 million came during each year until it was sharply curtailed by the Immigration Act of 1924.

One major exception in the aftermath of the Civil War was the coming of significant numbers of Asians, particularly Chinese contract laborers, who were recruited in large numbers to perform construction on the railroads and to work in the development of the west facilitated by those railroads. In general, the Republican Party championed open immigration, including Asian immigration, to support the growth of Northern industrialization and the prospects of expanded international trade. Of particular note were the negotiations with China leading to the Burlingame Treaty of 1868, which established formal trade and the free movement of Chinese into the United States.[118] Chinese immigration was strongly, often violently opposed by labor groups who saw them as undercutting native workers. In the West, where most Chinese were located, the issue became heated and the Democratic party in Western States grew in power by adopting an extremely hostile rhetoric and efforts to discourage Asian Immigration. Nevertheless, early in this period the national government, controlled by Republicans, resisted these exclusionary elements and in the decade of the 1870s, about 125,000 Chinese arrived and represented 4.4% of all immigrants.[119] By the late 1870s, popular discontent in the West forced the Republicans to reverse course and end almost all Chinese immigration in the Chinese Exclusion Act of 1882.[120]

Not only were the numbers much greater in these decades, but the countries of origin were different in the 4½ decades from 1881– 1924. Table 5.5 illustrates the changes. Prior to the 1880s, virtually all immigrants came from the English Islands, Germany, and Scandinavia, and the great majority were native English speakers. A large number came from Canada, most of whom were English speakers, though a substantial minority were French speaking. Germans continued to migrate in great numbers throughout this period, as they had throughout most of the 19th century, though their numbers dropped off significantly after 1890.

The most dramatic change was the very large number of immigrants from countries that heretofore had provided few if any immigrants to the United States. In the peak decade of 1901–1910, out of almost 9 million, more than two-thirds came from Eastern and Southern Europe. In the decade 1911-1920 they represented more than half of all immigrants, which is somewhat surprising given that the Eastern Europe was racked by war and related turmoil which made overland travel extremely difficult. Adding to the difficulty were naval blockades and submarine attacks on shipping, sometimes indiscriminate, which made sea travel dangerous.

The Italians made up the largest group of these immigrants, who numbered more than 4½ million. The figures in Table 5.5 for Italians are probably accurate, as most sailed from Italian ports and readily identified themselves as Italians. The immigration pool from Eastern Europe is not so easy to determine, because official statistics recorded the country of origin of immigrants and not their nationality, ethnicity, or religion. Before World War I, Eastern Europe was dominated by the Russian Empire, the Austro-Hungarian Empire, and Germany, all of which subsumed under their sovereignty a multitude of ethnicities and nationalities. The best estimates of ethnic background can be obtained from data collected on the mother tongue reported by immigrants. There was, for instance, no sovereign nation of Poland during this period; immigrants who reported Polish as their mother tongue in 1910 were listed as coming from Russia (418,370), Austria (329,000), or Germany (190,000). In all, some 943,781 people told immigration authorities that their mother tongue was Polish in the enumeration of 1910.[121]

Similarly, Jews who gave Yiddish or Hebrew as their mother tongue came largely from Russia, but also from Austria-Hungary, and in smaller numbers from many other countries such as Romania. In all, some 990,587 people gave Yiddish or Hebrew as their mother tongue in 1910.[122] Since immigration from Eastern Europe continued after 1910, though at a reduced pace, it is reasonable to estimate that the Poles and the Jews each contributed at least 1½ million immigrants to the United States in the period under discussion. Daniels gives a figure of 1.8 million for the Jews. Among the three largest of the new immigrant groups, however, the Jews had a very low rate of remigration back to their country of origin, probably in the range of 5%. In contrast, about a third of the Polish and almost one half of the Italian immigrants returned home. For that reason the Jews were not far behind the Italians in terms of their presence in the American landscape, and certainly outnumbered the Poles.[123] The Jews also differed in that the number of female immigrants, estimated at 45%, was much higher than for other groups, and this of course contributed to a relatively high fertility rate which swelled the ranks of first generation Jewish-Americans.[124] In addition, large numbers of other ethnic and national groups, such as the Greeks, Hungarians, and Slovaks participated in this mass movement of people, though their numbers are relatively small compared to the larger groups and many had very high rates of return migration.

The numbers from Asia are somewhat confusing in that in the decades 1901–1920, more than half of the immigrants classified as coming from Asia were from Turkey, since at the time Middle-East countries were categorized as Asian. About 300,000 people originating in Turkey arrived in those two decades, of whom an estimated two-thirds were ethnic Greeks who had been living under Turkish rule.[125] The others listed as coming from Asia were mostly from Japan, with very few coming from China. The numbers for Canada and Mexico continued to increase in the 1920s, since the Immigration Act of 1924 placed no restriction on immigration from the Americas.

The great majority of Jewish immigrants settled in the large cities of the Northeast and the upper Midwest. Many of the Jews came from the impoverished Jewish enclaves or "shtetles" of Eastern Europe. The situation of the Jews in Eastern Europe was the result of very high fertility rates, severe restrictions on where they could live and restrictions on the occupations open to them, especially in the oppressive regime of the Russian Tsar. As a consequence, most of the shtetle Jews did their best to eke out an existence as peddlers and petty shopkeepers catering to their even poorer Christian neighbors. A good

TABLE 5.5. MAJOR CONTRIBUTING COUNTRIES TO U. S. IMMIGRATION 1870–1930 (THOUSANDS)[126]

Region or country of last residence	1870–1879	1880–1889	1890–1899	1900–1909	1910–1919	1920–1929	Total
Italy	46,296	267,660	603,761	1,930,475	1,229,916	528,133	4,606,241
Austria-Hungary	60,127	314,787	534,059	2,001,376	1,154,727	60,891	4,125,967
Germany	751,769	1,445,181	579,072	328,722	174,227	386,634	3,665,605
Russia	35,177	82,698	450,101	1,501,301	1,106,998	61,604	3,337,879
United Kingdom	578,447	810,900	328,759	469,518	371,878	341,552	2,901,054
Canada	324,310	492,865	3,098	123,067	708,715	949,286	2,601,341
Ireland	422,264	674,061	405,710	344,940	166,445	202,854	2,216,274
Norway-Sweden	178,823	586,441	334,058	426,981	192,445	170,329	1,889,077
Asia	134,128	71,151	61,285	299,836	269,736	126,740	962,876
Mexico	5,133	2,405	734	31,188	185,334	498,945	723,739
Greece	209	1,807	12,732	145,402	198,108	60,774	419,032

number were involved in mining. Very few, almost none, worked as farmers. Those who lived in larger cities were involved in commerce and manufacturing. About half worked in clothing manufacture. Few of these Jews had professional training or training in trades outside of clothing production. In that regard they were quite different from the Jews living in Western Europe, many of whom were educated in skilled trades and professions. Nevertheless, about two-thirds of the men were literate, and about one-third of the women were as well.[127]

A great many of these Jewish immigrants to America, men and women alike, found work in the garment trade that, early in the 20th century, was becoming dominated by Jewish owned factories or "sweatshops." Many, in addition, became petty shopkeepers selling everything from groceries to umbrellas. The Jews distinguished themselves by their enthusiastic embrace of public education, due in part to their tradition of religious scholarship. The interest with education was also driven by a concern that their children learn English and make a rapid adjustment to America. Since very few Jews returned to Europe, most assumed America would be their permanent homeland.

The Jews' focus on education was strengthened by the fact that they had been preceded by the substantial number of German Jews already established in many cities, particularly New York. Many of these Jews, some well-off, provided resources and guidance to their coreligionists, at least in part, because they feared that the idiosyncrasies of the new immigrants might trigger an anti-Semitic backlash. For a variety of reasons, not least of which was undoubtedly their native intelligence, Jewish children succeeded in school, often spectacularly so. By the time these children reached college age in substantial numbers during the second decade of the 20th century, their scholastic prowess was becoming well known and in some circles resented. By the early 1920s many colleges and professional schools started putting Jewish quotas in place out of fear that without such limits the educational elite in the country would become overly Jewish in makeup.[128] They were, of course, correct in their assessment. When the quotas came down after World War II, the rise of the Jews in the academy and in the medical and legal professions was little short of astounding.

Before the 1880s, few Italians migrated to America, and of those who did, significant numbers came from northern Italy. Beginning in the 1880s, that changed and the vast majority came from southern Italy. The difference is important. Northern Italy was far more advanced economically than the south. Northern Italians tended to be better educated, to have more people with advanced skills and professions, and were more likely to have been landowners and entrepreneurs. According to Daniels, most of the Italians who immigrated during this early period "were artisans, merchants, businessmen, professional people, musicians, actors, waiters and seaman." They were also dispersed throughout the country with almost half of them living in the South. A good many went into agriculture in California and played an important part in the development of the wine industry in that state. [129]

Few of the southern Italians were educated or had advanced training. Part of this was due to the extreme poverty and economic backwardness of the south, but as Thomas Sowell explained, it also reflected a resistance, almost hostility, toward formal education. The southern Italians were a subject peasantry with an intense allegiance to family and local community. The region's tight class structure and its dire economic conditions provided little incentive to educate children who at a young age were needed to help provide for their families. In addition, the public schools were seen as intrusive elements of the state (and of Northerners) in their traditional patterns of living. The illiteracy rate in southern Italy was 70% in 1900, much higher than in northern Italy, and more than "ten times higher than in England, France and Germany at the same time." [130] The intense concern with family, coupled with extreme poverty, was reflected in a preoccupation with the virtue of female offspring. According to Sowell, "the illegitimacy rate in the region around Naples was about one-fifth what it was in the region around Rome." [131]

These social patterns persisted in America for some time after the Italians came to these shores. In particular, their children, who mainly attended public rather than Catholic schools, tended to leave school as soon as the law allowed. In the first decade of the 20th Century about 15% of Russian Jews and Germans graduated from high school in New York City but hardly any Italians did. Even as late as 1931, while 42% of all students in New York City graduated from high school, the figure for Italians was only 11%. This pattern was thought at the time, by many, to be indicative of lower intellectual ability. However, as measured since the 1950s, Italian IQ has been at parity with the national average. [132]

Given their background, Italian immigrants tended to gravitate to the lowest economic strata, largely doing the kind of work done by the Irish immigrants in earlier decades. They performed manual labor in construction, but also were employed as seasonal farm workers.

Much of this work was done under contract with *padrones* who arranged for their employment and often their transportation and housing. Most settled in the port cities of the East Coast, with a large contingent in Chicago. A majority of the immigrants were men, many of whom intended to, and did, return to Italy once they had accumulated sufficient capital to travel home and acquire farms and businesses in Italy.[133] In this regard they were similar to the Central Americans today who come, often illegally, with the intention of returning to their home villages with funds earned in American jobs.

The third large group of immigrants who came during this period identified themselves as Polish. Unlike the Italians or the Jews, Poles had a strong sense of nationality, even though their native Poland at the time had been partitioned and divided among Germany, Russia, and Austria-Hungary. Most were Catholic with a powerful commitment to their Church. About two-thirds of Polish children attended Catholic Schools. About one-third of Polish immigrants returned to Poland. Of those who stayed, many gravitated to areas near the Great Lakes and went into farming, though most settled in the industrializing cities of the Midwest. In 1920, 400,000 Poles were residing in Chicago and at least 100,000 in Pittsburgh, Buffalo, Milwaukee, and Detroit. In addition, a large number stayed in New York, which counted 200,000 Poles in 1920.[134]

Population growth in Poland, as in much of Europe, made land ownership prohibitively expensive and prompted emigration. The Poles were forced to seek work as laborers in the nascent industrial economies developing in Eastern Europe, and many migrated to the more advanced industrial societies of Western Europe and the United States. Many were employed in mining and related industries such as iron production. In the United States, they readily moved into mining, steel production, and the factory jobs in the fast growing industries in Midwestern cities where they settled. A good many took up work in the automobile plants that sprung up in the Detroit area. Being early entrants in many of these industries, they were able to move up the ladder, as it were, even without the benefit of the labor unions, which were not organized in these industries until the 1930s.

Social Consequences of the Mass Immigration of 1880–1924

From the end of the Civil War, the United States, especially in the North, was undergoing enormous industrial growth, with the Northeast having probably the most dynamic economy in the World by the end of the 19th century. World War I hastened the rise of the United States to the status as the world's preeminent industrial nation. During the initial phase of this expansion, prosperity was experienced in almost all sectors of the economy. According to Frederick Lewis Allen, wages in 22 industries had increased by 68% between 1860 and 1891 while wholesale prices had declined by 5%.[135] Huge fortunes were made in the railroad and steel industries and productivity soared as these industries were consolidated into huge combinations or trusts. Even with large-scale immigration, the expansion in these and other industries provided work for a wide range of workers. In the 1870s and 1880s, as discussed earlier, a large number of immigrants came as farmers who settled farms in the Midwest and benefited from growing markets for their produce.

During this time, the country had been transformed from a largely rural agricultural society to an urban industrial colossus. The large cities and smaller industrial towns were filled with people leaving rural areas and especially with immigrants from Europe. One could make a case that the great increases in productivity resulted not only from spectacular technical advances but also from the large supply of cheap immigrant labor that fueled this industrial growth. According to sociologist Nathan Glazer, the great majority of laborers during this period were immigrants. "The working force in the steel mills, the coal mines, the textile factories, the clothing shops, were overwhelmingly foreign-born…" Glazer cites government statistics showing that "in 21 branches of industry" about 75% were foreign-born or the children of the foreign-born.[136]

This economic progress was temporarily halted by a severe depression beginning in 1893 and lasting throughout most of the decade. According to George Mowry, the result was "thousands of business bankruptcies and millions of hungry and angry unemployed men walking the city streets." However, general prosperity resumed in 1898 and "industrial production increased steadily…farm prices rose and unemployment sank to more normal levels."[137] But the continuing prosperity did not trickle down to the urban working classes whose wages stagnated, at least initially. According to Mowry, "in only three years, from 1900 to 1912...was the average real wage above the 1890-99 average. During the other nine years, it was lower."[138] It should be stressed that during this decade, as was the case until the 1930s, unemployment was quite low by today's standards. Between 1900 and 1909 the unemployment rate was fewer than 4.5%, and this figure was inflated by a short-lived recession in 1908 in which unemployment shot up to 8%.[139] In fact, the average unemployment rate "was only 4.67% for the thirty years 1900 through 1929."[140]

The first three decades of the twentieth century witnessed extraordinary growth in industrial output, productivity, and rising living standards. The automobile industry, especially after the innovations introduced by Henry Ford, was probably the most spectacular example of this growth. The number of cars produced rose from about 18,000 in 1900 to 1.25 million in 1920–21. By 1930 more than 26 million cars were registered in the United States.[141] In effect there was about one car for every five inhabitants of the country, which meant that the typical family owned a car, whose real costs had fallen dramatically over the years. A related phenomenon was the growth in the production of farm tractors, which grew from 4,000 in 1910 to 200,000 by 1920.[142] The result was that American farming was transformed overnight, becoming the most productive in the world, raising farm earnings and lowering food costs. The phenomenal growth in industrial productivity was in large measure accelerated by the growth of electric power. The use of electric power in industry was only 2% in 1889, but that percentage grew to 31% in 1919.[143] And, of course, electricity became the primary source of most energy used in factories in subsequent years.

After the first decade of the 20th century, wages and living standards of urban workers in the crowded tenements and slums of the nation's largest cities grew, but not as much as would have been expected given the boost to productivity by the radical technological advances discussed above. The reason can be largely found in the influx of immigrant labor coming during this period. Most of these people settled in urban industrialized areas, and took unskilled jobs rather than moving west to establish farms. Cheap land was no longer readily available and many who came, particularly the Jews, had no tradition or experience in agriculture. The net result was a glut of unskilled workers that restrained wages and drove productivity up. The situation might have been even worse for workers had immigration not been curtailed by the war in Europe. Of course, for the majority of Americans, this situation allowed the prices of a wide range of manufactured goods to become affordable during the period. In particular, the phenomenal growth of retail chains such as Woolworth's Five & Ten and A&P grocery stores brought many of these new goods to market at lower cost, allowing the average American to benefit from the mass-production which had become the norm for American industry.[144]

During the enormous growth of the steel, railroad, and mining industries, labor conflict was common and often violent. The labor movement was weak and generally unpopular with most Americans, and many labor activities were ruled illegal under the Sherman anti-trust act of 1890. Early in this period work in steel and mining was arduous and dangerous, with long working days and little protection against the abuses of unscrupulous employers. Where unions attempted to organize workers "there were likely to be violent, headlong and bloody conflicts, with ferocious battles between rebellious workers on the one hand, and their implacable employers and the employers' scabs and perhaps the militia on the other hand."[145]

Since most of the workers in these industries were immigrants, it is hardly surprising that immigrants became, in the common mind, responsible for much of this strife, which was often attributed to the importation of radical foreign ideologies such as socialism and anarchism, neither of which had much appeal for most Americans. This perception was not altogether incorrect. According to Glazer, "[t]he biography of almost every immigrant labor leader or radical shows that the first contact with radicalism came in Europe."[146]

Many immigrant workers were drawn to the American Socialist Party, especially in the East, with many belonging to foreign-language federations of that organization. Its antiwar stance made it popular among those who opposed American involvement in Europe's War. However, after the United States' entry into that war, the Socialist position came to be seen as unpatriotic by most Americans.[147] While the absolute number of immigrants in radical groups was very small, their overrepresentation in them was viewed with growing alarm by large numbers of middle-class Americans. Various anarchist acts of violence during the War led to what has come to be called the *Red Scare*. In response to antiwar sentiment, according to Paul Johnson, President Wilson "signed the Espionage Act of 1917 and the Sedition

Act of 1918. The latter punished expressions of opinion which were 'disloyal, profane, scurrilous or abusive' of the American form of government, flag or uniform." Attorney General Mitchell Palmer, who was nearly killed by an Anarchist bombing, "led a nationwide drive against 'foreign-born subversives and agitators.'" In 1919 he presented a report to Congress which claimed that the "Department of Justice discovered upwards of 60,000 of these organized agitators of the Trotsky doctrine in the U. S." and that the government was in the process "of sweeping the nation clean of such alien filth."[148] While such talk was no doubt exaggerated, it reflected real concerns about the dangers of foreign ideas and not surprisingly fueled anti-immigration sentiment among the general public.

After the Communist Revolution in Russia, many Socialists in America gravitated toward the Communist movement. According to Nathan Glazer, "In late 1919, a group of East European foreign-language federations of the Socialist Party, along with some native American intellectuals and radicals, founded American Communism," and eventually became "part of the world-wide Communist Party centered in Moscow."[149] This pattern continued in the 1920s with the Communist party being "overwhelmingly composed of relatively recent immigrants. Probably only one in ten of the members was a native American."[150] The Communists did not support violence to forward their cause, but were often linked to anarchists who did. A particularly alarming incident of anarchist violence was the Wall Street bombing in 1920, in which 38 died and many were injured. In the minds of most Americans these violent acts were attributed to the foreign, un-American ideologies of Anarchism, Socialism and Communism.[151]

The association of immigration with these ideas tended to reinforce anti-immigration sentiment that had been growing in the early 1900s based in large part on the perception that massive immigration had begun to threaten traditional American patterns. As mentioned earlier, the population grew from 50 million at the start of the period in 1880 to 120 million by the late 1920s, with approximately half that increase attributable to the arrival of 30 million immigrants. Given their relatively high levels of fertility, immigrant communities were considerably larger than those figures suggest.[152] The country, furthermore, was being transformed from one composed overwhelmingly of Protestant English and North Europeans into one containing substantial numbers of Catholics and Jews from very different cultural backgrounds. Of course, for most rural Americans these changes were generally removed from their everyday affairs in the small cities and towns they inhabited, and rural farmers prospered with the growing demand for their agricultural output. Nevertheless, a growing unease was occasioned by these epochal changes; it would have been amazing had no such unease arisen.

Unlike the unrest about immigration prior to the Civil War that was dismissed by elite classes, at this time it was the elites who were most in earnest about the dangers of immigration. During this period, the most serious anti-immigration spokesmen came from the top rather than the bottom of the social system. The most influential group advocating immigration restriction was the Immigration Restriction League that was formed in 1894 and eventually had significant members in affiliated chapters in a large number of cities. The League was formed by three recent graduates of Harvard whose goal was to preserve the Northern European character of the United States by severely limiting immigration from other regions, including Eastern and Southern Europe. Its main political spokesman was Henry Cabot Lodge, a PhD graduate of Harvard in political science and Congressman from Massachusetts from 1887 until his death in 1924. The League's position on immigration was based in large measure on the best-selling work of it vice-president, Madison Grant, in his *The Passing of the Great Race*, first published in 1916.[153]

Grant was a wealthy and influential New York lawyer whose passions were eugenics and conservation. He was a prominent member of many scientific and philanthropic societies. He played a substantial role in the early movement to establish national parks and was the founder of the New York Zoological Society that eventually created the Bronx Zoo. He was also involved in an important organization aimed at wildlife preservation, and in this work became friends with Theodore Roosevelt.[154] In his book, he argued that world history can be understood in terms of the waxing and waning of the world's races, much as Gobineau had argued a half-century earlier. However, in the interim, the work of Charles Darwin had been published and gained widespread popularity among educated people. Grant advocated that the races differed in ability and temperament due to the conditions under which they evolved. This was, of course, much the same as the argument made by Charles Darwin in his *Descent of Man*. Such a view was common then, as it is today, among many educated people; the difference is that holding such a view was not then considered disreputable. In fact, by the first decade of the 20th century, the view that races differed in ability and temperament had become the dominant view in the social sciences.

The main reason for this was that by 1900 American social science was thoroughly imbued by Darwinian thinking. According to Pulitzer Prize-winning historian Carl Degler, "the study of human psychology in America began with the publication in 1890 of William James' *Principles of Psychology.*" James book was "built upon the Darwinian idea of the animal roots of human nature."[155] In particular, it was James' idea of the central place of instinct in explaining human nature that gained great popularity and was augmented by the influential work of social psychologist William McDougall. In all, between 1900 and 1920 more than 600 publications in England and America forwarded the instinct thesis.[156] It followed rather naturally that if human traits were in large measure the result of inheritance, then in humans, as in animals, selective breeding ought to be a way to improve the nature of human beings. This was the primary thesis of the eugenics movement which became increasingly popular in the early years of the 20th century and included among its supporters large numbers of highly influential Americans, including the leading sociologists of the time.[157]

A related view associated with the Darwinian perspective was the one proposed by Darwin himself, namely, that human groups that evolved in different environments would differ in their inherited characteristics. It became a matter of general consensus among educated Americans that the races differed in their abilities for genetic reasons. For instance, Edward Ross, who would go on to become the president of the American Sociological Society, wrote in 1907 that "I see no reason why races may not differ as much in moral and intellectual traits as obviously as they do in bodily traits."[158] There was more or less agreement on a hierarchy of the major races in ability, with Europeans standing at the top, with Asians and Africans falling at the lower rungs. But a large number of respected scientists also believed there were important differences among the ethnic groups making up the race of Europeans. This naturally led to concern with the ongoing mass immigration to America. According to Degler, Ross came out with a book of collected articles he had previously published under the title, *The Old World in the New,* in which he "deplored the declining quality of the population of the United States as a result of the increasing number of immigrants from Southern and Eastern Europe." Degler also quotes another psychologist that it "is commonly recognized that the immigrant received in this country since 1900... is distinctly inferior to the immigrant previously received."[159] Those views were seconded by the highly influential psychologist Lewis Terman (important in the development of IQ tests) who argued that the "immigrants who have recently come to us in such large numbers from Southern and Southeastern Europe are distinctly inferior mentally to the Nordic and Alpine strains which we received from Scandinavia, Germany, Great Britain and France."[160]

Grant, in his book, was therefore generally popularizing views common among scientists at the time. He did not specifically address differences among Europeans, Asians and Africans, but rather devoted his book to the differences within the white European race. Since very few immigrants were either of African or Asian descent, they were not of much concern to those worried about immigration. As a consequence, he devoted his book to the presumed differences between what he saw as the distinct races of Northern Europeans (Nordics), Middle-Europeans (Alpines), and Mediterraneans.

Grant acknowledged that the Mediterraneans were the equals to the Nordics in intellectual talent, and superior in many ways, especially in the arts. Aristotle, for instance, was quite clearly to him of the Mediterranean type. He thought, however, that the Nordics were superior in literature and science.[161] In addition, he argued that the Nordics were specifically "a race of soldiers, sailors, adventurers, but above all rulers, organizers and aristocrats in sharp contrast to the essentially peasant and democratic character of the Alpines."[162] In essence, he argued that the Nordics were superior in those heroic traits which, when they collided with other types, especially the early civilizations of the Mediterranean, created the glories of Greece and Rome. "In most cases the contact of the vigorous barbarians with the ancient civilizations created a sudden impulse of life and an outburst of culture..."[163] The persistent problem for the Nordics was that their martial, heroic qualities led to fratricidal war among them and they "possessed a blood mania to murder one another" that took its most recent form in the World War in Europe which he characterized as a "civil war."[164] Nevertheless the Nordics possessed traits uncommon to other groups that made them especially suited to organize and rule others, and particularly suited to a republic of independent spirits. These views were reflected in the comments of Albert John, chief author of the 1924

Immigration Act, "Today, instead of a nation descended from generations of freemen bred to a knowledge of the principles and practices of self-government, of liberty under law, we have a heterogeneous population no small proportion of which is sprung from races that, throughout the centuries have known no liberty at all..."[165]

The main problem with Grant's ideas, from a scientific point of view, was not the theory, which might have had some basis in fact. Rather the weakness lay in the lack of empirical support to confirm his hypotheses. Grant simply made no effort to determine whether the differences in traits he claimed existed could, in fact, be reliably measured and shown to exist in different quantities in Nordic, Alpine, and Mediterranean types. Contrary to the belief that intelligence and IQ testing played a role in his positions is the fact that he hardly ever mentions intelligence and makes no reference at all to mental testing. In fact, as previously mentioned, he was willing to grant creative and intellectual superiority to the Mediterranean type in many fields, which suggests that this was not of major concern to him. His attempt to restrict immigration seems, in retrospect, a rather extreme form of ethnocentrism and an unabashed love of his own ethnic background. As such, his views are unsavory from today's politically correct perspective, but were hardly perverse or surprising at the time, especially coming during the fratricidal war raging in Europe.

The trouble is that Grant went much further and advocated the most extreme and antidemocratic form of eugenics. For instance, he was an advocate of strict antimiscegenation laws in order to prevent the dilution and corruption of the Nordic race. In addition, he advocated the sterilization of mental defectives and other inferior people and hoped that such policies would lead over time to the extinction of "worthless race types."[166] Not surprisingly, Adolf Hitler praised Grant's work and, when in power, put into effect many of the eugenic practices Grant advocated, and did so far more brutally than Grant would have supported. For instance, Grant thought that a mental defective should be "nourished, educated and protected by the community during his lifetime" but should be sterilized so that "his line stops with him."[167] Such policies were, in fact, adopted by Canada and by most Scandinavian countries, and adopted in Germany in 1933 before Hitler came to power.[168] Hitler, once he took power, went much further and simply ordered the wholesale extermination of mental defectives and other types he thought detrimental to the purity of the Aryan race. Grant's advocacy of state-sponsored sterilization and Hitler's genocidal policies completely discredited the eugenics movement and rightly so. No society can be considered democratic or just that deprives people of their most fundamental biological imperative, and any nation that abrogates to itself the right to determine who can and who cannot procreate is properly condemned as totalitarian and vicious. Nazi practices, however, also undermined evolutionary psychology and the case for inherited group differences that do not necessarily lead to any particular policy prescriptions. Since these issues were discussed at length in Chapter 1, they need not be repeated here. For now it is enough to point out that the immigration restriction movement, with its theories of racial differences, was by the late forties inextricably linked to the eugenic ideas of Madison Grant and the horrors of Nazi genocide.

Nevertheless, during the last decades of the 19th century and the first decades of the 20th these views were popular among elites in the United States and Europe and undoubtedly played a prominent role in the sentiment to limit immigration, especially given the elite status of many of its main spokesmen. It was to play a role in later years in that it was the view accepted by many in the leadership of the United States armed forces and the State Department.[169] On the other side of the issue were also powerful elite elements, including most large industrial organizations and all the presidents of the United States until the 1920s. In addition, the restrictionist movement was opposed by a wide range of academics. Anthropologist Franz Boas, an ardent opponent of Grant's views, "was surely the most influential figure in the development of American anthropology," as well as the founder of the American Anthropological Association. His doctrines of cultural, as opposed to biological, causation became the official position of the American Anthropological Association, a position still officially espoused to this day by that organization.[170] Its most recent official position is that "physical variations in the human species have no meaning except the social ones that humans put on them."[171]

Most of small main street America were clearly concerned about the massive changes taking place, but it is doubtful how seriously they took these evolutionary arguments, given the clear distaste for Darwinian thinking among so many, especially religious, people. More likely they were moved by cultural and economic factors. For instance, all of the major labor unions, many of whose members were recent immigrants, were adamantly in favor of limiting immigration from their beginnings. They argued, quite correctly, that immigration was keeping wages lower than they would be without it. These concerns became acute during the economic depression of the 1890s and rose greatly at the close of World War I. The war created economic crises in all the nations of Europe, and when it came to an end, produced tremendous unemployment among the soldiers fortunate to have survived it. This situation gave rise to renewed massive immigration from Europe by the early 1920s.

In addition to these economic concerns, there were cultural fears. Largely Protestant small town America was alarmed by the tide of Catholics and Jews arriving during those years. Others saw the rise of an alien urban population whose evident problems might spill over into their rural enclaves. In addition, the war in Europe and the rise of radical regimes, especially the Communist takeover in Russia, disabused many Americans of the idea they had anything to gain from Europeans and what they viewed as their clearly dysfunctional philosophies. The most noteworthy expression of these sentiments was the rise of a new Ku Klux Klan, an organization founded on the fictional account of the original Klan of the reconstruction era depicted in D. W. Griffith's film, *The Birth of a Nation*. The movie was immensely popular and was endorsed by President Wilson who had treated the Klan in a favorable light in his earlier writings as a historian.[172] The new Klan, founded in 1915 was composed of local autonomous fraternal chapters and grew rapidly over the next ten years to an estimated 4 million members before eventually falling into disfavor. Its membership included a number of prominent politicians and was most influential in the South and Midwest, though it had many followers in the Northeast. At its height in the early 1920s it even managed to have President Warren Harding sworn in as a member in a ceremony in the White House.[173]

Its membership was almost exclusively Protestant and its stated aim was to preserve the moral character of the nation from the perceived threats from immigration and from the then accelerating migration of Southern blacks north in search of work. One of the main goals uniting the various disparate chapters was strong support for prohibition, and it managed to recruit large numbers (perhaps as many as 40,000) of fundamentalist ministers to its cause.[174] It was anti-Catholic, anti-Jewish, anti-immigrant, and antiblack. In imitation of *A Birth of a Nation*, members often gathered in large groups dressed in white robes and burned crosses to instill fear in those it held responsible for the problems caused by the rapid growth of the cities and the rise in crime and disorder that were viewed as the product of undesirable aliens. To its members it was a highly reputable expression of American morality and its large membership gave it particularly strong political influence.[175] If the elite Immigration Restriction League provided the intellectual underpinnings, the Klan provided the popular support that led Congress to reverse the liberal immigration policies that had prevailed until the 1920s.

Immigration Legislation and the Immigration Act of 1924

Until 1875, the United States had no specific federal policy regarding immigration and left the regulation of immigrants to the individual states having ports of entry for immigrants. The states tended to allow unrestricted immigration, and the United States had what has come to be called an *open-door* policy. This was changed by a Supreme Court ruling (Henderson v. Mayor of New York) which argued that "the laws which govern the right to land passengers in the United States from other countries ought to be the same in New York, Boston, New Orleans and San Francisco..." The Court decided that the issue was a national issue over which only congress had jurisdiction.[176] The first act of Congress under this new understanding was the *Chinese Exclusion Act* of 1882 which effectively halted all immigration from China. Such an act had been promoted by labor unions that were "in the forefront of decades-long efforts to exclude Chinese immigrants and expel Chinese residents from the United States."[177] The Chinese were being recruited in increasing numbers to take on difficult manual labor in the western states and were resented, and often harassed, by white workers to whom they represented serious economic competitors. Many Chinese were also quite successful in farming enterprises and were resented by white farmers who often found competing with them difficult. In general, the Chinese faced strong, often violent, hostility from whites who characterized the Chinese, in being nonwhite and non-Christian, as incapable of assimilating into American society.[178]

The hostility toward nonwhites was common at the time and both houses of Congress passed the Chinese Exclusionary Act overwhelmingly with little objection. According to Daniels, "Few national figures of any prominence had anything good to say for the Chinese."[179] The general bias against Asians was also reflected in new laws governing the naturalization of residents. The original (1790) Naturalization Act limited citizenship to "free white persons" of "good moral character" who had been resident in the country for two years.[180] In the wake of the Civil War, the 14th Amendment, ratified in 1868, extended citizenship to "all persons born or naturalized in the United States." Since this conflicted with the original statute limiting citizenship to whites, the Congress in 1870 changed the language from "free white persons" to "white persons and persons of African descent," language quite deliberately intended to exclude all resident Asians from possible citizenship. Those Asians resident in the United States at the time and all those who were to come later were classified as "aliens ineligible to citizenship."[181]

The general hostility toward Asians was also reflected in attempts to exclude the immigration of Japanese, who were also formidable economic competitors for whites, especially in California agriculture. California passed the "Alien Land Law of 1913" which barred the ownership of land to "aliens ineligible for citizenship," which meant all Asians.[182] In the preceding decades, a number of bills were introduced in the United States Congress to exclude Japanese immigrants. These efforts were strongly resisted by President Theodore Roosevelt who feared offending Japan, an important and growing Pacific power. The United States had recently acquired the Philippines, and Roosevelt did not wish to provoke Japan into actions threatening the American presence in Asia. The "Gentleman's Agreement" of 1908 was Roosevelt's way of resolving, if imperfectly, the conflict. Under this agreement, the Japanese agreed to drastically restrict the number of passports issued to laborers wishing to emigrate to the United States. In turn, the Americans agreed to allow the immigration of family members, mainly wives, of Japanese residing in America.[183]

The success of the anti-Asian measures was followed by continued and popular efforts to limit immigration in general. The earliest legislative efforts to limit general immigration were spearheaded by Henry Cabot Lodge and were, in comparison to later proposals, extremely moderate and reasonable. Arguing that America needed skilled workers and informed citizens, Lodge introduced a bill in 1895 to make literacy a basic requirement for immigration. The test proposed was extremely modest, the immigrant had to able to read a short passage in any language, including Yiddish or Hebrew.[184] The bill passed in the House, but not in the Senate. Lodge reintroduced the measure in 1897, where it passed in both House and Senate, but was vetoed by the President.

Lodge and the Immigration Restriction League introduced the literacy bill again in 1906. It passed in the Senate, but their efforts were foiled by the powerful speaker of the House Joseph Cannon, who opposed any attempt to restrict immigration. The bill was introduced by the House Committee on Immigration and Naturalization, but was amended to remove the literacy test and substituted the formation of a committee to study the issue. After months of negotiation between the House and the Senate conference committees, the result was that the Senate dropped the literacy requirement and Lodge and his allies were granted considerable influence in the commission formed to investigate the immigration issue. The commission was chaired by Lodge ally William Dillingham, after whom the commission was named.[185]

As explained by historian Daniel Tichenor, The Progressive era of the early twentieth century was marked by a desire to incorporate scientific findings in the formation of public policy and "the work of the Dillingham Commission was unprecedented, even by the standards of the Progressive era fact gathering and social engineering." The commission met for three years and "spent more than a million dollars, employed a staff that reached three hundred and ultimately published a hefty forty-two volume report."[186] The findings, not surprisingly, tended to mirror the positions of the Immigration Restriction League, in particular its view that recent immigrants from Eastern and Southern Europe were inferior to those of earlier immigrant groups from Northern Europe. Given the massive accumulation of data in the report it had enormous influence in the debates in the ensuing years. It included support for a literacy test, but in addition included a recommendation to restrict immigration on the basis of national origins.[187]

Lodge introduced the literacy bill again in 1913 and 1915 and it passed in both the House and the Senate, but was vetoed by the president. In 1917, it was passed and vetoed by President Wilson, but this time the veto was overturned, in part, according to Daniels, because of a rise in anti-European attitudes fostered by the debate over whether America should intervene in the European war.[188]

The episode is instructive in that this bill was heavily supported by the average citizen, gained large legislative support, but was resisted by Presidents of both parties. Most argued that any restrictions violated the nation's traditional moral stand on immigration. This argument conflicted, however, with those same presidents' support of extreme restrictions on Asian immigration. It seems more likely that the bills were opposed for the economic reasons given by the large industrialists who opposed any limitation on immigration on the grounds that it would drastically limit economic growth. One has to wonder whether, if this and other reasonable restrictions on immigration had been accepted at an early date, the extreme measures eventually adopted might have been avoided.

It is worth noting that even though IQ testing had gained considerable support within the scientific community, it played hardly any role in the immigration debate at the time. To a large extent this was because knowledgeable scientists who thought it wise to use available tools to shape immigration policy, were well aware of the wide variation within groups and objected to the exclusion of individuals based on race and ethnic disparities. The respected psychologist, Robert Yerkes, while supporting evidence of individual differences, questioned the validity of the assertions relating to IQ differences among European ethnic groups. Two important studies of the legislative record found little to suggest that IQ played an important role. According to Degler, the main concerns "were apprehensions about social cohesion and national unity...which the massive immigration of the previous two decades clearly aroused."[189]

In 1921 Congress passed the Emergency Quota Act, which was signed by President Harding. This was prompted by fears that the economic and political turmoil in Europe at the end of World War I would result in renewed and even greater immigration of destitute Europeans. The Red Scare, in addition, induced many industrial organizations such as the National Association of Manufacturers, which opposed immigration restriction in the past, to accept some limitation due to a concern about increased labor agitation by immigrants with socialist ideas. The bill also addressed the concern with the changing nature of the immigrants of the preceding four decades, especially those coming from Southern and Eastern Europe. It set up a quota for each nationality based on 3% of their foreign-born presence in the United States as enumerated in the census of 1910, and would have allowed approximately 350,000 immigrants from outside the Americas per year, which was about a third the number coming in previous decades. It placed no restrictions on immigration from either North or South America, regions from which about 1 million people had come in the decade 1910–1920. It kept the provisions of the Chinese exclusion Act. The bill was passed in the last days of Woodrow Wilson's presidency and he used the pocket veto to block it. Two months later it was reintroduced and passed overwhelmingly; in the Senate it passed 78 to 1. The newly elected President Warren Harding signed it into law as the Quota Act of 1921. The law was extended in 1922 for two years.[190]

In 1924, Congress took up the bill and passed the even more restrictive Immigration Act of 1924. It changed the quota to 2% and based it on the census of 1890 rather than of 1910. Its provisions allowed for approximately 165,000 annually or about 1.65 million per decade from outside the Americas, about 22% of what it had been in the decade 1900–1910 and about a third of what it had been in the years 1910-1920. In addition, by moving the quota basis to 1890, before the great bulk of immigrants from Eastern and Southern Europe had arrived, it greatly reduced the numbers, mainly of Jews, Poles, and Italians coming from those regions. It also extended the Asian exclusion, totally barring immigration from Japan. As in the 1921 Act, it placed no limitation of those coming from the Americas.[191]

This 1924 act was a compromise between two proposals as to the nature of the how the restrictions should be determined. One version was based on the national origins of the population of the United States and the other on the percentage of foreign-born. The difference was important since the proportion of foreign-born immigrants from Eastern and Southern Europe was considerably greater than the proportion of foreign born individuals from Western and Northern Europe. In effect, basing the quota on national origins gave greater favor to these latter groups since the country had a far greater proportion of people who could trace their origins to Northern and Western Europe. The compromise that resulted in the 1924 act set the quotas based on the foreign-born and with provision that after its expiration in 1927, it would be replaced by a system based on national origins, that were to be determined by a commission using data from the census of 1920 and historical data on national origin.[192]

In 1929 Herbert Hoover signed the National Origins Immigration Act based on this new formulation. In addition, it limited total annual immigration from outside the Americas to approximately 150,000, and kept the restrictions on Asian immigration. It continued to allow unlimited immigration from North or South America that had involved about 150,000 per year during the 1920s. This law remained in effect substantially unchanged until 1965.[193]

The true effect of the Act is difficult to determine since the depression of the 1930s, which was particularly severe in the United States, tended to reduce drastically immigration to this country. World War II also cut seriously into immigration. In the years immediately following the 1924 Act approximately 300,000 immigrants arrived every year as had been expected. Starting in 1931, immigration fell precipitously. In the fifteen years from 1930 to 1945 only 700,000 immigrants arrived, less than 50,000 each year and about one-third of those who could have come under the quotas of the 1929 Act. Among those 700,000 must be included a substantial number of immigrants from the Americas, mainly Canadians, Mexicans, and Caribbeans, so that the numbers coming from Europe were quite low.[194]

However, the reduced European immigration was also in large measure the result of the Department of State's efforts to limit immigration. As explained by Titchenor "what emerged in the 1930s and 1940s, was a two-tiered immigration bureaucracy." European immigration came under the control of the State Department which required immigrants to obtain visas and undergo investigation by consular officials in the home countries of potential immigrants, who were particularly hostile to immigrants from Eastern and Southern Europe and Jews in particular.[195] Restrictions became more severe during the depression, with President Hoover issuing an executive order that called for strict enforcement of the rule that barred immigrants likely to become public charges. According to Titchenor, Hoover sought to demonstrate to American workers in the 1932 election that tough enforcement of that clause "had resulted in a 94% underissue of available quota slots." According to Titchenor, "legal immigration plummeted from 242,000 in 1931 to 36,000 in 1932 (fewer than 3,000 visas went to Jews)."[196]

The second tier of the immigration bureaucracy involved immigration from the Americas, which was administered separately from European immigration by the Immigration Bureau and the Labor department. This was largely the result of Southern and Western interests who benefited from inexpensive Mexican farm labor. As Titchenor explains, "the two-tiered immigration bureaucracy that emerged was at once draconian toward overseas immigrants and strikingly tolerant toward the importation of temporary workers across the nation's Southern border."[197] The leniency toward Mexican immigrants, who were seen even less likely to assimilate than Eastern and Southern Europeans, was that they were not expected to assimilate, but rather to remain for short periods of seasonal work, and return home. This had been the general pattern until that time. Furthermore, they were not seen as undercutting union interests since they performed menial work not unionized at the time. However, with the coming of the Depression, many of these Mexican workers were deported and many left voluntarily as they were neither wanted nor needed.[198]

Consequences of the 1924 Act

Much has been written about the Immigration Act of 1924, almost all of it negative. It has been characterized as the product of nativist, anti-Semitic, and racist attitudes. There can be no doubt that such sentiments played an important part. However, as historian Otis Graham argued, a close reading of the Congressional Record revealed "that many of the advocates of restrictionist reform were keenly aware that charges of ethnic discrimination, even in 1920s America, threatened both political parties." The reason was, of course, the huge increase in the immigrant population in earlier decades that had significant voting clout and generally opposed restrictions on immigration. He argues that they took pains to avoid claims of Nordic superiority or claims that some groups were undesirable. Congressional proponents of reform claimed that the "Nordic superiority language" was coming from opponents, in an attempt to besmirch their motives. (For a modern reader, such a claim rings true, especially in light of half a century of ad hominem smears against opponents of unrestricted immigration).[199]

Representative William Vaile of Colorado argued that restrictionists were not claiming that Nordics or Anglo-Saxons were superior to others.

> Let us concede in all fairness, that the Czech is a more sturdy worker with a very low percentage of crime and insanity, that the Jew is the best businessman in the world, and that the

> Italian has a spiritual grasp and an artistic sense which have
> greatly enriched the world...which the Nordic rarely attains.

He stressed that a desire to limit immigration reflected no claim of racial superiority, but rather a desire to maintain America as it was shaped by its Anglo-Saxon founders. The other nationalities immigrated to a country that:

> [W]as already made as an Anglo Saxon commonwealth.
> They added to it, they often enriched it, but they did
> not make it, and have not yet greatly changed it. We are
> determined that they shall not. It is a good country. It suits
> us. And what we assert is that we are not going to surrender
> it to somebody else or allow other people, no matter what
> their merits, to make it something different."[200]

The public was strongly in favor of restriction. It was difficult for most citizens to imagine, probably correctly, that the immigration of some one million people every year could have continued indefinitely without causing serious economic and social difficulties. Even in the brief period in the late twenties before the Great Depression, about 5 million or more additional poor, unskilled laborers would have arrived without the restrictions of the 1924 Act. Certainly those numbers would have only added to the widespread unemployment and despair brought on by the economic catastrophe of the 1930s. Of course, none of the supporters of the Act could have anticipated the severity of the Depression. However, many thoughtful people were concerned about the consequences of a glut of labor should an economic downturn occur.

An analyst writing in a 1923 *Time* magazine article made the point that in most settled industrialized societies, such as those in Europe, agricultural workers acted as a labor reserve for the industrial sector. When labor demand was high during periods of industrial expansion those workers were drawn from the land by the promise of higher wages in factories, and they went back into agriculture when the economy contracted. Quoting that author:

> In America, which until about 20 years ago was a pioneer
> and not a settled country, the labor for expanding industries
> was drawn from Europe. Statistics show that the rate of the
> influx of immigrants and the rate of production, say of pig
> iron go up and down together. But labor from the European

peasantry to aid an American business boom cannot go back to Europe when the boom is over. It has to stay, be assimilated and Americanized. This was possible as long as there was free land to take up the slack. But that outlet is now gone, and the result for the last 20 years has been the abnormal crowding of cities with unassimilated and partially employed foreigners, with all the attendant political and social evils.[201]

The author maintained that the "best economists" argued that America would pay for the increased immigration with economic pain during the next downturn in the business cycle. If those economists were right, then the extreme severity and extraordinary unemployment of the Depression years may well have been the result, at least in part, of excessive immigration in the earlier period. A consequence of the 1924 Act may have been to make the Great Depression somewhat less severe than it might otherwise have been.

A second consequence was a much improved economic climate for American workers that accompanied the extraordinary industrial expansion that began in the 1940s with America's entry into World War II. Opponents of immigration restriction had argued that American industry could not thrive without the labor provided by immigration. According to Elbert H. Gary, Chairman of the U. S. Steel Corporation, the restrictions put into effect by the 1921 Act were "the worst thing that ever happened to this country economically."[202] To counter these assertions the then Secretary of Labor argued that since the restrictions were put in place "unemployment has been reduced to a minimum, wages everywhere are rising." He went on to say that given such conditions "it is inevitable that there should be agitation for the lifting of the immigration restrictions."[203] To those who supported the restrictions, such as an anonymous silk manufacturer quoted by *Time* magazine, the claims of a labor shortage were bogus. "We have a tremendous reservoir of labor in this country. We used to say, 'let George do it.' Now we say, 'Let Giovanni do it.' We can do it ourselves. Those who demand an unlimited labor supply have upon them the burden of proof not only that they need labor but that they need to get it outside the country."[204]

In fact, the boom times of the twenties continued unabated with much reduced levels of immigration from Europe under the 1921 Act and, of course, there was a glut of labor during the thirties. When

World War II arrived, industrial production increased enormously and did so even though some 11 million men were pulled out of the labor force for military duty. Women picked up much of the slack, as did a fair number of blacks. All of which suggests that, at least with regard to America's need for additional labor, the industrialists were wrong and the restrictionists were right.

A third consequence of the 1921 and 1924 Acts was greatly increased opportunities for black Americans. Approximately 90% of all blacks lived in the South in 1910, a percentage that had not changed appreciably since the Civil War.[205] Considering the extraordinary economic growth in the North during those decades, it is difficult to explain the lack of migration of blacks north to take advantage of higher paying industrial work. There are two obvious reasons. Blacks were not welcome in the North and were especially opposed by labor unions, for the same reasons they opposed heavy immigration; additional labor held down wages. Industrialists, who might have encouraged black migration, did not need to do so since massive immigration was clearly providing them with the low-priced labor they desired. That began to change during and after World War I. Immigration from Europe had declined sharply during World War I, but industrial production continued its robust growth and black workers could, and did, fill in for the Europeans who did not come. The 1921 restrictions prevented a return to previous levels of European immigration, so that opportunities for blacks continued. According to *Time* magazine, factory workers earned twice as much in the North as in the South. Georgia, in particular, was losing large numbers of black farm workers who were migrating north for better wages. "In Georgia a Negro farm worker gets about $1.25 a day; in the Pennsylvania steel mills he is offered $4.50 a day and 'all the overtime he wants.'"[206]

By 1920, the percentage of blacks living in the North rose to 15% and by 1930 to more than 20%. The northward migration came almost to a halt during the thirties, but resumed in the 1940s. By 1950, 33% of all blacks were living in the North, and the percentage rose to 47% in 1970, where it has stabilized.[207] Blacks made significant economic progress during this period and much of that progress is most simply explained by the fact that wages were higher in the North and opportunities for blacks greater. The wages for blacks, especially black males, have tended to stagnate since the 1960s, which is somewhat surprising given the new opportunities opened up to blacks by the Civil Rights movement.[208] Why this is so is complex and has many causes. However, the fact that the greatest advancement for blacks came during a lull in mass immigration suggests, though it does not prove, that blacks were major beneficiaries of the restrictive Immigration Acts of the 1920s, and may well be disadvantaged, at least in part, by the substantial immigration that resumed after the 1965 Immigration Act.

Perhaps the most tragic consequence of the 1921 and later immigration acts was that the restrictions kept many Jews in Europe who would surely have continued to migrate to the United States during the 1920s. With the Communist takeover in Russia, the social condition of the Jews in areas controlled by the communists improved considerably, and certainly reduced the oppression they had suffered under the Tsars, but many would have continued to emigrate. Whether the Jews of Eastern Europe would have continued to come in the 1930s despite the dismal economic prospects in the United States is difficult to say. The relatively small number of Jews living in Western Europe, however, would have gained little economically by migrating in the 1930s, and their favorable social situation prior to the rise of Hitler would have provided little incentive for them to do so. Obviously, after the Nazi takeover, many Jews would have migrated in the early 1930s, and almost all by the late 1930s, had they somewhere to go. Of course, any Jews who anticipated that Hitler would have been successful enough in war to come to rule almost all of Europe would have fled, but how many people could have anticipated such an outcome in the mid 1930s?

This opens one of the most distressing and most controversial issues in American history. For many, perhaps most analysts, the restrictions of the 1920s were clearly reflective of powerful anti-Semitic sentiments in the American population and those sentiments prevented any efforts to save the Jews of Europe once the Nazis came to power. From this, it is often inferred that those who promoted the restrictions in 1921 and 1924 were, at least in part, complicit in the genocide of the European Jews. There can be no doubt that many of the backers of the acts were anti-Semitic. It is equally obvious that many were anti-Catholic, and supported the limits on Italian immigration. The Ku Klux Klan was, after all, openly hostile to immigrants in general, whether Jews or Catholics.

It is by no means clear, however, that these were the motives of most of the Americans who overwhelmingly supported the restrictions. As discussed earlier, economic and cultural concerns were of overriding importance to a great many people. The sheer number of newcomers seemed overwhelming and created strains, especially in the cities, clear to all. The vast number of immigrants, in addition, clearly put downward pressure on wages. In 1921, many Americans were very much concerned about the Communist success in Russia, and a good deal of the restrictionist sentiment was based on fears that Europeans might bring in what most Americans viewed as dangerous ideologies. Indeed, the Red Scare was often invoked in the immigration debate. As in all complex social movements, a great many motives and sentiments are intertwined and it is rarely possible to determine which was of paramount significance. One thing is clear, and that is that virtually no one in 1921 could have anticipated the awful events that were to unfold 15 years later in Germany.

The charge, on the other hand, that anti-Semitic sentiments played a role in depriving Jews of refuge after Hitler came to power is impossible to dismiss. It is estimated that about 365,000 Jews lived in Germany at the time. In response to the rise of Nazis and their discriminatory laws and actions, Roosevelt in 1935 revoked Hoover's directive to use the most restrictive meaning of the clause barring those likely to become a public burden. According to historian Peter Novick, he also instructed the State department to "give refugees 'the most considerate and the most generous and favorable treatment possible under the Law.'" Unfortunately, "the new policy was not consistently implemented down the line."[209]

By 1938, 118,000 Jews had left Germany, of whom 50,000 went to England and some 15,000 to the United States.[210] In that same year a conference was held in Evian-les-Bains, France, on Lake Geneva, to consider the impact of Jewish refugees from Nazi Germany. Of the 32 nations attending, none, save the Dominican Republic, agreed that they could accommodate any displaced Jews. According to Jordana Horn, the "conference was later deemed by various historians to have given Hitler the explicit go-ahead for his Final Solution."[211]

At that point America could single-handedly have saved the German Jews by offering to accept about 250,000 people. Given the number of immigrants arriving in the late 1930s (about 50,000 a year) and the existing immigration quotas, this would hardly have put any particular strain on American resources. Why Roosevelt, with his enormous popularity, did not even attempt to offer such refuge must remain one of the most troubling enigmas in the history of the United States. It is especially ironic given Roosevelt's iconic status for most American Jews. The tragic voyage of the St. Louis, which left Germany in May of 1939 and carried about 900 Jews, is instructive. Most of these were on waiting lists and would have been eligible for entry within a few months or years under the quotas allotted to German nationals. The passengers had originally intended to land in Cuba and await their quotas for entry into the United States to come due, but they were turned away. Amid much news coverage, they sailed up the Atlantic coast hoping to disembark in New York, but they were not allowed to land. Roosevelt said and did nothing and refused to offer refuge: these 900 desperate people were simply turned away.[212]

It should be stressed that in the late 1930s unemployment had begun to rise to levels similar to what it had been earlier in the decade, and few people would have welcomed increased immigration for that reason alone. In addition, the earliest repressive measures by the Nazis targeted a variety of political opponents and communists, in particular, and Jews were not obviously the most threatened by internment in concentration camps. It wasn't until the infamous Kristallnacht in 1938 that the extent to which Jews, in particular, were threatened by Nazi policies became clear, but even then those policies seemed mainly designed to encourage Jewish emigration rather than physical elimination. In fact, it was not until the Germans had conquered Western Europe, that they began the grisly task of mass murder and extermination, largely in Eastern Europe after war with Russia had begun in 1941, and this went unreported in the Western press because very little was known about their existence at the time. Even the few reports of atrocities were generally dismissed as war propaganda by the British in their efforts to enlist American support. It was, by then, widely known that British propaganda during World War I about German atrocities had been wildly exaggerated and had contributed to America's involvement in the first war, an involvement which many, perhaps most, Americans in the 1930s saw as a mistake and wished to avoid a second time.

Once the war was underway, many millions of Jews were threatened, but by then it was far more difficult for them to leave, given the turmoil of war. Even then, if the United States had shown a willingness to accept Jewish refugees, especially those in Western

Europe, some might have made it to these shores. Unfortunately, no public offer of refuge was ever extended. This is not the place to attempt a fair treatment of the European tragedy and American indifference. It is raised here because of the implication that the immigration restrictions of the 1924 Act, and by extension, any attempt to restrict immigration today, are morally tainted by complicity with genocide. Put bluntly, it implies that the overwhelming majority of Americans who supported the restrictionist policy acted not out of concern with the effects of immigration per se, but rather out of xenophobic and anti-Semitic motives that were so intense as to make them indifferent to, or actually supportive of, the extermination of the Jews. This is such a serious charge that it is important to examine whether, in fact, it is supported by the facts.

According to David Wyman, author of the highly regarded *The Abandonment of the Jews*, "The American State Department and the British Foreign Office had no intension of rescuing large numbers of European Jews. On the contrary, they continually feared that Germany or other Axis nations might release tens of thousands of Jews into Allied hands." As a consequence of this fear "their policies aimed at obstructing rescue possibilities and dampening public pressure for governmental action."[213] Even though some Roosevelt administration figures wanted expanded refugee relief, the State Department remained adamantly opposed to such efforts. Treasury secretary Henry Morganthau, Jr. ordered his department to study the situation in 1943. The study produced a memo entitled "Report to the Secretary of the Acquiescence of this Government to the Murder of the Jews." It accused the State Department of "willful attempts to prevent action from being taken to rescues Jews from Hitler." Roosevelt issued very modest orders to the State Department as a result, but as Tichenor put it, "these interventions were too little, too late."[214]

Among the factors that contributed to the public's apparent indifference was the public's lack of awareness as to just what was going on. It was not until 1942 that knowledge of the mass murder of the Jews became available, but the major news sources tended to play down the reports, as did government officials. In general, Americans were unaware of the severity of the problem or of the State Department's resistance to changing its policies. Most people were focusing on the Pacific Campaign in the early phases of the War. It was not until 1944 when Congressional hearings led to the establishment of the *War Refugee Board* (WRB) that the issue finally received the full coverage in the American press.[215] Earlier reports had been treated with skepticism by the public who were, in effect, following the lead of the major newspapers, including the Jewish-owned *New York Times*, and government officials. Popular pressure for government action, earlier, might have made a difference, but that pressure did not come until very late. According to Wyman:

> Several factors hampered the growth of public pressure. Among them were anti-Semitism and anti-immigration attitudes, both widespread in American society in that era and both entrenched in Congress; the mass media's failure to publicize Holocaust news, even though wire services and other news services made most of the information available to them; the near silence of the Christian churches and almost all of their leadership; the indifference of most of the nation's political and intellectual leaders; and the President's failure to speak out on the issue.[216]

The failure, according to Wyman, was thoroughgoing in its depth and breadth. Even American Jewish leaders were in conflict over whether to make it a major issue. Some were worried that it would stoke anti-Semitism by fostering the idea that the war was a "Jewish war." It seems clear, however, that had President Roosevelt wished to offer refuge to the Jews he could have brought Americans in large majorities to his side, not-withstanding the real facts of anti-Semitism and anti-immigrant sentiment. To suggest that the actions taken by Congress in response to public concerns in 1924 were complicit in the genocide is to downplay the complicity at the highest levels of the American government and American leadership in the period 1938–1945. When the issue became common knowledge, the public was in favor of efforts to aid the Jews. A Gallup poll in April of 1944 revealed that 70% of the American people supported the idea for emergency refugee camps in the United States. According to Wyman there was widespread support for the proposal evidenced by "the large numbers of favorable letters, telegrams and petitions that were reaching the President, Congress and the WRB. Only a few letters of dissent turned up."[217] The claim, as made by many, that those who supported restrictions on immigration were motivated by xenophobia that doomed the Jews appears to be false in that those same Americans, or at least 70% of them, were not so xenophobic as to wish to deny refuge to the Jews of Europe once the truth was revealed to them.

Notes

1   J. M. Roberts, *The Penguin History of the World* (London: Penguin, 1995) 618–623.
2   Ibid, 625–626.
3   Paul Johnson, *A History of the American People* (New York: Harper Collins, 1997) 17–19.
4   Lee Miller, *Roanoke: Solving the Mystery of the Lost Colony* (New York: Penguin Books, 2000), 227–237.
5   Johnson, *A History of the American People*, 25; Wayne Andrews, ed., *Concise Dictionary of American History* (New York: Scribners, 1962) 734.
6   Roberts, *The Penguin History of the World*, 627.
7   Johnson, *A History of the American People*, 61–62.
8   Ibid., 126.
9   Roger Daniels, *Coming to America: A History of Immigration and Ethnicity in American Life, Second Edition* (New York: Harper Collins, 2002), 16–22; Marianne Sophia Wokeck, *Trade In Strangers: The Beginnings of Mass Migration to North America* (University Park, Penn.: Pensylvania State University Press, 1999), xxv–xxvi.
10 Johnson, *A History of the American People*, 28–32.
11 U. S. Census Bureau, Population Division/International Programs Center., Historical Estimates of World Population.
12 J. C. Russell, Population in Europe 500–1500, In Carlo M. Cipolla, ed., *The Fontana Economic History of Europe: The Middle Ages* (London: Collins/ Fontana Press, 1977), 36.
13 Fernand Braudel, *The Structures of Everyday Life: Civilization and Capitalism 15th Century–18th Century, Volume 1*, Translated from the French by Sian Reynolds (New York: Harper and Row, 1981), 42.
14 Brian M. Fagan, *The Little Ice Age: How Climate Made History 1300–1850* (New York: Basic Books, 2000). 101–112.
15 Ibid, 90–96.
16 Ibid, 84.
17 Ibid, 110–112, 181–194.
18 Ibid, 123–127.
19 Wokeck, *Trade in Strangers*, 59–112.
20 U. S. Department of Homeland Security, *2006 Yearbook of Immigration Statistics* (September 2007), Immigration by Region and Selected Country of Last Residence: Fiscal Years 1820–2004, Washington, D.C., 2007
21 Ibid, Table 2; U. S. Census Bureau, *Statistical Abstract of the United States*, Section 1, Population (2007), 7.
22 Ibid, Table 2.
23 Wokeck, *Trade in Strangers*, 1–9.
24 David Hackett Fischer, *Albion's Seed: Four British Folkways in America*

(London: Oxford University Press, 1989, 174–179.

25 Edmund S. Morgan, *The Puritan Family: Religion and Domestic Relations in Seventeenth-Century New England* (New York: Harper, 1966), 17–21.

26 James Axtell, *The School Upon a Hill: Education and Society in Colonial New England* (New York: Norton, 1976), 210–211.

27 Fischer, *Albion's Seed*, 16–17.

28 Fischer, *Albion's Seed*, 226–230; See also James Horn, Servant Immigration to the Chesapeake in the Seventeenth Century, in Thad W. Tate and David I. Ammerman, eds., *The Chesapeake in the Seventeenth Century: Essays on Anglo-American Society and Politics* (New York: Norton, 1979), 51–90.

29 Fischer, *Albion's Seed*, 212–220.

30 Ibid, 420–423.

31 Ibid, 434.

32 Ibid, 573–577.

33 Ibid, 431.

34 Ibid, 427.

35 Ibid, 601.

36 Ibid, 608–618.

37 James G. Leyborn, *The Scotch-Irish: A Social History*, (Chapel Hill, NC: University of North Carolina Press, 1988), 83–88.

38 Ibid, 99–107.

39 Ibid, 120–132.

40 Ibid, 158.

41 Ibid, 161.

42 Fischer, *Albion's Seed*, 626–632.

43 Leyburn, *The Scotch-Irish*, 305–308.

44 Ibid, 168–169.

45 Ibid, 174–178.

46 Ibid, 236–242.

47 Ibid, 194–224

48 Fischer, *Albion's Seed*, 662–668.

49 Ibid, 703–708.

50 Aaron Spencer Fogleman, *Hopeful Journeys: German Immigration, Settlement and Political Culture in Colonial America, 1717–1775* (Philadelphia Penn.: University of Pennsylvania Press, 1996), 17; Wokeck, Trade in Strangers, 2–4.

51 Fogleman, *Hopeful Journeys*, 18.

52 Wokeck, *Trade in Strangers*, 2–7.

53 Fogleman, *Hopeful Journeys*, 4–6.

54 Fogelman, *Hopeful Journeys*, 5–6.

55 Ibid, 19–21.

56 Fogelman, *Hopeful Journeys*, 23–31; Wokeck, *Trade in Strangers*, 7–9.

57 Wokeck, *Trade in Strangers*, 54.

58 Fogelman, *Hopeful Journeys*, 69–80. Wokeck, *Trade in Strangers*, 151–163.

59 Wokeck, *Trade in Strangers*, 157–163.

60 Fogleman, *Hopeful Journeys*, 80–86.

61 Ibid, 82–83.

62 Ibid, 86–92.

63 Ibid, 12.

64 Wokeck, *Trade In Strangers*, 45–46.

65 Daniels, *Coming to America*, 68.

66 Wokeck, *Trade in Strangers*, 150.

67 Daniels, *Coming to America*, 159–161.

68 Robert William Fogel, *Without Consent or Contract: The Rise and Fall of American Slavery* (New York: Norton, 1989), 18.

69 Daniels, *Coming to America*, 62.

70 Fogel, *Without Consent or Contract*, 33.

71 Ibid,18–21.

72 Toyin Falola, *Key Events in African History: A Reference Guide* (Westport Conn.: Praeger, 2002), 114–116.

73 Fogel, *Without Consent or Contract*, 129–130; Wokeck, *Trade in Strangers*, 54, gives a mortality figure of 3.8% for the ocean crossing, but these were for German immigrants arriving in America between 1727 and 1805. However these later figures do not include those who died in shipwrecks who never arrived in Philadelphia, nor does it include those who died during their journey from their homes in the Rhineland to their points of embarkation in English ports.

74 Fogel, *Without Consent or Contract*, 33.

75 U. S. Census Bureau. *Statistical Abstract of the United States*, Section 1, Population (2007), 14.

76 Daniels, *Coming to America*, 68.

77 Fogel, *Without Consent or Contract*, 115.

78 Daniels, *Coming to America*, 125.

79 Department of Homeland Security, *2006 Yearbook*, Table 2.

80 U. S. Census Bureau, *Statistical Abstract of the United States*, 2007. 14.

81 Ibid, 128.

82 Ibid, 136.

83 Ibid, 134.

84 Department of Homeland Security, *2006 Yearbook*, Table 2.

85 Daniels, *Coming to America*, 137–138.

86 Thomas Sowell, *Ethnic America* (New York: Basic Books, 1981), 119-120.

87 Daniels, *Coming to America*, 137–138.

88 Ibid., 150.

89 Department of Homeland Security, *2006 Yearbook*, Table 2.

90 Ibid, 152–155.

91 Ibid, 159–161.
92 Ibid, 158.
93 Ibid, 155–159.
94 Daniels, *Coming to America*, 164–183.
95 Department of Homeland Security, *2006 Yearbook*, Table 2.
96 Ibid, 166–172.
97 Ibid, 172–176.
98 Ibid, 176–183.
99 Fogel, *Without Consent or Contract*, 306–307.
100 Ibid, 304.
101 Ibid, 310–311.
102 Ibid, 360.
103 Ibid, 359.
104 Edward K. Spann, *Gotham at War: New York City, 1860–1865* (Wilmington: SR Books, 2002) 96.
105 Ibid, 95–96.
106 Ibid, 98–101.
107 Ibid, 101.
108 Fogel, Without Consent or Contract, 308–309.
109 Ibid, 364.
110 Ibid, 365.
111 Daniel J. Tichenor, *Dividing Lines: The Politics of Immigration Control in America* (Princeton, New Jersey: Princeton University Press, 2002), 62.
112 Jeffrey Rogers Hummel, *Emancipating Slaves, Enslaving Free Men: A history of the American Civil War* (Chicago: Open Court, 1996) 106–107.
113 Republican National Platform, Transcribed by Lloyd Benson from the Tribune Almanac, 1861, 30–31.
114 PBS Video Database Resource–*The Civil War*.
115 U.S. Bureau of the Census, *Statistical Abstract of the United States*, Census of 1830 and 1860.
116 PBS Video Database Resource–*The Civil War*.
117 Hummel, *Emancipating Slaves*, 351–356.
118 Titchenor, *Dividing Lines*, 92–94.
119 Ibid, 90.
120 Ibid, 106–107.
121 Daniels, *Coming to America,* 216.
122 Ibid, 217–218.
123 Ibid, 189, 202.
124 Ibid, 225.
125 Ibid, 202.
126 U. S. Department of Homeland Security, *2006 Yearbook*, Table 2.
127 Sowell, *Ethnic America*, 79.
128 Daniels, *Coming to America*, 230.

129 Ibid, 192–194.

130 Sowell, *Ethnic America*, 106.

131 Ibid, 106.

132 Ibid, 120–121.

133 Daniels, *Coming to America*, 194–196.

134 Ibid, 220–222.

135 Frederick Lewis Allen, *The Big Change: America Transforms Itself 1900–1950* (New York: Harper and Row, 1952), 45.

136 Nathan Glazer, *The Social Basis of American Communisn* (New York: Harcourt, Brace and World, 1961), 26.

137 George E. Mowry, *The Era of Theodore Roosevelt and the Birth of Modern America* (New York: Harper and Row, 1958), 3.

138 Ibid, 3–4.

139 Richard K. Veddeer and Lowell Eugene Gallaway, *Out of Work: Unemployment and Government in Twenthieth-Century America, Updated Edition* (New York: NYU Press, 1997), 55.

140 Ibid, 53.

141 Allen, *The Big Change*, 101, 110.

142 Ibid, 104.

143 Ibid, 102.

144 Ibid, 103.

145 Ibid, 48.

146 Glazer, *The Social Basis of American Communism*, 32–35.

147 Ibid, 21.

148 Johnson, *A History of the American People*, 668.

149 Ibid, 37.

150 Ibid, 38.

151 Kevin Baker, Blood on the Street, Book Review of Beverly Gage, *The Day Wall Street Exploded:The Story of America in its First Age of Terror* (New York: Oxford University Press, 2008),*The New York Times*, February 22, 2009; Lona Manning 9/16: Terrorists Bomb Wall Street, *Crime Magazine*, January 15, 2008.

152 U. S. Census Bureau. *Statistical Abstract of the United States*, Section 1, Population (2007), 7; Department of Homeland Security, *2006 Yearbook*, Table 2.

153 Madison Grant and Henry Fairfield Osborn, *The Passing of the Great Race Or the Racial Basis of European History* (New York: Charles Scribner's Sons, 1918.)

154 Nelson Rosit, Prescient Patrician, Review of Jonathan Peter Spiro, *Patrician Racist: The Evolution of Madison Grant.* (Ann Arbor: UMI Dissertation Services, 2000), *The Occidental Quarterly*, Vol 7, No. 2. 1–10, online.

155 Carl Degler, *In Search of Human Nature: The Decline and Revival of Darwinism in American Social Thought* (New York: Oxford University

Press, 1991), 33.

156 Ibid, 34–35.

157 Ibid, 44.

158 Ibid, 19.

159 Ibid, 48–49.

160 Ibid, 49.

161 Grant and Osborn, *The Passing of the Great Race*, 225–229.

162 Ibid, 228.

163 Ibid, 214–215.

164 Ibid, 230–231.

165 Daniels, *Coming to America*, 283.

166 Grant and Osborn, *Passing of the Great Race*, 47–51.

167 Ibid, 51.

168 Degler, *In Search of Human Nature*, 46.

169 Joseph W. Bendersky, *The Jewish Threat: Anti-Semitic Politics and the U.S. Army* (New York: Basic Books, 2000); Titchenor, *Dividing Lines*, 154–156.

170 Degler, *In Search of Human Nature*, 82.

171 John Paul Wright, *Inconvenient Truths: Science, Race and Crime*, in Anthony Walsh and Kevin Beaver, eds., *Biosocial Criminology: New Direction in Theory and Research* (New York: Routledge, 2009), 137–153, 137.

172 Wyn Craig Wade, *The Fiery Cross: The Ku Klux Klan in America* (New York: Simon and Schuster, 1986). 115–116, 126.

173 Ibid, 165.

174 Ibid, 171.

175 Ibid, 167–185.

176 Daniels, *Coming to America*, 272.

177 Sowell, *Ethnic America*, 137.

178 Ibid, 136–137.

179 Daniels, *Coming to America*, 271.

180 U.S. Congress, *An act to establish a uniform rule of naturalization,* passed by Congress, January 4, 1790.

181 Daniels, *Coming to America*, 271.

182 Sowell, *Ethnic America,* 163; Rechs Ann Pedersen, Internet Librarian, *Alien Land Laws*, Santa Cruz Public Libraries' Local History.

183 Sowell, *Ethnic America*, 163; Daniels, *Coming to America*, 255.

184 Daniels, *Coming to America*, 278.

185 Titchenor, *Dividing Lines*, 125–128.

186 Ibid, 129.

187 Ibid, 131.

188 Daniels, 276–277.

189 Degler, *In Search of Human Nature*, 53–54.

190 Ibid, 280–281; Daniel J. Tichenor, *Dividing Lines*, 142–143.

191 Ibid, 283–283.
192 Tichenor, *Dividing Lines*, 144–145.
193 Department of Homeland Security, *2006 Yearbook*, Table 2.
194 Department of Homeland Security, *2006 Yearbook*, Table 1 and Table 2.
195 Tichenor, *Dividing Lines,* 150–151.
196 Ibid, 156.
197 Ibid, 151.
198 Ibid, 172–173; Department of Homeland Security, *2006 Yearbook*, Table 2.
199 Otis L. Graham, *Unguarded Gates: A History of America's Immigration Policy* (Rowen and Littlefield, 2006) 48–49.
200 Ibid, 49.
201 *Time*, Reservoirs of Labor, April 28, 1923.
202 Ibid.
203 Ibid.
204 *Time*, Pro and Con, December 24, 1923.
205 Campbell Gibson and Kay Jung, *Historical Census Statistics on Population Totals by Race, 1790 to 1990, and by Hispanic Origin, 1970 to 1990, For the United States, Regions, Divisions, and States*, Population Division, U.S. Census Bureau, Washington D.C., Working Paper Series No. 56, September 2002.
206 Go North, *Time*, August 13, 1923.
207 Gibson and Jung, Historical Census Statistics.
208 Byron M. Roth, *Prescription for Failure: Race Relations in the Age of Social Science* (New Brunswick, New Jersey:Transaction Publishers,1994), 54–57.
209 Peter Novick, *The Holocaust in American Life* (New York: Houghton Mifflen, 2000), 49.
210 Martin Gilbert, *The Illustrated Atlas of Jewish Civilization* (New York: MacMillan, 1990) 161.
211 Jordana Horn, Strange Migration: An unlikely Haven for Refugees, *The Wall Street Journal, February 15, 2008, W11.
212 Deborah E. Lipstadt, *Beyond Belief: The American Press and the Coming of the Holocaust 1933–1945* (New York: The Free Press, 1993), 115–120.
213 David S. Wyman, *The Abandonment of the Jews: America and the Holocaust 1941–1945* (New York: Pantheon Books, 1985) xiv.
214 Tichenor, *Dividing Lines*, 167.
215 Wyman, *The Abandonment of the Jews*, 203–206.
216 Ibid, xiv–xv.
217 Ibid, 264.

Chapter 6

UNITED STATES IMMIGRATION SINCE 1965

Introduction

UNITED STATES IMMIGRATION POLICY remained largely unchanged from 1921 to 1965. The 1929 Immigration Act set in place national origins quotas based on the 1920 rather than the 1890 census, but the limited quotas for individual countries had the effect of greatly reducing immigration from all European regions except for Northern Europe. It continued the policy of excluding most Asians from immigration and naturalization, and, in addition, repealed the Gentlemen's Agreement with Japan even though the quota for Japan had been limited to about 200 people. It also left in place the policy of unrestricted immigration from the Western Hemisphere. It allowed, in total, for about 150,000 immigrants annually from all regions outside of the Americas.[1] The Great Depression of the 1930s and World War II, as well as the restrictionist actions of the State department, reduced immigration to a trickle until the late 1940s. During most of this period, annual immigration rarely exceeded 50,000 people. By comparison, more than 800,000 had arrived in 1921, the year in which the first restrictionist Emergency Quota Act was signed into law.[2]

During World War II, the existence of the Chinese Exclusion Act became an embarrassment to the State Department as it greatly offended an ally in the fight against Japan. It was repealed in 1943, and allowed for immigration from China and the naturalization of the

Chinese already residing in America. This allowed the many Chinese residing in America to bring in, without restriction, their spouses and children, and was the first significant change in the wholesale bias against Asians. It was, however, only intended as a symbolic gesture since it provided a yearly quota for all of China of only 105 people. In 1946, for similar foreign policy reasons, India and the Philippines were allotted symbolic quotas of 100 each.[3] In addition, the War Brides Act of 1945 allowed for the immigration and naturalization of the brides, including the Asian brides, of American serviceman who had married overseas. All of these measures breeched, modestly, what had been up to then the complete resistance to any Asian immigration.

World War II produced thousands of displaced persons who had been removed from, or had fled, their native countries. Most of these were returned to their native countries at the end of hostilities. However, there were significant numbers who could not reasonably return home, of whom many were being held in refugee camps under the control of the United States occupation forces. About 20% of these were Jews whose condition, after having survived the concentration camps, was particularly precarious. Many were being held in former German concentration camps and were dying in significant numbers from malnutrition and disease in the months immediately after the defeat of Germany. After receiving appeals from various Jewish agencies, the White House sent Earl Harrison to investigate the situation of the conditions of the Jews. He found their situation deplorable and claimed that "we appear to be treating the Jews as the Nazis treated them, except we do not exterminate them."[4] In response to this report Truman issued an executive order that resulted in 40,000 refugees gaining immediate access to the United States, most of whom were Jews.[5]

At the urging of President Truman, and an outpouring of concern from various religious and other organizations, Congress took up a bill to aid displaced persons in 1947. Of particular importance in this concern was the *Citizens Committee on Displaced Persons*, promoted by Jewish organizations, which was comprised of an impressive coalition of organizations promoting the admission of refugees. It included "Catholic and Protestant leaders, prominent members of the business community, social workers, public officials and academics... its national board boasted respected liberals like Eleanor Roosevelt, James Farley, Lehman, and LaGuardia." One of its most important achievements was to gain the support of the AFL, a labor organization that had in the past openly opposed liberalization of immigration policy. However, on the issue of refugees it took a sympathetic stance and at their convention in 1946 explicitly endorsed aid for displaced persons and specifically named Jews as in need of assistance. Nevertheless, intransigent restrictionists representing Southern Democrats and Southwest Conservatives held important chairmanships in both the House and the Senate and were able to bottle up the bill in committees and it never came to a vote.[6]

In 1948, these committee chairmen, after coming under intense pressure, allowed votes on a bill that allowed for 202,000 visas for displaced persons, but it included amendments which excluded refuge to most Jews. The president signed the bill but expressed disgust with its discriminatory and intolerant nature. Between the end of the war in 1945 and 1950, only 400,000 refugees were admitted through this bill, the president's executive order, and those coming under the existing country quotes.[7] However, by this time a great many of the displaced persons were those fleeing Communist rule in Eastern Europe, and the State department saw these people as valuable in its ideological struggles with the Soviet Union in the emerging Cold War. In 1950, the 1948 Act was extended to allow another 415,000 refugees or displaced persons during the following two years.[8]

It should be stressed that the displaced persons under discussion were those in the areas in Germany under United States military occupation. As stated previously, initially only about 20% were Jews, but the Jewish total increased as Jews were among the many fleeing Russian-dominated Eastern European countries, many of whose people were hostile to Jews. Jews were particularly unwelcome in Poland and many who returned to Poland after the war were attacked and hundreds killed. While most American Jewish organizations were vigorously concerned with providing asylum for their coreligionists, most desired that they be given asylum in Palestine which was under the control of the British government. In 1939, under pressure from Arab countries, Britain had issued the White Letter that set a limit of 100,000 Jews who would be allowed to immigrate to Palestine during the next 5 years, or fewer than 20,000 a year. This, of course, prevented many Jews who might have escaped Nazi control from going to the only place that wanted them. At the end of the War, the British government continued its policy of severely restricting Jewish immigration to

Palestine out of fear it would produce a military response from Arab governments, which Britain wished to avoid.[9]

The position of almost all Jewish organizations was that 100,000 Jews should be allowed immediate admission to Palestine for humanitarian reasons, a request backed by President Truman. Nevertheless, the British remained adamant in their refusal to change policy. American Jewish groups were split, however, between those who demanded that Britain honor its commitment under the Balfour Declaration to establish a Jewish homeland in Palestine and those Jewish organizations who opposed the establishment of a Jewish State. Eventually this issue was resolved by a UN resolution backed by the United States and the USSR creating a Jewish state in part of what had been the British Mandate in Palestine.[10]

It would be impossible, here, to do justice to the complications which led to this outcome, including the war waged by the Arab states that immediately broke out after the declaration of the Jewish state. It is pertinent to the issue of immigration that after 1948, Jewish refugees in European detention centers now had a place to go. After the successful establishment of the Jewish state, Jewish organizations, while still supporting the admission of displaced persons, saw the issue as somewhat less compelling for Jews. Another factor complicating the Jewish position was that among those claiming refugee status after 1950 were many ex-Nazis trying to escape harsh treatment by the Communist regimes established in Eastern Europe.[11] In the postwar years, according to Peter Novick, "about two-thirds of the Jewish survivors of the Holocaust who left Europe went to Palestine/Israel, one third to the United States," and by the early 1950s, some 100,000 had settled in the United States.[12]

The niggardly nature of the United States refugee measures was largely the result of the long-standing coalition of Southern Democrats and Southwestern Conservatives who held powerful chairmanships in both the House and Senate. They claimed that they were concerned about preserving jobs for the millions of servicemen returning to civilian life, a majority of whom expressed disapproval of greater refugee efforts, but the anti-Semitic nature of the legislation they fashioned was unmistakable.[13] In retrospect, it was the mean-spirited nature of these postwar actions which gave restrictionist sentiment the negative racist image it had in subsequent years. That image tainted the whole movement to limit immigration that had begun during the

1920s which was motivated by a host of concerns, most of which had little to do with anti-Semitism. In addition, the formation of the *Committee of Displaced Persons*, in response to Congressional inaction, served as the foundation of a coalition of interests that wished to end the restrictive national origins system. As a result of these wartime measures and the existing quotas, by the late 1940s immigration slowly increased and by the 1950s it had almost returned to the level of the late 1920s dictated by the 1924 act, averaging about 300,000 a year, with considerably less than half coming from Europe. It remained at that level until the mid-sixties, exceeding 300,000 in only three of those years.[14]

In 1952, Congress passed the McCarran-Walter Act that kept most of the 1924 provisions in place, and demonstrated the continued strength of the coalition of Southern Democratic and Southwestern conservatives on immigration. Its most significant change was the elimination of all formal Asian exclusion and, in addition, the naturalization of all Asians residing in the United States. It did so, however, grudgingly. It set the total yearly quota of 100 for those countries in what was called the Asia-Pacific Triangle. The act included a curious provision designed to limit Asian immigration from the Western Hemisphere of the many Asians who had, over the years, migrated into South America. To prevent these from immigrating to the United States, which had no quotas for the Western Hemisphere, Asian immigrants from South America were to be counted under the quotas (of 100) of their countries of origin, thereby severely limiting the immigration of Asians. However, by admitting existing Asian residents to citizenship, it allowed them to bring their spouses and children to the United States.[15] This last provision reflected, in some degree, the sense that the country had been mistaken to uproot Japanese citizens during the war and it sought to express appreciation for the contribution of Japanese men who had served in the American Army during the war. In all other respects, the act maintained the status quo and the limited immigration quotas of the 1929 Act.

Given the leading role of America in world affairs after World War II, the McCarran-Walter Act, which continued the enormous bias in favor of northern Europeans and people from the Americas, was an embarrassment and impediment to the foreign policy of the United States that, almost immediately after the war, was focused on the growing rivalry between the United States and the Communist regimes of the Soviet Union and China. President Truman, based on these concerns, vetoed the McCarran-Walter Act, but his veto was overridden by Congress, making clear its unwillingness to alter the immigration policies set in place in the 1920s.[16]

One feature of the McCarran-Walter Act is of significance for later developments. The law made it a felony to "willfully import, transport or harbor illegal aliens." In the Senate debates on this provision, Senator Paul Douglas proposed an amendment to stipulate that the hiring of illegal aliens would also be a criminal offense. The amendment was defeated through the efforts of Senator Eastland of Texas, who supported the interests of large-scale agriculture. The failure to criminalize the employment of illegal aliens became known as the "Texas Proviso."[17]

By the early 1960s, the struggle of black Americans to dismantle the Jim Crow laws of the South had gained the support of a majority of Americans. By that time, in addition, the full implications of the Nazi racial policies and the genocidal nature of that regime had entered into the consciousness of all Americans. The contradictions of the postwar revulsion to those racial policies and America's continued denial of full rights to black citizens could not reasonably be reconciled. In 1954, most Americans supported the Supreme Court in the Brown Decision that overturned the laws requiring racial segregation in the schools of the southern states. In addition, racial discrimination in America was a major hindrance in attracting Asian and African countries to the American side in its rivalry with the USSR and China. For these reasons, the Civil Rights Movement gained increasing support in the late 1950s and early 1960s. Furthermore, that support was widespread and included a majority of American and elite opinion, especially in the universities, in the foreign policy establishment, and among corporate executives with an interest in international markets.

The Civil Rights movement achieved fruition in the 1964 Civil Rights Act and the 1965 Voting Rights Act. Both acts were strongly endorsed by both political parties, with only the Democrats of the Deep South voting in the negative. In addition, the assassination of President Kennedy in 1963 had a galvanizing effect on efforts to move ahead with programs he had supported, among which had been efforts to reform race relations. His brothers, Robert and Edward, were in the forefront of these legislative efforts, as was the newly installed President Johnson. It should be noted that the acrimony between left and right which characterized the late 1960s as a result of the Vietnam War had not yet appeared in the early 1960s. In that period the political schism was between most of the country that supported the dismantling of Jim Crow and the recalcitrant Southerners who opposed those efforts.

The times were, therefore, propitious for the growing coalition of those who had long advocated a complete reform of immigration policy, especially as those policies could be characterized as racist in nature. But even those who saw nothing offensive in the existing quota system had reason to reconsider the McCarran-Walter Act. The Act was passed in anticipation of enormous numbers of people from war-ravaged Europe attempting to immigrate to the United States and especially in limiting those from eastern and southern Europe. In fact, this fear turned out to be unfounded. In the whole decade of the 1950s only 2.5 million immigrants arrived in the United States, and only 1.4 million (about 55%) were from Europe, less than would have been admitted under the quota system. The second-largest group (921,610) came from the Americas that had no quota restrictions. About 350,000 came from Canada and more than 60% from Central America, South America, and the Caribbean, with the largest number (about 250,000) coming from Mexico.[18]

In addition, the Act created especial hardships for recent immigrants from low-quota countries. People from countries with large quotas, such as England, France, and Germany, owing to their rapid recovery in the postwar years, did not fill their quotas. At the same time people from places like Poland, Italy and Greece were unable to bring in wives and children because the quotas created large backlogs in those countries. In addition, people from Eastern Europe, who were able to flee repressive Communist regimes, were blocked from coming because of the quotas. On the other hand, people from South and Central America, who were experiencing political turmoil and rapid population growth producing deteriorating economic conditions, came in increasing numbers, unhindered by quotas.[19] These anomalies led to a large number of Congressional bills to deal with individual hardship cases. According to Senator John F. Kennedy, writing in 1958, these private immigration bills "make up about half of our legislation today."[20]

Beyond those who came as immigrants to America, large numbers of people, primarily Mexicans, came to the United States as temporary agricultural workers. Many of these workers came under the *Bracero Program,* negotiated by the United States and the Mexican government, which authorized the orderly importation of temporary agricultural employees. However, large numbers of workers came as undocumented aliens outside of the *Bracero Program*; by the early 1950s, more than 500,000 illegal workers a year were being apprehended by the Immigration and Naturalization Service (INS); in 1954 the figure had risen to more than one million.[21] These numbers prompted many to call for better border enforcement, especially labor unions attempting to organize farm workers, since Mexican workers tended to undercut these efforts. Not surprisingly, large farm businesses, especially in Texas and California, opposed these attempts to reduce the supply of cheap labor. As long as the "Texas Proviso" remained in effect, employers had little incentive to cease hiring cheap illegal aliens whose status made them fearful of joining unions opposed by farmers. The *two-tiered* system discussed in the last chapter, restricting European immigration but ignoring Mexican immigration, became increasing difficult to justify.

In 1955, President Eisenhower, in response to public pressure, launched a major effort to remove these illegal workers in what became known as *Operation Wetback*. In that year, over one million people were apprehended and deported, mainly to Mexico. In an effort to placate the growers, the government increased the number of *Braceros* admitted to more than 400,000, doubling the number allowed earlier in the decade.[22] If these numbers are added to the 273,847 Mexicans who came as permanent immigrants, Mexico was at the time the major contributor of the foreign-born living in the United States during the 1950s.[23]

The Immigration Act of 1965

These changing patterns of immigration made many legislators receptive to rethinking immigration policy. From the very beginning those who urged change argued for replacing the national origins system with a system more suitable to the economic needs and foreign policy of the world's dominant democracy and leader of the Free World. In this formulation, discriminatory immigration policy was inconsistent with American ideals and the diplomatic demands of the Cold War, not to mention the needs of a booming postwar economy. Among the champions of this view was Senator John F. Kennedy who in 1958 had authored the book, *A Nation of Immigrants* that heralded the contributions of immigrants and advocated an end to what he viewed as the racist and morally compromised national origins policy. After he became President, Kennedy continued his support for change and in 1963 called on Congress to repeal the existing system, invoking the language of the Civil Rights Movement. In effect, his efforts to support an end to discrimination in immigration policy were an extension of his efforts to end discrimination against blacks in the United States.[24]

President Johnson continued Kennedy's effort for civil rights reform, signing the Civil Rights Bill in 1964 and the Voting Rights Act of 1965. He was, however, reluctant to support changes in the immigration status quo, especially those opposed by his supporters in Texas; as senator he had supported the McCarran-Walter Act. However, he eventually was convinced that immigration reform was a necessary corollary of the Civil Rights Act.[25] When the Immigration Act of 1965 came before him he signed it and in his speech at the signing ceremony he hailed it "as one of the most important acts of this Congress and this administration." He went on to say that it repairs "a very deep and painful flaw in the fabric of American justice. It corrects a cruel and enduring wrong in the conduct of the American Nation." Johnson elaborated:

> The system violated the basic principle of American democracy—the principal that values and rewards each man on the basis of his merit as a man. It has been un-American in the highest sense, because it has been untrue to the faith that brought thousands to these shores even before we were a country.[26]

Johnson's language reflected elite opinion at the time. Most Americans, on the other hand, saw nothing wrong with the existing immigration policy. When questioned, the public by a wide margin (58% to 24%) were "strongly opposed to easing of immigration law."[27] It is important to note the difference between elite and public opinion, since that has been a continuing feature of immigration policy. It is also important to note Johnson's tone in supporting the act, and casting those who might oppose the bill as "un-American" and in favor of a "cruel" and unjust policy. Such ad hominem attacks on those who wish to limit immigration have also been a continuing characteristic of those who support unrestrictive immigration policies.

Senators Sam Irvin of North Carolina and Robert Byrd of Virginia opposed the bill and questioned the premise that the current policy was cruel and unjust. Irvin saw nothing untoward in discrimination "in favor of national groups who historically had the greatest influence in building the nation." Byrd elaborated, arguing that the then current system was both just and wise and pointing out that "every other country that is attractive to immigrants practices selectively (in favor of their founding nationalities) and without apology." Byrd asked why the United States should be the only country "to develop a guilt complex concerning its immigration policies."[28] The bill's supporters insisted on framing it in moral terms, and in addition, argued that opponents were wrong in thinking it would change the ethnic makeup of the country. Senator Edward Kennedy claimed that under the bill neither the number nor ethnicity of immigrants would change appreciably. Quoting him, "the present level of immigration remains substantially the same. Secondly, the ethnic mix of this country will not be upset..."[29]

In effect, the bill's supporters seemed to be suggesting that the bill was largely symbolic and would not, in fact, change things very much. The limitation on immigration from outside the Western Hemisphere was little changed from the numbers existing under the 1952 McCarran-Walter Act. In addition it placed limits, for the first time, on immigration from the Americas. These facts no doubt explain the general acceptance of the new law by the general public. In addition, it had become clear by 1965 that the fear that Eastern and Southern Europeans would fail to assimilate was without foundation. There was little discernable difference in the relative success of the various ethnic groups, all of whom, including the Japanese, had made heroic contributions to the war effort. A final factor was that there had been very little immigration during the preceding 40 years, allowing for the thorough integration of most groups into the American mainstream.

It is important to understand the details of the law that Johnson signed, since it had consequences completely at odds with the effects predicted by its sponsors. The 1965 bill limited immigration from outside the Western hemisphere to 170,000 people, with no one country allowed more than 20,000. In addition, it limited immigration from the Western Hemisphere to 120,000. In 1978, these figures were combined so as to allow the admission of 290,000 people worldwide and to apply the 20,000 limit to all countries, including those of Central and South America. The bill would have allowed for immigration from Europe to reach the numbers common in the 1950s, and the supporters assumed, incorrectly, that such numbers would continue in future decades. Only Germany had sent more than 20,000 immigrants in the 1950s. The supporters of the bill thought that few Asians would come, basing that belief on the few applications for admittance by Asians during the 1950s and early 1960s. But, of course, with quotas set at 100 per Asian country, it would have been fruitless for Asians to apply for immigration visas. Based on the above assumptions, supporters argued that immigration would not increase very much, and would not alter the ethnic mix of the population appreciably.[30] Of course, these predictions assumed that the push factors driving people to immigrate would remain unchanged. It is difficult to understand why they would make such an assumption, as those factors had already begun to change during the 1950s. This was especially the case with regard to the large increases in people coming from Latin America.

Within the numerical limits, the bill specified a set of preferences strongly favoring the relatives of existing (and especially recent) residents and citizens. In addition, immediate family members (spouses, minor children and parents) of citizens were exempt from any numerical limits. For all others, visas were provided on a first-come basis according to the following system of preferences:

1. First Preference: Unmarried adult children of U. S. Citizens. (Maximum of 20%)

2. Second Preference: Spouses and unmarried adult children of resident aliens. (20% plus any not used in the first preference).

3. Third preference: Members of the professions and scientists and artists of exceptional ability. To be determined by the Department of Labor. (Maximum of 10%).

4. Fourth Preference: Married adult children of U. S. citizens. (10% plus any not used in the first three preferences).

5. Fifth Preference: Brothers and sisters of U. S. citizens. (24% plus any not needed in the first four preferences).

6. Sixth Preference: Skilled and unskilled workers in short supply as certified by the Department of Labor. (Maximum of 10%).

7. Seventh Preference: Refugees. (Maximum of 6%).

8. Eighth Preference: Applicants not entitled to any of the above.[31]

A number of questions arise when examining these preference requirements. First, is the low priority assigned to workers (Preferences 3 and 6). President Johnson in his signing remarks said that those wishing to immigrate "shall be admitted on the basis of their skills and their close relationship to those already here." But only 20% were to be admitted on the basis of needed skills and these needs were required to be certified by the Department of Labor. It was expected that labor unions would object to these visas as they had made clear their belief that no such provision was necessary. According to Roger Daniels, writing in 1990, "less than 4% in recent years" came under these two preferences.[32] The second question is the very low quota assigned to refugees which is curious given the claim that the bill was based in morality and compassion. A third question is why there was an absolute limit on the labor and refugee quotas, but no such limit on the family quotas. For instance, if only 10% of the applicants who applied did so on the basis of the first preference, as many as 30% would have been able to apply under the second preference, since they were entitled to 20% and could add the unused portion of the 10% in the first preference. However, no such accumulation is provided for preferences 3, 6, and 7. A fourth question concerns the very large preference provided for siblings, and the nonquota allowance for parents. In America and in Western European tradition, the primary family unit is the nuclear family. People living in such societies owe primary allegiance to spouses and children, and are not required by law or custom to show allegiance to siblings. In addition, the Western Tradition envisions the newly married couple as starting off anew and requires no legal or moral responsibilities toward parents beside those of affection. In many societies, to the contrary, especially in the Third-World, the extended family is the rule. In most Arab societies, for instance, the extended family or clan is the primary bond and takes precedence over immediate family loyalties. In many Asian societies, parental authority extends into the adult life of a child. Why should American immigration policy accommodate the extended family traditions alien to European and American patterns?

The full ramifications of this set of preferences were not discussed and presumably not examined. For instance, the bill strongly favored recent immigrants. People whose ancestors came before the 1920s, for example, were very unlikely to have any relatives who would qualify under this system of preferences. On the other hand, a recent immigrant was very likely to have parents and siblings and spouses who would qualify. If Europeans and other groups had continued to migrate according to their historic pattern, then the ethnic mix in America would not, indeed, have been affected. But Europeans were not immigrating in large numbers, while very large numbers were coming from Asia and Latin America. This change in the ethnic mix was exaggerated by the fact that the system allowed for a pattern of chain migration in which one individual could bring in large numbers of relatives within and outside the numerical limits. For instance, a person who came to work under the third preference could qualify as a legal resident after two years. He could then bring in his wife and children under the second preference. Once he became a citizen, he could then bring his parents (outside of any preference). He could also bring in his siblings under preference 5. His siblings would also qualify once his parents become resident aliens, under preference 2. Once his brothers and sisters become resident aliens, they could, in turn, bring their spouses and minor children without numerical limit. And so on. In his book, David Reimers demonstrated that it is highly feasible under these preferences, which remain in effect to this day, for one immigrant to bring in 18 others within 10 years. One consequence of the family unification provisions was that a great many more people were able to immigrate (with and without preference status) then law makers anticipated. In 1977, 1/3 of immigrants came outside any preference limitation under these family provisions. In that year 389,089 immigrants arrived, a figure considerably in excess of the 290,000 limit envisioned in the 1965 bill.

People from industrialized countries generally have small families and relatively few siblings, while people from Third-World countries often have very large families and therefore many siblings. In addition, people from industrialized societies have little economic incentive to immigrate, while just the opposite is true for Third-World people. For these reasons, the bill was heavily biased in favor of Third-World immigration. This is reflected in the immigration statistics. In the 1950s, approximately 2.5 million immigrants arrived, of whom 55% came from Europe and Canada. In the 1970s, after the bill took effect, immigration totaled about 4.3 million, of whom less than 25% came from Europe and Canada. In the 1990s total immigration had risen to almost 10 million, of whom about 16% came from Europe (mainly Eastern Europe) and Canada. In that decade about 5 million came from the Americas (excluding Canada), mainly from Mexico, Central America and the Caribbean, and almost 3 million from Asia. It should be stressed that these numbers are official statistics of immigrants of legal status, and do not include the very large number of illegal migrants who came into America every year. According to the Census Bureau in the year 2000, 10.4% of the population was foreign born, which begins to approach the figure of 14.7% in 1910, after the extraordinary wave of immigration late in the 19th and the early 20th Centuries. If one includes the people living illegally in the country and their offspring, who are not included in the official census data, the percentage of foreign born today is probably greater than it was in 1910.

Roger Daniels, who in his writings is extremely supportive of current immigration patterns is, nevertheless, highly critical of the legislators who passed the 1965 Bill, arguing that they "did not know what they were talking about and had not, obviously, paid close attention to what had been happening in immigration patterns in the United States."[33] The point is that, whether one approves of the current ethnic mix in immigration or not, the lawmakers who passed the bill were completely wrong in their estimates of its effect. Had any sound demographic modeling been done, this outcome could have been anticipated. As it was, the lawmakers voted in almost total ignorance of the consequences of their actions, and by any standard were grossly irresponsible. It is undeniable that the general public, who did not wish to see increased immigration, and did not desire these massive changes, were treated shabbily by their elected representatives.

Recent Immigration Legislation: Refugees and Reform

In 1965, when the Immigration Act was passed, the Cold War was at its height and the United States began to use immigration as a weapon in that war. The logic was simple: people fleeing Communist regimes and eager to come to the West and to America in particular, presented clear evidence of the superiority, both economically and morally, of the non-Communist West. When Fidel Castro announced that anyone who wished to leave Cuba was free to do so, large numbers of Cubans indicated a desire to migrate to the United States. Under the 1965 immigration law, a maximum of 6% were allowed admittance as refugees. Six percent of the total quota for the whole world would have meant that only 17,400 could be admitted as refugees. In order to get around this limitation, President Johnson claimed a "parole power," a power disputed by many legislators, to admit all Cubans who could make it to these shores. Congress regularized Johnson's action in the Cuban Refugee Adjustment Act of 1966 which granted special refugee status to all Cuban refugees, and placed them in a category outside the 1965 limits.[34] In the period between 1960 and 2000, some 750,000 Cubans arrived, which is less than the single country limit of 20,000 a year for Cuba, but these were outside the quota set for the Western Hemisphere.[35]

The fall of the South Vietnamese to the Communist North in the 1970s produced a continuing stream of refugees fleeing the harsh treatment they feared from the new Communist regime. Many of these had worked for or supported the United States during the Vietnam War and sought refuge in the United States. Subsequent upheaval in Indochina, not the least of which was the vicious regime of the Cambodian Communists, produced additional refugees. President Ford used the disputed parole power to bring many of them to this country and provided temporary assistance during their initial period of settlement. Subsequent Presidents continued to use their parole authority to settle additional refugees. By 1990, about 900,000 refugees from Indochina had been admitted.[36] Very large numbers continued to come after 1990. For instance, between 1970 and 1990, 322,000 Vietnamese arrived in the United States. Between 1990 and 2007, their number totaled 478,000.[37] Of course, these recent immigrants included many who came as relatives of those who had come earlier.

Political events in the Caribbean and Central America produced large numbers of people fleeing conditions made difficult by authoritarian regimes of the Left and Right. For instance, large numbers of people fled the dictatorial regime of Haiti for American shores. Since the United States supported Haiti's Duvalier regime at the time, these people were treated as illegal aliens who were viewed as coming for economic reasons, and therefore did not qualify as political refugees. However, domestic politics made their deportation problematic and most remained in the United States, with their status remaining undetermined until resolved by Congress in 1986.

In 1980, Congress attempted to regularize the treatment of refugees in the 1980 Refugee Act, and to gain more legislative control over the admission of refugees that had been, defacto, ceded to the executive branch. Many in Congress, as earlier mentioned, disputed the legitimacy of the parole power of the Presidency in that nowhere was such broad authority explicitly granted to the President.[38] The Refugee Act of 1980 raised the number of those admitted under the refugee preference to 50,000. However, the President was given the authority to exceed that number, after consultation with Congress, for either humanitarian reasons or reasons of national interest. In effect, Congress had increased the statutory limitation under the preference system from 290,000 to approximately 325,000. However, the 50,000 limit was exceeded in every year through 2001. Because of a backlog that had built up in the 1970s, almost 160,000 were admitted as refugees in 1980 and in 1981. The numbers fell off somewhat in the late 1980s, but averaged more than 100,000 in the early 1990s. Realistically, the 1980 Refugee act raised immigration to almost 400,000, not including those close relatives, spouses, children, and parents, admitted without limit.[39] The net result was that in the 1980s, legal immigration rose to an average of 600,000 a year, and rose to about 1 million a year in the 1990s.[40]

By the mid 1970s, the failure of the predictions of the supporters of the 1965 Immigration Act was perfectly clear. Not only were the numbers much greater than anticipated, but the assertion that the ethnic makeup of the United States would remain unchanged proved erroneous. The vast majority of immigrants were coming from Asia and the Americas, while few were coming from Europe. It was becoming perfectly clear that if these immigration trends were to continue, major changes in American demography were inevitable. Large majorities of Americans understood this reality, were unhappy about it, and favored curtailing immigration.

In addition to the concern with the scope of legal immigration, illegal immigration had become a major cause of concern for most Americans by the early 1970s. After *Operation Wetback* in the 1950s, the apprehension of illegal workers declined to approximately 50,000 people per year and though rising in the early 1960s, it never surpassed 100,000, and was not of major concern during the discussions leading up to the 1965 Act. However, one of the provisions of the 1965 Immigration act was the elimination of the *Bracero program*, with the result that there was no legal route of entry for seasonal agricultural workers. Since agricultural interests continued to desire cheap Mexican labor, there arose powerful incentives for workers to cross the border illegally and their numbers rose steadily after the act was passed in 1965. The number of illegal aliens rose from 86,597 in 1964 to over one million by the late seventies, reaching 1,767,400 in 1986.[41] According to *Time* magazine in 1977, "Some 80% of the illegal aliens now living in America came from Mexico, where population is growing at the rate of 3.4% a year, the jobless rate approaches 40% and a man lucky enough to find work may be paid $1 a day."[42] *Time* reported that the Mexicans were joined by large numbers of Haitians, Colombians, Jamaicans, Greeks, Filipinos, and Nigerians, and noted further that, "aliens used to do mainly farm work in the South and Southwest. But they have now established enclaves in major urban centers. According to the Immigration and Naturalization Service (INS) estimates, there are 50,000 illegal aliens in Washington D.C., more than 500,000 in Chicago and 1.3 million in the New York metropolitan area." *Time* went on to quote Leonard Chapman, the former INS commissioner; "We have become the haven for the unemployed of the world. I think its going to be catastrophic."[43]

The problem was directly the result of the fact that the INS was remarkably underequipped to deal with the situation. In 1979, the number arrested crossing the border in the area near Tijuana, Mexico had risen to more than 300,000, twelve times what it had been ten years earlier. To deal with these numbers, the INS had all of 40 men working that sector of the border. That they were able to apprehend almost 1,000 people a day is remarkable. It was clear, however, that the vast majority of illegal border-crossers were never apprehended. While many of these workers were transients and returned home, many remained in the United States. According to 1979 estimates by the INS, there were 3 million undocumented Mexican illegal aliens in the country and that number was augmented at the "rate of 500,000 to 800,000 a year."[44]

Throughout the 1970s, according to historian Otis Graham, Congressional liberals, sensitive to the concerns of the labor movement, attempted to overturn the "Texas Proviso" and criminalize the hiring of illegal aliens. These efforts were continuously blocked by Senator James Eastland, the author of the Texas proviso.[45] By the late 1970s, America was plagued by economic difficulties which were to become characterized as "stagflation." Unemployment was growing and would reach its highest rate since World War II in the early 1980s.[46] Massive legal and illegal immigration were seen as contributing to the problem. In 1977, 77% of Americans favored a ban on the hiring of illegal immigrants and supported sanctions on employers who violated the ban.[47] In 1980, 80% of Americans also wanted legal immigration reduced.[48] In that same year, 66% favored a complete halt to immigration whenever unemployment exceeded 5%.[49]

In 1980, newly elected President Reagan created a task force to study the immigration issue, appointing Father Theodore Hesburgh, President of Notre Dame University, to chair the task force. In its report, released in 1981, the task force acknowledged public misgivings about immigration, but failed to recommend any changes in the existing policy, except regarding illegal immigration. On this issue, it argued in favor of criminalizing the hiring of illegal aliens mainly as a way to avoid an expected popular backlash against all immigration.[50]

In 1981, the House and Senate opened joint hearings on the reform of the Immigration laws, chaired by Senator Alan Simpson and Representative Romano Mazzoli. Senator Simpson spoke for many Americans when he asserted:

> The American people are so fed up from being told—when they want immigration laws enacted which they believe will serve their national interest and when they also want the law enforced—that they are being cruel and mean-spirited and racist. They are fed up with efforts to make them feel that Americans do not have that fundamental right of any people—to decide who will join them here and help them form the future country in which they and their posterity will live...[51]

The joint hearings resulted in the Simpson-Mazzoli Bill that was introduced in both houses of Congress in 1981. Both sponsors had originally hoped to revise the 1965 Act so as to reduce the magnitude of immigration, a reduction the public overwhelmingly desired. Simpson, for instance, proposed eliminating the fifth preference for siblings that clearly exacerbated the problem of chain migration. On this proposal, Simpson argued that, "I do feel that family preference categories should be based on the United States concept and definition of a nuclear family and not on the definition of such a family as expressed in other nations."[52]

However, given the respected stature of Father Hesburgh, the sponsors chose to limit their proposals to deal solely with illegal immigration as was recommended by the task force he chaired. Both sponsors hoped to tackle the larger problems caused by the 1965 Act at a later date. The very limited Simpson-Mazzoli Bill was introduced in 1981. It passed in the Senate, but failed to pass in the House in 1981 and again in 1982. It was reintroduced in 1983 and once again passed in the Senate but died in the House. It didn't come up again until 1986, when it was, in fact, enacted as the Immigration Reform and Control Act of 1986.

The resulting law reflected a host of compromises among various powerful interests. On the one hand, there was the general public who by a very large majority wanted to end the flow of illegal aliens. A poll commissioned by the Federation of Americans for Immigration Reform (FAIR) found that a substantial majority of blacks and even Hispanics favored improved border controls and employee sanctions. In the case of Hispanics, this result is hardly surprising, since undocumented Hispanic workers were in direct competition with legal Hispanic immigrants and citizens.[53] Blacks favored control of illegal immigration for similar reasons.

A powerful coalition of interest groups opposing the public's preferences was made up of the numerous immigrant advocacy agencies and other nonprofit organizations, most supported by large foundations, and religious organizations and other groups who opposed any measures that might threaten illegal aliens residing in the country. The idea of government sweeps to round up and deport illegal aliens, as had been done in *Operation Wetback,* was strongly opposed by these groups and had little popular political support or support in Congress. Such actions had become unpalatable because of the changed nature of illegal immigration. In the early 1950s, most illegal aliens were male farm workers who intended to go home voluntarily after their seasonal work was done. By the 1980s, however, large numbers of illegal aliens were regularly employed in urban settings and women and children made up a sizable portion of these individuals. Also, by the 1980s, television was almost universal in American homes and the primary source of news for most people. Images of federal agents dragging women and children from their homes and deporting them en masse would have been widely deplored and would have conjured up images of the Nazi roundups during World War II. Such actions, however, would have been unnecessary with better border security and real and enforceable sanctions on businesses hiring illegal aliens. Without the lure of employment, far fewer would have come and many would have left voluntarily.

A second powerful coalition opposing restrictions was composed of those industries, such as agriculture, the hospitality and other service industries, that benefited from a supply of inexpensive labor. These industries found allies among the many teachers and welfare workers who directly benefited from additional students and clients. Added to these were the considerable and growing number of upper middle-class and wealthy households who increasingly employed illegal immigrants as maids and nannies, and who employed the services of landscapers and home cleaning firms in which illegal immigrants kept wages low and prices in check. Finally, there were the lawmakers themselves, many of whom welcomed this or that group, out of the simple belief that they might provide additional voters, once regularized, who could be expected to gratefully return them to office. It should be stressed that recent immigrants, especially Hispanics, did not at the time represent a significant voting block since many had not yet been naturalized and could not vote. However, in recent years, this changed and Hispanics became increasingly important in electoral politics.

The law satisfied the desire for a humane solution for resident illegal aliens by granting amnesty to those who had been resident in the country for at least 4 years. Under this provision any illegal alien who could demonstrate that he had been continuously resident in the country before December 31, 1981, could apply for temporary residency, which could be converted to permanent resident status within 18 months. Once permanent residency was established, the person could then apply for citizenship.

The law included, for the first time in the history of immigration law, a civics provision listed under the heading "Basic Citizenship Skills." The law stipulated that the immigrant must demonstrate a "minimal understanding of ordinary English and a knowledge and understanding of the history and government of the United States," or "is satisfactorily pursuing a course of study (recognized by the Attorney General) to achieve such an understanding of English and such a knowledge and understanding of the history and government of the United States."[54]

The law made a disingenuous attempt to satisfy the general public with promises of greater border security and penalties for employers who hired illegal aliens. It was disingenuous because it gave employers great leeway in avoiding prosecution for hiring illegal aliens. As no national ID existed or was proposed under the law, an employer was merely required to attest that he had examined a small number of a long list of documents, such as a social security card, a birth certificate or a driver's license indicating that an employee was in the country legally. Almost immediately an industry grew up for the sale of these readily forged documents. The law specifically stated that an employer was in compliance with the document verification clause if "the document reasonably appears on its face to be genuine." In addition, in order to prevent discrimination against recent legal immigrants, it made it "an unfair immigration-related employment practice" to discriminate on the basis of national origin.[55] In fact, the bill spends almost as much time talking about preventing discrimination as it does preventing the hiring of illegal aliens. In practice this meant that if an employer questioned the legitimacy of a worker's document, such as a driver's license or birth certificate that "on its face appears to be genuine," he could be charged with unfair discrimination.

To satisfy agricultural interests, Congress created, at the last minute and almost as an afterthought, a second path to legal status for seasonal farm workers who could obtain permanent resident status "if they could demonstrate that they had 60 days agricultural work experience in qualifying crops from May 1985 to May 1986."[56] This amendment for "special agricultural workers" or SAW was passed without hearings and was curious indeed. As representative James Sensenbrenner pointed out at the time, while nonagricultural workers applying for legalization had to prove "that they have lived and worked in the U. S. since 1982," these agricultural workers "only have to account for 60 days, with documents which would be difficult to, if not impossible to verify, and easy to draw up." While immigrants under the normal provisions were required to meet the English and history requirements, these requirements did not apply to SAW applicants. Another extraordinary benefit to agricultural interests was that INS agents were prohibited from questioning workers on a farm without first obtaining a search warrant or the farm owner's consent.[57] No such provision was provided for nonagricultural businesses. These provisions meant that, in effect, agricultural employers were exempt from the law.

In the final analysis, most interests were satisfied by the 1986 Act except for those of the general public. Approximately 1.7 million resident aliens obtained legal status under the general (non-SAW) provisions, and 1.4 million under the SAW provisions, or 3.1 million in all. Approximately 90% of these people were from the Americas, with 70% from Mexico. As in the 1965 Act, the legislators got their numbers completely wrong in this bill. They had claimed that only about 250,000 people would apply under the SAW provision, rather than the 1.4 million who actually applied. In addition, far fewer nonagricultural unauthorized workers applied for legal residency than expected, which meant that many illegal aliens remained illegal. Furthermore, there were no clear provisions made for the removal of those who arrived after 1982. Betsy Cooper and Kevin O'Neil, authors of a 2005 report by the Migration Policy Institute argued "these people became the nucleus of the unauthorized population today."[58]

When it came to stemming the flow of illegal immigrants, the law was totally ineffective. The employer sanctions provided very few incentives to reduce the hiring of illegal aliens, since documents "which on their face appear genuine" were easy to obtain, and questioning those documents opened an employer to charges of discrimination. Efforts to secure the border were minimal, at best. The law stipulated that "sufficient funds shall be available to provide for an increase in the border patrol personnel of the Immigration and Naturalization Service so that the average level of such personnel in each of fiscal years 1987 and 1988 is at least 50 percent higher than such level for fiscal year 1986."[59] But given the total inadequacy of the border patrol at the time, a 50% increase was, at best, a token increase and totally inadequate to meaningfully reduce the flow of those wishing to enter without authorization. In fact, the number of apprehensions reported by the INS fell initially from the high figure of 1986, but by 1992 apprehensions had grown to what they had been in 1984 and by 2000 surpassed the 1986 number.[60] An intensive study of migratory patterns among Mexicans in the late 1980s concluded that "In none of these analyses could we detect any evidence that IRCA [Immigration Reform and Control Act] has significantly deterred undocumented migration from Mexico."[61]

1990 Immigration Act

In 1990 Congress addressed the immigration issue again. This was prompted by three developments. The first was the economic prosperity of the late 1980s, which created demands from business interests for the greater immigration of skilled workers. The second was a large pool, estimated at 100,000 illegal aliens from Ireland who had migrated to America during an economic recession in Ireland during the 1980s. Most of these people came after 1982 and could not apply for legalization under the 1986 law. Furthermore, few Irish could be sponsored as relatives under the preference system, since few had close relatives in the country. As mentioned earlier, American citizens of European decent had few opportunities to sponsor relatives under the relative preferences. The third factor was that many people who had arrived before 1982, and qualified for amnesty, had brought spouses and children into the country after 1982, who were not qualified for legalization.

As usual, the final bill required a compromise between those who wished for basic changes, especially regarding family unification, and those who wished to maintain or even expand the family preferences. Business interests and immigrant-support organizations favoring greater immigration were in direct conflict with the American public who quite clearly wanted reduced immigration. As in past legislation, the desire of the majority of Americans was simply ignored. The law raised overall immigration to 675,000, with an additional 25,000 during the first three years. It responded to the concerns of immigrant-support groups by raising the total admitted under the family preferences to 480,000. It responded to business interests by raising the number admitted under the preference for skilled workers to 140,000, a rise of 100,000 over the previous 40,000 limit. It did not change in any way the numbers permitted for immediate family members that were admitted outside any preference provisions. It will be recalled that the 1965 Act had limited immigration to 290,000 per year under the various preferences, so that this bill more than doubled permitted immigration, completely at variance with the wishes of the electorate.

The bill created a new "diversity" category of 40,000 (to be raised to 55,000 after three years) specifically reserved for the European countries that were unable to take advantage of the family preference provisions of 1965 Act. This provision created a lottery in which 40,000 (later 55,000) visas would be issued on a first come, first served basis to the citizens of mainly European countries. To deal specifically with the Irish illegal aliens it set aside, for the first three years, 16,000 of these "diversity visas" for Ireland. In addition, the law made a variety of relatively minor changes in the existing laws. It raised the individual country limit from 20,000 visas to about 25,000. It also raised to 10,000 the number of persons who could receive residency under the asylum provision. This provision allowed someone illegally in the United States to apply for asylum on the basis that he might be persecuted if returned to his homeland.[62]

Perhaps the most perverse aspect of the Act was the way it dealt with those individual family members of amnestied individuals who came after 1982. According to Cooper and O'Neil, "The INS originally held that legalized migrants should wait until receiving permanent residency and then apply to sponsor family members through normal channels."[63] Under normal channels, the spouses and children of Mexicans, for instance, would have had to return to Mexico and be admitted under quotas that had a large backlog of applications. In the 1990 Act, Congress resolved the dilemma by allowing these families members to stay and work in the United States and apply for legal status while doing so.[64] This, of course, created the anomaly, some would say injustice, whereby an illegal Mexican immigrant who brought his family in during the interim period could remain with his family, while the legal immigrant would have to wait for his sponsored family members who were queuing up behind the long line of those waiting for admission.[65]

It is important to stress that the law did not change the family preference provisions, including the unlimited immigration of spouses, children, and parents, nor the preference for siblings. Nor did it change the numbers admitted under the refugee preference, which had been targeted at 50,000 in the 1980 Refugee Act, but actually averaged about 100,000 (due to the leeway allowed Presidents in defining refugee status). The figure of 675,000 in the 1990 bill approximated the actual number of immigrants admitted in the mid 1980s, before the large numbers were granted permanent resident status by the amnesty provisions of the 1986 act. In other words, instead of attempting to correct the law so as to limit immigration to the numbers specified in the 1986 law, as most people wanted, it merely raised the number to be in line with actual immigration.

The act also created a new category for temporary workers under what was termed the H-1B visa. This was separate from the preference for skilled workers that was raised to 140,000 individuals. Under the H-1B visa, a maximum number of 65,000 workers with at least a BA degree could apply for a 3-year visa that could be renewed for an additional 3 years. Such a worker could bring in his spouse and minor children during the duration of his employment. The increases in the skilled worker preference and the H-1B visas were motivated by a concern expressed by the National Science Foundation that predicted a shortage of technical workers, especially scientists and engineers in coming years. This provision is complicated and has stirred considerably controversy, and for that reason will be dealt with in a separate section further on.

Recent Legislative Actions

In 1994, the Congress passed a little-understood amendment, Section 245(i) that reinstated the provision allowing for the legalization of illegal aliens under the 1990 act that had expired by 1994. This provision was to last from 1995 and expire on September 30, 1997. However, it was extended in 1998 and again in 2000, and set to expire on April 30, 2001.[66]

Amendment 245(i) did not merely reinstate the legalization provision, but changed it in important ways. Under the original 1986 provision, an individual had to demonstrate that he had entered the country legally and had remained in permanent residence since some specified date, and in addition would have to have been eligible for legal immigration under one of the preference provisions. Under the new, amended version he did not have to demonstrate that he had arrived legally or had resided permanently for any specified time. The only condition was that he qualified because of one of the preference provisions. In practice this meant that a person, a brother of an United States citizen, for instance, who had entered the country illegally without a visa, or who had come as a tourist and overstayed his visit, could apply for 245(i) status if sponsored by his brother.[67]

The applicant was required to pay a $1,000 processing fee and undergo a background check for criminal violations. If his application was approved he was granted the right to remain in the country without fear of deportation, though he was not supposed to obtain employment. If there was a backlog of applications for visas in his native country, as there was, for instance in Mexico, he would have to join the waiting list and apply for an "adjustment" to permanent resident status once he became eligible under the quota system, all the while remaining in the country, and in all likelihood working, given the lax enforcement of the employment ban.

The law has been widely attacked as incoherent and in contradiction of the elaborate procedures set up for legal immigration. Under those routine procedures a person had to apply for immigration in his native country, provide a sponsor under the family or work preference provisions, join a list of other approved applicants and then wait until the quota provisions for his country allowed him to immigrate. Given that many countries had large backlogs of applicants, the waiting period could be many years. Taking a hypothetical example, suppose a Mexican citizen had a brother who had immigrated to America and eventually acquired citizenship. Under the normal procedures he would have to wait approximately seven years (for his brother to become a U. S. citizen) before he could be sponsored by his brother and would then have to join the backlogged line of those who had applied before him. Practically speaking he might have to wait ten or more years, after his brother immigrated, to qualify for legal immigration.

Under 245(i), however, such a person could enter the United States without authorization as soon as his brother became a citizen and could then be granted 245(i) status that would allow him to settle in America immediately. If he were willing to risk the small likelihood of being detected and deported, he could come even before his brother achieved citizenship, and wait until his brother did so. It is hard to imagine a more perverse incentive for illegal entry. It is hardly surprising that the numbers following the illegal route to citizenship grew considerably while this provision remained in effect. In addition, even after the provision expired it continued to act as an incentive for others to enter illegally given the not unreasonable expectation that it might be reinstated in the future as it had on two previous occasions.

In addition to 245(i), a number of other laws were passed in the late 1990s and early 2000s, allowing those who had entered without legal visas to adjust their status to permanent residency and eventually citizenship. One such act, passed in 1997, entitled the Nicaraguan Adjustment and Central American Relief Act (NACARA) was designed to regularize the status of Central Americans who had fled the war and political turmoil of the region during the 1980s and 1990s and settled in the United States illegally. It is estimated that this applied to almost one million people.[68]

In 1998, Congress passed the "Haitian Refugee Fairness Act Amnesty," which regularized the status of some 125,000 illegal aliens who had fled Haiti. In 2000, Congress passed a law granting the right to apply for legalization to approximately 400,000 people who had filed lawsuits claiming they were unfairly denied permanent resident status under the provisions of the 1986 law.[69] In that same year, as discussed earlier, Congress reinstated the 245(i) provision allowing individuals to apply during the four months from January through April of 2001. This act was passed as the "Immigration through the Legal Immigration Family Equity Act (LIFE) of 2000.[70]

All of these various amnesty provisions added large numbers of permanent residents and citizens. In addition to granting residency to previously illegal aliens, it also increased the numbers of those eligible to gain entry through the family preference provisions. In four of the first six years of the new century, the annual numbers admitted exceeded one million. In 2006, the most recent year reported by the Department of Homeland Security, the number was 1,266,265, or almost if not quite double the ceiling of 675,000 envisioned under the 1990 law. These numbers, furthermore, do not include the estimated 100,000 to 200,000 individuals who enter the country illegally every year. A breakdown of the people gaining admittance in 2006 under the various provisions is given in Table 6.1. Their regions of origin are given in Table 6.2.

TABLE 6.1. TOTAL LEGAL IMMIGRATION IN 2006

Family Sponsored Preferences	222,229
Employment-Based Preferences	159,081
Immediate Relatives	580,483
Refugees	99,609
Asylum	116,845
Diversity	44,471
Others	43,546
Total	1,266,264[71]

TABLE 6.2. THE REGIONAL ORIGINS OF IMMIGRANTS IN 2006

Africa	112,108
Asia	411,795
Europe	169,197
North America	338,439
Central America	74,258
South America	136,149
Oceania	8,001
Total	1,266,262[72]

It was clear throughout this period that the Immigration Act of 1965 had produced results altogether at variance with its supporter's predictions. Furthermore, by the mid-1970s, at the latest, it was clear that the vast majority of Americans wanted a reduction in legal as well as illegal immigration. Congress, nevertheless, failed even to address the question of legal immigration and in fact increased the number. It made minimal, window-dressing efforts to halt illegal immigration, and in fact enacted a long list of confusing alphabet-soup titled laws that were bound to increase the incentives for illegal immigration. Demographer Jeffrey Passel remarked

> [b]y the mid-1990s...unauthorized population was growing rapidly. In 2006, an estimated 11.5 to 12 million illegal immigrants were living in the United States, compared with 3 million to 5 million at the passage of IRCA (Immigration Reform and Control Act of 1986) 20 years earlier.[73]

To address this problem and the considerable concern of the populace, Congress passed the "Secure Fence Act of 2006" that directed the Secretary of Homeland Security to take all actions necessary to secure the land and maritime borders of the United States and stipulated that it should include the following:

> [S]ystematic surveillance of the international land and maritime borders of the United States through more effective use of personnel and technology, such as unmanned aerial vehicles, ground-based sensors, satellites, radar coverage, and cameras; and physical infrastructure enhancements to prevent unlawful entry by aliens into the United States

and facilitate access to the international land and maritime borders by United States Customs and Border Protection, such as additional checkpoints, all weather access roads, and vehicle barriers.[74]

The act specifically required the construction of about 700 miles of "at least 2 layers of reinforced fencing, the installation of additional physical barriers, roads, lighting, cameras and sensors."[75] Eighteen months after the passage of the Secure Fence Act, the Secretary of Homeland Security reported to Congress, as required by law, that efforts to secure a 28 mile section of the southern border with a "virtual fence" had failed, and that meaningful border security would not be feasible until at least three years in the future. The 700 miles of "double reinforced fencing" had not even been begun.[76]

H-1B Visa Program

As previously discussed, the 1990 immigration act not only raised the preference for skilled workers, but in addition created the H1-B program allowing for 65,000 skilled or professional workers to take up temporary residence for three years with the provision that their residency could be extended for an additional three years. One of the features of this act was that a temporary worker could simultaneously apply for immigration status on the basis of the skilled worker preference. In effect, a person who applied for a place in the queue for immigration under the skilled worker preference could take up residency, along with his spouse and children, under the H-1B provision, with the hope that sometime during his 6 year stint as a H-1B worker he would become eligible for permanent resident status and eventual citizenship. A separate provision of the 1990 Act created, in addition to H-1B visas, a category with a cap of 66,000 for "H-2B nonimmigrant visas for nonagricultural temporary or seasonal workers…who are employed in a variety of fields including hospitality, construction, sports and entertainment."[77]

In 1998, during the height of the dot-com boom and in anticipation of problems arising in computer systems due to the beginning of the new century, the information technology sector claimed a pressing need for more workers. In response, Congress increased the limit for H-1B workers from 65,000 to 115,000 for the years 1999 and 2000. Under this act the ceiling was to be reduced to 105,500 in 2001 and to revert to 65,000 in 2002. The law required that the foreign worker be paid the prevailing wage existing for his position, which had been part of the 1990 law, but also required that such workers also receive the same benefits as native workers. It also added language that strengthened the provision of the 1990 law that the employer must *attest* to the fact that the foreign worker would not displace native workers.[78]

However, in 2000 Congress expanded the limit to 195,000 H-1B visas for the years 2001, 2002, and 2003, after which the ceiling was set to revert to the 65,000 limit. Congress did not alter these new ceilings even after the downturn in the technology sector reduced demand for information technology workers beginning in 2000, and even though there were widespread reports that United States workers were being laid off and replaced with H1-B applicants.[79] In addition, the bill eliminated "the per-country ceilings for employment-based [non-H-1B workers] immigrants."[80] In effect this meant that one or a few countries could fill most of the slots allotted to the employment-based immigration preference. In addition, in 2002, the H-1B act was amended to allow for a worker to extend his stay in one year increments beyond 6 years while his application for permanent status under the skilled-worker preference provision was pending.[81]

In 2004, the cap reverted to the 65,000 limit. There were, however, a wide range of statutory exemptions to the cap.

> Specifically, the H-1B cap does not apply to H-1B workers employed by institutions of higher education, related or affiliated nonprofit research or governmental research organization. The cap also does not apply to H-1B extensions of status with the same company, a petition for a second H-1B, transfers from one H-1B cap-subject employer to another H-1B employer...

In 2004 Congress passed the Visa Reform Act which "provided exemptions from the H-1B cap for up to 20,000 foreign nationals who graduated from U. S. universities with master's or higher degrees."[82] Given these exemptions the actual number of workers admitted since 1999 has greatly exceeded the H-1B cap in every year. For instance, even after the cap had reverted to 65,000, some 266,000 H-1B petitions were approved in 2005.[83] Ruth Wassem, in her 2007 Constitutional Research Service report to the Congress, noted that the largest percentage of H-1B workers (49%) came from India and "that nearly three-fourths of all systems analysts and programmers are from India."[84]

The reader is to be excused, as is the author, if he admits to some confusion over these provisions. Why would Congress add to the competition for American workers, when that competition was already being increased by massive legal and illegal immigration? Workers at the bottom of the ladder were being squeezed by Mexican legal and illegal migrants, while those at the top were being squeezed by highly talented Asian immigrants. Could it really be the case that American citizens and legal residents would have been unable to fill the desirable and well-paying jobs in the fields of computer programming and information technology? Why, when manufacturing jobs were in decline, and Americans were told that they could replace those losses by training for jobs in technical areas, were they burdened by additional competition in those very areas? How well was the Department of Labor doing its job of assuring that H-1B workers were not displacing American workers? In addition, was it not obvious to the legislators that importing large numbers of workers in technical fields would depress wages in those fields? If there actually were shortages in, for instance, computer programmers, couldn't that be corrected by market forces driving up wages so that more students would enroll in programs to fill those jobs?

In fact, there is considerable evidence that the program was being abused for the express purposes of keeping wages down. Norman Matloff, in an extensive review of the H-1B program, discussed numerous studies demonstrating that there was, in fact, no shortage of workers in the computer science fields and that employers were merely using the program to reduce costs.[85] He argued that companies saved costs by hiring foreign H-1B workers, who were generally younger and needed and accepted lower salaries, than native, especially older workers.[86] Matloff suggested that even in the middle of the dot-com boom "there were a number of people who just weren't able to get work, and these were generally people who were over 40, many well qualified in the classical sense—years of significant experience. It was clear that what the industry wanted was cheap labor."[87]

These problems continue to this day. According to Ron Hira, public policy professor at the Rochester Institute of Technology, "the H-1B visa program is thoroughly corrupted and needs to be cleaned up immediately. Loopholes enable employers to hire H-1B workers at below-market wages, and bypass American workers, never even entertaining their applications." He argued that they often replace American workers with foreign nationals and sometimes require "their American workers to train their foreign replacements." Hira, author of the book *Outsourcing America*, argues

> contrary to conventional wisdom, the program actually speeds up the offshoring of American jobs.... In 2008, Infosys, Wipro, Satyam and Tata Consultancy, all offshore outsourcing firms, were the top H-1B recipients. They use H-1B...programs to facilitate the offshoring of American jobs to low-cost countries like India. Companies achieve this by bringing foreign workers to the U. S. for training and rotating them back to their home country, with improved skills.[88]

John Miano, a lawyer and computer programmer, argued that normal immigration channels are "wide open to the best minds in the world—both for permanent residency and for guest workers. For high skilled workers with distinguished ability, the United States has 'O' temporary guest-worker visas, for which there is no numerical limit." He further argued that "according to the latest visa bulletin from the State Department, there is currently no backlog for employment based green cards for the highest skilled workers." He thinks that the H-1B visas are filled by employees who are "not extremely high-skilled workers. A college degree from a correspondence school can qualify someone for an H-1B visa.... In short, H-1B is a cheap labor program being marketed as a program for the highly skilled."[89] A serious consequence of the program is that it discourages students from pursuing degrees in computer science and related fields since they are unlikely to find work, and if they do, it is likely to be underpaid.

From its inception, the program was ripe for abuse. According to William Branigan, writing over a decade ago, employers who use H-1B workers

> to keep them from seeking higher pay elsewhere...frequently dangle the promise of sponsoring them for 'green cards' denoting much-coveted status as legal permanent residents. This gives the company enormous leverage, since the process is a lengthy one and must be started over from scratch if the worker moves to another employer."

Obviously such workers are unlikely to complain about poor conditions or pay for fear of being fired and forced to leave the country. "Besides receiving lower starting pay, H-1B workers complain of getting fewer and smaller raises, remaining mired in relatively menial jobs, and, as salaried employees, having to work long hours without overtime." Branigan made the point that this makes it difficult for

American workers, especially older ones, who have to compete "with foreigners who are willing to accept lower wages and work longer hours."[90] Amendments to the H-1B program have attempted to reduce these abuses, but seem to have had little affect.

It is not only in computer programming that H-1B stipulations have harmed American students, but also in advanced training, especially doctoral training, where large numbers of PhD students in science and engineering are now foreign. The 2004 provision that excluded 20,000 foreign advanced degree graduates from the 65,000 H-1B cap, has had the effect of encouraging foreign students to pursue advanced training in the United States and then remain to take jobs in industry and academia. Even in 2002, before this amendment to the 2004 amendment, foreign students represented "35.4% of all graduate students in the physical sciences and 57.8% of those in engineering." The situation for postdoctoral students in science and engineering is equally skewed "with almost 60% coming from outside the United States."[91] According to the eminent scholars Ralph Gomory and Harold Shapiro, this has had fairly obvious consequences. "The competition of foreign students for positions in Unites States graduate schools has also contributed to making scientific training relatively unattractive to United States students, because the rapidly increasing supply of students has diminished the relative rewards of this career path." Gomory and Shapiro make the point that "shortcomings in primary education are sometimes cited as a factor in the loss of technological jobs in the United States...however, there seems to be little basis for the idea that there is a shortage of U. S. citizens who are interested in science." They argue that "there are more students entering college with intent of majoring in science or engineering than the nation could ever use. However, many of them switch, perhaps opting for more attractive careers."[92]

The 2004 change merely exacerbated the problem since not only are foreign students attracted to the United States for advanced training, but they can also expect to work here in these fields upon graduating. However, many of them return to their home countries, which benefit enormously from their valuable experience. The upshot is that America suffers from a loss of local scientific talent, especially among those with actual work experience, and American competitiveness in the global economy will invariably suffer, especially as opportunities and living standards in the home countries of foreign scientists improve and more go home. Similar problems are likely to arise in the fields of biology and medicine. Gomory and Shapiro conclude, "globalization is an ever-increasing force.... It is driven by the profitability it affords companies and as such, globalization is insensitive to effects on individual countries."[93] Put in other words, multinational companies clearly benefit from an oversupply of scientists, but very likely to the detriment to U. S. scientists and American competitiveness.[94]

The H-1B program was not wanted by most people and in fact was not needed. The original act in 1990 was based in large part on a study, never made public, by a research group of the National Science Foundation that claimed that there would be a severe shortage of engineers and scientists in the coming years. By 1992, it had become clear that the study was severely flawed. The author of the study acknowledged that the study was hypothetical and did not consider the influence of shortages on supply. In other words, it ignored the fact that if shortages did arise, wages would rise and more people would gravitate toward technical fields. Representative Howard Wolpe, chairman at the time of the Oversight Subcommittee of the House Committee on Science, Space and Technology, held hearings on the NSF claim in which many scientists argued that, in fact, there was no shortage. Rustin Roy, a scientist at Pennsylvania State University, claimed that the numbers in the study were very bad, and "we probably need a few less" scientists and engineers. Richard Ellis, director of manpower studies at the American Association of Engineering Societies reported "if we produced more engineers, there would be no work for them to do." Chairman Wolpe asserted that he was "absolutely stunned" and claimed that the study was "intentionally misleading."[95] As discussed earlier, any shortage of homegrown talent could easily have been accommodated through regular immigration channels.

Yet even after these allegations were confirmed, Congress not only did not eliminate the program, but enlarged it. The only beneficiaries have been information technology firms in the form of a cheaper and more docile labor force, highlighting in stark form the corruption of American immigration policy by the massive lobbying efforts of corporate interests. It has resulted in severely reduced opportunities for American citizens in jobs that pay relatively good salaries at a time when opportunities in manufacturing are declining. It also exacerbated the problem of outsourcing, eroding even further the opportunities for citizens.

The utter contempt that the Government had toward the desires of the American people regarding immigration and its impact on employment was glaringly exposed by the 2009 economic stimulus bill designed to create some 2 million construction jobs in infrastructure projects. The House version of the bill included a provision requiring that all employers receiving government funds confirm the citizenship status of all employees hired for these projects through the E-Verify system. The Senate version did not include this provision and the bill signed by the President did not include it. It is projected by both immigrant restriction advocates and immigrant advocacy groups that about 300,000 of those 2 million jobs will probably be filled by undocumented workers.[96] They also voted to let the highly successful and easy to use E-Verify program, discussed in Chapter 1, expire in 2009. It should be borne in mind that many, perhaps most, of those jobs will be filled by single men who would probably return home if they failed to find employment. And this is occurring during a period when the unemployment among American workers was increasing by more than half a million a month.

Demographic Repercussions of the 1965 Act

In 2008 the Pew Research Center released a study of population projections for the United States through 2050. The authors of that study, Jeffrey Passel and D'Vera Cohn, based their estimates on expected immigration to remain at about current levels (both authorized and unauthorized) of 1.4 million per year, and rising gradually to 2.1 million by 2050. They assumed a general convergence of fertility rates as immigrant populations adjusted to the economic conditions of life in the United States. Under those conditions they projected that population will rise to 438 million in 2050, or an increase of almost 50% above the 2005 level of 296 million. Under a lower immigration scenario they projected the population will grow to 385 million, and if immigration were higher, to 496 million. By 2050, based on the middle projection, more than one quarter of the population, or 117 million people, will be immigrants or the children of immigrants. In addition, "The foreign-born share of the nation's population will exceed historic highs sometime between 2020 and 2025, when it reaches 15%. The historic peak share was 14.7% in 1910 and 14.8 in 1890."[97]

Passel and Cohn provide the percentage (rounded) of the projected population in terms of ethnic makeup for the next four decades, assuming the moderate estimate resulting in a total U. S. population of 438 million. These numbers are given below in Table 6.3

These projections do not take into account factors and events that might alter the basic assumptions over the next four decades. They do not take into account international events involving the United States which could alter the numbers. At this point it is unclear, for instance, how things will resolve themselves in Iraq, but if political turmoil and civil war erupts in that country and produces large numbers of refugees, the world community would put enormous pressure on the United States to take these people in, given our direct responsibility for their situation. Another problem is the growing violence in Mexico between the Government and drug cartels that in 2009 threatened to tear the country apart.[98] Should Mexico fall into chaos, how many people will flee across the border into the United States to escape the escalating violence? It is almost impossible to anticipate other international events that could bring refugees to these shores.

Other factors could reduce the migratory flow to the United States. One such factor would be an extreme economic downturn or some other circumstance that created a popular backlash against such massive immigration. But such a backlash would have to be of a magnitude to produce a political realignment not unlike the one that preceded the Civil War that replaced the Whig with the Republican Party. What such realignment would look like is difficult, at this time, to envision. What is perfectly clear from the series of actions taken by Congress and all administrations since 1965 is that neither party has had the slightest intention of responding to the public's disapproval of large-scale immigration and an open-border policy, coupled with amnesty provisions that encouraged and continues to encourage massive illegal immigration.

TABLE 6.3. PERCENTAGE OF UNITED STATES POPULATION

Ethnicity	1960	2005	2050
Asian	0.6%	5%	9%
White	85.0%	67%	47%
Hispanic	3.5%	14%	29%
Black	11.0%	13%	13%

Roberto Suro, the son of a Puerto Rican father and Ecuadorian mother, has written an extremely well-researched book, published in 1998, on Hispanic immigrant groups, and has painted a highly sympathetic portrait of them. Toward the end of his book he argues that illegal aliens seriously undermine the Hispanic (he prefers the term Latino) community since, among other things, it "prolongs the transitory nature of barrio life by maintaining a segment of the population that is largely unable to help forge constructive links to American institutions such as police departments and U. S. political parties." He makes the point that "Latinos have the most to gain by gradually but deliberately closing the doors of their homes, businesses, and communities to illegal aliens."[99] It is for this reason that he expresses extreme concern with the way government has handled the illegal alien issue. He is worth quoting at length:

> Illegal aliens are easy to castigate. Their presence in large numbers encourages abuses in the workplace, weakens sovereign control of the borders, undermines law enforcement, and convolutes the process by which immigrant communities establish their place in American society. But illegal aliens are the wrong target for public rage. The real culprits are the officials of both political parties who have refused to make hard choices.[100]

Suro later makes the point that when lawmakers passed immigration laws that "have a huge impact on the land, no one felt obliged to explain the whys and wherefores to the American people. This became standard practice," and "in the circumscribed world of immigration policy-making, the absence of reasoning has never been an impediment to action."[101]

The political leadership of the country has acted with gross incompetence, utter contempt for the public, and with monumental dishonesty. They have compounded their betrayal of the public by a cavalier attitude toward the threat of terrorist infiltration that is invited by undefended borders. Claims that the borders cannot be controlled are patently disingenuous, and truly absurd. Estimates of the cost of a truly effective border barrier vary widely. The Congressional Budget office estimated the cost at $3 million per mile. The Congressional Research Service claimed that the fence under construction in the San Diego area will end up costing $9 million per mile. However, these estimates do not account for maintenance. The Army Corps of engineers estimated that "the combined cost of building and maintaining the fence over a 25-year life cycle would range from $16.4 million to $70 million per mile." This would mean that the cost for a state of the art 2,000 mile barrier would range between $32 billion to $140 billion, but this would be spread over a 25 year period, or something in the range $1.28 billion to $5.6 billion per year.[102] These cost estimates are based on the sort of barrier envisioned by Congress in the Secure Fence Act, consisting of "at least 2 layers of reinforced fencing, the installation of additional physical barriers, roads, lighting, cameras and sensors."[103] But, of course, a much simpler fence, made up of those concrete structures on many highways to reduce road noise in urban neighborhoods, would greatly facilitate policing of the border at a fraction of the cost cited here. It would substantially reduce the smuggling of drugs and thereby reduce the influence of Hispanic gangs. And perhaps, most important, reduce the potential for terrorists to infiltrate into the U. S. across the southern border. It makes little sense to wage war against radicals in Afghanistan, at great cost, while leaving the border undefended. Terrorists do not possess ballistic missiles or airplanes. They can only damage the United States if they can find their way into the U. S. This logic seems hardly to influence administrative decision making. Why are we willing to spend billions on wars to deal with potential terrorists in far–off lands, but refuse to spend a fraction of that on securing the border?

Even if one assumes the highest cost estimate of $70 million per mile, and assumes, in addition, that the largest portion of the cost of building such a barrier would come during its initial construction, this cost would be spread over an estimated five years needed for its completion. In other words, the cost, even assuming the highest estimate and assuming that it all would be spent simply to build the fence, would be less than $30 billion per year over five years. Such a figure pales besides the cost of the wars in Iraq and Afghanistan, not to mention the cost of the financial bailouts of 2009, and a projected national budget in excess of three trillion dollars. Against this estimate must be balanced the savings of reduced illegal immigration. Robert Rector of the Heritage Foundation has done an exhaustive analysis of the federal and state financial burdens of some 4.5 million low skilled immigrant families and came to an estimate of approximately $20,000 per family, based on various costs and subtracting out the taxes paid by those families. Much of this cost involves education and health care and a variety of welfare benefits (many of which are not denied to illegal aliens), and includes the additional costs incurred for incarceration of a population overrepresented in criminal activity. This gives a figure of some $90 billion dollars per year for those 4.5 million families. Rector estimates that about 40% of these families are illegal immigrants, and therefore they cost taxpayers a total of roughly $36 billion per year. While some have disputed the size of this figure, few doubt the integrity or scholarship of Robert Rector, or the legitimacy of the Heritage Foundation for which he works. No one disputes that the costs are high, and reducing the flow of illegal immigrants by an effective barrier would produce savings that must be considered in reckoning the overall costs of building such a barrier. Yet three years after Congress authorized a modest beginning of a barrier, nothing meaningful has been done, during which time the illegal population has grown by an estimated 500,000 per year, or 1.5 million in that three-year period.

As if to highlight this lack of concern with illegal immigration, the Department of Homeland Security under the new administration, reversed the policy created under the previous administration authorizing local police to enforce federal immigration law. According to Miriam Jordan, writing in the Wall Street Journal in July of 2009 "the new guidelines sharply reduce the ability of local law enforcement to arrest and screen suspected illegal immigrants." The new guidelines are designed "to prevent sheriff and police departments from arresting people 'for minor offenses as a guise to initiate removal proceedings...'" One has to wonder why the Department of Homeland Security, which lacks the manpower to effectively deal with illegal aliens at the local level, should make it all but impossible for local agencies to deal with the problem. The only conceivable answer to that question is that the federal government is not interested at all in reducing illegal immigration.[104]

The failure to deal with illegal aliens creates serious moral problems. The first is that there are many millions of poor people throughout the world whose lives are as difficult, or more difficult, than those in Mexico and Central America, who would very much like to immigrate to America. If it really is the case that the United States needs millions of low skilled workers, why not raise the quotas worldwide to allow these people to come to America? It seems grossly unfair to give people from the Americas the opportunity to come merely because they are fortunate to live geographically close to America. With secure borders, this fundamental unfairness could be eliminated.

Of course, it is highly questionable whether, in fact, the United States needs low skilled workers. Most of the evidence suggests otherwise. The present laxity about border security benefits mainly those who employ unskilled workers. Why is it wiser to allow poor Mexicans to cross the borders to harvest tomatoes rather than merely importing tomatoes from Mexico? Mexico would benefit from the export of agricultural crops to America, and save Americans the considerable costs of providing services to the families of the illegal aliens who pick tomatoes. The second problem is that when employers, such as farmers, builders, or lawn care providers, for instance, use illegal aliens, they undercut employers who behave properly and only hire legally resident workers. To stay in business, otherwise law-abiding employers are often forced to hire illegal aliens, turning them into lawbreakers, often very much against their will. Government policies that provide great incentives to break the law are not only perverse, but profoundly immoral.

Since 1965 Congress and the administrations of both parties have conspired to guarantee—there is no other appropriate word—a steady stream and a growing presence of illegal aliens. When the numbers become so large and the costs to local communities so great as to prompt a popular outcry, the response has been to claim that these illegal aliens must be legalized on humanitarian grounds. Those who point out that such humanitarian action would be unnecessary, with properly controlled borders and sanctions against employers of illegal immigrants, are characterized by the country's elites as uninformed, mean-spirited, xenophobic bigots.

Immigrant Groups: Adjustment to Life in the United States

Given these historically high levels of immigration, it is important to determine how well immigrants, and more importantly, their children, are adjusting to life in the United States. The question of assimilation is critical both for the immigrant groups and the future of the United States. Since recent immigrants come from such a wide range of societies, differing in ethnicity, culture and political experience, it would be surprising if the various immigrant groups do not have different experiences in this country. An objective measure of the adjustment of various groups is found in the statistical data provided by various government agencies on marriage patterns, education, employment, income, and criminal behavior. These statistics are often broken down into the broad groups: blacks, whites, Asians/Pacific Islanders, Hispanics, and the group defined as Native Americans that includes American Indians, Eskimos and Aleuts.

The group classified as "Hispanic" includes Mexicans (the largest group), but it also includes Cubans, Puerto Ricans, and people from the countries of Central and South America. Most recent immigrants in the Hispanic category are either Amerindians or those of mixed heritage; few are of unmixed European ancestry. For instance, only 9% of Mexicans are of unmixed European heritage and very few of these migrate to America.[105] Most immigrants from the Americas arrive with very low levels of education and include few with professional training or advanced skills.

The category of Asian/Pacific Islanders generally includes people from China, India, Vietnam and the Philippines (the largest group of immigrants), and various other countries. This is an extremely diverse group in ethnicity and race, derived from countries with large differences in economic performance. Large numbers of immigrants from Asian countries are of Chinese ethnic background, known as the *Overseas Chinese,* whose ancestors migrated to various Asian countries at an earlier time. Many of the immigrants in the Asian/Pacific Islander category come with advanced education and many have professional experience and advanced technical skills.

These people usually gain entrance through the quota limits for their countries and the quotas for skilled workers. Many come under H1-B visas and others as postgraduate students who, as discussed earlier, are permitted to remain and find employment in their fields of expertise. Relatively few enter as illegal aliens, since most rely on air travel to migrate to the U. S. Asians, therefore, are usually a fairly select group compared to those who come, for instance, from Central America. Immigrants from India seem to be particularly talented compared to those who remain in their home country. According to Jason Richwine, writing in *Forbes* magazine, "despite constituting less than 1% of the U. S. population, Indian-Americans are 3% of the nation's engineers, 7% of its IT workers and 8% of its physicians and surgeons." They are the most economically successful group among those classified as Asians, having median household income, according to Richwine, of "approximately $83,000, compared with $61,000 for East Asians and $55,000 for whites." He reports that based on the digit span subtest used in some IQ measurements, they performed at a level suggesting an IQ in the range of 110. While this figure is admittedly speculative, it may explain why Indian youngsters seem extraordinary gifted in spelling competitions, having won six of the top spots in the last ten years.[106] As will be seen in Chapter 7, Indian immigrants in England are also quite successful compared to most other groups.

For more detailed information about the progress of specific groups, one must rely on a variety of sources, not all of which are of equal value, as they range from serious statistical analyses to almost purely anecdotal reports. The government's statistical data, therefore, represent at best an initial tool for estimating, at least in broad outline, relative patterns of adjustment. The following discussion includes American–born whites and blacks for purposes of comparison. Native American Indians are not included since they are relatively few in number and when identifiable are often parts of groups or tribes desirous of maintaining their traditional cultures and are not, for that reason, expected to fully assimilate into American culture.

Educational Attainment

As mentioned earlier, there are major differences among immigrant groups in the average educational level of the individuals when they arrive in the United States. In addition, there are major differences in the extent to which individuals from various groups speak English. For instance, most immigrants from the Indian subcontinent learned English in their native land, whereas this is not the case for large numbers of immigrants from Asia and Central America. Both of these factors play an important role in the adjustment of individuals to American society and in their economic success once they get here. More important, however, for the long-range adjustment of the individuals from various groups is how well their children fare in American schools. The following data generally address this latter question, in terms of their performance on standardized tests, high school graduation and dropout rates, college attendance and the attainment of higher degrees and specialized training. (The groups "Asians/Pacific Islanders" are abbreviated as "Asian" in the following tables.) The first one (Table 6.4.) summarizes the highest educational attainment by the various groups.

TABLE 6.4. HIGHER EDUCATION ACHIEVEMENT

	High School Graduates	College or More
All Groups	85.5%	28.0%
Asian	87.4%	49.7%
White	86.1%	28.4%
Hispanic	59.3%	12.4%
Black	80.7	18.5

The statistics in Table 6.4 include all members of the groups including foreign-born immigrants. Since many immigrants come with little education, it is more valuable to look at the educational attainment of young people in the U. S. education system, many of whom are native born or came at a very young age. Table 6.5 presents data for individuals 18-24 years old.

TABLE 6.5. EDUCATIONAL STATUS 18-24-YEAR-OLDS (2005)[107]

Race/Ethnicity	H.S. Dropoouts	H.S. Graduates	Attending College
Asian	3.1%	93.7%	60.6%
White	7.0%	87.8%	42.8%
Hispanic	12.9%	79.2%	32.7%
Black	27.3%	66.0%	24.8%

As would be expected, the younger cohort has more education than the general population. High school graduation rates and college attendance is clearly higher for all groups, though it is unclear from these data how many will graduate from college, or with what degrees. The high dropout rate for young Hispanics is troublesome. Even more disturbing is that this pattern continues for second and third generation Hispanics who have dropout rates considerably higher than whites and somewhat higher than blacks. In addition, the number of college graduates among Hispanics does not markedly improve over generations, with only about 11% of second and third-generation Hispanics earning college degrees, a percentage somewhat below blacks.[108]

Differences in academic performance between groups are present in the early years of schooling. The U. S. Department of Education measures performance in 4th grade and 8th grade through the National

Assessment of Educational Progress (NAEP) testing program. Tables 6.6 and 6.7 present the percentage of students who achieved the basic level and those who achieved proficiency for various groups.[109] It should be kept in mind that many of these children come from homes where English is not spoken. For children 5 to 17, fully 63.4% of Asians and 67.4% of Hispanics fit into this category.[110]

TABLE 6.6. 4TH GRADE NAEP REPORT (2005)

Race/Ethnicity	Reading		Mathematics	
	Basic	Proficiency	Basic	Proficiency
Asian	73%	42%	90%	55%
White	76%	41%	90%	40%
Hispanic	46%	16%	68%	19%
Black	42%	13%	60%	13%

TABLE 6.7. 8TH GRADE NAEP REPORT (2005)

Race/Ethnicity	Reading		Mathematics	
	Basic	Proficiency	Basic	Proficiency
Asian	80%	40%	81%	47%
White	82%	39%	80%	39%
Hispanic	56%	15%	52%	13%
Black	52%	12%	42%	9%

High school graduation and college attendance rates provide only part of the educational picture. Perhaps more important is the quality of education children receive as well as their ability to turn that education into valuable skills. Some high schools and colleges are far more likely to provide high levels of intellectual resources than others. An important indication of the quality of schooling is the academic ability or preparedness of students as quantified in SAT scores. Historically, SAT scores are normalized with a mean of 500 and a standard deviation of 100. For 2007, the actual standard deviations fell between 100 and 106. The College Board reports Mexicans separately from Puerto Ricans and other Hispanics, but these differences are minimal and only the Mexican scores are given below.

As can be seen, black students score almost one standard deviation below whites and Asians on most measures. This pattern has remained largely unchanged since the 1970s. Hispanics fare somewhat better, but still significantly below Asians and whites. The gap between Asians and all other groups on the mathematics section is notable. It is hardly surprising that the nation's leading scientific and engineering schools are greatly overrepresented by Asians relative to their proportion of the general population.

TABLE 6.8. SAT SCORES OF 2007 COLLEGE-BOUND SENIORS.[111]

	Critical Reading	Mathematics	Writing
All Students	502	515	494
Asian	514	578	513
White	527	534	518
Mexican	455	466	450
Black	433	429	425

Perhaps most striking is the educational disparity of the Asians and Hispanics, both of whom arrived in large numbers after the 1965 Immigration Act, and as mentioned above, both groups come from homes where English is often not spoken. As with many of the statistics that will be reviewed in what follows, Asians tend to perform considerably above the national average and Hispanics considerably below. In the case of Academic performance, these results are completely consistent with the worldwide distribution of IQs discussed in Chapter 3.

Fertility and Marriage Patterns

Hispanics tend to have higher fertility rates than other groups. The replacement fertility rate for the United States population, given current mortality rates, is 2.110. This is the rate that is necessary for the group to maintain its current population level. In 2004, whites, blacks, and Asians tended to have rates slightly below the replacement level, with rates of 2.054, 2.033, and 1.898, respectively. Hispanics tended to exceed the replacement rate by a considerable amount at 2.825.[112] This no doubt reflects the peasant origins of the majority of Hispanic immigrants. It is expected that this figure will trend in the direction of the other groups as Hispanics adjust to life in urban environments.

Table 6.9 below presents figures for teenage and out of wedlock births for various groups. Both types of birth put mothers at risk both educationally and economically. The families of unmarried women almost invariably fall behind others in income, if for no other reason than that today, so many married couples rely on two salaries. In addition, a teenage or out of wedlock birth often interferes with the education of young women.

TABLE 6.9. PERCENT OF BIRTHS TO TEENS AND
UNMARRIED MOTHERS (2004)[113]

	Teenage Women	Unmarried Women
Total U. S..	10.3%	35.8%
Asian	3.3%	15.5%
White	9.3%	30.5%
Hispanic	14.3%	46.4%
Black	16.8%	68.8%

Steven Camarota of the Center for Immigration Studies has broken down illegitimacy rates for Immigrants and native-born residents. The table below is derived from his analysis.

TABLE 6.10. PERCENT OF BIRTHS TO UNMARRIED
MOTHERS (2003)[114]

	Immigrant Women	Native Women
All Groups	31.5%	35.4%
Asian	11.0%	29.9%
White	11.8%	24.4%
Hispanic	41.9%	49.6%
Black	39.4%	72.5%

Out of wedlock births are lower, across the board, for immigrant women. In general this is explained by the fact that many immigrant women are already married when they arrive. In addition, they tend to be past their late teenage years and early twenties, when women are at heightened risk for unwed pregnancies. The reader should be cautioned regarding the figures for Asians. As mentioned previously, census data do not distinguish East Asians, mainly those whose ethnic background is Chinese and Korean, from those from South Asia. Nevertheless, the pattern shown in Table 6.10 is not reassuring, and suggests that in the case of immigrant families, assimilation to native patterns is, at least in the area of sexual behavior, negative. In all likelihood this is the result of the fact that illegitimacy is less frowned upon in the United States than in many of the rural communities from which immigrants come. Whatever the cause, however, it does not bode well for the economic advancement of those groups with high levels of illegitimacy.

The alarm over the above figures should be tempered by the fact that many women who have out of wedlock births eventually marry the father of their children. This is reflected in the table below which gives the family structure for the children of immigrants and natives. From Table 6.11, it is fairly clear that most white and Asian children are being raised in two-parent households, while the opposite is the case for black children. It is not reassuring for the future success of Hispanic children that almost half are not benefiting from a two-parent upbringing.

TABLE 6.11. PERCENTAGE OF CHILDREN IN MARRIED PARENT HOUSEHOLDS[115]

	Children of Immigrants	Children of Natives
Asian	86.0%	83.0%
White	83.3%	78.7%
Hispanic	70.2%	55.6%
Black	58.9%	37.7%

Criminal and Incarceration Rates

Unlike other government agencies, the FBI in its *Uniform Crime Reports* (UCR) does not include the category Hispanics in its statistics for criminality and victimization, but does include the category of Asian/Pacific Islander. The FBI data is based on information provided by law enforcement authorities at the local, state and national level on reported crimes. The Justice department, in its *National Crime Victimization Survey* (NCVS) also fails to provide information about Hispanics, but only for whites and blacks, and the general category *other*. It does not list the category of Asian. The Justice Department statistics are based on reported incidents of crime victimization in a nationwide survey of households. The statistics of the FBI and the Department of Justice differ for a number of reasons, most prominently because many victims of crimes, for various reasons, do not report those crimes to police.[116] In both reports, most crimes committed by Hispanics are classified as crimes committed by whites. The reason is that Mexico, which provides the bulk of the Hispanic immigrants, has few people of African descent. Ninety percent of Hispanics identify themselves as white when asked to indicate their race.[117]

Table 6.12 is based on the FBI's Uniform Crime Report and gives some indication of the prevalence of criminality. It is provided to give the reader some estimate of the extent of crime among Asians, whites (Hispanic and non-Hispanic) and blacks.

TABLE 6.12. PERSONS ARRESTED (2005)[118]

	White	Black	Asian/Pacific
All Arrests	7,117,000	2,830,800	106,000
Serious Crimes	1,075,900	510,300	20,000
Murder	5,000	4,900	100
Forcible Rape	2,000	6,000	200
Robbery	35,800	47,700	800
Aggravated Assault	208,400	113,100	3,600
Burglary	151,800	62,000	1,900
Larceny/Theft	586,400	236,600	1,900
Auto Vehicle Theft	67,600	37,500	1,400
Arson	9,000	2,500	100

Based on the statistics in Table 6.12, blacks (of whom a small percentage were Hispanics) who made up 13% of the population accounted for 27% of all arrests and for 32% of arrests for serious crimes. Whites, including most Hispanics, accounted for 73% of all arrests and 68% of those for serious crimes. In addition, blacks accounted for about one half of all murders and significantly more than half of all robberies. Asian/Pacific Islanders, by contrast, who made up 5% of the population, made up only 1% of those arrested for all crimes as well as for serious crimes. If they were the same size as the black population they would make up about 2.6% of all arrests. It should be stressed that the Asian figure includes groups whose home societies have fairly disparate rates of criminal behavior. As discussed earlier Korea has very low rates of crime, whereas the Philippines have relatively high rates.

Reports on rates of incarceration, reported by the Bureau of Justice, are an exception in that they *do* include the categories of Hispanics, non-

Hispanic whites and non-Hispanic blacks. These data do not include a separate category for Asian/Pacific Islanders, but given their very low rates of arrest, one can reasonably assume that they would represent a relatively small percentage of the total. Table 6.13 is based on inmates in state and federal prisons in 2006 who had been sentenced for terms of more than 1 year.

TABLE 6.13. PRISON POPULATION IN STATE AND FEDERAL CUSTODY IN 2006[119]

	Number	Percent	Rate per 100,000
All Groups	1,502,200	100.0%	501
Males	1,399,100	93.1%	943
White Males	478,000	31.8%	487
Black Males	534,200	35.6%	3,042
Hispanic Males	290,500	19.3%	1,261
Females	103,100	6.9%	68
White Females	49,100	3.3%	48
Black Females	28,600	1.9%	148
Hispanic Females	13,000	1.2%	81

Given the above statistics, it is clear that the overwhelming majority of prisoners, and by extension of lawbreakers, are men. Blacks make up approximately 37% of those in prison, while whites and Hispanics taken together make up the remaining 63%. These figures are reasonably close to the arrest data given in the previous table. Black men are 6.2 times as likely as white men to be imprisoned. The ratio of Hispanic men to white men is 2.6. It is important to note, however, that Hispanics are far more likely to be recent immigrants than either whites or blacks, and immigrants have much lower rates of incarceration than native born-individuals. Kristin Butcher and Anne Piehl were able to determine the statistics comparing immigrant and native-born incarceration rates. Their data is given in the Table 6.14. As can be seen, native-born individuals are some 5 times as likely as immigrants to be incarcerated. Even among immigrants, however, blacks and Hispanics have higher rates than either whites or Asians.

TABLE 6.14. PERCENTAGE OF POPULATION INSTITUTIONALIZED IN 2000[120]

	Native-Born	Immigrants
Asian/Pacific	2.53%	0.37%
White	1.70%	0.39%
Hispanic	6.59%	0.79%
Black	11.32%	1.79%
All	3.45%	0.68%

The black to white ratio among native-born Americans is 6.6 to 1, somewhat higher than the overall rate noted above. However, the ratio of Hispanic to white incarceration is about 3.9 to 1 among the native-born, considerably higher than the 2.6 to 1 ratio cited for all Hispanic residents. The one somewhat surprising figure is the higher rate for native-born Asian/Pacific Islanders than for whites which, given most other statistics, is somewhat of an anomaly. However, a glance back at the statistics for out of wedlock births reveals a similar pattern for native-born individuals of Asian/Pacific origin. This can be accounted for by the fact that the Asian category, more than any other, includes a wide variety of racial, ethnic, and national groups, with very different intellectual and temperamental profiles. The World Health Organization reports very low homicide rates for Korea (2 per 100,000 inhabitants), but much higher rates for the Philippines (14 per 100,000 inhabitants).[121] Those countries are both important sources of Asian immigration to the United States.

One explanation for the native-born versus immigrant criminality is that many immigrants are adults socialized in their home countries. They often come from rural settings where parental supervision is fairly extensive. Since a majority of immigrants settle in urban settings in America, their children are often not nearly as well supervised as they were. Furthermore, the United States tends to tolerate a higher degree of youthful antisocial behavior, especially in cities, than the countries from which the immigrants came. Ethnic groups, whose young men exhibit high rates of antisocial behavior, often have higher rates of illegitimacy among their young women. This suggests that recent immigrants in the United States have a difficult time regulating the behavior of their offspring. In the absence of such parental regulation or control, males tend to higher rates of criminality and females tend to higher rates of teenage pregnancy and out of wedlock births. Put another way, without strong and effective oversight, children, and especially teenagers, tend to more fully express their natural predispositions. The research reviewed in Chapter 3 suggest that these predispositions reflect a combination of genetic and cultural influences. What the data suggest, in addition, is that many immigrant children are assimilating to American underclass culture and not to traditional American middle-class culture. Part of the explanation for the disparities between immigrants and native-born individuals may be that immigration in most cases is somewhat selective and immigrants differ in a variety of ways from those who remain behind. For instance, black immigrants from the Caribbean tend to perform fairly well in American society relative to native blacks.[122] Perhaps the behavior of their children reflects in some degree regression to the mean of their respective groups.

The pattern of criminality among native-born Hispanics is particularly troublesome since their numbers are likely to grow, with the Hispanic proportion of the population expected to more than double in the next 40 Years. Another cause for concern is that a group's proportion of the prison population underrepresents the criminal behavior of the youthful, rapidly growing Hispanic population. Many of the whites and blacks currently in prison are men in their 40s and 50s who were sentenced for crimes committed in their 20s, the age at which criminality peaks. Since there were far fewer Hispanics 20 or 30 years ago, there tend to be fewer older Hispanic inmates than older inmates of other groups. However, their number will grow in the coming years as current Hispanic inmates age behind bars. For these reasons, a better index of current crime rates for various ethnic groups is given by incarceration rates for younger individuals. Table 6.15 provides incarceration rates for males in the age group 18 to 34.

TABLE 6.15. MALE INMATES BY AGE AND RACIAL GROUP[123]

	All Ages	Percent	18–34	Percent 18–34
Whites	478,000	34%	201,300	29%
Blacks	534,200	38%	276,600	40%
Hispanics	290,500	21%	164,700	24%
Other	96,400	7%	49,700	7%
Total	1,399,100	100%	692,300	100%

Given the fact that Hispanics have surpassed blacks in the general population, these figures suggest that rates of criminality among Hispanic males is about 50% the figure for black males. Given that the Hispanic proportion of the population is projected to more than double in the next four decades, while the proportion of blacks is projected to remain the same, it is likely that sometime during that period Hispanics will surpass blacks as the largest ethnic group in prison and, by extension, the most common perpetrators of crime.

The above figures may understate the problem of Hispanic crime as they may not accurately reflect criminal behavior, often gang related, among illegal aliens. Such gangs often target recent immigrants and illegal aliens and use tactics of intimidation that dissuade many victims from reporting crimes to police. Crimes that are not reported cannot be prosecuted and their perpetrators, therefore, do not end up in prison. Furthermore, those illegal aliens who commit serious crimes can return to their country of origin if they expect that they will become suspects. Mexican nationals, in particular, if they operate close to the border, can slip into Mexico and avoid arrest and potential imprisonment. However, even criminal elements coming from countries lacking a common border with the United States, such as El Salvador, Nicaragua, and the Caribbean islands can freely move back and forth between the United States and their home countries because of regular air connections.

The most conspicuous feature of recent Hispanic criminality has been the growth of gang violence. Before the influx of Hispanics, most urban gangs were composed of blacks engaged in the drug trade and various other criminal enterprises. But black gang dominance over drugs has been wrested away by more recently established Hispanic gangs. In Los Angeles, a virtual war of attrition between black and Hispanic gangs has broken out and what seems to be a process of ethnic cleansing is underway. The Hispanic gangs, of which *Mara Salvatrucha* or MS-13 is the most notorious, are better organized and have ties with criminal elements in Central America and Mexico. Their international character allows for a vertical organization of the drug trade and other illegal smuggling operations. As such, they represent the very real potential to align themselves with terrorist organizations wishing to infiltrate the United States. MS-13 is a large organization. *Newsweek* reporter Arian Campo-Flores estimates that in 2005 it had "8,000 to 10,000 members in 33 states in the United States...and tens of thousands more in Central America."[124] As discussed in an earlier chapter, criminal violence is endemic to Mexico and Central America, and to many countries of the Caribbean and South America such as Jamaica, Columbia and Brazil. Almost 60% of all immigrants in 2000 came from such countries. According to the United States Department of State, almost all of the countries from which these immigrants come are dangerous places for residents and tourists alike.[125]

Gangs, of whatever ethnicity, recruit members from the large pool of disaffected young males lacking employable skills. While Los Angeles is considered the gang capital of the United States, gangs have formed wherever there is a sizable number of such young men, most of whom are black and Hispanic. The Department of Justice estimates that, in 2004, there were 24,000 gangs spread out in America with 760,000 members. 85% of these gangs were located in large cities and their suburbs.[126] A survey in 1999 revealed that 47% of gang members were Hispanic, 31% were black, 13% were white and 7% Asian.[127] Given that the white population is about five times the black and Hispanic populations, a very small percentage of whites are gang members. Asians, on the other hand, are a third as numerous as blacks and Hispanics, and they are far more likely to be gang members than whites but considerably less likely than either blacks or Hispanics.

Given the size and makeup of the Hispanic and black gangs, their activities are prone to spill over into random violence and mayhem which can terrorize communities. In Los Angeles and Chicago, more than 50% of homicides are gang related.[128] To a large extent this is an example of the effects of the "youth bulge" discussed earlier and is exacerbated by the poor economic prospects among many blacks and Hispanics. The end result is that middle-class people flee such areas; neighborhoods deteriorate, and in the end provide even fewer opportunities for unskilled and uneducated young men. Today, as a consequence, America's urban schools are more segregated by race than at any time since they were formally desegregated in the 1960s.

Economic Performance

Given the relatively low levels of education and relatively high rates of criminal involvement, especially among native-born blacks and Hispanics, it is not surprising that they are more frequently unemployed than whites or Asians. This is reflected in table 6.16. These figures reveal a number of patterns. In the first case, foreign-born workers have, overall, a higher labor participation rate and lower unemployment rate than native-born workers. The lower participation rate of native-born is to be expected on two grounds: native-born individuals will be older and include a higher percentage of retirees and, in addition, are more likely to have accumulated or inherited wealth that allows them to avoid paid labor.

The higher unemployment rate of native-born workers is difficult to understand, but is probably related to their having a greater willingness to refuse undesirable or low paying jobs especially if they have established families they can rely on temporarily. The greater unemployment rates for blacks and Hispanics relative to whites and Asians is best explained by their lower educational attainment which is a major factor driving unemployment rates.

TABLE 6.16. LABOR PARTICIPATION AND UNEMPLOYMENT STATUS (2006)[129]

	% Labor Participation Rate	% Unemployment Rate
FOREIGN BORN		
Whites	61.4	3.5
Blacks	73.7	5.5
Asians	67.6	2.8
Hispanics	71.5	4.5
NATIVE BORN		
Whites	60.7	3.9
Blacks	63.0	9.4
Asians	61.5	3.8
Hispanics	65.6	6.2

Education level also explains the occupations to which various groups gravitate. Bureau of Labor Statistics data indicate that both blacks and Hispanics are underrepresented in more remunerative occupations such as in management and the professions and overrepresented in service and production activities. Particularly notable is the overrepresentation of Hispanics in construction and maintenance industries. In those industries in 2006, about 25% of the workers were Hispanic and only about 7% were black, even though both have about the same population size. This pattern confirms the general impression that the housing boom of the 1990s and most of the 2000s provided opportunities for Hispanics (both legal and illegal) who were able to outbid other groups in these fields, since they often lived in group homes and were not supporting families in America.[130]

The type of work people do determines in large measure their incomes. Table 6.17, giving the weekly earnings of various groups, is instructive and confirms the general impression from anecdotal experience. Asians are the best-paid workers and Hispanics the worst paid. In percentage terms, whites earn 88%, blacks 70% and Hispanics 62% of what Asians earn. These disparities are particularly striking in light of the fact that virtually all the Asians in the country are either immigrants or the children of immigrants, since as recently as 1965 Asians made up about 0.5% of the total U. S. population.

TABLE 6.17. WEEKLY EARNINGS (2006)[131]

	All Workers	Male	Female
White	$690	$761	$609
Asian	$784	$882	$699
Black	$554	$591	$519
Hispanic	$486	$505	$440

The earnings given in Table 6.17 are, not surprisingly, reflected in family income and poverty levels given in Table 6.18.

TABLE 6.18. FAMILY INCOME AND POVERTY[132]

	Median income	% below Poverty Level
All Families	$56,194	12.6%
White	$59,317	10.6%
Asian	$68,957	11.1%
Black	$35,464	24.9%
Hispanic	$37,867	21.8%

The figures in Table 6.18 reflect not only earnings, but also all money benefits in welfare payments. The income distribution is very much affected by family type. Married-couple families had median income of $65,906, while female-headed families had median income of $27,244, or about 40% of the income of married couple-families.[133] The fact that blacks and Hispanics have a higher proportion of single parent families than whites or Asians explains a large part of the above disparities. Table 6.19 gives the income distribution for the various groups.

TABLE 6.19. INCOME DISTRIBUTION (2006)134

	Below $35,000	$35,000 to $75,000	More Than $75,000
All Families	29.6%	34.9%	35.3%
White	27.0%	35.7%	37.3%
Asian	22.5%	31.5%	46.0%
Black	49.4%	31.1%	19.4%
Hispanic	46.2%	32.6%	18.2%

Given the large number of low income black and Hispanic families it is to be expected that these groups should make greater use of welfare benefits than Asian or white families. In fact, Hispanics and blacks are about two and half times more likely to receive Medicaid and food stamps. In addition, since Hispanics are less likely to have health insurance, they are more likely to use hospital emergency rooms for health care.[135] Hospitals may not refuse emergency care under a 1985 federal law that requires that they provide care to any who present themselves regardless of citizenship or legal resident status. Those hospital costs, however, are uncompensated by the federal government and therefore must be made up in some way, either by passing them on in higher costs to other patients or to the general population in the form of higher state taxes. But sometimes the costs cannot be made up. Madeleine Cosman, writing in the *Journal of American Physicians and Surgeons* in 2005, reports that "between 1993 and 2004, 60 California hospitals closed because half their services became unpaid. Another 24 California hospitals verge on closure." She reports that ambulances from Mexico bring poor patients to American emergency rooms since federal law "requires accepting patients who come *within 250 yards of a hospital.*"[136]

Assimilation and Residential Integration

Assimilation into America has typically been thought of as the process by which immigrants (and to a more important extent, the children of immigrants) speak the common language of English, think of themselves as Americans, and abide by the American version of the "Protestant Ethic," which is usually defined as being "self-reliant, hardworking and morally upright." [137] If individuals assimilate in this way, as almost all did in prior waves of immigration, they will find that they can blend into any community of Americans, for the simple reason that they will be seen as desirable neighbors. Of course, there were individuals in the past that did not fit this pattern, but no one ethnic group had a disproportionate number of ne'er-do-wells or antisocial types, at least after the first generation. This definition of assimilation is neither uniquely American nor Protestant, but would hold for most industrialized countries, and any European country. Two major objective measures of assimilation under this definition are residential integration and intermarriage among the children, and especially the grandchildren, of immigrants of various ethnic groups.

Immigrants, in the American historical pattern, in their initial residence, generally congregated in neighborhoods with their coethnics. They did so for fairly straightforward reasons, among which are ease of communication, familiar customs, and the likely support of relatives and friends. The children of immigrants through public education mastered the English language and acquired the skills allowing for a broad range of employment in the new country. A good many of these people moved out of ethnic enclaves and settled in areas among people of similar social class, but often with different ethnic backgrounds. Nevertheless, there continued to be high levels of homogeneity in the original ethnic enclaves, due to the continued flow of immigrants and the appeal of ethnic homogeneity to many individuals, especially among those of limited upward mobility, where ethnic relations provided jobs in often quite specific, often civil service occupations. Even after the cessation of mass immigration in the 1920s, these enclaves continued to maintain their character well into the 1960s, especially in large cities. However, the grandchildren of the original immigrants were fairly widely dispersed in the population, especially those in a position to take advantage of the educational and occupational choices that opened up in the wake of World War II.

Since all of these groups were Europeans and of very similar genetic makeup, they tended to look alike and made similar economic advances, and as a consequence there tended to be high rates of intermarriage. The clearest exception to this pattern were the Jews who, while often physically indistinguishable from others, and fully competitive economically, resisted intermarriage for religious reasons for a longer period than other groups. By the end of the 20th century, however, this distinction had all but disappeared, with a majority of Jews marrying outside their religion. It was this pattern which gave rise to the model of assimilation as a "melting pot." In recent decades one is very unlikely to come across people of European descent who do not have parents and grandparents representing a variety of ethnicities.

The most glaring exception to this ethnic mixing was the case of Americans of African descent. During the great migration of blacks out of the south beginning in the 1920s and accelerated in the 1950s and 1960s, blacks tended to congregate in black neighborhoods, for all the reasons that immigrants gravitated to their own ethnic enclaves. However, the pattern of movement out of black neighborhoods and the taking up residence in more integrated settings was, and continues to be, much less pronounced for blacks than for immigrant groups. In addition, outmarriage is very low. Obviously, their racial distinctiveness explains much of this. In addition, however, the very limited upward mobility among blacks severely limits their residential choices. Poor people must, of necessity, live in less expensive neighborhoods and cheaper houses than others. But that does not explain why poor blacks rarely live in integrated neighborhoods with other poor people, but continue to live in highly homogenous communities. Why, in other words, do there continue to be black "ghettoes?"

This last question is among the most hotly debated in American social science and, in addition, has been addressed by a host of government desegregation efforts since the 1960s. Part of the reason, perhaps the most important part, is the emergence among poor blacks of what has come to be called an underclass. An underclass is usually defined as a subpopulation characterized by high unemployment, low income, poor educational performance, high rates of illegitimacy, and high levels of crime, especially violent crime. While many of these phenomena are associated with the relatively low IQ of poor blacks, not all of these behaviors can be accounted for by IQ alone. Low income whites also tend to have lower IQs and higher rates of underclass behavior, but not to the same extent as low income blacks. When comparing blacks and whites of similar IQ, black-white disparities in, for instance, illegitimacy and crime, decline, but they are still substantial.[138] However, a far larger percentage of the black population exhibits the low IQs associated with social difficulty than is the case for whites.

An important factor in preventing the rise of a distinctive white underclass is that poor whites are a relatively smaller percentage of the white population and tend to be spread more evenly around the country and many live in rural areas that are far less conducive to unchecked antisocial behavior. Poor blacks, a substantial portion of the black population, have tended to congregate in large numbers in neighborhoods in a relatively small number of Northern cities. Underclass behavior in such neighborhoods produces a high degree of social pathology. Looked at historically, the "white flight" which characterized the 1960s and 1970s was the rational response of middle-class and poor whites to the massive migration of blacks out of the rural South into Northern cities, which produced a host of ills, especially declining schools and burgeoning crime. It was that migration, and the attendant white flight, which brought so many urban white ethnic enclaves to an end. It also emptied many cities of their middle-class inhabitants, both black and white. Many cities, both large and small, never recovered. Detroit is perhaps the most notorious example. Today many of these cities are among the poorest and most crime-ridden in the nation. People who could, fled to the safety and better schools in the suburbs.

The high concentration of poor blacks in the inner cities, and especially in public housing, was thought to be a contributing factor in explaining the persistence of underclass patterns. The federal government attempted to address this problem by creating what is known as "Section 8" housing, which provides vouchers to public housing residents enabling them to afford to move to nearby suburbs. Unfortunately, suburban areas that attracted a substantial number of section 8 residents saw a burgeoning of crime. Sociologist Phyllis Betts and her husband, criminologist Richard Janikowski, found a high degree of overlap between Section 8 housing and rising crime rates. It seems that it is the residents of high-rise public housing that create crime and not the high-rises themselves.[139]

The important question related to immigration is to what extent residential segregation exists for various groups and whether any group is likely to mimic the patterns found in black underclass neighborhoods. Two studies examining ethnic residential segregation found that segregation from whites is greatest for blacks, somewhat less for Hispanics, and lowest for Asians.[140] This is hardly surprising in light of the income, education, and crime data given earlier. Asians income allows them to afford to live in housing similar to middle-class whites. They are also likely to associate with whites in college and in the workplace, given the similarity of their income and education. In addition, their low crime rates do not threaten to undermine middle-class neighborhoods. What segregation exists for Asians tends to be greatest among recent immigrants living in urban ethnic enclaves. Since Asians, generally, are represented in the occupational and income structure in a way that mimics whites, there is likely to be a high degree of interaction. Such interaction, when coupled with assortative mating, is conducive to a high degree of exogamy among Asians. By 1990 a majority of Asians married non-Asians and that figure rises for younger Asian-Americans. Almost two-thirds of Asian women younger than 25, in 1990, married interracially.[141]

It appears that Asians are following the historic pattern of European immigrants. It is important to emphasize that this is happening even though Asians are clearly physically distinct as a racial group. It is also important to emphasize that the census category of Asians/Pacific Islanders includes people from a wide variety of cultures and ethnic groups, and it is unlikely that integration will be equal among these various groups.

Most Hispanics as a group are not as easily identifiable as are Asians, and are considerably more homogenous both genetically and culturally. The figures for education, income, illegitimacy, and crime among Hispanics, however, especially native-born Hispanics, suggest that integration is less likely to be as smooth as it is for most Asian groups. Given their education and income, Hispanics are unlikely to afford homes in desirable white neighborhoods and their relatively high crime rates make them undesirable in such neighborhoods. Their very high participation in gang activity makes them even more undesirable. The neighborhoods they can afford often are occupied by lower and middle-income blacks who, if they have the means, move to more suburban areas. As discussed earlier, the tensions between poorer Hispanics and those blacks who cannot leave their neighborhoods have in many places become severe, often breaking out in open warfare among rival gangs.

Since Hispanics tend to live in more segregated settings and occupy the lower rungs of the socioeconomic ladder, they are less likely to mingle with and marry non-Hispanics. Also, as the number of Hispanics increases in the population their likelihood of finding a suitable mate among other Hispanics is growing. In 1977, 31% of Hispanics married non-Hispanics. By 1998 that had dropped to 28%.[142] Furthermore, given the number of Hispanic children being raised in single-parent homes, many Hispanic women do not marry at all, thus precluding an important step toward integration and assimilation. Jacob Vigdor of the Manhattan Institute developed an "assimilation index" based on economic and cultural factors. Based on that index he concluded that Mexicans, who represent the bulk of the Hispanic population "show evidence of assimilating very slowly in comparison with other contemporary immigrant groups" or other earlier immigrant groups.[143]

Particularly troubling is the large percentage of Hispanics who evidence patterns of behavior common to an underclass. While this percentage is smaller than among blacks, it is much higher than among Asians and whites. Should a Hispanic underclass develop and persist in urban and suburban communities, it is to be expected that "white (and Asian) flight" will occur, but on a larger scale due to the expected growth in the Hispanic population. To some extent this is already happening. Much of the opposition to illegal immigration is fueled by growing Hispanic populations in many of the suburbs of major cities where residents witness a very clear degradation in Hispanic neighborhoods and fear an eminent decline in their quality of life. The rise of Hispanics to majority status in some states such as California and those of the Southwest has produced an outmigration of whites and middle-class individuals of all races in search of safer communities and better schools for their children.

Assimilation and Multiculturalism

All of the above raises the question of the impact of the doctrine of multiculturalism on the assimilation of immigrant groups. It appears, at least given the different patterns found between Asians and Hispanics, that it is a far less potent force than economic mobility. The effect of the efforts to "Americanize" newcomers in the late 1800s and early 1900s may have had less effect than is generally thought by the opponents of multiculturalism. It is well to recall that those efforts by a host of private and governmental agents, especially the schools, to impose an American identity on the children of immigrants were often resisted by the parents of those same children. Almost all immigrants wished to maintain their traditional cultures and made powerful emotional demands on their children in their attempt to do so. Perhaps the most powerful of these was the attempt to restrict the marital choice of children to coethnics. Nowhere was this more powerful than among Jews, as is evidenced by their high rates of endogamy well into the late 20th century.

But against these social and cultural pressures against assimilation are arrayed the more powerful forces of human nature—of the desire to live as well and marry as well as one's natural resources allow. To satisfy those desires in a modern industrialized society requires that one fit in and satisfy the economic requirements demanded by such a society. In acquiring those skills and finding employment, the children of immigrants naturally find themselves side by side with people of abilities and propensities similar to their own. Equally naturally, they will marry people among those with whom they interact.

Parents with strong ethnic identities will attempt to restrict those choices to co-ethnics and in many cases they succeed. However, the power of sexual selection operates in the opposite direction, driving people to strike the best marriage bargain they can and, in doing so, reject the limiting choices some parents and cultures would impose. The net result, as the historical data clearly reveal, is that in a highly mobile, geographically and economically modern society, such cultural pressures lose out, in a generation or two, to the biological imperatives driving mate choice. In practical terms, an individual member of an ethnic group that comprises only 5% of the population would have to eliminate 95% of the population from his prospective pool of marital choices. That is a very high biological price to pay in the name of ethnic solidarity. As the data indicate, most people are unwilling to pay that price, if they can avoid it.

However, cultural and ethnic allegiance is not the only factor operating to prevent universal random (panmictic) marriage. Native ability is an even greater impediment, due, as earlier discussed, to assortative mating preferences. If two groups are equally represented in all ability levels, as are Asian and white Americans, than any individual in one group can find a potential mate of similar ability in the other ethnic group. If one group is very small, then the likelihood of outmarriage is magnified. Most whites are unlikely to find an Asian mate, but this is also true for Asians. Not surprisingly, many Asians marry non-Asians.

On the other hand, if two groups exhibit large differences in ability, their economic and social standing will not overlap nearly as much. Such is the case with whites and blacks. Blacks represent 13% of the population, but they are seriously underrepresented in the top rungs of the socioeconomic ladder, and overrepresented in the bottom rungs. A white person in the upper rungs, who sets out to marry a black person, if he followed the dictates of assortative mating, would have a hard time doing so. A poor white could have a much easier time finding a mate among blacks of similar status, but would be severely hindered by the extreme segregation of poor blacks from white society and the tendency for poor black women to have children out of wedlock. In other words, a poor white man who wanted to marry a black woman of similar status would have difficulty meeting such a woman. Most such opportunities would take place in the workplace, since they would rarely live in close proximity to each other. Even if he did meet such a woman, she might, as do a great many poor black women, already have children and men are often reluctant to marry women in such circumstances.

A similar problem arises in the marital choices of Hispanics and whites, though since their social stratification overlaps to a greater degree than for whites and blacks, they have more opportunity to mate assortatively than blacks, but less so than Asians. The data given above is consistent with this interpretation. In short, racial solidarity or prejudice may explain, in part, why intermarriage is not greater than it is, but native abilities and socioeconomic stratification seems to be more important. The very high outmarriage rate among young Asian women suggests that this is the case.

While the doctrine of multiculturalism does not seem to impede in any serious way the assimilation of Asians, the same cannot be said with regard to the assimilation of Hispanics. In order to understand why, it is important to think clearly about what multiculturalism means in practice and not merely in theory. The doctrine arose in the 1970s at the time when two powerful forces were at work in American society, namely, the civil rights movement and immigration reform. Was multiculturalism a response to the entry of new immigrants or to the demands of the civil rights movement? A very strong case can be made that it was primarily a response to the civil rights movement, or more specifically, to the disappointing outcomes of that movement. As Charles Murray demonstrated in his seminal book, *Losing Ground*, blacks had been making significant gains throughout the 1950s and 1960s. After passage of the Civil Rights Act of 1964, however, those trends started to reverse and the emergence of a black underclass became unmistakable. Welfare dependency, illegitimacy, school failure, and crime all increased dramatically throughout the 1970s.[144]

Concurrent with these developments a new militancy developed among black leaders, which took its most extreme form in the Black Power Movement. At the same time there arose a host of explanations for the poor academic performance of black children. Such explanations included many plausible causes such as poor school funding and low expectations for black children among white educators. Also cited were the debilitating effects of past segregation and prejudice on the current motivations of black children. How could black children be expected to work hard in school when they would be denied the fruits of those labors by discriminating employers? At the same time, less plausible explanations were introduced such as the need to recognize Black English as a respectable variant of Standard English. It was also argued that the Eurocentric emphasis in American education was less relevant to the interests and learning style of black children and interfered with their acquisition of useful skills and knowledge. Black children would perform better, it was argued, if their education took on an Afrocentric emphasis.[145]

As the more plausible arguments were undermined by experience and empirical research, the less plausible arguments took on greater importance, especially the argument about the detrimental effect of Eurocentrism. In direct response to this claim, The New York State Department of Education in the early 1990s revised its social studies curriculum in the direction of a "curriculum of inclusion." It based this revision on a report issued by a task force entitled, "One Nation, Many Peoples: A Declaration of Cultural Independence." The report argued that "the systematic bias toward European culture and its derivatives has a terribly damaging effect on the psyche of young people of African, Asian, Latino and Native American descent" and explained why "large numbers of children of non-European descent are not doing as well as expected."[146] Other school systems around the country soon followed in due course and multiculturalism became the reigning doctrine in educational circles. The problem is that no empirical evidence was brought forth by the New York Task Force to substantiate its claims, and to date no serious empirical support has come to light. It was a highly implausible claim to begin with, and was contradicted at the time by the stellar performance of Asian children in New York schools. As a reality check, it is well to note that since the installation of this doctrine, the black-white educational gap has remained unchanged, and the performance of Hispanic children has also not improved.[147]

The doctrine of multiculturalism was not a response to Asian or Hispanic parents' complaints or requests for more Asian and Hispanic history in the curriculum, but rather to the claims of what was at best a fringe element in black educational circles. It did have one extremely negative effect in that it created a climate where it was difficult to impose normal standards on minority group children in that these standards were henceforth defined as "white" and "Eurocentric." A similar attitude had taken hold two decades earlier in the administration of social welfare among the poor. White social workers were admonished not to attempt to impose their "white middle-class standards" on poor black people. It would be incorrect, for instance, to attempt to argue for such standards in the sexual realm.[148] One consequence of this cultural tolerance was that black illegitimacy skyrocketed from about 25% in the mid sixties to 65% over the next two decades.

When that type of social "tolerance" permeates the classroom, as it does in many urban schools, the net result is a disastrous breakdown in discipline and order that makes education all but impossible. That permissive atmosphere now permeates almost all schools with heavy minority, including Hispanic, representation. Its practical effect has been to create two parallel school systems, one geared to whites and Asians, where discipline is maintained and education is largely successful, and one geared to blacks and Hispanics, with just the opposite dynamics. For the brightest blacks and Hispanics this has been an unmitigated disaster, since they cannot benefit from the education they could certainly acquire as long as they are forced to attend the typical urban school. Those living in the suburbs, or fortunate enough to attend Catholic or private schools, are spared the debilitating effects of urban public schooling. But sadly they are in the minority. It hardly needs saying that the high rates of educational failure among Hispanics documented in the statistics presented earlier are a major hindrance to their assimilation into the American mainstream.

In the earlier wave of immigration before the mid-1920s very few people objected to the imposition of middle-class European standards on students in schools. Among the values of middle-class America at the time were those consistent with restraint in sexual behavior and public demeanor that were widely accepted. Then, as today, the adoption of such standards and values enabled individuals to attain the skills necessary for economic self-sufficiency. Without such self-sufficiency—there was no government welfare support at the time—achieving assimilation would have been difficult indeed.

A major difference between those times and today is the significance of formal education. Before the 1960s, most jobs did not require advanced training since there were a wide range of occupations that could be learned on the job, including many which required very limited skills. High school graduation was clearly advantageous, but was not necessary to obtain a reasonable wage able to support a family. Today, of course, the situation is drastically different. A high school diploma is a necessity for entry into most jobs. The high dropout rate among Hispanics (27%) guarantees that many Hispanics will fail to achieve the economic status which allows for full assimilation. In addition, because of the decline in educational standards in poor neighborhoods, even high school graduation no longer signifies that an individual has acquired the tools necessary for economic self-sufficiency. The prospects for those who fail to attain a meaningful high school education are bleak indeed. All of these developments have particularly serious consequences for Hispanics and blacks, especially given the sizable number of people in those groups with below average IQ. As the authors of a *Perfect Storm* warned, these problems are likely to grow worse in a globalized economy that demands more, rather than less, advanced training.

The income gap between whites and Asians, on the one hand, and blacks and Hispanics, on the other, will continue to grow unless the educational system can be made more effective in dealing with less capable children. As discussed in an earlier chapter, sizable income differences in recognizably different racial groups do not bode well for societal harmony. Most people think that a decent government ought to help those who have economic difficulties not of their own making, including those with lower abilities. This sentiment comes up against the reality of just how much the better-off part of the population can be taxed to support a growing number of people in poverty. How much government revenue can be diverted to public support before basic infrastructure (in transportation and energy production), education, health provision and criminal justice, not to mention national security, are seriously compromised? A nation's productivity is largely dependent on such things and at some point it may simply be impossible to maintain the current level of support for the poor without impoverishing the nation as a whole. Social harmony is not furthered if the racial groups in need of government aid attribute their difficulties to discrimination and enmity on the part of those racial groups providing the support. The problem is compounded if the better-off groups are required to divert more of their resources toward protecting themselves from predatory crime and attempting to put distance between themselves and a growing underclass population. Numerous examples from around the world, and historical experience, suggest that the scenario outlined here is a sure prescription for group strife and societal instability.

Notes

1   Roger Daniels, *Coming to America: A History of Immigration and Ethnicity in American Life*, Second Edition (New York: Harper Collins, 2002), 383.

2   United States Department of Homeland Security. *2006 Yearbook of Immigration Statistics,.* Table 1. Persons Obtaining Legal Permanent Resident Status: Fiscal Years 1820 to 2006 (Washington D.C.: U. S. Department of Homeland Security. Office of Immigration Statistics, 2007).

3   David M. Reimers, *Still the Golden Door: The Third World Comes to America, 2nd Edition* (New York: Columbia University Press, 1992), 14–16.

4   Daniel J. Titchenor, *Dividing Lines: The Politics of Immigration Control in America* (Princeton New Jersey: Princeton University Press, 2002), 182.

5   Ibid, 182; Peter Novick, *The Holocaust in American Life* (New York: Houghton Mifflen, 2000), 81.

6   Titchenor, *Dividing Lines*, 183–185.

7   Ibid, 187–188.

8   Daniels, *Coming to America*, 331.

9   Allis Radosh and Ronald Radosh, *A Safe Haven: Harry S. Truman and the Founding of Israel* (New York: HarperCollins, 2009), 36–60.

10 Ibid, 36–60; Peter Novick, *The Holocaust in American Life*, 63–84.

11 Ibid, 89.

12 Ibid, 79, 82.

13 Titchenor, *Dividing Lines*. 181–182.

14 Department of Homeland Security, *2006 Yearbook,* Table 1, Table 2, Persons Obtaining Legal Permanent Resident Status by Region and Selected Country of Last Residence (Washington DC: U. S. Department of Homeland Security. Office of Immigration Statistics, 2007).

15 Reimers, *Still the Golden Door*, 16–20.

16 Ibid, 20.

17 Otis L. Graham, *Unguarded Gates: A History of America's Immigration Policy* (Rowen and Littlefield, 2006), 106.

18 Department of Homeland Security, *2006 Yearbook,* Table 2.

19 Daniels, *Coming to America*, 334.

20 John F, Kennedy, *A Nation of Immigrants* (New York, Harper Perennial, 2008), 47.

21 Reimers, Still the Golden Door, 50.

22 Ibid, 53–54.

23 Department of Homeland Security, *2006 Yearbook,* Table 2.

24 Graham, *Unguarded Gates*, 87–88.

25 Titchenor, *Dividing Lines*, 211–213.

26 President Lyndon B. Johnson, Remarks at the Signing of the Immigration Bill, Liberty Island, New York. October 3, 1965, Lyndon Baines Johnson Library and Museum, National Archives and Record Administration.

27 Graham, *Unguarded Gates*, 88–89.

28 Ibid, 90.

29 Lawrence Auster, *The Path to National Suicide: An essay on Immigration and Multiculturalism* (Charles Town, West Virginia: Old Line Press, 1990), 12.

30 Ibid, 14.

31 Daniels, *Coming to America*, 342.

32 Ibid, 344.

33 Ibid, 344.

34 Graham, *Unguarded Gates*, 99–100.

35 Department of Homeland Security, *2006 Yearbook*, Table 2.

36 Reimers, *Still the Golden Door*, 182.

37 Department of Homeland Security, *2006 Yearbook*, Table 2.

38 Graham, *Unguarded Gates*, 99.

39 Department of Homeland Security, *2006 Yearbook, Table 2.*

40 Ibid, Table 2.

41 Ibid, Table 34.

42 *Time Magazine*, Getting Their Slice of Paradise, May 2, 1977.

43 Ibid.

44 *Time Magazine*, The Desperate Ones. October 8, 1979, online.

45 Graham, *Unguarded Gates*, 106.

46 Sam Allis, Maureen Dowd and Bonnie Bartok, Losing Control of the Borders, *Time Magazine*, June 13, 1983, 47.

47 Graham, *Unguarded Gates*, 108.

48 James Kelly, Closing the Golden Door, *Time*, May 18, 1981.

49 Graham, *Unguarded Gates*, 108.

50 Ibid, 107.

51 Ibid, 107. Graham cites Roberto Suro, *Watching America's Door: The Immigration Backlash and the New Policy Debate* (Twentieth Century Fund, 1996) p.33.

52 Daniels, *Coming to America*, 392.

53 Reimers, *Still the Golden Door,* 243.

54 Immigration Reform and Control Act of 1986. 8USC 1101 note.

55 Ibid.

56 Betsy Cooper and Kevin O'Neil, *Lessons from the Immigration Reform and Control Act of 1986* (Washington, DC: Migration Policy Institute, August 2005), No. 3, 5.

57 Reimers, *Still the Golden Door*, 247–248.

58 Cooper and O'Neil, *Lessons*, 5.

59 Immigration Reform and Control Act of 1986. 8USC 1101 note.

60 *2006 Yearbook of Immigration Statistics*, Table 34.

61 Katherine M. Donato, Jorge Durand and Douglas S. Massey, Stemming the Tide? Assessing the Deterrent Effects of the Immigration Reform and Control Act. *Demography,* 29, 2 May 1992.
62 Reimers, *Still the Golden Door,* 259–261.
63 Cooper and O'Neil, *Lessons,* 5.
64 Reimers, *Still the Golden Door,* 249.
65 Ibid, 253–255.
66 What Section 245(i) actually does, *Numbers USA.*
67 Ibid.
68 U. S. Amnesties for Illegal Aliens, *Numbers USA,* online at numbersusa.
69 Ibid.
70 U. S. Citizenship and Immigration Services, Immigration through the Legal Immigration Family Equity Act (LIFE) of 2000.
71 Department of Homeland Security, *2006 Yearbook, Table 6.*
72 Department of Homeland Security, *2006 Yearbook, Table 2.*
73 Jeffrey S. Passel and D'Vera Cohn, *U. S. Population Projections: 2005–2050,* (Washington D.C.: Pew Research Center, February 11, 2008), 36.
74 U. S. Citizenship and Immigration Services, Pub. L 109–367 Secure Fence Act of 2006.
75 Ibid.
76 Tony Blankley, Border Insecurity, *Townhall.com* March 5, 2008.
77 Prakesh Khatri, Recommendation from the CIS Ombudsman to the Director, USCIS, August 28, 2005, Office of the Citizenship and Immigration Service Ombudsman, U. S. Department of Homeland Security.
78 Ruth Ellen Wasem, CRS Report for Congress, Immigration: Legislative Issues on Nonimmigrant Professional Specialty (H–1B) Workers, May 23, 2007 (Washington D.C.: Congressional Research Service, 2007), 17.
79 Ibid, 1.
80 Ibid, 18.
81 Ibid, 21.
82 Khatri, Recommendation from the CIS Ombudsman.
83 Wasem, CRS Report for Congress, 5.
84 Ibid, 9.
85 Norman Matloff, On the Need For Reform Of the H-1B Non–Immigrant Work Visa in Computer-Related Occupations (Invited Paper). *University of Michigan Journal of Law Reform,* Fall 2003, Vol. 36, Issue 4, 815–914, 19–31. The paper was downloaded from Mattloff's Website, pagination is that in PDF version of that paper.
86 Ibid, 2–3.
87 Patrick Thibodeau, Norman Matloff Tells What's Wrong with the H-1B Visa program, *Computer World,* September 8, 2008.
88 Ron Hira, Do we Need Foreign Technology Workers? *The New York Times, Room For Debate,* April 8, 2009, online.

89   Ibid.
90   William Branigan, Visa Program, High–Tech Workers Exploited Critics Say, Visa Program Brings Charges of Exploitation, *The Washington Post, July 26, 1998, A1*. Published online in 2000 Eugene Katz Award for Excellence in the Coverage of Immigration (Center for Immigration Studies, June 2000).
91   National Academy, Brain Mobility, *Issues In Science and Technology*, Winter 2006.
92   Ralph E. Gomory and Harold T. Shapiro, Globalization: Causes and Effects, *Issues in Science and Technology*, Summer 2003.
93   Ibid.
94   For a succinct discussion on the challenges confronting America in the global economy, see Robert D. Atkinson, Deep Competitiveness, *Issues In Science and Technology*, Winter 2007, online at issues.org.
95   National Science Foundation, NSF Shortage Study Called 'Bad Science', *Science News*, May 2, 1992.
96   William M. Welch, Illegal Immigrants Might Get Stimulus Jobs, Experts Say *USA Today*, March 8, 2009.
97   Passel and Cohn, *Population Projection*, 8–11.
98   Joel Kurtzman, Mexico's Instability Is a Real Problem: Don't Discount the Possibility of a Failed State Next Door, *The Wall Street Journal*, January 16, 2009.
99   Robert Suro, *Strangers Among Us: How Latino Immigration is Transforming America* (New York: Alfred A. Knopf, 1998), 316.
100 Ibid, 102.
101 Ibid, 102
102 Tyche Hendricks, Study: Price for Border Fence Up to $49 Billion, *San Francisco Chronicle*, January 8, 2007.
103 U. S. Citizenship and Immigration Services, Pub. L 109–367 Secure Fence Act of 2006.
104 Miriam Jordan, New Curbs Set on Arrests of Illegal Immigrants, *The Wall Street Journal*, July 11, 2009.
105 Central Intelligence Agency, *The World Factbook: Statistics and Analysis for Every Country on the Planet* (New York: Barnes and Noble, 2006), 396.
106 Jason Richwine, Indian Americans: The New Model Minority, *Forbes Magazine*, February 24, 2009.
107 U. S. Census Bureau, Statistical Abstract, 2008, 158.
108 New Century Foundation, *Hispanics: A Statistical Portrait*, Oakton, Virginia, September 2006, 6.
109 National Assessment of Educational Progress, 2005, Washington D.C.: U. S. Department of Education, Reading, 4–5, Mathematics, 4–5.
110 U. S. Census Bureau, *Statistical Abstract*, 2008, 148.
111 College Board, *2007 College Bound Seniors, Total Group Profile* (New

York, College Board, 2007)

112 U. S. Census Bureau, *Statistical Abstract*, 2008, 66.

113 U. S. Census Bureau, Statistical Abstract, 2008, 67.

114 Steven A. Camarota, *Illegitimate Nation: An Examination of Out of Wedlock Births Among Immigrants and Natives*. (Washington, D.C.: Center for Immigration Studies, 2007), 7.

115 Camarota, *Illegitimate Nation*, 20.

116 U. S. Census Bureau, *Statistical Abstract*, 2008, 189–190.

117 Barry Holman, *Masking the Divide: How Officially Reported Prison Statistics Distort the Racial and Ethnic Realities of Prison Growth*, (Alexandria, Virginia: National Center on Institution and Alternatives, May 2001), 2.

118 U. S. Census Bureau, *Statistical Abstract*, 2008, 202.

119 William J. Sabol, Heather Couture, and Paige M. Harrison., *Bureau of Justice Statistics Bulletin, Prisoners in 2006, NCJ 219416* (revised 5/12/09), (Washington D.C.: U. S. Department of Justice, December 2007), 6,8.

120 Kristin F. Butcher and Anne Morrison Piehl, *Why Are Immigrants' Incarceration Rates So Low: Evidence on Selective Immigration, Deterrence and Deportation*. WP 2005–19 (Chicago Illinois: Federal Reserve Bank of Chicago, November), 2005, 38.

121 Etienne G. Krug et al., eds. World Report on Violence and Health (Geneva: World Health Organization, 2002), 308-313.

122 Thomas Sowell, *Ethnic America* (New York: Basic Books, 1981), 216–220.

123 Sabol et. al., *Prisoners in 2006* 23. The category "other" includes, according to the authors, "American Indians, Alaskan Natives, Asians, Native Hawaiians, other Pacific Islanders, and persons identifying two or more races."

124 Arian Campo–Flores, The Most Dangerous Gang in America, *Newsweek*, March 28, 2005.

125 U. S. Department of State, Bureau of Consular Affairs.

126 Arlen Egley, Jr. and Christina E. Ritz, *Highlights of the 2004 National Youth Gang Survey* (Washington, U. S. Department of Justice, April 2006).

127 U. S. Census Bureau, *Statistical Abstract*, 2008, 66; Arlen Egley, Jr. *National Youth Gang Survey Trends from 1996 to 2000*. (Washington, D.C.: U. S. Department of Justice, February, 2002).

128 Egley and Ritz, *Highlights of the 2004 National Youth Gang Survey*.

129 U. S. Census Bureau, *Statistical Abstract*, 2008, 375.

130 Ibid, 388–391.

131 Ibid, 415.

132 Ibid, 449, 458.

133 Ibid, 450.

134 Ibid, 449.

135 New Century Foundation, *Hispanics: A Statistical Portrait*, Oakton, Virginia, 2006.

136 Madeleine Pelner Cosman, Illegal Aliens and American Medicine, *Journal of American Physicians and Surgeons*. 10:1, Spring 2005, 6–10. The law referred to is Emergency Medical Treatment and Active Labor Act of 1985.

137 Peter D Salins, *Assimilation, American Style* (New York: Basic Books, 1997), 6, 244–5. Cited in Samuel P. Huntington, *Who Are We: The Challenges to America's National Identity*, (New York: Simon and Schuster Paperbacks, 2004), 183.

138 Richard J. Herrnstein and Charles Murray, *The Bell Curve: Intelligence and Class Structure in American Life* (New York: The Free Press, 1996), 331, 339.

139 Hanna Rosen, American Murder Mystery, *Atlantic Monthly*, July/August 2008.

140 Erika Stienmetz and John Iceland, Racial and Ethnic Residential Housing Patterns in Places: 2000. Paper presented at the Annual Meetings of the *Population Association of America*. Minneapolis, MI. May 1–3, 2003; Michael J. White, Catherine Bucker and Jennifer E. Glick, The Impact of Immigration on Residential Segregation Revisited. Paper presented to the *American Sociological Association*, August, 2002.

141 Eric Lin, *The Accidental Asian: Notes of a native Speaker* (New York: Random House, 1998) 188, cited by Huntington, *Who we Are*, 298.

142 Samuel P. Huntington, *Who Are We: The Challenges to America's National Identity* (New York: Simon and Schuster Paperbacks, 2004), 240.

143 Jacob L. Vigdor, *Measuring Immigrant Assimilation in the United States, Civic Report No. 53*, May 2008 (New York: Manhattan Institute, 2003) 20.

144 Charles Murray. *Losing Ground: American Social Policy1950–1980* (New York: Basic Books, 1984).

145 Byron M. Roth, *Prescription for Failure: Race Relations in the Age of Social Science* (New Brunswick, New Jersey :Transaction Publishers,1994), 273–292.

146 Arthur M. Schlesenger, Jr., *The Disuniting of America: Reflections on a Multicultural Society* (New York: W.W. Norton, 1992, 88.

147 Roth, *Prescription for Failure*, 289–292.

148 Personal experience of the author during a 16 month employment with the New York City Department of Welfare in 1964–1965.

Chapter 7

EUROPEAN IMMIGRATION IN THE POSTWAR ERA

Introduction

THE MOST SALIENT FACT about the history of immigration in Europe is that, prior to the mid-twentieth century, immigration was limited and consisted almost exclusively of people moving from one country in Europe to another. As discussed in Chapter 5, throughout the 1800s Europe was a major exporter of people; millions of Irish, English, Italians, and Germans left their homelands to settle in the United States, and to a lesser extent in the other overseas colonies of the European states. The reasons, already discussed, were the enormous population pressures in Europe at the time. Europe was experiencing the front end of the demographic transition brought on by industrialization. From the end of the Napoleonic Wars until 1914 Europe enjoyed almost a century of relative peace and prosperity. This, along with improvements in agriculture and public health, promoted significant population growth. Europe's population increased from 180 million in 1800 to some 390 million by 1900. Even the rapid growth of cities during this time and the advent of the industrial revolution could not accommodate Europe's population explosion. This explains the massive movement of people out of Europe, and also explains why European countries were not, generally, desirable destinations for migrants seeking a better life.[1]

The movement of people out of Europe at the time was especially remarkable in light of the fact that it was during this period that

Europe was experiencing extraordinary economic growth. According to historian Samuel Huntington, the West's share of the world's manufacturing output dramatically increased during the second half the nineteenth century and peaked at 84% in 1928. It was during this time that Europe controlled almost one half of the world's landmass.[2]

In August of 1914, Europe entered into World War I with devastating results. It was followed by 20 years of economic and political turmoil, culminating in the even more devastating Second World War, which was in many ways a continuation of the first. These years of war and social and economic turbulence exhausted Europe and led to the rapid decline of European world dominance. By mid-century European states were in desperate straits in the need to rebuild their ruined infrastructure. They could hardly afford to maintain their overseas empires or their earlier military superiority. Their former dominant world position was taken over by the United States whose industrial capacity had grown substantially during World War II and whose infrastructure had been unscathed in the war.

The cataclysmic effect of the wars and economic turmoil and the massive loss of life taken by those wars and by Communist rule in Russia had surprisingly little lasting demographic effect. As in the United States, a postwar baby boom returned European populations to their prewar levels in a fairly short time. European population rose to 547 million by the mid-20th century, a figure 40% higher than at the beginning of the century, and in 2000 it had risen to 728 million, almost double what it had been 100 years earlier.[3] Equally surprising was that these events had little impact on European patterns of immigration. While the war created millions of refugees and displaced persons, most who survived returned to their native villages and cities. A major exception were the large numbers of people who fled the Communist regimes emerging in Eastern Europe and settled in Western Europe and the United States, but relative to the native populations, their overall numbers were small. Perhaps the most notable demographic change was the movement of many of the surviving European Jews to the newly established state of Israel or to other countries outside Europe.

In the immediate postwar years Western Europe began to rebuild its devastated infrastructure and experienced robust economic expansion. In many ways this recovery was aided by the benign treatment by the United States of those it had defeated. Europe's recovery was aided significantly by the Marshall plan, and the U. S.'s relatively open trading policies in relation to Europe. The French refer to the period between

1945 and 1975, as the "thirty glorious years." The Western European countries that experienced the most rapid growth were confronted by labor shortages, especially of manual labor, and in the 1950s welcomed the migration of foreign workers to fill the native gap. Most of these workers came from the less robust economies of Southern Europe, especially Italy, Spain, and Portugal. Somewhat later migrant workers arrived from the Balkans and North Africa. A very large number came from Turkey and settled in various European countries, but with Germany as their primary destination.[4]

It should be stressed that these *gastarbeiters* or "guest workers" were mainly men who were expected to return to their native countries when the work shortages ended and were not seen as prospective citizens of the host countries. According to Craig Parsons and Timothy Smeeding, "At no point did substantial groups or policymakers in Europe intend for most of these postwar immigrants to settle permanently."[5] Many of the temporary workers did, in fact, go home, but a substantial number did not, and by the 1970s they began bringing families and creating immigrant communities in European cities.[6] This was especially notable in Germany where Turkish communities, almost exclusively Muslim, tended to remain distinct from the native population and rarely intermarried. Workers from European countries, such as Italy and Spain, often went home and, if they did not, were not nearly as segregated and the men frequently married native women.[7]

During the 1970s economic growth slowed considerably, influenced in part by the oil crisis of 1973-1974. In addition, industrial production began its decline and a number of regions in Europe became rust-belts similar to developments at that time in the United States. Also, as in the United States the process of moving production overseas to lower-cost labor markets and various technological improvements reduced demand for unskilled labor. This period brought major changes in the way European governments viewed immigrants. According to Marco Martiniello, "Until then, immigration had been seen largely as an essentially economic resource to be mobilized according to precise labor requirements. Generally speaking, the presence of immigrants was supposed to be temporary. In the case of unfavorable economic conditions, they were expected to go home."[8] In response to the economic downturn in the 1970s, most governments developed policies to halt immigration, but "European governments somehow never seemed able or inclined" to follow through with their restrictionist pronouncements. Workers continued to come and many workers brought in wives and children under family unification provisions. The southern European countries of Italy, Spain, and Greece, which had been countries exporting population, found themselves attracting migrants from Third World countries.[9]

The postwar labor shortage was only one of many factors driving immigration in Europe. Equally important were political developments resulting from the waning of European colonialism and the rise of national movements in colonial countries. This was especially true for England and France, both of which encouraged migrants from colonies, both before and after they had achieved independence. For England, the biggest source of immigrants was those fleeing the turmoil on the Indian Subcontinent and former African colonies. For France, the major sources were its former colonies in North Africa and particularly Algeria in the aftermath of the Algerian War and the resulting independence of Algeria.[10]

Until 1960 all citizens of British Commonwealth nations—for example India, South Africa, Pakistan, Australia, etc.—were not subject to immigration control and as holders of British passports could freely enter the countries of England, Wales, Scotland and Northern Ireland, which together make up the United Kingdom. Legislation in 1962 removed this advantage for Commonwealth citizens, who thereafter were treated as any foreigner seeking immigration to the United Kingdom. However, because of family reunification policies and the existence of social networks in Great Britain, large numbers of immigrants from former colonies continued to immigrate. In 1971 the government placed further restrictions on immigration by favoring those of European descent from the former colonies of Australia, New Zealand, Canada, and South Africa.[11] This legislation was largely a response to racial problems and was transparently designed to limit non-European (nonwhite) immigration. For numerous reasons these attempts to limit immigration were ineffective and large numbers of people continued to arrive in the United Kingdom from its former colonies.

Immigration in France during the 1960s was greatly augmented by the bitter Algerian War, which ended in 1962 under the presidency of Charles de Gaulle. At the time, France had a policy of open immigration for people from Algeria. Many who came were ethnic French colonists who could not safely remain in the new Algeria. Many were Algerians who had sided with the French in the bloody struggle for independence and who were equally threatened under the new regime. According to Kimberly Hamilton, Patrick Simon, and Clara Veniard, writing for the Migration Immigration Source, "In 1962, about 350,000 so-called 'French Muslims' were counted in France. The number of Algerians rose to 470,000 in 1968 and 800,000 in 1982." A similar, though far less frequent, pattern occurred after the defeat of France and the loss of its colonies in Indochina. While the French attempted to limit further immigration, according to the authors cited above, "immigration continued and diversified over the following decades."[12]

Similar, but smaller, migrations from former colonies were experienced by the Dutch from Indonesia and the Belgians from the Belgian Congo. It should be stressed, firstly, that all the European countries experienced high levels of immigration from a host of countries and in most instances, Britain and France being notable exceptions, these immigrants outnumber those from former colonies. A primary reason for this was Europe's extreme openness to refugees seeking asylum, an openness supported, and in many cases required, by the EU and the European Court of Human Rights. An additional factor, especially for Spain and Italy, was the large number of illegal aliens who arrived by overseas travel from various African countries, the Balkans, and Turkey who, after some time, were allowed to take up legal residency. Once they had established legal residency they were, under the human rights rulings, entitled to bring family members to live with them.[13]

A second point, mentioned earlier, is that roughly half of all immigrants to European countries come from other European countries. It should be stressed that most of the movement between European countries (and immigration from other advanced societies such as the U. S.) takes place for occupational reasons, in ways not much different from movement within the various states of the United States. Many of these people are professionals or in managerial positions and are often more highly educated and skilled than the natives of the country to which they move. Since the recent enlargement of the EU to 27 countries, to include many from Eastern Europe, internal migration has increased considerably. Most of the concerns Europeans express about immigration have, in most cases, little to do with these European immigrants, but rather concern those of Third-World origin who are viewed as having values and customs foreign to Europe. This point must be borne in mind when examining statistics on immigration that often do not distinguish between European and Third World immigrants.

Today, as is the case in the United States, the force driving immigration is the explosive population growth in countries close to Europe with poor economic prospects, often-dangerous political instability, and many with oppressive governments. Europe has become a magnet for people fleeing poverty and oppression. One prominent reason is that European Union directives have become increasingly influential in shaping the ways countries deal with the immigration problems. These directives are shaped by international laws to which most European nations subscribe, and limit considerably their ability to shape their own national immigration policies.[14] This is especially the case in regard to the treatment of asylum seekers, which makes it difficult and often costly to simply deport illegal entrants claiming asylum.[15] In addition, the EU recognizes UN conventions dealing with rights of family reunification that require nations to allow the immigration of spouses and minor children of migrant workers and those granted asylum.[16]

For these reasons immigration continued and grew even as national policies became more restrictive regarding legal immigrant flows. According to Hugo Brady, writing for the think-tank, Centre for European Reform, "Europe is currently absorbing 2 million migrants each year—more as a proportion of its population than any other part of the world, including North America." It should be noted, however, that since approximately half of these immigrants are Europeans, the proportion of Third World immigrants into Europe with a population of about 500 million, is somewhat smaller than their proportion into the United States with a population of about 300 million. Brady also reports that there are approximately 8 million illegal immigrants in the EU, "and that this number increases by 500,000 to 1 million every year."[17]

Not surprisingly, the native populations of all European countries find this troublesome. As in the United States, almost all polls show that large majorities of EU citizens oppose this influx of immigrants, especially those from Third World countries. European elites, especially the officials of EU institutions, have been as unresponsive, perhaps even more unresponsive, to those concerns as American elites.[18]

Table 7.1 provides an estimate of the number of foreign-born in various European states. The table is based on estimates made for the OECD (Organization for Economic Co-operation and Development) in 2006 by Georges Lemaitre and Cecile Thoreau. It should be emphasized that not all the people in the foreign-born population are immigrants in the sense that they wish to establish citizenship and reside permanently in the host country. Many are resident in a country for reasons of business or education and expect to return home. This is more likely to be true for people from the more affluent industrialized nations of Europe and the Americas, and even many of those from the poorer regions of Eastern Europe. Those who come from Third World countries usually come with the intention of taking up permanent residency.

TABLE 7.1. FOREIGN POPULATION (ROUNDED) IN SELECTED COUNTRIES AND PERCENT OF TOTAL POPULATION19

Country	Foreign Population	% of Total
Austria	1,059,100	13.00%
Belgium	1,185,500	11.40%
Denmark	343,400	6.30%
Finland	166,400	3.20%
France	5,862,200	10.00%
Germany	10,620,800	12.90%
Greece	1,122,900	10.30%
Ireland	443,000	11.00%
Italy	1,446,700	2.50%
Luxembourg	149,600	33.10%
Netherlands	1,736,100	10.60%
Norway	361,100	7.80%
Portugal	704,400	6.70%
Spain	2,172,200	5.30%
Sweden	1,100,300	12.20%
Switzerland	1,737,700	23.50%
United Kingdom	5,552,700	9.30%
Total	35,764,000	

Table 7.2 gives the proportion of immigrants in each country and their continent of origin. As can be seen, large numbers come from other European countries with, however, considerable variation from country to country. Relatively few migrants come from the Americas, and many of those are from the U. S. and Canada. Notable exceptions

are Spain and Portugal both of which attract migrants from South and Central America. In the case of the Netherlands, more than 80% of those coming from the Americas are from the Netherlands Antilles in the Caribbean and Suriname, both former colonies. About half the migrants from America to the United Kingdom are from former colonies in the Caribbean, predominantly from Jamaica, and about half come from the Unites States and Canada.[20]

TABLE 7.2. PROPORTIONS OF THE IMMIGRANTS' CONTINENTS OF ORIGIN 2000[21]

Country	Europe	Americas	Africa	Asia	Unknown
Austria	77.1%	1.6%	1.6%	1.9%	17.8%
Belgium	75.9%	2.3%	16.0%	2.8%	3.0%
Denmark	49.4%	4.6%	8.7%	28.5%	8.8%
Finland	71.4%	4.5%	8.0%	15.9%	0.2%
France	47.6%	2.7%	40.8%	7.3%	1.6%
Germany	79.0%	2.9%	3.4%	10.2%	4.4%
Greece	61.2%	12.7%	7.3%	16.0%	2.8%
Italy	37.8%	9.4%	30.1%	18.5%	4.3%
Luxembourg	93.4%	2.9%	1.6%	1.6%	0.6%
Netherlands	38.4%	16.3%	17.0%	21.8%	6.4%
Norway	62.5%	7.4%	5.7%	19.6%	4.9%
Portugal	27.3%	17.6%	45.1%	2.6%	7.5%
Spain	40.9%	23.9%	26.1%	6.1%	3.0%
Sweden	63.7%	7.4%	4.4%	21.5%	3.0%
Switzerland	84.4%	3.6%	2.4%	4.9%	4.8%
United Kingdom	34.7%	12.5%	14.8%	28.6%	9.4%

When examining immigration patterns from Africa it is important to distinguish those from North Africa, of whom the overwhelming majority are Muslim Arabs, and those from sub-Sahara Africa, the great bulk of whom are black Africans, many of whom are also Muslims. The pattern of migration from Africa for each European country is very much dependent on past relations with that region. Almost 80% of African migrants to France, for instance, are from Arab countries of northern Africa such as Algeria, Morocco and

Tunisia, with the remaining coming from a variety of black African countries, especially former colonies. A similar pattern explains the sizable African population in the United Kingdom, but almost all (about 90%) came from former colonies in sub-Saharan Africa.[22]

A large percentage of the African migration to Belgium, Italy, the Netherlands, Portugal, and Spain consists of Moroccans. Morocco was a colony jointly administered by France and Spain from 1912 to 1956, which explains the sizable migration of Moroccans to those two countries. In addition, Morocco signed labor agreements with Belgium and the Netherlands in the 1960s, which resulted in those two countries receiving a large number of Moroccan migrants. About two-thirds of the relatively large African immigrant population in Italy comes from Northern Africa, with the largest portion from Morocco, largely because of geographic proximity. In addition, a sizable portion of the migration to Italy from the Arab countries in recent years has been unauthorized, but many of these migrants were subsequently regularized (granted amnesty) in a series of acts by the Italian government. Finally, the extremely large number of Portuguese immigrants from Africa is also primarily Moroccans who began to arrive in substantial numbers beginning in the mid-1990s.[23]

The pattern of migration from Asia is also complex and varied. Turkey and the subcontinent of India provide the bulk of immigrants classified as Asian. For the United Kingdom, the primary sending nations are India, Pakistan, and Bangladesh, and a much smaller but a substantial number of immigrants come from various countries and former colonies in the Far East, such as Hong Kong. For Germany, over two-thirds of those classified as Asians come from Turkey. Immigrants from Turkey are the largest immigrant group in Europe comprising almost 4 million people with considerable presence in many European nations.[24] In the case of the Netherlands, more than half of those coming from Asia are from Turkey. For Italy, the two largest contributors of Asians are Mainland China and the Philippines. The relatively high percentage of Asians in the Scandinavian countries (though small in absolute numbers) comes from a wide variety of places, with a majority from West Asian and Middle Eastern countries and relatively few from the Far East. A large number of these people are Muslim in religion.

In fact, a fairly sizable portion, perhaps as many as a half, of the non-European immigrant population in Europe is of the Muslim faith. It is difficult to determine the exact percentage, however. This has to do with the way various European countries count foreigners. Some countries, like the United States, count all those born on American soil as citizens. France, on the other hand, counts the children (under 18) of nonnaturalized residents as foreigners. Once they turn 18 years of age, they are reclassified as French citizens. Germany counts as foreigners all those people who have not received citizenship, even those who may have been resident in Germany for two or three generations. Until recently, German citizenship was not easy to arrange, unless one could demonstrate that one was of German heritage, usually coming from Eastern Europe, whereupon citizenship was routinely conferred. Table 7.3 lists the number of Muslims residing in various countries. While it was compiled by a Muslim organization that might have an interest in exaggerating the size of the Muslim population, it seems, in general, reasonably accurate and consistent with various reports on the Muslim population from a number of sources. In fact, the organization stresses that its information is obtained from official government and other generally reliable sources.

It should be noted that Table 7.3 does not include the recently admitted countries of Eastern Europe that bring the EU total to 27. However, in most cases those countries are not at present important destinations for Muslims.

In addition to Muslim groups, most of whom come from the Middle East and the subcontinent of India (India, Pakistan and Bangladesh), there is also a sizable number of sub-Saharan Africans and Eastern Asians within the immigrant population. Exact numbers, here, are also difficult to come by, as not all countries classify citizens by race or ethnicity. France, for instance, has made it illegal for any government agency to gather statistics on race or religion for reasons of public policy. This contrasts markedly with the practice in the U. S. and the United Kingdom, both of whose governments amass detailed statistics on various ethnic and racial groups and their differential experience on a wide range of social indices, such as school performance, crime rates, unemployment rates and income.

TABLE 7.3. ESTIMATE OF MUSLIM POPULATION FOR SELECTED
COUNTRIES, 2006 (IN MILLIONS)[25]

Country	Total Population	Muslim Population	Percent Muslim
EU (15 countries)	380.4	14.49	3.81%
Austria	8.2	0.18	2.23%
Belgium	10.5	0.38	3.60%
Denmark	5.4	0.16	3.02%
Finland	5.2	0.01	0.18%
France	60.7	6.12	10.00%
Germany	82.5	3.05	3.70%
Greece	11.0	0.17	1.50%
Ireland	4.1	0.00	0.01%
Italy	59.0	1.42	2.40%
Luxembourg	0.5	0.01	1.10%
Netherlands	16.3	0.89	5.40%
Norway	4.6	0.05	1.04%
Portugal	10.6	0.05	0.50%
Spain	45.5	0.55	1.20%
Sweden	9.0	0.28	3.10%
Switzerland	7.4	0.23	3.10%
United Kingdom	60.1	1.51	2.50%

Indices of Social Adjustment

Education

Table 7.4 provides data on the academic performance of the children of immigrants in Europe, but no indication of race or ethnicity is provided. This is unfortunate, since such information for American immigrants, for instance, provides powerful evidence that immigrants are not an undifferentiated mass and different ethnic groups respond in very different ways to the struggle with assimilation. If this is true for European immigrants, then the reluctance of some countries to acquire and provide such data complicates the task of determining the best ways to facilitate assimilation. It also makes the task of cross-cultural comparisons very difficult. It is important to keep these caveats in mind when examining the information provided in the tables presented below.

TABLE 7.4. STUDENT PERFORMANCE (MEANS)[27]

	Native Students		Second Generation		First Generation	
	Math	Reading	Math	Reading	Math	Reading
Austria	515	501	459	428	452	425
Belgium	546	523	454	439	437	407
Denmark	520	497	449	440	455	454
France	520	505	472	458	448	426
Germany	525	517	432	420	454	431
Netherlands	551	524	492	475	472	463
Norway	499	505	460	446	438	436
Sweden	517	522	483	502	425	433
Switzerland	543	515	484	462	453	422
U. S.	490	503	468	481	453	453
Canada	537	534	543	543	530	515
Australia	527	529	522	525	525	517

The OECD (Organization of Economic Co-operation and Development) has created the *Program for International Student Assessment* (PISA) based on the testing of various academic skills in the member countries of the OECD. Table 7.4 presents data on the reading and mathematics performance for a sample of students (15 years old) of European OECD nations in 2003. Luxembourg is omitted because of its small population and highly unrepresentative foreign-born population. These tests are similar to those used in the United States in the NAEP studies reported on in Chapter 6. PISA tests have a mean of 500 and a standard deviation of 100. The table includes a comparison of the performance of native students with foreign-born students (first-generation students) and students born in their country of residence (second-generation students) whose parents are foreign. Results for the United States, Australia and Canada are included for purposes of comparison. The United Kingdom is a member state of the OECD but, for reasons not given by the authors, was not included in the study. It is important to keep in mind that these students include many whosee parents are first- and second-generation immigrants, both of whom are of European origin. In addition, many of the students described as native are the children of non-European immigrants.

The authors of this study report that almost all of the differences between native children and foreign children are statistically significant, with the notable exceptions of Australia and Canada. Somewhat disappointing is the fact that few of the differences between first- and second-generation students are large enough to reach statistical significance. In looking for the reasons for these differences, none of the variables tested by the authors seemed, in their analysis, particularly important. Immigrant children expressed the same, or higher, level of desire to learn and the same or more positive attitudes toward schooling as did native children. Controlling for socioeconomic differences (such as income) reduced the differences, but they, nevertheless, remained important.[26]

The strikingly better performance of the immigrants in the Canadian and Australian schools was noted, but not explained, even though the explanation is obvious enough. Some 60% of immigrants to Australia come from Europe, New Zealand and the Americas, and are overwhelmingly of European descent. About 33% come from Asia. Relatively few come from the Middle East, Western Asia or Africa. Very similar figures hold for Canada. About 46% of immigrants come from the United States and Europe and about 36% come from Asia, many from the Far East. Very few come from the Middle East or Africa. Put another way, more than 90% of the immigrants to Australia and more than 80% to Canada are Europeans and Asians, both groups known to perform well academically. In the case of the European countries participating in this study, the largest percentage of non-Europeans came from the Middle East and West Asia, a percentage that is even greater if one looks only at school-age children.[28]

The OECD student assessment program classifies students in six proficiency levels ranging from the most basic level 1 to the highest level 6, and is defined similarly to the 5 levels discussed by the authors of the *Perfect Storm* described in Chapter 1. Level 2 (a PISA score of at least 420) in mathematics is considered essential for the effective use of mathematics. By comparison, a PISA score above 730 is necessary to achieve level 6. According to the authors of the study, students "who are classified below level 2 are expected to face considerable challenges in terms of their labor market and earning prospects as well as their capacity to participate fully in society." While few native students fail to surpass level 2, more than 40% of first-generation students and more than 25% of second-generation students failed to achieve this level in many European countries. In Germany more than 40% of second-generation students performed below level 2, while in Austria, Belgium, Denmark and Norway, more than 30% failed to reach this level. It is important to remember that the above figures do not distinguish between European and non-European immigrant students. It seems reasonable to assume, however, that the minimal level is not achieved by an even greater percentage of students with non-European backgrounds, but no such data is available to confirm this assumption.[29]

It is instructive, in this regard, to examine the educational performance of English students, especially since ethnic membership *is* included in the data. Table 7.5 provides information about the basic educational level attained by various ethnic groups.

TABLE 7.5. PERCENTAGES ACHIEVING SCORE OF 5 OR MORE A*-C ON GCSE SCORES, 2006[30]

Race/Ethnic Group	Performance		
	Male	Female	Female-Male Differences
White British	47%	57%	10%
White Irish	54%	62%	8%
Mixed	45%	55%	10%
Indian	62%	72%	10%
Pakistani	38%	52%	14%
Bangladeshi	41%	55%	14%
Black Caribbean	27%	44%	17%
Black African	36%	48%	12%
Other Black	29%	43%	14%
Chinese	70%	79%	9%
Other Ethnic Groups	43%	54%	11%

Specifically, the table gives the percentage in each group that had achieved five or more grades of A* -C or Level 2 of the General Certificate of Secondary Education (GCSE). The grade A* is equivalent to an A+ in American schools. A C grade is the minimal passing grade. Students usually take these nation-wide examinations in their eleventh year of school at age 16. Generally students who perform well in the

GCSEs will be expected to advance to A level study in their twelfth and thirteenth year of school in preparation for more advanced study, and if they perform well in those years, move on to advanced academic and professional training.

It is extremely interesting that in no case did males outperform females, and in many cases the male-female gap was considerable. This may have special ramifications for the Pakistani and Bangladeshi (mainly Muslim) communities whose customs prescribe female submissiveness and often reflect a reluctance to allow women the freedom to gain professional advancement. It is important to stress that at this level of education, motivation and temperament may play an important role in academic performance, as important perhaps as intellectual ability. This is the usual explanation for the superior performance of girls in American schools at this age level. It is also important to point out that students in the U. K. have some latitude in the choice of subject matter in the examinations they take. Since the subject matter varies in difficulty, students' differing interests and vocational aspirations may account for some of the above differences.

Both the male and female Chinese students outperformed most other groups by wide margins. Indian students (mainly Hindus and Sikhs) ranked second and were clearly more successful in school than their native British counterparts. Pakistani and Bangladeshi boys scored well below native British, but this was not true for the girls from these groups. Blacks in general performed below all other groups; those from the Caribbean performed the least well, whereas blacks from Africa scored considerably better, almost on par with Pakistanis. These figures reflect important features of life in the United Kingdom. Theodore Dalrymple reports that Indians, who represent fewer than 2% of the population, "make up a quarter of all British medical students, 12 times their proportion in the population. They are likewise overrepresented in the law, sciences and economics faculties of our universities."[31]

The above educational outcomes are mirrored in data on the sort of behavioral problems that result in a student being permanently excluded from school, what in the United States is termed expulsion. Blacks had exclusion rates of approximately 40 pupils per 10,000, while whites had rates of 14 per 10,000, and Chinese and Indian students had exclusion rates of only 2 or fewer per 10,000.[32] These figures are remarkably similar to patterns in US schools, except that in Europe, Muslims are the dominant immigrant group as opposed to Hispanics in the United States. Both perform similarly in relation to other groups.

These educational results are, furthermore, broadly consistent with the IQ data for the student's respective home countries. The main exception is the Indians who perform better in English schools than would be expected based on the average IQ for India. This can be partly explained by the fact that India is extremely heterogeneous both culturally and genetically, much more so than most other countries. In addition, the number of Indians of Sikh faith in the United Kingdom is very high relative to their numbers in India. Sikhs in India account for only about 2% of the population, but make up about 32% of the Indians who migrate to the United Kingdom. Many Sikhs had been resident in Africa as entrepreneurs before their expulsion from that continent by African dictators. In addition, a large proportion of the Indian migrants to the United Kingdom speak English, while fewer than 5% of Indians speak English in their native country.[33] According to the CIA in their *World Factbook*, "English is the most important language for national, political, and commercial communication."[34] These factors suggest that the Indians who migrate to the United Kingdom are a fairly select group relative to the Indian population as a whole. This also seems to be the case for the Indian immigrants in the U. S. as discussed in Chapter 6, though their educational performance in the U. S. is not given separately in government statistics.

Employment

Given the educational differences noted above, it would be surprising if these did not translate into different patterns of participation in the labor force and unemployment. In general, the greater a person's educational attainment, the higher he is able to rise in the employment hierarchy. In addition, those higher in that hierarchy tend to have higher rates of participation in the labor force and lower levels of unemployment. Those with limited educational attainment tend to fall in the lowest, unskilled levels in the job market and to suffer disproportionately high unemployment or to drop out of the labor market completely. In Austria, Belgium, Denmark, and the Netherlands the proportion of the foreign born workers with the lowest educational levels in 2000 was about 50%; in France it is 55%.[35] This problem is exacerbated in most European societies whose generous welfare policies often reduce the advantage of working for those at the bottom of the job market. It should also be noted that the unemployment rate for those in the 15-25 year age group is, in most countries, much higher than what it is for the general population. In France, according to a report of the Open Society Institute, some 20% of people between 19 and 29 are unemployed. The children of immigrants are unemployed at the higher rate of 30%. "When the parents are natives of Algeria or Morocco, the unemployment rates are approximately 40%."[36] These young people often find themselves depending on government support. The reasons for this youth unemployment problem and some of its serious ramification for assimilation will be taken up in due course.

Table 7.6 gives the unemployment rate for various European countries.

TABLE 7.6. UNEMPLOYMENT RATES FOR NATIVE-BORN AND FOREIGN-BORN WORKERS IN SELECTED EUROPEAN COUNTRIES 2003[37]

	Native-born	Foreign-born
Austria	4.2%	8.3%
Belgium	6.4%	17.8%
Denmark	4.0%	8.7%
France	8.2%	15.8%
Germany	9.1%	15.7%
Netherlands	2.9%	8.9%
Norway	3.9%	9.0%
Sweden	4.8%	11.1%
Switzerland	2.9%	8.0%

Without a breakdown by ethnic, or by European versus non-European status, these figures provide limited information. As is clear in the data, foreign-born individuals exhibit rates of unemployment two to three times those for native-born. It is probable, though unclear, that rates for the non-European foreign-born are higher than the average for all foreign-born.

Here again, the United Kingdom, with its much more detailed reporting, gives more insight. It should be clear that the British figures may not reflect the Europe-wide pattern, but they do provide an indication as to whether some groups are faring better than others. Table 7.7 below presents the unemployment rate for the major ethnic groups in the United Kingdom. Clearly blacks, along with mixed-race individuals, Pakistanis, and Bangladeshis have the highest unemployment rates. Whites have the lowest rates, while the Chinese and Indians are at an intermediate level. Unemployment rates tell only part of the employment story, since in order to be classified as unemployed an individual must be in the labor market and actively seeking work. Table 7.8 presents figures on the percentage of individuals in each ethnic group that is in the United Kingdom labor market.

TABLE 7.7. UNITED KINGDOM UNEMPLOYMENT RATE[38]

Ethnic Group	Males	Females
White British	5%	4%
White Irish	5%	4%
Mixed	12%	11%
Indian	7%	8%
Pakistani	11%	20%
Bangladeshi	12%	N/A
Black Caribbean	14%	9%
Black African	12%	11%
Chinese	9%	7%
Other Ethnic Groups	5%	4%

TABLE 7.8. UNITED KINGDOM LABOR MARKET PARTICIPATION RATES[39]

Ethnic Group	Males	Females
White British	84%	75%
White Irish	84%	75%
Mixed	78%	65%
Indian	74%	65%
Pakistani	75%	31%
Bangladeshi	72%	25%
Black Caribbean	82%	75%
Black African	75%	65%
Chinese	63%	58%
Other Ethnic Groups	84%	75%

With the exception of Caribbean blacks, nonwhites are less likely to enter the labor market, with Chinese men having the lowest rate of participation. The authors of this report point out that the low rate of the Chinese can be accounted for by the fact that Chinese tend to pursue advanced education and are therefore unavailable for work. Quite striking are the very low participation rates of Pakistani and Bangladeshi women, especially in light of their academic performance that is almost on par with white women. In large measure, this is explained by the fact that most of these women are Muslim and many are at home caring for young children. According to a government report, Muslims have the largest proportion of population under 16 among all religious groups (34%).[40] This explains, in part, that overall only 32% of Muslim women are in the workforce. Muslim men also have the lowest labor participation rate among men (70%) compared to other groups, the Chinese excepted. In addition, Muslim men and women have the highest unemployment rate of any religious group with rates of 14% for men and 15% for women.[41]

As is to be expected, many recent immigrants work in low-skilled occupations. However, Indians (35%) and Chinese (38%) were more likely than those in the general population to be employed in managerial and professional occupations. About 4% of Indian men were medical practitioners, 10 times the rate of white British men. Blacks, on the other hand, were least likely, at about 20%, to be employed in professional and management occupations. A large number of people in ethnic communities are self-employed, very often in small businesses such as restaurants. This is particularly the case for Pakistanis, Bangladeshis, and Chinese. Not surprisingly, large numbers of people in these groups work in the distribution, hotel, and restaurant industries. Three out of five Bangladeshis worked in such jobs, as did just under 50% of the Chinese. Blacks are least likely to be self-employed. More than 50% of black working-women were employed in public administration, education and the health sector. One out of 10 black African working-women was employed as nurses, and 1 in 7 women classified as "Other Asian" was also so employed. Black men worked in a variety of skilled and unskilled occupations.[42]

Given the above employment patterns, it is to be expected that immigrants would make fairly heavy use of government welfare benefits. In most European countries these can be substantial and can include income supplements, health benefits, free public transportation and housing supplements for poorer families. France, in an attempt to boost fertility, has extremely generous benefits for pregnant women and families (either single- or dual-parent families) with children. These benefits are particularly helpful to Muslims, whose cultural practices encourage early marriage and large families. This is an additional factor helping to explain the very low labor participation rates of Muslim women.[43]

Criminal Behavior

The impression that crime has become a serious problem in recent years is widely held by the public and commonly attributed to the massive influx of immigrants. As J. F. O. McCallister, writing in *Time* magazine in 2002 put it, "A specter is haunting Europe—crime. Voters are mad as hell about it, and they've made it clear to their elected officials that they're not going to take it anymore."[44] During the summer of 2008, London newspapers were headlining a series of murders caused by stabbing and decried the epidemic of "knife crime" among adolescents. While the government claimed that such attacks were falling, "Casualty doctors believe knife crime is far more widespread in the country than official figures suggest because scores of victims who seek treatment in hospitals leave without making a formal complaint to police."[45]

Theodore Dalrymple reports that in Paris, "it is the private complaint of everyone…that the police have become impotent to suppress and detect crime." Dalrymple blames the problem on the "notorious" laxity of the French criminal justice system. He gives examples of the police letting assailants free because they were convinced that even fairly blatant crimes committed by young people were unlikely to be prosecuted and even if they were convicted, the "judge would give no proper punishment."[46]

Table 7.9 provides convincing evidence that the common perceptions about crime are correct. Data for the U. S. are provided for purposes of comparison. The figures for 1995 and 2005 for the European countries are unprecedented with rates 3 to more than 5 times what they had been in the 1960s. All Western societies saw rising crime rates beginning in 1965, but while these tended to level off in the United States in the 1980s and in fact began to decline after 1995, this was not the case for the European countries. In these countries, the figures continued to rise into the 1990s and have continued to rise, though at a reduced rate, in France and Great Britain, while falling somewhat in Germany after 1995. These years were chosen since they coincide with the rapid rise in immigration to Europe in this period.

TABLE 7.9. CRIMES REPORTED TO THE POLICE IN GERMANY, FRANCE, ENGLAND (INCLUDING WALES), AND THE UNITED STATES FROM 1965 TO 2005 (IN THOUSANDS)[47]

Year	Germany	France	England	United States
1965	1,789	660	1,133	4,739
1975	2,919 (1.63)	1,912 (2.89)	2,106 (1.85)	11,257 (2.38)
1985	4,215 (2.35)	3,579 (5.42)	3,611 (3.19)	12,430 (2.62)
1995	6,669 (3.72)	3,665 (5.55)	5,100 (4.50)	13,862 (2.92)
2005	6,392 (3.57)	3,727 (5.64)	5,555 (4.90)	11,556 (2.43)

Note: the numbers in parentheses give the multiple for that year over 1965.

Part, but only part, of the explanation for this rise in almost all Western Societies was the baby boom in the aftermath of WWII. Since young males disproportionately commit crime, the dramatic rise in their numbers could very well explain the rising rates of crime in 1965 when the first of the postwar cohort reached 20 years of age. Though the baby boom came to an end in the 1960s, and the cohort of young males as a percentage of the population born to native women declined beginning in the 1980s, this age group continued to grow due to the large-scale immigration experienced by all these countries after the 1960s. However the increase in the size of the youthful male cohort, while considerable, could not by itself explain the explosive growth of crime in this period.

One reason for the difference between the U. S. and the European countries was their different approaches to the problem. This will be discussed more fully later, but for now it is enough to point out that beginning in the 1980s and accelerating in the 1990s, the United States took fairly drastic measures to remove criminals from the streets. These measures clearly were effective but at the cost of a greatly expanded prison population. The European countries, by contrast, continued more or less with the same policies and continued to experience rising crime rates.

TABLE 7.10. PRISON POPULATION BY ETHNICITY 2005[48]

Ethnicity	N	% Prison Population	% UK Population	Likelihood of Incarceration
White	56,824	74.58%	92.10%	0.81%
Mixed	2,157	2.83%	1.20%	2.36%
Bangladeshi	308	0.40%	0.50%	0.81%
Pakistani	1,418	1.86%	1.30%	1.43%
Other Asian	1,627	2.14%	0.40%	5.34%
Indian	1,211	1.59%	1.80%	0.88%
African	2,692	3.53%	0.80%	4.42%
Caribbean	6,264	8.22%	1.00%	8.22%
Other Black	2,214	2.91%	0.20%	14.53%
Chinese	301	0.40%	0.40%	0.99%
Other	562	0.74%	0.40%	1.84%
Not Recorded	613	0.80%		
Total	76,191	100%	100%	

That crime exploded in an unprecedented way in European societies cannot be denied. There remains, however, the question of whether the popular conception tying immigration to crime is correct. It is extremely difficult to get an accurate assessment of this question since most European countries either do not collect data on the race, ethnicity, or nationality of those arrested and imprisoned, or if they do gather such information, they often do not release it to the public. Britain is again the exception. Table 7.10 presents the prison population of England and Wales in 2005, in terms of ethnicity. As indicated in this table, some groups are more likely to have members incarcerated than others. This is indicated by the last column, which gives a likelihood estimate that a member from a particular ethnic group will be incarcerated as a ratio of the percentage in prison as a function of their percentage of the general population. A number of 1.00 would indicate that the prison population reflects the ethnic population in the general society. The figure of 0.81 for whites suggests that they are somewhat underrepresented, as do the figures for Indians, Chinese and the Bangladeshis. The figures for Pakistanis are relatively high, while those for the category *Other Asians* (this term is undefined in the report), are extremely high. This group probably includes a large proportion of young people born in the United

Kingdom whose origins are West Asian. Unfortunately, the government statistics are silent on this question. Perhaps most extraordinary is the figure for blacks, especially those from the Caribbean, who are 8 times as numerous in the prison population as in the population as a whole. The category *Other Blacks* is clearly disturbing and it is troubling that this category is not better defined in the government statistics. It may be that these people, like those termed *Other Asians*, are blacks born in the United Kingdom who, as will be discussed later, do not appear to be adjusting well to life in England. It should be stressed that the age structure of the various ethnic groups is not the same and that some groups have more individuals in the crime-prone group of young males. While this undoubtedly gives the impression that some ethnicities are more crime prone than is, in fact, the case, the numbers present an accurate picture of the incidence of crime by immigrant groups at the present time. In other words, while some groups, such as blacks, may contain an elevated number of young males, this in no way changes the fact that blacks commit considerably more crime than would be expected given their proportion in the general population. It is important to remember that if immigration continues at present levels, this youthful cohort will remain large or grow larger in future years.

The above table does not report on the religion of the inmates. However, almost all of the people from Pakistan are Muslim, and that is likely to be the case for those classified as *Other Asians*. In addition, large portions of African blacks are Muslim by birth, and an unknown number of blacks convert to Islam while in prison. Jack Straw, Secretary of State for Justice, reported to Parliament on March 17, 2008, that Muslims made up about 11% of the prison population. Straw gave the then current Muslim population as 3% of the total UK population, which would mean that Muslims are incarcerated at about 3.67 times more frequently than their numbers in the population.[49]

The over-representation of Muslims in English prisons is a very general phenomenon throughout Europe. Since these figures are not generally available from government officials, one is forced to rely upon independent researchers who can offer, at best, reasonable estimates. The Open Society Institute, funded by George Soros, includes the EU Monitoring and Advocacy Program that published a series of papers on the status of Muslims in European countries. These studies are published online at the web site *EUMAP*. Two of these, one dealing with Belgium and the other with the Netherlands, report data on incarceration rates. According to the Institute, foreign Moroccans and Turks, who are virtually all Muslims, make up 15.9% of all inmates even though they account for only about 2% of the general population, making them about 8 times as likely to be incarcerated as would be expected from their numbers in the population. It should be stressed that this figure does not include those people in Belgium of Moroccan and Turkish ancestry who have acquired citizenship and who are defined merely as Belgians.[50] In their report on the Netherlands, the Institute reports that "20% of the prisoners describe themselves as Muslims." Among youth prisoners, 26% identified themselves as Muslims. Since Muslims are estimated to be between 5% and 6% of the population, they are about 4 to 5 times as likely to be incarcerated as would be expected by their numbers in the general population.[51]

There are other reports that also indicate a disproportionate representation of Muslims in European prisons. The Danish newspaper *Kristeligt Dagblad* quotes Jon Olsen, a sociologist of religion, who reported that 20% of Danish prisoners were Muslim.[52] The Islamic Committee of Spain claims that 70% of Spanish prisoners are Muslim.[53] The Italian newspaper *Il Sole 24 Ore*, reported that, according to the Italian penitentiary administration, almost 40% of prisoners were foreign, of whom a substantial number were Muslims from North Africa.[54] Without precise government figures, it is quite impossible to determine the accuracy of such reports.

The problem of obtaining accurate figures is highlighted by a Washington Post story on the Muslim presence in French prisons. Reporter Molly Moore was unable to gather any information from government statistics (as discussed earlier, France does not allow the collection of such data) and prison officials "declined to discuss any such numbers." In an attempt to get more information, she made various attempts to visit prisons in France and was repeatedly denied access for what, on their face, were trivial reasons. After much effort she was able to gain access to a detention center in Northern France, which she found to be majority Muslim.[55] According to Moore, somewhere between 60% and 70% of all French prisoners are Muslim. She bases that estimate on reports of "Muslim leaders, sociologists and researchers." According to these figures, Muslims, who make up about 10% of the French population, are 6 to 7 times overrepresented in the prisons.[56] Moore's report is consistent with an earlier report (2001) in the *San Francisco Chronicle* claiming that more than half of French inmates were Muslim.[57] Craig Smith, writing in the *New*

York Times, reports similar numbers.[58] It would be valuable to know what proportion of inmates are black, whether Muslim or not, but this information is simply unavailable.

The above figures may understate the problem of immigrant crime. Police generally solve fewer than half of all crimes, and sometimes far fewer, and have a more difficult time in poor and immigrant communities. In England, for instance, only 28% of all crimes are solved.[59] Crime tends to be underreported in immigrant communities, and when reported, to result in fewer arrests and prosecutions than in the general population. People in immigrant communities often do not report crimes out of fear of retribution and also because of a general wariness of criminal justice officials. For similar reasons, and due to the extent and concentration of crime in these communities, apprehensions and convictions are harder to obtain. Many areas, especially those dominated by militant Muslims, are places where non-Muslims are not welcome. Police in these areas find segments of the population, particularly young males, especially hostile and uncooperative. This problem is common in most large English cities.[60]

It is also common in France and Germany. According to Stephen Brown, writing in *Front Page* magazine in 2008, police on routine checks in immigrant neighborhoods in Germany's major cities "are met with angry crowds and often risk assault." Sometimes residents swarm the police when they try to make an arrest. "Overall, Germany's police union records an average of 26,000 such occurrences in recent years, an increase of 60% over 1980."[61] In French suburbs or *banlieues* (suburban housing projects) surrounding major French cities, police are regularly confronted with violent attacks when they enter to quell the rioting that breaks out episodically. Immigrants from North Africa and sub-Saharan Africa inhabit these *banlieues* almost exclusively. Two-thirds of the black African immigrants in France live in the Paris area.[62]

The riots in the Paris suburbs in November of 2007 resulted in 77 injuries among police officers, with five having been sent to the hospital in critical condition. In this outbreak, involving widespread arson against hundreds of cars, numerous businesses, and public buildings, police were attacked with projectiles, Molotov cocktails, baseball bats, and, in a few instances, firearms.[63] Similar hostile enclaves exist in many European countries. Steve Harrigan of Fox News reports that in the Swedish city of Malmo, for instance, where 25% of the population is Muslim, there are "parts of the city where buses refuse to go for fear of safety. Firemen, policemen and ambulance drivers have been attacked in certain sections when trying to do their jobs."[64] Obviously, under such conditions, police are loath to enter known hostile neighborhoods unless they must, and are unlikely to probe too deeply in their search for lawbreaking. In addition, as discussed earlier, French police often do not arrest individuals for what they consider minor offenses. As a consequence, crime is almost certainly underreported in such enclaves and therefore many criminals are never arrested and tried, and never appear in the numbers of those imprisoned.

Two types of crime involving Muslim perpetrators are particularly troubling: namely, rape and anti-Semitic incidents. These are disturbing, in and of themselves, but also because they may involve deep-seated and powerful anti-European attitudes and motives. The anti-Semitic instances speak for themselves in that they involve attitudes completely unacceptable in Europe, but ubiquitous in the Muslim Middle East. Attacks, particularly in France, on synagogues and other Jewish institutions are common, as is vandalism of Jewish cemeteries.[65] While there have been some spectacular crimes against Jews, in general there is simple routine harassment of Jews and assaults against Jewish students by Muslim students.[66] The situation in Paris has become so serious that Jews are advised to refrain from wearing scull caps and other symbols of Judaism so as to avoid attack. Similar problems have arisen in England, Germany, and Sweden, and they appear to be common features associated with the influx of Muslims into European Society.[67]

Equally troubling is the growing problem of rape, especially gang rape by young Muslim men. The authorities have downplayed this because it is so glaringly an indication of the failure of assimilation, especially with regard to European standards on the relations between the sexes. The rape of women charged with immorality is sanctioned in many Muslim societies, but it is altogether abhorrent to Europeans. These rapes can be broadly broken into two categories. On the one hand, there is the rape of Muslim girls deemed immodest and too Europeanized by Muslim standards. On the other, there is the rape of European women by Muslim men who claim that European women, by their dress and demeanor, invite sexual predation. The first involves the importation of alien values into Europe while the second is a direct assault on the European way of life.

While long suppressed by the media, Muslim rape has become so common and violent that it can no longer be ignored. The Swedish blogger, Fjordman, writing in *Front Page* magazine, reports that charges of rape in Sweden have tripled during the last 20 years. He reports that Crime

Prevention Council statistics show that those born abroad are four times as likely to commit rape as natives, with almost half of all perpetrators being immigrants. In addition, he claims "in Norway and Denmark, we know that non-Western immigrants...are grossly over represented on rape statistics." He reports that in Oslo, Norway, immigrants accounted for 2 out of 3 rape charges made in 2001.[68] Daniel Pipes and Lars Hedegaard report that in Denmark, where Muslims make up 4% of the population, "they make up a majority of convicted rapists" and that "practically all of the female victims were non-Muslim."[69]

According to *Time* magazine in a 2002 article, court convictions for rapes in France have "soared by 61% between 1995 and 2000.... Specialists and victim's groups say violence against women is especially acute in the *banlieues* because of cultural attitudes toward women." *Time* reported that since 1999, in those projects rapes "have increased by 15% to 20% *every* year" (italics added). Much of this was brought to public awareness by the publication of a book *Dans L'enfer des Tournantes*, which is roughly translated as *In the Hell of Gang Rape,* written by Samira Bellil, an Algerian immigrant. She argued that gangs of young men brutalize, rape, and torment young women who choose to adopt French manners and clothing. *Time* quotes her:

> As children of immigrants, we receive a strict upbringing and are judged very harshly if we stray from it.... From the moment a girl steps outside, guys think they have the right to pass judgment and treat us differently. In extreme cases, this leads to violence or aggression.

Time reports, further, that such attacks are becoming more common, or at least more commonly reported and prosecuted. "Over the past year, nearly a score of highly publicized gang rapes have been reported or brought to trial across the country, some involving victims and perpetrators as young as 11." *Time* quotes Gilbert Collard, a lawyer in a gang rape case, "We've allowed a subculture to develop with its own codes and references that have made sexual violence a banality"[70]

Bellil argues that Muslim young men "adopt the lifestyles of other French youth—pop music, fast cars and pornography—but they also frequently embrace traditional prejudices...any neighborhood girl who smokes, uses makeup, or wears attractive clothes is a whore." Since most victims know their assailants, "intimidation often suffices to ensure that charges are never lodged...and that both they and their families will be threatened if they speak up." *Time* quotes Paris judge Marc Trevidic that in the *banlieues*, people don't like seeing girls "living according to the rules of French society. For many the slightest affront is a declaration of war." *Time* reports on two particularly shocking murders of young Muslim girls and quotes judge Trevidic who commented "The worst elements of the *banlieues* have no respect for human lives."[71]

A similar problem has arisen in England. Sorious Samura, a black immigrant and journalist, undertook an investigation of gang rape in the wake of two sensational trials in 2008 involving gang rapes. To his dismay he found that no separate figures were compiled nationally on the crime. However, London's Metropolitan Police force had recently started recording such incidents, which are defined as involving 3 or more perpetrators. "In 2008 alone, they received reports of 85 gang rapes." Samura was able to obtain specific data on 29 cases resulting in convictions during the period January 2006 to March 2009, in which a total of 92 individuals, mainly young men, were found guilty.

According to Samura, "One fact stood out. Of those convicted, 66 were black or of mixed race, 13 were white and the remainder [13] were from other countries including Afghanistan, Iraq, and Libya." He quotes a social worker from the black neighborhood of Brixton:

> We've got a generation that looks at sex as if it's nothing, and treats disrespecting women as if it's nothing. These guys are like 13, 14, and 15, and their actual attitudes towards young girls—towards sex—is mind-blowing. It's actually leaving you asking; where are their morals, where are their values?[72]

It is worth noting that, since many of these rapes involve gang members known to retaliate against *snitches*, the actual incidence of this crime is likely grossly underreported.

In reading through the voluminous literature on crime among immigrants, some from reputable sources and others more anecdotal, one is struck by the absence of sound government statistics. It is quite impossible to know if such reports are exaggerations or are merely hinting at much more common and serious problems. From the official statistics reported at the beginning of this section, it is clear that crime has risen dramatically in the last few decades in all European countries. However, without more precise government data, it is difficult to determine exactly the full extent and pattern of immigrant crime, the motivation of the perpetrators, and the significant correlates, if any, that might help explain it.

An important factor impeding crime prevention is rooted in political correctness. As in America, the disproportionate involvement of minority group individuals with the criminal justice system gives rise to charges of police racism and xenophobia. This charge is made despite the fact that governments in all European countries have acted to reduce official prejudice. In England, there have been extraordinary efforts by police departments to root out racism in the wake of the MacPherson report, which accused United Kingdom police of widespread "institutional racism." The report was an inquiry into the (apparently) racially motivated murder of a black man, and the failure of the police to obtain convictions in the case. The primary recommendations of the report dealt with the need for better monitoring of racially motivated crime and the need to make police forces more sensitive to minority community concerns.[73] In many regards the report is reminiscent of the Kerner Commission report on the causes of the riots in U. S. black communities in the 1960s, in that it insisted on interpreting as racist misconduct on the part of police actions that might otherwise have been characterized as simple incompetence.[74] As in the United States, the main problem was not the "unwitting racism" (the term used by the MacPherson report), but the extraordinarily high crime rates in the black community. The MacPherson Report, by stressing the need for racial sensitivity on the part of police, made dealing with black crime much more difficult by discouraging police from confronting unruly immigrant adolescent males.

The Relevance of the American Crime Experience

To understand the crime patterns in England and other European countries, it is useful to examine the situation in the United States, which experienced a dramatic increase in crime, especially among blacks, beginning in the 1960s. As discussed in the last chapter, there was a large-scale movement of blacks out of the rural South in the aftermath of World War II, propelled primarily by the booming economy in the North. This migration resulted in very noticeable demographic changes in which rural blacks began to displace working-class ethnic whites in most major northern cities. With these changes came rising rates of crime and deteriorating public schools, which served to hasten what had come to be called "white flight." The rise in black crime is to a large degree explained by the fact that the black community had large numbers of young adolescent males, who, in general, had a lower average IQ than those they replaced. Being young, male, and having a low IQ are powerful, in fact the most powerful, predictors of antisocial behavior.[75] These factors would themselves have produced a rising crime rate as neighborhoods became black, even if one discounts completely any temperamental characteristics of blacks which may predispose them to criminal activity. However, other factors were at work to exacerbate the problem.

In the rural communities in the South from which they came, young men were under constant surveillance by parents and other adult authorities. In addition, the harsh and repressive Jim Crow regimes of the Deep South had a major deterrent effect on black antisocial behavior. In the Northern cities, neither of these conditions existed. Urban streets provided anonymity and Northern police forces were more circumspect in their dealing with black delinquents than had been their counterparts in the rural South, especially after the Civil Rights Act of 1964, and even more so after the publication of the Kerner Commission Report in 1968. Given the greatly increased level of crime, it would have been reasonable for Northern cities to have responded with much more aggressive policing and the required expansion of police forces. Such a response, however, was out of favor at the time. Most criminologists had by then rejected theories of crime which located the source of crime in criminal personality types. In place of those theories, criminologists sought the causes of crime in social factors such as poverty, prejudice, discrimination, and "institutional racism" that resulted in underfunded public schools and social services. In the common view of the time, pointing the finger at the criminal as the source of crime was to "blame the victim" and was not only coldhearted but also racist in intent. The "root causes" of crime had to be addressed if one seriously wished to solve the crime problem. This was the position taken by the Kerner Commission, which investigated the widespread rioting in black communities in the 1960s.[76]

Beginning in the 1960s, the federal government embarked on large-scale programs to address these issues and continues to do so to this day. The "War on Poverty" was launched, affirmative action policies enacted, and school busing instituted to overcome segregation in northern public schools. In addition to those measures, the government extended its efforts to eliminate prejudice and discrimination, increased spending for urban schools, and initiated a host of other programs designed to improve the nutrition and educational prospects for black children as, for instance, with the

Headstart program.[77] In spite of these efforts, black crime and other social pathologies continued to grow in subsequent decades and the emergence of a black "underclass" became unmistakable. For instance, illegitimacy among black women climbed from about 25% during the 1960s to 65% in the 1980s. Drug use and academic failure became endemic. These developments should have been the occasion for a second thought among social scientists about their theories, but instead they recommended more of the same.[78]

One of the few dissenters to this orthodoxy was Harvard political scientist James Q. Wilson, who put forth his alternative explanation in the seminal book, *Thinking about Crime*. Wilson argued that the breakdown in the black community was the direct result of the absence of official authority to reign in unruly young black men. The problem was compounded by the breakup of the black family, one consequence of which was that adult black men played a diminishing role in the discipline of adolescent males. The result of this failure of authority was that black neighborhoods came to be dominated by young males who engaged in a variety of antisocial behaviors, often violent, which drove out the more law-abiding citizens who had the economic means to leave. The net result was a downward spiral of social pathology and ever more depressed neighborhoods.[79]

Wilson argued that most criminologists at the time had the causation backward. Rather than poverty, poor schooling, and deteriorating living conditions being the cause of crime, it was unchecked crime, which produced these undesirable conditions. His prescription was simple and straightforward. Cities must begin to reassert their authority over young males by aggressive policing and the swift punishment of wrongdoers, even for minor offenses. He put forward his now famous "broken windows" analogy with minor law violations. Petty crimes, when they go unaddressed, are like broken windows in a building that are not repaired. They are a signal that nobody cares and nobody is in charge, and that additional windows can be broken and, by analogy, crimes committed, with impunity. Over time, young people who engage in petty crime will graduate to more serious misbehavior. Wilson argued that a much higher police profile was required to break this pattern and that judges had to follow through by making clear to young offenders that even minor misbehavior was taken seriously and would result in punishment. He was widely criticized at the time for oversimplifying so complex a problem as crime, and for suggesting that black males be targets for greater scrutiny, i.e., to be racially profiled. His response to the latter charge was that if one wished to reduce crime, one had to go to the source of most crime and in most large American cities, that was young black males.[80]

In the early 1990s, the newly elected mayor of New York City, Rudolf Guilliani, and his Police Commissioner, William Bratton, inaugurated a crime reduction strategy consciously grounded in Wilson's ideas. The plan included a far more visible street presence for police officers, and specific attempts to target young males suspected of carrying weapons or dealing in drugs. The results of the implementation of this strategy were startling. Within a few years, the number of murders in New York City which had been steadily climbing and had reached a figure of significantly more than 2,000 per year was reduced to approximately 700 murders. Crime in all categories exhibited equally swift and dramatic downturns. Even the Mayor's most outspoken critics had to admit to the remarkable success of his approach. Indeed, it is difficult to recall any other social science theory receiving such a resounding confirmation in so short a time in a real-life empirical test.[81]

Part of the success of the program, and its continuing effectiveness in succeeding New York administrations, was that large numbers of repeat offenders, who commit a disproportionate percentage of all crime, were removed from the streets and placed in prison. Wilson had foreseen this effect, since his research had indicated that antisocial types are fairly indiscriminate in their offending; they commit large numbers of crime of both a petty and serious nature. When the police began to arrest young men for minor offenses, such as jumping subway turnstiles to avoid paying fares, they found that such men often had many outstanding arrest warrants for more serious crimes. The strategy not only deterred young men from misbehavior in the first place, but it also resulted in the incarceration of many who could not be so easily deterred.

In general, the experience of New York City confirms the commonsense view that if you replace a population of people with another that is less law-abiding for whatever reason, the police must modify their responses to take account of the change. Not to do so will result, inevitably, in more crime and, depending on the nature of the new population, sometimes more serious crime. Unfortunately, the mayors of any number of U. S. cities with large black populations have not taken this lesson to heart. Cities like Washington, Baltimore, Newark, and Detroit, to name just a few, continue to suffer tragically high crime rates due to an unwillingness to recognize or acknowledge that the source of crime lies in the character of the criminal and not his social circumstances.

Cities in Europe are in the midst of rapidly rising crime rates due to major demographic changes and a concomitant failure to make the necessary adjustments in crime prevention strategies. Since these demographic changes are likely to continue and grow more pronounced as the immigrant population grows, Europeans can expect crime rates to continue to rise until they modify their responses to crime. It is difficult to be sanguine in this matter, given the attitudes expressed by the overwhelming majority of European leaders and their academic advisers, who seem intent on denying the existence of ethnic differences in the propensity for antisocial behavior, no matter what the cost to European citizens.

As in the United States, not all ethnic groups in Europe exhibit the same degree of adjustment. Blacks in the United Kingdom seem to have the most serious problems in terms of education, income, and crime. On the other hand, like their counterparts in America, the Chinese and Indians in England seem to adjust quite readily in terms of major social indices. In America, Hispanics are faring better than blacks, but still exhibit considerable difficulties in adjustment. A similar pattern emerges for Muslims in Europe, most of whom come from Third World countries of North Africa and the Indian subcontinent. As was suggested earlier, adjustments in education, income, and criminal behavior are the main drivers of assimilation. Groups that have difficulties in these areas are going to find it hard to blend in, or achieve equal status, relative to the general population, which is, in effect, the operational definition for assimilation.

Residential Segregation

Non-Western immigrants in European countries tend to live in the poorest neighborhoods and make heavy use of public, government-supported housing. In general, they tend to be concentrated in areas among their own ethnic groups. In most cases, they are concentrated in the major cities, living in inner city areas or in near suburbs, and almost always in the least desirable neighborhoods.

The reasons for these housing patterns are fairly straightforward. Non-Western immigrants tend to have less education and fewer employment opportunities than natives, and, as the data previously presented indicate, have lower salaries and higher unemployment rates than natives. Their economic condition necessitates their seeking out the least expensive housing which by definition is the least desirable. For the same reason, they often resort to government-supported housing developments. Furthermore, they tend to cluster in groups among coethnics for social support and protection. In addition, their differences from the native populations in customs and practices result in a certain level of discrimination by native owners of rental housing, though it is unclear how widespread such practices are. All EU countries, following directives by the European Court, have established laws and policies to make it unlawful to practice discrimination in employment and housing. Nevertheless, there is considerable ethnic clustering in almost all European communities.

Ethnic residential segregation of immigrants was, and continues to be, a common phenomenon in the United States. The historical pattern in America was for the children of immigrants, especially those on an upwardly mobile course, to move out of those enclaves into the larger society. However, sufficient numbers remained in ethnic neighborhoods, augmented by more recent arrivals, to allow them to maintain their distinctive character for extended periods. In America, those enclaves, especially in large cities, did not really begin to disintegrate until the 1970s, almost fifty years after immigration was severely curtailed in the 1920s.

In Europe, which continues to have sizable immigration, these enclaves continue to grow and sustain themselves. Since a majority of non-European immigrants in Europe are Muslim, their enclaves tend to have features very distinct from others of similar social class. Muslims are hardly alone in living in areas among their own ethnic group; as such concentrations are common for all recent non-Western immigrants. The question is whether these areas will become true ghettoes in the sense that they maintain their ethnic makeup for more than a few generations. Most blacks in America continue to live in impoverished segregated enclaves some 40 years after racial discrimination was prohibited by law.

The reasons for this segregation, as discussed in the previous chapter, have to do with education, income, and, most important, criminal behavior. As expected, blacks, who achieve moderate economic success leave such neighborhoods for more desirable areas. The consequence is that black neighborhoods, or ghettoes, deteriorate further with falling performance in schools, increased social disorder, crime, and family decomposition. They, in effect, become "underclass" communities that become even more isolated from the larger society. More successful people of all races and ethnicities avoid such neighborhoods, primarily out of a concern with crime and the undesirable quality of the schools.

Many black and Muslim communities in Europe have begun to resemble black underclass communities in America for much the same reasons. Most such communities are now composed of second- and third-generation ethnics, many of whom continue to occupy the lowest educational and economic positions in their respective societies, and as discussed earlier, exhibit high rates of crime and disorder, especially among those born in Europe. The *banlieues* in France are the most notorious examples, but similar enclaves exist in almost all European cities. Blacks, for instance, are concentrated in certain boroughs in central London. According to Lee Jasper, Chairman of the National Assembly against Racism and an adviser to the Mayor of London, London's black areas have become underclass communities (although he does not use that term). Writing in 2002, Jasper commented:

> Around 45 per cent of London's unemployed are black. Failure rates among black schoolchildren are the silent catastrophe of London. The black prison population in Britain has doubled since 1994.... Teenage pregnancy rates are the highest in Europe and the number of single parents is going through the roof.[82]

According to Jasper, himself a black man, "Black neighborhoods have become free trade zones for all kinds of drugs and illegal contraband, including guns." He argues that a gangster mentality has taken hold over many young blacks whose creed is to "live rich, live fast and don't give a damn about society."[83] A report by Lord Ouseley, former chairman of the Commission for Racial Equality, on conditions in the city of Bradford in north central England, was critical of these insular enclaves and their residents' unfamiliarity with those from different groups. According to Ouseley, who is black, the consequences are segregated schools and "serious fear of harassment, violence and crime." In addition, it leads to resentment since, "different communities believe they get nothing while the others get all the benefits."[84]

The development of separate enclaves or ghettoes is especially noteworthy in London where so many immigrants live. Somewhat of a stir was caused when Michael Nazir-Ali, Bishop of Rochester, and of Pakistani descent, argued that many immigrant enclaves, especially Muslim enclaves, were effectively "no-go" zones for non-Muslims. In his view the problem was caused by the doctrine of multiculturalism coupled with "the world resurgence of the ideology of Islamic extremism." Quoting the Bishop:

> One of the results of this has been to further alienate the young from the nation in which they are growing up and also to turn already separate communities into 'no-go' areas where adherence to this ideology has become a mark of acceptability. Those of a different faith or race may find it difficult to live or work there because of hostility to them and even the risk of violence.[85]

In most European countries, Muslims make up the bulk of non-European immigrant groups, and many have, even after two or three generations, continued to live in highly segregated communities, which are beset by similar problems. In France, 56% percent of immigrants were living in government housing and most of these were non-Europeans, mainly Muslims and blacks, living in segregated conditions with serious social problems.[86] As discussed earlier, they have come to exist as semiautonomous areas dominated by young males who are often quite violent. Though the French government does not define these areas as specifically Muslim, it recognized that these districts required special attention and in a 1996 act (Décret n°96-1156 du 26/12/1996) designated these areas as sensitive urban zones (zones *urbains sensibles*) or ZUS, for special assistance. These are officially defined as urban districts

> characterized by the presence of dilapidated high-rise developments or housing areas and by an accentuated imbalance between housing and employment.... In these areas, the government, local authorities, and associations implement urban renewal programs and specific operations (education, job creation, health, culture, etc.).... New businesses are also encouraged to set up and move to these districts by...tax exemptions.[87]

There are now 751 of these sensitive zones located in all large and many small cities all over France. A list of these areas with maps and street names can be found at a French government web site under the title, *Atlas des Zones Urbains Sensibles*, which can be accessed with any web browser. While the French government never uses the terminology, Paul Belien, writing in the *Washington Times*, describes them as no-go zones and they include all of the *banlieues* surrounding Paris. The riots that racked France in 2005 started in the Paris ZUS, but then spread to other similar areas throughout the country. According to Belien, citing the noted French criminologist Xavier Raufer, these are centers of drug trafficking and are often controlled by criminal organizations. "People get mugged, even murdered, in the ZUS, but the media prefer not to write about it."[88]

In Germany, a similar pattern exists among the Muslim population, most of whom are of Turkish origin. In most cases in German cities, Muslims, even when they have the means, tend to remain in their ethnic enclaves and use their resources to try to improve them, but are not often successful. In the Muslin area of the Neukolln district in Berlin, for instance, a pattern among the children of immigrants "leads to a subculture with its own value systems and ways of behavior...formed by youth gangs." The segregation of this community does not appear to be diminishing, and may, in fact, be growing.[89] The district has the highest percentage of welfare recipients and the highest use of housing benefits. In March of 2006 the Neukolln district received wide media coverage when the head of a secondary school "wrote a desperate letter to the Senator for Education, asking for immediate help, because violence in the school had made the lessons unbearable." Eighty percent of the students are of Muslim immigrant background.[90]

In Denmark, 70% of non-European ethnic groups, largely Muslim, live in and around the city of Copenhagen in government supported housing in poor neighborhoods, with large numbers of people subsisting on welfare benefits. The concentration of ethnics in these housing developments is increasing, due to natural increase, the arrival of new immigrants, and the departure of native Danes from such areas.[91] The mainstream Danish media refer to these areas as "ethnic ghettos." These neighborhoods are depicted as having high rates of unemployment, high rates of youth crime and violence, high rates of school dropouts, lack of social integration, domestic violence, and the oppression of women. In one particular housing complex, the population is 93% ethnic minorities who came in the 1980s from Lebanon, Palestine, Turkey, and Pakistan. In response to a series of arson cases in 2004, "the whole residential quarters are installed with 230 close-circuit cameras and remains under constant surveillance and frequent police patrolling."[92]

In the Netherlands, 30% of the inhabitants of Amsterdam, Rotterdam, Utrecht, and The Hague (the largest cities), are of non-

European extraction, primarily Muslim from a number of Third World countries. A large proportion of these people live in neighborhoods with 50% or more non-European inhabitants. These neighborhoods are "characterized by deterioration, and less social cohesion. Inhabitants are often victims of crime and feel less safe." The author of the EUMAP report predicts that "the concentration of underprivileged Immigrants will increase in the major cities" due to the movement of native Dutch and middle-class immigrants out of cities into suburbs. Two thirds of the people of non-Western background are born in these four major Dutch cities and in the near future this is "expected to have significant effects on the school population and the labour markets in those cities."[93]

Non-European immigrants in Sweden tend to be concentrated in the close-in suburbs of the three largest cities of Stockholm, Goteborg and Malmo. Because of their "precarious situation in the labour market," people of Arab and African background are the "most disadvantaged groups in Swedish society." Large proportions live in large-scale government housing developments, which, like most disadvantaged areas, are places of "anonymity, lack of security, low-quality standards, lack of services, and transit, etc." These projects were built in the 1960s and 1970s to deal with an anticipated housing shortage for native Swedes. The housing was in most cases better than existing housing at the time and the program was deemed a success. However, this was "rather short-lived. The areas were quickly subjected to a stigmatization process, which today has taken on an ethnic dimension."[94] As described in the previous section, many of these areas have become crime-ridden no-go zones for native Swedes.

Similar patterns are evident in all European countries with significant non-European populations. Many immigrant areas are coming to resemble underclass communities in the U. S. The German political scientist Volker Eichener is reported to fear "an Americanization of the German cities" and the "danger of social disintegration and exclusion."[95] The evidence presented in this section suggests that the danger is hardly limited to Germany. Two points must be stressed. The first is that substantial numbers of non-Europeans are economically successful and manage to fully integrate in European society. It is difficult to tell how many do so, since if they are not racially distinct, they and their children would be hard to identify. This is especially the case with those who intermarry with native individuals. Of course, this would only be true of those, especially Muslim women, who abandon traditional Muslim attire.

The second point is that nowhere in the literature on immigration are similar patterns of segregation for immigrants of European descent reported, with the noteworthy exception of the Roma or Gypsies. This is not to deny that earlier immigrants from the poorer countries of Europe did not form ethnic, namely, Italian, Portuguese, Spanish, etc., neighborhoods. The difference is that they did not remain segregated much beyond the first generation of immigrants. Whether current immigrants from the poorer countries of Eastern Europe will follow this pattern is an open question, but it appears highly likely that they will not remain segregated beyond the first generation. The fact that all Europeans share a common racial and religious background, and that all share similar abilities makes assimilation almost automatic, once the language barrier is overcome, as it always is for the children of immigrants born in the host country. It is far more difficult to predict the future course of assimilation for non-Europeans who lack that commonality with Europeans. The material reviewed in this section is hardly likely to make one sanguine.

Muslim Attitudes and the Influence of Saudi Wahhabism

A major impediment to the assimilation of the large number of Muslim immigrants has been the growth of Islamic mosques and schools funded and sponsored by Arab states and Islamic organizations which spread beliefs often at variance with those promoting assimilation and identification with the nationality of host nations. As political scientist Jonathan Laurence explains, this was the result of the initial notion that most Muslims would return to their homelands. When it became apparent in the 1970s that this was unlikely to happen, governments acknowledged the deep desire of Muslim immigrants to practice their faith. They were therefore, open to the support of mosques and schools funded and guided by the countries from which many Muslims came, particularly Algeria, Morocco, and Turkey. These countries were anxious to maintain the allegiance of their overseas nationals, and to keep them within the fold of the forms of Islamic faith as practiced in those countries. This concern was bolstered by the growth of pannational Muslim organizations, such as the Muslim Brotherhood that often spread very fundamentalist versions of the Islamic faith and openly challenge the legitimacy of Arab governments and their state controlled religious organizations.

According to Laurence, European governments were ambivalent about the permanence of the Muslim presence and maintained a "fiction of the eventual 'return home' for migrants and even their locally-born children."[96] This ambivalence was particularly strong in Germany as evidenced by its reluctance to grant citizenship to its Turkish inhabitants and their children. As mentioned earlier, many of these people in Germany are still officially designated as foreign nationals, though in the 1990s Germany changed this position and became more receptive to granting citizenship to non-German ethnics. Nevertheless, the existing reality was that Muslim communities existed and wished to practice their faith. Most of these local communities were poor "and given the legal and political difficulties of providing public funding, European governments encouraged the use of foreign funds for religious practice." This funding often came not only from the sending countries but also from countries with few European migrants, particularly Egypt and Saudi Arabia, that were recognized centers of Muslim authority. "The large, classical mosques that were planned and built across Europe during this period were justified as a fix for the practical needs of local Muslims."[97]

The European nations welcomed this *official Islam* promoted by foreign governments because they "attended to the housekeeping of combating extremism in their own national interests."[98] Not to be overlooked in this accommodation to foreign influence was that "European governments were eager to be on good terms with regional powers in the Arab world, which were the source not only of immigration but also oil."[99] One example of *official Islam* is the Turkish directorate for religious affairs, a Turkish government entity, that "lays claim on all Turkish citizens living abroad; it underwrites prayer spaces and religious education for Turks living abroad through local offices...often staffing them with diplomats from Turkish consulates." The organization, which operates local offices in many European nations, "indirectly controls half of all Turkish mosques in Europe. In 1995 it employed 760 imams in Germany, who were hired as Turkish civil servants receiving "a salary from the Turkish state."[100]

By the late 1980s, as it became clear in Europe that its Muslim population was not going home, but was rather growing rapidly due to family unification and natural increase, these foreign organizations were seen as impeding the assimilation of Muslims and operating at cross-purposes with the desire to foster a sense of European national identity among immigrants. National governments at that point began to promote the development of Muslim organizations that would promulgate religious faith compatible with national allegiance to the host nations. The idea was to create a means by which governments could involve Muslim citizens in order to resolve growing tensions between the Muslim community and the secular modern states of Europe. This involved the organization of various state-sponsored Muslim committees or councils to act as intermediaries to the Muslim communities in their midst. This often included questionable practices of state funding for religious institutions and tolerance for practices that ran counter to traditional state-church relations in most European countries, but which were seen as necessary to promote assimilation.[101] England's acceptance of *sharia* courts is one example of this phenomenon. Another is the leasing of state-owned land at minimal rents to facilitate the building of mosques and schools. Of course, these efforts required negotiating with and accommodating the existing Muslim establishment which had grown up over the years.

A major problem in these efforts to co-opt Muslim religious leaders has been the continuous growth of pannational Islamic movements and, more important, the growing influence of Saudi Wahhabism. By 1990, Saudi Arabia had established a vast network of mosques and schools with the express purpose of expanding the influence of the Wahhabi version of Islam, the state religion of Saudi Arabia. In Saudi Arabia, both the legal and educational systems are under almost complete control of Muslim Wahhabi clerics. While the Wahhabi version of Islam is a minority view among all Muslims, the stated goal of the Saudi government is to make it the dominant form, and it has expended an estimated 75 billion dollars in a worldwide effort to this effect. None of this would be troubling were it not for the fact that Wahhabism is stridently fundamentalist and preaches a doctrine of hatred and disdain for all other faiths. It demands a literal interpretation of the Koran and strict adherence to *sharia* law. It is the version of Islam espoused by Osama Bin Laden and it is noteworthy that 15 of the 19 hijackers involved in the attacks that brought down the World Trade Center were citizens educated in Saudi schools.[102]

Saudi Arabia has been roundly criticized by human rights organizations for its strict limitation of women's rights and freedoms and the harshness of its penal codes. It dictates beheading for murder, rape, and drug smuggling. It dictates amputation of limbs for theft and flogging for selling alcohol. It is especially harsh in its treatment of sexual offenses, including the flogging of homosexuals and in some cases death for similar transgressions. This was brought glaringly to light by the execution of a Saudi princess and her lover for having an unapproved sexual relationship in the early 1980s.[103]

According to a report by the respected Center for Religious Freedom, the curriculums of state sponsored schools' in Saudi Arabia "encourages violence toward others, and misguides pupils in believing that in order to safeguard their own religions, they might violently repress and even physically eliminate the 'other.'" A study of textbooks used in state schools found that the "Saudi government continues to propagate an ideology of hate toward the 'unbeliever' which includes Christians, Jews, Shiites, Sufis, Sunni Muslims who do not follow Wahhabi doctrine, Hindus, atheists, and others." [104]

The textbooks examined "command Muslims to 'hate' Christians, Jews, polytheists and other 'unbelievers'…" They also teach that "the Crusades never ended" and claim that the Western and Christian education, health, and social service efforts and campaigns for women's rights are part "of the modern phase of the Crusades." In addition, students are taught "not to 'greet', 'imitate', show loyalty to or 'respect' non-believers." They are especially hostile toward Jews and teach that the fraudulent *Protocols of the Elders of Zion* is in fact an historically accurate depiction of the Jewish plan of world domination.[105]

The educational system calls for violent jihad, or war, against infidels of different faiths who are depicted as "morally inferior and even evil" and that "peaceful coexistence with so-called 'infidels' is unattainable and violence to spread Islam is not only permissible, but an obligation." In a textbook used in the twelfth grade it acknowledges that "one of the meanings of jihad is self-perfection," but it does not deny the more militant meaning of the term. "In fact, in repeated statements, it justifies a militant jihad for the purpose of spreading the faith." "Jihad is the path of God—which consists of battling against unbelief, injustice and those who perpetrate it—is the summit of Islam. This religion arose through jihad" and engaging in jihad is "one of the most magnificent acts of obedience to God."[106] Of course, anyone familiar with the spread of Islam throughout history, as surely these students are, knows that Islam grew and spread by bloody war, accompanied by the wholesale slaughter, enslavement, and forced conversion of the conquered peoples, throughout the Middle East and

India. Such wars continue in various forms in countries in Africa, Asia, and the Balkans, wherever there are sufficient Muslim populations to mount successful military campaigns and terrorist attacks against infidels of all sorts.[107]

It must be stressed that these doctrines are spread in the thousands of schools (*madrassas*) and mosques throughout the world which are built and supported by Saudi wealth, both of the government and individual Saudis and Saudi organizations, especially in Pakistan, but also in the United States, Europe, and India. Since these institutions are of relatively recent origin, they are likely to influence newer Muslim immigrants and the children of immigrants who came in the immediate postwar period. Recent polls reflect these developments.

Three recent polls, two conducted in England and one in Germany, highlight the problem. The British polls were commissioned by the conservative think tank, Policy Exchange and were conducted in 2006. One poll involved telephone and Internet interviews with 1,003 Muslims and 1,025 people from the general population. The second poll consisted of 40 face-to-face interviews with younger Muslims in the 16–24 year-age group who were either university students or recent graduates of universities.

Both polls found that religion played a very important part in Muslim's identity. Fully 86% of the Muslim sample felt that "my religion is the most important thing in life." This is in marked contrast with native Britons for whom religious identity is not particularly salient; only 11% of native Britons stressed the importance of religion.[108]

The researchers found significant differences in attitude between Muslims and other groups, but these differences were especially pronounced among the young, educated Muslims. The study revealed that 37% of Muslim 16–24 year olds expressed a preference for living under *sharia* law, while only 17% of those older than 55 did so. Fully 74% of the 16–24 age group prefer women to wear the veil, as opposed to only 28% of the older group. Perhaps most disturbing is that 36% of 16–24 year old Muslims "believe that if a Muslim converts to another religion they should be punished by death, compared to 19% of 55+ year olds." In addition, 13% of the younger cohort expressed admiration for organizations like Al-Qaeda "that are prepared to fight the West." Only 3% of 55+ age individuals expressed such admiration. This is particularly disturbing coming in the wake of the terrorist attack on British buses and subways in London on July 7, 2005 that resulted in 52 deaths and hundreds of injuries. Even if the 13% figure is wildly inflated by youthful braggadocio, with the Muslim population in England well over 1.5 million, it suggests that there is a sizable group of young Muslims who feel it is acceptable to kill and maim fellow citizens in the name of religion. On reflection, it suggests that these individuals, whose exact number is unknown, do not see native Britons as "fellow citizens."[109]

The poll of younger United Kingdom Muslim university students found that almost a third thought that killing in the name of Islam could be justified, and an equal number supported the creation of a worldwide Muslim State or *Caliphate*. Fully 40% of Muslim students felt it "was unacceptable for Muslim men and women to associate freely."[110] The growing identification with Muslim practices among a substantial minority of young Muslims attending universities, most of whom were born in England and educated in British schools suggests, at least for the minority expressing such views, a serious estrangement from mainstream British values. Furthermore, this estrangement does not seem to stem from any perception of discrimination toward Muslims in England, with fully 84% saying that they have been treated fairly in British Society.[111]

The German poll of some 1700 people, conducted by the Federal Ministry of the Interior begun in 2004, gave results surprisingly similar to those of the British poll. The Muslim population in Germany, which numbers well over three million people, consists primarily of Turkish workers who came in the 1960s, and their children and grandchildren, many of whom were born in Germany. The sample included 1,000 Muslims chosen at random, 500 students between 14 and 18 years old, 150 university students and 60 male members or activists in Islamic associations, mosques, etc. Researchers personally interviewed this latter group of 60. As in England, religion was very important to the people in the general sample of 1,000 individuals. "Over 85% described themselves as 'religious' or 'very religious.'" In addition, the percentage of "those who attend mosque at least once a week has increased between 2000 and 2005 from 30.7% to 41.6%." Almost all Muslims, even those not regularly attending mosques, take the Koran very seriously, with 79.6% agreeing "completely" that the Koran is "the true revelation of God." Almost half of the people in this group claimed that the "observance of the commandments of my religion...(is) more important for me than democracy." While most expressed a belief in religious freedom, some 30% agreed "completely" or "somewhat" that it "should be forbidden to persuade

Muslims to change their religion." Among this group, only about a third were German citizens and "only 12.2% defined themselves as German." Significantly, more than half could be described as "poorly" or "moderately" integrated into German society, and only about 12% could be described as "well-integrated." [112]

Their attitudes toward religious violence were somewhat ambivalent. "More than 90% reject the killing of other people in the name of God as unjustifiable." On the other hand, "44% agreed 'somewhat' or 'completely' that Muslims who die fighting for the faith will enter 'into paradise'" and about 40% consider "the use of physical violence as a reaction to the threat presented to Islam by the West as legitimate." [113]

Among the 14 to 18 year old students, religious commitment is also quite high, in fact slightly higher than in the general sample. A fourth of these students "affirms its own readiness to exert corporal violence against unbelievers in the service of the Islamic community." It should be noted that while 77% of these students were born in Germany, only 40% were German citizens. Fully 27.2% of these students felt bound to the country of their origins, and only 10% expressed a "primary cultural identification with Germany." A considerable majority (63%) have few or "no German friends at all."

Only 45% believe that they should adapt to German culture, as opposed to 82% of the general Muslim population, and expect acceptance on their own terms. This contrasts sharply with the views of young people of German origins, among whom about half think that immigrants should integrate and that those "who are unable or unwilling to accommodate themselves should leave Germany." The author makes the point that in this difference "lies a considerable potential for conflict." [114]

The 150 university students sampled expressed less attachment to religion than the general sample, but even here 76.7% describe themselves as religious (with 20% claiming to be very religious), and two thirds consider the Koran to be the true revelation of God. About 18% thought that the commandments of the Koran were more important than democracy. Especially noteworthy among the university students was their perception of themselves as victims of discrimination, with more than half citing the police and administrative agencies as being discriminatory against foreigners. While the great majority of these students (80%) reject religious violence, it is difficult to determine whether that rejection is based, at least in part, on their knowledge of the sensitivity of the German authorities on this topic. These students are, by virtue of attending a university, quite well educated. The authors of the report argue that even among highly educated young Muslims, a significant minority adopts a religious attitude that involves "a strong devaluation of the West" and a perception that the world's Muslim population suffers from "discrimination and oppression."[115]

Among the 60 male activists interviewed, this sense of worldwide victimhood was especially intense. The researchers comment, "striking were the frequently exaggerated reports about a climate of prejudices, hostilities, rejection and discrimination against Muslims in Germany," but point out that in most instances these perceptions could not be tied to any personal experience with discrimination. The younger of these activists are "self-assured Muslims" who "demand they be given recognition" and "have the vision of forming a kind of political or even economic avant-garde." In addition, they express ambivalence toward the personal liberties of German society. They praise Germany for its religious tolerance, but reject absolutely the right of Muslim women to marry non-Muslims and barely accept it for men. In addition, they have "the expectation that the German state should introduce special rights for Muslims" and believe in "the application of Islamic law" for Muslims through the establishment of a "parallel legal society." The researchers report "religiously and politically motivated violence is almost never openly promoted or approved." But, of course, to express such views in Germany is to subject oneself and one's organization to possible prosecution by the state. The authors argue that the activists extreme views toward Islamic law and their rejection of religious liberty for female Muslims, along with their powerful sense of victimization, make them likely candidates for radicalization.[116]

In summarizing their report the researchers noted that about 6% of the Muslims in Germany show an affinity for violence, and if one adds those who show a low regard for democracy and the rule of law, the figure rises to approximately 14%. When put in the perspective of the Muslim population of about 3 million people, even 6% represents almost 200,000 individuals who support violence to further religious aims. The authors are particularly concerned with the large numbers of Muslims with a fundamentalist orientation, which they describe as follows:

> Fundamentalist orientations that combine a close religious attachment, a high relevance of religion in daily life, and a strong orientation on religious rules and rituals with a tendency to exclude Muslims who do not observe these, as well as with the tendency generally to heighten the value of Islam and to derogate Western, Christian-influenced cultures show an enormous dissemination. In the general population, about 40% are to be assigned to such a pattern of orientation.[117]

The strong identification with religion expressed by most Muslims would not in itself be cause for concern were Islam similar to the other major monotheistic religions, Judaism and Christianity. But Islam differs from these in very important ways. For one, it has not evolved a doctrine acknowledging a clear distinction between faith and governance. The Jews in Europe never attained sufficient numbers to attempt to impose their faith on others through government fiat, and have not done so in the state of Israel, even though Israel defines itself as a Jewish country and makes religious holy days state affairs. It does not, however, attempt to impose Judaism on its Muslim citizens, and provides them full rights of citizenship, with the exception of service in the armed forces. In large measure, this is the result of the fact that secular Jews, many of whom were socialist in ideology, founded Israel. Christianity, on the other hand, once it came to dominance in Europe, became the official religion of all states and was highly intolerant of religious deviation throughout most of its history. This religious intolerance came to a head with the rise of various Protestant movements and led to centuries of bloody conflict that finally came to an end during the Enlightenment. From that point on most governments finally granted religious freedom and equal rights to all citizens, though official discrimination against Jews continued in many states into the 20th century.

The situation for Islam is entirely different and in most countries, especially in the Arab states, non-Muslims do not possess equal rights as citizens, and in many states, such as Saudi Arabia and Iran, cannot openly express their faith. Saudi Arabia and other states absolutely forbid the building of non-Muslim places of Worship. This state of affairs is largely the result of Muslim, especially Wahhabist, doctrine which has remained virtually unchanged for over one thousand years and which does not recognize any distinction between religious *sharia* law and state law. Of course, in practice, few countries with Muslim majorities abide by this doctrine with strict adherence, though some, such as Iran, do. It is, nevertheless, a strong conviction among ardent believers that *sharia* should, in fact, govern all aspects of life including the legal practices of Muslim states. Furthermore, even fairly secular states incorporate *sharia* principles in such things as governing the relations between the sexes, and in their penal codes.[118]

That is the reason why it is troubling that large numbers of young European-born Muslims favor the adoption of *sharia* law and would impose it if they had the power to do so. According to Wahhabist principles non-Muslims, or infidels, are deeply flawed morally and pose an existential threat to the rightful ascendance of Islam in the world. As such they must be converted to Islam by argument or, if that fails, by force. In this worldview the infidel living among Muslims may be killed for failure to convert, or may be left in peace as long as he accepts an inferior status as a "*dhimmi*" and agrees to abide by specific rules and pay special taxes.[119]

Where Muslims are in the minority they are required, under Wahhabism, to spread the faith among nonbelievers and in time convert their new society into an Islamic one. Islamic tradition requires jihad, war against infidels to spread Muslim power, and has a long and bloody history of conquest. For many adherents, the use of terror is considered a legitimate tool in the effort to convince others of the need to convert to Muslim faith and abide by its dictates. Needless to say, Wahhabism is a radical utopian faith promoting the idea that in time Islam will dominate the world, but it is a faith that is growing, in large part due to the support of the Saudis and their enormous oil wealth.[120]

As discussed earlier, communities in England with large Muslim populations have already established *sharia* courts with state sanction. This poses serious problems for some countries where Muslims may soon make up a majority of the population in major cities. Some of those cities might enact statutes based on Islamic law, such as requiring separation of the sexes in schools, the banning of alcohol and pork, or requiring the traditional covering of women. Of course, such acts would, in most cases, violate national laws, but given the general tolerance of most European politicians, they might well go unchallenged. This is especially the case if Muslim populations rise to a level where Muslim political parties might be essential in the formation of controlling coalitions in national parliaments. Such a scenario, while almost unimaginable at present, may become real if current demographic trends continue. The results would be catastrophic, since most secular Arabs and non-Muslims would refuse to accept such rules which if actually enforced would cause them to abandon those cities. In effect, these cities would become Islamic enclaves embedded in secular states totally at variance with the laws and values of the European population.

Would visitors to those cities be required to abide by those rules? In Washington D.C., for instance, where the carrying of a firearm is unlawful, a citizen of neighboring Virginia that has no such restriction can be arrested if he drives into the city and forgets to leave his gun at home. Would a European visiting a Muslim-dominated city be arrested if his car contained a case of wine? Of course, such a possibility seems preposterous, but given the rapid rise of fundamentalist Islam and the growing Muslim populations of some cities, such as Oslo, it cannot entirely be dismissed. It should also be obvious that if such enclaves were to arise, they would serve as ideal territories for the spread of radical doctrine and the recruitment of young people for terrorist activities. A fuller discussion of the ramifications of such developments will be postponed until the concluding chapter, but are raised at this point to suggest the real dangers posed by the attitudes expressed by a great many young Muslims living in Europe.

Role of European Institutions in Immigration Policy

Considering the problems outlined in the preceding sections, it is hardly surprising that many European countries have attempted to curtail immigration from Third World countries as desired by their citizens. These efforts are opposed by the European Union, the European Court of Justice, the European Court of Human Rights, and a large number of nongovernmental organizations (NGOs) and industrial interests who are supportive of more generous immigration policies and greater immigrant rights. It is not merely a bureaucratic struggle over prerogatives, but a very real struggle between those who wish to preserve national sovereignty and maintain their distinctive national and ethnic character and those who take a more international or supranational stance and who, especially on immigration, wish to erode those national goals in the name of a more peaceful and just human order.

In many ways the situation is similar to that in the United States, where local authorities are burdened by the needs of immigrants, often illegal, and try to reduce their numbers through various legal stratagems. In doing so they are, as outlined in previous sections, responding to the overwhelming wishes of their constituents. The national government, business interests, and a variety of immigrant advocacy groups, who often forward their efforts by court action, oppose these efforts, and courts have often been very sympathetic to those views.

In both Europe and the United States, the conflict over immigration clearly reflects left-right philosophical and political differences, where the left demands a universalistic and egalitarian stance on immigration and the right (at least the nationalist right) argues for the national interest in preserving ethnic solidarity. In Europe, as in America, the left has been able to frame the argument as one between humanitarian and egalitarian interests, on the one hand, and mean-spirited, racist motivations, on the other. In Europe this comes down to a struggle over how much authority should be granted to the EU and its courts in immigration matters. As in the United States, European courts very often attempt to expand control given them by interpreting statutes more broadly than had been intended by their authors.

All European nations are bound by the European Convention on Human Rights, which requires that states provide for family unification, especially between spouses and children. In effect this means that people who have established legal residency in Europe have the right to marry, live together, and found families without state interference. This has been interpreted to mean that once an individual establishes residency in a country, even as a migrant worker, he is entitled to bring his spouse and children to live with him. In practice this has come to mean that an individual can arrange to marry someone from outside the EU, who will then have the right to establish residency in the EU. Among Muslim groups, and non-Muslims from India, who have a tradition of arranged, often cousin-cousin or uncle-niece, marriage, it is quite common for men and women to enter into an arranged marriage with someone from his own native country, or his or her parent's native country. A recent study, in the English city of Bradford, found that 48% of Pakistani men and 60% of Bangladeshi men married spouses from the Indian subcontinent, as did 40% of the women from both groups. The figures for Indians were somewhat lower at 38% for men and 15% for women. Such families find it harder to assimilate since they contain at least one adult member who is a new immigrant. According to Lord Ouseley,

> Many of the children arrive at school with little or no English. Many of those who come from overseas have little education and do not possess skills which are transferable to a Western economy. The high family size means that overcrowding will be a persistent problem.[121]

These arranged marriages account for a significant number of new Third World immigrants to the EU. In many cases the right to marry is abused by people entering into fraudulent marriage arrangements merely to gain residency in a European country. For both of these reasons, several member states try to restrict them. Ireland, for instance, denied residency to any new spouse who came from a non-EU country.

Denmark took a different tack and made it a requirement that both partners in such a marriage be at least 24 years old. The Danes argued that many such marriages are forced marriages, which European countries are obligated to prevent under the International Covenant on Civil and Political Rights. They also argued that such a measure would limit unwanted immigration and promote assimilation of those living in Denmark. These are all legitimate reasons and not unlawful under European regulations. The idea here was that someone in their mid-twenties would be in a better position to avoid a forced marriage than would someone in their teens. Arranged marriages are, in almost all countries, seen as a serious impediment to assimilation, especially for the children of such unions.

An unstated reason, but also quite reasonable, is that arranged marriages are alien to the Western belief that marriages should be based in mutual affection and not be part of the larger aims of the family or social group. From this point of view, it is difficult to understand why two people, living in different countries, would freely choose to marry someone they had never met out of purely personal choice. Perhaps more important, such a practice is likely to import into Europe attitudes toward the place of women that most Europeans find repugnant.

In July of 2008, the European Court of Justice (the EU's highest court) overturned the Irish law on the grounds that it violated the right to family life provisions of the Human Rights Convention. Four

African men who had married Irish women but were subsequently refused residency permits brought the case.[122] Denmark's government is concerned that the ruling may foretell a court ruling against its 24 year-old age rule for overseas spouses and has announced its intention of defending that law if challenged, as is likely to be the case. An adviser to the former Prime Minister of Denmark argued, in the newspaper *Jyllands-Posten*, that the "EU court is doing the job of elected politicians.... This practice is a democratic problem.... Political decisions that ought to be the responsibility of elected representatives are left with the court."[123] As in the United States, proimmigration groups in Europe use the courts to forward their agenda and can often find judges sympathetic to their views.

A second major source of immigration in recent years is composed of people who enter an EU country and claim refugee status. According to London School of Economics political scientist, Eiko Thielemann, "from the early 1980s, the number of asylum seekers in Europe increased almost tenfold to 970,000 in 2001."[124] In the EU, once a person claims refugee status, he cannot be summarily deported, but must be allowed to stay until his claim can be justified. All European states are signatories to the UN Convention on Refugees adopted in 1951 and subsequently amended in 1967. The original policy granted asylum status to those displaced by World War II and the subsequent turmoil in Eastern Europe, and specifically dealt with events occurring before January 1, 1951. It specifically left to the signatory nations whether they chose to limit its effect to "events occurring in Europe" or "events occurring in Europe or elsewhere." Refugee status was conferred on an individual who "owing to well-founded fear of being persecuted for reasons of race, religion, nationality, membership of a particular social group or political opinion, is outside the country of his nationality and is unable, or owing to such fear, is unwilling to avail himself of the protection of that country..."[125] In 1967 this policy was amended to apply to events in general and not merely those in Europe before 1951. In addition, the European Court of Human Rights, which had ruled against the use of torture or degrading treatment, extended that doctrine by ruling that it was illegal to deport someone to a country where such abuses were common. Once an individual is granted the status of a refugee, he is entitled to take advantage of the family unification rule, meaning he can bring in members of his immediate family to join him in the country of refuge.

Many of these laws and court rulings have allowed for considerable abuse. The vagueness of the refugee law means that many people who migrate for purely economic reasons feign refugee status, and it is difficult to deport them without going through fairly elaborate legal proceedings to determine whether they are entitled to refugee status. According to Eiko Thielemann, an industry has grown up around the desire to gain residency in Europe by this means. Substantial sums are acquired through fees for such things as "smuggling across borders, arranging forged documents and visas, organizing employment and lodging." He estimates that "more than 70 percent of asylum seekers make use of such services."[126] In addition, they can seek and are often given legal help by organizations that support large-scale immigration.

According to Melanie Philips, the British courts interpreted asylum provisions very broadly and made it increasingly difficult to deport people who claimed asylum status on what were evidently frivolous grounds. In addition, the English courts expanded the human rights doctrine defending the right to family life in such a way as to, for instance, require the state to provide welfare support to asylum seekers who arrived with families, or who acquired families by marrying while waiting for rulings in their cases.[127] The net result is that large numbers of people came to the United Kingdom, claimed refugee status and remained while their claims were being investigated. In 90% of the cases their claims were denied, although about 20% of those were given permission to remain under special exemptions, so that a majority, 70%, was ordered to leave the country.[128] But owing to lax enforcement, those denied asylum or special exemptions were rarely deported. In 2006, the British Home Office disclosed that there was a backlog of some 450,000 cases of asylum claimants, many of which had never been processed. In addition, many of those who had been denied asylum had never been tracked and deported. The government promised to complete work on these cases by 2011. Many of the claimants had been in the United Kingdom for a long time, however, and had started families that protected them from deportation.[129]

Major sources of immigration into the EU are migrants who enter a country illegally and take up work in the underground economy. The number of illegal residents working off the books became so great in Italy and Spain that both countries granted amnesty to these people in order to bring them out of the underground economy. In the last 20 years Italy has had five amnesties and Spain six. In Spain's most recent amnesty, Spain granted legal residency and work status to 700,000 illegal entrants. In 1998 Italy granted amnesty to 308,000. Other countries have granted amnesties to regularize underground workers. In 1998, Greece granted amnesty to 397,000 people and France regularized 152,000. One of the primary reasons for these amnesties is the extraordinary expense required under EU guidelines to deport illegal residents. Dominic Casciani, writing for the BBC, reports that it can cost as much as 11,000 British Pounds to deport *one* individual.[130] These amnesties have the affect of encouraging further illegal entry by individuals who hope to acquire regular status in some future amnesty.

Once these individuals become legal residents, they can bring into the EU their spouses and children and can begin the process of obtaining citizenship, if that was not granted in the original amnesty. Another important consequence, especially for other EU countries, is that once a person acquires citizenship in one EU state, he is free to move and work in any EU country. This is a result of a series of agreements (the Schengen agreements) guaranteeing freedom of movement among EU states. In 1985, France, Germany, Belgium, Luxembourg and the Netherlands met near the town of Schengen in Luxembourg and agreed to the elimination of all border controls between member states. The policy was put into practice in 1990. Other countries quickly followed in joining in these agreements. In 1997, the EU, in the Treaty of Amsterdam, incorporated the Schengen provisions for all EU states who chose to participate (the United Kingdom, Ireland, and Denmark chose to opt out) and the EU Council of Ministers assumed decision making in these matters.[131] It should be stressed that the Amsterdam Treaty does not allow legal EU residents to work or take up residence in any country, it only stipulates that they can travel freely. However, under current EU rules a *citizen* of any EU country is entitled to take up residence and work in any other EU country that ratified the treaty. But this is not the case for legal residents without citizenship or what are called "Third Country Nationals" (TCNs). However, the European Council in 1998 issued a directive urging that such rights be granted to all those with legal residence, including TCNs. In the language of the Council, "A more vigorous integration policy should aim to grant them [third country nationals] rights and obligations comparable to those of European Union citizens."[132] The EU member states have so far rejected this recommendation since it would seriously undermine their ability to set individual state immigration policies. There is considerable concern that the European Court of Justice might intervene in this matter and grant such rights by the back door, as it were, in a ruling tangentially related to free movement, such as those which guarantee basic civil rights for all EU legal residents.[133]

The elimination of border and passport checks within Europe meant that EU residents and authorized visitors could freely move between EU countries unimpeded. But it also meant that illegal entrants could also move about without hindrance. This meant that securing the external borders of the EU was critical for immigration and security purposes. However, the EU member states have not agreed on EU-wide measures to do so. As a consequence, countries bordering on the Mediterranean—and especially those with island possessions close to Africa, such as Spain and Italy—became magnets for African migrants seeking illegal entrance into the EU. Once a migrant gains access to an island of an EU nation, he cannot be simply sent home, but had to be individually processed for deportation, a time-consuming and costly process. In many cases individuals simply leave shelters and detention centers and spread out into the countryside, and many travel to the mainland of other European states. In Spain and Italy, as discussed earlier, most illegal migrants were allowed to remain, and eventually granted amnesty to bring them out of the underground economy.[134]

The migration of desperate people trying to find a better life in Europe has produced enormous tragedy. Most of these migrants are from sub-Saharan Africa and make the long trek to the North African coast in hopes of finding passage to a European Island. Others leave from the African coast close to the Spanish Canaries on rickety boats that often capsize and all aboard are drowned. Nobody knows how many are lost in this way. If they are lucky enough to reach an island, they will often disable their boats so that they cannot be turned back, since they know the coastal patrol will take them ashore rather than let them drown. Those who reach the Italian Island of Lampedusa, which lies 70 miles off the coast of North Africa, will "be flown to other parts of Italy where immigration officials will interview them and where they can press claims for asylum or try to sneak away before being sent home."[135]

Many reach Spain by way of the Spain's southernmost city of Tarifa, less than ten miles from North Africa. The civil guard can turn them away while still at sea but thousands make it to the Spanish coast. A member of the civil guard explains "Our job is basically to apprehend them and guide them safely to shore. It's a treacherous journey if it's a short one." Most illegal migrants, however, come by airplane. As Katya Adler of the BBC explains, "They enter the European Union legally on short-term work or holiday visas and never leave."[136]

In summary, what started out as an attempt to fill labor shortages during the reconstruction of Europe by labor agreements with various countries such as Turkey and Morocco, has resulted in millions of immigrants making their way into Europe. Initially this was the result of inattention; few people anticipated these small communities of workers would grow to the extent they eventually did. They grew because of the growing body of humanitarian law and policies making it difficult to deport workers who had resided for lengthy times. This was compounded by EU policies requiring that families be united by bringing spouses and children into the host country of the workers.

In addition, the implementation of the laws on refugees created conditions where many non-Europeans looked to gain access through legitimate and nonlegitimate claims for asylum. As it became clear that most European countries had no real intention of deporting those whose refugee claims were denied, others simply entered illegally in the hopes that they, too, could avoid deportation. EU policies, in fact, made it unlikely that they would be deported, and the repeated amnesties of various states encouraged more to make the attempt to migrate, sometimes by extremely dangerous and costly means. The parallel to what is happening in America could not be clearer. On both sides of the Atlantic, public officials, no matter what they say to their electorates, are quite simply unwilling to stem the flow of immigration. That the vast majority of EU citizens oppose this massive migration seems beside the point. As Craig Parsons and Timothy Smeeding aptly put it, this result was the product of "non-majoritarian institutions—constitutional guarantees of human rights and courts—that protected this movement against restrictions by elected officials."[137] But this begs the question why the elected officials of all European countries who, after all, design and implement EU policies and who still control the scope of the EU, have acquiesced in these widely unpopular developments.

Public Attitudes and Official Responses

Given the above findings and the data dealing with education, employment, welfare dependency, and crime, it is hardly surprising that large majorities of Europeans have grave misgivings about the current level of immigration from Third World countries. Migration Watch, a United Kingdom policy think tank, commissioned a poll conducted in 2007 by the international organization YouGov to sample the attitudes of the British Public. Overall, 81% thought immigration should be substantially reduced, with 57% agreeing "strongly" and 24% tending to agree. Only 14% disagreed. Fifty-four percent of the public saw no economic benefit from immigration and fully 85% thought "immigration is putting too much pressure on public services."[138]

Similar results were found by a more recent poll sponsored by the British television station, Channel 4, and used in its three-part series, *Immigration: The Inconvenient Truth.* Eighty-four percent of the national sample favored either reducing immigration or halting it altogether, with 83% believing that there is an "immigration crisis" in Britain, with 44% being "definite" in this belief. Eighty-five percent felt there is less community spirit in Britain today than ten years ago, and 58% felt that British culture was being damaged or diluted because of immigration. On economic issues, 59% thought that immigrants receive more in public benefits than they pay in taxes, and 69% thought that ordinary British people are losing out because of special benefits for immigrants, with 66% believing that immigrants in terms of employment and wages were undercutting British workers. Sixty percent of Britons believe that immigration is "making Britain a dangerous place in which to live" with 41% agreeing that there are "some dangerous 'no-go' areas near where I live as a result of immigration."[139]

Political scientists Jack Citrin and John Sides analyzed a 2002 European Social Survey of the attitudes of residents of 20 countries in Europe in an attempt to understand the resistance of Europe's population to large-scale immigration. Their findings indicate that most people were not opposed to immigration per se, but rather with the size of the immigrant flow; most people favored *some* immigration. Somewhat surprisingly, given the common charge of xenophobia and racism, they report "Europeans were not significantly more likely to welcome immigrants from within Europe as opposed to outside Europe, or to welcome immigrants from richer countries as opposed to poorer countries...." The authors note that there may be a bit of political correctness in these responses. The authors argue "these results demonstrate that intensely exclusionary attitudes are not the dominant view." However, they add the caveat that this inference depends "on how one interprets the ambiguous word 'some.'" The authors interpret the category of *some* "as an acceptance of a modest level of immigration."[140]

Not surprising, given the evidence reviewed earlier, the greatest concern about immigration involved crime, and that "69 percent of all respondents believe that immigrants make crime 'worse.'"[141] In addition, most individuals were more negative toward asylum seekers than regular immigrants, with 64% thinking their own countries "had more than a fair share of people applying for refugee status." In addition a substantial plurality (47% to 22%) thought that most refugees weren't "in real fear of persecution in their own countries."[142]

Citrin and Sides performed a comprehensive analysis of many factors associated with views about immigration. According to the authors, "although both cultural attitudes and economic concerns matter, these data suggest cultural factors are more potent. Immigration is opposed when immigrants are perceived as a threat to one's 'way of life'"[143] Even though the poll did not specifically ask questions dealing with Muslim immigration, the authors made the point that their analysis suggests that Islam is viewed as a threat to cherished European values. "Despite the declining significance of religion in most European countries...there seems little doubt that the cultural as well as the political dimension of Islam increasingly is viewed as a threat to European attitudes toward women, family and homosexuals. If to be European is to be postmodern and postnational, immigration may well threaten European as well as national identity."[144]

Given these public attitudes, it is hard to explain most governments' continued support of large-scale immigration from Third World countries. In 2004, in a major address, and his first on immigration, Tony Blair, then Prime Minister of the United Kingdom, argued that immigration was economically vital and essential due to serious worker shortages. Such utterances are common among European leaders. Anthony Browne, the respected environmental editor of the *London Times* and frequent critic of the government, has made a very strong case that the economic argument is deeply flawed and disingenuous, at best. He cited the fact that only "10% of manufacturers said a shortage of skilled labor affected output, and 3% said shortages of other (semi-skilled and unskilled) was a constraining factor."[145] As discussed earlier, most immigrants are working at unskilled labor. In the case of the Muslims, only 28% of their total population in England are employed, and very high percentages are supported by government subsidies. It is difficult to make an economic argument that unskilled Muslim labor compensates for the large public expenditure in support of the Muslim community. This situation is common to most European countries with large Muslim immigrant communities.

Browne pointed out that there are large numbers of people in Britain who remain outside the workforce, as is true in many European countries. According to him "one in four men between 50 and 65—nearly 1.3 million people—are economically inactive, often involuntarily prematurely retired." He added that there are 2.7 million people "on sickness and disability benefits with no obligation to look for work, even though many are perfectly capable of work." He argued that while the official unemployment rate is given at 4.8%, in reality, "11.5% of those of working age want a job in the United Kingdom." He noted that London, where large numbers of immigrants live, has the highest unemployment rate in the country with an official rate of 6.8%, and in many London boroughs the rate is more than 10%. He suggested that for many low-skilled individuals, the difference of relying on work or on public benefits is so small as to act as a disincentive to work. Since high levels of immigration tend to suppress wages for unskilled work, he argued that reduced immigration would cause wages to rise and induce many of the unemployed to enter the labor market.[146] Much the same can be said about the situation in France.

European governments spend massive funds on social services for immigrants, and on the crime prevention necessitated by high levels of immigration. If a fraction of these funds were devoted to efforts designed to move native Europeans into the workforce, it could easily provide the relatively small number of workers needed. Such arguments are so cogent that most governments do not attempt to refute them but, rather, simply fail to respond in any coherent fashion to such criticism. In similar fashion, governments uniformly deny that problems in the educational area, or in crime, or in unemployment have anything to do with immigration, although even modest examination of government statistics gives the lie to these positions.

Summary

When considering existing immigration policy in the United States and in the European Union, there are considerable similarities and noteworthy differences. The similarities result from the fact that elites in all Western societies have adopted wholeheartedly an extreme form of the multicultural doctrine. It is extreme in that it denies historical and scientific evidence that people differ in important biological and cultural ways that makes their assimilation into host countries problematic. It is also extreme in the viciousness with which it attacks those who differ on this issue. These attacks are accompanied by a very generalized and one-sided denigration of Western traditions and Western accomplishments, and claims that a collective guilt should be assumed by all Europeans (whites) for the sins of their forebears. In the United States those sins include the displacement and destruction of the indigenous cultures of the Americas, the evils of American slavery, and its continued discrimination against blacks and other minority groups. In Europe those sins include the excesses of colonialism and, perhaps even more, the acquiescence of Europeans in the Holocaust.

In the semireligious formulation of this view, expiation of these sins can only come through an absolute benevolence toward the poor of the world whose suffering is claimed to be the result of the white race and its depredations. In practical terms this can only be accomplished through aid to Third World peoples and generous immigration policies that allow large numbers of people to escape the poverty of the Third World.

The policies of all Western governments reflect these sentiments and while numerical limits are set for legal immigration, very weak border controls and a variety of rulings have made it almost impossible to remove immigrants who arrive without authorization. In addition, family unification and asylum policies add to the growing immigrant communities. The final outcome of these policies is inevitable and predictable: by the end of the 21st century, in virtually all Western societies, white Europeans will find themselves minorities in their ancestral homelands. The motivations that drive these ideas and policies will be examined in the concluding section, but there can be no doubt as to the power of this elite ideology.

This multicultural ideology is based on a huge distortion of history and is alien to the vast majority of citizens. It can only be maintained by ignoring the wishes of the majority and by increasingly coercive means to silence dissent. This coercion takes the form of insult and social ostracism in the United States, and in Europe it is supplemented by civil and criminal sanction against dissenters. This distinction may well evaporate if the United States Supreme Court comes to be dominated by people who accept the multicultural doctrine, an outcome that seems likely given the near unanimous liberal ideology of the major law schools and of the profession in general.

There are, however, two very important differences between the United States and the European Union. The first involves differences in the political structure of these societies, with immigration policy in the EU far less responsive to popular pressure than in the United States. Five institutions that have confusing and intertwined powers that have changed over the years by various treaties and agreements determine the policies of the EU. First, The European Council is made up of the heads of state of all member states, and has very general power to establish and define the functions of the EU, but it plays a fairly limited role in the actual functioning of the EU and meets irregularly only three or four times a year.[147]

Second, the Council of Ministers is the most important legislative branch, and is made up of 27 members appointed by the member states. According to Elizabeth Bomberg and Alexander Stubb "alone or (increasingly) with the Parliament, it decides which EU legislation is adopted, and in what form." Most important votes are taken by *qualified majority voting*, in which member states' votes depend on the size of their population. However, according to Bomberg and Stubb, most issues never come to a vote. "Consensus is...widely sought in the Council and votes are seldom forced.... Whatever decision method is used, these meetings and votes still take place behind closed doors."[148] The seclusion of the decision process "makes consensus and agreement easier to achieve, but it makes the Council one of the few—if not the only—legislative bodies in the democratic world that makes its main decisions behind closed doors."[149]

Third, there is the European Parliament, the other legislative branch of the EU. It is made up of 726 members elected for 5-year terms by citizens in member countries, but has considerably less power than the council of Ministers. "It does not have the right to initiate legislation, and its control over the EU's purse strings is limited." However, it does have the power to veto decisions of the Council of Ministers. It has the right of "supervision or control over the European Commission and the Council through its right to question, examine and debate the large number of reports produced by these two bodies. According to Bomberg and Stubb, its power has grown over the years, but it still is quite weak when compared to almost any national parliament or to, for instance, the House of Representatives in the United States.[150] This is probably why voter interest in European Parliament elections tends to be weak. According the Wall Street Journal, "Turn-out has declined six straight times since the first elections in 1979. It was 45.5% in 2004."[151] In the elections held in June of 2009, only about 43% of eligible voters actually went to the polls, continuing the decline in voter interest.[152]

Fourth, the executive branch of the EU is the European Commission, made up of one member appointed by each of the 27 states in the EU, but it controls a very large bureaucracy to interpret and implement the legislation of the EU. As in the United States, legislation made by the Council of Ministers and approved by the European Parliament is often purposefully vague. For that reason, the Commission and its bureaucratic arm have considerable power in the everyday functioning of the EU, much as do the various federal bureaucratic entities in the United States.

Finally, the European Court of Justice acts as the judicial branch of the EU and is somewhat comparable to the United States Supreme Court. As explained earlier, it has tended to interpret the legislation of the EU quite liberally, much as the American Supreme Court of the United States has tended to liberally interpret the U. S. Constitution. It does have the power, interestingly, to "impose fines against member states" who violate its rulings, and can, in some cases, overrule national legislation and the decisions of national courts. Like the U. S. Supreme Court, its rulings "have raised fundamental questions about the proper limits of judicial activism and the role of courts in democratic societies."[153]

The EU suffers what is often called a *democratic deficit* since much of EU policy is determined by unelected bodies such as the Council of Ministers or the European Court of Justice and the

European Commission, none of which are directly elected by the populace. In addition, the European Parliament, which is made up of elected representatives, is generally unresponsive to the wishes of the people in any particular nation, since each country has only a limited number of seats in the Parliament.[154] According to John Loughland, writing at the *Brussels Journal*, EU governance is favored by most EU member governments since it favors the executive branch over their respective legislative branches. "It increases their power and their room for maneuver. How much easier it is to pass laws in a quiet and secret meeting with your twenty-seven colleagues than it is in front of a fractious parliament.... How much better to be able to vote for an unpopular law and then blame 'Europe' for it instead."[155]

While the executive branches of most European countries favor the current structure of the EU, they do not agree about the power that EU agencies should have over individual member states. According to Adam Luedthe, "Member state governments did not originally anticipate the degree to which the EU's central institutions... would eventually gain policy-making authority as the EU evolved."[156] According to Luedthe, the European Union is split between two camps which he characterizes as supranationalist and intergovernmentalist. The former wish to consolidate the power of the European Court, Commission, and Parliament over the policies of individual states, while the latter, especially in regard to immigration, desire to maintain the power of the individual nations. Luedthe argues that "the European Commission, Parliament and Court of Justice have advocated the expansion of immigrant rights and freedoms, while most national governments have preferred a restrictive line."[157]

The issue at the present time that has the greatest salience in distinguishing these camps concerns the rights of Third Country Nationals (TCNs), discussed previously. The supranationalists want to adopt the recommendations of the Tampere Council in 1999 that urged giving the right of free movement and all social benefits to TCNs and, in addition, prohibit individual states from giving priority in employment to their own citizens. These provisions in the EU deliberations were supported by France, Finland, and Sweden, but strongly opposed by Germany, Greece, Italy, and Austria.[158] The United Kingdom, Denmark, and Ireland did not participate in these discussions, since they had opted out of the 1997 Amsterdam Treaty that regularized the Schengen accords. They would be expected, in any parliamentary vote, however, to be in opposition to giving greater rights to TCNs. It should be noted that the draft EU Constitution, which failed to pass, would have "made immigration an area of full EU control."[159] In addition, over the years the EU has "passed binding immigration laws in a variety of areas, which now commit national governments to implement EU immigration policy."[160]

It is difficult at this point to predict how this argument will end, but one suspects that in the end the supranationalists will win out, either through a direct vote of the Council of Ministers and the acquiescence of the Parliament, the adoption of a reformulated European Constitution, or usurpation of the issue by the European Court of Justice. Should any of these actions come to pass, it would mean that individual countries would lose almost all control over immigration. In effect, the majority of citizens of all European states, who oppose unlimited immigration by wide margins, would have no influence whatsoever over who came to reside in their countries. In that case, the current democratic deficit, especially on immigration matters, would become a democratic chasm, with unelected bureaucrats in Brussels having complete control over immigration. It is worth noting, if only parenthetically, that a substantial number of European leaders have supported the encroachment of EU powers over immigration for the simple reason that it removes an extremely volatile issue from electoral concern. In other words, European elites that oppose restrictions on immigration are quite happy to have unelected bureaucrats take actions that are widely opposed by most electorates, rather than take actions themselves that reap the wrath of the electorate.

In the United States the situation is different because immigration policy is directly in the hands of elected representatives in Congress. The problem, of course, has been that Congress has continued to act in ways that seemed to reflect public concerns, but which, in the final analysis, failed to do so. Nevertheless, if the public is sufficiently aroused, its wishes can be influential. Roberto Suro, former director of the Pew Hispanic Research Center, whose book *Strangers Among Us* was discussed in Chapter 6, lamented the influence of the "new media," in being able to "amplify discrete sectors of public opinion to help block legislative action" in the immigration debates in 2006 and 2007. Quoting Suro, "In the first act of this drama, the Spanish-Language media helped mobilize huge crowds to protest legislation passed by the House that would have mandated an unprecedented crackdown on unauthorized migrants..." According to Suro, the new media had an even bigger impact in the second act. "In 2007, conservative voices on cable television news shows, talk radio, and the internet mobilized opposition to provisions of a Senate bill that would have offered legal status, or 'amnesty' as it was labeled, to unauthorized migrants."[161] Suro points out that the first measure involved very harsh measures, including imprisoning illegal aliens on felony charges that were not supported by most Americas, even those who strongly supported immigration restrictions. The second amnesty measure was defeated by Republican Senators, even though it had the support of Republican President George Bush, because it was overwhelmingly opposed by most Republican voters. It should be added that Senator McCain's support of that measure may have cost him the Presidential election in 2008, because it alienated so many in the conservative Republican base. The point, however, is that voters in the United States, if sufficiently aroused, can influence policy on immigration, whereas their European counterparts rarely have much of an influence on EU policies.

The second important difference between the United States and the European Union is the size of the immigrant population and its ethnic makeup. As discussed earlier, about half of all European immigrants are themselves European. The other half come from a wide range of Third World countries and the legal entrants comprise a relatively small percent of the overall population. Even if one takes into account illegal immigrants, whose exact numbers are unknown, it is unlikely that non-European ethnics make up more than 10% of Europe's population. Furthermore, unlike the United States, Europe had very few non-European ethnics prior to the postwar period. In the United States, on the other hand, non-Europeans, including blacks, Hispanics, and Asians, make up about a third of the population. Of course, if current trends continue these percentages in the European Union and the United States are likely to grow, but Americans of European descent will likely find themselves in a minority by 2050, whereas this is unlikely to be the case in the European Union. However, as will be discussed in the next chapter, this may also occur in some individual European countries, and certainly in a number of major European cities, by 2050. By the end of the century, however, Europeans may also find themselves a minority in their native lands if current demographic trends continue.

It is important to emphasize that even though the relative size of the non-European population in the EU is smaller than in the United States, it is highly homogenous in religious, essentially Muslim, character. For that reason, as already discussed, the problems of assimilation are very different in the U. S. and the EU. In the former, the main problem of assimilation will be the ability of immigrants to assimilate and not so much, except in special cases, with their desire to do so. In Europe the problem is twofold in that it must deal with an immigrant population that may have difficulty in assimilating, but also includes many who have expressed a resistance to doing so for religious reasons that are profoundly important to them.

Notes

1   Paul Demeny, Europe's Immigration Challenge in Demographic Perspective, In Craig A. Parsons, ed, *Immigration and the Transformation of Europe* (Cambridge, Cambridge University Press, 2006), 30.

2   Samuel P. Huntington, *The Clash of Civilizations: Remaking of World Order* (New York: Simon and Schuster, 1996), 84, 87.

3   Demeny, Europe's Immigration Challenge, 31–32.

4   Craig A. Parsons and Timothy M. Smeeding, "What's Unique about Immigration in Europe, in Parsons, *Immigration and the Transformation of Europe,* 6–7; Open Society Institute, Muslims in EU Cities, Cities Report, Germany, EU Monitoring and Advocacy Program, 2007, 39, 39–41.

5   Parsons and Smeeding, "What's Unique about Immigration in Europe, 7.

6   Ibid., 7; Kemel Kirisci, Turkey: A Transformation from Emigration to Immigration, Country Profiles, *Migration Information Source*, November 2003.

7   Parsons and Smeeding, What's Unique, 7.

8   Ibid., 300–303.

9   Ibid, 304.

10 Kimberly Hamilton, Patrick Simon with with Clara Veniard, The Challenge of French Diversity, Country Profiles, *Migration Information Source*, Migration Policy Institute, November 2004.

11 Dhananjayan Sriskandarajah and Francesca Hopwood Road, United Kingdom: Rising Numbers, Rising Anxieties, Country Profiles, *Migration Information Source*, November 2003.

12 Hamilton, The Challenge of French Diversity, *Migration Information Source*.

13 Martin Baldwin-Edwards, The Changing Mosaic of Mediterranean Migrations, *Migration Information Source*, January 2003; Kathleen Newland, Troubled Waters: Rescue of Asylum Seekers and Refugees at Sea, Country Profiles, *Migration Information Source*, June 2004; Hein de Haas, Trans-Saharan Migration to North Africa and the EU: Historical Roots and Current Trends, *Migration Information Source*, November 2006; Soeren Kern, Spain's Bluster Masks and Immigration Crisis, *American Thinker*, August 16, 2007.

14 Parsons and Smeeding, What's Unique, 7.

15 Marco Martiniello, The New Migratory Europe: Toward A Proactive Immigration Policy? in Parsons, *Immigration and the Transformation of Europe*, 300–301.

16 International Organization for Migration, International Law and Family Reunification, online at iom.int/jahia: European Commission; The Right of Family Reunification for Third–Country Nationals Recognized by a Directive.

17 Hugo Brady, *EU Migration Policy: An A-Z* (London: Centre for European Reform, February 2008), 1, 27.

18 Adam Luedte, The European Union Dimension: Supranational Integration, Free Movement and Immigration Policies, in Parsons, *Immigration and the Transformation of Europe*, 421.

19 Georges Lemaitre and Cecile Thoreau, Estimating the Foreign-Born Population on a Current Basis, *Organization for Economic Co-operation and Development*, December 2006, 13.

20 Migrants and their countries of origin are provided by the Migration Policy Institute in considerable detail at their *Data Hub*.

21 Peder J. Pedersen, Mariola Pytikova and Nina Smith, Migration into OECD Countries 1900–2000, in Parsons, *Immigration and the Transformation of Europe*, 56,57.

22 Migration Policy Institute, *Data Hub*, Country and Comparative Data, France: Stock of Foreign Population by Country of Nationality, United Kingdom: Stock of Foreign-born Population by Country of Birth.

23 Migration Policy Institute, *Data Hub*; Hein de Haas, Morocco: From Emigration Country to Africa's Migration Passage to Europe, *Migration Information Source*, October 2005.

24 Maurice Crul and Hans Vermeulen, Immigration, Education, and the Turkish Second Generation in Five European Nations: A comparative Study, in Parsons, *Immigration and the Transformation of Europe*, 236.

25 Muslim Population. Data based on a variety of government and other sources. Online at Islamicpopulation.org. The same data were presented for 2003 in Parsons and Smeeding, What's Unique, 8.

26 Ibid, 7–11.

27   OECD, based on Table 2.1a and Table 2.1b in *Where Immigrants Students Succeed, A Comparative Review of Performance and Engagement in PISA 2003,* OECD Publishing, 2006, 183.

28   Migration Policy Institute, *Data Hub,* Country and Comparative Data, Australia: Stock of Foreign Population by Country of Birth, Canada: Stock of Foreign-born Population by Country of Birth.

29   OECD, *Where Immigrant Students Succeed,* 8–9.

30   Office of National Statistics, United Kingdom, Education: Chinese pupils have best GCSE results.

31   Theodore Dalrymple, Choosing to Fail, *City Journal,* Winter 2000.

32   Office of National Statistics, United Kingdom, Education: Chinese pupils have best GCSE results.

33   Samuel P. Huntington, *The Clash of Civilizations: Remaking of World Order,* New York: Simon and Schuster, 1996, 62.

34   CIA, *The World Factbook* (New York: Barnes & Noble, 2006), 279.

35   OECD, *Where Immigrant Students Succeed,* 177.

36   *Open Society Institute,* Muslims in EU Cities, Cities Report, France. EU Monitoring and Advocacy Program, *Open Society Institute,* 2007.

37   Ibid, 177.

38   Office of National Statistics, United Kingdom, Ethnicity and Identity: Labour Market, Non-White Unemployment Highest.

39   Ibid.

40   Office of National Statistics, United Kingdom, *Focus on Religion,* (2001), 3.

41   Ibid., 13.

42   Office of National Statistics, United Kingdom, Ethnicity and Identity: Employment Patterns, Pakistanis most likely to be self–employed.

43   CLEISS, The French Social Security System, III-Family Benefits.

44   J. F. O. McAllister, A Shock to the System, *Time* Magazine, November 24, 2002.

45   Stephen Wright and Nicola Boden, Thugs Committing 350 Knife Assaults Every Day, as Blade Menace Spreads to Rural Areas, *Daily Mail,* July 17, 2008.

46   Theodore Dalrymple, The Barbarians at the Gates of Paris: Surrounding the City of Light are Threatening Cities of Darkness, *City Journal,* Autumn 2002.

47   Table compiled from information obtained from the European Union Eurostat website, Crimes Recorded by the Police: Historical Data (Total Crime) 1950-2000; data for 2005 from Crimes Reported by the Police: Historical Data, 2005; U.S. Data from the Statistical Abstract of the United States, 1977, 1982-83, 2008.

48 Home Office, United Kingdom, Statistics on Race and the Criminal Justice System United Kingdom–2005, 87.

49 The United Kingdom Parliament, House of Commons Hansard Written Answers for 17 Mar 2008 (pt 0032).

50 *Open Society Institute,* Muslims in EU Cities, Cities Report, Belgium. EU Monitoring and Advocacy Program, *Open Society Institute*, 2007, 36.

51 Open Society Institute, Muslims in Europe, Cities Report, Netherlands, 29.

52 Kristeligt Dagblad, February 28, 2008, online at kristligt-dagblad.dk.

53 Government of Dubai, Department of Islamic Affairs.

54 AdnKronos, Italy: 40 Percent of Prisoners are Immigrants, Says Report, AdnKronos International Italy.

55 Molly Moore, Field Note: How I Got the Story, *Washington Post*, April 28, 2008.

56 Molly Moore, In France, Prisons Filled With Muslims, *Washington Post*, April 29, 2008.

57 Frank Viviano, French Prisons: Extremist Training Grounds, *San Francisco Chronicle*, November 1, 2001.

58 Craig S. Smith, Islam in Jail: Europe's Neglect Breeds Angry Radicals, *New York Times*, December 8, 2004.

59 Home Office, United Kingdom, Crime in England and Wales 2007–2008.

60 Jonathan Wynne-Jones, Bishop of Rochester Reasserts "No–Go" Claim, *Telegraph.uk*, Aril 18, 2008; Shiraz Maher, Muslim Britain is Becoming One Big No-Go area. *The Sunday Times,* January 13, 2008; John Cornwall, Are Muslim Enclaves No-Go Areas, Forcing Other People Out, Asks Historian John Cornwall, *The Sunday Times,* March 16, 2008.

61 Stephen Brown, Germany's Intifada, *Front Page Magazine*, August 1, 2008.

62 Open Society Institute, Muslims in EU Cities, Cities Report, France. EU Monitoring and Advocacy Program, *Open Society Institute*, 2007, August 19, 2008, 17.

63 Bruce Crumley, French Riots Enter a Second Night, *Time*, November 27, 2007, online at time.com; *Agence France Press*, Scores of Police Injured in New French Riots, November 25, 2007.

64 Steve Harrigan, Where Buses Won't go, *Fox News*, October 22, 2004.

65 Peter Ford, France's Angry Young Muslims, *The Christian Science Monitor*. April 17, 2002; Craig S. Smith, Anti-Semitism at Ground Level in France, *International Herald Tribune,* March 23, 2006.

66 Colin Nickerson, Anti-Semitism Seen Rising among French Muslims,

The Boston Globe, March 13, 2006.

67 Chris McGreal, Rising United Kingdom Anti-Semitism Blamed on Media, *The Guardian*, January 25, 2005; Bjorn Hengst and Jan Friedmann, Insults Against Jews on the Rise, *Spiegel Online*, August 12, 2006; Arnold Beichman, Anti-Semitism in Sweden, *The Washington Times*, October 28, 2003.

68 Fjordman, Muslim Rape Wave in Sweden, *Front Page Magazine*, Dec 15, 2005.

69 Daniel Pipes and Lars Hedegaard, Something Rotten in Denmark? Capitalism Magazine, September 16, 2002.

70 Bruce Crumley and Adam Smith, Sisters in Hell, *Time*, November 24, 2002.

71 Ibid.

72 Sorious Samura, Gang Rape: Is it a Race Issue, *The Independent*, June 21, 2009.

73 *BBC News*, Sir Willian MacPhersons Inquiry into the Matters Arising from the Death of Stephan Lawrence on 22 April 1993 to Date, in order particularly to Identify the Lessons to be Learned for the Investigation and Prosecution of Racially Motivated Crimes.

74 David G. Green, ed., *Institutional Racism and the Police: Fact or Fiction* (London: Institute for the Study of Civil Society, 2000); Otto Kerner, *Report of the National Advisory Commission of Civil Disorders* (New York: Bantam, 1968).

75 Robert A. Gordon, "Scientific Justification and the Race-IQ-Delinquency Model," in Timothy Hartagel and Robert A. Silverman (Eds.) *Critique and Explanation: Essays in Honor of Gwynne Nettler* (New Brunswick, New Jersey: Transaction Books, 1986).

76 Otto Kerner, *Report of the National Advisory Commission of Civil Disorders* (New York: Bantam, 1968).

77 Byron M. Roth, *Prescription for Failure: Race Relations in the Age of Social Science*. New Brunswick, New Jersey :Transaction Publishers,1994), 229–238.

78 Ibid., 238–247.

79 Ibid., 245–249.

80 Ibid., 240–242.

81 U. S. Census Bureau. *Statistical Abstract, 1993, 998, 2008*. New York's murder rate dropped from 29.3/100,000 people in 1991to 13.4/100,000 in 1996 and stood at 6.6/100,000 in 2005. The total violent crime rate fell from 2,318/100,000 in 1991 to 1344/100,000 in 1996 and was 671 per 100,000 in 2005.

82 Lee Jasper, Breaking Out of the Black 'Gangsta' Ghetto, *Guardian*, United Kingdom, February 17, 2002.

83   Ibid.

84   *BBC News*, Blueprint for 'Divided' Bradford, *BBC News*, July 12, 2001.

85   Michael Nazir-Ali, Extremism Flourished as United Kingdom Lost Christianity, *Telegraph*, Jan 11, 2008.

86   *Open Society Institute*, Muslims in EU Cities, Cities Report, France, 51, online at eumap.org.

87   Sensitive urban zones and free urban zones, Geoportail, an official website of the French government.

88   Paul Belien, Sensitive Urban Areas, *Washington Times*, January 16, 2008.

89   *Open Society Institute*, Muslims in EU Cities, Cities Report, Germany, 39–41.

90   Ibid., 64–67.

91   *Open Society Institute*, Muslims in EU Cities, Cities Report, Denmark, 24.

92   Ibid., 48.

93   *Open Society Institute*, Muslims in EU Cities, Cities Report, The Netherlands, 24.

94   *Open Society Institute*, Muslims in EU Cities, Cities Report, Sweden, 2.

95   *Open Society Institute*, Muslims in EU Cities, Cities Report, Germany, 39–41.

96   Laurence, Jonathan. Managing Transnational Islam: Muslims and the State in Western Europe, in Parsons, *Immigration and the Transformation of Europe, 264.*

97   Ibid., 264.

98   Ibid., 265.

99   Ibid., 266.

100   Ibid., 262.

101   bid., 266–269.

102   Nina Shea, Saudi *Arabia's Curriculum of Intolerance: With Excerpts from the Saudi Ministry of Education Textbooks for Islamic Studies,* (Washington D.C.: Center for Religious Freedom, Freedom House, 2006), 9.

103   Frank Gardner, Analysis: Saudi Rough Justice, *BBC News*, March 28, 2000.

104   Shea, Saudi Arabia's Curriculum of Intolerance, 11–12.

105   Ibid., 13–14.

106   Ibid., 29.

107   Serge Trifkovik, *The Sword of the Prophet: Islam, History, Theology, Impact on the World* (Boston: Regina Orthodox Press, 2002), 209–262.

108   Munira Mirza, Abi Senthilkumaran and Zein Ja'far, Living apart

together (London: Policy Exchange, 2007), 37.

109 Ibid., 5–7.

110 *Times on Line*, A third of Muslim students back killings, July 27, 2008.

111 Mirza, Senthilkumaran and Ja'far, Living Apart Together, 6.

112 Christine Schirrmacher, Muslims in German: A Study Conducted by the Federal Ministry of the Interior, Results of the Study-A Summary; Institute of Islamic Studies of the German Evangelical Alliance e. V., April 2008, 1–4.

113 Ibid., 1–4.

114 Ibid., 5–7.

115 Ibid., 7–9.

116 Ibid., 9–11.

117 Ibid., 11–12

118 Trifkovik. *The Sword of the Prophet*, 143–208.

119 Ibid

120 Ibid.

121 *Migration Watch*, Transnational Marriage and the Formation of Ghettoes, Briefing Paper 10.12, September 22, 2005.

122 *BBC News*, Court Backs EU Citizens' Spouses, July 25, 2008.

123 Lisbeth Kirk, Danish Immigration Law Under Fire after EU Court Ruling, *EU Observer*, July 29, 2008.

124 Eiko R. Thielemann, The Effectiveness of Governments' attempts to control unwanted immigration, in Parsons, *Immigration and the Transformation of Europe*, 442.

125 United Nations Convention Relating to Status of Refugees and Stateless Persons, Office of the High Commissioner for Human Rights, Adopted 28 July 1951.

126 Thielemann, The Effectiveness of Governments, 468.

127 Melanie Philips, *Londonistan* (New York: Encounter Books, 2006), 19–23.

128 Alistair McConnachie, Assylum Policy: Restoring Integrity.

129 *British National Party*, British National Party News Team, Another Labour Act of Betrayal: Quarter Million Failed Asylum Seekers Get Secret Deal to Stay, July 25, 2008.

130 Dominic Casciani, An Illegal Immigration Amnesty, *BBC News*, June 14, 2006.

131 Julia Gelatt, Migration Fundamentals: Schengen and Free Movement of People across Europe, *Migration Information Source*, October 2005.

132 Adam Luedte, The European Union Dimension: Supranational integration, Free Movement and Immigration Policies, in Parsons, *Immigration and the Transformation of Europe*, 433.

133 Ibid, 438.

134 Dominic Casciani, An Illegal Immigration Amnesty.

135 Frank Bruni, Wave Of Immigrants Breaks Against Italian Island's Shore, *New York Times*, July 11, 2003.

136 Katya Adler, Spain Stands By Immigrant Amnesty, *BBC News*, May 5, 2005.

137 Parsons and Smeeding, "What's Unique about Immigration in Europe, 7.

138 *Migration Watch,* YouGov pic, Immigration, Fieldwork Dates: 6th–8th November 2007.

139 *Channel4,* Poll conducted by YouGov for use in a three part television program, Immigration: The Inconvenient Truth, aired April 7, April 14 and April 21, 2008.

140 Jack Citrin and John Sides, European Immigration in the People's Court, in Parsons, *Immigration and the Transformation of Europe*, 331–332.

141 Ibid., 334.

142 Ibid., 337.

143 Ibid., 349.

144 Ibid., 353–354.

145 Anthony Browne, Response to Tony Blair's First Speech on Immigration, *Civitas* Background Briefing.

146 Ibid.

147 Elizabeth Bomberg and Alexander Stub, *The European Union: How Does It Work* (New York: Oxford University Press, 2003), 55–56.

148 Ibid., 49–51.

149 Ibid., 52.

150 Ibid., 56–57.

151 John W. Miller and Alistair MacDonald, European Parliament Elections Loom as Political Bellwether, *The Wall Street Journal*, May 30–31, 2009, A14.

152 Reuters, Right Advances in Europe Amid Voter Apathy, *The Independent*, June 8, 2009.

153 Ibid., 60–62.

154 Ibid., 157–158.

155 John Loughland, Why Europe's National Politicians Sign Away National Sovereignty, *The Brussels Journal*, December 19, 2007.

156 Adam Luedthe, The European Union Dimension, 419.

157 Ibid., 426.

158 Ibid., 435

159 Ibid., 420.

160 Ibid., 420.

161 Banu Akdenizli, E. J. Dione, Jr., Martin Kaplin, Tom Rosenstiel and Roberto Suro, *Democracy in the Age of New Media: A report on the Media and the Immigration Debate* (Washington D.C.: Governance Studies at Brookings, September 25, 2008). Suro is quoted from his Executive Summary of the Report, vi–ix.

Chapter 8

IMMIGRATION AND THE FUTURE OF THE WEST

Introduction

AMONG THE REASONS THE MAJORITY of the population of the United States and the European Union give for their discomfort with mass immigration, perhaps the most prominent and most often expressed is a concern about preserving their way of life and traditional customs. In sociological terms this comes down to the question of people wishing to preserve their culture. It is the position taken in this book that a culture reflects the needs and the character of the people who inhabit a society. Those who take an opposing view, and support large-scale immigration, argue that human beings do not differ in any fundamental way; thus this concern about immigration is misplaced. Those with this second perspective assert that since cultures depend on a set of principles and ideals, they can be preserved regardless of the particular inhabitants who take up residence in this or that society. In this view, America, in particular, is a "propositional" nation, based on a set of values, associated with constitutional democracy, free enterprise, self-reliance, to name but the most prominent of core American values. These values were set in place by the founding fathers, and while they have evolved over time, they still remain paramount. In this view, the United States, since it has had such an extensive history of immigration, cannot be viewed, as can most other nations, as based in a shared ethnic history. In that sense America is exceptional. In recent years, similar views have begun to be expressed about the EU, in that Europe is composed of so many different ethnic and national groups, the idea is becoming more common that Europe is also a propositional entity. For that reason, European intellectuals view Western civilization as in no way threatened by large numbers of newcomers. These views are opposed by a relative small number of intellectuals who argue, to the contrary, that mass immigration is altering both the U. S. and the EU in fundamental ways, and they are both in the midst of committing a sort of cultural suicide presaging the death of the West.

There can be no doubt that there are many, especially among intellectual elites, who express little concern with the preservation of Western civilization and, in fact, would welcome its disappearance from the world stage. However, this is clearly a minority view and most people, whether favoring or opposing mass immigration, claim to cherish the cultural heritage of Western civilization. This raises the question about the very meaning of a culture and the definition of the good society. What, in fact, makes the Western way of life so valuable that people should be concerned with its preservation? After all, the great contributions of Western civilization would not disappear from the Earth if the West were to be overtaken by another population from a different civilization. Western science and art are now nearly universal, and would not cease to exist and evolve in the absence of the West as a living culture. Classical Greek and Roman civilizations have long since vanished from the earth, but the contributions they made live on.

Of course, if a culture alien to the West were to overwhelm western countries, it might be derelict in preserving Western Civilizations material manifestations, such as its great architectural achievements and magnificent representational art. If an openly hostile culture, such as one based in fundamentalist Islam, should come to power in a Western Country, it might well deface or even destroy some of these achievements, if it found them offensive to its faith. That would be a terrible loss to the human heritage. Nevertheless, the essential contributions of the West in the form of ideas and discoveries are now possessed by all mankind.

The question, then, that must be answered is why should people be concerned with preserving their heritage, especially if it requires sacrifices of one sort or another, in an increasingly materialistic and egoistic age? B. F. Skinner asked this question directly in his book

Beyond Freedom and Dignity and responded "that the only honest answer to that question seems to be this: 'There is no good reason why you should be concerned, but if your culture has not convinced you that there is, so much the worse for your culture.'"[1] Many contemporary commentators have remarked on the individualism and hedonistic nihilism so common in the West, and of the loss of faith in any transcendent values. Many attribute this to the decline of religious faith, while others attribute it to the lack of moral certitude brought on by the doctrine of moral relativism that permeates the educational system and is promoted by elites in all Western societies. Both have some basis in truth. To those explanations must be added that the wealth of modern Western societies allows most people to live lives freed of the abject misery that often induced people to hunger for transcendent reasons in religion or the continuities of family or tribe or nation. Even those who found no solace in religion often took comfort in the sense that they were part of a larger whole, part of a culture that came before and would extend beyond their mortal existence that would place the suffering they endured as part of a transcendent scheme of things.

Without such a transcendental frame of reference, people are thrown back on their immediate existence and a pressing concern with their own or their families' welfare. In the past, such an individual might have also been concerned with the well-being of his local group, but given the mobility and fragmentation of modern life, few people have profound attachments to their local communities. In fact, the mark of "postmodern" individuals is their disdain for the local as parochial and inconsistent with the cosmopolitan stance so many embrace. Put another way, if a culture places such a high value on the satisfaction of individual desires, to many people, perhaps a majority, it might seem foolish to make sacrifices to preserve their culture. A thoroughgoing individualist, according to Skinner, "has refused to be concerned with the survival of his culture and is not reinforced [given solace] by the fact that the culture will long survive him...he has denied the contributions of the past and must relinquish all claim upon the future."[2]

Changes in culture can have very negative consequences for large numbers of the people who were born and adapted to the older displaced culture, as well as for their descendants. This opens up a number of issues that require examination. For one, there is the profoundly moral question of what obligations one generation owes to future generations? Would the new culture which arose be suitable and comfortable to the progeny of the Europeans who will live in it? A second question is whether the transformation of the West could be so great as to make it very inhospitable for the current generation so that they would attempt to flee? Finally, is it possible under current immigration policies for Western cultures to be transformed peaceably?

Considering the first question, it is useful to turn to the thoughts of Edmund Burke who argued that a society is a contract between members, a partnership as it were, but unlike a normal contract between parties for mutual benefit, it is of a very different sort.

> It is a partnership in all science; a partnership in all art; a partnership in every virtue, and in all perfection. As the ends of such a partnership cannot be obtained in many generations, it becomes a partnership not only between those who are living, but between those who are living, those who are dead, and those who are to be born.[3]

Failure to recognize an obligation to past and future generations is one of the characteristics of the nihilistic individual. Should such a mentality come to be widespread, the consequence could be catastrophic to a society, especially one threatened by a hostile and potential aggressor state. Even one not infected by such individualism would have to think twice about putting his life on the line to defend a society, especially if he suspected that few would honor or even remember his sacrifice.

Anyone who has had occasion to visit the American military cemeteries that dot the European continent and is not profoundly moved by the sight of the thousands of grave markers of the young Americans who were sacrificed in war in the pursuit of causes (even causes which may have been, in retrospect, of dubious value), is hardly one who can be expected to much concern himself with the fate of future generations. As mentioned in an earlier chapter, nations often place terrible burdens on their members, which could not be endured were those burdens to be forgotten by mindless, self-absorbed future generations. Even when not required to make such extreme contributions, all citizens are expected and often gladly contribute to the well-being of their society through volunteer work and other charitable efforts, and act in myriad ways with a concern for their fellow citizens. It is worth quoting Burke at length on what would ensue if any generation, which is only a temporary possessor of its society, forgets its fiduciary responsibility and was to become:

> unmindful of what they have received from their ancestors, or of what is due to their posterity, should act as if they were the entire masters; that they should not think it amongst their rights to cut off the entail, or commit waste on the inheritance, by destroying at their pleasure the whole original fabric of their society; hazarding to leave to those who come after them, a ruin instead of a habitation...[4]

One can make a case that those who are plunging Western societies headlong into great changes under massive immigration, whose consequences are, at best, unknown, are profoundly amoral and astoundingly arrogant in indulging "at their pleasure" in policies that gain their force from the sense of moral superiority that comes from the almost religious faith that all men are equal in all regards, and all can live comfortably in any social arrangement.

This leads directly to the second question of whether, in fact, all men can live comfortably in any social arrangement. The argument throughout this book is that this assertion is almost certainly false, and it is worth repeating and amplifying the reasons why the multiculturalist position is flawed. Multiculturalism is often incorrectly confused with the doctrine of cultural relativism that was formulated by anthropologists early in the 20th century. Cultural relativism, which continues to be a central principle in anthropological research, did not argue that all cultures are equal, but rather that every culture had to be understood in terms of its needs and ecological circumstances, including its knowledge and technology. The concept did not include the position taken throughout this book, however, that cultures also reflect the particular idiosyncrasies of their inhabitants including, especially, their abilities and temperamental characteristics. For instance if a society has a great many people of an aggressive temperament, its methods of regulating antisocial behavior are likely to be very different from one in which very few people exhibit such tendencies. Likewise, a society composed of people with few high IQ members is likely to be structured very differently from one with a substantial number of intellectually gifted individuals.

To take a contemporary example from the field of education, it is worth considering the failures of so many of the nation's urban schools. Those failures can, in part, be explained by the fact that, in general, school procedures are set at the state, rather than the local, level. The rules governing discipline and curricular content are therefore the same for children from the poorest, often black and Hispanic, neighborhoods in the inner cities as they are for those from the wealthiest suburban communities. This is bound to create disastrous consequences for the urban schools, given the differences in ability and perhaps in temperament between the two populations. The consequence is that poor black and Hispanic children are required to study things they often find unfathomable, and must attempt to do so in disorderly and dangerous environments. It is hardly surprising that the dropout rates in urban schools are alarmingly high. Christopher Swanson analyzed the graduation rates of the schools in the 50 largest U. S. cities and found an overall average graduation rate of only 52%. In the worst case, Detroit, only 25% graduate. In 10 of the worst performing cities, including New York, Los Angeles, Dallas and Atlanta, fewer than 46% graduate. In Baltimore, Cleveland and Indianapolis the figure is fewer than 35%.[5] Linda Gottfredson made the point

> that the black-white differences among children from the *same social class* is no larger than the mean difference (about 12 IQ points) between siblings brought up in the same household.... Most families, however, neither expect nor demand that all siblings perform to the same level, and most believe it is inappropriate for parents to treat children who have different needs in an identical manner. It is likewise unwise for a nation to insist that all its subgroups perform to the same average level. [emphasis added][6]

Gottfredson was, in this case, discussing the education of black American students that have an average IQ of 85. She did not deal with temperamental differences, but the same logic would apply, if such temperamental differences do in fact exist.

The point is that what works well in one population may fail in a different population. If a group of people making up a society is to survive, it must, at the least, provide the basic necessities of existence. It must also organize itself for defense against enemies and order the relations between individuals so that they do not destroy their society in intrasocietal violence. In other words, they must have a set of practices and values which enable them to survive and prosper. Necessarily, differences in populations and circumstances are likely to produce very different societal solutions, as is evidenced by the extraordinary cultural variation revealed by anthropological studies. As discussed earlier, large numbers of immigrants to the EU and the U. S. come from societies with average IQs of about 90, while the average IQ in the West is about 100. Practically, this means that while 50% of the population of Western societies has IQs above 100, that figure drops to approximately 25% for those from societies with a mean IQ of 90. The question immediately arises as to whether there is some threshold for IQ required for the smooth functioning of a democratic republic. The work of Tatu Vanhanen discussed in Chapter 4, strongly suggests that this is the case. As mentioned in the first chapter, it may well be that the autocratic regimes, and lack of democratic forms, that are so common in the many countries from which immigrants come are the result of their populations lacking the intellectual resources to create democratic republics. One extremely important feature of Western democracies is the rule of law and trial by juries. Is there some threshold below which such systems cannot effectively function? In other words, can a jury of people with an average IQ of 85 to 90 be expected to understand the nuances of law and come to sound judgments as to how they should be applied in complex cases?

The above question is not merely conjectural. Before it revised its tort laws in 2004, Mississippi was, according to its governor, Haley Barbour, "America's No. 1 judicial hellhole for jackpot jury verdicts.... For trial lawyers, this was the state you wanted to come to if you wanted to sue someone." According to Stephen Moore, writing in the *Wall Street Journal*, "One of the worst places, in terms of frivolous lawsuits, was Jefferson Country...it had more plaintiffs than residents." Jefferson County was sought out by lawyers who "shopped around" for favorable courts. "In one legendary case against a pharmaceutical company that sold the diet pill *Pondimin*...a Jefferson County Jury awarded $1 billion to the family of a woman who had taken the drug."[7] What is rarely mentioned in the discussions dealing with Mississippi's tort problem is that Mississippi ranks near the bottom of all states in educational attainment. In fact, its NAEP scores in mathematics for eighth-grade students in 2007 were the lowest of all the states in the nation: only the District of Columbia had lower scores.[8] Part of the reason is that Mississippi has a large minority population; in 2000 approximately 39% of its population was nonwhite. Jefferson County's population was 86% black.[9] Put bluntly, it seems that juries in Jefferson County lacked the intellectual substance and mathematical acumen, in particular, to determine what to most people would seem to be reasonable awards in such cases.

A primary thesis of this book is that human societies are primarily the product of the genetic nature of human beings who make them up. In this view, contrary to the one prevailing today in the social sciences, the human element is far more important than the physical or ecological conditions confronting societies. Put another way, a people living in an environment rich in natural resources may not be able to exploit those resources if they lack the human capital to do so. On the other hand, societies with greater human capital can prosper in places with only meager natural resources. An important element of this thesis is the recognition that culture-gene interaction is a two-way street; genes affect cultures, but cultures, in turn, affect genes. It is important, however, to recognize that the effect of genes on culture is likely to operate quite quickly, while the effects of culture on genes require a much longer time to take place. In other words, changes in the demographic makeup of a population will have almost immediate effects, whereas the evolutionary impact of a society on its inhabitants will take centuries, at the least, to take effect. From this rather simple, and to some extent, rather self-evident thesis, it follows that current immigration patterns are likely to change quite quickly the societies to which immigrants go. It will also change those countries, especially those with small populations, from which immigrants come. The nature of these changes is likely to be wide-ranging and is, without exaggeration, of world-historical significance that will affect future generations for centuries to come.

The population of the world will grow by some 2.5 billion people during the first half of the 21st century, and most of that growth will occur in the poorest countries on earth.[10] Significant evidence, previously reviewed, shows that differences in wealth, both within nations and among them, are profoundly influenced by the human capital of their inhabitants, especially as measured by IQ. Human capital, in addition, is influenced by values associated with productivity, wealth accumulation and a respect for the rule of law, all of which appear to be, at least in part, influenced by genetics. If these associations are accurate reflections of reality, and it is hard to argue that they are not, than the explosion of technological advances leading to rapid industrialization in most of the world will likely serve to exacerbate the income differentials that currently exist. This is so, since the exploitation of those technological advances will be highly dependent on human intellectual capital. Not only will the income gap within nations grow, but the gap between the richer and poorer nations will also grow. Nations with large numbers of people with talent will prosper relative to those with fewer talented people. Likewise, nations that import immigrants of high human capital will likely prosper and undergo little, if any, major civil and social problems, though obviously they will undergo cultural changes as the new immigrants bring their ways to their new societies. Just the opposite is likely for those states that import significant numbers of individuals with less human capital.

In addition, immigration will have important effects on donor countries. This is so because immigration is almost always selective and, in general, is undertaken by people who hope to improve their lot in receiving countries. One consequence is that donor countries that have a lower proportion of talented individuals, such as those in Africa and South Asia, such as the Philippines, and especially the smaller countries that export large numbers of people, which will suffer from the loss of talented individuals, and for that reason suffer declining productivity and wealth relative to world standards.

The questions posed by the potential relations between intellectual competence and temperamental differences, and the social and political structure of societies, have not even begun to be studied. It is unlikely that any progress will be made in this area as long as the intellectual climate in the scientific community tends to suppress intensive and unhindered research in these topics. If and when a time arrives that such research can be carried out, it is safe to say that it will transform the social sciences, including political science and history, in revolutionary ways. Clearly these topics cannot possibly be fairly treated in this book, since so little is yet known. But the questions raised here are so important when considering the consequences of large-scale immigration that they will be discussed, though necessarily in abbreviated fashion.

In what follows, much is necessarily speculative in that it assumes population projections based on current patterns, and such patterns can change. It should also be emphasized that it assumes that IQ estimates of immigrant populations are reasonably accurate and stable. On this issue one can feel relatively confident. The following discussion, however, also makes reference to potential temperamental differences between immigrant populations and host populations, especially in regard to potential problems in dealing with antisocial behavior and the social responses to the problem of crime. One must be very cautious about these possibilities. While it is becoming clear that there are genetic correlates associated with antisocial behavior, the research in this area is extremely recent and little has been confirmed with any degree of certainty. In addition, though it seems likely that different populations differ in the incidence of these genes, virtually no information is currently available on such differences, and any assertions in this area are, at this point in time, almost completely speculative. Having said that, it should be stressed that this research is proceeding at a rapid pace and it is not unreasonable that within a relatively short period of time a better understanding of any such relations will begin to take shape.

United States: Domestic Impact

Statistical projections, reviewed earlier, indicate that the U. S. population in 2050 will consist of 13% blacks, 29% Hispanics, 47% Whites and 9% Asians. Asian immigrants consist of two quite different population groups. There are those of North Asian descent from China, Korea, Japan and Taiwan with IQs in the 105 range. By contrast, Asian immigrants from South and West Asia come from countries, such as India, the Philippines, Indonesia and other Pacific Islands, where IQs range between 82 and 90. It is important to stress, however, that immigration is selective and that the immigrants from south Asia may have IQs substantially higher, with some exceptions, than those of their home country. As mentioned in Chapter 7, Indian immigrants to England tend to be a highly select group; it is likely that Indian immigrants to America are equally select. Furthermore, many of the immigrants from South Asian countries are professionals and many come under educational and H-1B visas and eventually establish permanent residency status. The educational data reviewed in Chapter 6 suggests that for the most part, Asians, whatever their home countries, perform above other groups, including native-born European

Americans. The education results, on the other hand, for second- and third-generation Hispanics suggest that Hispanic immigration is less selective, at least in regard to intellectual ability. It is clearly selective in that most Hispanics are law-abiding, ambitious, and hardworking. However, the effects of regression to the mean may diminish some of these qualities in later generations. Criminal data reviewed in Chapter 6 suggest that this may well be the case.

The net result of these patterns is that the demographic profile of the U. S. in 2050 will consist of two distinct ability groups: about 56% will be whites and Asians with average IQs of about 100 or somewhat higher, whose cultural background and ability are highly predictive of economic success. The other group of about 42% will consist of blacks and Hispanics, whose collective average IQ is likely to be somewhere between 85 and 90, and who seem to possess fewer characteristics consistent with economic advancement. (The remaining 2% are made up of various small groups who do not fit into these categories). Population projections and IQ estimates for various groups suggest that the overall IQ of the U. S. population will probably fall from about 96 today to about 93 by mid-century.

This drop in average IQ of about 3 points is quite modest and would hardly be noticeable in the general population. However, it is in the upper tail of the bell curve that these changes are bound to have economic and social effects. If we use the rough IQ figure of 110 as necessary for meaningful education at the level of college graduation, then the percentage of the population in this group in the United States will fall to approximately 13% from the percentage of about 17% today. In addition, the people who fall in the lower two rungs of the proficiency levels outlined in Chapter 1 will grow considerably and these people will find it difficult to find remunerative employment.

The economic consequences of this decline are rather straightforward. The number of college-capable individuals will drop by about 24% at a time when advanced training becomes more crucial for the country's economic dynamism. It should be stressed that many current college graduates fall below the 110 threshold. The reasons for this are plain. It is well known that the education establishment has promoted enormous growth largely by dramatically lowering admissions and graduation standards, often in the name of affirmative action, but just as often out of simple avarice. In this they were aided and abetted by government programs that encouraged students to attend college and by employers that use the attainment of a college degree as a proxy for job fitness. College graduation provides proof of a certain temperament and of sufficient intelligence for jobs that often do not actually require advanced education. People familiar with higher education know that the BA degree has been seriously devalued since the 1960s.[11] Charles Murray has suggested that relatively easily designed certification exams could be used in the selection of suitable employees instead of college degrees and would save a large number of young people the expense of pursuing college degrees, including the loss of income, time, and practical on-the-job training.[12] Such certification exams would obviously be resisted by colleges and might run into difficulty with discrimination laws due to their likely disparate racial impact. For these reasons, college degrees will likely remain important tickets for many jobs.

One likely consequence of a reduction in talented individuals is that the demand for such individuals will exceed their number. This is especially the case in the more demanding professions, such as medical doctors, research scientists, and others who make substantial contributions to innovation and who contribute disproportionately to a nation's economic prosperity. These jobs require a threshold IQ of perhaps 120, where the proportion above this threshold will drop from about 5.5% to 3.6%, a drop of about 35%.[13] This problem can be addressed by attempting to recruit competent immigrants, but that would require a complete reorganization of current immigration policy, especially the preference given for relatives and the interpretation of the Constitution granting automatic citizenship to anyone born on American soil. A second problem is that as the donor nations grow more prosperous, the appeal of emigration, especially for more competent individuals, will decline.[14]

In practice, the United States will most likely attempt to cope with the shortage by filling these positions with less capable people. This would almost certainly reduce the economic competitiveness of the U. S. relative to other advanced nations. To some extent this is already happening under affirmative action policies.[15] A shortage of high IQ individuals may have other consequences, for instance, such as influencing the career choices of a declining fraction of intellectually competent individuals. Some may gravitate to higher paying positions, creating shortages in those that are less economically rewarding. If the United States moves in the direction of nationalized health care that limits the salaries of physicians, a trend already underway, the country's medical care will undoubtedly suffer.[16] Similar changes could effect other professions, but in ways difficult to predict at this point. The higher demand for this pool of individuals will likely drive up their incomes, increasing economic disparities that are already troublesome.

In all likelihood the decline in human capital will not necessarily lead to a decline in actual living standards for most Americans, as they can be compensated for by modest increases in productivity which is likely to continue over the next 40 years. In a static world environment nothing much would change. However, the current world economy is hardly static, and will be greatly influenced by globalization and the rise of India and China as leading industrial powers. To drive home the significance of this somewhat modest decline of about 3 points in the IQ of the U. S. population, it is valuable to compare the future demographics of the United States with the demographics of India and China. The U. S. population is expected to reach about 400 million by 2050 and by then China's population will be about 1 billion 400 million, while India's population is expected to reach 1 billion 600 million. In China, with an average estimated IQ of 105, approximately 37% of population will exceed the IQ threshold of 110, as compared to about 13% of the population in the U. S. Based on the current population estimates, this mean that 520 million Chinese will be college-capable compared to 52 million Americans, or a ratio of about 10 to 1. Even if we use Lynn and Vanhanen's lowest sample IQ from the 10 samples reported for the Chinese, which was an IQ of 102, some 30% of China's population, or about 420 million people, will exceed the 110 threshold, or about 8 times the number of Americans exceeding that threshold.[17] Put another way, China will have more people in this high IQ group, even using the lowest estimate of China's IQ, than the total projected population of the entire United States. Of course, China may not be able to provide advanced training for those many millions in the next four decades, but they will certainly be able to provide it in ever greater numbers, especially if they make it a high state priority, as appears to be the case. Looking at those people with IQs above 120, again using the lowest estimate, China will have some 160 million people in this category as opposed to about 14.4 million in the United States, a ratio of 10 to 1.[18]

The upshot is that the gap in the potential for innovation and economic growth between China and the U. S. will grow enormously and begin to have its effects in the very near future. The situation for India is somewhat different, given that the current IQ for India, estimated to be 82, is much lower than that of China. In India, therefore, the percentage of people above 110 will be about 3.2%. However, with a projected population of 1600 million people, this would give a total of about 50 million people exceeding the 110 threshold, not much fewer than the number in that category in the United States. Furthermore, if the Indian IQ is suppressed by poor nutrition and limited schooling, as appears to be the case, than the number of talented Indians should be sufficient to propel the economic progress of India and eliminate current nutritional and educational deficiencies, perhaps by mid-century. This would mean an even larger proportion of Indians would fall into the college-capable group. To fully explore the meaning of these changes would require a book many times the size of this one. Nevertheless, a few of these effects are so obvious and so important that they will be touched on, though necessarily in a very limited fashion.

The most obvious effect of the demographic changes in the United States will be a decline in relative standards of living for most Americans and this will be felt quite differently for different segments of the country's population. Tensions between groups with divergent economic success will likely be most pronounced in states and regions with large numbers of Hispanics and blacks. The Hispanic population in the states of the southwest is growing rapidly and may soon constitute a majority in many of those states. Samuel Huntington argues that Miami had, by the late 1970s, become a majority Hispanic city dominated by the successful Cuban community where Spanish had become the de facto official language and assimilation became unnecessary for normal economic activity. He points out that the original Cuban immigrants contained large numbers of professionals and entrepreneurs who turned Miami into "an international economic dynamo, with expanding international trade and investment." The economic growth of Miami and its Hispanic character attracted large numbers of poorer, less-educated Hispanics. By the late 1980s, Miami had become a center of the drug trade and one of the most violent cities in America. Much of the violence was drug related, but a good deal involved rivalries among various Hispanic factions.[19]

Huntington asks,

> is Miami the future for Los Angeles and the southwest generally? In the end, the results could be similar: the creation of a large, distinct, Spanish-speaking community with economic and political resources sufficient to sustain its own Hispanic identity apart from the national identity of other Americans...[20]

Of course, a major difference is that few of the Hispanic immigrants to the American southwest are entrepreneurs and professionals as were the Cubans; most are poorly educated. In addition, later generations have not demonstrated the sort of social advancement common to earlier groups of immigrants or current immigrants from Asia. As the number of Hispanics grows in those states, they may in time create enclaves that recreate the cultures of their Mexican and Central American origins, and eventually they may come to political dominance in those states. If future generations remain poor they could very well develop resentments that could be used to political advantage by various stripes of political demagogues, some of whom may take radical stances and agitate for independence from the United States.[21] The desire for ethnic groups to control the culture and policies of areas they dominate is so pervasive worldwide, that the possibility of secession cannot be discounted offhandedly. Would the people of the United States support a second civil war to prevent such an attempt?

Patrick Buchanan reports that the college organization MEChA, which translates as the Chicano Student Movement of Aztlan, has more than 400 chapters on campuses throughout the nation. *Aztlan* is the name given by this group to refer to the ancestral home of the Aztec peoples. The group openly advocates the retaking of the lands taken by the Europeans. Buchanan quotes from the plan of the group, "*Aztlan* belongs to those who plant the seeds, water the fields, and gather the crops and not to foreign Europeans. We do not recognize capricious frontiers on the bronze continent," and translates the slogan of the group as "For the race, everything. For those outside the race, nothing."[22] The web site of the organization includes the document "*El Plan Espiritual De Aztlan*" that includes among its goals the establishment of "A nation autonomous and free—culturally, socially, economically, and politically—will make its own decisions on the usage of our lands, the taxation of our goods, the utilization of our bodies for war..."[23] In its *"El Plan De Santa Barbara,"* it explains:

> For decades Mexican people in the United States struggled to realize the ''American Dream.'' And some, a few, have. But the cost, the ultimate cost of assimilation, required turning away from *el barrio* and *la colonia.* In the meantime, due to the racist structure of this society, to our essentially different life style, and to the socio-economic functions assigned to our community by Anglo-American society as suppliers of cheap labor and dumping ground for the small-time capitalist entrepreneur the *barrio* and *colonia* remained exploited, impoverished, and marginal. As a result, the self-determination of our community is now the only acceptable mandate for social and political action; it is the essence of Chicano commitment.[24]

Of course, this radical student movement is hardly representative of the great majority of Hispanics residing in America. Nevertheless, it is well-organized and is, after all, an organization of university students, many members of whom will no doubt take up leadership positions in their community and in the United States in general. It is worth pointing out that Antonio Villaraigosa, the current mayor of Los Angeles, was at one time the chairman of the UCLA chapter of *MEChA*.[25] Its emphasis on racial identity is not unique; the largest, and probably the wealthiest Hispanic organization in America calls itself the *National Council of La Raza* (the race), and as discussed in Chapter 1, enjoys considerable support from foundations as well as millions of dollars in federal grants. From 1998-2004, it counted among its members Judge Sonia Sotomayor, who has recently been seated on the Supreme Court of the United States.[26] As the Hispanic population grows, these sentiments may well take the form of a movement for secession, or for uniting several states with Mexico.

Unlike Hispanic organizations, Black Nationalist and separatist political movements have generally not been attractive to most black Americans. Blacks are a relatively small minority in most states and are spread widely throughout the country. For that reason, separatist movements, in particular, have gained very little support. In addition, with the exception of many cities, blacks have not been in a position to achieve political dominance.

Hispanics, on the other hand, are much more concentrated geographically and are rapidly growing by continued immigration and natural increase, while the black population is projected to stabilize at its current proportion. For that reason Hispanic political movements could gain traction in the Southwest, some of which might have radical goals and may resort to organized violence to forward their ends, perhaps in imitation of Muslim radicals in the use of terror tactics. This problem would be exacerbated if criminal gangs grow in size and attempt to influence politicians to limit police action against their control of the drug trade and human trafficking as is common in Mexico and other Central American countries. Much of the civil strife currently afflicting Mexico is the result of the government's attempt to reduce gang influence over law enforcement.[27]

Political Consequences

The political consequences of such developments would be enormous for the United States as a whole. The rise of Hispanic enclaves or states with cultures closer to that of Central America may make the idea of secession more palatable to many Americans, and given the proximity to Mexico, may result in portions of the Southwest reuniting with Mexico. Hispanics, however, are not limited only to the Southwest, but are spread throughout the United States, as is the case with blacks.

In many United States communities the presence of an economically depressed ethnic majority living in areas alongside a much more prosperous minority, most of whom are of different ethnicity, is a sure prescription for ethnic resentment and hostility as was demonstrated by Amy Chua in her *World on Fire*.[28] At the very least, such resentment could lead to demands for greater social support and enlarged affirmative action in education and employment. In fact, one of *MEChA's* claims is that America is racist in its relations with Hispanics, thus *MEChA* calls for greater support for higher education among Hispanics. It could also take the form of random acts of criminal violence. Such responses are clearly evident in cities with large black populations, though it is almost impossible to determine the extent to which black crime is racially motivated.

Given the income, crime and education data reviewed in earlier chapters, this suggests that the social problems currently confronting many communities in the United States will likely grow, perhaps to alarming proportions. Stagnant or declining living standards relative to the rest of the world and increasing economic disparities will only exacerbate these problems. As already stated, this is a clear recipe for political and social turmoil. The most likely consequence will be a growing segregation between the more successful and less successful ethnic communities. The reasons will be those that usually drive segregation, even in ethnically homogenous societies, namely the desire of successful people to live in orderly, well-maintained communities, protect themselves from random violence and their property from predatory crime, and assure their children safe and well-functioning schools.

This may well lead to a major political realignment along ethnic lines. Today, the Democratic Party is favored by liberal elites on both coasts and by ethnic minorities throughout the country, who benefit from a powerful central government that can expand income transfers and enforce affirmative action policies unpopular with whites. Both groups tend to support liberal immigration policies. Rank-and-file Democrats, on the other hand, including successful immigrants, often find themselves in competition with new immigrants and tend to be less supportive of liberal immigration. In addition, the elites in this group, especially the intellectuals, have a distaste for traditional American values that they see as retrograde and nationalistic.

The Republican Party, for the most part, draws votes from middle-class whites and, to a modest degree, from successful members of minority groups, especially Asians, who bear the burden of higher taxes and the personal costs of affirmative action, especially as it affects the opportunities of their children. In general, these people tend to support more restrictive immigration policies, and generally support more conservative traditional American values.

There are certain fundamental inconsistencies in the political affiliations of many of the supporters of both parties, particularly in terms of economics. Democratic elites, especially those who live in the Northeast and West Coast, are plagued by high living costs requiring high salaries, and therefore find themselves burdened by high marginal tax rates. In addition, if these elites work in large cities with weak public schools, they are forced to commute long distances from suburbs with better schools or send their children to private schools. Their need for protection from predatory crime also drives them to safer suburbs or high-priced neighborhoods in buildings with expensive security provisions. In voting for Democrats who support current public school policies and more lenient criminal justice policies, they vote against their own economic interests and the safety of their families. In other words, they seem willing to pay a fairly high price for their liberal world view. If continued massive immigration exacerbates social problems and drives up taxes, many liberal whites may gradually, if reluctantly, gravitate toward the Republican Party.

Working class whites who benefit from liberal government support and who currently vote for Democrats may gravitate toward the Republicans who seem more responsive to their concern with competition from immigrants, both legal and illegal. Lower income whites may become increasingly unhappy with Democratic support for affirmative action that increasingly benefits a growing Hispanic population. These trends may benefit the Republican Party, but only if it takes a much more energetic approach to immigration limitation.

Conservative middle-class Americans who tend to support the Republican Party also face dilemmas. Such individuals, who generally support fiscal prudence and limits on immigration, find themselves supporting a Republican Party that supports a very expansive foreign policy and has been totally unresponsive to their concerns about immigration. It should be noted that, prior to the Cold War, traditional conservatives opposed expansionist policies, with many being isolationist in the 1930s and opposed to American involvement in World War II before the Pearl Harbor attack. In addition, middle-class Americans find themselves threatened by H1B visas for skilled workers that most rank and file Republicans overwhelmingly oppose, but which have been supported by the Republican Party. In addition, Republicans have failed to voice opposition to the outsourcing of skilled work, which severely undercuts middle-class wages. These immigration and economic policies have tended to alienate a significant number of conservative voters, resulting in significant losses for the Republican party in the 2006 and 2008 elections. Many traditional Republican voters simply stayed home on Election Day. It seems that only by moving in the direction of greater fiscal prudence and more restrictive immigration policies can the Republican Party bring these voters back into their corner.

All of which suggests that Republicans will have to respond to these concerns and in effect become the champions of white and

Asian middle-class Americans, or find themselves marginalized as was the Whig Party in the 1850s. In addition, the Democratic Party will become increasingly identified as the party of an uneasy alliance of various minority ethnic groups and even more ardent supporters of affirmative action and unrestrictive immigration policies. Put another way, current trends suggest that political affiliation will, while retaining its economic dimension, also be determined even more than it currently is, by ethnic identification.

What may emerge from these realignments and demographic patterns is that the United States will move in the direction of Central and South American oligarchic politics common to those regions. A number of factors make this a reasonable assertion. For one, a likely decline in the productivity of the laboring classes will undoubtedly increase demands for greater government support. Rising crime rates and threats from terrorism will demand greater government spending on law enforcement. The attempt to maintain the current world military dominance will add to that burden. All of which will drive up taxes on the shrinking proportion of the population who pay the overwhelming portion of those taxes. Given the huge number of unknowns, it is almost impossible to predict how these changes will play out in the political arena. A growing lower class, including an expanded underclass, coinciding with a diminishing middle class and a concentration of wealth in a declining privileged class, certainly suggest a political climate similar to many of the autocratic regimes of Central and South America. A similar parallel is suggested by the ethnic makeup of the social classes, with blacks and Hispanics dominating the poorer classes and whites and Asians dominating the wealthier classes. As discussed earlier, oligarchies arise when the poor so outnumber the well-off, that democracy becomes a palpable threat to the well-being of the upper classes.

Whether American institutions can forestall the sort of autocratic politics of Central and South America remains to be seen, but a rising population not accustomed to those traditional institutions and whose multicultural education in American schools tends to disparage traditional American values, makes it difficult to remain sanguine about the future of American democracy and its European cultural heritage.[29]

None of the above developments are in any sense inevitable. Reduced immigration would allow the United States to assimilate existing immigrant groups more effectively. That would allow the

United States to remain a relatively open and safe society and maintain its current, or even more generous education and social welfare provisions, provided there continue to be quite modest increases in productivity. The United States would no doubt have to deal with declining industrial and military power, relative to the rest of the world, but would still be able to sustain a very comfortable standard of living for its population, much as the European nations have done, at least until now, in the face of declining world influence.

United States: Foreign Relations

Leslie Gelb, President Emeritus of the Council of Foreign Relations, wrote recently in *Foreign Affairs* that, "The United States is declining as a nation and a world power, with mostly sighs and shrugs to mark this *seismic* event." (emphasis added) Gelb goes on to explain "The decline starts with weakening fundamentals in the United States. First among them is that the country's economy, infrastructure, public schools, and political systems have been allowed to deteriorate. The result has been diminished economic strength, a less vital democracy, and a mediocrity of spirit."[30] While Gelb seems correct in his assessment, he chose not to provide any explanation for this decline, but limited himself to what he argues is the second reason for the decline in American influence, namely, "how ineffectively the United States has used its international power, thus allowing its own and others' problems to grow and fester."[31]

He argues that America's position can be much improved by a more reasonable foreign policy. This is a sanguine view indeed, given the demographic evidence previously stated. Those demographics suggest that in the future American educational performance will decline, social trust, harmony, and faith in American institutions will decline, as will economic productivity. All of these factors will necessarily reduce American influence in the world, no matter how wise our leaders are in directing our foreign policy.

Most of these problems arise out of the massive immigration of the last four decades and are unlikely to be reversed. As discussed earlier, it is reasonable to expect an IQ decline from an average of 96 to 93 over the next 40 years. The distinguished political scientist Samuel Huntington, in his acclaimed *Clash of Civilizations*, argues that the end of the Cold War has resulted in the emergence of a new world order in which national coalitions will tend to form along the lines of the world's major civilizations. The exigencies of the Cold War produced alliances between nations having little in common other than their commitment or opposition to Communism. The West found itself in alliances with various regimes in the Middle East, Asia, and Africa, whereas the Communist coalition also found itself tied up in the same places and in an uneasy alliance between the Soviet Union and China.

Huntington argues that the end of the Cold War meant that countries have begun to align themselves along lines of religion and other cultural affinities. He says the world is quickly becoming a multipolar world composed of eight major civilizations.[32] These are listed in Table 8.1 along with their proportion of the world's territory in 1993 and projected proportion of the world's population in 2025 (the category *Other* includes a variety of small independent societies not associated with any major civilization):

TABLE 8.1. THE MAJOR WORLD CIVILIZATIONS

Civilization	% of Territory	% of Population[33]
Western	24.2%	10.1%
African	10.8%	14.4%
Sinic	7.5%	21.0%
Hindu	2.4%	16.9%
Islamic	21.1%	19.2%
Japanese	0.3%	1.5%
Latin America	14.9%	9.2%
Orthodox	13.7%	4.9%
Other	5.2%	2.8%

The category *Western* includes Western Europe, the United States, and those countries such as Australia and Canada settled by Europeans. By *Sinic* civilization, Huntington includes China and closely related societies. *Orthodox* civilization refers to those countries whose primary religious tradition is orthodox Christianity, including Russia and much of Eastern Europe. Huntington argues that three of these, namely, the Western, Sinic, and Islamic civilizations, will dominate world affairs, based on their share of world population and their wealth, and that world peace will be dependent on relations between them. Hindu civilization has a very large population, but controls very little territory and is primarily situated in India, and will be hindered in its influence because of the enormous heterogeneity of India's population, including a large Muslim minority. The other civilizations are unlikely to play dominant roles, according to Huntington, and will influence world affairs mainly in their tendency to join with one or another of the three major civilizations in times of conflict based, in large measure, on their momentary interests or by their conquest by one of the major civilizations. For instance, it is difficult to determine how much independence Japan will be able to maintain given its small population and its proximity to the colossus that China is becoming. In Huntington's words, the "dangerous clashes of the future are likely to arise from the interaction of Western arrogance, Islamic intolerance, and Sinic assertiveness."[34]

In addition, Huntington points out that Western Civilization is aging and has begun to lose the dynamism that drove its growth for 500 years. In contrast, both China and the Muslim world are undergoing dynamic change, with Muslim populations growing rapidly and possessing a large number of people in the youth bulge. The dynamism of Muslim societies is unlikely to be based on the rapid economic progress that China and India will likely undergo, but rather on its fervent attachment to Militant Islam, its large youthful and restive population and its ambition to reassert itself after its dominance and colonization by the West, a domination it continues to view with considerable resentment.[35]

In contrast to Islam, Chinese civilization does not have a history of expansionism beyond its immediate sphere of influence, but rather was generally content to maintain its hegemony in the Far East. Whether that tradition will continue in a resurgent China remains to be seen. One factor which may play a role in this is the extraordinary sex imbalance that has developed in China since it began enforcing its "one child" policy in the 1980s. The normal sex ratio at birth for humans is about 108 males to 100 females. Eric Caculinao, writing in 2004, reported that the ratio in China had reached 120 to 100, resulting from prenatal sex determination and selective abortion. Data from the 2000 census indicated that there were 19 million more boys than girls in the 0–15 age group. Caculinao cites the work of scholars that "the vast army of surplus males could pose a threat to China's stability. Low status adult males unable to marry are "much more prone to attempt to improve their situation through violent and criminal behavior in a strategy of coalitional violence."[36] While not mentioned in the article, it hardly needs saying that such a large army of young bachelors would welcome the opportunity to venture abroad in search of women, whether in overseas peaceful activities or as part of a conquering army. In any case, it suggests that China may develop a more expansionist posture, if only to maintain peace within its own borders.

Whether it moves in that direction or not, China is likely to react quite powerfully to any interference with its Asian hegemony by any competing civilization. According to Huntington, the main source of world disorder in the coming century is likely to come from Muslim civilization. This prediction is based on the recent history of conflicts in the world, the majority of which have involved conflicts between Muslim states and civil disorders in states with large Muslim minorities. According to Huntington, "Muslims make up about one-fifth of the world's population, but in the 1990s they have been far more involved in intergroup violence than the people of any other civilization. The evidence is overwhelming."[37] Huntington provides numerical evidence for this assertion and, in addition, demonstrates that Islamic societies tend to be much more militaristic than other civilizations in terms of the proportion of their population in military service and the proportion of their wealth devoted to military ends.[38]

Given the changing world order envisioned by Samuel Huntington, the United States will find it difficult to maintain its expansive foreign policy in the face of the rising military power of China. This concern may come to a head if serious military confrontations are threatened by potential conflicts with China over the status of Taiwan, over China's increasing economic expansion in Africa and China's attempt to woo Middle East tyrants in an effort to assure their huge and growing energy needs. The United States will be poorer and less able to support such a policy. It may also be smaller, in population and geography, if some of the Southwestern States secede as independent nations or rejoin Mexico. Such concerns have given rise in some circles to the idea of the formation of a North American Union, composed of the United States, Canada, and Mexico in order to bolster the industrial base of the United States and its ability to sustain its military superiority. Such a North American Union would have a population of almost 600 million by 2050, but it would only exacerbate the current income and educational disparities among racial groups, and in any case would have less than half the population of China, and with far fewer individuals with strong intellectual capacities. The most obvious consequence of these demographic changes in the world is that any attempt by the United States to maintain its current economic and military dominance in the world will be futile; counterproductive at best, disastrous at worst.

Writing in *Foreign Affairs*, Andrew Krepinevich argues that the U. S. will have to seriously rethink its military preparedness and strategy in a world with declining American influence. In particular, it must eliminate *wasting assets* designed for the Cold War and devote its resources to confront the new dangers America faces, especially from growing Chinese strength and irregular forces such as terrorist organizations.[39] Furthermore, the United States will be unable to receive much assistance from other states with which it is allied. "Even absent the global economic crisis, U. S. allies such as France, Germany, Japan, and the United Kingdom are saddled with aging populations and burdensome social welfare systems, leaving ever fewer resources available for contributing to collective security."[40] In other words, the defense of the West will rest almost entirely on the shoulders of the United States. But the declining relative wealth of the United States may make that defense increasingly unlikely and its foreign policy is likely to become more restrained and directed mainly in the defense of its own homeland. Europe may find that if it comes into conflict with any other major civilization it will have to rely more on its own resources.

This new set of circumstances means that American policy makers will have to reorient government priorities to avoid the potential for serious social disorder among its disparate ethnic groups in ways that are sure to be resisted by important and powerful interest groups. For instance, the military would have to be reduced and its main task redefined in terms of deterring foreign attack. Almost all overseas bases would have to be closed and military intervention abroad ended. Failure to do so would lead to an enormous reduction in the funds necessary for important social programs. In addition, the shape of social programs will have to undergo vast changes and wasteful programs in education, for instance, dramatically reduced. Social welfare provisions, such as Social Security and Medicare, will in all likelihood have to be means–tested, and limited to the very poor. The United States will simply lack the resources to make do on all the promises it has made This will be true even if the current economic downturn of 2008–2009 is short-lived. If it remains persistent, then the need for policy reorientation will be even more severe and onerous, and action will be needed sooner. Failure to take such actions in an attempt to maintain current levels of expenditure will almost certainly produce high levels of inflation that will only exacerbate problems, driving up the cost of living in large measure since so much domestic spending is on imported goods that will rise in price with a devalued dollar.

Failure to recognize the changes needed in current national priorities could produce disastrous consequences even if the United States had a highly homogeneous population. One hardly needs reminding that Communism and Fascism arose out of the economic disaster produced by World War I. While ethnic conflict played a role in the rise of those tyrannies, they arose, especially in Germany and Italy, in countries that were among the most advanced on Earth, and both were ethnically homogenous. (The Jews in Germany represented a minuscule part of the population). The consequences of economic decline for a multicultural society could be much more severe. The reason is that growing economic disparities will tend to fall along ethnic lines, creating the potential for resentments that may well be expressed violently. As discussed earlier, such violence was a prominent feature of the riots in Los Angeles where black and Hispanic rioters targeted the businesses of Asians and Koreans, in particular. It is also apparent in the violent rivalry between black and Hispanic gangs in many major cities with large black and Hispanic populations.

European Union: Domestic Impact

The difficulties Europe faces are very different from those faced by the United States. Whereas the United States is home to a very large percentage of non-European individuals who make up about one third of the population, with 27% being either black or Hispanic, the number of non-Europeans in Western Europe is a much smaller percentage of their total population. In the 15 countries of Western Europe, only about 18 million are non-European.[41] This is fewer than 5% of the total in these 15 countries, of whom a majority (15 million) is Muslim and make up about 4% of the population.[42] In addition, large numbers of immigrants come from nations with various cultural and political traditions, such as India, Pakistan, Turkey, Morocco, Algeria, and a variety of sub-Saharan African countries. One consequence of this is that Europe lacks a large population from a single neighboring country as is the case in United States in relation to Mexico, with radical Hispanic spokesman expressing a desire to establish sufficient control in some states that might allow them to secede or join in union with Mexico. While secession may be an unlikely possibility in the United States, no such possibility exists, at least at present, in Europe.

The main problem confronting European countries is the difficulty of assimilating Muslim immigrants and their children, many of whom express no desire to adapt to European practices and values. This has proved especially troublesome in France, with a Muslim population of six million people or 10% of the total population. But it has also created problems in countries such as England, Germany, the Netherlands, and the Scandinavian countries with much smaller Muslim populations, in the range of 3%. Part of the problem, as demonstrated in Chapter 7, is the overall poor educational and economic performance and high crime rates among Muslims. In comparison, the Muslim population in the United States of about 3 million people represents only about 1% of the total. The problem is compounded in Europe by the aggressive stance taken by Muslim leaders in their efforts to preserve the religious values of their faith, especially their attitudes about the place of women and a tendency to see European values and Europeans as enemies of Islam. The attitudes of Muslims reviewed in Chapter 7 suggest that a sizable number of young Muslims hold such negative views and are unwilling to accept assimilation.

This problem is likely to grow under European Union policies that promote continued Muslim immigration and make it difficult for individual countries to control their own immigration policies. Even were these policies to be reversed, the proportion of Muslims in Europe would continue to grow significantly, due mainly to large differences in fertility rates between Muslims and Europeans. Even should Muslim fertility decline, it is unlikely to match the extremely low levels for Europeans. Furthermore, the Muslim population of Europe will grow enormously if Turkey is admitted to the EU, an idea currently supported by many EU leaders, and also promoted by the United States.[43] Turkey has a population of about 75 million, 99% of whom are Muslim, which is five times the current Muslim population of Europe. Furthermore, Turkey's population is projected to rise to more than 100 million by the year 2050, while Europe's native European population is expected to decline.[44] With the admission of Turkey, the Muslim population of the EU would come to represent about 20% immediately and would grow considerably over the next four decades. This is the main reason that most European citizens express a strong disapproval of the admission of Turkey. In 2007, a poll of French voters showed that only 16% supported the admission of Turkey to the EU.[45]

With the admission of Turkey, and high Muslim fertility rates, the Muslim minority in Europe may well exceed the proportion of Hispanics in the United States by mid-century. Currently, 40% of the newborns in France are born to Arab and African immigrants.[46] As reported earlier, the great majority of these are Muslim. In England the Muslim birthrate is three times the rate for native Englishmen and Mohammad is likely to be the most popular boys name in London in the near future.[47] It is also already the most popular boy's name in the nation of Belgium, and the cities of Amsterdam and Malmo, Sweden. In the Dutch city of Rotterdam, 40% of the current population is Muslim.[48] By the end of the century the EU, or at least a number of EU countries, may well contain a majority Muslim population, meaning that those who have expressed fear of the Islamization of Europe are hardly paranoid lunatics. A continuation of current trends, in conjunction with the admission of Turkey to the EU, makes this eventuality almost a certainty by the end of the century. This trend is exacerbated by a growing tendency of native Europeans to emigrate to countries such as Australia, New Zealand, Canada, and the United States. Paul Belien, writing in the *Washington Times* in 2007, reported that 200,000 English, 155,000 Germans, 130,000 Dutch, and 50,000 Swedes left Europe as emigrants during the preceding year. High taxes and lack of opportunity is often cited as a reason to leave, but as in important is a sense of alienation from the changing culture of Europe brought on by the massive immigration of recent decades.[49] These emigration figures are hardly trivial. The Netherlands has a total population of 16.4 million people, and Sweden a population of 9 million.[50] This is especially serious because the people leaving are generally young in their childbearing years, meaning that the demographic trends of this phenomenon exaggerate an already serious problem.

The admission of Turkey would especially compound the problems of those nations attempting to reduce Muslim influence, since as EU citizens, Turkish Muslims would, under the Amsterdam Treaty, have the right to settle and establish citizenship in any EU country. Denmark, for instance, with a population of only 5 million people, which has been trying to limit Muslim immigration, could be transformed into a Muslim-dominated country. Such an apparently unlikely outcome could become a reality if radical and influential Muslim leaders target small countries like Denmark, and promote extensive immigration to them with the express purpose, one often openly stated, of establishing Muslim outposts in Western Europe governed by *sharia* law. These possibilities, while they are very troublesome, even feared, by most Europeans, seem to be of no concern to the bureaucrats, judicial authorities, and politicians who control EU policies, and include the full support of left-wing European academics. On the issue of the admission of Turkey, for instance, European leaders see benefits in "future economic growth, a stronger EU foreign policy, and energy security." The general public, on the other hand, whose oppose the admission of Turkey, fear "the loss of jobs, the threat of terrorism, and the weakening of national culture."[51]

In the face of popular opposition, European elites continue in their efforts to limit the ability of individual countries to control immigration and are increasingly autocratic in dealing with those who oppose these policies. As reviewed in Chapters 1 and 7, any such criticisms are open to various legal restrictions on both civil and criminal grounds, and the ruling parties have attempted to delegitimize those political parties supporting immigration restrictions, such as the BNP in England and the *Vlamms Belang* in Belgium. A good part of these policies appear designed to appease Middle East regimes because of energy dependence. In addition, it is difficult to deny that the enormous wealth controlled by many individuals in that region can influence European politicians.

The appeasement by many Western governments of the militant Islam preached in local mosques also represents an attempt to appease the potentially violent Muslims in their cities. It is hard, otherwise, to explain the tolerance of civil anarchy which is a regular feature of Muslim riots in the *banlieues* in various French cities. During the invasion of Gaza by Israel, in late 2008, a very large number of Muslim protest rallies took place in many European cities and a number of these turned violent and revealed an extraordinary degree of anti-Semitism. In the city of Nice in France, for instance, protestors rioted and looted cars and business establishments in a massive demonstration of civil disorder. Police responded fairly weakly, as is common in France.

What is perhaps most indicative of the views of French authorities was that the Prefect of Alps-Maritimes denied permission for a rally in Nice organized to protest the inaction of the authorities to the riots of the previous week. The rally, to be held under the name "Masters in our Own Land," was disallowed on the grounds that it was likely to lead to civil disorder.[52]

It is important to emphasize that the growing Muslim presence and influence in Western Europe has not as yet had much effect in Eastern Europe, in the region that Huntington defines as the home of Orthodox civilization, though of course the breakup of Yugoslavia has led to the rise of the Muslim dominated areas and states in the Balkans. It is too early to tell if Eastern Europe will also become a magnet for Muslim immigration, but it may well become one if its economy grows in strength. It should be noted, however, that the conflict between the Muslim and Christian Orthodox civilizations has a long and bloody history. Open conflict between Islam and Eastern Orthodox Europe continued long after it had come to an end in Western Europe. Spain conquered its Muslim population in 1492, while as recently as 1683, the Muslim world made a concerted effort, in the siege of Vienna, to invade the eastern heart of Europe. It is difficult to determine what influence Russia will have on the region's immigration policies. Russia itself, which continues to grapple with Muslim populations in regions such as Chechnya, is unlikely to welcome Muslim immigration.

Most elites in Europe argue that there is no fundamental contradiction between the maintenance of a strong religious attachment to Islamic beliefs and full assimilation into European society. Many argue that, over the course of time, future generations will gradually assimilate into the European states, and that will be accompanied by a liberalization of Muslim attitudes and practices, much as have the Jews in the course of the 20th century. The Jews during that century divided themselves into three distinct groups: the Orthodox, the Conservative and the Reform movements, with only the Orthodox maintaining strict adherence to traditional practices. Why should this pattern not be followed by Muslim immigrants? What would prevent Muslims from maintaining their religious identity and at the same time adopting a powerful allegiance to their countries of residence and its secular values and practices, which has been the common pattern among Jews in Europe and the United States? There are a number of reasons, however, why this parallel may not be appropriate.

In this regard, it is important to note that Judaism has undergone centuries of revision, codified in the lengthy texts and commentaries of the Talmud, and studied by all serious orthodox Jews, which defines their everyday practice and also the relationship of Jews with the civil authorities in the nations in which they reside. During these centuries of revision, most of the barbaric practices prescribed in ancient texts, such as the stoning of women for adultery and the right to polygamy by men, were revised and are no longer sanctioned by even the most fundamentalist Jews. In Israel, where they have considerable influence, the orthodox religious parties are severely curtailed by secular authority, since they have never managed to achieve widespread support among the voting populace. They maintain control over marriage and funeral practices, for instance, but have no control over the sale of nonkosher food items, or the enforcement of Sabbath rules, and virtually no influence on judicial practice or criminal punishment. There is little doubt that they would attempt to control everyday life in Israel if they could attain majority status, but that is a very remote, almost impossible, outcome.

There are other differences between Jews and Muslims, which make the Jewish experience in the West an unlikely example of the fate of Muslim immigrants. For one, the Jewish population never made up more than a tiny fraction of the population of any nation. Even where Jews have great influence, such as in America, they make up perhaps 3% of the population; almost all of them are either completely secular or of Conservative or Reformed faith. A second factor is that the Muslim religious tradition is of more recent origin and its sacred texts have not been reconstructed as have Jewish texts. Muslim religious practice has remained virtually unchanged over the centuries, even though Muslims are divided into a variety of competing branches, such as the Sunnis and the Shiites, which differ in their interpretations of the holy texts. Those differences are very narrow, however, and very few of them could be said to have been liberalized to the extent that has been the case among the Jews. The harsh dictates of *sharia* law, which many view as barbaric by modern standards, have remained basically unaltered, and are fully sanctioned by highly regarded religious authorities. Sexual transgressions and apostasy are still punishable by death, and polygamy is tolerated, as are a host of limitations on the freedom of women in Islamic states governed in whole or in part by *sharia* law. Furthermore, the overwhelming majority of Jews follow teachings that recognize fully the distinction between church and state. Islam, in contrast, recognizes no such distinction. Of course, large numbers of Muslims do not practice their religion and do not attend services at mosques. But as the polls discussed in Chapter 7 indicate, a majority of Muslims take their religion very seriously and the tendency to do so increases among younger Muslims, many of whom were born on European soil.

Another important distinction between Jewish and Muslim populations is that prior to the establishment of Israel there was no nation supporting Jewish communities worldwide and even today, while Jews have a high regard for Israel, it has only limited ability to influence the practices of Jewish communities outside of Israel. Just the opposite is the case for Muslims, who dominate a very large number of countries with a total population of more than one billion people. Many states, such as Saudi Arabia and Iran, have large populations that are expected to reach respectively 50 million and 80 million people by 2050. Both of these states are dominated by rulers who support fundamentalist Islam and promote the spread of fundamentalist doctrines. Saudi Arabia supports mosques and religious schools throughout the world with enormous amounts of money. It is no secret that Iran is supportive of terrorist organizations worldwide, nor is it a secret that almost all the terrorists who attacked the world Trade Center were Saudis. Pakistan, with powerful fundamentalist elements, has a population of about 160 million which is expected to grow to more than 300 million by 2050. Indonesia, a Muslim country, is projected to have a population of 285 million by 2050.[53] In all of these countries there are large fundamentalist constituents who follow the Islamic doctrine of Jihad that requires the spread of the Islamic faith, by force, if necessary, and who would certainly welcome the conversion of European countries to Muslim control.

The Koran recognizes a fundamental distinction between the Land of Peace, controlled by Muslims (*Dar al-Islam*) and the Land of War (*Dar al-Harb*) controlled by non-Muslim infidels. According to Serge Trifkovic, "this is the most important legacy of Mohammad. Ever since his time, Islam has been a permanent challenge to all non-Muslim polities around it."[54] According to Trifkovic, fundamentalist imams preach that Islam is at war with the non-Muslim world and fighting violently for the spread of the Dar al-Islam is a spiritual requirement and dying in the effort opens the gates of heaven to all such martyrs. This is why almost all countries with sizable Muslim populations are invariably torn by religious strife and religiously motivated terrorism.[55] This was the point made by Samuel Huntington cited earlier.[56] While very few Muslims answer the call to Jihad, many otherwise peaceful Muslims sympathize with this violent impulse in their coreligionists. The polls reported in Chapter 7 indicate the extent of this sympathy among many young Muslims living in Europe. In contrast, the Jewish faith does not encourage or support efforts to proselytize among non-Jews and, in fact, its orthodox adherents make conversion a difficult process. Christians, of course, do proselytize but have long since abandoned efforts to convert non-Christians by coercive practices.

A last important distinction between Jews and Muslims is that Jews maintained their fundamentalist practices mainly in those European communities where they were severely repressed by civil authorities. Wherever those restrictions were limited, Jews prospered mightily, and in Western Europe and the United States in the 20th century, especially, this tended to promote assimilation, with most Jews eventually abandoning orthodoxy. Where orthodox practice conflicted with social and economic mobility, most Jews chose social mobility, especially in liberal democracies where Jews ceased to fear persecution and no longer felt the need for protective communities. The case among most Muslims is different. As already discussed, many Muslims lack the human resources to achieve economic success and that severely limits their ability to fully assimilate into Western societies. That lack of success can be used, and is used, by religious demagogues to argue that Muslims suffer discrimination and must band together as a group for reasons of social advancement. A consequence of these preachings, especially common among Wahhabi Imams and supported by Saudi Arabia, is to create hostility to the West and a resistance to assimilation.

For all these reasons, the modern Jewish pattern of assimilation is an unlikely model for Muslim assimilation. Muslim populations in Europe are growing rapidly and an openly Muslim separatist movement will, given current trends, become a palpable threat. In fact, as discussed in Chapter 7, separatist sentiments are already common in various European Muslim communities.

All of which begs the question of where Europe is headed. Under its current leadership, the EU seems destined to become more and more influenced by a growing Muslim presence and these are trends very much unwelcomed by most Europeans. It needs to be stressed that as the Muslim population grows, the average IQ of the EU will decline, bringing with it problems in education already apparent in the data presented in Chapter 7. With declining educational levels, productivity will not rise as rapidly as it would otherwise. So far, immigration restrictionists, and others who oppose EU policies, have been entirely unsuccessful in gaining political influence. However, it should be kept in mind that the coming world dominance of China will have similar effects in Europe as in the United States, especially in the economic sphere. Unless Europe and the United States can drastically improve their productivity, they will, to an increasing extent, be reliant on China, and to a lesser extent on India and other emerging market producers for most of their advanced industrial goods. As these economies strengthen, and their wealth grows, so will their standard of living, and this is turn will mean rising wages and an increase in the cost of the consumer goods they export to the West. This will necessarily mean declining purchasing power on the part of Europeans and Americans and a declining relative, if not absolute, standard of living.

To the extent that the EU continues to encourage the immigration of poor Middle-Easterners who compete directly with European workers, the result will be increased discontent and civil unrest, which would be intensified in periods of economic recession and rising unemployment. Furthermore, as the cost to support the large families of immigrants grows, taxes may need to be raised, which will further undercut the living standards of the average European, one consequence of which is continued or increased emigration from Europe. For those unable to emigrate, resistance to immigration is likely to grow and, in some countries, may lead to the ascendance of restrictionist parties who will promise to respond to these concerns, but will be stymied in their efforts by EU rules and directives. This is likely to lead some countries (Denmark seems a leading candidate) to demand autonomy in immigration matters as a basis for remaining in the EU. If such demands are not met, the pressure to withdraw from the EU will become almost irresistible. The alternative, perhaps the only alternative to the eventual Islamization of a number of European countries, will be withdrawal from the EU, presaging the dissolution of the EU itself. If, as is likely, there is a growing concern about the preservation of national values among more and more citizens, one can expect an increased sense of national identity among Europeans. One very dangerous possibility is that Fascist-type movements may come to power, especially in those nations where Muslims make increasing demands for autonomy in, for instance, major cities such Amsterdam and Rotterdam, where Muslim populations are growing very rapidly, and may become majorities in the next decade. Such Fascist movements are much more likely during periods of economic stress. In addition, if crime rates among Muslims continue at current levels and civil disorders become more common, the rise of nationalistic law and order candidates might well become inevitable, especially if the current political elites continue to ignore and suppress the desires and interests of the populace. The result may be the sort of ethnic civil strife that broke out in Yugoslavia and brought the dissolution of that multiethnic state.

It is quite unfathomable why the EU leadership fails to anticipate these potentially catastrophic possibilities, and fails to respond to popular concerns with more moderate immigration policies. One possible explanation for these perverse policies that has been put forward by highly regarded scholars, such as Samuel Huntington, is that the current leadership of the EU is composed of left-wing authoritarians who are enemies of the Western liberal tradition. According to Huntington, "Multiculturalism is in its essence anti-European... "and opposes its civilization.[57] The official repression of dissent and pursuance of unpopular policies by undemocratic means suggests that such ideologues wish to turn the EU into a centrally controlled empire similar to the Soviet Union. If that is the case, then their current policies make a good deal of sense, in that they flood the continent with people who have lived under autocratic regimes and never lived in democratic republics. Such people may well be willing to tolerate repressive regimes provided they can maintain a moderate standard of living and their own traditional religious practices. As Huntington points out, imperial regimes often promote ethnic conflict among their minority citizens to strengthen the power of the central authority, with the not unrealistic claim that a powerful central authority is essential to maintain civil order.[58] But if that is the case, then Europe will be transformed into an authoritarian and illiberal multiethnic empire, undemocratic, economically crippled and culturally retrograde. Is it any wonder that so many see Europe as committing suicide and its end coming "not with a bang, but a whimper?"[59]

European Union: Foreign Relations

Muslim Immigration not only threatens social harmony in Europe, but it complicates foreign policy. The danger to Europe in this area comes from two sources, both of which relate to communication in the modern world. Modern media, television in particular, vividly portrays the problems of people in various parts of the world and draws out the sympathy of related groups of people. This is clear in the enormous and near unanimous sympathy that Muslims, including almost all in Europe, have toward the problems of the Palestinians and their clear anger at the United States for its military involvement in Iraq and Afghanistan. For this reason, any conflict between Europe and any Muslim country is likely to draw out sympathy and support for the Muslim side by many, perhaps most, of the Muslims in Europe. Put bluntly, in any military conflict between Europe and some state in the Muslim world, Europe has to deal with the threat of a potentially dangerous third column in its midst. The second source of danger to Europe is that actions taken against Muslim citizens in Europe are likely to produce powerful reactions in the Muslim world. An example of this second danger was the violent reaction to the Danish cartoon episode (which included the destruction of a Danish embassy) and the showing of the Geert Wilders film *Fitna*, both of which were seen as major insults to the basic tenets of Islamic faith.

These incidents were provoked by the work of individuals and in no way represented official actions on the part of any EU state, and in fact were repudiated by most European leaders. Europe has to be concerned about the likely consequence of European state actions or laws which are seen as oppressive by their Muslim inhabitants, such as banning the *burka* (the total covering of the female, including the face) to promote assimilation or for reasons of security. In 2004, France passed a law banning any conspicuous religious symbols, such as headscarves or crosses, from state schools and government offices. In the summer of 2009, the French parliament was debating a ban on the *burka* in any public place and had the full support of French President Sarkozy.[60] The ban on headscarves drew complaints from some Muslim countries, but these have resulted in no major protests or other actions by them. However, if Muslim fundamentalism should grow in Europe, a greater number of Muslims may see the ban on fundamentalist dress as a constraint on their religious practice. This might result in more serious reactions in the Muslim countries of the world, such as those produced by the Danish cartoons. Additional problems could arise if European countries take more vigorous action to suppress the criminal activity of young Muslims or place greater restrictions on inflammatory rhetoric by Muslim clerics, or engage in greater surveillance of Muslims to detect terrorist activities, all of which might be viewed as oppressive by the Muslim community. Such concern would receive sympathetic responses among the people in Muslim countries, many of whom have relatives living in Europe, and it might result in protests in the form of mass demonstrations, boycotts of European products, and attacks against European residents in Muslim countries. The generally muted response of French authorities to the rapes, riots, and arson common in the Muslim *banlieues* may well reflect these concerns.

It is, furthermore, difficult to understand why Europe fails to consider the potential of a resurgent Islam and its potential to threaten Europe militarily. According to Samuel Huntington, writing in the mid-1990s, Islam and the West were already engaged in what he called a *quasi war*. It is a "quasi war because...it has been fought with limited means: terrorism on the one side and air-power, covert action, and economic sanctions on the other."[61] It is also a quasi war because "it has involved intermittent actions by one side that provoke responses by the other."[62] Huntington points out that "participants employ much more violent tactics against each other than the United States and the Soviet Union employed against each other in the Cold War. With rare exceptions, neither superpower purposely killed civilians or even the military belonging to the other." He cites U. S. Defense Department statistics showing that between 1980 and 1995 "the United States engaged in seventeen military operations in the Middle East, all of them directed against Muslims."[63] Huntington wrote those words before the bombing of the World Trade Center in September of 2001, the terrorist acts in London and Madrid, and the prolonged conflicts in Iraq and Afghanistan.

The clear hostility between Muslim civilization and Western civilization is a quasi war rather than a hot war because the Muslim Nations are simply incapable of mounting a creditable shooting war with the Western powers. In the parlance common today, the conflict is referred to as asymmetric warfare. The clearest example is the ongoing conflict between Israel and the Palestinians. The Palestinians attack Israel with primitive missiles and terror bombings, while Israel responds with modern tanks and aircraft. Israeli tactics are largely unsuccessful because they cannot eliminate the threat without severely harming the population who support the attacks and within whom the militants are embedded. Similar problems arise in the U. S. military efforts in Iraq and Afghanistan. In their various interventions in the Middle East, the West insists that it is not making war on Muslims per se, but rather against radical Muslim Islamist renegade groups and regimes who are not representative of the majority of Muslims. But as Huntington points out, there is no evidence for this view. "Protests against anti-Western violence have been totally absent in Muslim countries." Muslim countries, even those apparently friendly to the West, "have been strikingly reticent when it comes to condemning terrorist acts against the West."[64] According to Huntington, Trifkovic, and other knowledgeable observers, the enemy of the West is not "radical Islam" but Islam itself, whose core beliefs requires expanding dominion over unbelievers.

The open hostility toward the West explains the West's adamant resistance to the acquisition of nuclear weapons by Iran, and the very real concern about the stability of Pakistan, a huge Muslim nation with a sizable nuclear arsenal. In the eyes of most Muslims and most of their leaders, Western resistance to nuclear weapons in the Muslim Middle East, while it accepts a nuclear-armed Israel, is seen as a specific attempt to limit the power of the Islamic states, as indeed it is. Should Iran acquire nuclear weapons, it is likely that Saudi Arabia will soon follow in its footsteps and would have no difficulty doing so given its enormous wealth. In due course other Muslim countries would likely follow.[65]

One also has to reckon the potential that Turkey, which could become much less secular under an openly Islamic party, would also acquire nuclear weapons. Turkey has remained a secular state, due largely to the influence of the military and more moderate elements in the judiciary. For instance, it banned the wearing of any head covering in a university, including the *burka*, the *chador* (which is a hood that covers the neck) and even a simple headscarf tied under the chin. It has recently, under popular pressure, removed the last ban and allowed the wearing of simple headscarves.[66] However, the government's lifting of the ban was overruled by Turkey's Constitutional court.[67]

Popular sentiment in Turkey favors the Islamic parties and has often resulted in the military takeover of elected governments. In 2008, the Turkish Supreme Court ruled by a narrow majority against outlawing the ruling Justice and Development Party (AKP) led by Prime Minister of Turkey, Recep Erdogan. The Party, which won a landslide victory with 47% of the popular vote in 2007, was charged by state prosecutors on the grounds it included Islamist elements that threatened to undermine Turkey's secular constitution.[68] Given the worldwide Islamic resurgence, Turkey might well become an Islamic state. Perhaps this explains why EU leaders are attempting to bring Turkey into the European fold. This attempt to make Turkey European runs contrary to the sentiment of the Turkish population which clearly identifies itself as Muslim. Ironically, the same EU leaders who wish to admit Turkey insist that its admission requires that Turkey promote reforms so as to make it more democratic, a move that in all likelihood will lead to its Islamization. Europe's relation to Turkey is therefore fraught with difficulties. If, as many EU leaders desire, Turkey enters the EU, it will dramatically change European demographics and irrevocably undermine the Christian nature of Europe. If Turkey remains outside the EU, it could become a formidable enemy in some unforeseeable future conflict between Europe and the Muslim World.

The West claims that its opposition to nuclear weapons in the Middle East is based in a concern that they might find their way into terrorists' hands, which is clearly a legitimate concern. But perhaps even more of a concern is that Islamic states with nuclear arms would neutralize the overwhelming military superiority currently enjoyed by the West. It is not inconceivable that sometime in the not too distant future, alliances of Muslim states, including a major state such Iran, Pakistan, or Turkey, could pose a very real threat to large areas of Europe. Pakistan already has nuclear weapons, Iran is attempting to obtain them and Turkey could certainly do so if it wanted. All three countries have large and growing populations, and perhaps more important, large youthful populations. In addition, in any struggle between a Muslim country and a country in Europe, the huge populations of Muslim North Africa would be openly sympathetic with their Muslim brothers and many of their young men could be expected to volunteer in a holy war against the West. Against such a threat, an aging European population could not possibly match the manpower of Muslim armies, especially as the population gap between the Muslim and European civilization grows in the coming decades. In addition, the current overwhelming technological advantage of European armies over their Muslim counterparts cannot help but be eroded in the future. Already those armies are becoming increasingly effective, in large part through military assistance from China, which might see a benefit from a weakened Europe.

Such a conflict between Islam and the West could be triggered by any number of events. A conflict between Greece and Turkey over the status of Cypress is one. Another would be an attempt to expel the United States from Iraq and Afghanistan, if the United States, as seems likely at present, maintains military garrisons in those states well into the future. Or it could be triggered by Muslim extremism in European enclaves which brings down harsh reactions from European governments. While open war between the Muslim Middle East and Europe seems far-fetched at the current moment, it is the business of governments to anticipate all such contingencies and prepare for them. It is hard to believe that military analysts in Europe have not been playing out various scenarios which might threaten European security and the threat from the Middle East is, since the fall of the Soviet Union, clearly the most palpable of those threats. European leaders, after all, blundered into both World Wars and were totally unprepared for either their duration or their destructiveness. Are Europe's leaders today any more prepared than their predecessors?

Given their tolerance of a growing Muslim presence in their midst, the conclusion must be drawn that they are not. How would France, for instance, if involved in a war with a Muslim state, deal with an insurrection in their *banlieues* with large numbers of young men ready to die in the name of Islam, aided and abetted with arms from one or a number of Muslim states? They would be confronted with an intifada similar to the one undertaken by the Palestinians against the Israelis and they would be faced with the same dilemmas confronting Israel. How does one fight an enemy embedded in a civilian urban enclave? Hand-to-hand street fighting would produce enormous casualties on both sides, including many women and children. What part can tanks and airpower play in such a battle? Would French authorities be willing to level entire neighborhoods, killing large numbers of civilians? The Israelis have concluded that their only solution is to withdraw from Palestinian areas, and adopt a defensive military posture against hostile and aggressive enclaves on its borders. Would the French secede from the *banlieues* around Paris, effectively giving over authority in those areas to hostile and alien quasi governments, whose leaders would have a difficult time preventing militants from launching missiles into the heart of Paris?

The above possibilities have not been completely ignored by European authorities. Journalist Thomas Landen, writing in the *Brussels Journal*, repored, in 2008: "European security analysts were closely watching the Gaza War to see how Israel dealt with a hostile enclave from which rocket attacks are launched on Israeli territory within a 25 mile radius of Gaza." Landen goes on to comment:

> the center of Paris is within this radius from several surrounding ZUS [sensitive urban zones] surrounding the French capital. The Muslim-dominated district of Rosengard in the Swedish city of Malmo is just 21 miles from the Danish capital of Copenhagen... Denmark does not exclude the possibility that in the coming decades it may be compelled to raid Rosengard, as Israel was raiding Gaza earlier this year.[69]

The very possibility of such a scenario seems so absurd as to be almost laughable. But if actual military hostilities between some coalition of Muslim states and a nation such as Greece in southwestern Europe should arise, bringing in other nations under the NATO accords, the above scenario becomes not only possible, but likely, especially if the Muslim population should grow to encompass fully 25% of the French population, a not unlikely figure, given current trends. However unlikely such a nightmare scenario might currently appear, it is important to reiterate that European leaders managed to allow equally unimaginable nightmares to occur twice in the last century.

The Emerging World Order and the Place of Africa

There is a moral dimension that must be acknowledged in any discussion of immigration. Voluntary migration almost always involves people attempting to improve their lot. That is a human striving which is universally recognized and, almost as universally, one with which people sympathize. There is no physical reason why all the billions of the world's poor could not be accommodated by the world's wealthiest nations. Many rich nations, such as Australia, Canada, and New Zealand, are vastly underpopulated. Even the United States could accommodate a much larger population. The problem is whether those countries would remain wealthy and whether their inhabitants, both new immigrants and natives, would experience a better way of life. The position taken in this book is that such a massive migration would be impractical and would have primarily negative consequences. In any case, that is not the pattern common today. Rather, what is currently happening are very large internal and international migrations driven by population growth and by advanced inexpensive transportation.

The important question in this circumstance is whether the wealthier nations should limit immigration and whether they should be more selective in their immigration policies. It is clear from the data provided in earlier chapters that great majorities of people in the West desire reduced, more selective immigration, while governments, and the elites influencing governments, promote policies totally at variance with these desires.

The current wave of immigration to advanced countries, as large as it is, does not have a major impact on the great majority of the world's poor. However, most of the world's regions are making important economic advances which suggest that the gaping differences between developed and Third-World countries is likely to narrow. One major exception has been sub-Saharan Africa. Since Europe abandoned its African colonies, the African standard of living has deteriorated markedly and its infrastructure has fallen into disrepair. Researchers for the National Bureau of Economic Research argue that "there should be no doubt that the worst economic disaster of the 20th century is the dismal growth performance of the African Continent"[70] The authors point out that the economic performance of all of Africa, including North Africa, has been abysmal, but the performance of sub-Saharan Africa has been even worse. According to the authors, "today, per capita GDP for sub-Saharan Africa is 200 dollars smaller than it was in 1974, a decline of nearly 11% over a quarter of a century."[71]

Furthermore, even though world population grew rapidly in this period, "the total number of poor in the world declined from 1.3 billion in 1975 to 900 million in 2000. During this period of overall improvement, however, Africa's poor increased from fewer than 140 million in 1975 to more than 360 million in the year 2000." In addition, while poverty was in the past essentially an Asian problem, today it is largely an African one with about 42% of the poor of the world living in North and sub-Saharan Africa.[72] The primary reason for this decline, according to the authors, was a very low rate of private investment in Africa, largely because of the very low rate of return on investment, some one-third less than elsewhere.[73] The authors cite the endemic violence, corruption, and limited human capital resulting from very high disease rates and very low involvement in education. "Sub-Saharan Africa had a primary school enrollment of 40% in 1960, whereas North Africa had an average rate of 56%.... This contrasts with nearly 100% rate in OECD countries or East Asia."[74]

Not discussed in the report was the decolonization of Africa by Europeans. As long as Africa was controlled by Europeans, they were willing to invest in Africa since they knew their investments were protected by European force. Since decolonization and the loss of European control, such investment became far more risky and for that reason tended to dry up. The exceptions were, of course, South Africa and Southern Rhodesia (now Zimbabwe) which remained under European control until late in the 20th century and experienced robust growth. The end of European dominance in Zimbabwe has been nothing short of disastrous and current trends in South Africa suggests a similar fate may await that country.

Never mentioned in the economic problems of Africa is the very low average IQ of the continent that can produce very few people capable of innovation and entrepreneurial development. It means that African countries cannot develop sizable middle-class and well-educated populations, factors generally considered crucial for the development of democratic republican forms. In fact, most African states are autocratic, corrupt regimes led by intelligent but generally cruel dictators that in many respects resemble the early African states described in Chapter 4. They are rife with tribal rivalries that often result in genocidal war between groups, with male children often forced into fighting factions and where the killing is widespread and indiscriminate. Women come in for particularly brutal treatment; they are raped, tortured, horribly mutilated, and murdered for the clear purpose of terrorizing rival tribes and driving them from their territories.[75] Of course, this does not occur everywhere at all times, but it is, without question, an endemic element of life in many African countries.

The difference in the success of various countries in the transition to the industrial way of life is very much related to national IQ. Richard Lynn and Tatu Vanhanen, in their *IQ and Global Inequality*, calculated a correlation coefficient or $r = 0.68$ between IQ and per capita GDP (Gross National product) for the 113 countries for which they had direct measures of national IQ.[76] This is a remarkably large relationship for research in the social sciences. It is even more remarkable when one considers that many of the countries with high average IQ, such as China, were economically crippled by Communist policies, which have only recently, in large part, been abandoned. It also includes countries from the Middle East, for instance, with relatively low IQs and very high GDPs resulting from oil wealth. Lynn and Vanhanen argue that the relationship between IQ and wealth holds "because the intelligence of a population determines the efficiency with which work is performed throughout the economy." In addition, they expect this relationship to be magnified in the modern era because "nations with highly intelligent populations can make and market complex technological goods like computers, aircraft, televisions, automobiles, etc. that sell well in world markets." On the other hand, countries with fewer high IQ people are limited to marketing "less cognitively demanding goods such as clothing, and agricultural products for which there is a world surplus, and hence command only low prices in world markets."[77]

The population of sub-Saharan Africa (excluding the North African Arab countries) in 2009 was approximately 800 million.[78] Given the average IQ of the natives of that continent, which is approximately 70, this means that, given the normal distribution or bell curve, only about 0.5% of Africans will surpass an IQ of 110, which was previously defined as the threshold for college success. This represents a total of about 4 million people. By way of comparison, the United States, with an average IQ of 96and with one third the population of Africa, has approximately 52 million people who surpass the 110 threshold. Many talented Africans, furthermore, never achieve their full potential because of the limited educational opportunities in Africa, especially in those countries torn by civil strife, and the very limited educational opportunities for women. The actual number of people receiving advanced training is, therefore, only a fraction of 4 million, the size of which is very difficult to determine, but it is not likely to exceed 1 million. This is the pool of people from which almost all leaders, professionals, businessmen and competent bureaucrats, teachers and engineers must be drawn in a continent fast approaching a population of 1 billion. A large number of this very limited pool of talented people is induced to escape the disorder and corruption in African countries by migrating to the more advanced countries of the West. According to Richard Lynn, poor nutrition and other environmental factors account for a good part of the very low African IQ; he estimates that it would rise to about 80 if Africans grew up in an environment similar to Europeans.[79] However, given the current misrule and civil strife in Africa, it is difficult to see how this nutritional deficit can be appreciably reduced. The evidence is, in fact, that nutrition has been falling in the postcolonial era. It is difficult to see how Africa can possibly advance given this set of circumstances.

The most humanitarian solution for Africa might well be the return of colonialism to restore order and reasonable administration to those countries thereby facilitating a vast growth in foreign investment. Future historians may view Europe's abandonment of their African colonies as one of the crueler consequences of Europe's fratricidal wars in the twentieth century. Among Western elites, however, the idea of a return of colonialism is viewed as an obscenity and there is hardly any possibility it will be tried by any Western nation, even in the unlikely case that the African people should be amenable to such a movement.

It is important to emphasize that the northern tier of black African states bordering on the Arab states of North Africa, including the northern coasts of East and West Africa, are almost all Muslim in their population. For instance, Somalia on the east coast is 100% Muslim and the Sudan, bordering on Egypt, is 70% Muslim. Mauritania and the Western Sahara on the west coast are almost completely Muslim. A major exception in the north is Ethiopia with a 30% Muslim population. Nigeria, the largest country in Africa, with 130 million people, is 50% Muslim. This makes it virtually impossible for Europeans to play much of a role in these states, but it is not unlikely that Arab Muslim countries may take on a quasi colonization role, though according to the report discussed above, the Muslim North Africans have hardly performed well and would be unlikely to improve conditions in black Africa.

On the other hand, the countries in the southern portion of Africa, including the Congo, Angola, Zambia, Zimbabwe, and South Africa have very few Muslims, and might more easily undergo something akin to a new colonial movement.[80] Current trends suggest that China, which has much to gain by African colonies, may take on such a role. China is currently greatly expanding its economic activities in Africa, but has been doing so by accommodating African leaders, including some with Muslim leadership, engaging in a form of crony capitalism.[81] As the Chinese presence grows, as it surely will, China may take a more active political role through the installation and support of less corrupt African leaders. Such foreign rule by proxy may in time find adherents among Africans if it markedly improves their economic circumstances, reduces disease, and the endemic violence in the continent that makes life for so many Africans one of great suffering. Such a Chinese expansion in Africa is likely to be resisted by a resurgent Islam expanding into Africa from the North.[82]

In other words, central Africa may be a fault line (to use Huntington's terminology) between the growing and rival civilizations of China and Islam. China's overwhelming technological advantages over the Muslim countries may not be sufficient to deter a nuclear-armed Muslim world filled with angry young men hoping for martyrdom. For China, such a war on the African continent would offer an outlet for its millions of young bachelors hungry for wives. What part, if any, would Europe with a large, possibly majority, Muslim population play in such a conflict? Where would Indonesia and Pakistan fit in? And lastly, what part, if any, would the United States play? While such a potential world-encompassing conflict appears remote at present, it may not seem so remote in a rapidly industrializing world competing for what may be declining essential raw materials, of which Africa is a primary repository.

Conclusions

If the United States and Europe continue with the policies that have been outlined in the sections above, it will mean that Western civilization will go into inexorable decline and may eventually cease to exist in any meaningful way. This returns us to the question posed at the very beginning of this book: why is this happening and why is it happening now? The answer given throughout this book is that the reasons lie in the influence of patently false ideas, ideas promoted by intellectuals for a variety of reasons, not least of which have been a desire to increase their influence on world affairs and thereby their own power. In effect it has been a *Treason of the Intellectuals,* the name of the 1927 book by the French writer, Julien Benda. The treason to which he was referring was the abandonment by the intellectual class of the disinterested search for truth in favor of using scholarship to promote political ends. When he wrote in 1927, those political ends involved promoting the passionate nationalism and ethnic identity that led to World War I and which, he predicted, would result in even greater violence in the future. The intellectual's greatest crime was the abandonment of the ideals of the enlightenment that had promoted the idea that there were universal truths which could become known to men by disinterested research and the replacing of those universal ideals with a Nietzschean *will to power* and a nihilism that only recognized the utility of knowledge to advance political ends.

According to Benda, intellectuals demonstrated a "desire to debase the values of knowledge before the values of action."[83]

He was particularly critical of the intellectuals' efforts to politicize almost all issues, and to enlist the masses in the antidemocratic mass movements of Fascism and Communism. "It may be said that to-day there is scarcely a mind in Europe which is not affected—or thinks itself affected—by a racial or class or national passion, and most often by all three."[84] Since Benda's time the power of intellectuals has grown, as has their political agenda, and today, as much as in his time, they have adopted a much more open stance that the truth must take second place to what they view as virtuous political ends. This is, of course, what we know today as political correctness. As discussed in the first chapter, this phrase came into use under Communism and meant simply that all ideas must conform to and support the agenda of the Communist movement. History and philosophy were the first to be forced into line. But as is clear from the career of the biologist Trofim Lysenko, science was also made to conform. Psychiatry and psychology were corrupted so that those who dissented from the ideas of Communist doctrine were judged to be psychologically imbalanced and confined to mental institutions.

Today, of course, the ruling ideology of the intellectuals is an absolute egalitarianism which recognizes no idea, work of art, or historical analysis as better than any other. It argues that all histories are *narratives* fabricated for some class or race advantage. Many argue that even science is corrupted by its patriarchal and European roots and serves to justify the subjugation of one group by another. This all-encompassing egalitarianism gives rise to a nihilistic relativism in which no work of art, no cultural value or practice is better or worse than any other, and to suggest otherwise is to be intolerant of human difference and demonstrate an unwillingness to show due respect to the *other,* to illegitimately *privilege* certain groups, ideas, and artistic works above others.

Of course, for the average person such ideas make no sense, are in fact nonsense, yet in intellectual and academic circles, and among political elites, they are overarching truths. Thus the attack on Eurocentric ideas, and the claim that the time-honored works of art and literature are merely the products of narrow-minded, dead white men and have no more significance than the incoherent ranting of modern scribblers or the grotesque productions of talentless artists, especially if they are produced by women or members of this or that victimized minority group. The greatest sin in this prevailing orthodoxy is to question the absolute equality of all humans and human groups. From the noble idea that all men are equal in the eyes of god and should therefore be treated as equals under the laws of man, the modern multiculturalist insists that all men are, *in fact*, equal in all ways, and all cultures equally worthy in all respects. This, of course, was the fatal error that Aristotle saw would undermine democracy, namely: that since men are equal in some regard, they are therefore equal in all regards.

Such extreme egalitarianism produces, necessarily, the anomalies discussed earlier. If Islam is the equal of Christianity in all ways, then to criticize it is to commit the sin of intolerance. If an artist such as Geert Wilders creates a film highlighting the unequal treatment of women under *sharia* law, he must be prosecuted for "inciting hatred." His sin, of course, is pointing out the absurdity of a cult of tolerance which requires a thoroughgoing critique of Western injustices but makes it a crime to criticize the injustices of any other culture. Extreme egalitarianism also induces a profound nihilism, since if all things are equal, than there can be no value or moral code that can justify one's commitment or any sort of personal sacrifice. By similar logic no one can claim that a certain standard of behavior is superior to another, and there can be no justification for any attempt to impose such a standard on another. This is, of course, the foundation upon which the cult of multiculturalism is based. It explains the paralyzing ambivalence of Western societies about immigrant assimilation and tolerance of the maintenance of alien traditions. A specific problem for Europe is that it welcomes Muslim immigrants, and Muslims categorically reject this view, correctly recognizing its nihilism, and see it as far inferior to their own faith and the way of life it prescribes.

Whether Western elites really believe these things is less important than the benefit they gain from its promulgation. The primary benefit is that it paralyses the popular preferences for national preservation by characterizing opposition to elite doctrines as immoral, indecent, and inhumane. It allows unelected elites to aggrandize their own power by obliterating national sovereignty and nullifying democratic accountability. Many are, without exaggeration, true totalitarians that have no regard for the well-being of those they control, since the only way they can consolidate their dystopian plans is through brute state power. While there is no doubt that many well-meaning individuals join their efforts, they are the sort of "useful idiots" who excused and covered up Communist atrocities during most of the 20th Century.

Since the smooth assimilation of an ever-growing immigrant population, especially of Muslims in Europe, seems unlikely, the only possible way to avoid the negative outcomes outlined above is an immediate and complete moratorium on any further immigration, or very limited immigration for those immediate family members of adult legal residents, meaning existing spouses and dependent (under 18 year old) children. This is such a remote possibility that one hesitates even to consider how it might come about. It would not be remote, at all, if modern democracies reflected the wishes of their citizens regarding immigration. Such a change of policy would be supported by overwhelming majorities in all Western nations. It would also be extremely beneficial in economic and cultural terms in helping to promote a sense of civic unity among current citizens. Indeed, if such a change were to be enacted today, the negative effects of the massive immigration of recent decades would be greatly ameliorated in that current immigrants would be more likely to assimilate and less likely to be segregated into separate communities. After all, at the present time only about 5% of Europe's population is non-European, and these people should present a manageable, though difficult, problem to integrate into European society. A moratorium on immigration would also allow time for the adjustment in policies in, for instance, education and law enforcement, that would encourage assimilation without major insults to democratic principles. The same can be said about the current Hispanic immigrant population in the United States of some 13%, who could be readily assimilated with the right policies, especially if a halt to immigration prevents the growth of self-sustaining ethnic communities such as that in Miami.

However, a major limitation of immigration is a remote possibility because the elites and the special interests that control all the major institutions in Western societies would strongly resist any such change. The history of the past three decades makes it clear that they will not be moved by popular sentiment unless faced by a very unlikely set of circumstances which threaten their own positions of power. It would require a popular revolt of enormous proportions against the existing order. Under present circumstances the problems outlined above are unlikely to create such a revolt, for the simple reason that the population is intentionally denied, by the government and all the major media, the knowledge and information that would enable them to fully comprehend the inevitable long-term consequence of current policies. This ignorance is reinforced by the legal and social repression of any individual willing to voice opposition to those policies.

The only way the public could be moved to a major reaction against current policies would be events of such a catastrophic nature that they would force an increase in the saliency of the costs of current policies to almost everyone and demonstrate the need for immediate action. Two calamities could bring that about, though both are very unlikely. The first would be an economic depression as severe as that of the 1930s. The second, even less likely, would be a dramatic rise in terrorist activity which produces panic in the general population. This second is unlikely for the simple reason that the Islamic radicals who wish to impose their ways in Europe are currently being accommodated by European elites and can foresee their program being implemented by immigration without the resort to violence. They are unlikely to promote widespread terrorism that might threaten that accommodation, though random acts of terroristic violence are bound to be carried out by various renegade Muslim groups. This means that the only real possibility of a popular revolt against current European autocrats would be a drastic 1930s–like economic depression affecting all Western societies.

The near panicked response of most major governments in the West to the economic meltdown of late 2008 indicates that many recognize the danger which they would face if this situation should grow much worse than is currently anticipated. The massive spending and government intervention in response to the 2008 downturn is unprecedented and suggests that the characterization of governmental responses as panicked is not unreasonable. A severe depression driving unemployment rates to the range of 20% to 25% would make it immediately apparent to the average person how much their personal well-being is threatened by continued uncontrolled immigration.

Given these economic realities, governments will face the Hobbsian choice between major cutbacks in social welfare spending or risking very high rates of inflation. Raising taxes sufficient to pay for increases in social support would not be possible in a time of high unemployment and asset depreciation. It is hard to imagine any other choices. Either of these choices will cause discontent, even fury, among large constituent classes. In the globalized economy, workers will find it almost impossible to demand wages to keep up with inflation. People on fixed incomes would be impoverished. People currently dependent on government assistance will find their payments diminished at a time of steeply rising prices. The almost certain result would be conflict between those damaged by inflation and those damaged by reduced government assistance. Since large numbers of the latter are non-European, significant ethnic tensions between native Europeans and United States citizens and immigrant populations are very likely.

One result of an economic depression would be the return of some recent immigrants to their home villages where they could expect support from relatives. Even a subsistence, peasant existence might seem more desirable than extreme deprivation in the cities of Western Europe or the northern United States with their bitterly cold winters, even without open and potentially violent hostility directed toward them. Not all immigrants, however, will be able to exercise such an option, since many governments may reject the return of impoverished immigrants who would add to their own problems, and represent a phalanx of people familiar with Western ways who might well form a revolutionary vanguard in the repressive regimes of their home countries.

Democratic governments will only be able to survive by a harsh crackdown on violence of all sorts and a halt to immigration which will, by then, be seen as obviously adding to the economic difficulties they face. If such moves are blocked by EU directives, such directives will be ignored and some countries may simply withdraw from the EU to prevent their own collapse. If this senario were to occur today rather than 30 or 40 years from now, the non-European population will be too small to engage in civil war with the majority population and public order will be much easier to restore, especially if economic conditions show promise of improving.

The situation in America is likely to be much more peaceful than in Europe, but the outcome regarding immigration is likely to be the same, namely, a moratorium on immigration and a real effort to secure the borders against illegal entry. The reason is that the United States government, especially the House of Representatives, is much more responsive to voter sentiment than European governments. This was demonstrated by the House's rejection of the amnesty proposals of the Bush administration in 2007 under protests by large numbers of citizens. In addition, freedom of expression is much less restricted in the United States than it is in Europe. Political correctness is not nearly as coercive as it is in Europe, and is regularly mocked by popular commentators, especially those in the center and on the right of the ideological spectrum. Politicians who call for a moratorium on immigration will not be threatened by hate laws and, given the overwhelming popular sentiment favoring immigration restriction, will probably be rewarded by voters, even if they lost the financial support of special interests.

With an end to massive immigration, the western democracies will cease to grow, but they need not become poor. Economic growth in terms of GNP is not a meaningful measure of the well-being of citizens. *Per capita* GNP is far more important and can continue to grow with modest increases in productivity. Western nations could maintain a relatively high standard of living and remain pockets of democracy in a largely undemocratic world. In addition, if they maintained a prudent foreign policy and recognized the legitimate interests of competing civilizations, there is reason to believe they will be left in peace, especially if they maintain a military deterrence sufficient to make their conquest too costly. Tiny Switzerland managed to avoid invasion by Germany by such realistic deterrence.

Of course, a worldwide depression is a nightmare scenario. That such a nightmare might be necessary to reverse Western immigration policies that, in the long run, promise the demise of Western civilization, is a great tragedy. All of which would be unnecessary if elites adopted more sensible approaches to immigration and more prudent fiscal policies. It is difficult to decide, on reflection, whether the enormous human pain of such a depression would be worth the advantage of a reversal of current policies. The dilemma is moot, since such a nightmare scenario seems very unlikely, and the current downturn will probably be turned around without major unrest. In that case, things will continue on their current course with all the negative consequences outlined above.

Sometime during the last half of the 21st century the world will be very different from what it is today. China will undoubtedly be the World's dominant power and will likely bring all of Asia into its orbit. Islam will become the most common religion in the world with considerably more adherents than Christianity or any other religion. Relations between Europe and the Muslim Middle East may be one of fairly constant low-level conflict, especially, as is likely, if Muslim countries develop nuclear arms and mass immigration to Europe continues. However, this tension is likely to be affected, in currently unpredictable ways, by the growing power of China in Africa. In a Muslim-dominated Mediterranean, there will be no place for a Jewish state and the fate of its inhabitants will necessarily be grim. The future of Indonesia, a Muslim country in the heart of Asia, will be problematic at best and may well become a flashpoint in a conflict between China and the Muslim world. The future of India is equally problematic. It will be bordered by Muslim States and has a significant Muslim minority which may prove a dangerous third-column should its Muslim neighbors attempt its conquest.

The United States may well join a North American alliance including Mexico and Canada, and include most Central American and Caribbean nations. The relative wealth of such a Union would clearly fall behind that of the Asian countries, but its per capita GNP might continue to rise and its standard of living could remain comfortable. Of course, if the U. S. enters into a North American Union it will be difficult for it to maintain its European heritage. Furthermore, with such a diverse population, many features of American democratic traditions will probably be abandoned. South America may become a flashpoint between the United States and China. The small, Western dominated societies in the Pacific will be able to maintain their European traditions, but only if they resist the multiculturalists' demands for massive non-Western immigration which, to date, they have failed to do. Their ability to maintain their traditions will also depend on the willingness of China to accept their continued independence. If they are able to maintain their Western character they will become appealing destinations for those of European origins who feel uncomfortable, or are placed in a disadvantaged position, by the growing presence of Muslims in Europe.

It is difficult for those who cherish the Western heritage not to be saddened by these prospects, but they are almost inevitable given current trends. The survival of Western traditions would also depend on the prudence of what may become an isolated multicultural United States, or North American Union. Should it attempt to maintain its current world dominance and refuse to acknowledge the legitimate interests of its Muslim and Chinese rivals, the result could well be a worldwide catastrophic conflict in which it would be unlikely that North America would prevail. What will arise out of the ashes I leave to the reader to surmise.

All of which could surely be avoided if the West's liberal elites rejected the totalitarian impulses of many among them and came to acknowledge their responsibilities to their own countrymen. This might result in their abandonment of multiculturalist doctrine in favor of the more reasonable cultural relativism of the early 20th century. Cultural relativism was based on the notion that cultures reflected the distinctive needs and ecological conditions confronting particular peoples. What was missing in the early formulation was the human element. It has been the recurrent theme of this book that cultures reflect not merely the ecological conditions they confront but must, in addition, accommodate the talents and sensibilities of their human participants. From this perspective no culture is better than any other in any absolute sense. Rather each culture, necessarily, sees itself as the best and most suitable for its own people. World harmony need not be threatened by the cultural differences which exist and the sense of superiority that most people feel for their way of life. The danger arises when one culture sees itself as possessing a way of life that is superior and suitable for all the world's peoples and seeks to impose its way of life on others either out of benign motives or for merely predatory gain under the guise of benign motives.

If leaders accept these realities, relative peace between different civilizations can be maintained if they adopt prudent policies and remain ever vigilant in their efforts to protect their societies from encroachment by more ambitious and aggressive rivals. This simple truth was self-evident to the founders of the American republic who fervently desired to avoid the errors of their European forebears. Sadly, their progeny failed to heed their admonitions even in their dealings with each other. Neither were they able to avoid the dangers of foreign entanglements against which their first president warned. It would require a total ignorance of history to suppose that these simple truths would be endorsed by all, or even most, of the world's leaders. It may not be too much to hope, however, that American leaders, confronting the new world order unfolding before them, may return to the vision of their founders. That, of course, would require that there remain sufficient numbers of Americans who still honor those founders and their vision. That may be a foolish hope, but striving to realize that hope is the absolute obligation that the adult members of living generations have to their own children and to those of generations yet to come.

Notes

1   B. F. Skinner, *Beyond Freedom and Dignity* (New York: Bantam Books, 1972), 131.

2   Ibid. 201.

3   Edmund Burke, *Reflections of the Revolution in France* (1790) published in one volume along with Thomas Paine, *The Rights of Man* (Garden City, New York: Doubleday, 1961), 110.

4   Ibid., 108.

5   Christopher B. Swanson, Cities in Crisis: A Special Analytic Report on High School Graduation (Bethesda, Maryland: Editorial Projects in Education, April 1, 2008).

6   Linda S. Gottfredson, Implications of Cognitive Differences for Schooling within Diverse Societies. In Craig L. Frisby and Cecil R. Reynolds, eds. *Comprehensive Handbook of Multicultural School Psychology.* (Hoboken, New Jersey: Wiley and Sons, 2005) 517–554, 548.

7   Stephen Moore, Mississippi's Tort Reform Triumph, *The Wall Street Journal,* May 10, 2008.

8   National Center for Education Statistics, State Comparisons, 2007.

9   U. S. Census Bureau, Mississippi by Country.

10 United Nations, *World Population Prospects: The 2009 Revision.*

11 John Stossel, The College Scam, *Townhall Online,* January 28, 2009, online. See also Charles Murray, *Real Education: Four Simple Truths for Bringing America's Schools Back to Reality* (New York: Random House, 2008).

12 Charles Murray, For Most People, College is a Waste of Time, *The Wall Street Journal,* August 13, 2008.

13 Estimates for thresholds for varying occupations are based on: Linda Gottfredson, Why g Matters: The Complexity of Everyday Life, *Intelligence,* 24:1, 1997, 79–132. Similar estimates are taken from: Arthur R. Jensen, *Bias in Mental Testing* (New York: Free Press, 1980), 110–114.

14 Timothy J. Hatton and Jeffrey G. Williamson, Vanishing Third World Emigrants? February 2009 draft paper.

15 Edwin S. Rubenstein and the Staff of NPI, *Cost of Diversity: The Economic Costs of Racial and Cultural Diversity* (Augusta, Georgia: National Policy Institute), Issue Number 803, October 2008.

16 Bruce Landes, Letter to the Editor; Eric Ruth, Letter to the Editor, Price Fixing Explains Shortage of General Surgeons, *Wall Street Journal,* January 24–25, 2009, A10.

17 Richard Lynn and Tatu Vanhanen, *IQ and Global Inequality: A Sequel*

to IQ and the Wealth of Nations (Augusta, Georgia: Washington Summit Publishers, 2006), 297.

18   The IQ estimate for China may be an overestimate in that it reflects measures taken among Overseas Chinese and more developed regions within China and may be based on fewer samples from the backward interior of China. In these areas, IQ may be somewhat depressed by poorer nutrition and other environmental factors. However, as China's economy grows, this hypothetical difference may be eliminated. In any case such an adjustment in IQ for China would not appreciably change the overall pattern under discussion. This is why I have included the lowest estimate of 102 from Lynn and Vanhanen's work. It is based on a sample of more that 5,000 students, 6 to 15 year old, and is by far the largest sample for China.

19   Samuel Huntington, *Who Are We: the Challenges to America's National Identity* (New York: Simon and Schuster, 2004), 248–251; Suro, Robert, *Strangers Among Us: How Latino Immigration is Transforming America,* New York: Alfred A. Knopf, 1998, 159–178.

20   Huntington, *Who Are We.,* 252.

21   Samuel P. Huntington, *The Clash of Civilization and the Remaking of the World Order* (New York: Simon and Schuster, 1997), 206.

22   Patrick Buchanan, *The Death of the West: How Dying Population and Immigrant Invasions Imperil Our Country and our Civilization* (New York: St. Martin's Press, 2002), 130.

23   El Plan Espiritual De Aztlan, which can be found at the website of the California State University chapter of MEChA.

24   El Plan De Santa Barbara, which can be found at the website of California State University chapter of of MEChA online at calstatela. edu/orgs/mecha/documents.htm. A fuller statement of the plan can be found at the official website of MEChA.

25   Buchanan, *The Death of the West,* 130.

26   Robert M. Engstrom, Sotomayor's La Raza Uses Taxpayer Money for Radical Agenda, *Human Events,* June 15, 2009; Jeremy P. Jacobs, Sotomayor a Former Member of La Raza, The Hill's Blog Briefing Room, June 4, 2009. Jacobs cites Sotomayor's response to the Senate questionnaire where she listed her membership in the organization as lasting from 1998 to 2004.

27   Mark Hosenball and Dan Ephron, The Mexican Problem: Homeland Security Secretary Janet Napolitano says Washington is stepping up its efforts to assist in Mexico's war on drug cartels, *Newsweek,* March 14, 2009.

28   Amy Chua, *World on Fire: How Exporting Free Market Democracy Breeds Ethnic Hatred and Global Instability* (New York: Anchor Books,

2003).

29   Huntington, *Who are We*, 173–177.

30   Leslie H. Gelb, Necessity, Choice, and Common Sense: A Policy for a Bewildering World, *Foreign Affairs*, May/June 2009, 56.

31   Ibid., 57.

32   Huntington, *The Clash of Civilization*, 84–85.

33   Ibid.,

34   Ibid., 183.

35   Ibid., 116–120.

36   Eric Baculinao, China Begins to Face Sex–Ratio Imbalance, *MSNBC*, September 14, 2004.

37   Ibid., 256.

38   Ibid., 257–258.

39   Andrew F. Krepinevich, Jr., The Pentagon's Wasting Assets: The Eroding Foundations of American Power, *Foreign Affairs*, July/August 2009, 18–33.

40   Krepinevich, The Pentagon's Wasting Assets, 28.

41   George Lemaitre, and Cecile Thoreau, Estimating the Foreign–Born Population on a Current Basis, *Organization for Economic Co–operation and Development*, December 2006, 13; Peder J. Pedersen, J., Mariola Pytikova and Nina Smith, Migration into OECD Countries 1900–2000. In Craig A. Parsons (Ed) *Immigration and the Transformation of Europe* (Cambridge, Cambridge University Press, 2006), 56–57.

42   Islampopulation.org, Muslim Population. Online at islampopulation. org; Craig A. Parsons and Timothy M. Smeeding, "What's Unique about Immigration in Europe, In Parsons, *Immigration and the Transformation of Europe*, 8.

43   *BBC News*, Obama Reaches Out to Muslim World, April 6, 2009.

44   United Nations, *World Population Prospects: The 2004 Revision*, 34–39.

45   Katinka Barysch, What Europeans Think about Turkey and Why, Briefing Note, August 2007, *Centre for European Reform*.

46   Paul Belien, Europeans' Flight from Europe, *The Washington Times*, June 6, 2007.

47   Helen Nugent and Nadia Menuhin, Mohammad Is No 2 Boy's Names, *Times Online*, June 6, 2007.

48   Michael Freund, Right On!: Say Goodbye to Europe, *The Jerusalem Post*, January 9, 2007.

49   Barysch, What Europeans Think About Turkey.

50   Central Intelligence Agency, *The World Factbook: Statistics and Analysis for Every Country on the Planet* . (New York: Barnes and Noble, 2006) 427, 569.

51 Barysch, What Europeans Think About Turkey, 2.

52 Tiberge, Nice Rally Banned, *Gallia Watch,* January 16, 2009.

53 United Nations, *World Population Prospects.*

54 Serge Trifkovik, *The Sword of the Prophet: Islam, History, Theology, Impact on the World* (Boston: Regina Orthodox Press, 2002), 50.

55 Ibid., 50–53.

56 Huntington, *The Clash of Civilization*, 256.

57 Huntington, *Who Are We*, 171.

58 Ibid., 143.

59 T. S. Eliot, *Collected Poems 1909–1962* (New York: Harcourt, Brace, 1963), The Hollow Men, 82.

60 Charles Bremner, Burka Makes Women Prisoners, Says President Sarkozy, *Times Online*, June 23, 2009.

61 Huntington, *The Clash of Civilizations*, 216.

62 Ibid., 216.

63 Ibid., 217.

64 Ibid., 217.

65 Krepinevich, The Pentagon's Wasting Assets, 27.

66 *BBC News*, Turkey Eases Ban On Headscarves, February 9, 2008, online.

67 Bremner, Burka makes women Prisoners.

68 Sabrina Tavernise and Sebnem Arsu, Turkish Court Call Ruling Party Constitutional, *New York Times,* July 31, 2008.

69 Thomas Landen, From the Ivory Tower: Newsweek Sees No Danger, *The Brussels Journal,* July 16, 2009.

70 Elsa V. Artadi and Xavier Sala–i–Martine, The Economic tragedy of the 20th Century: Growth in Africa, Working Paper 9865, *National Bureau of Economic Research*, Cambridge MA, July 2003, 1.

71 Ibid., 2.

72 Ibid., 6–7.

73 Ibid., 10.

74 Ibid., 11.

75 Michelle Faul, Congo Women Speak Out About Rape: Victims Shatter Local Taboos Around Talking About Violence Against Civilians, *Associated Press*, March 16, 2009. Online at www.msnbc.com.

76 Richard Lynn, and Tatu Vanhanen, *IQ and Global Inequality: A Sequel to IQ and the Wealth of Nations* (Augusta, Georgia: Washington Summit Publishers, 2006), 102.

77 Ibid., 251–252.

78 United Nations, *World Population Prospects*, 1, 38–42. The population figure for sub–Saharan Africa was calculated by the author by subtracting

from the total for Africa the populations of Algeria, Egypt, Libya, Morocco, Tunisia, Western Sahara, and the Sudan. The population of the Sudan, it should be noted, is approximately 50% black African.

79   Richard Lynn, *Race Differences in Intelligence: An Evolutionary Analysis* (Augusta Georgia: Washington Summit Publishers, 2006, 69–71. Lynn gives an estimate of the phenotypic IQ of 67 in this book, somewhat lower than the figure of 70 I used in this discussion which was the estimate given for sub–Saharan Africa by Lynn and Vanhanen, *IQ and Global Inequality*, 63. The difference is the result of slightly different samples used. The Lynn and Vanhanen book came out after Lynn's book and I therefore used the latter estimate.

80   Central Intelligence Agency, *The World Factbook*.

81   Princeton N. Lyman, China's Rising Role in Africa, *The Council on Foreign Relations*, July 21, 2005.

82   Norimitsu Onishi, Rising Muslim Power in Africa Causes Unrest in Nigeria and Elsewhere, New York Times, November 1, 2001.

83   Julien Benda, *The Treason of the Intellectuals: with a New Introduction by Roger Kimball* (Edison, New Jersey: Transaction, 2006), xii. Quotation is cited by Roger Kimball in his introduction.

84   Ibid., 3.

BIBLIOGRAPHY

Adler, Katya. Spain Stands By Immigrant Amnesty. *BBC News*, May 5, 2005.

AdnKronos. Italy: 40 Percent of Prisoners are Immigrants, Says Report. AdnKronos International Italy.

Aftenposten. Oslo Rape Statistics Shock. September 5, 2001.

Agence France Press. Scores of Police Injured in New French Riots. November 25, 2007. Akdenizli, Banu, E. J. Dioone, Jr.,

Martin Kaplin, Tom Rosenstiel and Roberto Suro. *Democracy in the Age of New Media: A report on the Media and the Immigration Debate.* Washington D.C.: Governance Studies at Brookings. September 25, 2008.

Allen, Frederick Lewis. *The Big Change: America Transforms Itself 1900–1950.* New York: Harper and Row, 1952.

Allis, Sam, Maureen Dowd and Bonnie Bartak. Losing Control of the Borders. Time Magazine, June 13, 1983.

Andrews, Wayne, ed. *A Concise Dictionary of American History.* New York: Scribner's, 1962.

Appiah, K. Anthony. The Limits of Pluralism, *In Multiculturalism and American Democracy.* Eds. Arthur M. Melzer, Jerry Weinberger and M. Richard Zinman. Lawrence, Kansas: University Press of Kansas, 1998.

Artadi, Elsa V. and Xavier Sala-i-Martine. The Economic tragedy of the 20th Century: Growth in Africa, Working Paper 9865. National Bureau of Economic Research, Cambridge, Mass., July 2003.

Atkinson, Robert D. Deep Competitiveness, *Issues in Science and Technology.* Winter 2007.

Auster, Lawrence. *The Path to National Suicide: An essay on Immigration and Multiculturalism.* Charles Town, West Virginia: Old Line Press, 1990.

Axtell, James. *The School Upon a Hill: Education and Society in Colonial New England*. New York: Norton, 1976.

Baculinao, Eric. China Begins to Face Sex-Ratio Imbalance. *MSNBC*, September 14, 2004.

Bailey, Ronald. Born to Be Wild. *Reason Magazine*. August 7, 2002.

Baker, Hugh D. R. *Chinese Family and Kinship*. New York: Columbia University Press, 1979.

Baker, Kevin. Blood on the Street, Book Review of Beverly Gage. *The Day Wall Street Exploded: The Story of America in its First Age of Terror*. New York: Oxford University Press, 2008. *The New York Times*, February 22, 2009.

Baldwin-Edwards, Martin. The Changing Mosaic of Mediterranean Migrations. *Migration Information Source*, January, 2003.

Barash, David. *The Whisperings Within: Evolution and the Origins of Human Nature*. New York: Harper and Row, 1979.

Barnett, Susan M. and Wendy Williams. National Intelligence and the Emperor's New Clothes. *Contemporary Psychology*, 2004, 49:1, 389–396.

Bateson, Patrick. Optimal Outbreeding. *In Mate Choice*. Patrick Bateson, ed. Cambridge, Mass.: Cambridge University press, 1983, 257–278.

Baumeister, Roy F., Jennifer D. Campbel, Joachim I. Krueger, and Kathleen D. Vohs. Does High Self-esteem Cause Better Performance, Interpersonal Success, Happiness or Healthier Lifestyles. *Psychological Science in the Public Interest,* 4:1, (2000), 1–44.

Bawer, Bruce. *While Europe Slept: How Radical Islam is Destroying the West from Within*. New York: Doubleday, 2006.

BBC News. Sir Willian MacPhersons Inquiry into the Matters Arising from the Death of Stephan Lawrence on 22 April 1993 to Date, in Order Particularly to Identify the Lessons to be Learned for the Investigation and Prosecution of Racially Motivated Crimes, February 1999.

BBC News. Blueprint for 'Divided' Bradford. *BBC News.* July 12, 2001.

BBC News. Bardot Fined for "Race Hate Book. June 10, 2004.

BBC News. Court Rules Vlaams Blok is Racist. September 11, 2004.

BBC News. Turkey Eases Ban on Headscarves. February 9, 2008.

BBC News. Court Backs EU Citizens' Spouses. July 25, 2008.

BBC News. Obama Reaches Out to Muslim World. April 6, 2009.

BBC News, South African Rape Survey Shock. June 18, 2009.

Beaver, Kevin M. *The Nature and Nurture of Antisocial Outcomes.* El Paso, Texas: Scholarly Publishing LLC, 2008.

Beaver, Kevin M., Matt DeLisi, Michael G. Vaughn and J.C. Barnes, Monoamine Oxidase A Genotype is Associated with Gang Membership and Weapon Use. *Comprehensive Psychiatry,* 2009, Article in Press.

Becroft, A. J. Maori Youth Offending: Paper Addressing Some Introductory Issues by His Honor Judge A. J. Becroft, Principal Youth Court Judge. *Ngakia Kia Puawai Conference,* 8–10 November, 2005.

Beichman, Arnold. Anti-Semitism in Sweden. *The Washington Times,* October 28, 2003.

Belien, Paul. Europeans' Flight from Europe. *The Washington Times.* June 6, 2007.

Bell, Ruth and Ehsan Masood, Ehsan. 'Race and IQ' Psychologist in Inquiry over Teaching Conduct. *Nature,* 381, 6578, (1996), 105.

Bellil, Samira. *Dans L'enfer Des Tournantes.* Paris: Editions Flammarion, 2003.

Benda, Julien. *The Treason of the Intellectuals: With a New Introduction by Roger Kimball.* Edison, New Jersey: Transaction, 2006.

Bendersky, Joseph W. *The Jewish Threat: Anti-Semitic Politics and the U.S. Army.* New York: Basic Books, 2000.

Bernstein, Nina. In Secret, Polygamy Follows Africans to N.Y. *New York Times*, March 23. 2007.

Bertram, Brian C. R. The Social System of Lions. *Scientific American*, 232, (1975), 54–65.

Betzig, Laura. L. *Despotism and Differential Reproduction.* New York: Aldine, Hawthorne, 1986.

Bill and Melinda Gates Foundation. Grants.

Biddis, Michael D. *Gobineau: Selected Political Writings*. New York: Harper and Row, 1970.

Biro, Dora, Norika Inoue-Nakamura, Rikako Tonooka, Gen Yamakoshi, Claudia Sousa, and Tetsuro Matsuzawa. Cultural Innovation and Transmission of Tool Use in Wild Chimpanzees: Evidence from Field Experiments. *Animal Cognition*, 6:4. (2003).

Bittles, Allen H. and James V. Neel. The Costs of Human Inbreeding and Their Implications for Variations at the DNA Level. *Nature Genetics*, 8 (1994) 117–121.

Blair, R. J. R. Neurocognitive Models of Aggression, the Antisocial Personality Disorders and Psychopathy. *J. Neurol. Neurosurg. Psychiatry*, 71 (2001) 727–731.

Blair, R. J. R., J. S. Morris, C. D. Frith, D. I. Perrett and R. J. Dolan. Dissociable Neural Responses to Facial Expressions of Sadness and Anger. *Brain*. 122, (1999), 883–893.

Blankley, Tony. Border Insecurity. *Townhall.com*, March 5, 2008.

Blinder, Alan S. Offshoring: The Next Industrial Revolution. *Foreign Affairs*, March/April. (2006).

Boe, Erling E. and Sujie Shin. Is the United States Really Losing the International Horse Race in Academic Achievement? *Phi Delta Kappan*, 86, 9 (May 2005), 688–695.

Bomberg, Elizabeth and Alexander Stub. *The European Union: How Does It Work*. New York: Oxford University Press, 2003.

Brady, Hugo. *EU Migration Policy: An A-Z*. London: Centre for European Reform, February 2008.

Branigan, William. Visa Program, High-Tech Workers Exploited Critics Say, Visa Program Brings Charges of Exploitation. The Washington Post, July 26, 1998.

Braudel, Fernand. *The Structures of Everday Life: Civilization and Capitalism 15th Century - 18th Century, Voume 1*. Translated from the French by Sian Reynolds. New York: Harper and Row, 1981.

Bremner, Charles. Burka Makes Women Prisoners, Says President Sarkozy, *Times Online*, June 23, 2009.

Breuer, Thomas, Mireille Ndoundou-Hockemba and Vicki Fishlock. First Observation of Tool Use in Wild Gorillas. *PLoS Biol* 3:11 (2005) e380.

Brimelow, Peter. *Alien Nation: Common Sense about America's Immigration Disaster*. New York: Harper Collins, 1996.

British National Party News Team. Another Labour Act of Betrayal: Quarter Million Failed Asylum Seekers Get Secret Deal to Stay. July 25, 2008.

Brown, Stephen. Germany's Intifada. *Front Page Magazine*, August 1, 2008.

Browne, Anthony. Response to Tony Blair's First Speech on Immigration. *Civitas* Background Briefing, 2004.

Bruni, Frank. Wave Of Immigrants Breaks Against Italian Island's Shore. *New York Times*, July 11, 2003.

Buchanan, Patrick J. *State of Emergency: The Third World Invasion and Conquest of America*. New York: St. Martin's Press, 2006.

Bunting, Madeleine. Immigration is Bad for Society, But Only Until a New Solidarity is Forged. *The Guardian,* June 18. 2007.

Burdick, Katherine E., Todd Lencz, Birgit Funke, Christine T. Finn, Philip R. Szeszko, John M. Kane, Raju Kucherlapati, and Anil K. Malhotra. Genetic Variation in DTNBP1 Influences General Cognitive Ability. *Human Molecular Genetics* 15:10 (2006), 1563–1568.

Burke, Edmund. *Reflections on the Revolution in France,* published in one volume along with Thomas Paine, *The Rights of Man*. Garden City, New York: Doubleday, 1961.

Buss, David M. *Evolutionary Psychology: The New Science of the Mind, 2nd Ed*. Boston, Mass.: Pearson, 2004.

Camarota, Steven A. Illegitimate Nation: An Examination of Out of Wedlock Births Among Immigrants and Natives. Washington, D.C.: Center for Immigration Studies, 2007.

Campo-Flores, Arian. The Most Dangerous Gang in America. *Newsweek*, March 28, 2005.

Carr, Laurie, Marco Iacoboni, Marie-Charlotte Dubeau, John C. Mazziotta and Gian Luigi Lenzi. Neural Mechanisms of Empathy in Humans: A Relay from Neural Systems for Imitation to Limbic Areas. *PNAS*, 100:9 (April 29, 2003) 5497–5502.

Carrell, Jennifer Lee. *The Speckled Monster: A Historical Tale of Battling Smallpox*. New York: Penguin Group, 2004.

Casciani, Dominic. An Illegal Immigration Amnesty. *BBC News*, June 14, 2006.

Caspi, Avshalom, Joseph McClay, Terrie E. Moffitt, Jonathan Mill, Judy Martin, Ian W. Craig, Alan Taylor, and Richie Poulton. Role of Genotype in the Cycle of Violence in Maltreated Children. *Science* 297:5582 (2002) 851–4

Caspi, Avshalom and Terrie E. Moffitt. Gene-Environment Interactions in Psychiatry: Joining Forces with Neuroscience. Nature reviews: *Neuroscience*. 7, (2006) 583–590.

Cavelli-Sforza, L. Luca. The Chinese Human Genome Diversity Project. *Proceedings of the National Academy of Science*, 95, September 1998 11501–11503.

Ceci, Stephen, Douglas Peters and Jonathan Plotkin. Human Subjects Review, Personal Values, and the regulation of Social Science Research. *American Psychologist*, Vol. 40, No. 9, (1985), 994–1002.

Ceaser, James. Multiculturalism and American Liberal Democracy. In Arthur M. Melzer, Jerry Weinberger and M. Richard Zinman, eds. *Multiculturalism and American Democracy*. Lawrence, Kansas: University Press of Kansas, 1998, 139–56.

Central Intelligence Agency. *The World Factbook: Statistics and Analysis for Every Country on the Planet*. New York: Barnes and Noble, 2006.

Chagnon, Napolian A. *Yanomamo: The Fierce People*. New York: Holt, Rinehart and Winston, 1977.

Channel4. Poll conducted by YouGov for use in a three part television program, Immigration: The Inconvenient Truth. Broadcasted April 7, April 14 and April 21, 2008.

Chua, Amy. *World on Fire: How Exporting Free Market Democracy Breeds Ethnic Hatred and Global Instability*. New York: Anchor Books, 2003.

Civil War, The. Directed by Ken Burns. Written by Ken Burns, Ric Burns, and Geoffrey C. Ward. PBS Home Video, 1990.

Clark, Gregory. *A Farewell to Alms: A Brief Economic History of the World*. Princeton, New Jersey: Princeton University Press, 2007.

CLEISS. The French Social Security System, III—Family Benefits.

Cochran, Gregory, Jason Hardy, and Henry Harpending. Natural History of Ashkenazi Intelligence. *Journal of Biosocial Science*. 38, (2006) 659–93.

Cochran, Gregory and Henry Harpending. *The 10,000 Year Explosion: How Civilization Accelerated Human Evolution*. New York: Basic Books, 2009.

College Board. 2007 College Bound Seniors, Total Group Profile. New York, College Board, 2007.

Collins, D. Anthony, Curt Busse and Jane Goodal. Infanticide in two populations of mountain gorillas with comparative notes on chimpanzees. In Glen Hausfater and Sara Blaffer Hrdy, eds. *Infanticide: Comparative and Evolutionary Perspectives*. New York: Aldine, 1984, 193–216.

Cooper, Betsy and Kevin O'Neil. Lessons From the Immigration Reform and Control Act of 1986. Washington, D.C.: Migration Policy Institute, August 2005. No. 3, 5.

Cornwall, John. Are Muslim Enclaves No-Go Areas, Forcing Other People Out, Asks Historian John Cornwall. *The Sunday Times,* March 16, 2008.

Cosman, Madeleine Pelner. Illegal Aliens and American Medicine. *Journal of American Physicians and Surgeons*. 10:1, Spring 2005. 6–10.

Courtois, Stephane, Nicolas Werth, Jean-Louis Panne, Andrezej Paczkowski, Karel Bartosek and Jean-Louis Margolin. *The Black Book of Communism: Crimes, Terror, Repression*. Translated by Jonathan Murphy and Mark Kramer. Cambridge, Mass., Harvard University Press, 1999.

Craven, Avery O. *The Coming of the Civil War*. Chicago: University of Chicago Press, 1966.

Crockett, Carolyn M. and Ranka Sekulic. Infanticide in Red Howler Monkeys. In Glen Hausfater and Sara Blaffer Hrdy. eds. *Infanticide: Comparative and Evolutionary Perspectives*. New York: Aldine, 1984, 173–192.

Crul, Maurice and Hans Vermeulen. Immigration, Education, and the Turkish Second Generation in Five European Nations: A comparative Study. In Parsons, ed. *Immigration and the Transformation of Europe, 235–250*.

Crumley, Bruce. French Riots Enter a Second Night. *Time* Magazine, November 27, 2007.

Crumley, Bruce and Adam Smith. Sisters in Hell. *Time* Magazine, November 24, 2002.

Dalrymple, Theodore. The Barbarians at the Gates of Paris: Surrounding the City of Light are Threatening Cities of Darkness, *City Journal*, Autumn 2002.

Dalrymple, Theodore, Choosing to Fail, *City Journal*. Winter 2000.

Daly, Martin and Margo Wilson. Violence Against Stepchildren. *Current Directions in Psychological Science*, 5, (1996).

Daniels, Roger. *Coming to America: A History of Immigration and Ethnicity in American Life, Second Edition*. New York: Harper Collins, 2002.

Davidson, Richard J., Katherine M. Putnam, and Christine L. Larson. Dysfunction in the Neural Circuitry of Emotion Regulation - A Possible Prelude to Violence. *Science*, 280, 5479, (2000), 591–594.

Dawkins, Richard. *The Selfish Gene, New Edition*. Oxford: Oxford University Press, 1989.

Dawkins, Richard. *The Extended Phenotype*. Oxford: Oxford University Press, 1982.

Degler, Carl N. *In Search of Human Nature: The Decline and Revival of Darwinism in American Social Thought*. New York: Oxford University Press, 1991.

DeLisi, Matt. Neurosceince and the Holy Grail: Genetics and Career Criminology. In Anthony Walsh and Kevin Beaver, eds. *Biosocial Criminology: New Direction in Theory and Research*. New York: Routledge, 2009. 207–224.

de Haas, Hein. Morocco: From Emigration Country to Africa's Migration Passage to Europe. *Migration Information Source*, October 2005.

de Haas, Hein, Trans-Saharan Migration to North Africa and the EU: Historical Roots and Current Trends, *Migration Information Source*, November 2006.

Demeny, Paul, Europe's Immigration Challenge in Demographic Perspective, In Craig A. Parsons (Ed), *Immigration and the Transformation of Europe*. Cambridge, Cambridge University Press, 2006, 30–42.

Diamond, Jared. *Guns, Germs and Steel: A Short History of Everybody for the Last 13,000 Years*. London: Vintage, 2005.

Dick, Danielle M., Fazil Aliev, John Kramer, Jen C. Wang, Anthony Hinrichs, Sarah Bertelsen, Sam Kuperman, Marc Schuckit, John Nurnberger Jr., Howard J. Edenberg, Bernice Porjesz, Henri Begleiter, Victor Hesselbrock, Alison Goate and Laura Bierut. Association of *CHRM2* with IQ: Converging Evidence for a Gene Influencing Intelligence. *Behavior Genetics*, 37, 2, March 2007.

Dillon, Sam. 'No Child' Law is Not Closing a Racial Gap. *New York Times*, April 28, 2009.

Dobbs, Lou. *The War on the Middle Class*. New York: Penguin, 2006.

Donato, Katherine M., Jorge Durand and Douglas S. Massey. Stemming the Tide? Assessing the Deterrent Effects of the Immigration Reform and Control Act. *Demography*, 29, May 2, 1992.

Doughty, Steve. Britain has 85 Sharia Courts: The Astonishing Spread of the Islamic Justice behind Closed Doors. *Mail Online*, June 29, 2009.

Duchesne, Richard. Asia First? *The Journal of the Historical Society*, VI:1, (2006), 69–91.

Durham, William H. *Coevolution: Genes, Culture and Human Diversity*. Stanford CA: Stanford University Press, 1991.

Dutch News—Radio Netherlands Worldwide—English. Wilders' Freedom Party leads Polls, March 1, 2009.

Egley, Arlen Jr. National Youth Gang Survey Trends from 1996 to 2000. Washington, D.C.: U.S. Department of Justice, February 2002.

Egley, Arlen Jr. and Christina E. Ritz. *Highlights of the 2004 National Youth Gang Survey*, Washington, U.S. Department of Justice, April 2006.

Eliot, T. S. *Collected Poems 1909–1962*. New York: Harcourt, Brace, 1963.

Ellis, Lee and M. Ashley Ames. Neurohormonal Functioning and Sexual Orientation: A Theory of Homosexuality-Heterosexuality. *Psychological Bulletin*, Vol. 101, No. 2 (1987), 241–251.

Elwood, Robert W. and Malcolm C. Ostermeyer. Infanticide by Male and Female Mongolian Gerbils: Ontogeny, Causation and Function. In Glen Hausfater and Sara Blaffer Hrdy, eds. *Infanticide: Comparative and Evolutionary Perspectives*. New York: Aldine, 1984, 367–386.

Engstrom, Robert M. Sotomayor's La Raza Uses Taxpayer Money for Radical Agenda. *Human Events*, June 15, 2009.

Ervik, Astrid Oline. IQ and the Wealth of Nations, Book Review. *The Economic Journal*, June 2003, F406–F408.

Eswaran, Vinayak, Henry Harpending and Alan R. Rogers. Genomics Refutes an Exclusively African Origin of Humans. *Journal of Human Evolution*. 49:1 (2005) 1–18.

European Commission. The Right of Family Reunification for Third-Country Nationals Recognized by a Directive. Online at ec.europa.eu/justice_home.

European Union Eurostat.

Evans, Patrick D., Sandra L. Gilbert, Nitzan Mekel-Bobrov, Eric J. Vallender, Jeffrey R. Anderson, Leila M. Vaez-Azizi, Sarah A. Tishkoff, Richard R. Hudson, Bruce T. Lahn. Microcephalin, a Gene Regulating Brain Size, Continues to Evolve Adaptively in Humans. *Science*, 309: 5741, (2005), 1717–1720.

Fagan, Brian M. *The Little Ice Age: How Climate Made History 1300–1850.* New York: Basic Books, 2000.

Falola, Toyin. *Key Events in African History: A Reference Guide.* Westport, Conn.: Praeger, 2002.

Farahany, Nita and William Bernet. Behavioral Genetics in Criminal Cases: Past, Present, and Future. *Genomics, Society and Policy*, 2:1 (2006), 72–79.

Faul, Michelle. Congo Women Speak Out About Rape: Victims Shatter Local Taboos Around Talking About Violence Against Civilians. Associated Press, March 16, 2009.

Ferguson, Niall. *The House of Rothschild.* London: Penguin Books, 1998.

Ferguson, Niall. *The War of the World: Twentieth Century Conflict and the Descent of the West.* New York: The Penguin Press, 2006.

Fish, Stanley. Boutique multiculturalism. In Arthur M. Melzer, Jerry Weinberger and M. Richard Zinman, eds. *In Multiculturalism and American Democracy.* Lawrence, Kansas: University Press of Kansas, 1998, 69–88.

Fischer, David Hacket. *Albion's Seed: Four British Folkways in America.* New York: Oxford University Press, 1989.

Fisher, Ronald A. *The Genetical Theory of Natural Selection.* New York: Dover Publications, 1958.

Fitna. Written and Directed by Geert Wilders. LiveLeak, 2008.

Fjordman. Muslim Rape Wave in Sweden, *Front Page Magazine*, Dec 15, 2005.

Fjordman. Political Correctness: The Revenge of Marxism. *Gates of Vienna*, June 14, 2006.

Fjordman. Norwegian Authorities Still Covering Up Muslim Rapes. *Gates of Vienna*, July 27, 2006.

Flynn, James. Beyond the Flynn Effect: A Lecture by James Flynn. Psychometrics Centre, University of Cambridge, April 17, 2009.

Fogel, Robert William. *Without Consent or Contract: The Rise and Fall of American Slavery.* New York: Norton, 1989.

Fogel, Robert William and Stanley L. Engerman. *Time on the Cross: The Economics of American Negro Slavery.* Boston: Little, Brown, 1974.

Fogleman, Aaron Spencer. *Hopeful Journeys: German Immigration, Settlement and Political Culture in Colonial America, 1717–1775.* Philadelphia Penn.: University of Pennsylvania Press, 1996.

Foley, Debra L, Lindon J. Eaves, Brandon Wormley, Judy L. Silberg, Hermine H. Maes, Jonathan Kuhn, and Bruce Riley. Childhood Adversity, Monoamine Oxidaze A Genotype, and Risk for Conduct Disorder. *Archives of General Psychiatry,* 61:7 (2004) 738–744.

Ford Foundation. Database, Grants.

Ford, Peter. France's Angry Young Muslims, *The Christian Science Monitor.* April 17, 2002. Online at csmonitor.com; Craig S. Smith, Anti-Semitism at Ground Level in France. *International Herald Tribune,* March 23, 2006.

Fossey, Dian, Infanticide in Mountain Gorillas (Gorilla gorilla beringei). In Hausfater and Hrdy, *Infanticide,* 217–236.

Frank, T. Race Mixture in the Roman Empire. *American Historical Review,* 21:4 (1916), 689–708.

Frazzetto, Giovanni, Giorgio D. Lorenzo, Valeria Carola, Luca Proletti, Ewa Sokolowska, Alberto Siracusano, Cornelius Gross, and Alfonso Troisi. Early Trauma and Increased Risk for Physical Aggression During Adulthood: The Moderating Role of MAOA Genotype. PLoS One 2:5 (2007), e486.

Freedman, Daniel G. *Human Infancy: An Evolutionary Perspective,* Hillsdale, New Jersey: Lawrence Erlbaum, 1974.

Freud, Sigmund. *Civilization and its discontents.* New York: Norton, 1961.

Freund, Michael. Right On!: Say Goodbye to Europe. *The Jeruselem Post,* January 9, 2007.

Frisby Craig L. and Cecil R. Reynolds, ed. *Comprehensive Handbook of Multicultural School Psychology.* Hoboken, New Jersey: Wiley and Sons, 2005.

Fukuyama, Francis. *Trust: The Social Virtues and the Creation of Prosperity.* New York: Free Press, 1995.

Fukuyama, Francis. Identity and Migration. *Prospect Magazine*, 131, February, 2007.

Frank Gardner. Analysis: Saudi Rough Justice. *BBC News*, March 28, 2000.

Gay, Peter. *The Enlightenment: An Interpretation, Volume 2, The science of freedom.* New York: W. W. Norton, 1969.

Gelatt, Julia. Migration Fundamentals: Schengen and Free Movement of People across Europe. *Migration Information Source*, October, 2005.

Gelb, Leslie H. Necessity, Choice, and Common Sense: A Policy for a Bewildering World. *Foreign Affairs*, May/June, 2009, 56.

George, Rose. "Revolt Against the Rapists." *Guardian Unlimited*. April 5, 2003.

Ghiglieri, Michael P. The Social Ecology of Chimpanzees. *Scientific American*, 252:6, 110–119.

Gibson, Campbell and Kay Jung. Historical Census Statistics on Population Totals by Race, 1790 to 1990, and by Hispanic Origin, 1970 to 1990, For the United States, Regions, Divisions, and States. Population Division, U.S. Census Bureau, Washington D.C., Working Paper Series No. 56, September, 2002.

Gilbert, Martin. *The Illustrated Atlas of Jewish Civilization.* New York: MacMillan, 1990.

Glazer, Nathan. *The Social Basis of American Communism.* New York, Harcourt, Brace and World, 1961.

Glazov, Jamie. Symposium: The Death of Multiculturalism? *FrontPage Magazine*, September 8, 2006.

Goldsmith, Rosie. France in shock over gang rape. *BBC News*, July, 26, 2001.

Gomory, Robert E. and Harold T. Shapiro. Globalization: Causes and Effects, *Issues In Science and Technology*, Summer 2003.

Gordon, Robert A. Scientific Justification and the Race-IQ-Delinquency Model. In Timothy Hartagel and Robert A. Silverman, eds. *Critique and Explanation: Essays in Honor of Gwynne Nettler.* New Brunswick, New Jersey: Transaction Books, 1986.

Gordon, Robert A. Everyday Life As an Intelligence Test: Effects of Intelligence and Intelligence Context. *Intelligence*, 24(1), (1997) pp. 203–320.

Gottfried, Paul. E. *The Strange Death of Marxism: The European Left in the New Millennium.* Columbia, Missouri : University of Missouri Press, 2005.

Gottfredson, Linda S. Why g Matters: The Complexity of Everyday Life. *Intelligence*, 24:1, (1997), 79–132.

Gottfredson, Linda S. Implications of Cognitive Differences for Schooling Within Diverse Societies. In Craig L. Frisby and Cecil R. Reynolds, eds. *Comprehensive Handbook of Multicultural School Psychology*. Hoboken, New Jersey: Wiley and Sons, 2005, 517–554.

Graham Otis L. *Unguarded Gates: A History of America's Immigration Policy*. Rowen and Littlefield, 2006.

Grant, Madison and Henry Fairfield Osborn. *The Passing of the Great Race*. New York: Charles Scribner's Sons, 1918.

Gray, Jeremy, and Paul M. Thompson. Neurobiology of Intelligence: Science and Ethics. *Nature Reviews: Neuroscience*, 5, (2004), 471–482.

Gray, P. Misuse of Evolutionary Theory to Advocate for Racial Discrimination and Segregation: A Critique of Salter's On Genetic Interests. *Human Ethology Bulletin*, 20,2 (2003) 10–13.

Green David G., ed. *Institutional Racism and the Police: Fact or Fiction*. London: Institute for the Study of Civil Society, 2000.

Guillemette, Yvan and William B. P. Robson. No Elixir of Youth: Immigration Cannot Keep Canada Young (*Backgrounder*, No. 96, September 2006), Ottawa, Canada: The C.D. Howe Institute, 2006.

Guttentag, Marcia, and Paul Secord. *Too Many Women: The Sex Ratio Question*. Beverly Hills, Calif.: Sage, 1983.

Haas, Hein de. Morocco: From Emigration Country to Africa's Migration Passage to Europe. *Migration Information Source*, October 2005.

Hamilton, Kimberly, Patrick Simon and Clara Veniard. The Challenge of French Diversity. *Migration Information Source*, November 2004.

Hamilton, William D. The Genetical Evolution of Social Behavior, I, II. Journal of Theoretical Biology 7 (1964) 1–52. Reprinted in W. D. Hamilton. *Narrow Roads of Gene Land: The Collected Papers of William. D. Hamilton*. Oxford: W. H. Freeman, 1995.

Hamilton, William D. *Narrow Roads of Gene Land: The Collected Papers of William D. Hamilton*. W. H. Freeman, Oxford, 1995.

Harpending, Henry and Gregory Cochran. In Our Genes. *PNAS*, 99:1 (2002) 10–12.

Harrigan, Steve. Where Buses won't Go. *Fox News*, October 22, 2004.

Harris, Paul. "Gang Mayhem Grips LA." *Observer*, March 18, 2007.

Hatton, Timothy J. and Jeffrey G. Williamson. Vanishing Third World Emigrants? February 2009 draft paper.

Hausfater, Glen and Sara Blaffer Hrdy, eds. *Infanticide: Comparative and Evolutionary Perspectives*. New York: Aldine, 1984.

Hawkins, William R. *Importing Revolution, Open Borders and the Radical Agenda*. Monterey, Virginia: The American Immigration Control Foundation, 1994.

Hawks, John and Milford H. Wolpoff. Sixty Years of Modern Human Origins in the American Anthropological Association. *American Anthropologist*, 105, 1 (2003), 87–98.

Hawks, John. Why Human Evolution Accelerated. JohnHawks.net. December 12, 2007.

Hendricks, Tyche. Study: Price for Border Fence Up to $49 Billion. *San Francisco Chronicle*, January 8, 2007.

Hengst, Bjorn and Jan Friedmann. Insults Against Jews on the Rise. *Spiegel Online,* August 12, 2006.

Hedegaard, L. Interview: A Continent of Losers. *Sappho*, 2007.

Herrnstein, Richard J. and Charles Murray. *The Bell Curve: Intelligence and Class Structure in American Life*. New York: Free Press, 1994.

Herrnstein, Richard J. Still an American Dilemma. *The Public Interest*. No. 98, Winter (1990) 3–17.

Hickley, Mathew. Islamic Sharia Courts in Britain are Now 'Legally Binding'. *Mail Online,* September 15, 2008.

Hira, Ron. Do We Need Foreign Technology Workers? *The New York Times, Room For Debate*, April 8, 2009.

Ho, Christina. Gang Rapes and the 'Cultural Time Bomb.' Review of Paul Sheehan, *Girls Like You; Four Young Girls, Six Brothers and a Cultural Time Bomb*. Sydney, Australia: Pan Macmillan, 2006. *Australian Review of Public Affairs*, September, 25 2006.

Holman, Barry. *Masking the Divide: How Officially Reported Prison Statistics Distort the Racial and Ethnic Realities of Prison Growth*. Alexandria, Virginia: National Center on Institution and Alternatives, May 2001, 2.

Home Office, UK. Crime in England and Wales 2007-2008.

Home Office, UK. Statistics on Race and the Criminal Justice System UK - 2005, 87.

Horn, James. Servant Immigration to the Chesepeake in the Seventeenth Century. In Thad W. Tate and David I. Ammerman, eds. *The Chesepeake in the Seventeenth Century: Essays on Anglo-American Society and Politics.* New York: Norton, 1979, 51-90.

Horn, Jordana. Strange Migration: An Unlikely Haven for Refugees. *The Wall Street Journal,* February 15, 2008.

Hrdy, Sara Blaffer. Assumptions and Evidence Regarding the Sexual Selection Hypothesis: A Reply to Boggess. In Glen Hausfater and Sara Blaffer Hrdy, eds. *Infanticide: Comparative and Evolutionary Perspectives.* New York: Aldine, 1984, 315–319.

Huizinga, D., Haberstick, B. C., Smolen, A., Menard, S., Young, S.E., Corley, R. P., Stallings, M. C., Grotpeter, J. and Hewitt, J. K. Childhood Maltreatment, Subsequent Antisocial Behavior, and the Role of Monoamine Oxidase A genotype. *Biological Psychiatry,* 60, 7, (2006) 677–83.

Human Rights Watch. Leave None to Tell the Story: Genocide in Rwanda, 1999.

Hummel, Jeffrey Rogers. *Emancipating Slaves, Enslaving Free Men: A history of the American Civil War.* Chicago: Open Court, 1996.

Hunt, James, ed. *Selected Readings in Sociobiology.* New York: McGraw-Hill, 1980.

Hunt-Grubbe, Charlotte. The Elementary DNA of Dr. Watson. *The Sunday Times,* October 14, 2007.

Huntington, Samuel P. *The Clash of Civilizations: Remaking of World Order.* New York: Simon and Schuster, 1996.

Huntington, Samuel P. *Who Are We? The Challenges to America's National Identity.* New York: Simon and Schuster Paperbacks, 2004.

Independent. Brigitte Bardot Fined for Racism. June 3, 2008.

International Hapmap Project. RefSNP rs760761.

International Hapmap Project. RefSNP rs1115781.

International Organization for Migration. International Law and Family Reunification.

IRIN, News.org. Pakistan: Honour Killings Continue, Despite Law. March 8, 2007. IRIN is identified as the Humanitarian News and Analysis Service of the UN Office for the Coordination of Humanitarian Affairs.

IRIN, News.org, Jordan: Honour Killings Still Tolerated. March 11, 2007.

Islampopulation.org, Muslim Population.

Jacobs, Jeremy P. Sotomayor a Former Member of La Raza. *The Hill's Blog Briefing Room*, June 4, 2009,

Jacoby, Tamar. Defining assimilation for the 21st century. In Tamar Jacoby ed. *Reinventing the melting pot: The new immigrants and what it means to be American*. Basic Books, New York, 2004, 3–16.

Jasper, Lee, Breaking Out of the Black 'Gangsta' Ghetto. *Guardian*, UK, February 17, 2002.

Jeffreys, Kelly and Randall Monger. *Annual Flow Report: U.S. Legal Permanent Residents: 2007*. U.S. Department of Homeland Security, Office of Immigration Statistics, March 2008.

Jensen, Arthur R. How Much Can We Boost IQ and Scholastic Achievement? *Harvard Educational Review* 39 (1969), 1–123.

Jensen, Arthur R. *Bias in Mental Testing*. New York: Free Press, 1980.

Johnson, President Lyndon B. Remarks at the Signing of the Immigration Bill, Liberty Island, New York. October 3, 1965, Lyndon Baines Johnson Library and Museum, National Archives and Record Administration.

Johnson, Paul. *A history of the modern world from 1917 to the 1980s*. London: Weidenfeld and Nicolson, 1983.

Johnson, Paul. *A History of the Jews*. New York: Harper and Row, 1987.

Johnson, Paul. *Modern Times: A History of the World from the 1920s to the Year 2000*. London, Phoenix Press, 1997.

Johnson, Paul. *A History of the American People*. New York: Harper Collins, 1997.

Johnson, Paul. *Intellectuals: From Marx and Tolstoy to Sartre and Chomsky*. New York: Harper Collins, 2007.

Jones, Garett and W. Joel Schneider. Intelligence, Human Capital, and Economic Growth. *Journal of Economic Growth*, 11(1), (2006) 71–93.

Jordan, Miriam. New Curbs Set on Arrests of Illegal Immigrants. *The Wall Street Journal*, July 11, 2009.

Kaufman, Michael T. Idi Amin, Murderous and Erratic Ruler of Uganda in the 70s, Dies in Exile. *New York Times*, August 17, 2003.

Keeley, Lawrence. H. *War before Civilization: The Myth of the Peaceful Savage*. Oxford: Oxford University Press, 1996.

Kelly, James. Closing the Golden Door. *Time Magazine*, May 18, 1981.

Kennedy, John F. *A Nation of Immigrants*. New York: Harper Perennial, 2008.

Kern, Soeren. Spain's Bluster Masks an Immigration Crisis. *American Thinker*, August 16, 2007.

Kerner, Otto. *Report of the National Advisory Commission on Civil Disorders*. New York: Bantam, 1968.

Khatri, Prakesh. Recommendation from the CIS Ombudsman to the Director, USCIS, August 28, 2005. Office of the Citizenship and Immigration Service Ombudsman, U.S. Department of Homeland Security.

Kim-Cohen, J., Caspi, A., Taylor, A., Williams, B., Newcombe, R., Craig, I. W. and Moffitt, T. E. MAOA, Maltreatment, and Gene-Environment Interaction Predicting Children's Mental Health: New Evidence and a Meta-Analysis. *Molecular Psychiatry*, 11 (2006), 903–913.

Kirk, Lisbeth. Danish Immigration Law under Fire after EU Court Ruling. *EUobserver*, July 29, 2008.

Kirisci. Kemel. Turkey: A Transformation from Emigration to Immigration. Country Profiles, Migration Information Source, November 2003.

Kirsch, Irwin, Henry Braun and Andrew Sum, and Kentaro Yamamoto. America's Perfect Storm: Three Forces Changing Our Nation's Future. Princeton, New Jersey: Educational Testing Service, 2007.

Kohut, Andrew, Richard Wike, and Juliana Menasce Horowitz. World Publics Welcome Global Trade—But Not Immigration: 47 Nation Pew Global Attitudes Survey. *The Pew Global Attitudes Project*.

Krepinevich, Andrew F. Jr. The Pentagon's Wasting Assets: The Eroding Foundations of American Power. *Foreign Affairs*, July/August 2009, 18–33.

Kristeligt Dagblad. Prisons to Screen Muslim Clerics, February 28, 2008.

Krug, Etienne G., Linda L. Dahlberg, James A. Mercy, Anthony B. Zwi, and Rafael Lozano. eds. *World report on violence and health*. Geneva: World Health Organization, 2002.

Kurtz, Stanley. Not Without a Fight, *The New Criterion, Special Pamphlet, Free Speech in an Age of Jihad: Libel Tourism. Hate Speech" & Political Freedom*. Summer 2008.

Kurtzman, Joel. Mexico's Instability Is a Real Problem: Don't Discount the Possibility of a Failed State Next Door. *The Wall Street Journal*, January 16, 2009.

Lamb, Kevin. Forced Out: The Price of Speaking Freely in Multicultural America. *Middle American News*, June 2005.

Lancaster, John. Pakistan Court Will Reopen Rape Case: Fresh Inquiry is Ordered As Suspects are Detained. *Washington Post*, June 29, 2005.

Landen, Thomas. From the Ivory Tower: Newsweek Sees No Danger. *The Brussels Journal*, July 16, 2009.

Laurence, Jonathan. Managing Transnational Islam: Muslims and the State in Western Europe. In Craig A. Parsons, ed. *Immigration and the Transformation of Europe*. Cambridge, Mass.: Cambridge University Press, 2006.

Leland, Lysa, Thomas T. Struhsaker and Thomas M. Butynski. Infanticide by Adult Males in Three Primate Species of Kibale Forest, Uganda: A test of Hypotheses. In Glen Hausfater and Sara Blaffer Hrdy. *In Infanticide: Comparative and Evolutionary Perspectives*. New York: Aldine, 1984, 151–172.

Lemaitre, George and Cecile Thoreau. *Estimating the Foreign-Born Population on a Current Basis*. Organization for Economic Co-operation and Development, December 2006.

Lessing, Doris. Questions You Should Never Ask a Writer. New York Times, June 26, 1992, Reprinted by the New York Times, October 13, 2007.

Levine Louis. *Biology of the Gene, Third Edition*. St. Louis, Missouri: C.V. Mosby Company, 1980.

Lewis, P. The World Today. *ABC Radio* (Transcript) August 9, 2006.

Leyborn, James G. *The Scotch-Irish: A Social History*. Chapel Hill, North Carolina: University of North Carolina Press, 1989.

Lin, Eric. *The Accidental Asian: Notes of a Native Speaker*. New York: Random House, 1998, 188. Cited by Huntington, *Who Are We?*, 298.

Lind, William S. *Political Correctness: A Short History of an Ideology,* Free Congress Foundation, 2004.

Lindemann, Albert, S. *Esau's Tears: Modern Anti-Semitism and the Rise of the Jews.* Cambridge: Cambridge University Press, 2000.

Lipshitz, Cnaan. Dutch MP Behind Film on Radical Islam: Decision to Prosecute Me is Political. *Haaretz,* January 23, 2009.

Lipstadt, Deborah E. *Beyond Belief: The American Press and the Coming of the Holocaust 1933–1945.* New York: The Free Press, 1993.

Loughland, John. Why Europe's National Politicians Sign Away National Sovereignty. *The Brussels Journal,* December 19, 2007.

Loomis, Louise Ropes, ed. Aristotle, *On Man in the Universe.* New York: Walter J. Black, 1943.

Lovejoy, Arthur A. *The Great Chain of Being: The Study of the History of an Idea.* Cambridge, Mass: Harvard University Press, 1960.

Lloyd, John. Study Paints Bleak Picture of Ethnic Diversity. *Financial Times,* October 8, 2007.

Luedthe, Adam. The European Union Dimension: Supranational integration, Free Movement of Persons and Immigration Politics. In Craig A. Parsons, ed. *Immigration and the Transformation of Europe,* Cambridge, Massachusetts: Cambridge University Press, 2006.

Lyman, Princeton N., China's Rising Role in Africa, The Council on Foreign Relations, July 21, 2005.

Lynn, Richard. *Race Differences in Intelligence: An Evolutionary Analysis.* Augusta, Georgia: Washington Summit Publishers, 2006.

Lynn, Richard. *The Global Bell Curve: Race, IQ, and Inequality Worldwide.* Augusta, Georgia: Washington Summit Publishers, 2008.

Lynn, Richard and Tatu Verhanen. *IQ and the Wealth of Nations.* Westport: Conn. Praeger, 2002.

Lynn, Richard and Tatu Vanhanen. *IQ and Global Inequality: A Sequel to IQ and the Wealth of Nations.* Augusta, Georgia: Washington Summit Publishers, 2006.

MacDonald, Kevin. *A People That Shall Dwell Alone: Judaism As a Group Evolutionary Strategy, with Diaspora Peoples.* Lincoln Neb.: Writers Club Press, 2002 (1994).

MacDonald, Kevin. *Separation and Its Discontents: Toward an Evolutionary Theory of Anti-Semitism*. Bloomington Ind.: Firstbooks Library, 2004 (1998).

MacDonald, Keven. *The Culture of Critique: An Evolutionary Analysis of Jewish Involvement in Twentieth-Century Intellectual and Political Movements*. Bloomington Ind.: Firstbooks Library, 2002 (1998).

MacEoin, Denis. *Sharia Law or One Law for All*. London: Civitas: The Institute for the Study of Civil Society, 2009.

Maher, Shiraz. Muslim Britain is Becoming One Big No-Go Area. *The Sunday Times*, January 13, 2008.

Mahoney, Daniel J., 1968 and the Meaning of Democracy. *The Intercollegiate Review*, 43:2, Fall 2008, 4–13.

MALDEF. 2003–2004 Annual Report.

Mann, Jonathan. Muslim Women Rebel in France. CNN.com transcript of feature aired on May 24, 2004.

Manning, Lona. 9/16: Terrorists Bomb Wall Street. *Crime Magazine*, January 15, 2006.

Marco Martiniello, The New Migratory Europe: Toward A Proactive Immigration Policy? in Craig A. Parsons (Ed) *Immigration and the Transformation of Europe*.

Martinon-Torres, M., Bermudez de Castro, J. M., Gomez-Robles, A., Arsuaga, J. L., Carbonell, E., Lordkipanidze, D., Manzi, G. and Margvelashvili, A. Dental Evidence on the hominin dispersals during the Pleistocene. *Proceedings of the National Academy of Science*, 2007.

Matloff, Norman. On the Need For Reform Of the H-1B Non-Immigrant Work Visa in Computer-Related Occupations (Invited Paper). *University of Michigan Journal of Law Reform*, Fall 2003, Vol. 36, Issue 4, 815–914.

McAllister, J. F. O., A Shock to the System. *Time Magazine*, November 24, 2002.

McConalogue, James. Immigration: Heaping Up the Funeral Pyre. *Brussels Journal*, Aug 8, 2006.

McConnachie, Alistair. Asylum Policy: Restoring Integrity. *Sovereignty*, April 2005.

McGreal, Chris. Rising UK Anti-Semitism Blamed on Media. *The Guardian*, January 25, 2005.

McKinsey & Company. The Economic Impact of the Achievement Gap in America's Schools. April 2009, 17.

McNeill, William H. *The Rise of the West: A History of the Human Community.* Chicago: Chicago University Press, 1963.

McNeill, William. *Plagues and Peoples.* Garden City, New York: Doubleday, 1976.

McNeill, William H. The Steppe. *Encyclopedia Britannica*, 2007, 5.

Mealey, Linda. The Sociobiology of Sociopathy: An Integrated Evolutionary Model. *Behavioral and Brain Science* 18:3, (1995), 523–599.

Meggitt, Mervyn. *Blood is Their Argument: Warfare Among the Mae Enga Tribesman of the New Guinea Highlands.* Palo Alto, California: Mayfield, 1977.

Mekel-Bobrov, Nitzan, Sandra L. Gilbert, Patrick D. Evans, Eric J. Vallender, Jeffrey R. Anderson, Richard R. Hudson, Sarah A. Tishkoff, Bruce T. Lahn. Ongoing Adaptive Evolution of ASPM, a Brain Size Determinant in Homo Sapiens. *Science* 309: 5741 (2005), 1720–1722.

Melzer, Arthur M., Jerry Weinberger and M. Richard Zinman, eds. *Multiculturalism and American Democracy.* Lawrence, Kansas: University Press of Kansas, 1998.

Meyer-Lindenberg, Andrea, Joshua W. Buckholtz, Bhaskar Kolachana, Ahmad R. Hariri, Lukas Pezawas, Giuseppe Blasi, Ashley Wabnitz, Robyn Honea, Beth Verchinski, Joseph H. Callicott, Michael Egan, Venkata Mattay and Daniel R. Weinberger. Neural mechanisms of genetic risk for impulsivity and violence in humans. *PNAS* 103:16 (March 28, 2006), 6269–6274.

Miano, John. Do We Need Foreign Technology Workers? *The New York Times, Room For Debate*, April 8, 2009.

Middle East Times. Saudi Gang Rape Victim Faces 90 Lashes. March 5, 2007.

Migration Watch. Transnation Marriage and the Formation of Ghettoes, Briefing Paper 10.12, September 22, 2005.

Migration Watch. YouGov pic, Immigration, Fieldwork Dates: 6th - 8th November 2007.

Migration Watch. Public 'Don't Believe' Government on Immigration. January 30, 2007.

Miller, A. The UK, BNP and the Modern McCarthyism. *The Brussels Journal*, 22 July, 2008.

Miller, Edward M. Paternal Provisioning Versus Mate Seeking in Human Populations. *Personality and Individual Differences,* 17:2 (1993) 27–255.

Miller, John W. and Alistair MacDonald. European Parliament Elections Loom as Political Bellwether. *The Wall Street Journal,* May 30–31, 2009, A14.

Miller, Lee. *Roanoke: Solving the Mystery of the Lost Colony.* New York: Penguin Books, 2000.

Mirza, Munira, Abi Senthilkumaran and Zein Ja'far. *Living Apart Together: British Muslims and the Paradox of Multiculturalism.* London: Policy Exchange, 2007.

Moffitt, Terrie, Avshalom Caspi, Nigel Dickson, Phil Silva and Warren Stanton. Childhood-Onset versus Adolescent-Onset Antisocial Conduct Problems in Males: Natural History for Ages 3 to 18 Years. *Development and Psychopathology* 8 (1996), 399–424.

Moore, Stephen. Mississippi's Tort Reform Triumph. *The Wall Street Journal,* May 10, 2008.

Moore, Molly, Field Note: How I Got the Story. *Washington Post,* April 28, 2008.

Moore, Molly. In France, Prisons Filled With Muslims. *Washington Post,* April 29, 2008.

Morgan, Edmund S. *The Puritan Family: Religion and Domestic Relations in Seventeenth-Century New England.* New York: Harper, 1966.

Mowry, George F. *The Era of Theodore Roosevelt and the Birth of Modern America,* New York Harper and Row, 1958.

Mullen, John D and Byron M. Roth. *Decision-Making: Its Logic and Practice.* Savage, Maryland: Rowman and Littlefield, 1991.

Murdock, George P., and Douglas R. White. Standard Cross-Cultural Sample. *Ethnology,* 8 (1969) 329–369.

Murray, Charles. *Losing Ground: American Social Policy 1950-1980.* New York: Basic Books, 1984.

Murray, Charles. *Real Education: Four Simple Truths for Bringing America's Schools Back to Reality.* New York: Random House, 2008.

Myers, David G. *Psychology, 3rd Ed.* New York: Worth publishers, 1992.

Charles Murray. For Most People, College is a Waste of Time. *The Wall Street Journal*, August 13, 2008.

Myrdal, Gunnar with Richard Sterner and Arnold Rose. *An American Dilemma: The Negro Problem and Modern Democracies, 20th Anniversary Edition*. New York: Harper and Row, 1962.

National Academy. Brain Mobility, *Issues In Science and Technology*, Winter 2006.

National Assessment of Educational Progress, 2005. Washington DC: U.S. Department of Education Reading, 4–5, Mathematics, 4–5.

National Council of La Raza, 2007 Annual Report.

National Science Foundation. NSF Shortage Study Called 'Bad Science.' *Science News*, May 2, 1992.

Nazir-Ali, Michael. Extremism Flourished as UK Lost Christianity. *Telegraph*, Jan 11, 2008.

Nickerson, Colon. Anti-Semitism Seen Rising Among French Muslims. *The Boston Globe*, March 13, 2006.

Neisser, Ulric, Gwyneth Boodoo, Thomas J. Bouchard, A. Wade Boykin, Nathan Brody, Stephen J. Ceci, Diane F. Halpern, John C. Loehlin, Robert Perloff, Robert J. Sternberg, and Susana Urbina. Intelligence: Knowns and Unknowns. *American Psychologist*, 31:2, (1996), 77–101.

New Century Foundation. *Hispanics: A Statistical Portrait*, New Century Foundation, Oakton, VA 2006.

Newland, Kathleen. Troubled Waters: Rescue of Asylum Seekers and Refugees at Sea. Country Profiles, Migration Information Source, June 2004.

New Zealand Herald. Maori Crime Rate Concerns Government. October 28, 2005.

NIH/National Institute of Mental Health. Dopamine-dampening gene linked to prefrontal inefficiency, schizophrenia. *Science Daily*, May 29, 2001.

Nilsson, Kent W, Richard L. Sjoberg, Mattias Damberg, Jerzy Leppert, John Ohrvik, Per Olof Alm, Leif Lindstrom and Lars Oreland. Role of Monoamine Oxidase A Genotype and Psychosocial Factors in Male Adolescent Criminal Activity. *Biological Psychiatry*, 59:2 (2006) 121–127.

Novick, Peter. *The Holocaust in American Life*. New York: Houghton Mifflin, 2000.

Nugent, Helen and Nadia Menuhin. Mohammad is No. 2 Boy's Names. *Times Online*, June 6, 2007.

Numbers USA. What Section 245(i) actually does.

Numbers USA. U.S. Amnesties for Illegal Aliens.

Office of National Statistics, UK. Education: Chinese Pupils Have Best GCSE Results.

Office of National Statistics, UK. Ethnicity and Identify: Employment Patterns, Pakistanis Most Likely to be Self-employed, March 2005.

OECD. *Where Immigrants Students Succeed, A Comparative Review of Performance and Engagement in PISA 2003*. OECD Publishing, 2006.

Onishi, Norimitsu. Rising Muslim Power in Africa Causes Unrest in Nigeria and Elsewhere. *New York Times*, November 1, 2001.

Open Society Institute. 2006 Annual Report.

Open Society Institute. Muslims in EU Cities, Cities Report. EU Monitoring and Advocacy Program, 2007.

Packer, Craig. and Anne E. Pusey. Infanticide in carnivores. In Glen Hausfater and Sara Blaffer Hrdy. *Infanticide: Comparative and Evolutionary Perspectives*. New York: Aldine, 1984, 31–42.

Passel, Jeffrey S. and D'Vera Cohn. U.S. Population Projections: 2005-2050. Washington D.C.: Pew Research Center, February 11, 2008.

Pangle, Lorraine. Multiculturalism and Civic Education. In Arthur M. Melzer, Jerry Weinberger and Richard Zinman. *Multiculturalism and American Democracy*. Lawrence, Kansas: University Press of Kansas, 1998, 173–98.

Parsons, Craig A., ed. *Immigration and the Transformation of Europe*. Cambridge, Cambridge University Press, 2006.

Parsons, Craig A. and Timothy M. Smeeding. What's Unique about Immigration in Europe. In Craig A. Parsons Ed. *Immigration and the Transformation of Europe*. Cambridge, Cambridge University Press, 2006, 1–29.

Pedersen, Peder J., Mariola Pytikova and Nina Smith. Migration into OECD Countries 1900-2000. In Craig A. Parsons, ed. *Immigration and the Transformation of Europe*. Cambridge, Cambridge University Press, 2006.

Phillips, Melanie. *Londonistan*. New York: Encounter Books, 2006.

Pinker, Steven. *The Blank Slate: The Modern Denial of Human Nature*. Penguin Books, New York, 2003.

Pipes, Daniel and Lars Hedegaard, Something Rotten in Denmark? *Capitalism Magazine*, September 16, 2002.

Pryce-Jones, David. Heil Haider?, *National Review*, May 6, 2000.

Putnam, Robert D. E Pluribus Unum: Diversity and Community in the Twenty-First Century, The 2006 Johan Skytte Prize Lecture. *Scandinavian Political Studies*, 30:2, (2007).

Quixote, Darth. 10 Questions for Steven Pinker. Gene Expression, July 4, 2006, 2006.

Randall, Colin. Migrant Polygamy Helped Cause Riots. *Telegraph*, November 17, 2005.

Rampey, Bobby D., Gloria S. Dion and Patricia L. Donahue. The Nation's Report Card: Trends in Academic Progress in Reading and Mathematics. National Center of Education Statistics, U.S. Department of Education., April 2009.

Rapoport, Anatol and Albert M. Chammah. *The Prisoner's Dilemma: A Study of Conflict and Cooperation*. Ann Arbor, Michigan: University of Michigan Press, 1969.

Rauch, Jonathan. The Truth Hurts: The Humanitarian Threat to Free Speech. *Reason,* April 1993.

Rechs Ann Pedersen, Internet Librarian. *Alien Land Laws*. Santa Cruz Public Libraries' Local History.

Regalado, Antonio. Head Examined: Scientist's Study of Brain Genes Sparks a Backlash. *Wall Street Journal.* June 16, 2006, A1.

Reid, Sue. Polygamy UK: This Special Mail Investigation Reveals How Thousands of Men are Milking the Benefits System to Support Several Wives. *Daily Mail,* February 24, 2009.

Reimers, David M. *Still the Golden Door: The Third World Comes to America, 2nd Edition*. New York: Columbia University Press, 1992.

Republican National Platform, Transcribed by Lloyd Benson from the Tribune Almanac, 1861, 30-31. Downloaded from the website of Gil Troy, McGill University, History 301.

Richwine, Jason. Indian Americans: The New Model Minority. *Forbes*, February 24, 2009.

Ridley, Matt. *The Red Queen: Sex and the Evolution of Human Nature*. New York: Penguin, 1993.

Rindermann, Heiner. The G-Factor of International Cognitive Ability Comparisons: The Homogeneity of Results in PISA, TIMSS, PIRLS and IQ-Tests Across Nations. *European Journal of Psychology*, August 8, 2007, 667–706.

Roberts, J. M. *The Penguin History of the World*. London: Penguin, 1995.

Roelofs, Joan. *Foundations and Public Policy: The Mask of Pluralism*. Albany, New York, State University of New York Press, 2003.

Rosit, Nelson. Prescient Patrician. Review of Jonathan Peter Spiro. *Patrician Racist: The Evolution of Madison Grant*. Ann Arbor: UMI Dissertation Services, 2000. *The Occidental Quarterly*, Vol. 7, No. 2. 1–10.

Rose, David. Lives of Crime. *Prospect Magazine*, 125. (2005)

Rosen, Hanna. American Murder Mystery. *Atlantic Monthly*, July/August 2008.

Rosenberg, Noah, A., Jonathan K. Pritchard, James A. Weber, Howard M. Cann, Kenneth K. Kidd, Lev A. Zhivotovski and Marcus W. Feldman. Genetic Structure of Human Populations. *Science*. 34:1 (2002), 2381–2385.

Roth, Byron M. *Prescription for Failure: Race Relations in the Age of Social Science*. New Brunswick, New Jersey: Transaction Publishers, 1994.

Roth, Byron M. Crime and Childrearing. *Society*, 34:1, (1996), 39–45.

Roth, Byron. M. Self-esteem, Ethnicity and Academic Performance Among American Children. In Craig L. Frisby and Cecil R. Reynolds, eds. *Comprehensive Handbook of Multicultural School Psychology*. Hoboken, New Jersey: Wiley and Sons, 2005, 577–611.

Rowe, D. C. *The Limits of Family Influence*. New York: Guilford Press, 1994.

Ruark, Eric. *Immigration Lobbying: A Window Into the World of Special Interests*, Washington, DC: Federation for American Immigration Reform, January 2008.

Rubenstein, Edwin S. Cost of Diversity: *The Economic Costs of Racial and Cultural Diversity*, Number 803. Augusta Georgia: National Policy Institute, 2008, October 2008.

Rubenstein, Edwin S. National Data: September Data Shows Immigrants Displacing American Workers – Especially Blacks. *Vdare*, October 5, 2008.

Russell, J. C. *Population in Europe 500–1500*. In Carlo M. Cipolla, ed. *The Fontana Economic History of Europe: The Middle Ages*. London: Collins/ Fontana Press, 1977.

Rushton, J. Philippe. *Race, Evolution and Behavior: A Life History Perspective*. New Brunswick, New Jersey: Transaction Publishers, 1995.

Rushton, J. Philippe and Arthur R. Jenson. Thirty years of research on race differences in cognitive ability. *Psychology, Public Policy, and Law*. 1:2, (2005) 235–294.

Rushton, J. Philippe, David W. Fulker, Michael C. Neale, David K. B. Nias and Hans J. Eysenck. Altruism and Aggression: The Heritability of Individual Differences. *Journal of Personality and Social Psychology*, 50 (1986), 1192–1198.

Sailer, Steve. Cousin Marriage Conundrum: The Ancient Practice Discourages Democratic Nation-Building. *The American Conservative*. January 13, 2003, 20–22.

Sailer, Steve. America's Minoirty Mortgage Meltdown/ Diversity Recession: The Smoking Gun. *Vdare*, October, 10, 2008.

Sailer, Steve. The Minority Mortgage Meltdown (Contd.): How the Community Reinvestment Act Fits In. *Vdare*, February 1, 2009.

Salins, Peter, D. *Assimilation, American Style*. New York: Basic Books, 1997, 6, 244–5. Cited in Samuel P. Huntington, *Who Are We: The Challenges to America's National Identity*. New York: Simon and Schuster Paperbacks, 2004, 183.

Salter, Frank. *On Genetic Interests: Family, Ethnicity and Humanity in an Age of Mass Migration*. New Brunswick, New Jersey: Transaction Publishers, 2007.

Samuel, Henry. France to Consider Banning the Burka. *Telegraph.co.uk*, June 19, 2009.

Samura, Sorious. Gang Rape: Is it a Race Issue. *The Independent*, June 21, 2009.

Sarich, Vincent and Frank Miele. *Race: The reality of Human Differences*. Boulder, Colorado: Westview Press, 2004.

Sawhill, Isabel and John E. Morton. Economic Mobility: Is the American Dream Alive and Well. Washington D.C.: The Pew Charitable Trusts, 2007.

Schirrmacher, Christine. Muslims in Germany: A Study Conducted by the Federal Ministry of the Interior, Results of the Study – A Summary. Institute of Islamic Studies of the German Evangelical Alliance e. V., April 2008, 1–4. Online at europenewsdk.

Schlesenger, Arthur M. Jr. *The Disuniting of America: Reflections on a Multicultural Society.* New York: W.W. Norton, 1992.

Schnapper, Dominique. *Relativisme in Commentaire,* 31:121 (Spring 2008) 126–130.

Scruton, Roger. Roger Scruton on Immigration, Multiculturalism and the Need to Defend the Nation State. Speech by Roger Scruton, Antwerp, 23 June, 2006. *Brussels Journal,* July 8, 2007. Online at Brusselsjournal.com.

Semeno, Ornella, Giuseppe Passarino, Peter J. Oefner, Alice A. Lin, Svetlana Arbuzova, Lars E. Beckman, Giovanna De Benedicta, Paolo Francalacci, Anastasia Kouvatsi, Svetlana Limborska, Mladen Marcikiae, Anna Mike, Barbara Mika, Dragan Primorac, A. Svetlana Santachiera-Benerecetti, L. Luca Cavalli-Sforza, Peter A. Underhill. The genetic legacy of Paleolithic Homo sapiens in extant Europeans: A Y Chromosome Perspective. Science, 290, (2000) 1155–9.

Shea, Nina. *Saudi Arabia's Curriculum of Intolerance: With Excerpts from the Saudi Ministry of Education Textbooks for Islamic Studies.* Washington D.C.: Center for Religious Freedom, Freedom House, 2006.

Shorter, Edward. *The Making of the Modern Family.* New York: Basic Books, 1977.

Shreeve, James. *The Neandertal Enigma: Solving the Mystery of Modern Human Origins.* New York: Avon, 1995.

Singer, S. Fred and Dennis T. Avery. *Unstoppable Global Warming.* Rowman and Littlefield, New York, 2007.

Singer, Tania, Ben Seymour, John O'Doherty, Holger Kaube, Raymond J. Dolan and Chris D. Frith. Empathy for Pain Involves the Affective But Not the Sensory Components of Pain. *Science,* 303:5661, (2004), 1157–1162.

Sigmund, Karl. *Games of life: Explorations in Ecology, Evolution and Behavior.* Penguin Books, London, 1993.

Sjoberg, Richard L., Francesca Ducci, Christina S. Barr, Timothy K. Newman, Liliana ll'Osso, Matti Virkkunen and David Goldman. A Non-Additive Intereaction of a Functional MAO-A VNTR and Testosterone Predicts Antisocial Behavior. *Neurpsychopharmacology* (2008) 33, 425–430.

Skinner, B. F. *Beyond Freedom and Dignity.* New York: Bantam Books, 1972.

Slezkine, Yuri. *The Jewish Century.* Princeton, New Jersey: Princeton University Press, 2004.

Smith, Craig S. Islam in Jail: Europe's Neglect Breeds Angry Radicals. *New York Times,* December 8, 2004.

Smith. Craig S. Anti-Semitism at Ground Level in France. *International Herald Tribune,* March 23, 2006.

Smith, John Maynard. *The Theory of Evolution.* Cambridge, UK: Cambridge University Press, 1975.

Smith, John Maynard. *Evolution and the Theory of Games.* Cambridge, UK: Cambridge University Press, 1982.

Smith, Nicola. Dutch Minister Bans Burka to 'Boost Tolerance.' *The Australian,* November 20, 2006.

Sobol, Willian J., Heather Couture, and Paige M. Harrison. Bureau of Justice Statistics Bulletin, Prisoners in 2006, NCJ 219416. Washington D.C.: U.S. Department of Justice, December 2007, 6, 8.

Southern Poverty Law Center. 2007 Annual Report.

Southern Poverty Law Center. *The Intelligence Project.*

Solomon, Eldra P, Linda R. Berg and Diana W. Martin. *Biology, 6th Edition.* Toronto: Brooks/Cole, 2002.

Sowell, Thomas. *Ethnic America.* New York: Basic Books, 1981.

Spann, Edward K. *Gotham at War: New York City, 1860–1865.* Wilmington, Del.: SR Books, 2002.

Spiro, Jonathan Peter. *Patrician Racist: The Evolution of Madison Grant.* Ann Arbor: UMI Dissertation Services, 2000.

Sriskandarajah, Dhananjayan and Francesca Hopwood Road, United Kingdom: Rising Numbers, Rising Anxieties. Country Profiles, Migration Information Source, November 2003.

Stanford, Craig. B., Caleb Gambaneza, John Bosco Nkurunungi and Michele L. Goldsmith. Chimpanzees in Bwindi-Impenetrable National Park, Uganda, Use Different Tools to Obtain Different Types of Honey. *Primate,* 41.3 (2003) 337–341.

Stienmetz, Erika and John Iceland. Racial and Ethnic Residential Housing Patterns in Places: 2000. Paper presented at the annuals meeting of the Population Association of America. Minneapolis, Michigan. May 1–3, 2003.

Steyn, Mark. *America Alone: The End of the World as We Know It.* Washington, D.C.: Regnery, 2006.

Steyn, Mark. The Lamps are Going Out. *The New Criterion, Special Pamphlet, Free Speech in an Age of Jihad: Libel Tourism, "Hate Speech" & Political Freedom.* Summer 2008, 32–33.

Stossel, John. The College Scam. *Townhall,* January 28, 2009.

Strock, Margaret. Attention Deficit Hyperactivity Disorder. Public Information and Communications Branch, National Institute of Mental Health (NIMH), 1996.

Sullum, Jacob. Brain Storm: Can We Talk About Sex Differences in Math and Science Aptitude Without Yelling? *Reason,* January 21, 2005.

Suro, Robert. *Strangers among Us: How Latino Immigration is Transforming America.* New York: Alfred A. Knopf, 1998.

Sykes, Brian. *The Seven Daughters of Eve,* New York: Norton, 2001.

Tate, Thad W. and David L. Ammerman, eds. *The Chesapeake in the Seventeenth Century: Essays on Anglo-American Society and Politics,* New York: Norton, 1979.

Tavernise, Sabrina and Sebnem Arsu. Turkish Court Call Ruling Party Constitutional. *New York Times,* July 31, 2008.

Taylor, Charles, The Politics of Recognition. In Charles Taylor, ed. *Multiculturalism: Examining the Politics of Recognition.* Princeton, New Jersey: Princeton University Press, 1994, 25–74.

Taylor, Charles, ed. *Multiculturalism: Examining the Politics of Recognition.* Princeton, New Jersey: Princeton University Press, 1994.

Talmon-Garber, Yonina G.. *Family and community in the kibbutz.* Cambridge, Mass.: Harvard University Press, 1972.

Tancredo, Tom. *In Mortal Danger: The Battle for America's Border and Security.* Nashville, Tenn.: Cumberland House, 2006.

Theilemann, Eiko R. The Effectiveness of Governments' attempts to control unwanted immigration. , In Craig A. Parsons (Ed) *Immigration and the Transformation of Europe,* Cambridge, Cambridge University Press, 2006.

Thernstrom, Steven. Rediscovering the Melting Pot - Still Going Strong. In Tamar Jacoby, ed. *Reinventing the Melting Pot: The New Immigrants and What It Means to be American.* Basic Books, New York, 2004. Pp. 47–60.

Thibodeau, Patrick. Norman Matloff Tells What's Wrong with the H-1B Visa Program. *Computer World,* September 8, 2008.

Thomas, Hugh. *World History, Revised Edition.* New York: HarperCollins, 1996.

Thorne. Alan G. and Milford Wolpoff. The Multiregional Evolution of Humans, revised paper. *Scientific American,* 13, 2 (2003), 46–53.

Thornycroft, Peta. Invaders Cripple Zimbabwe Farms. *Telegraph.co.uk,* October 7, 2001.

Thornycroft, Peta. Robert Mugabe's Mobs Invade Last White Farms *Telegraph.co.uk,* April 18, 2008.

Tiberge, Nice Rally Banned. GalliaWatch, January 16, 2009.

Tichenor. David J. *Dividing Lines: The Politics of Immigration Control in America.* Princeton, New Jersey: Princeton University Press, 2002.

Tiger, Lionel, and J. Shepher. *Women in the Kibbutz.* New York: Harcourt, Brace and Jovanovich, 1975.

Time Magazine. Reservoirs of Labor. April 28, 1923.

Time Magazine. Pro and Con. December 24, 1923.

Time Magazine. "Go North." August 13, 1923.

Time Magazine. The Desperate Ones. October 8, 1979.

Time Magazine. Getting Their Slice of Paradise. May 2, 1977.

Times Public Wants Much Harsher Immigration Policy, says poll. August 20, 2006.

Times A Third of Muslim Students Back Killings. July 27, 2008.

Trivers, Robert L. The Evolution of Reciprocal Altruism. *Quarterly Review of Biology,* 46, (1971) 35–57. Reprinted in James H. Hunt, eds. *Selected Readings in Sociobiology.* New York: McGraw-Hill, 1980. 38–68.

Trifkovik, Serge. *The Sword of the Prophet: Islam, History, Theology, Impact on the World.* Boston: Regina Orthodox Press, 2002.

TVNZ. "Police Tackling Maori Crime Rates. November 10, 2005,

United Kingdom Parliament, House of Commons Hansard Written Answers for 17 Mar 2008 (pt 0032).

United Nations Office on Drugs and Crime. *Eighth United Nations Survey of Crime Trends and Operations of Criminal Justice Systems, Covering the Period 2001–2002*, (2003).

United Nations. World Population Prospects: The 2008 Revision.

United Nations Convention on the Status of Refugees and Stateless Persons. Adopted 28 July 1951.

U. S. Census Bureau. *Statistical Abstract of the United States*, 1977.

U. S. Census Bureau. Statistical Abstract of the United States, 1982–84

U. S. Census Bureau. *Statistical Abstract of the United States*, 1993.

U. S. Census Bureau. *Statistical Abstract of the United States*, 2008.

U. S. Census Bureau. Population Division/International Programs Center. Historical Estimates of World Population.

U. S. Department of Homeland Security. *2006 Yearbook of Immigration Statistics*. Immigration by Region and Selected Country of Last Residence: Fiscal Years 1820–2004. Washington, D.C., 2007.

U. S. Congress. *An act to establish an uniform rule of naturalization,* passed by Congress, January 4, 1790. Online at Harvard University Library, Page Delivery Service.

U. S. Department of Labor. Bureau of Labor Statistics , Household Data, Annual Averages. Table 10, Employed Persons by Occupation, Race, Hispanic or Latino Ancestry and Sex.

Van den Berghe, Pierre L. *Human Family Systems: An Evolutionary View.* Prospect Heights, Illinois: Waveland Press, 1990.

Vanhanen, Tatu. *The Limits of Democratization: Climate, Intelligence, and Resource Distribution.* Augusta, Georgia: Washington Summit Publishers, 2009.

Veddeer, Richard K. and Lowell Eugene Gallaway. *Out of Work: Unemployment and Government in Twentieth-Century America, Updated Edition.* New York: NYU Press, 1997.

Viding, Essi, R. James R. Blair, Terrie E. Moffitt and Robert Plomin. Evidence for Substantial Genetic Risk for Psychopathy in 7-Year-Olds. *Journal of Child Psychology and Psychiatry.* 46:6 (2005), 592–597.

Viding, Essi and Uta Frith. Genes for Susceptibility to Violence Lurk in the Brain. *Proceedings of the National Academy of Sciences.* 103:16 (2006) 6085–86.

Vigdor, Jacob L. Measuring Immigrant Assimilation in the United States, Civic Report No. 53, Mat 2008. New York: Manhattan Institute, 2003

Viviano, Frank. French Prisons: Extremist Training Grounds. *San Francisco Chronicle,* November 1, 2001.

Voight, Benjamin F., Sridhar Kudaravalli, Xiaoquan Wen and Jonathan K. Pritchard, A Map of Recent Positive Selection in the Human Genome. *PLoS Biol* 4:3 (March 2006), 446–458.

Wade, Wyn Craig. *The Fiery Cross: The Ku Klux Klan in America.* New York: Simon and Schuster, 1986.

Wade, Nicholas. *Before the Dawn: Recovering the Lost History of Our Ancestors.* New York: Penguin Press, 2006.

Wade, Nicholas. Humans Have Spread Globally, and Evolved Locally. *The New York Times,* June 26, 2007.

Walker, Jonathan. Call for Probe into Police after Apology to Channel 4. *Birmingham Post,* May 15, 2008.

Walsh, Anthony and Kevin Beaver. eds. *Biosocial Criminology: New Direction in Theory and Research.* New York: Routledge, 2009.

Wang, Eric T., Greg Kodama, Pierre Baldi, and Robert K. Moyzis, Global Landscape of Recent Inferred Darwinian Selection for Homo Sapiens. *PNAS,* 103:1 (2006), 135–140.

Washington Times. Battling Censorship, Editorial, July 20, 2007.

Wasem, Ruth Ellen. CRS Report for Congress. Immigration: Legislative Issues on Nonimmigrant Professional Specialty (H-1B) Workers, May 23, 2007. Washington DC: Congressional Research Service, 2007.

Webb, James. *Born Fighting: How the Scots-Irish Shaped America.* New York: Random House, 2004.

Welch, William M. Illegal Immigrants Might Get Stimulus Jobs, Experts Say. *USA Today,* March 8, 2009.

Wen, Bo, Hui Li, Daru Lu, Xifeng Song, Feng Shang, Ungang He, Feng Li, Yang Gao, Xianyun Maoo, Liang Zhang, Ji Qian, Jingze Tan, Jianzhong Jin, Wei Huang, Ranjan Deka, Bing Su, Ranajit Chakraborty, and Li Jin. Genetic Evidence supports Demic Diffusion of Han Culture. *Nature*, 431, September 16, 2004, 302–305.

Weston, Louis. Zimbabwe's Last White Farmer Forced to Quit. *Telegraph. co.uk*, June 26, 2008.

Wheeler, Mark. Study Gives More Proof that Intelligence is Largely inherited: UCLA Researchers Find that Genes Determine Brain's Processing Speed. USLA *Newsroom*. March 17, 2009.

White, Douglas R. and Michael L. Burton. Causes of polygyny: Ecology, Economy, Kinship and Warfare. *American Anthropologist*. 90:4 (1988), 871–887.

White, Michael J., Catherine Bucker and Jennifer E. Glick. The Impact of Immigration on Residential Segregation Revisited. Paper Presented to the American Sociological Association, August, 2002.

Widom, C. S. and L. M. Brzustowicz. MAOA and the Cycle of Violence: Childhood Abuse and Neglect, MAOA Genotype, and Risk for Violent and Antisocial Behavior. *Biological Psychiatry*, 60(7), (2006) 684–9.

Wike, Richard and Juliana Menasce Horowitz. World Publics Welcome Global Trade – But Not Immigration: 47-Nation Pew Global Attitudes Survey, The Pew Global Attitudes Project, October 4, 2007.

Wilford, John Noble. In Ruin, Symbols on a Stone Hint at a Lost Asian Culture. *New York Times*, May 13, 2001.

Williams, George C. *Sex and Evolution*. Princeton, New Jersey: Princeton University Press, 1975.

Williamson, Scott, Melissa J. Hubisz, Andrew G. Clark, Bret A. Payseur, Carlos D. Bustamante, and Rasmus Nielson. Localizing Recent Adaptive Evolution in the Human Genome. *PLoS Genetics* 3:6 (2007).

Wills, Christopher. *The Runaway Brain: The Evolution of Human Uniqueness*. London: Harper Collins, 1994.

Wilson, Edward O. *Sociobiology: The New Synthesis*. Cambridge Mass.: Belknap Press, 1975.

Wilson, Edward O. *Sociobiology: The Abridged Edition*. Cambridge, Mass.: Belknap Press, 1980.

Wilson, James Q. *Thinking About Crime.* New York: Vintage Books, 1985.

Wilson, James Q. and Richard J. Herrnstein. *Crime and Human Nature.* New York: Simon and Schuster, 1985.

Wokeck, Marianne Sophia. *Trade In Strangers: The Beginnings of Mass Migration to North America.* University Park, Penn.: Pennsylvania State University Press, 1999.

Wolf, Susan, Comment. In Charles Taylor, ed. *Multiculturalism: Examining the Politics of Recognition.* Princeton, New Jersey: University Press, 1994, 75–86.

Wolpoff, Milford H., Bruce Mannheim, Alan Mann, John Hawks, Rachel Caspari, Karen R. Rosenberg, David W. Frayer, George W. Gill and Geoffrey Clark. Why *Not* the Neandertals? *World Archaeology* 36:4 (2004) 527–546.

Wright, John Paul. Inconvenient Truths: Science, Race and Crime. In Anthony Walsh and Kevin Beaver, eds. *Biosocial Criminology: New Direction in Theory and Research.* New York: Routledge, 2009. 137–153.

Wright, John Paul, Danielle Boisvert, Kim Dietrich, and M. Douglas Ris. The Ghost in the Machine and Criminal Behavior: Criminology for the 21st Century. In Anthony Walsh and Kevin Beaver, eds. *Biosocial Criminology: New Direction in Theory and Research.* New York: Routledge, 2009, 73–89.

Wright, Stephen and Nicola Boden. Thugs Committing 350 Knife Assaults Every Day, as Blade Menace Spreads to Rural Areas. *Daily Mail,* July 17, 2008.

Wyman, David S. *The Abandonment of the Jews: America and the Holocaust 1941-1945.* New York: Pantheon Books, 1985.

Wynne-Jones, Jonathan. Bishop of Rochester Reasserts "No-Go" Claim. *Telegraph.UK,* April 18, 2008.

Ye'or, Bat. *Eurabia: The Euro-Arab Axis.* Madison, New Jersey: Fairleigh Dickinson University Press, 2005.

Young, Susan E., Andrew Smolen, John K. Hewitt, Brett C. Haberstick, Michael C. Stallings, Robin P. Corley, and Thomas J. Crowley. Interaction Between MAO-A Genotype and Maltreatment in the Risk for Conduct Disorder: Failure to Confirm in Adolescent Patients. *American Journal of Psychiatry.* 163, (2006), 1019–1025.

Zerjal, Tatiana, Yali Xue, Giorgio Bertorelle, R. Spencer Wells, Weidong Bao, Suling Zhu, Raheel Qamar, Qasim Ayub, Aisha Mohyuddin, Songbin Fu, Pu

Li, Nadira Yuldsheva, Ruslan Ruzibakiev, Juijin Xu, Qunfang Shu, Ruofu Du, Huanming Yang, Methew E. Hurles, Elizabeth Robinson, Tudevdagva Gerelsaikhan, Bumbein Dashnyam, S. Qasim Mehdi, and Chris Tyler-Smith. The Genetic Legacy of the Mongols. *American Journal of Human Genetics*, 72, 2003, 717–721.

Zinkstok, Janneke R., Odette de Wild, Therese AMJ van Amelsvoort, Michael W. Tanck, Frank Baas, and Don H. Linszen. D.H. Association Between the DTNBP1 Gene and Intelligence: A Case-Control Study in Young Patients with Schizophrenia and Related Disorders and Unaffected Siblings. *Behavioral and Brain Functions* 3:19 (2007).

INDEX

A

A Cry in the Silence (Bardot) , 33
Abandonment of the Jews (Wyman), 300
absentee landlords, 247
ad hominem argument, 16, 27, 293, 319
Adler, Katya, 440
adolescent-onset delinquency, 166–167
affectionate marriage, 208
affirmative action, 10, 128, 219–220,
221, 471, 472, 477, 478, 479
Afghanistan, 35, 348, 412, 496, 497, 499
Africa:
    Chinese expansion in 484, 505;
    economic problems of,
    502–505; and homicide rates,
    126;
    and IQ, 60, 125, 203, 215;
    immigrants to Europe, 392–393,
    409, 439;
    kingdoms, 186–190;
    origins of human races,
    128–133, 146–152;
    population of, 1;
    Watson on, 26.
    See also African slaves; North
    Africa
African Eve theory, 128
African slaves, 11, 233, 240, 241, 253,
254, 255
aggressiveness, 12, 60, 150, 154, 182, 184

agriculture:
    and classical civilizations,
    190–194;
    and cultural innovation,
    135–136;
    and sickle cell anemia, 143–144
Aid el-Kebir, 34
air travel, 125, 242, 351
Al Qaeda, 33, 427
Albion's Seed, 243
Alexander the Great, 184
ALFRED genetic database, 157
Algeria, 388, 389, 392, 400, 423, 486
Alien Land Law, 288
Allen, Frederick Lewis, 277
Alms for Jihad (Collins), 32
Alpine region, 238
Alpine strain or race, 283–284
Altria corporation, 49
altruism, 99–104;
    universal, 113.
    See also reciprocal altruism
America Alone (Steyn), 32
America, North. *See* North America
American Anthropological Association,
285
American Association of Engineering
Societies, 344
American Civil Liberties Union (ACLU),
46, 47
American Federation of Labor (AFL),
313
American Federation of State, Local and
Municipal Employees, 50   American

B

C

E

F

H

I

J

K

T

U

V

W

ABOUT THE AUTHOR

BYRON M. ROTH is Professor Emeritus of Psychology, Dowling College. He received his BA from Rutgers University and his Ph.D. from the Graduate Faculty of the New School for Social Research. His work has appeared in *The Journal of Conflict Resolution, The Public Interest, Academic Questions* and *Encounter.* His previous books include, *Decision Making, Its Logic and Practice*, co-authored with John D. Mullen and *Prescription for Failure: Race Relations in the Age of Social Science.* The latter was described by the editors of the *Journal Political Psychology* as "a book of major importance to the science and the applications of political psychology."

CPSIA information can be obtained at www.ICGtesting.com
Printed in the USA
BVOW05s1300180216

437041BV00011B/125/P